国家出版基金项目
NATIONAL PUBLICATION FOUNDATION

国际海事组织海员行为示范

MODEL COURSE 3.12

海员评估、考试与发证
（第二册：纲要）

ASSESSMENT, EXAMINATION AND CERTIFICATION OF SEAFARERS（2000） Volume 2: Compendium

中华人民共和国海事局 译

中英对照

大连海事大学出版社
DALIAN MARITIME UNIVERSITY PRESS

国际海事组织1992年第一次出版

4 Albert Embankment, London SE1 7SR

Ⓒ 中华人民共和国海事局　2016

图书在版编目(CIP)数据

海员评估、考试与发证. 第二册, 纲要：汉英对照 /
国际海事组织著；中华人民共和国海事局译. — 大连：
大连海事大学出版社, 2016.6
（国际海事组织海员行为示范）
书名原文：ASSESSMENT, EXAMINATION AND
CERTIFICATION OF SEAFARERS Volume 2: Compendium
ISBN 978-7-5632-3346-5

Ⅰ. ①海… Ⅱ. ①国… ②中… Ⅲ. ①海员 – 管理 –
国际条约 – 技术培训 – 教材 – 汉、英 Ⅳ. ①D998.2

中国版本图书馆CIP数据核字(2016)第141910号

大连海事大学出版社出版

地址：大连市凌海路1号　邮编：116026　电话：0411-84728394　传真：0411-84727996
http://www.dmupress.com　　E-mail:cbs@dmupress.com

大连住友彩色印刷有限公司印装　　　　　　　　　大连海事大学出版社发行

2016年6月第1版	2016年6月第1次印刷
幅面尺寸：210 mm×297 mm	印数：1～3000册
印张：43.75	字数：1358千
出　版　人：徐华东	策　　划：徐华东
责任编辑：张　华　杨玮璐	责任校对：张　冰　宋彩霞
封面设计：解瑶瑶	版式设计：孟　冀　解瑶瑶

ISBN 978-7-5632-3346-5　　　　　　　　　　　　　　　　　定价：109.00元

国际海事组织海员行为示范
编审委员会

主　任：郑和平
副主任：林　浦　　葛同林
委　员：刘正江　　杨万里　　张安富　　周明顺
　　　　朱可欣　　于洪江　　陆立明　　陈永忠
　　　　王玉洋　　王长青　　陈国忠　　唐春辉
　　　　韩杰祥　　毛洪鑫　　李蕙兰　　饶滚金
　　　　石万里　　王兴琦

《海员评估、考试与发证》(第二册：纲要)
翻　译：金国柱
审　校：王凤武　　胡甚平

CONTENTS

Preface iv
Part 1   Introduction to the Revised STCW Convention 2
Part 2   Process Overview 46
Part 3   International Obligations 58
Part 4   Authority and Organization 116
Part 5   Quality Standards System 138
Part 6   Certificate Requirements 162
Part 7   Assessing Applications 190
Part 8   Regulation I/6: Training and Assessment 200
Part 9   Approved Training 236
Part 10   Training and Assessment 260
         Part 10-1:   Introduction to competence-based training 264
         Part 10-2:   Competence-based assessment 292
         Part 10-3:   Methodologies in standards development 320
         Part 10-4:   Setting criteria for required performance 330
         Part 10-5:   Collecting evidence of competence 348
         Part 10-6:   Matching evidence to standards 368
         Part 10-7:   Review and follow-up 388
         Part 10-8:   Quality assurance 392
         Annex 10-1   Development of standards: an example (Australia) ... 404
Part 11   Developing Written Tests 420
Part 12   Invigilation of Tests 442
Part 13   Scoring Tests 448
Part 14   Oral and Practical Tests 464
Part 15   Shipboard Assessment System 492
Part 16   Performance Criteria for Shipboard Assessment 510
Part 17   The Assessment Process 530
Part 18   Developing Performance Improvement Plan 554
Part 19   Maintenance of Standards 564
Part 20   Administration 596
         Annex 20-1   Formal investigation of sinking of ANTACUS 618
         Annex 20-2   Development of an electronic database for Certification Registration 660
Part 21   Training and Certification of Seafarers on High Speed Craft 682
Part 22   Group Evaluation 690

目录

前言		v
第1章	经修订的STCW公约介绍	3
第2章	进程概述	47
第3章	国际义务	59
第4章	机构与组织	117
第5章	质量标准体系	139
第6章	发证要求	163
第7章	评估申请	191
第8章	公约规则I/6：培训与评估	201
第9章	认可的培训	237
第10章	培训与评估	261
第10-1章	适任培训介绍	265
第10-2章	适任评估	293
第10-3章	制定标准的方法	321
第10-4章	设定实操的评判标准	331
第10-5章	适任证据的收集	349
第10-6章	证据与标准的匹配	369
第10-7章	复查与跟踪	389
第10-8章	质量保证	393
附件10-1	标准的制定：范例（澳大利亚）	405
第11章	笔试设计	421
第12章	监考	443
第13章	考试评分	449
第14章	口试和实操考试	465
第15章	船上评估体系	493
第16章	船上评估的实操标准	511
第17章	评估过程	531
第18章	制订操作改进计划	555
第19章	标准的维护	565
第20章	主管机关	597
附件20-1	关于"ANTACUS"号沉没的正式调查报告	619
附件20-2	证书登记数据库的开发	661
第21章	高速船船员的培训与发证	683
第22章	分组评估	691

Preface

This compendium has been compiled for use as a textbook during the presentation of the IMO model course on Assessment, Examination and Certification of Seafarers. It will also serve as a source of reference material for use in the development of national legislation or administrative instructions and guidelines for those responsible for the conduct of assessments and examinations leading to the issue of certificates of competency which are in compliance with the International Convention on Standards of Training, Certification and Watchkeeping (STCW), 1978, as amended in 1995. In its use, care should be taken to ensure that national and international laws referred to have not been revoked or revised.

Since its inception, IMO has given high priority to maritime training, recognizing the critical importance of well trained and competent personnel to the safe and efficient operation of shipping.

The demonstration of competency by passing appropriate examinations and the assessment of evidence obtained from various approved assessment methods conducted by or on behalf of Administrations is the central requirement of the STCW Convention. The training, certification and documentation of ship's personnel is also governed by certain conventions and recommendations adopted under the aegis of the International Labour Organisation (ILO). The training and certification of personnel of ship stations and ship earth stations is governed by the provisions of the International Telecommunication Union (ITU) Radio Regulations and by the STCW Convention.

Whilst this compendium provides a certain amount of information on these aspects of a system of training, assessment, examination and certification for merchant ship personnel, the main emphasis of the course and this compendium is on the implementation of the 1978 STCW Convention, as amended in 1995, associated resolutions and the IMO/ILO Document for Guidance, 1985.

Assessment and examination methods and practices vary from country to country, and the aim of the course is to provide training in a typical examination process and in the preparation and use of examination material of various types in current use in general education, some of which have been successfully applied in maritime subjects.

Through the kind co-operation of the Maritime Administration of the Republic of Singapore, detailed information is provided on their examination provisions and processes.

Other sources of information are taken from the Internet websites of various Maritime Administrations, in particular, that of the United States Coast Guard (USCG), as well as shore-based training organizations.

前　言

　　在讲解关于海员评估、考试和发证的IMO示范课程时,本纲要作为教材使用。在履行依照STCW78/95公约签发适任证书所要求的评估考试而制定国内立法或行政指令和指南时,本纲要也可作为参考资料使用。使用本纲要时,须注意确保所参考的国内和国际法律是没有被废除或修改过的。

　　由于意识到受过良好培训和适任的人员对航行安全和效率具有极大的重要性,因此IMO自成立之初就对航海培训给予高度的优先权。

　　STCW公约的核心要求是通过主管机关进行的或代表主管机关进行的适当考试和各种认可的方法进行评估来确定海员的适任能力。同时,船舶人员的培训和发证也受国际劳工组织(ILO)通过的某些公约和所采纳的建议案的约束。而船岸电台人员的培训和发证则受国际电信联盟(ITU)无线电规则的规定和STCW公约约束。

　　本纲要提供有关船员培训、评估、考试和发证制度方面的一些信息,课程和纲要的主要侧重点是实施1978年STCW公约1995年修正案、相关决议以及1985年IMO和ILO的指导文件。

　　各国评估和考试的方法与做法各不相同,本课程的目的是在典型的考试方法和普通教育中用到的各种考试材料组织和使用方法方面提供培训,其中一些已在海事主题中成功应用。

　　新加坡海事局与IMO进行了友好合作,并提供了他们的考试规则和方法的详细资料。

　　其他资料来源于各国海事局的网站,特别是美国海岸警卫队(USCG),以及岸上培训机构的网站。

3.12 MODEL COURSE

Part 1
Introduction to the Revised STCW Convention

The 1995 amendments to the International Convention on Standards of Training, Certification and Watchkeeping for Seafarers (STCW), 1978

Background

Since its inception in 1959 IMO has endeavoured not only to improve the safety of ships and their equipment but also to raise the standards of the seafarers which man them.

Among the many resolutions adopted in 1960 at the International Conference on the Safety of Life at Sea was one which called upon Governments to take all practicable steps to ensure that the education and training of seafarers in the use of aids to navigation, ships' equipment and devices was sufficiently comprehensive and was kept satisfactorily up to date. It also recommended that IMO and the International Labour Organisation should co-operate with each other and with interested Governments in achieving these ends.

In response to this recommendation, the Governing Body of ILO and IMO's Maritime Safety Committee (MSC) established a Joint Committee on Training. This Committee had its first meeting in 1964 and prepared the *Document for Guidance 1964*. This Document gave guidance on the education and training of masters, officers and seamen in the use and operation of aids to navigation, life-saving appliances, devices for the prevention, detection and extinction of fires, and other ship's equipment contributing to safety at sea.

The Document was subsequently amended, expanded and supplemented by the Joint Committee in 1975, 1977 and 1985. Despite the success of this Document, the IMO Council in 1971 decided that still further measures were needed to strengthen and improve standards and it requested the MSC to give urgent consideration to international standards of watchkeeping, training and certification.

The IMO Assembly, which also met in 1971, decided to convene a conference to adopt a convention on the subject. Preparatory work was carried out by the IMO Sub-Committee on Standards of Training and Watchkeeping, which prepared the text of a draft convention, an annex containing requirements for watchkeeping, training and certification and a number of draft recommendations.

The 1978 STCW Convention

The conference met in 1978 and was attended by delegates from 72 countries. It was the largest conference ever held by IMO and the Convention which resulted was regarded as one of the most important maritime safety conventions ever developed.

第1章
经修订的STCW公约介绍

《1978年海员培训、发证和值班标准国际公约》1995年修正案

背景

  自1959年成立以来,IMO不但致力于提高船舶的安全和改善船舶的装备,而且致力于提高船舶配员的标准。

  1960年海上人命安全国际大会通过了若干决议。其中之一是要求政府采取所有可行的措施,在助航仪器、船舶设备与装置的使用方面确保船员教育与培训有足够广泛的内容和及时具备更新的知识。同时也建议,为实现这一目标,IMO和国际劳工组织(ILO)应相互合作,并且也应与有关国家的政府合作。

  为响应这一建议,ILO主管机关和IMO海上安全委员会(MSC)建立了联合培训委员会。该委员会在1964年召开第一次会议并形成1964年指导文件。该文件对船长、高级船员和普通船员在使用和操作助航仪器、救生设备、防火装置、探火装置、灭火装置和有助于海上安全的其他船舶设备的教育与培训方面提供了指导。

  该文件由联合委员会分别在1975年、1977年和1985年进行了修改、扩充和补充。尽管这个文件很成功,但是为了加强和提高教育与培训标准,IMO委员会在1971年决定采取进一步的行动,它要求MSC紧急考虑制定值班、培训和发证国际标准。

  1971年召开的IMO大会决定召开专门的会议通过有关该主题的公约。IMO培训和值班标准分委会开展筹备工作,起草公约草案,包括值班、培训和发证要求的附则以及若干建议案草案。

1978 STCW公约

  1978年IMO召开了由72个国家代表参加的、规模最大的一次大会。该大会通过了STCW公约,它被认为是历来制定的最重要的海上安全公约之一。

The Convention was the first attempt to establish global minimum professional standards for seafarers. Previously the standards of training, certification and watchkeeping of officers and ratings were established by individual governments, usually without reference to practices in other countries. As a result standards and procedures varied widely, even though shipping is the most international of all industries.

The Convention prescribes minimum standards which countries are obliged to meet or exceed. In the majority of established maritime countries, standards are often higher than those stipulated in the Convention. In some countries, however, standards are not so high and by ratifying or accepting the Convention Governments undertake to implement and enforce its requirements. The effect of the Convention's entry into force was therefore to raise standards in the world as a whole.

STCW 78
Intentions not achieved

- Good principles
- Not detailed
- Not explicit
- Not sufficient basis for control

The Convention does not deal with manning levels: IMO provisions in this area are covered by regulation 13 of chapter V of the International Convention for the Safety of Life at Sea (SOLAS), 1974, whose requirements are backed up by resolution A.481(XII) which was adopted by the IMO Assembly in 1981.

The requirement for entry into force of the Convention was the same as for the International Convention for the Safety of Life at Sea: acceptance by 25 countries whose combined fleets of merchant shipping represent at least 50 per cent of world tonnage. This target was reached on 27 April 1983 and the Convention entered into force one year later, on 28 April 1984. The Convention has been accepted by 114 States with fleets aggregating 94.99% of the world merchant shipping tonnage.

When the Convention entered into force, it was expected that its requirements would ensure the competence of masters, officers and ratings of all seagoing ships and their safe operation through efficient watchkeeping. As with all IMO Conventions it reflected the highest practicable standards which could be globally agreed at the time of its adoption.

But despite its broad global acceptance, it was realized by the late eighties that the Convention was not achieving its purpose. Instead it was gradually losing credibility as its acceptance widened. The main cause for this appeared to be the general lack of precision in its standards, the interpretation of which was left "to the satisfaction of the Administration". This resulted in widely varying interpretation of standards and many Parties failed to effectively administer and enforce Convention requirements. STCW certificates could no longer be relied upon as evidence of competence.

公约首先尝试建立全球海员最低职业标准。在这以前,高级船员和普通船员培训、发证和值班标准由各政府自己确定,通常没有参考其他国家的做法。结果造成国际化程度最高的航运业在其标准和程序上存在广泛的差别。

公约规定了最低标准,各国有义务满足或超过这个标准。通常大多数海运国家使用的标准高于公约的规定。虽然一些国家使用的标准不太高,但他们的政府通过批准或承认公约的方式,承诺履行和实施公约的要求。因此本公约生效的结果是提高了世界整体标准。

该公约没有涉及船舶配员标准:1974年《国际海上人命安全公约》(SOLAS公约)第5章第13条规则对这一方面做了规定,1981年IMO大会通过的A.481(XII)决议也支持IMO在该方面的要求。

本公约生效的必要条件与《国际海上人命安全公约》相同:至少得到25个国家接受,其商船总和至少占世界吨位的50%。这一目标在1983年4月27日达到。一年后,即1984年4月28日,该公约正式生效。该公约目前有114个国家接受,其商船总和占世界商船吨位的94.99%。

本公约生效时,人们期望公约的要求可确保所有海船船长、高级船员和普通船员的适任能力以及通过有效的值班达到作业安全性。与所有IMO公约一样,本公约反映了通过之时世界公认的最高可行标准。

尽管它得到全球广泛的认可,但是在20世纪80年代后期,人们意识到该公约未能实现其目标。相反,随着更多国家的接受,它正逐渐失去可信度。其主要原因似乎是它的标准普遍缺乏准确性——对标准的解释只要令"主管机关满意"即可。这导致对标准的解释有较大的差异,而且各缔约国不能有效地执行公约的要求。STCW证书不再作为证明适任的依据。

Other factors had reduced the effectiveness of the 1978 Convention such as the reliance placed on seafaring skills and competence being acquired through service on board ship or in machine shops. The Convention had prescribed minimum periods of seagoing or other appropriate service and specified knowledge requirements without defining the skills and competence required. Crew reductions, faster turn-rounds, more frequent crew changes and the mix of differing education and training backgrounds resulting from multinational manning, undermined the effectiveness of this on-board training.

Since the development of the Convention in the seventies, many changes had taken place in the structure of the world merchant fleet and in the management and manning of ships. Emerging economies had acquired greater maritime expertise and expanded their fleets. The fleets of traditional maritime countries had declined and the major sources of supply of seafarers had also shifted.

In response to these changes IMO technical co-operation projects had strengthened the maritime administrations and maritime education and training capabilities of developing countries, by improving their facilities and equipment and enhancing their expertise by training their administrators and educators at the World Maritime University in Malmö, Sweden.

The traditional organization of duties and responsibilities on board ship was also changing. Some felt that management response to emerging safety, efficiency and career development needs and expectations had become hampered by the traditional departmental structure upon which the 1978 Convention had been exclusively based. Within the industry, the need for greater flexibility in the training and certification of seafarers became a significant force in the demand for change.

The loss of credibility of the Convention and political and public concern regarding human related causes of shipping disasters, generated growing criticism not only of the Convention itself but also of IMO, which some claimed to be ineffective and unresponsive to the safety needs of the traveling public and the protection of the marine environment from accidental pollution.

A limited review of Convention provisions was already in hand, when the Maritime Safety Committee decided, in May 1993, to give high priority to its comprehensive review. On the suggestion of Mr. William A. O'Neil, the Secretary-General of IMO, the comprehensive review was accelerated by having consultants prepare a revised text under the direction of the Sub-Committee on Standards of Training and Watchkeeping (STW). The original date for completing the revision at sub-committee level was 1996, meaning that the revision conference would probably not have been held until 1998. Under the accelerated programme the conference was brought forward to June-July 1995.

The use of consultants and four sessions of an Inter-Sessional Working Group of the STW Sub-Committee allowed basic texts to be approved by IMO and circulated for the 1995 Diplomatic Conference within a two year period. Although the group of consultants was kept small to allow speedy completion of its work, all regions were represented in its membership. All consultants acted as independent experts and were sponsored by Germany, The Netherlands, Mexico, Korea, Spain, the United Kingdom and the United States.

其他因素,例如通过船上或机器车间服务获得的航海技能和适任能力的可信度不足,也降低了1978年公约的有效性。公约规定了最短的海上资历或其他合适的资历和具体的知识要求,却没有规定要求的技能和适任能力。船舶配员的减少、更快速的周转、更频繁的船员轮换以及来自不同教育和培训背景的多国籍船员混配等因素削弱了船上培训的有效性。

自20世纪70年代该公约制定以来,世界商船的结构、船舶管理及船舶配员等方面已经发生很多的变化。新兴经济体已经获得了更广泛的航海技能并扩大了它们的船队。传统海运国家的船队已减少,海员的主要来源地也已随之转移。

为适应这些变化,IMO技术合作项目加强了针对发展中国家的海事管理、海事教育和能力培训。这些合作项目包括:改善发展中国家的设施和设备;在瑞典马尔默市的世界海事大学,通过培训发展中国家的海事管理人员和教育工作者提高他们的专门知识。

船上传统的职能结构也在不断变化。有些人觉得,完全根据1978年公约设置的传统的部门结构已限制了应对新出现的安全、效率和职业发展需要及期望所需要的相应管理。在本行业内,在海员培训和发证方面较大灵活性需求成为要求变革的重要力量。

公约可信度降低以及政府和公众对海运灾难中人为原因的担忧使人们不仅对公约本身而且也对IMO产生越来越多的批评。有些人声称公约对大众旅游的安全需求和对保护海上环境免遭事故污染没有效率和不适应。

1993年5月,海上安全委员会决定对公约的全面审查给予高度优先考虑时,对公约中各项规定的有限审查实际已在进行中。在IMO秘书长William A. O'Neil先生的建议下,在培训和值班标准(STW)分委会的指导下,由IMO的顾问人员起草修订文本。分委会层次完成修订工作的原定日期是1996年,意味着修订大会可能要到1998年才能召开。通过加速计划,大会提前到1995年6至7月召开。

由于使用了顾问人员并召开了四次STW分委会会议间工作小组会议,使基本文本能够在短短两年的时间内获得IMO批准并在1995年外交大会上分发。尽管为了能够快速完成工作而保持小规模的顾问组,但世界各地区均有成员参加。所有顾问都作为独立专家行使职责,并受到德国、荷兰、墨西哥、韩国、西班牙、英国和美国的资助。

Organizations in consultative status, including the International Shipping Federation and the International Confederation of Free Trade Unions also contributed to the work as did the Arab Maritime Transport Academy, Dalian Maritime University, the National Maritime Academy of Singapore, Singapore Polytechnic and the World Maritime University. The ease of acceptance of the basic text by the Conference in June/July 1995 reflected the quality of the preparatory work.

The main aims of the revision were:

.1 to transfer all detailed technical requirements to an associated Code;
.2 to clarify the skills and competence required;
.3 to require Administrations to maintain direct control over and endorse the qualifications of those masters, officers and radio personnel they authorize to serve on their ships;
.4 to make Parties to the Convention accountable to each other, through IMO, for their proper implementation of the Convention and the quality of their training and certification activities; and
.5 to have the amendments enter into force for all Parties to the Convention with the least possible delay.

The 1995 amendments

For procedural reasons, it was decided not to amend the articles of the Convention. This can only be done by the "positive acceptance" procedure, meaning that any amendments adopted would require the acceptance of two-thirds of Parties before entering into force, a process which would have taken many years. By concentrating simply on the technical annex, it was possible to make use of the Convention's "tacit acceptance" provisions, under which amendments adopted by the Conference can enter into force within a minimum of one year (and a maximum of two years) unless they are rejected in the meantime by sufficient Parties.

The amendments entered into force under this procedure on 1 February 1997.

Until 1 February 2002, however, Parties may continue to issue, recognize and endorse certificates which applied before that date in respect of seafarers who began training or seagoing service before 1 August 1998.

STCW 95

• Competence
• Detailed and explicit
• Clearly defined responsibilities
• Extensive control regime

以顾问身份参与的机构组织,包括国际航运联盟和自由贸易联盟国际大会,它们与阿拉伯海运院校、大连海事大学、新加坡国立海事院校、新加坡理工大学和世界海事大学一样也对该项工作做出了贡献。基本文本在1995年6月/7月的大会上轻松获得通过,反映了筹备工作的质量。

修订的主要目标为:

.1 把所有详细的技术要求转化成相应规则;
.2 阐明所要求的技能和适任能力;
.3 要求主管机关对其批准在船上服务的船长、高级船员和无线电人员的资历保持直接的监督和签注;
.4 使缔约国通过IMO相互督促各自对公约的正确履行以及培训和发证活动的质量;及
.5 尽快在所有缔约国开始实行该修正案。

1995修正案

由于履约的程序原因,决定不修改公约的原条款。因为若修改条款,修正案只有通过"绝对的接受"程序才能生效。即,已通过的修正案需要三分之二的缔约国接受才能生效,这是一个需要很多年的过程。若仅集中于技术附则,则可以利用公约的"默认"规定。根据该规定,除非有足够多的缔约国同时抵制,则大会通过的修正案在最短一年(和最长两年)的时间内可以生效。

按"默认"程序,修正案于1997年2月1日已经生效。

然而,对于在1998年8月1日之前开始参加培训或海上服务的船员,在2002年2月1日以前申请证书,缔约国可继续签发、认可和签证。

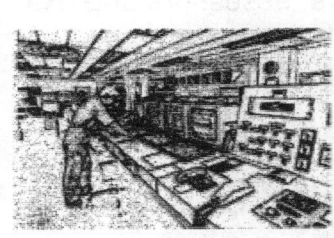

Overview of STCW 1995

The 1995 amendments cover three important areas:

■ *Responsibilities of shipping companies.* Shipping companies are responsible for ensuring that:
  — seafarers under their employment meet minimum international standards of competence;
  — their ships are manned according to the flag state requirements; and
  — detailed records of their seafarers are kept.

A shipping company is also required to ensure that a seafarer undergo familiarization on board when he is assigned a ship.

Further, port state control officers have greater authority in checking on the operational competence of seafarers.

■ *Uniform standards of competence.* Through the STCW Code, there is, for the first time, uniform standards of competence in various maritime functions. The phrase "to the satisfaction of the administration" frequently mentioned in the 1978 Convention has been replaced by more specific terms. Each element of competence contains specific criteria for standards of knowledge, understanding and proficiency, methods of demonstrating competence, and criteria for evaluating them.

■ *Implementation by governments.* Under the revised Convention, Parties to the Convention are required to submit to IMO evidence that they are implementing STCW requirements and that they are issuing certificates to seafarers if they meet the minimum competence standards.

In support of the above major areas, the revised Convention includes new provisions like qualifications of trainers, assessors and examiners and quality standards systems.

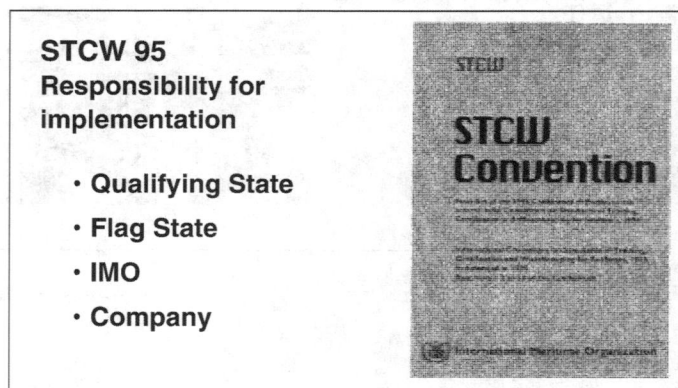

STCW 1995 概述

1995年修正案涉及三个重要领域：

- 航运公司的责任。航运公司负责确保：
  — 公司雇用的船员满足国际最低适任标准；
  — 公司的船舶按船旗国要求配员；及
  — 保存公司船员的详细记录。

  也要求航运公司确保在船员被派上船时，船员有熟悉船舶的过程。

  而且，港口国检查官有更大的权力检查船员操作方面的适任能力。

- 统一的适任标准。STCW规则使各种海上职能第一次有了统一的适任标准。1978年公约频繁提到的短语"令主管机关满意"已被更明确的用语所代替。每一项适任能力都包含知识、理解和熟练标准的明确判定依据、表明适任的方法和评价适任的标准。

- 政府的履约。经修订的公约要求缔约国向IMO提交证据，证明他们正在履行STCW的要求，并证明他们签发的证书满足最低的适任标准。

为了支持上述主要规定，经修订的公约制定了许多新规定，比如教员、评估员和主考官的资格以及质量标准体系。

Structure of the revised Convention

The revised Convention consists of:

- 17 Articles, these are the same as for the 1978 Convention.

- Regulations, divided into eight chapters. Chapters VII and VIII are new, the others have been substantially revised. These are:

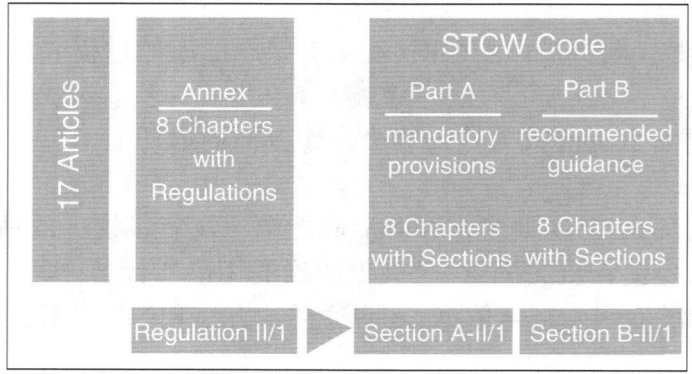

    — Chapter I: General Provisions
    — Chapter II: Master and Deck Department
    — Chapter III: Engine Department
    — Chapter IV: Radiocommunication and Radio Personnel
    — Chapter V: Special Training Requirements for Personnel on certain types of ships
    — Chapter VI: Emergency, Occupational Safety, Medical Care and Survival functions
    — Chapter VII: Alternative Certification
    — Chapter VIII: Watchkeeping

- STCW Code, also with eight chapters, each corresponding to the respective chapter in the Regulations.

  The STCW Code is divided into two sections:
  — Part A containing mandatory requirements; and
  — Part B containing recommendatory guidance.

- 14 Resolutions.

The articles

The articles (which, as was explained above, were unchanged by the 1995 amendments) contain the legal provisions of the Convention while the technical content is incorporated in the annex. The articles deal with entry into force provisions, amendment procedures, denunciation and various other matters.

经修订的公约的结构

经修订的公约由下面各项内容组成：

- 17条条款与1978年公约相同。

- 公约规则，分成8章。第Ⅶ章和第Ⅷ章是新的，其他各章也做了实质性的修订。各规则如下：

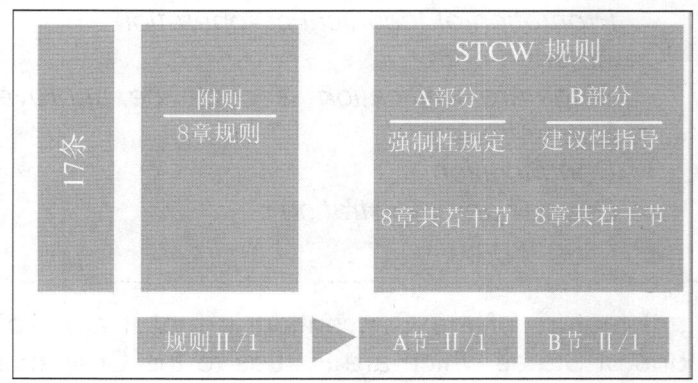

— 第Ⅰ章：总则
— 第Ⅱ章：船长和甲板部
— 第Ⅲ章：轮机部
— 第Ⅳ章：无线电通信和无线电人员
— 第Ⅴ章：特定类型船舶的船员特殊培训要求
— 第Ⅵ章：应急、职业安全、医护和救生职能
— 第Ⅶ章：可供选择的发证
— 第Ⅷ章：值班

- STCW规则，也有8章，每章与公约规则各章对应。

  STCW规则分为两部分：
  — A部分为强制性标准；及
  — B部分为建议性指导。

- 14个决议。

条款

条款（如上所述，1995年修正案没调整条款数量及编排）包含了公约的法律规定，而技术内容则编入附则。条款涉及生效的规定、修正的程序、退出和其他事宜。

Article I	*General obligations under the Convention*
Article II	*Definitions*
Article III	*Application*
Article IV	*Communication of information*
Article V	*Other treaties and interpretation*
Article VI	*Certificates*
Article VII	*Transitional provisions*
Article VIII	*Dispensation*
Article IX	*Equivalents*
Article X	*Control*
Article XI	*Promotion of technical co-operation*
Article XII	*Amendments*
Article XIII	*Signature, ratification, acceptance, approval and accession*
Article XIV	*Entry into force*
Article XV	*Denunciation*
Article XVI	*Deposit and registration*
Article XVII	*Languages*

One especially important feature of the Convention is that it applies to ships of non-party States when visiting ports of States which are Parties to the Convention. **Article X** requires Parties to apply the control measures to ships of all flags to the extent necessary to ensure that no more favourable treatment is given to ships entitled to fly the flag of a State which is not a Party than is given to ships entitled to fly the flag of a State that is a Party. The difficulties which could arise for ships of States which are not Parties to the Convention is one reason why the Convention has received such wide acceptance.

Certificates, each authorizing the holder to serve in a stated capacity, are the basic control provision of the Convention and **article VI** requires that they be issued only to those who meet the requirements of the Convention. Article X states that ships (with some exceptions, such as warships and fishing vessels) are subject, while in the ports of a Party, to control by officers duly authorized to verify that personnel on board hold the required certificates.

Deficiencies are required to be reported to the master and to the authorities of the flag State. If the deficiencies are such that they are judged to pose a "danger to persons, property or the environment, the Party carrying out the control shall take steps to ensure that the ship will not sail unless and until the Convention requirements are met to the extent that the danger has been removed."

Although one aim of the Convention is that in future all certificates shall ultimately be issued in accordance with its requirements, the need for transitional provisions is recognized in **article VII**. It states that certificates issued before entry into force of the Convention for a Party shall remain valid, no matter what the standards may have been. After the entry into force of the Convention for a Party, its Administration may continue to issue certificates of competence in accordance with its previous practices for a period not exceeding five years. This provision will enable the requirements of certificates to be updated in line with technical and other changes.

第1条	公约的一般义务
第2条	定义
第3条	适用范围
第4条	资料交流
第5条	其他条约与解释
第6条	证书
第7条	过渡规定
第8条	特免
第9条	等效
第10条	监督
第11条	促进技术合作
第12条	修正案
第13条	签字、批准、接受、核准和加入
第14条	生效
第15条	退出
第16条	保管和登记
第17条	语言

公约特别重要的一个特点是它适用于到访缔约国港口的非缔约国船舶。**第10条**要求缔约国对悬挂各国国旗的船舶采取一定程度的必要的检查措施,确保不给予有权悬挂非缔约国国旗的船舶比有权悬挂缔约国国旗的船舶以更为优惠的待遇。解决非缔约国船舶造成的管理困扰是该公约得到如此广泛接受的一个原因。

证书(授权证书持有者具有所列明的能力)是公约基本的监控规定。**第6条**要求证书仅发给满足公约要求的人员。而且,第10条规定,船舶(除了例外船舶,例如军舰和渔船)在缔约国港口时要接受经正式授权的官员检查,以核实船上人员是否持有所要求的证书。

要求把缺陷报告提供给船长和船旗国主管机关。如果断定存在对人员、财产和环境会产生危险的缺陷,实施检查的缔约国应采取措施确保该船不出航,直到该船消除了危险并满足了公约要求为止。

虽然公约的一个目标是最终都将按本公约的要求签发所有证书,但还是认识到在**第7条**中给出的过渡规定的需要。它规定某一缔约国在本公约生效之前不管按何标准签发的证书仍保持有效。本公约在某缔约国生效之后,其主管机关可继续在不超过5年的期间内,按其以前的做法签发适任证书。该规定将使发证要求能够随着技术和其他变化而得到更新。

Article VIII describes how, in circumstances of exceptional necessity, dispensations may be granted to enable seafarers to serve in capacities for which they do not hold appropriate certificates, but no such dispensation is permitted in the case of a radio officer or operator.

The Convention also incorporates in **article XII** a "tacit acceptance" procedure similar to that included in the 1974 SOLAS Convention. Under this procedure amendments to the STCW Convention or its annex may be adopted by IMO's Maritime Safety Committee, expanded to include all Contracting Parties, some of whom may not be members of the Organization. Amendments to the STCW annex will normally enter into force one and a half years after being communicated to all Parties unless, in the meantime, they are rejected by one-third of the Parties or by Parties whose combined fleets represent 50 per cent of world tonnage.

Article XI of the Convention deals with technical co-operation and it requires Parties to promote support for Parties which request technical assistance in such matters as training.

The regulations and the STCW Code

One of the major features of the revision is the adoption of a new STCW Code, to which many technical regulations have been transferred. Part A of the Code is mandatory while Part B is recommended. Dividing the regulations up in this way makes administration easier and it will also make the task of revising and updating them more simple: for procedural and legal reasons there is no need to call a full conference to make changes to Codes.

Chapter I (General Provisions)

Chapter I has been strengthened to better ensure proper implementation, monitoring and enforcement of the Convention.

Communication of information to IMO

Another important change means that for the first time IMO itself is given some authority over individual Parties. Under Chapter I, **regulation I/7** Parties will be required to provide detailed information to IMO concerning administrative measures taken to ensure compliance with the Convention, education and training courses, certification procedures and other factors relevant to implementation.

This information will be used by the Maritime Safety Committee (MSC), IMO's senior technical body, to identify Parties that are able to demonstrate that they can give full and complete effect to the Convention.

This regulation is regarded as particularly important because it means that Governments will have to establish that they have the administrative, training and certification resources necessary to implement the Convention. No such proof was required in the original Convention (or in any other IMO instrument), leading to complaints that standards differed widely from country to country and certificates could therefore not always be relied on.

第8条规定：在特殊需要的情况下，可签发特免证明，准许船员担任他们并未持有相应适任证书的职位；但对于无线电报务员或无线电话务员，不允许签发特免证明。

本公约也把"默认"程序编入**第12条**，它与1974年SOLAS公约包含的"默认"程序相类似。根据此程序，STCW公约的修正案或它的附则可由IMO海上安全委员会通过，进而扩大到所有缔约国（包括一些非IMO成员的缔约国）。一般地，除非有1/3的缔约国或其船队总和等于世界吨位的50%的缔约国同时抵制修正案，否则STCW附则的修正案将在修正案送达所有缔约国一年半之后生效。

公约的**第11条**涉及技术合作，它要求缔约国促进对那些诸如培训事务方面要求技术援助的缔约国的支持。

公约规则和STCW规则

修正案的主要特征之一是，在继承了许多原来的技术规则的基础上制定新的STCW规则。规则划分为A部分和B部分：A部分是强制性规定，而B部分是推荐性要求。这种方式的划分更便于管理，也将使得修订和更新工作更便利，即在程序和法律上可以不必召开全体大会就可对规则进行修改。

第Ⅰ章（总则）

第Ⅰ章着重更好地确保公约的正确履行、监督和实施。

与IMO的资料交换

另一个重要的变化是IMO自身第一次被授予一些管理各缔约国的权力。根据**公约规则I/7**，缔约国应向IMO提交详细资料。这些资料涉及为保证遵守公约而采取的管理措施、教育和培训课程、发证程序以及与实施公约有关的其他要素。

海上安全委员会（MSC）、IMO的高级技术机构将利用这些资料确定哪些能够证明能全面和有效地履行本公约的缔约国。

本条规则被认为具有特别重要的意义，因为它意味着各缔约国政府需要证实他们具备实施本公约所必需的行政、培训和发证资源。原公约（或IMO其他文件）没有要求提供这些证据，这导致各国之间执行标准有很大差别，因而发放的证书有时也不可信。

The regulation is backed up by section A-I/7 of the STCW Code which requires the information to be submitted to IMO by 1 August 1998 and says that it must include the following:

1. the name, postal address and telephone and facsimile numbers and organization chart of the ministry, department or governmental agency responsible for administering the Convention;

2. a concise explanation of the legal and administrative measures provided and taken to ensure compliance, particularly with regulations I/6 (training and assessment) and I/9 (medical standards and the issue and registration of certificates);

3. a clear statement of the education, training, examination, competency assessment and certification policies adopted;

4. a concise summary of the courses, training programmes, examinations and assessments provided for each certificate issued pursuant to the Convention;

5. a concise outline of the procedures followed to authorize, accredit or approve training and examinations, medical fitness and competency assessments, required by the Convention, the conditions attaching thereto, and a list of the authorizations, accreditations and approvals granted;

6. a concise summary of the procedures followed in granting any dispensation under article VIII of the Convention; and

7. the results of the comparison carried out pursuant to regulation I/11 and a concise outline of the refresher and upgrading training mandated.

Section A-I/7 also requires the Secretary-General to maintain a list of competent persons approved by the MSC who may be called upon to assist in the preparation of the report required by regulation I/7. Meetings of those on the list may be held at the discretion of the Secretary-General and their views shall be taken into account in the report submitted to the MSC.

Quality standards system

Regulation I/8 of the Convention requires a quality standards system to be used where training, assessment of competence, certification, endorsement and revalidation activities are carried out. Further provisions covering this point are contained in section A-I/8 of the Code.

Other important amendments to Chapter I (General Provisions) include the following:

STCW规则第A-Ⅰ/7节对本条公约规则做了进一步详述。它要求资料应不迟于1998年8月1日递交给IMO。而且这些资料需包括下列内容：

1. 负责主管该公约的部委、司局或政府机构的名称、通信地址、电话和传真号码以及组织结构图；

2. 为确保履行公约，特别是遵行公约规则Ⅰ/6（培训和评估）和Ⅰ/9（健康标准和证书签发及登记）而制定并采用的法律和行政措施的简要介绍；

3. 对所采取的教育、培训、考试、适任评估以及发证方针的明确说明；

4. 对按公约签发的每种证书规定的课程、培训计划、考试及评估安排的简明摘要信息；

5. 按公约要求所进行的培训和考试、健康检查、适任评估进行授权、认可或批准所遵行的程序和相应附加条件的简明概要，以及已获得授权、认可或批准的项目一览表；

6. 按公约第Ⅷ条要求发放特免证书的应遵行程序的简要说明；及

7. 对照公约规则Ⅰ/11所做的比较结果，以及强制性更新知识培训的概要说明。

第A-Ⅰ/7节也要求秘书长保存一份经MSC批准的顾问人员名单，这些人具备帮助起草公约规则Ⅰ/7要求提交的报告的资格。由秘书长决定召开顾问会议，在递交给MSC的报告中应考虑他们的观点。

质量标准体系

公约规则Ⅰ/8要求，在实施培训、适任评估、发证、签证和证书再有效工作时，要采纳质量标准体系。STCW规则第A-Ⅰ/8节涉及这方面的更多规定。

第Ⅰ章（总则）的其他重要修正包括：

- Enhanced procedures concerning the exercise of port State control under Article X of the Convention have been developed to allow the competence of seafarers in carrying out watchkeeping to be assessed and to permit intervention in the case of deficiencies deemed to pose a danger to persons, property or the environment (regulation I/4). This can take place if certificates are not in order or if the ship is involved in a collision or grounding, if there is an illegal discharge of substances (causing pollution) or if the ship is manoeuvred in an erratic or unsafe manner, etc.

- Parties are required to establish procedures for investigating acts by persons to whom they have issued certificates that endanger safety or the environment. Penalties and other disciplinary measures must be prescribed and enforced where the Convention is not complied with.

- Technical innovations, such as the use of simulators for training and assessment purposes have been recognized. Simulators will become mandatory for training in the use of radar and automatic radar plotting aids.

- Parties will be required to ensure that training, certification and other procedures are continuously monitored by means of a quality assurance system (regulation I/8).

- Every master, officer and radio operator shall be required at intervals not exceeding five years to meet the fitness standards and the levels of professional competence contained in Section A-I/11 of the STCW Code.

- In order to assess the need for revalidation of certificates after 1 February 2002, Parties must compare the standards of competence previously required with those specified in the appropriate certificate in part A of the STCW Code. If necessary, the holders of certificates may be required to undergo training of refresher courses (regulation I/11).

- Provisions covering the use of simulators, in particular radar and automatic radar plotting aids equipment, are contained in regulation I/12 (and section A-I/12 of the STCW Code).

The following table summarizes the major changes to Chapter I.

- 按公约第10条实施港口国检查的程序得到加强。该程序扩展到允许港口国检查官评估在值船员的适任能力;并且,如果认为存在的缺陷会危及人员、财产和环境(公约规则 I/4),如证书不齐备、船舶发生碰撞或搁浅、非法排放污染物质或船舶操纵方式不正确或不安全等,允许港口国检查官干预。

- 要求缔约国建立程序,以对持有该国签发证书的人员危及安全或环境的行为进行调查。对不遵守公约的行为,应当规定并实施罚款和其他惩戒措施。

- 认可诸如使用模拟器进行培训和评估等方面的技术革新。模拟器将强制用于雷达和自动雷达标绘仪使用技能训练。

- 要求缔约国借助质量保证体系(公约规则 I/8),保证连续地监控培训、发证和其他程序。

- 要求每位船长、高级船员和无线电操作员,应在所持证书有效的5年时限内,符合健康标准和满足STCW规则第A-I/11节规定的专业适任水平。

- 为了2002年2月1日后评估证书再有效的需要,缔约国必须把过去所要求的适任标准与STCW规则A部分所规定相应证书的适任标准做比较。如果必要,可要求证书持有人接受知识更新课程培训(公约规则 I/11)。

- 公约规则 I/12(和STCW规则第A-I/12节)包含了使用模拟器(特别是雷达和自动雷达标绘模拟设备)的规定。

下表概括了第 I 章的主要修订内容:

Regulation	Summary of main changes
I/1–Definitions and clarifications	Some definitions changed. New definitions and clarifications added.
I/2–Certificates and endorsements	The regulation requires that the certificates referred to be endorsed by the flag State. Endorsement format revised.
I/3–Principles governing near-coastal voyages	Reporting requirement included.
I/4–Control procedures	Safe Manning compliance and ability to maintain watchkeeping standards may be checked through port State control.
I/5–National provisions	Incompetency to be investigated. Penalties to be imposed for Convention infractions.
I/6–Training and assessment	The regulation requires that trainers and assessors be qualified, whether on board or ashore.
I/7–Communication of information	Parties report by 1 August 1998 on Convention implementation.
I/8–Quality standards	Quality standards apply to all training and certification activities. Independent evaluation required every five years.
I/9–Medical standards-Issue and registration of certificates	The regulation requires that Parties establish medical standards. Registers of certificates have to be maintained and accessible.
I/10–Recognition of certificates	The regulation requires the flag State to confirm that standards are met and to issue endorsement or own certificate.
I/11–Revalidation of certificates	Requirements harmonized. Parties compare old new standards. Need for refresher training to be determined.
I/12–Use of simulators	Standards regarding performance and use for mandatory training, assessment or demonstration of competence.
I/13–Conduct of trials	No change.
I/14–Responsibilities of companies	Crew certification, familiarization and ability to co-ordinate activities. Manning compliance.
I/15–Transitional provisions* * Regulation I/15 concerns existing certificate and endorsement provisions only. All other requirements apply from 1 Feb. 1997.	1 Feb. 1997—All requirements apply. 1 Feb. 1997—Tonnage limits may be replaced. 1 Aug. 1998—New entrants meet new standards. 1 Feb. 2002—All candidates meet new standards.

公约规则	主要修订概要
Ⅰ/1—定义和说明	修订了一些定义,增加新定义和说明。
Ⅰ/2—证书和签证	公约规则要求有关证书由船旗国签证。签证的格式做了修改。
Ⅰ/3—关于近岸航行的原则	包括了报告的要求。
Ⅰ/4—监督程序	可通过港口国监督检查船舶安全配员和船员保持值班标准的能力。
Ⅰ/5—国家规定	对不适任进行调查,对违反公约的进行惩罚。
Ⅰ/6—培训和评估	公约规则要求船上或岸上的培训员和评估员都应具有合格的资格。
Ⅰ/7—资料交流	缔约国不迟于1998年8月1日提交关于实施公约的报告。
Ⅰ/8—质量标准	质量标准应用于所有培训和发证事务。 要求每5年进行一次独立评审。
Ⅰ/9—健康标准证书的签发和登记	公约规则要求缔约国制定健康标准。 须保持证书登记并可接受随时查询。
Ⅰ/10—证书确认	公约规则要求船旗国确认证书满足标准,并签发背书或证书。
Ⅰ/11—证书再有效	协调规定的各项要求。各缔约国须比对新老标准,并确定是否需要知识更新培训。
Ⅰ/12—模拟器的使用	有关性能标准,在强制培训、评估或适任能力演示中的使用。
Ⅰ/13—试验的实施	没变化。
Ⅰ/14—公司的责任	船员证书、熟悉船舶岗位和事务的协调能力、遵守配员规定。
Ⅰ/15—过渡规定 *公约规则Ⅰ/15仅涉及现有的证书和签证规定。其他所有要求自1997年2月1日起适用。	1997年2月1日起——实施所有要求。 1997年2月1日起——吨位限制可变更。 1998年8月1日起——新进入者满足新标准。 2002年2月1日起——所有证书申请者满足新标准。

Tonnage

Tonnage is a parameter used in the shipping laws to regulate a vessel according to its size. The traditional system used for measuring a vessel to determine its tonnage (called the "*regulatory measurement system or Gross Register Tonnage* (GRT)") consists of the standard, dual, and simplified measurement systems. The regulatory measurement system (with the exception of the simplified system used primarily for smaller vessels) provides for a complex series of internal measurements and exemptions to arrive at gross tonnage. Over time, this system has become increasingly susceptible to manipulation because the system allows vessel designers to use features, such as excessive framing and tonnage openings, solely to reduce the gross tonnage of the vessel artificially. In this manner, increasingly larger vessels can be designed to fall within the tonnage bounds of their class.

In response to this development, the International Convention on the Tonnage Measurement of Ships, 1969 was initiated, which establishes a worldwide system of measurement that provides a genuine representation of a vessel's size. Under the *convention measurement system*, gross tonnage (GT) is based on a logarithmic function of the total enclosed volume of the vessel and is not subject to manipulation by the use of tonnage reduction techniques. Because convention measurement does not allow for artificial tonnage reduction techniques, vessels measured using this system often are greater in tonnage than vessels measured using regulatory measurement.

STCW regulation I/15, paragraph (3), explicitly allows an Administration to change 200 GRT (under the national tonnage system) to 500 GT (under the international tonnage system), and 1600 GRT to 3000 GT.

Regulation I/15 Transitional Provisions

3   Where a Party, pursuant to regulation I/11, reissues or extends the validity of certificates originally issued by that Party under the provisions of the Convention which applied immediately prior to 1 February 1997, the Party may, at its discretion, replace tonnage limitations appearing on the original certificates as follows:

   .1   "200 gross registered tons" may be replaced by "500 gross tonnage"; and

   .2   "1,600 gross registered tons" may be replaced by "3,000 gross tonnage".

Mariners holding licenses limited to 200 GRT would automatically be eligible for a license limited to 500 GT. Mariners holding licenses limited to 1,600 GRT would automatically be eligible for a license limited to 3,000 GT.

There is no change in the engine power limiting requirements for engineers' licenses. These remain at 750 kW and 3,000 kW.

吨位

吨位在海运法中是根据船舶尺度来管理船舶的一个参数。用以丈量船舶确定其吨位的传统方法〔称"规范的丈量方法或总登记吨位(GRT)"〕包括标准、复式和简化三种丈量方法。规范的丈量方法（主要用于较小船舶的简化丈量方法除外）应用一系列复杂的内部丈量和免除规则来获得总吨位。随着时间的推移，该方法日益易受操控。因为该方法允许船舶设计者仅仅为了减少船舶的总吨位而使用特殊的船舶结构特征，诸如过多的构架和吨位开口。用这种方式，越来越多较大的船舶能够通过设计使其仍处在较低的吨位范围之内。

为应对这种趋势，1969年国际船舶吨位丈量公约被制定。该公约规定了一套全球性的丈量方法，真实地表示船舶的大小。按照公约的丈量方法，总吨位(GT)是基于船舶总封闭容积的对数函数，不会受上述的吨位减少的技术手段影响。公约丈量是不认可人为减少吨位的技术手段。所以，用这种方法丈量的船舶吨位通常比用常规丈量方法丈量的结果要大。

STCW公约规则Ⅰ/15第3款明确规定：主管机关可将200总登记吨（按国内吨位丈量方法）改为500总吨（按国际吨位丈量方法），以及将1600总登记吨改为3000总吨。

公约规则Ⅰ/15过渡规定

3　　缔约国在按照公约规则Ⅰ/11节规定重新签发原先根据1997年2月1日以前适用的公约规定发放的证书或延长其有效期时，可自行更改出现在原证书上的吨位限制：

　　.1　　"200总登记吨"可改为"500总吨"；及

　　.2　　"1600总登记吨"可改为"3000总吨"。

持有限于200总登记吨的证书的船员自动取得限于500总吨的证书资格；持有限于1600总登记吨的证书的船员有资格自动取得限于3000总吨的证书资格。

轮机员证书的主机马力限制要求没变化，仍然是750千瓦和3000千瓦。

The remaining chapters are as follows:

Chapter II: Master and deck department

The watchkeeping provisions contained in chapter II of the 1978 STCW Convention have been transferred to a new chapter VIII and the revalidation requirements for masters and deck officers have been consolidated with those for engineer officers and radio operators in new regulation I/11. The revised arrangement of chapter II regulations and the main changes made are shown in the table below.

Regulation	Summary of main changes
II/1—Mandatory minimum requirements for certification of officers in charge of a navigational watch on ships of 500 gross tonnage or more	Approved education and training required in all cases. Not less than one year seagoing service documented in approved training record book or three years seagoing service. The candidate to hold appropriate radio certificate and meet competence standard in the STCW Code.
II/2—Mandatory minimum requirements for certification of masters and chief mates on ships of 500 gross tonnage or more	All reductions of sea service for special training eliminated. Minimum service for chief mate reduced to 12 months in charge of a navigational watch. The regulation requires that candidates meet competence standard in the STCW Code.
II/3—Mandatory minimum requirements for certification of officers in charge of a navigational watch and of masters on ships of less than 500 gross tonnage	Near-coastal ships—Officer in charge of watch: Approved education and training required. The regulation requires that candidates hold appropriate radio certificate and meet competence standard in the STCW Code. Master: Approved education and training required. The regulation requires that candidates meet competence standard in the STCW Code.
II/4—Mandatory minimum requirements for certification of ratings forming part of a navigational watch	The regulation requires that candidates be duly certificated and meet competence standard in the STCW Code.

Chapter III: Engine department

The watchkeeping provisions previously contained in chapter III have been transferred to a new chapter VIII and the revalidation requirements for engineer officers have been consolidated with those for masters and deck officers and radio operators in new regulation I/11. The revised arrangement of chapter III regulations and the main changes made are shown in the table below.

第1章 经修订的STCW公约介绍

余下各章介绍如下：

第Ⅱ章：船长和甲板部

1978年STCW公约第Ⅱ章包含的值班规定已调整到新增加的第Ⅷ章，在新规则Ⅰ/11中已将船长和驾驶员的证书再有效要求与轮机员和无线电操作员的相应要求合并。修正后第Ⅱ章公约规则的安排和所做的主要修订如下表所示：

公约规则	主要修订概要
Ⅱ/1——对在500总吨及以上船舶上负责航行值班的高级船员发证的强制性最低要求	在任何情况下都要求经过认可的教育和培训。在认可的培训记录簿中载明的海上资历不少于1年，或3年的海上资历。申请人持有适当的无线电证书并且满足STCW规则的适任标准。
Ⅱ/2——对500总吨或以上船舶的船长和大副发证的强制性最低要求	取消所有因特殊培训而减少的海上资历。申请大副证书的最低海上资历减少到12个月的航行值班。公约规则要求申请人满足STCW规则的适任标准。
Ⅱ/3——对在小于500总吨的船舶上负责航行值班的高级船员发证的强制性最低要求	近岸船舶——负责值班的高级船员：需要经过认可的教育和培训；公约规则要求申请人持有适当的无线电证书并且满足STCW规则的适任标准。 船长：需要经过认可的教育和培训；公约规则要求申请人满足STCW规则的适任标准。
Ⅱ/4——对组成航行值班部分的普通船员发证的强制性最低要求	规则要求给申请人签发合适的证书并要求其满足STCW规则的适任标准。

第Ⅲ章：轮机部

以前第Ⅲ章包含的值班规定已调整到新增加的第Ⅷ章，在新公约规则Ⅰ/11中对轮机长和轮机员的证书再有效要求已与船长、驾驶员和无线电操作员的相应要求相合并。修正后第Ⅲ章公约规则的安排和所做的主要修订如下表所示：

Regulation	Summary of main changes
III/1—Mandatory minimum requirements for certification of officers in charge of an engineering watch in a manned engine-room or designated duty engineers in a periodically unmanned engine-room	Six months minimum of seagoing service. Thirty months approved education and training which includes on-board training documented in approved training record book as well as training in workshop skills. The regulation requires that candidates meet competence standard in the STCW Code.
III/2—Mandatory minimum requirements for certification of chief engineer officers and second engineer officers on ships powered by main propulsion machinery of 3,000 kW propulsion power or more	The regulation requires that candidates have completed approved education and training and meet competence standard in the STCW Code.
III/3—Mandatory minimum requirements for certification of chief engineer officers and second engineer officers on ships powered by main propulsion machinery of between 750 kW and 3,000 kW propulsion power	The regulation requires candidates to have completed approved education and training and meet competence standard in the STCW Code.
III/4—Mandatory minimum requirements for certification of ratings forming part of a watch in a manned engine-room or designated to perform duties in a periodically unmanned engine-room	The regulation requires that candidates be duly certificated. Shore experience plus seagoing service option eliminated. Two months seagoing service now required with special training option as an alternative to seagoing service of six months duration. Candidates to meet competence standard in the STCW Code.

Chapter IV: Radiocommunication and radio personnel

The revalidation requirements for GMDSS radio personnel have been consolidated with those for masters and deck officers and engineer officers in new regulation I/11. The revised arrangement of chapter IV regulations and the main changes made are shown in the table below.

Regulation	Summary of main changes
IV/1—Application	Certification of radio personnel on ships not subject to SOLAS chapter IV now included.
IV/2—Mandatory minimum requirements for certification of GMDSS radio personnel	The regulation requires candidates to have completed approved education and training and to meet competence standard in the STCW Code.

Chapter V: Special training requirements for personnel on certain types of ships

Special requirements have been introduced concerning the training and qualifications of personnel on board ro-ro passenger ships. Previously the only special requirements in the Convention concerned crews on tankers. This change was made in response to proposals made by the Panel of Experts set up to look into ro-ro safety following the capsize and sinking of the ferry Estonia in September 1994. Crews on ro-ro ferries will have to receive additional training in technical aspects and also in crowd and crisis management and human behaviour. The revised arrangement of chapter V regulations and the main changes made are shown in the table below.

公约规则	主要修订概要
Ⅲ/1—对在有人值班机舱负责轮机值班的高级船员或在周期无人值班机舱指定值班的轮机员发证的强制性最低要求	6个月的最低海上资历。 30个月经认可的教育和培训,其中包括在认可的培训记录簿上载明的船上培训和车间技能培训。公约规则要求申请人满足STCW规则的适任标准。
Ⅲ/2—对主推进动力装置为3000千瓦或以上船舶的轮机长和大管轮发证的强制性最低要求	公约规则要求申请人完成认可的教育和培训,并满足STCW规则的适任标准。
Ⅲ/3—对主推进动力装置为750至3000千瓦船舶的轮机长和大管轮发证的强制性最低要求	公约规则要求申请人完成认可的教育和培训,并满足STCW规则的适任标准。
Ⅲ/4—对在有人值班机舱参与值班的或指定在周期无人值班机舱履行值班职责的普通船员发证的强制性最低要求	公约规则要求对申请人签发合适的证书。取消可选择岸上经验加海上资历的规定。 现在需要由两个月的海上资历加上选择的专门培训替代6个月的海上服务期限。申请人须满足STCW规则的适任标准。

第Ⅳ章:无线电通信和无线电人员

在新公约规则Ⅰ/11中,GMDSS无线电人员的再有效要求已与船长、甲板部高级船员和轮机部高级船员的再有效要求相合并。修正后第Ⅳ章公约规则的安排和所做的主要修订如下表所示:

公约规则	主要修订概要
Ⅳ/1—适用范围	现规则包括了不受SOLAS公约第Ⅳ章限制的船舶上无线电人员发证的规定。
Ⅳ/2—对GMDSS无线电人员发证的强制性最低要求	公约规则要求申请人完成认可的教育和培训,并满足STCW规则的适任标准。

第Ⅴ章:特定类型船舶的船员特殊培训要求

提出了有关滚装客船人员培训和资格的特殊要求。修订前的公约仅有的特殊培训要求是针对液货船船员的。1994年9月渡船Estonia倾覆并沉没,IMO对事故成立了专家组以调查滚装船的安全。这一变化就是根据他们的建议而做出的。公约要求不仅在技术方面,而且在密集人群管理、危机管理和人的行为方面,滚装渡船的船员应接受补充培训。修正后第Ⅴ章公约规则的安排和所做的主要修订如下表所示:

Regulation	Summary of main changes
V/1–Mandatory minimum requirements for the training and qualification of masters, officers and ratings on tankers	An appropriate certificate or endorsement of an existing certificate is now required.
V/2–Mandatory minimum requirements for the training and qualifications of masters, officers, ratings and other personnel on ro-ro passenger ships	Additional familiarization and training required, in accordance with capacity, duties and responsibilities, in: .1 crowd management, .2 extra safety training, .3 passenger safety, cargo safety and hull integrity, .4 crisis management. (Certain refresher training is also required)

Chapter VI: Emergency, occupational safety, medical care and survival functions

New provisions have been added regarding familiarization and basic safety training and instruction, training in fast rescue boats, training in advanced fire fighting, training in medical first aid and training in medical care on board ship. The revised arrangement of chapter VI regulations and the main changes made are shown in the table below.

Regulation	Summary of main changes
VI/1–Mandatory minimum requirements for familiarization, basic safety training and instruction for all seafarers	Familiarization training for all except passengers. The regulation requires that those with safety or pollution-prevention duties in the operation of the ship provide evidence that they met or retained the standard of competence in basic training within the previous five years.
VI/2–Mandatory minimum requirements for the issue of certificates of proficiency in survival craft, rescue boats and fast rescue boats	The regulation requires that candidates meet the standard of competence for issue of a certificate of proficiency. Separate standard of competence established for certificate of proficiency in fast rescue boats.
VI/3–Mandatory minimum requirements for training in advanced fire fighting	The regulation requires that candidates for certification provide evidence of having met the standard of competence within the previous five years.
VI/4–Mandatory minimum requirements relating to medical first aid and medical care	The regulation requires that candidates for certification provide evidence of having met the standard of competence. The regulation also requires that those designated to take charge of medical care provide documentary evidence of having met the standard of competence of the STCW Code.

公约规则	主要修订概要
Ⅴ/1—液货船船长、高级船员和普通船员培训和资格的强制性最低要求	现要求适当发证或对现有证书签证。
Ⅴ/2—滚装客船的船长、高级船员、普通船员和其他人员培训和资格的强制性最低要求	按照职位、职责和责任要求对下面各项进行补充熟悉和培训： .1　密集人群管理， .2　特别安全培训， .3　乘客安全、货物安全和船体完整， .4　危机管理（也要求一定的知识更新培训）。

第Ⅵ章：应急、职业安全、医护和救生职能

已经增加了关于熟悉、基本安全培训和训练、快速救助艇培训、高级消防培训、急救培训和船上医护培训的新规定。修正后第Ⅵ章规则的安排和所做的主要修订如下表所示：

公约规则	主要修订概要
Ⅵ/1—所有海员熟悉、基本安全培训和训练的强制性最低要求	除乘客外，所有人员应接受熟悉安全培训。公约规则要求，在船舶操作中负有安全或防止污染职责的人员，提供近5年内满足或保持基本培训适任标准的证据。
Ⅵ/2—签发救生筏、救助艇及快速救助艇熟练操作证书的强制性最低要求	公约规则要求申请人满足签发熟练操作证书的适任标准。为快速救助艇熟练操作证书建立独立的适任标准。
Ⅵ/3—高级消防培训的强制性最低要求	公约规则要求证书申请人提供近5年内已满足适任标准的证据。
Ⅵ/4—急救和医护的强制性最低要求	公约规则要求证书申请人提供已满足适任标准的证据。公约规则也要求被指定负责医护的人员提供已满足STCW规则适任的书面证据。

Chapter VII: Alternative certification

Regulations regarding alternative certification (also known as the functional approach) have been included in a new Chapter VII. This involves enabling crews to gain training and certification in various departments of seafaring rather than being confined to one branch (such as deck or engine room) for their entire career. Although it is a relatively new concept, the Conference was anxious not to prevent its development. At the same time, the new chapter is intended to ensure that safety and the environment are not threatened in any way. The use of equivalent educational and training arrangements is permitted under article IX.

This new chapter will allow those Parties wishing to do so to issue appropriate certificates to those candidates who have met all requirements for certification as officer in charge of a navigational watch or as officer in charge of an engineering watch and, in addition, have been found duly qualified in a function or functions of another discipline. The functions are identified in the competence tables of chapters II, III and IV of the STCW Code.

In the same way, Parties wishing to do so may issue appropriate certificates to those candidates who have met all requirements for certification as master or as chief engineer officer and in addition have been found duly qualified in a function or functions of the other discipline.

Summaries of the main changes introduced by the new chapter VII regulations are shown in the table below.

Regulation	Summary of main changes
VII/1–Issue of alternative certificates	Party to first inform IMO of relevant provisions. Same education, training and competence required as under chapters II, III and IV. Equivalent seagoing service as per STCW Code. Radio certificate for navigational watchkeeping. Meets regulation I/9 and chapter VII of the STCW Code.
VII/2–Certification of seafarers	The regulation requires that seafarers hold an appropriate certificate to perform all functions at the operational level or above referred to in either chapters II or III.
VII/3–Principles governing the issue of alternative certificates	Equivalent level of safety and pollution prevention is required. The regulation requires that chapter II, III, IV and VII certificates or endorsements be "interchangeable" and the competency of officers not be reduced. Alternative certification not to be used in itself to reduce size of crew, to de-skill individual crew members or to justify the assignment of combined deck and engineering duties during any particular watch.

第Ⅶ章:可选择的发证

关于可选择发证的公约规则(也称作按功能发证方法)已包括在新增加的第Ⅶ章中。依照该方法,同一个船员将可以获得船上不同部门的培训和证书,在不同部门(比如甲板部或轮机部)工作将不再受限制。功能发证方法虽然是一个相对新的概念,但大会不想阻碍其发展。同时,新的第Ⅶ章意图确保安全和环境在任何情况下不受威胁。根据第Ⅸ章,允许使用对应的教育和培训安排。

对于已满足负责航行值班或轮机值班的高级船员证书的所有要求并且对另一个部门的一项或多项职能具有适当的资格的申请人,新增加的第Ⅶ章允许愿意采用功能发证方法的缔约国给这些申请人签发合适的证书。这些功能根据STCW规则第Ⅱ、Ⅲ和Ⅳ章的适任表确定。

同样地,对于已满足船长或轮机长证书的所有要求并且对另一个部门的一项或多项职能具有适当资格的申请人,愿意采用功能发证方法的缔约国也可给这些申请人签发合适的证书。

新第Ⅶ章公约规则所做的主要修订由下表概括表示:

公约规则	主要修订概要
Ⅶ/1—可供选择的证书的签发	缔约国须首先将有关规定通知IMO。与第Ⅱ章、第Ⅲ章和第Ⅳ章要求相同的教育、培训和适任要求。与STCW规则要求相当的海上资历。 航行值班无线电证书。 满足公约规则Ⅰ/9和STCW规则中的第Ⅶ章的规定。
Ⅶ/2—对海员的发证	公约规则要求海员持有一张适当证书,以履行第Ⅱ章或第Ⅲ章所涉及的操作级及以上的所有职能。
Ⅶ/3—签发可供选择的证书的原则	要求相当的安全和防污染水平。 公约规则要求按第Ⅱ章、第Ⅲ章、第Ⅳ章和第Ⅶ章签发或签证的证书具有互换性,并且不降低高级船员的适任能力。 可供选择证书本身并非用于:减少船员的数量、降低船员的技能,或用以证明在任何特定的值班时段同一船员同时兼管甲板和轮机职能是合适的。

Chapter VIII: Watchkeeping

All watchkeeping provisions previously contained in chapters II and III and the basic guidelines and operational guidance relating to safety radio watchkeeping adopted by the 1978 Conference have been incorporated into this new chapter. New provisions have been added regarding hours of rest for watchkeeping personnel. Part B of the STCW Code also contains recommendations on drug and alcohol abuse. Administrations are required to establish and enforce rest periods for watchkeeping personnel and to ensure that watch systems are so arranged that the efficiency of watchkeeping personnel is not impaired by fatigue. The arrangement of chapter VIII regulations and the main changes they introduce are shown in the table below.

Regulation	Summary of main changes
VIII/1–Fitness for duty	Hours of rest.
VIII/2–Watchkeeping arrangements and principles to be observed	Voyage planning.
	Watchkeeping at sea. Watchkeeping in port.

The STCW Code

The regulations contained in the Convention are supported by sections in the STCW Code. Generally speaking, the Convention contains basic requirements which are then enlarged upon and explained in the Code.

Part A of the Code is mandatory. The minimum standards of competence required for seagoing personnel are given in detail in a series of tables. Chapter II of the Code, for example, deals with standards regarding the master and deck department. An extract is given below.

Specification of minimum standards of competence for masters and chief mates of ships of 500 tons gross tonnage or more

Competence	Knowledge, understanding and proficiency	Methods for demonstrating competence	Criteria for evaluating competence
Establish watchkeeping arrangements and procedures	Thorough knowledge of content, application and intent of the International Regulations for Preventing Collisions at Sea. Through knowledge of the content, application and intent of the Principles to be Observed in Keeping a Navigational Watch. Effective bridge teamwork procedures.	Examination and assessment of evidence obtained from one or more of the following: .1 Approved in-service experience .2 Approved simulator training, where appropriate.	Watchkeeping arrangements and procedures are established and maintained in compliance with international regulations and guidelines so as to ensure the safety of navigation, protection of the marine environment and the safety of the ship and persons on board.

第Ⅷ章：值班

新增加的第Ⅷ章合并了第Ⅱ章和第Ⅲ章包含的所有值班规定和1978年大会采纳的有关无线电安全值班的基本原则及操作指导,并增加了有关值班人员休息时间的新规定。STCW规则B部分也包含针对吸毒和酗酒的建议。主管机关被要求规定和实施值班人员休息时间,并确保值班制度的安排能使值班人员的效率不致因疲劳而削弱。第Ⅷ章公约规则的安排和所做的主要修订如下表所示：

公约规则	主要修订概要
Ⅷ/1—适于值班	休息时间
Ⅷ/2—值班安排和应遵守的原则	航次计划
	海上值班。港口值班

STCW规则

公约包含的各项规则由STCW规则各节表述。一般来说,公约仅包含基本的要求,这些要求在规则中进行详细说明和解释。

规则A部分是强制性的。对海上人员要求的最低适任标准列明在一系列适任表中。例如,规则第Ⅱ章涉及关于船长和甲板部的标准,摘录如下。

500总吨及以上船舶的船长和大副的最低适任标准

适任	知识、理解和熟练	表明适任的方法	适任的标准
确立值班安排和程序	关于《国际海上避碰规则》的内容、适用范围和目的的全面知识。 航行值班中应遵守的基本原则的内容、适用范围和目的的全面知识。 有效的驾驶协作程序。	从下列一项或多项中获得的考试和评估证明： .1 认可的工作经历 .2 如合适，认可的模拟器培训。	按照有关国际规则和指南,制定并保持值班安排和程序,从而保证航行安全、保护海洋环境以及船舶和船上人员的安全。

Tables of competences are covered in detail in Part 9.

Part B of the Code contains recommended guidance which is intended to help Parties implement the Convention. The measures suggested are not mandatory and the examples given are only intended to illustrate how certain Convention requirements may be complied with. However, the recommendations in general represent an approach that has been harmonized by discussions within IMO and consultation with other international organizations.

The following table shows the relationship between the Regulations and the Code.

Regulation	Code Part A	Code Part B
Regulation I/4 *Control procedures*	Section A-I/4 *Control procedures*	Section B-I/4 *Guidance regarding control procedures*
1 Control exercised by a duly authorized control officer under article X shall be limited to the following: .1 verification in accordance with article X(1) that all seafarers serving on board who are required to be certificated in accordance with the Convention hold an appropriate certificate or a valid dispensation, or provide documentary proof that an application for an endorsement has been submitted to the Administration in accordance with regulation I/10, paragraph 5; .2 verification that the numbers and certificates of the seafarers serving on board are in conformity with the applicable safe manning requirements of the Administration; and .3 assessment, in accordance with section A-I/4 of the STCW Code, of the ability of the seafarers of the ship to maintain watchkeeping standards as required by the Convention if there are clear grounds for believing that such standards are not being maintained because of any of the following have occurred:	1 The assessment procedure provided for in regulation I/4, paragraph 1.3, resulting from any of the occurrences mentioned therein shall take the form of a verification that members of the crew who are required to be competent do in fact possess the necessary skills related to the occurrence. 2 It shall be borne in mind when making this assessment that on-board procedures are relevant to the International Safety Management (ISM) Code and that the provisions of this Convention are confined to the competence to safely execute those procedures.	*Introduction* 1 The purpose of the control procedures of regulation I/4 is to enable officers duly authorized by port States to ensure that the seafarers on board have sufficient competence to ensure safe and pollution-free operation of the ship. 2 This provision is no different in principle from the need to make checks on ships' structures and equipment. Indeed, it builds on these inspections to make an appraisal of the total system of on-board safety and pollution prevention.

涉及详细的适任能力的各个表格包含在第9部分。

规则B部分包含建议性指导以有助于各缔约国实施本公约。所建议的措施不是强制性的，所给出的例子仅为了说明如何遵守本公约的某些要求。然而，通过IMO内部讨论和与其他国际组织的磋商，这些建议在总体上体现协调的结果。

下表说明公约规则和STCW规则规定之间的关系。

公约规则	STCW规则A部分	STCW规则B部分
公约规则Ⅰ/4 监督程序	第A-Ⅰ/4节 监督程序	第B-Ⅰ/4节 关于监督程序的指南
1 经正式授权的监督官员按第X条规定所行使的监督应仅限于下列各项： .1 按照X(1)款查核根据本公约要求应持证的所有船上工作的海员所持有的适任证书或有效特许证书，或依照公约规则Ⅰ/10第5段要求提交给主管机关申请签证而提供的证明文件； .2 核实在船上服务的海员的人数和证书是否符合主管机关的适当的安全配员要求；及 .3 如果因为发生了下列任一情况而有明显理由表明未能保持值班标准时，则根据STCW规则第A-Ⅰ/4节，对船上海员保持公约的值班标准的能力进行评估：	1 公约规则Ⅰ/4第1.3段规定的评估作业，在遇到本段中所提到的任何事件时，应核查要求应适任的船员实际上是否确实具有与该事件有关的必要技能。 2 当进行此种评估时应切记，船上的评估程序与国际安全管理(ISM)规则有关，而本公约的规定应限于安全实施那些程序的适任能力。	介绍 1 公约规则Ⅰ/4监督程序的目的是使港口国正式授权的官员能够确保船上的海员充分适任，以保证安全和船舶操作无污染。 2 此项规定与对船舶结构和设备所要求的检查在原则上并无差别。实际上，通过这些检查可以对船上安全和防止污染的整个体系进行评估。

Regulation	Code Part A	Code Part B
Regulation I/4 *Control procedures*	Section A-I/4 *Control procedures*	Section B-I/4 *Guidance regarding control procedures*
.3.1 the ship has been involved in a collision, grounding or stranding, or .3.2 there has been a discharge of substances from the ship when underway, at anchor or at berth which is illegal under any international convention, or .3.3 the ship has been manoeuvred in an erratic or unsafe manner whereby routeing measures adopted by the Organization or safe navigation practices and procedures have not been followed, or .3.4 the ship is otherwise being operated in such a manner as to pose a danger to persons, property or the environment. 2 Deficiencies which may be deemed to pose a danger to persons, property or the environment include the following: .1 failure of seafarers to hold a certificate, to have an appropriate certificate, to have a valid dispensation or to provide documentary proof that an application for an endorsement has been submitted to the Administration in accordance with regulation I/10, paragraph 5; .2 failure to comply with the applicable safe manning requirements of the Administration; .3 failure of navigational or engineering watch arrangements to conform to the requirements specified for the ship by the Administration; .4 absence in a watch of a person qualified to operate equipment essential to safe navigation, safety radiocommunications or the prevention of marine pollution; and	3 Control procedures under this Convention shall be confined to the standards of competence of the individual seafarers on board and their skills related to watchkeeping as defined in part A of this Code. On-board assessment of competency shall commence with verification of the certificates of the seafarers. 4 Notwithstanding verification of the certificate, the assessment under regulation I/4, paragraph 1.3 can require the seafarer to demonstrate the related competency at the place of duty. Such demonstration may include verification that operational requirements in respect of watchkeeping standards have been met and that there is a proper response to emergency situations within the seafarer's level of competence. 5 In the assessment, only the methods for demonstrating competence together with the criteria for its evaluation and the scope of the standards given in part A of this Code shall be used.	*Assessment* 3 By restricting assessment as indicated in section A-I/4, the subjectivity which is an unavoidable element in all control procedures is reduced to a minimum, no more than would be evident in other types of control inspection. 4 The clear grounds given in regulation I/4, paragraph 1.3 will usually be sufficient to direct the inspector's attention to specific areas of competency, which could then be followed up by seeking evidence of training in the skills in question. If this evidence is inadequate or unconvincing, the authorized officer may ask to observe a demonstration of the relevant skill. 5 It will be a matter for the professional judgement of the inspector when on board, either following an incident as outlined in regulation I/4 or for the purposes of a routine inspection, whether the ship is operated in a manner likely to pose a danger to persons, property or the environment.

公约规则		STCW 规则 A 部分		STCW 规则 B 部分	
公约规则 Ⅰ/4 监督程序		第 A-Ⅰ/4 节 监督程序		第 B-Ⅰ/4 节 关于监督程序的指南	
.3.1	船舶发生碰撞、搁浅或触礁,或	3	本公约的监督程序应限于在船上的海员个人的适任标准,以及本规则 A 部分规定的与海员值班有关的技能。船上对适任能力进行的评估应以核实海员的证书开始。		评估
.3.2	船舶在航、锚泊或靠泊时,违反任一国际公约而非法排放物质,或			3	通过第 A-Ⅰ/4 节所述的有限制的评估,各种监督程序中不可避免的主观性可减少到最低限度,不致大于其他种类的监督检查中的主观性。
.3.3	以不稳定或不安全方式操纵船舶,从而未遵循本组织采纳的定线措施或安全航行方法和程序,或	4	尽管核实了证书,在按公约规则 Ⅰ/4 第 1.3 段进行评估时,可以要求海员演示与其岗位有关的适任能力。这种能力的演示可包括核查是否符合值班标准方面的操作要求,以及该海员对紧急情况是否能做出与其适任级别相适应的适当反应。	4	公约规则 Ⅰ/4 第 1.3 段所述的明显理由通常足以引起检查官员对适任能力特定范围的注意,继而可查找有疑问的技能培训的证据。如果证据不足,或不可信,授权官员可以要求观看有关技能的演示。
.3.4	以其他危及人员、财产或环境的方式操作船舶。				
2	可被认为危及人员、财产或环境的缺陷包括下列各项:				
.1	要求持有证书的海员未持有合适的证书或有效的特免证明,或未能提供依照公约规则 Ⅰ/10 第 5 段要求提交给主管机关申请签证的证明文件;	5	在评估时,只应采用本规则 A 部分中的演示适任能力的方法以及适任评估标准的适用范围。	5	对于船舶是否以对人身、财产或环境构成危险的方式操作,不论是发生了公约规则 Ⅰ/4 所述的事件后,或是在日常的检查中,都是船上的检查官员做出专业判断的事情。
.2	未符合主管机关的适当安全配员要求;				
.3	不符合主管机关规定要求做出航行或轮机值班安排;				
.4	缺少合格人员值班以进行安全航行、安全无线电通信或防止海洋污染必要设备的操作;及				

Regulation	Code Part A	Code Part B
Regulation I/4 *Control procedures*	Section A-I/4 *Control procedures*	Section B-I/4 *Guidance regarding control procedures*
.5 inability to provide for the first watch at the commencement of a voyage and for subsequent relieving watches persons who are sufficiently rested and otherwise fit for duty. 3 Failure to correct any of the deficiencies referred to in paragraph 2, in so far as it has been determined by the Party carrying out the control that they pose a danger to persons, property or the environment, shall be the only grounds under article X on which a Party may detain a ship.		

The scope of control measures in regulation I/4 of the revised STCW Convention is much broader than that in the 1978 Convention. It allows Port State Control Officers (PSCOs) to verify that the numbers and certificates of seafarers serving on board are in conformity with the safe manning requirements of the Administration. The master, officers and radio operators will have to hold appropriate certificates.

In accordance with section A-I/4, any operation of a ship in a manner deemed to pose a danger to persons, property or the environment will provide clear grounds for assessing the ability of the seafarers of the ship to maintain the prescribed watchkeeping standards.

Section B-I/4 gives further guidance on the need to minimize subjectivity (inherent in all control measures), "clear grounds" and "professional judgement" in dealing with "whether the ship is operated in a manner likely to pose a danger to persons, property or the environment".

It can be seen that while the regulations outline general requirements and part A of the STCW Code contains mandatory elaboration, part B of the STCW Code provides additional guidance and advice.

The following table illustrates the relationship between the articles and the STCW Code.

Article	Code Part B
Article IX—Equivalents	Section B-IX Guidance regarding equivalents
(1) The Convention shall not prevent an Administration from retaining or adopting other educational and training arrangements. including those involving seagoing service and shipboard organization especially adapted to technical developments and to special types of ships and trades, provided that the level of seagoing service, knowledge and efficiency as regards navigational and technical handling of ship and cargo ensures a degree of safety at sea and has a preventive effect as regards pollution at least equivalent to the requirements of the Convention.	1 Naval certificates may continue to be accepted and certificates of service may continue to be issued to naval officers as equivalents under article IX, provided that the requirements of the Convention are met.

公约规则	STCW规则A部分	STCW规则B部分
公约规则Ⅰ/4 监督程序	第A-Ⅰ/4节 监督程序	第B-Ⅰ/4节 关于监督程序的指南
.5 未能提供为航次开始第一个班次和其后接班经过充分休息并适于值班职责的人员。		
3 未能纠正第2段所提及的任何缺陷,只要实施监督的缔约国确认这些缺陷危及人员、财产或环境,便构成缔约国按本公约第Ⅹ条滞留船舶的唯一理由。		

经修订的STCW公约规则Ⅰ/4监督措施的范围比1978年公约要广泛得多。它允许港口国检查官(PSCO)核查在船上工作的船员数量和证书是否符合主管机关的安全配员要求。船长、高级船员和无线电操作员须持有合适的证书。

根据第A-Ⅰ/4节,用对人员、财产或环境造成危险的方式操作船舶,将构成对船上海员是否具备保持规定的值班标准的能力进行评估的明显依据。

第B-Ⅰ/4节给出了最小化主观性(所有监督措施中固有的)的进一步指导,以便确定"船舶是否以可能对人员、财产或环境构成危险的方式操作"的"明显依据"和"专业判断"。

可以看到,公约规则概要说明一般的要求,而STCW规则A部分包含详尽的强制性要求,STCW规则B部分则提供补充的指导和建议。

下表说明公约条款和STCW规则之间的关系。

公约条款	STCW规则B部分
第Ⅸ条——等效	第B-Ⅸ节:关于等效的指导
(1) 本公约不应妨碍主管机关保留或采取其他教育和培训的安排,包括涉及专门适应技术发展和特种船舶及贸易的海上服务和船上组织的教育和培训的安排,但是,就船舶和货物在航海和技术操作方面的海上服务、知识与效率的水平,应保证海上安全的程度和防止污染的效果至少相当于本公约的要求。	1 假如满足公约要求,可继续承认海军船的证书,并且也可继续签发服务证书给符合公约第Ⅸ条等效条款要求的海军船高级船员。

Article	Code Part B
(2) Details of such arrangements shall be reported as early as practicable to the Secretary-General who shall circulate such particulars to all Parties.	

Resolutions

It is expected that the need to provide information to IMO and the powers given to the MSC to assess the actions of national Governments will greatly strengthen the effectiveness of the Convention. But it is also recognized that it will be difficult for some Governments to comply with the amendments without assistance.

One of the resolutions adopted by the Conference recognizes the importance of education, training and appropriate experience for all seafarers. It also recognizes that "in some cases, there may be limited facilities for obtaining the required experience and providing specialized training programmes, particularly in developing countries".

It says that "the promotion of technical co-operation at an inter-governmental level will assist those States not yet having adequate expertise or facilities for providing such training and experience to implement the revised STCW Convention requirements".

The resolution "strongly urges Parties to provide, or arrange to provide, in co-operation with IMO, assistance to those States which have difficulty in meeting the improved requirements of the STCW Convention and which request such assistance".

Another resolution recognizes the contribution made by the World Maritime University in raising standards and notes that it can help deal with the need for personnel in the international maritime field by "assuming a leading role for the transfer of maritime education and knowledge through its activities and the networking of advanced maritime training establishments".

In a further resolution, IMO itself is called upon to revise and update the model training courses that have been developed over the years to provide core curricula for use in maritime academies and similar institutions.

Other resolutions adopted by the Conference dealt with:

- training in crisis management and human behaviour for personnel on board ro-ro passenger ships and training of personnel on passenger ships

- monitoring the implications of alternative certification

- development of international standards of medical fitness for seafarers

- promotion of the participation of women in the maritime industry.

公约条款	STCW规则B部分
(2) 应尽早将这种安排的详情报告秘书长,秘书长则应将这种详情通报所有缔约国。	

决议

按公约规定,缔约国需要给IMO提供信息,而IMO授权MSC评估缔约国政府的行动措施。人们期望,这将大大增强公约的有效性。但是,人们也认识到,某些政府在没有外界帮助的情况下,将很难履行修正案。

大会通过的一个决议确认了教育、培训和适当的资历对全体海员的重要性。决议也承认"在某些情况下,尤其在发展中国家,可能存在限于设备而不能获得所要求的资历和不能提供专门的培训服务的情况"。

决议提到"促进政府间的技术合作,有助于那些不具备足够的专门知识或设备提供这类培训和经验的国家履行经修订的STCW公约的要求"。

决议"强烈呼吁各缔约国协作IMO,向有困难履行已修订的STCW公约要求的国家和这方面请求帮助的国家提供帮助"。

另一个决议对世界海事大学在提高标准方面所做的贡献表示赏识,并注意到世界海事大学"通过其活动及其先进的海事培训机构网络为传播海事教育和知识担当主要角色",因而可以帮助解决对国际海事领域专业人员的需求。

在其后的一个决议中,大会呼吁IMO自己来修订和更新已制定多年的示范培训课程,以便作为海事院校和类似机构的核心课程。

大会通过的其他决议涉及:

- 关于滚装客船上服务的人员在危机管理和人的行为方面的培训

- 监督选择发证的建议

- 制定海员健康国际标准

- 促进妇女参与海事行业活动。

Responsibility of companies

Reference is made in regulation I/14 to the International Safety Management (ISM) Code, which was adopted by IMO in 1993 and was made mandatory under the May 1994 amendments to the International Convention for the Safety of Life at Sea (SOLAS), 1974. The regulation details further company responsibilities for manning, certification etc. Part 5 deals with STCW requirements for companies, and compares the requirements of ISM Code and the revised STCW Convention.

International Convention on Standards of Training, Certification and Watchkeeping for Fishing Vessel Personnel (STCW-F)

While the amendments to the STCW Convention were being considered, a separate conference running concurrently adopted a new International Convention on Standards of Training, Certification and Watchkeeping for Fishing Vessel Personnel (STCW-F).

Because of the nature of the fishing industry it is extremely difficult to develop regulations for other sections of the shipping industry which can be applied without modification to fishing vessels as well. The Convention will apply to crews of seagoing fishing vessels, generally of 24 metres in length and above. The Conference was attended by delegates from 74 countries.

It was originally intended that requirements for crews on fishing vessels should be developed as a Protocol to the main STCW Convention, but after careful consideration it was agreed that it would be better to adopt a completely separate Convention. The Convention is the first attempt to make standards of safety for crews of fishing vessels mandatory.

The STCW-F Convention is comparatively short and consists of 16 Articles and several chapters contained in an annex. Chapter I contains General Provisions and Chapter II deals with Certification of Skippers, Officers, Engineer Officers and Radio Operators.

Previously efforts to improve the training, certification and watchkeeping standards of fishing vessels' personnel have been adopted as recommendations in Assembly resolutions and the Document for Guidance on Fishermen's Training and Certification produced jointly by IMO and the Food and Agriculture Organization (FAO) and the International Labour Organisation (ILO).

The Convention will enter into force 12 months after being accepted by 15 States.

公司的责任

公约规则Ⅰ/14参考了国际安全管理(ISM)规则。《国际安全管理规则》1993年被IMO采纳，并被编入1974年《国际海上人命安全公约》(SOLAS公约)1994年5月的修正案而成为强制性规定。公约规则Ⅰ/14进一步详述公司对配员、证书等方面的责任。第5部分涉及STCW对公司的要求，并对ISM规则和经修订的STCW公约的要求进行比较。

渔船人员培训、发证和值班标准国际公约(STCW-F)

STCW公约修正案在酝酿的同时，召开了独立大会并通过了一个新的渔船人员培训、发证和值班标准国际公约(STCW-F)。

由于渔业的性质，很难制定不需做修改也能适用于渔船的海运规则。本公约适用于海上渔船(一般指长24米及以上)的船员。大会由74个国家的代表参加。

最初的计划是，把对渔船船员的要求制定成STCW公约主体的附属议定书。但经仔细考虑后，认为制成一个完全独立的公约更为适宜。该公约首次做出了使渔船船员的安全标准成为强制性标准的尝试。

STCW-F公约相对较短小，由16条条款和一个包含数章内容的附则组成。第Ⅰ章为总则，第Ⅱ章涉及对船长、驾驶员、轮机员和无线电操作员的发证。

为提高渔船人员培训、发证和值班标准的努力成果已在较早前被采纳成为大会决议和由IMO、世界粮农组织(FAO)以及国际劳工组织(ILO)联合制定的渔民培训和发证指导文件。

本公约将在15个国家承认后的12个月内生效。

Part 2
Process Overview

Introduction

1. While a number of differing processes may be employed to satisfy the requirements of the revised STCW Convention, all must ensure that candidates for certificates of competency purporting to be issued under that Convention meet all requirements of international and national law. The requirements laid down specify minimum age, medical fitness, experience and training.

International law

2. Requirements of international law are contained in conventions and protocols; these may be bilateral in certain instances but in the main are multilateral treaties between States.

3. States become Parties to these conventions and protocols by ratifying them or by accepting them. In so doing they bind themselves to comply with all requirements of such conventions and to take all steps that may be necessary to give full effect to them.

National legislation

4. International law is given effect by the States concerned incorporating all necessary measures into their national law, rules, regulations, administrative orders and instructions.

5. It is therefore essential to a process of training, examination and certification that the national legislation provides all necessary authority to ensure that certificates are only issued to those who are properly qualified and further prohibits ships from sailing without a requisite complement of certificated personnel.

6. Examples of national laws which typically provide the necessary legal framework covering the documentation, training, examination and certification of merchant marine personnel may be consulted on application to any maritime administration.

Competency

7. The objective of requiring merchant marine personnel to hold appropriate certificates is to ensure that they are competent to safely carry out all tasks associated with the positions they fill on board ship.

8. Competency is defined as the ability to do a task adequately, and in the case of seafarers the range of tasks which may be involved is considerable.

第2章
进程概述

序言

1. 要满足经修订的STCW 95公约要求,可以使用很多不同的方法。但这些方法必须保证按公约申请适任证书的申请人满足国际法和国内法的所有要求。公约的要求详细规定了最小年龄、身体条件、资历和训练。

国际法

2. 公约和议定书包含了国际法的要求;这些要求在某些情况下可以是双边协议,但在多数情况下为多国之间的多边协议。

3. 各国通过批准或接受这些公约和议定书而成为缔约国。各缔约国保证遵守这些公约的所有要求,并采取所有必要的步骤进行贯彻执行。

国内立法

4. 有关国家通过国内立法,把所有必要的议案编入国内法律、法规、条例、行政命令和指令,从而使国际法生效。

5. 国内立法提供所有必要的权力,确保证书不授予不具备适当资格的人员。此外,国内立法应禁止没配齐必要持证人员的船舶开航。所以,国家必须立法规范培训、考试和发证程序。

6. 所提供的国内法的范例给出了有关船员的文件、培训、考试和发证所必需的典型法律框架。这些范例适合于所有海事部门参考。

适任

7. 要求船员持有适当证书的目的是确保他们能够安全地执行与他们船上担任的岗位相关的任务。

8. 适任定义为能够适当完成任务的能力,就船员而言还应考虑可能涉及的任务范围。

9. Before anyone can evaluate the competency of any seafarer we must know as precisely as possible exactly what we are evaluating. In most countries the syllabuses for the examination of seafarers for certificates of competency have in the past been drawn up simply on the basis of experience, through listing a series of topics, without a great deal of attention being necessarily expended on defining the precise level of knowledge, the degree of skill and the type of behaviour which should be required of candidates to ensure that they will safely and efficiently perform the duties that they will be called upon to undertake.

Job analysis

10. A modern approach to training is first to carry out a job analysis, so as to clearly identify the specific tasks involved. The areas and levels of knowledge and the types and degrees of skill necessary to perform each task competently are then identified.

The STCW Convention

11. The revised STCW Convention introduced the concept of "competence" for various functions at each level of certification as the basis for certification. The knowledge, proficiency and understanding required for each competence are specified.

The 1978 Convention did not specify the required knowledge in detail. For example, Regulation III/3 provides only that, "Every candidate shall possess sufficient elementary theoretical knowledge to understand the basic principles involved in the following subjects: ..." No mention was made on how this is to be achieved, nor the criteria for evaluation. It is also noteworthy that the prime objective of the Convention is to achieve the highest practicable level of safety and the avoidance of pollution. The ability of the ship's complement to manage the ship efficiently as a commercial enterprise receives little attention.

The new STCW Code addresses this shortcoming by establishing, for the first time, uniform standards in particular maritime skills. The revised Convention contains specific criteria detailing the standards of knowledge, understanding and proficiency to be achieved in each element of competence, for example:

STCW Code, Chapter III

Section A-III/3:

Mandatory minimum requirements for certification of chief engineer officers and second engineer officers on ships powered by main propulsion machinery of between 750 kW and 3,000 kW propulsion power

Standard of competence

1 Every candidate for certification as chief engineer officer and second engineer officer of seagoing ships powered by main propulsion machinery of between 750 kW and 3,000 kW power shall be required to demonstrate ability to undertake, at management level, the tasks, duties and responsibilities listed in column 1 of table A-III/2.

9. 在对海员进行适任评估之前,必须尽可能准确地了解要评估的内容。过去,大多数国家在制定海员适任证书考试大纲时仅以经验为基础,列出了一系列的主题,但对于准确规定证书申请者以确保其安全有效地履行被要求承担的职责所必要的知识水平、技能熟练程度和行为规范不够重视。

工作任务分析

10. 现代培训方法要求首先进行工作分析以明确所涉及的具体任务。然后,确定适任地执行每一项任务所必需的知识范围和水平、技能类型和熟练程度。

STCW公约

11. 经修订的STCW公约引入了对于每一等级证书不同功能的"适任"概念并以此作为发证的基础。规定了每一项适任所需的知识、理解和熟练的程度。

    1978年公约没有详细规定所需的知识。例如,公约规则Ⅲ/3仅提供:"每个申请人必须具有足够的基本理论知识,以便理解下列科目中的基本原理:……"。不但没有提及如何取得,也没有提及评估标准。很明显,公约的主要目标是达到安全和防止污染的最高可行水平。作为一个商业企业,船上人员在船舶效益管理方面的能力几乎不受重视。

    新的STCW规则首次制定了各项海上技能的统一标准,克服了上述不足。经修订的公约包含具体的准则,详述每项适任要素应达到的知识、理解和熟练,例如:

    STCW规则,第Ⅲ章

    第A-Ⅲ/3节:

    对主推进动力装置为750~3000千瓦船舶的轮机长和大管轮发证的强制性最低要求

    适任标准

    1   每个主推进动力装置为750~3000千瓦船舶的轮机长和大管轮证书申请人,应表明承担表A-Ⅲ/2第1栏所列的管理级的任务、职责和责任的能力。

2   The minimum knowledge, understanding and proficiency required for certification is listed in column 2 of table A-III/2. This incorporates, expands and extends in depth the subjects listed in column 2 of table A-III/1 for officers in charge of an engineering watch in a manned engine-room or designated duty engineers in a periodically unmanned engine-room.

3   Bearing in mind that a second engineer officer shall be in a position to assume the responsibilities of the chief engineer officer at any time, assessment in these subjects shall be designed to test the candidate's ability to assimilate all available information that affects the safe operation of the ship's machinery and the protection of the marine environment.

4   The level of knowledge of the subjects listed in column 2 of table A-III/2 may be lowered but shall be sufficient to enable the candidate to serve in the capacity of chief engineer officer or second engineer officer at the range of propulsion power specified in this section.

5   Training and experience to achieve the necessary level of theoretical knowledge, understanding and proficiency shall take into account the relevant requirements of this part and the guidance given in part B of this Code.

6   The Administration may omit knowledge requirements for types of propulsion machinery other than those machinery installations for which the certificate to be awarded shall be valid. A certificate awarded on such a basis shall not be valid for any category of machinery installation which has been omitted until the engineer officer proves to be competent in these items. Any such limitation shall be stated on the certificate and in the endorsement.

7   Every candidate for certification shall be required to provide evidence of having achieved the required standard of competence in accordance with the methods for demonstrating competence and the criteria for evaluating competence tabulated in columns 3 and 4 of table A-III/2.

Near-coastal voyages

8   The level of knowledge, understanding and proficiency required under the different sections listed in column 2 of table A-III/2 and the requirements of paragraphs 2.1.1 and 2.1.2 of regulation III/3 may be varied for officers of ships engaged on near-coastal voyages, as considered necessary, bearing in mind the effect on the safety of all ships which may be operating in the same waters. Any such limitation shall be stated on the certificate and in the endorsement.

Tables of competences are dealt with in more detail in Part 9.

12. It should also be observed that the revised STCW Convention does not prescribe minimum levels of manning. It deals solely with the qualifications of shipboard personnel. International provisions for manning are contained in IMO Assembly resolution A.890(21), Principles of Safe Manning. The resolution was presented to the IMO Assembly in 1999 and supercedes Resolution A.481(XII).

2 发证所要求的最低知识、理解和熟练列于表 A-Ⅲ/2 第 2 栏中,其内容包括、扩大和加深了表 A-Ⅲ/1 第 2 栏列出的对于有人值班机舱负责轮机值班的高级船员或周期性无人值班机舱指定值班的轮机员的对应科目。

3 切记大管轮随时有可能承担轮机长的职责,对这方面科目的评估应重点考查证书申请人掌握有关船舶机械安全操作和保护海洋环境方面所有可用知识的能力。

4 表 A-Ⅲ/2 第 2 栏所列科目的知识水平可以降低,但证书申请人应满足本节规定的推进功率范围内的轮机长或大管轮职位的服务要求。

5 为达到必要的理论知识、理解和熟练而进行的培训和体验,应考虑规则本部分的有关要求和 B 部分提供的指导。

6 主管机关可删除不属于所发证书对应机械装置的其他类型推进装置的知识要求。据此所发的证书也因此对上述其他种类的机械装置无效,除非该轮机部高级船员能证明自己符合相应要求。任何这种限制性条件应在证书上和签注中载明。

7 每个证书申请人应按照表 A-Ⅲ/2 第 3、4 栏所列的表明适任的方法和评价适任的标准,提供已达到所要求的适任标准的证明。

近岸航行

8 如认为必要,对于从事近岸航行船舶的高级船员,表 A-Ⅲ/2 第 2 栏各部分对知识、理解和熟练的要求,以及公约规则 Ⅲ/3 第 2.1.1 和 2.1.2 段的有关要求,可以有所变动。但要注意这种改变对在同一水域航行的所有船舶安全可能造成的影响。由改变引起的任何限制性条件应在证书上和签注中载明。

关于适任表,在第 9 章有更详细的论述。

12. 也应注意到,经修订的 STCW 公约没有规定最低配员水平。它仅涉及船上人员的资格,有关配员的国际规定则包含在 IMO 大会决议 A.890(21)——安全配员的原则中。该决议于 1999 年提交给 IMO 大会并取代决议 A.481(Ⅻ)。

Training and assessment

13. Under the revised STCW Convention regulation I/6 and section A-I/6, all training and assessment of seafarers is required to be administered, supervised and monitored. Moreover, the trainers and assessors have to be appropriate qualified. Further, regulation I/8 and section A-I/8 require quality standards to be applied to all training and assessment activities. Training and assessment is dealt with in greater detail in Part 10.

Administration of examinations

14. It is of critical importance that any examination process be properly administered. It must be seen to be fair, just and up to date and to have clear practical application to the job which is to be performed at sea.

    Uniformity of standards must be attained as far as practicable and every care taken to ensure that the examination process is not compromised in any way, whether by accident or by malfeasance of office.

Provisions for appeals

15. Failure in an examination for a certificate of competency brings with it a real or perceived economic penalty for the candidate as well as giving rise to emotional stress. It is therefore essential that a means of appealing against the decisions of the examiner is provided. The fact that an appeal procedure is provided for assists greatly in establishing the credibility of the system.

Revocation of certificates

16. Inevitably, situations will arise or incidents will occur which call into question the continuing competence of the lawful holders of certificates. Some of these incidents will be shipping casualties but others may be of an entirely different nature but still serious enough to warrant the withdrawal, suspension or revocation of the certificates of the holders concerned. The certification process must therefore provide an easily administered procedure for revocation of certificates which at the same time adequately protects the rights of the individual.

Revalidation

17. The examination process that is established must provide for periodic revalidation of the certificates issued. The purpose of this provision is to ensure that the knowledge of certificate holders is kept up to date.

    Regulation I/11 *Revalidation of certificates* spell out clearly the steps a Party has to take to revalidate certificates.

    In order to assess the need for revalidation of certificates after 1 February 2002, Parties must compare the standards of competence previously required with those specified in the appropriate certificate in part A of the STCW Code. If necessary, the holders of certificates may be required to undergo training or refresher courses (regulation I/11)

培训和评估

13. 根据经修订的STCW公约规则Ⅰ/6和STCW规则第A-Ⅰ/6节,要求管理、监督和监控所有的海员培训和评估,并且要求培训和评估人员要有适当的资格。而且,公约规则Ⅰ/8和STCW规则第A-Ⅰ/8节要求所有的培训和评估活动要采用质量标准。关于培训和评估,第10章有更详细的论述。

考试管理

14. 正确管理考试非常重要。考试必须公平、合理和保持更新,并针对海上工作实际。

    只要可行,必须制定统一的标准,并且注意确保不因任何事故或失职而危及考试。

申诉的规定

15. 适任证书考试不合格给申请人带来实际的或感觉上的经济损失,并造成心理压力。因此,提供因不同意主考官决定而申诉的途径很重要。提供申诉程序非常有利于树立制度的可信性。

证书的注销

16. 由于发生某些情况或事故,证书的法定持有人继续适任的能力不可避免地会受到怀疑。这些事故中有些造成海运人员伤亡,有些可能具有完全不同的性质,但事故都很严重,有理由收回、中止或注销所持有的证书。因此,发证程序中必须规定便于管理的证书注销程序,同时应正确地保护当事人的权利。

证书的再有效

17. 制定的考试程序必须包含证书的定期再有效规定。此规定的目的是保证证书持有人掌握的知识保持最新。

    公约规则Ⅰ/11证书的再有效,清楚地说明了为使证书再有效缔约国立采取的措施。

    为了在2002年2月1日之后评估证书再有效的需要,缔约国必须将过去的适任标准要求与STCW规则A部分对应证书的规定标准进行比较。如有必要,可要求证书持有人参加培训或知识更新课程(公约规则Ⅰ/11)。

The examination syllabus and examination material must also be revalidated periodically so as to ensure that the examination process continues to reflect the knowledge, skills and experience that are necessary to carry out the functions concerned in a competent manner.

Security

18. Considerable attention should be paid to measures for maintaining the confidentiality of examination content. This is particularly true if the examination data base is small, but, even where a large data base has been built up, it is still essential that the precise content of the test series actually used should not be divulged prior to the test.

Approved courses

19. The process must require the successful completion of certain courses which have been approved by the Administration. The process of approval of training courses should be such as to ensure that standards are maintained and adjustments made in the course syllabus to reflect any changes made in the certification requirements.

    The approval of many activities in the assessment, examination and certification of seafarers has been made mandatory in the revised STCW Convention. This is dealt with in the Part 8.

Medical standards

20. Medical standards are contained in regulation I/9. Certificates have to be issued showing that levels of fitness have been met, particularly regarding eyesight and hearing.

    Every master, officer and radio operator shall be required at intervals not exceeding five years to meet the fitness standards prescribed in regulation I/9 and the levels of professional competence contained in section A-I/11 of the STCW Code. Medical standards are dealt with in Part 4.

Qualification Process

21. The revised STCW Convention gives a range of possibilities with regards to the qualification process. In theory, a seafarer may complete his education in State A, do his sea service and/or participate in-service training in State B, get his certificate from State C, and serve aboard a ship in State D. Such a qualification process will only work if the different states involved are confident that the education and training systems in other states are compliant.

22. There is a need for a common standard to make the qualification process work in accordance with the STCW 95 intentions. Such a recognised standard may serve as a basis for acceptance from other States with regards to the maritime educational and training system as such. The standard could also facilitate delegation of responsibility to the individual MET institution. Moreover, agreements on co-operation may be facilitated.

为了保证考试方法始终反映履行有关职能所必需的知识、技能和经验,考试大纲和考试材料也必须周期性更新。

安全

18. 应当充分注意保证考试内容机密性的措施。如果考试数据库较小,尤其需要保密;但是,即使已建立大的数据库,在考试前依然要对实际使用的考试系列试题的确切内容保密。

认可的课程

19. 程序要求必须学完主管机关认可的某些课程。培训课程的认可程序应能够保证标准的维护以及调整课程大纲以反映发证要求的变化。

    在经修订的STCW公约中,对海员评估、考试和发证的许多事务的核准已成为必要程序。在第8章有关于这方面内容的论述。

健康标准

20. 健康标准包含在公约规则Ⅰ/9中。满足健康标准的应签发相应证书,特别是关于视力和听力。

    要求每位船长、高级船员和无线电操作员在不超过5年的时间内满足公约规则Ⅰ/9规定的健康标准和STCW规则第A-Ⅰ/11节包含的专业适任标准。在第4章有关于健康标准的论述。

资格认可程序

21. 经修订的STCW公约给出了关于资格认可程序的可能范围。在理论上,一位海员可在A国完成教育,在B国从事海上服务和/或参与在职培训,从C国获得证书,并在D国上船工作。因此,只有所涉及的不同国家确信其他国家的教育和培训制度也符合规定,才能运作这样的资格核准程序。

22. 要运作资格核准程序,需要根据STCW 95制定一个共同的标准。这种公认的标准可作为接受其他国家有关海上教育和培训制度的基础。该标准也更便于主管机关给各航海教育培训(MET)机构授权。而且,合作也会更便利。

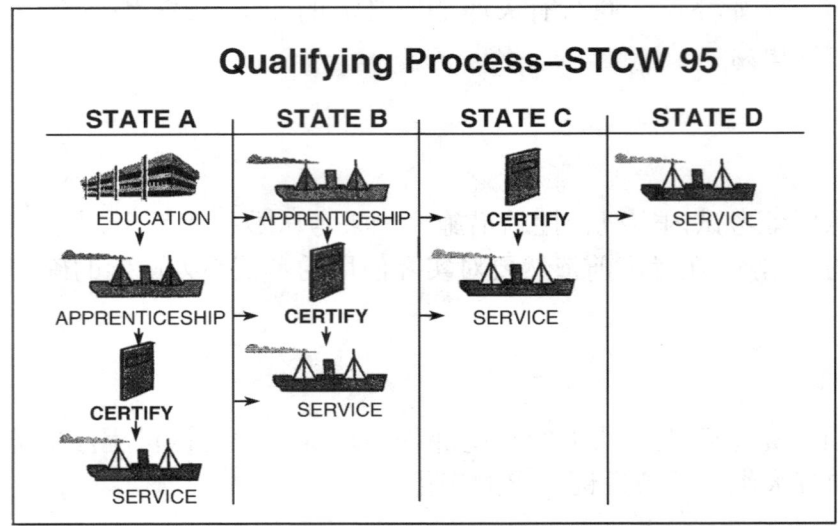

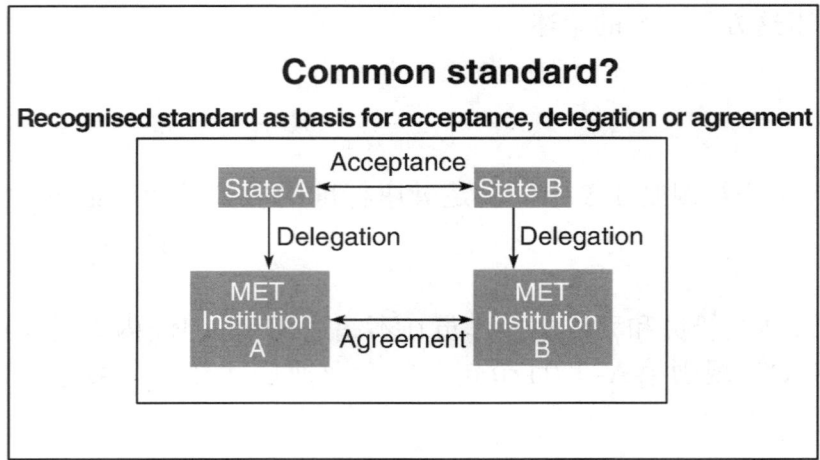

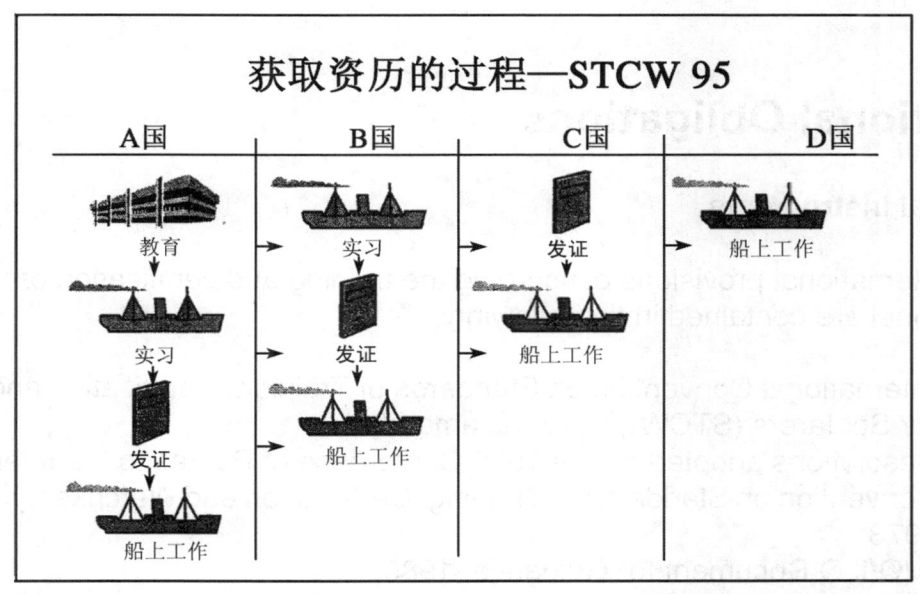

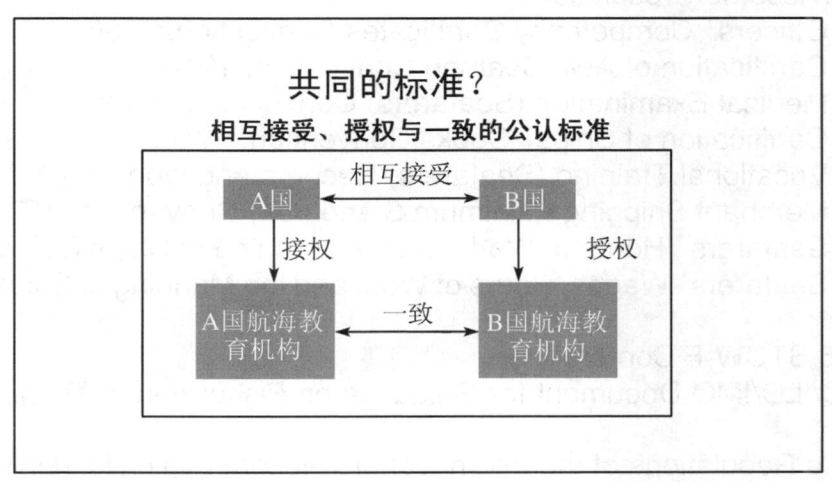

Part 3
International Obligations

International instruments

1. The international provisions concerning the training and certification of seagoing personnel are contained in the following:

    .1 International Convention on Standards of Training, Certification and Watchkeeping for Seafarers (STCW), 1978, as amended;
    .2 Resolutions adopted by the 1995 Conference of Parties to the International Convention on Standards of Training, Certification and Watchkeeping for Seafarers, 1978;
    .3 IMO/ILO Document for Guidance, 1985;
    .4 IMO Assembly resolutions;
    .5 ILO Officers' Competency Certificates Convention, 1936;
    .6 ILO Certification of Able Seamen Convention, 1946;
    .7 ILO Medical Examination (Seafarers) Convention, 1946;
    .8 ILO Certification of Ships' Cooks Convention, 1946;
    .9 ILO Vocational Training (Seafarers) Recommendation, 1970;
    .10 ILO Merchant Shipping (Minimum Standards) Convention, 1976;
    .11 ILO Seafarers' Hours of Work and the Manning of Ships Convention, 1996;
    .12 ILO Seafarers' Wages, Hours of Work and the Manning of Ships Recommendation, 1996;
    .13 1995 STCW-F Conference;
    .14 FAO/ILO/IMO Document for Guidance on Fishermen's Training and Certification; and
    .15 Radio Regulations of the International Telecommunication Union.

STCW Convention

2. Basically, the revised STCW Convention applies to seafarers serving on board sea-going merchant ships—see Article III of the Convention—and lays down mandatory minimum requirements regarding their minimum age, medical fitness, training, examination and certification.

    Note that under Article II(h) the Convention excludes vessels used for catching fish, whales, seals, walrus or other living resources of the sea. Vessels not engaged in the catching activity cannot enjoy such exclusion, and under Article III(d) the Convention excludes all wooden ships of primitive build, including junks.

    Article II—Definitions

    For the purpose of the Convention, unless expressly provided otherwise:
    (a)...(g)...etc.
    (h) "Fishing vessel" means a vessel used for catching fish, whales, seals, walrus or other living resources of the sea;

第3章
国际义务

国际法律文件

1. 有关航海人员培训和发证的国际规定如下：

    .1 经修订的《1978年海员培训、发证和值班标准(STCW)国际公约》；
    .2 1995年缔约国大会通过的对《1978年海员培训、发证和值班标准国际公约》的决议；
    .3 1985年IMO/ILO指导文件；
    .4 IMO大会决议；
    .5 1936年ILO高级船员适任证书公约；
    .6 1946年ILO一级水手证书公约；
    .7 1946年ILO健康检查(海员)公约；
    .8 1946年ILO船舶厨师证书公约；
    .9 1970年ILO职业培训(海员)建议案；
    .10 1976年ILO商船运输(最低标准)公约；
    .11 1996年ILO海员工作时间和船舶配员公约；
    .12 1996年ILO海员工资、工作时间和船舶配员建议案；
    .13 1995年STCW-F大会；
    .14 FAO/ILO/IMO渔民培训和发证指导文件；及
    .15 国际电信联盟无线电规则。

STCW公约

2. 经修订的STCW公约主要适应在商船上工作的海员——参考公约第Ⅲ条——规定有关最低年龄、身体条件、培训、考试和发证的强制性最低要求。

    应注意，根据第Ⅱ(h)条，公约不适用于捕捞鱼类、鲸鱼、海豹、海象或其他海洋生物资源的船舶，但不从事捕捞活动的船舶不能免责。根据第Ⅲ(d)条，公约不适用于所有构造简单的木船，包括舢板。

    第Ⅱ条——定义

    除另有明文规定外，就本公约而言：
    (a)……(g)……等。
    (h) "渔船"系指用于捕捞鱼类、鲸鱼、海豹、海象或其他海洋生物资源的船舶；

Article III—Application

The Convention shall apply to seafarers serving on board seagoing ships entitled to fly the flag of a Party except to those serving on board:

(a) warships, naval auxiliaries or other ships owned or operated by a State and engaged only on governmental non-commercial service; however, each Party shall ensure, by the adoption of appropriate measures not impairing the operations or operational capabilities of such ships owned or operated by it, that the persons serving on board such ships meet the requirements of the Convention so far as is reasonable and practicable;

(b) fishing vessels;
(c) pleasure yachts not engaged in trade; or
(d) wooden ships of primitive build.

The revision of the STCW regulations

3. When the 1978 International Convention on Standards of Training, Certification and Watchkeeping entered into force in 1984 it was expected that it would ensure the competence of crews of all seagoing ships. This was not realized. Instead, the Convention was gradually lost credibility as its acceptance widened. The main cause for this appeared to be the general lack of precision in its standards. This resulted in widely varying interpretation of standards and many Parties failed to effectively administer and enforce Convention requirements.

   A limited review of the STCW Convention was already in hand when the MSC decided, in May 1993, to give high priority to a comprehensive review.

4. The various deck and marine engineering certificates prescribed by the Convention, their associated prerequisites and their rights and privileges are summarized or referenced in Tables in Part 6 of this compendium.

STW Conference resolutions

5. The resolutions are not of mandatory effect but are recommendations that have been agreed by all States participating in the conference and that represent global opinion on the matters dealt with.

ITU Radio Regulations

6. The International Telecommunication Union (ITU) is the United Nations Specialized Agency charged with the responsibility for all telecommunication matters, including management of the radio spectrum. The provisions of the Radio Regulations govern the use of the radio spectrum.

第Ⅲ条——适用范围

本公约适用于在有权悬挂缔约国国旗的海船上工作的海员,但在下列船上工作的海员不在此列:

(a) 军舰、海军辅助舰船或者由国家所有或经营并只从事政府非商业性服务的其他船舶;但是各缔约国应采取适当措施无损于其所有或经营的此类船舶的作业或作业能力,以保证在此类船上服务的人员在合理可行的范围内符合本公约的要求;

(b) 渔船;

(c) 非营业的游艇;或

(d) 构造简单的木船。

STCW公约规则修正案

3. 《1978年海员培训、发证和值班标准国际公约》在1984年生效之时,人们期望,该公约能保证所有海船船员的适任能力,但是这个愿望没有实现。相反,随着公约被更多国家接受,它逐渐失去可信性。主要的原因似乎是公约的标准普遍较笼统。这导致对标准的解释有较大的出入,许多缔约国未能有效地执行公约的要求。

当1993年5月MSC决定给予特别优先以全面评估STCW公约时,部分研究工作已在进行中。

4. 本纲要第6章以表格的形式给出了公约规定的各种甲板和轮机证书及其相关条件、权利和特免的说明或其他参考内容。

STW大会决议

5. 决议没有强制作用,但它们是经所有参加大会的国家达成的建议案,并代表处理相关事务的全球性意见。

ITU无线电规则

6. 国际电信联盟(ITU)是一个联合国的专门机构,负责所有电信事务,包括管理无线电频段管理。《无线电规则》规定无线电频谱的使用。

The International Maritime Organization, in co-operation with ITU, the International Maritime Satellite Organization (INMARSAT), the COSPAS-SARSAT Partners, the World Meteorological Organization (WMO) and the International Hydrographic Organization (IHO) considered the existing arrangements for maritime distress and safety communications. It was decided that a new global maritime distress, to improve distress and safety, radiocommunications and procedures, should be established which, in conjunction with a co-ordinated search and rescue infrastructure, would incorporate recent technical developments and significantly improve the safety of life at sea.

The new system, known as the Global Maritime Distress and Safety System (GMDSS) came into force on 1 February 1999. This is a global communications service based upon automated systems, both satellite based and terrestrial, to provide distress alerting and promulgation of maritime safety information for mariners.

Basic Concept of the GMDSS

7. The basic concept of the GMDSS is that search and rescue authorities ashore as well as shipping in the immediate vicinity of the ship, or persons, in distress, will be rapidly alerted to a distress incident so they can assist in a co-ordinated search and rescue operation with the minimum delay. The system also provides for urgency and safety communications and the promulgation of maritime safety information (navigational and meteorological warnings and forecasts and other urgent safety information). In other words, every ship is able, irrespective of the area in which it operates, to perform those communication functions, which is essential for the safety of the ship itself and of other ships operating in the same area. To this end each Government contracting to the amendments to the 1974 SOLAS Convention concerning Radiocommunications for the GMDSS undertake to make available appropriate shore-based facilities for space and terrestrial radio communications services, as recommended by the International Maritime Organization, and all ships, while at sea, must be capable of:

   .1 Transmitting ship-to-shore distress alerts by at least two separate and independent means, each using a different radio-communication service;
   .2 Receiving shore-to-ship distress alerts;
   .3 Transmitting and receiving ship-to shore distress alerts;
   .4 Transmitting and receiving search and rescue co-ordinating communications;
   .5 Transmitting and receiving on-scene communications;
   .6 Transmitting and receiving signals for locating;
   .7 Transmitting and receiving maritime safety information;
   .8 Transmitting and receiving general radiocommunications from shore-based radio systems or networks; and
   .9 Transmitting and receiving bridge-to-bridge communications

8. Recognizing that the different radio sub-systems incorporated in the GMDSS system have individual limitations with respect to the geographical coverage and services provided, the equipment required to be carried by ships is determined in principle by the ship's area of operation, which is designated as follows:

第3章 国际义务

国际海事组织,在ITU、国际海事卫星组织(INMARSAT)、COSPAS-SARSAT合伙人、世界气象组织(WMO)和国际水道测量组织(IHO)的协作下,评估了海上遇险和安全通信的现有安排。为了改善遇险和安全、无线电通信和程序,决定建立新的全球遇险系统。该系统与经过协调的搜救基础设施结合,吸收了最近的技术发展成果,极大地提高了海上人命安全。

这一新的系统,被称为全球海上遇险与安全系统(GMDSS),于1999年2月1日生效。它是一种基于自动系统(卫星和陆地)的全球通信服务系统,提供遇险警告并为航海者提供海上安全信息广播。

GMDSS的基本概念

7. GMDSS的基本概念是它将迅速地向岸上搜救主管机关以及遇险船舶或人员附近的船舶发送遇险警报,以便他们能在最短的时间内参与经协调的搜救作业。该系统也能提供紧急和安全通信以及发布海上安全信息(航海和气象的警告及预报,以及其他紧急安全信息)。换句话说,每艘船舶,不论在什么区域,都能够使用这些通信功能。这对船舶本身和在同一区域作业的其他船舶的安全来说很重要。为实现这个目标,签署有关GMDSS无线电通信的1974年SOLAS公约修正案的每个政府将按国际海事组织的建议,保证给空中和陆上无线电通信服务提供适当的岸基设施,并且,所有船舶在海上时,必须能够:

   .1 以至少2种独立的方法并用不同的无线电通信设施,发送船对岸的遇险警报;
   .2 接收岸对船遇险警报;
   .3 发送和接收船对岸遇险警报;
   .4 发送和接收搜寻和救助协调通信;
   .5 发送和接收现场通信;
   .6 发送和接收定位信号;
   .7 发送和接收海上安全信息;
   .8 发送一般无线电通信和接收来自于岸基无线电系统或网络的一般无线电通信;及
   .9 发送和接收驾驶台对驾驶台的通信。

8. 考虑到并入GMDSS系统的不同无线电分系统在地理覆盖范围和所提供服务方面有各自的局限性,要求船舶安装的设备原则上按船舶航行区域确定,规定如下:

Sea area A1   an area within the radiotelephone coverage of at least one VHF coast station in which continuous DSC[1] alerting is available, as may be defined by a Contracting Government;

Sea area A2   an area, excluding sea area A1, within the radiotelephone coverage of at least one MF coast station in which continuous DSC alerting is available, as may be defined by a Contracting Government;

Sea area A3   an area, excluding sea areas A1 and A2, within the coverage of an INMARSAT geostationary satellite in which continuous alerting is available, and;

Sea area A4   an area outside areas A1, A2 and A3.

In all areas of operation the continuous availability of alerting is required.

Operational details

9. The worldwide communication coverage of the GMDSS is achieved by a combination of satellite (INMARSAT) and terrestrial systems. Based on the range limitations of each system, the four sea areas have been defined according to the coverage of VHF, MF, HF Coast Radio Services and INMARSAT services. The type of radio equipment to be carried by a vessel is therefore determined by its area of operation.

Area description	Distance	Radio	Frequencies	EPIRB	Survival Craft
A1 within range of shore-based VHF stations	Depends on antenna height at shore-based VHF station, about 20–50 nm	VHF	156.525 MHz (Ch 70) for DSC or 156.8 MHz (Ch 16) RT	Either L-Band (1.6 GHz) or 406 MHz COSPAS-SARSAT or VHF EPIRB	9 GHz radar transponder (SART); VHF portable radio (Ch 16 and one other frequency)
A2 within range of shore-based MF stations	About 50–400 nm	MF VHF As above, plus 2187.5 kHz DSC[1], 2182 kHz RT, 2174.5 kHz NBDP[2], 518 NAVTEX[3]	L-Band(1.6 GHz) or 406 MHz COSPAS-SARSAT	As above	

---

1 *Digital Selective Calling system—a technique using digital codes which enables a radio station to establish contact with, and transfer information to another station or group of stations, and complying with the relevant recommendations of the ITU Radiocommunication Sector (name changed due to Article 1 of the International Telecommunication Constitution, 1992)*

2 *Narrow-Band Direct-Printing; automated telegraphy system as used by the NAVTEX system and telex-over-radio*

3 *Narrow-Band Direct-Printing telegraphy system for transmission of navigational and meteorological warnings and urgent information to ships*

海区 A1　在至少一个VHF岸台无线电话有效范围之内并且能够获得连续DSC警报的区域,该区域可由缔约国政府规定;

海区 A2　海区A1除外,在至少一个MF岸台无线电话有效范围之内并且能够获得连续DSC警报的区域,该区域可由缔约国政府规定;

海区 A3　海区A1和A2除外,在INMARSAT同步卫星覆盖范围之内并且能获得连续警报的区域,及;

海区 A4　海区A1、A2和A3以外的区域。

在所有的作业区域中,要求能获得连续警报。

运作细节

9. 全球GMDSS通信由海事通信卫星(INMARSAT)和陆地系统联合实现。基于每个系统的作用距离限制,按照VHF、MF、HF岸上无线电服务和INMARSAT服务的有效范围,规定了4类海区。船舶安装的无线电设备的类型由其作业区域确定。

区域种类	距离	无线电设备	频率	EPIRB	救生艇用设备
A1 岸基VHF电台的作用范围之内	20~50海里(取决于岸基VHF电台的天线高度)	VHF	DSC:156.525 MHz (Ch 70) 或RT:156.8 MHz (Ch 16)	L波段(1.6 GHz)或406 MHz COSPAS-SARSAT或VHF EPIRB	9 GHz雷达应答器(SART); VHF手持式无线电设备(Ch 16和一个其他频率)
A2 岸基MF电台的作用范围之内	50~400海里	MF, VHF同上, 加上2187.5 kHz DSC[1] 2182 kHz RT, 2174.5 kHz NBDP[2], 518 NAVTEX[3]	L波段(1.6 GHz)或406 MHz COSPAS-SARSAT	同上	

1　数字选择性呼叫系统——使用数字编码和遵守ITU无线电通信部分的相关建议案的一种技术,该技术能够使一个无线电台与另一个无线电台或电台组建立联系并传递信息(由于1992年国际电信法规第1条而改变名称)
2　窄带直接印字电报;NAVTEX系统和无线电电传使用的自动电报系统
3　发送航海、气象警告和舰船紧急信息的窄带直接印字电报系统

Area description	Distance	Radio	Frequencies	EPIRB	Survival Craft
A3 within geo-stationary satellite (i.e. INMARSAT)	70°N–70°S	HF or Satellite MF VHF	As above, plus 1.5–1.6 GHz alerting or as A1 and A2 plus all HF frequencies	L-Band (1.6 GHz) or 406 MHz COSPAS-SARSAT	As above
A4 other areas (i.e. beyond INMARSAT range)	North of 70°N or South of 70°S	HF MF VHF		406 MHz COSPAS-SARSAT	As above

Minimum GMDSS Carriage Requirements

Equipment	Sea Area A1	Sea Area A2	Sea Area A3	Sea Area A4
VHF with DSC	X	X	X	X
SART (2)	X	X	X	X
NAVTEX	B	B	B	B
EGC[1] Receiver	X	X	X	C
VHF Portable (2–3)	X	X	X	X
MF R/T+DSC		X	X	X
plus				
INMARSAT-A, -B or -C			X	
HF R/T with DSC and Telex				X

Notes:

A required only in those areas where the NAVTEX service is available

B Required only in those areas where the NAVTEX service is NOT available; also, the EGC receive facility is included in the standard INMARSAT-C terminal

C 406 MHz COSPAS-SARSAT EPIRB

Training of Radio Operators

10. The GMDSS was introduced into the regulations annexed to the SOLAS 74 Convention as the revised Chapter IV at the 1988 GMDSS Conference held in London in November 1988. The revised Chapter IV came into force on 1 February 1992 and is applicable to cargo ships of 300 gross tonnage and upwards and to passenger ships irrespective of their gross tonnage.

---

1 Enhanced Group Calling

区域种类	距离	无线电设备	频率	EPIRB	救生技术
A3 在静止卫星(即INMARSAT)作用范围之内	70°N~70°S	HF或卫星 MF VHF	同上,加1.5~1.6 GHz警报或如A1和A2加所有HF频率	L波段(1.6 GHz)或406 MHz COSPAS-SARSAT	同上
A4 其他区域即INMARSAT作用范围以外)	70°N以北或70°S以南	HF MF VHF		406 MHz COSPAS-SARSAT	同上

GMDSS最低安装要求

设备	海区A1	海区A2	海区A3	海区A4
带有DSC的VHF	X	X	X	X
SART(2)	X	X	X	X
NAVTEX	B	B	B	B
EGC¹接收器	X	X	X	C
手持式VHF(2-3)	X	X	X	X
MF R/T+DSC		X	X	X
加				
INMARSAT-A,-B或-C			X	
带有DSC和电传的HF R/T				X

注释:
A 仅在有NAVTEX服务的区域要求
B 仅在没有NAVTEX服务的区域要求;EGC接收设施也包括在标准INMARSAT-C终端
C 406 MHz COSPAS-SARSAT EPIRB

无线电操作员培训

10. 1988年12月在伦敦召开的1988年GMDSS大会把GMDSS作为修正后的第Ⅳ章列入SOLAS 74公约规则内容。修正后的第Ⅳ章于1992年2月1日生效,适用于300总吨及以上的货船和任何吨位的客船。

---

1 强化群呼

In view of this change, IMO published two Model Courses to assist maritime training institutes in organising and conducting appropriate training in accordance with the training recommended in annexes to the IMO Assembly resolution A.703(17):

— Annex 3 Recommendation on Training of Radio Operators related to the General Operator's Certificate (GOC)
  GOC for the GMDSS—Model Course 1.25 plus compendium; and

— Annex 4 Recommendation on Training of Radio Operators related to the Restricted Operator's Certificate (ROC).
  ROC for the GMDSS—Model Course 1.26 plus compendium

Whilst the relevant requirements and administrative procedures vary from country to country, the following extracts from the Radio-Communication regulations of the Telecommunication Authority of Singapore provide a typical example of the type of arrangements necessary to give effect to the implementation of GMDSS.

TELECOMMUNICATION AUTHORITY OF SINGAPORE ACT (CHAPTER 323)

Under the Radio-communication (Certificates of Competency for Ship Station Operators) Regulations, 1998 of the Telecommunication Authority of Singapore Act, the Authority may issue a Certificate of Competency in radio-communications on being satisfied after examinations that the candidate is qualified to hold such a Certificate under these Regulations. The Certificate of Competency is graded as follows:
(a) General Operator's Certificate (GOC) of Competency; and
(b) Restricted Operator's Certificate (ROC) of Competency.
In order to qualify for a GOC, a candidate shall give proof to the Authority by examinations that he has the following knowledge and qualifications:
(a) detailed practical knowledge of the operation of all the sub-systems and equipment of the GMDSS;
(b) an ability to send and receive correctly by radio telephone and by direct-printing telegraphy;
(c) detailed knowledge of the Radio Regulations relating to radio-communications, knowledge of the documents relating to charges for radio-communications an of those provisions of the International Convention for the Safety of Life at Sea which relate to radio-communications;
(d) sufficient knowledge of the English language to be able to express himself satisfactorily both orally and in writing; and
(e) he has satisfied the standard of competence specified in section A-IV/2 of the STCW Code.

The holder of a GOC is authorised by the Authority to operate the radio-communication service of licensed ship station equipment with radio-communication apparatus in accordance with the procedures laid down in the Radio Regulations for the GMDSS.

In order to qualify for a ROC, a candidate shall give proof to the Authority by examinations that he has the following knowledge and qualifications:

考虑到这一变化,IMO出版了两本示范课程,以帮助海上培训机构根据IMO大会决议A.703(17)附录的建议案组织和实施适当的培训。

— 附录3 有关通用操作员证书(GOC)的无线电操作员培训建议案
　　GMDSS的GOC——见示范课程1.25和纲要;及

— 附录4 有关限用操作员证书(ROC)的无线电操作员培训建议案
　　GMDSS的ROC——见示范课程1.26和纲要

不同国家相关要求和管理程序也有所不同,以下摘录的《新加坡电信管理法案》无线电通信规则提供了有效实施GMDSS所需的各种安排的典型案例。

新加坡电信管理法案(第323章)

根据《新加坡电信管理法案》1998年无线电通信(船舶电台操作员适任证书)规则,在申请人考试后,主管机关确信其有资格持有证书时,可签发无线电通信适任证书。适任证书分级如下:
(a) 通用操作员适任证书(GOC);及
(b) 限用操作员适任证书(ROC)。

为了有资格获得GOC,申请人须通过考试向主管机关证明自己具备下列知识和资格:
(a) 完整的操作GMDSS各分系统和设备的实际知识;
(b) 能够用无线电话和直接印电报正确地发送和接收信息;
(c) 完备的无线电通信规则知识、无线电信收费文件知识和《国际海上人命安全公约》有关无线电通信规定的知识;
(d) 充分的英语语言知识,具备合适的口头和书面表达能力;及
(e) 已满足STCW规则第A-Ⅳ/2节规定的适任标准。

主管机关授予GOC持有人可按照GMDSS无线电规则规定的程序操作经许可的船舶电台无线电通信设备的职权。

为具备获得ROC的资格,申请人须通过考试向主管机关证明,他具备下列的知识和资格:

(a) practical knowledge of the operation of all the sub-systems and equipment of the GMDSS which is required while the ship is sailing within the range of Very High Frequency coast stations;
(b) an ability to send and receive correctly by radio telephone;
(c) knowledge of the Radio Regulations relating to radiotelephony communications and specifically of the part of those regulations relating to the Safety of Life;
(d) an elementary knowledge of the English language to be able to express himself satisfactorily both orally and in writing; and
(e) he has satisfied the standard of competence specified in section A-IV/2 of the STCW Code.

The holder of a ROC is authorised by the Authority to operate the radio-communication service of licensed ship station equipment with radio-communication apparatus in accordance with the procedures laid down in the Radio Regulations for the GMDSS.

In accordance with Regulation IV/16 (Radio Personnel) of SOLAS 74, ships fitted with GMDSS equipment are required to carry personnel qualified for distress and safety radiocommunication purposes, any one of whom shall be designated to have primary responsibility for radiocommunications during distress incidents. These personnel are required to hold appropriate certificates according to their Radio Regulations.

Example of the carriage requirements of radio personnel:

Sea Areas	No. of Personnel and Qualifications
A1	One person (non-exclusive*) holding at least a ROC
A1+A2	One person (non-exclusive*) holding a GOC
A1+A2+A3	Minimum two persons (non-exclusive*) holding GOC; or one person (exclusive**) holding a GOC

* "non-exclusive" means the person is not employed exclusively for the purpose of carrying out duties of distress and safety radiocommunications and other routine radiocommunications. However, if two are carried, one of them shall be designated to have primary responsibility for radiocommunications during distress incidents.

** "exclusive" means the person is employed exclusively for the purpose of carrying out duties of distress and safety radiocommunications and other routine radiocommunications. The person shall have the primary responsibility for radiocommunications during distress incidents.

Document for Guidance

11. *The Document for Guidance, 1985*, is a joint publication of the International Labour Organisation and IMO. It is not of mandatory effect but provides in a single publication a summation of the 1978 STCW mandatory minimum requirements and related 1978 STW Conference resolutions and IMO Assembly resolutions dealing with the training of seafarers.

The IMO/ILO Document for Guidance 1985 is out-of-date and requires review to take account of developments in the last two decades. There are currently no plans to undertake such a review.

(a) 操作在甚高频岸台作用范围之内船舶航行所要求的 GMDSS 各分系统和设备的实际知识;
(b) 能够用无线电话正确地发送和接收信息;
(c) 无线电通信规则的知识,特别是有关人命安全的规则部分的知识;
(d) 基本的英语语言知识,具有令人满意的用口头和书面表达的能力;及
(e) 已满足 STCW 规则第 A-IV/2 节规定的适任标准。

主管机关授予 ROC 的持有人可按照 GMDSS 无线电规则规定的程序操作经许可的船舶电台无线电通信设备的职权。

依照 SOLAS 74 规则 IV/16(无线电人员),装有 GMDSS 设备的船舶要求配备具备遇险和安全无线电通信资格的人员,并指定其中一人为遇险事故期间无线电通信的主要负责人。根据无线电规则,这些人员都必须持有合适的证书。

通信人员持证要求示例:

海区	人员和资格
A1	一人(非专职*),至少持有 ROC
A1+A2	一人(非专职*),持有 GOC
A1+A2+A3	最少两人(非专职*),持有 GOC;或一人(专职**),持有 GOC

* "非专职"指该人不是专门担任履行遇险和安全无线电通信和其他日常无线电通信的职责。然而,如果有两人,其中的一位应被指定为遇险事故期间无线电通信的主要负责人。

** "专职"指该人专门担任履行遇险和安全无线电通信和其他日常无线电通信的职责。此人为遇险事故期间无线电通信的主要负责人。

指导文件

11. 《指导文件 1985》是国际劳工组织和 IMO 的联合出版物。它不具备强制作用,但是它以专门出版物的形式对 1978 年 STCW 公约的强制性最低要求和有关的 1978 年 STW 大会决议以及有关海员培训的 IMO 大会决议进行了概要说明。

考虑到最近二十年的发展情况,1985 年 IMO/ILO 指导文件已过时,它需要审核,但当前没有这项审核的计划。

IMO training-related requirements and recommendations

12. In response to the concerns expressed by the Chairmen of the MSC and the MEPC that it had become difficult for Administrations, designers, shipyards and other interested parties to identify, from the various IMO instruments in force, which requirements and recommendations applied at a given time, to certain or all types of ships, the MSC at its sixty-sixth session, instructed the Secretariat to prepare a list of safety-related requirements and recommendations.

    The first list of IMO safety-related requirements and recommendations applicable to all ships and certain types of ships (MSC/Circ.815 dated 13 November 1998) would be updated and disseminated annually be means of an MSC circular.

    It should be noted that IMO Assembly resolutions on maritime training and certification are not of mandatory effect but stipulate a globally recommended standard and format of training in the field concerned. Those instruments dealing with training are listed in the following tables.

第3章 国际义务

IMO有关培训的要求和建议

12. MSC和MEPC主席担心，主管机关、设计师、船厂和其他有关各方想从IMO生效的各种文件中确定哪项要求和建议在某一给定的时期适用于哪种类型或所有类型的船舶，会变得很困难。为了应对MSC和MEPC主席所表示的担心，MSC在其第66次会议上指示秘书处起草一份有关安全要求和建议的清单。

    适用于所有船舶和某些类型船舶(MSC/815号文件，日期为1998年11月13日)的IMO有关安全要求和建议的首份清单会以MSC文件的形式每年更新并发布。

    应注意，有关海上培训和发证的IMO大会决议没有强制性，但是它们规定了有关领域培训的全球推荐性标准和形式。有关培训的文件在下表中列出。

CONVENTIONS

	Name of the instrument	Ship types to which the requirements are applicable	Reference to relevant regulations in Conventions, as appropriate	Application date
1	International Convention for the Safety of Life at Sea, 1974 (SOLAS) as amended. including:			25.05.80
.1	1988 amendments (GMDSS) (Conference resolution 1)	Cargo ships[1]; passenger ships;	SOLAS ch II-1, II-2, III, IV and V	01.02.92
	1994 amendments (1994 SOLAS Conference resolution 1)			
	• Annex 1 (new Ch X-Safety measures for high-speed craft)	High-speed craft; cargo ships; passenger ships	SOLAS ch. X	01.01.96
	• Annex 2 (new Ch IX-Management for the safe operation of ships)	High-speed craft; bulk carriers; passenger ships; oil tankers; gas carriers	SOLAS ch. IX	01.07.98
		Cargo ships; mobile offshore drilling units		01.07.2002
2	Protocol of 1978 relating to the International Convention for the Safety of Life at Sea, 1974, (1978 SOLAS Protocol) as amended, including	Cargo ships; passenger ships	SOLAS ch I and reg. II-1/1, 2, 29. II-2/1, 3, 55, 60, V/12, 19 19-1 and 19-2	01.05.81
.1	1988 amendments (GMDSS) (Conference resolution 1)	Cargo ships; passenger ships	SOLAS ch. II-1/1, 2. 29 II-2 and V	01.09.84
3	International Convention on Standards of Training, Certification and Watchkeeping for Seafarers. 1978 (STCW) as amended, including:	Cargo ships; passenger ships		28.04.84
.1	1991 amendments (GMDSS and trails) (res. MSC.21(59))			01.12.92
.2	1994 amendments (res. MSC.33 (63)) (special training requirements for personnel on tankers)	Tankers		01.01.96
.3	1995 amendments (1995 STCW Conference resolution 1)	Cargo ships; passenger ships		01.02.97
.4	1997 amendments (res. MSC.66(68)) (minimum requirements for the training of masters, officers, ratings and other personnel on passenger ships)	Passenger ships		01.01.99
.5	1995 STCW Code (1995 STCW Conference resolution 2) including:	Cargo ships; passenger ships		01.02.97
	• 1997 amendments (res. MSC.67 (68)) (minimum requirements for the training of masters, officers, ratings,and other personnel on passenger ships)	Passenger ships		01.01.99
4	International Convention on Standards of Training, Certification and Watchkeeping for Fishing Vessel Personnel, 1995 (STCW-F)	Fishing vessels		Not in force

1 throughout the list, the term "cargo ships" means cargo ships as defined in SOLAS regulation I/1 (g), i.e. ships which are not passenger ships

第3章 国际义务

公约

	文件名称	适用规定要求的船舶类型	涉及的有关公约规则	实施日期
1	经修订的1974年《国际海上人命安全公约》(SOLAS),包括:			25.05.80
.1	1988年修正案(GMDSS)(大会决议1) 1994年修正案(1994年SOLAS大会决议1)	货船[1];客船;	SOLAS公约第Ⅱ-1、Ⅱ-2、Ⅲ、Ⅳ和Ⅴ章	01.02.92
	• 附件1(新的第Ⅹ章——高速艇安全措施)	高速艇;货船;客船	SOLAS公约第Ⅹ章	01.01.96
	• 附件2(新的第Ⅸ章——船舶安全操作管理)	高速艇;散货船;客船;液货船;液化气船	SOLAS公约第Ⅸ章	01.07.98
		货船;移动式近海钻井装置		01.07.2002
2.	经修订的1974年《国际海上人命安全公约》1978年议定书(1978年SOLAS议定书),包括:	货船;客船	SOLAS公约第Ⅰ章和规则Ⅱ-1/1, 2, 29, Ⅱ-2/1, 3, 55, 60, Ⅴ/12, 19 19-1和19-2章	01.05.81
.1	1988年修正案(GMDSS)(大会决议1)	货船;客船	SOLAS公约第Ⅱ-1/1, 2, 29 Ⅱ-2和Ⅴ章	01.09.84
3.	经修订的《1978年海员培训、发证和值班标准国际公约》(STCW),包括:	货船;客船		28.04.84
.1	1991年修正案(GMDSS和试验)〔res.MSC.21(59)〕			01.12.92
.2	1994年修正案〔res.MSC.33(63)〕(液货船人员特别培训要求)	液货船		01.01.96
.3	1995年修正案(1995年STCW大会决议1)	货船;客船		01.02.97
.4	1997年修正案〔res.SMC.66(68)〕(客船船长、高级船员、普通船员和其他人员培训最低要求)	客船		01.01.99
.5	1995年STCW规则(1995年STCW大会决议2),包括:	货船;客船		01.02.97
	• 1997年修正案〔res.MSC.67(68)〕(客船船长、高级船员、普通船员和其他人员培训最低要求)	客船		01.01.99
4	1995年《渔船人员培训、发证和值班标准国际公约》(STCW-F)	渔船		尚未生效

1 在本表中,"货船"一词指SOLAS公约规则Ⅰ/1(g)规定的货船,也就是指不是客船的船舶。

ASSEMBLY RESOLUTIONS

Name of the instrument	Ship types to which the requirements are applicable	Reference to relevant regulations in Conventions, as appropriate	Application date
A.157(ES.IV) Recommendation on the use and testing of shipborne Navigational equipment	Cargo ships; passenger ships	SOLAS reg.V/12	24.11.68
A.222(VII) Performance standards for navigational radar equipment (refer to res.A.477(XII))	Cargo ships; passenger ships	SOLAS reg.V/12	12.10.71 for equipment installed before 01.09.84
A.224(VII) Performance standards for echo-sounding equipment	Cargo ships; passenger ships	SOLAS reg.V/12	12.10.71
A.275(VIII) Recommendation on performance standards for mechanical pilot hoists	Cargo ships; passenger ships	SOLAS reg.V/17	20.11.73
A.278(VIII) Supplement to the recommendation on performance standards for navigational radar equipment (symbols for controls on marine navigational radar equipment)	Cargo ships; passenger ships	SOLAS reg.V/12	20.11.73
A.280(VIII) Recommendation on performance standards for gyro-compasses	Cargo ships; passenger ships	SOLAS reg.V/12	20.11.73
A.342(IX) Recommendation on performance standards for automatic pilots	Cargo ships; passenger ships	SOLAS reg.V/19	12.11.75 for equipment installed before 01.01.99
A.380(X) Standard Marine Navigational Vocabulary	Cargo ships; passenger ships	STCW ch. II	14.11.77
A.382(X) Magnetic compasses: carriage and performance standards (Annex I is incorporated in SOLAS reg.V/12(b))	Cargo ships; passenger ships	SOLAS reg.V/12	14.11.77
A.384(X) Performance standards for radar reflectors	All ships less than 100 gross tonnage operating in international waters and adjacent coastal areas	SOLAS ch. III; COLREG rule 6 (b)(iv)	14.11.77
A.415(XI) Improved steering gear standards for passenger and cargo ships	Cargo ships; passenger ships	SOLAS regs.II-1/29 and 30	15.11.79
A.416(XI) Examination of steering gears on existing tankers	Tankers	SOLAS regs.II-1/29 and 30	15.11.79

大会决议

文件名称	适用规定要求的船舶类型	涉及的有关公约规则	实施日期
A.157(ES.Ⅳ) 有关船上导航设备使用和试验的建议案	货船;客船	SOLAS 公约 reg. Ⅴ/12	24.11.68
A.222(Ⅶ) 航海雷达设备性能标准〔参考决议 res. A.477(Ⅻ)〕	货船;客船	SOLAS 公约 reg. Ⅴ/12	12.10.71 (对于 1984 年 9 月 1 日之前安装的设备)
A.224(Ⅶ) 测深设备性能标准	货船;客船	SOLAS 公约 reg. Ⅴ/12	12.10.71
A.275(Ⅷ) 引航员机械升降装置性能标准建议案	货船;客船	SOLAS 公约 reg. Ⅴ/17	20.11.73
A.278(Ⅷ) 对导航雷达设备性能标准建议案的补充 (航海雷达设备控制符号)	货船;客船	SOLAS 公约 reg. Ⅴ/12	20.11.73
A.280(Ⅷ) 陀螺罗经性能标准建议案	货船;客船	SOLAS 公约 reg. Ⅴ/12	20.11.73
A.342(Ⅸ) 自动舵性能标准建议案	货船;客船	SOLAS 公约 reg. Ⅴ/19	12.11.75 (对于 1999 年 1 月 1 日之前安装的设备)
A.380(Ⅹ) 标准航海用语	货船;客船	STCW 公约第 Ⅱ 章	14.11.77
A.382(Ⅹ) 磁罗经:支架和性能标准〔附件 Ⅰ 编入 SOLAS 公约 reg. Ⅴ/12(b)〕	货船;客船	SOLAS 公约 reg. Ⅴ/12	14.11.77
A.384(Ⅹ) 雷达反射器性能标准	100 总吨以下、在国际水域和毗邻沿岸水域作业的所有船舶	SOLAS 公约第 Ⅲ 章;COLREG 规则第 6 条(b)项第(Ⅳ)款	14.11.77
A.415(Ⅺ) 经改进的客船和货船舵机标准	货船;客船	SOLAS 公约 regs. Ⅱ-1/29 和 30	15.11.79
A.416(Ⅺ) 现有液货船舵机检验	液货船	SOLAS 公约 regs. Ⅱ-1/29 和 30	15.11.79

Name of the instrument	Ship types to which the requirements are applicable	Reference to relevant regulations in Conventions, as appropriate	Application date
A.415(XI) Performance standards for automatic radar plotting aids (ARPA) (refer to res.A.823(19))	Cargo ships; passenger ships	SOLAS regs.V/12	15.11.79 for equipment installed before 01.01.97
A.424(XI) Performance standards for gyro-compasses	Cargo ships; passenger ships	SOLAS regs.V/12	15.11.79
A.425(XI) Performance standards for differential Omega correction transmitting stations	Cargo ships; passenger ships	SOLAS regs.V/12	15.11.79
A.431(XI) Recommendation concerning vessels restricted in their ability to manoeuvre when engaged in an operation for the maintenance of safety of navigation in a traffic separation scheme	Cargo ships; passenger ships	COLREG rule 10	15.11.79
A.474(XII) Proper use of VHF channels at sea	Cargo ships; passenger ships	SOLAS ch. IV	19.11.81
A.477(XII) Performance standards for radar equipment (refer to res. A.222(VII) and MSC.64(67))	Cargo ships; passenger ships	SOLAS reg.V/12	19.11.81 for equipment installed after 01.09.84 and before 01.01.99
A.478(XII) Performance standards for devices to indicate speed and distance (refer to res. A.824(19))	Cargo ships; passenger ships	SOLAS reg.V/12	01.09.84 for equipment installed before 01.01.97
A.479(XII) Performance standards for shipborne receivers for use with differential Omega	Cargo ships; passenger ships	SOLAS ch.V	19.11.81
A.481(XII) Principles of safe manning	Cargo ships; passenger ships	SOLAS reg.V/13	19.11.81
A.484(XII) Basic principles to be observed in keeping a navigational watch on board fishing vessels	Fishing vessels	STCW-F reg.IV/1	19.11.81
A.485(XII) Training, qualifications and operational procedures for maritime pilots other than deep-sea pilots	Cargo ships; passenger ships		19.11.81
A.488(XII) Use of the Standard Marine Navigational Vocabulary	Cargo ships; passenger ships	SOLAS reg.V/13.3; STCW regs. II/1, II/5.16 and IV/2	19.11.81
A.524(13) Performance standards for VHF multiple watch facilities	Cargo ships; passenger ships	SOLAS reg. IV/14	17.11.83

文件名称	适用规定要求的船舶类型	涉及的有关公约规则	实施日期
A.415(XI) 自动雷达标绘仪(ARPA)性能标准〔参考决议res.A.823(19)〕	货船;客船	SOLAS公约reg.V/12	15.11.79(对于1997年1月1日之前安装的设备)
A.424(XI) 陀螺罗经性能标准	货船;客船	SOLAS公约reg.V/12	15.11.79
A.425(XI) 差分奥米伽改正发射台性能标准	货船;客船	SOLAS公约reg.V/12	15.11.79
A.431(XI) 有关操纵能力受限制的船舶在分道通航制水域从事航行安全的维修作业时的建议案	货船;客船	COLREG规则第10条	15.11.79
A.474(XII) VHF频道在海上的正确使用	货船;客船	SOLAS公约第IV章	19.11.81
A.477(XII) 雷达设备性能标准〔参考res.A.222(VII)和MSC.64(67)〕	货船;客船	SOLAS公约reg.V/12	19.11.81(对于1984年9月1日之前安装的设备)
A.478(XII) 速度和距离指示装置性能标准〔参考res.A.824(19)〕	货船;客船	SOLAS公约reg.V/12	01.09.84(对于1997年1月1日之前安装的设备)
A.479(XII) 船上使用的带有差分奥米伽的接收器的性能标准	货船;客船	SOLAS第V章	19.11.81
A.481(XII)安全配员原则	货船;客船	SOLAS公约reg.V/13	19.11.81
A.484(XII) 渔船航行值班应遵守的基本原则	渔船	STCW-F公约reg.IV/1	19.11.81
A.485(XII) 海上引航员(深海引航员除外)培训、资格和操作程序	货船;客船		19.11.81
A.488(XII) 标准航海用语的使用	货船;客船	SOLAS公约reg.V/13.3; STCW公约regs.II/1、II/5.16和IV/2	19.11.81
A.524(13) VHF多频道值守设备性能标准	货船;客船	SOLAS公约reg.IV/14	17.11.83

Name of the instrument	Ship types to which the requirements are applicable	Reference to relevant regulations in Conventions, as appropriate	Application date
A.526(13) Performance standards for rate-of-turn indicators (ROTI) (refer to res. A.281 (VIII)	Cargo ships; passenger ships	SOLAS reg.V/12	17.11.83 for equipment installed on or after 01.09.84
A.529(13) Accuracy standards for navigation	Cargo ships; passenger ships	SOLAS reg.IV/14	17.11.83
A.538(13) Maritime safety training of personnel on mobile offshore units	MODUs	1995 STCW Conference resolution 10	17.11.83
A.539(13) Certification of skippers and officers in charge of a navigational watch on fishing vessels of 24 metres in length and over	Fishing vessels	STCW-F regs.II/1 and 2	17.11.83
A.561(14) Translation of the text of certificates (refer to MSC/Circ.704)	Cargo ships; passenger ships		20.11.85
A.568(14) Use of the COSPAS-SARSAT low polar orbiting satellite EPIRB system	Cargo ships; passenger ships	SOLAS ch. IV	20.11.85
A.576(14) Standards for skippers and officers in charge of a navigational watch on fishing vessels of less than 24 metres in length operating in unlimited and limited waters	Fishing vessels	SOLAS reg. V/13; FAO/ILO/IMO Document for Guidance on Fishermen's Training and Certification	20.11.85
A.600(15) IMO ship identification number scheme	Cargo ships; passenger ships	SOLAS regs.I/12, 1/13 and XI/3	01.01.96
A.601(15) Provision and display of manoeuvring information on board ships (supersedes res. A.209(VII))	Cargo ships; passenger ships	SOLAS regs. II-1/28; STCW reg./1	19.11.87
A.606(15) Review and evaluation of the GMDSS	Cargo ships; passenger ships	SOLAS ch.IV	19.11.87
A.609(15) Performance standards for shipborne VHF radio installations capable of voice communication and digital selective calling (refer to res. A.803(19))	Cargo ships; passenger ships	SOLAS reg.V/14.1	19.11.87 for equipment installed before 23.11.96
A.610(15) Performance standards for shipborne MF radio installations capable of voice communication and digital selective calling (refer to res.A.804(19))	Cargo ships; passenger ships	SOLAS reg. V/14.1	19.11.87 for equipment installed before 23.11.96
A.612(15) Performance standards for float-free VHF EPIRBs (refer to res.A.805(19))	Cargo ships; passenger ships	SOLAS reg.V/14.1	19.11.87 for equipment installed before 23.11.96

文件名称	适用规定要求的船舶类型	涉及的有关公约规则	实施日期
A.526(13) 船舶转头速率指示器性能标准(ROTI)〔参考res.A.281(Ⅷ)〕	货船；客船	SOLAS公约 reg. Ⅴ/12	在 01.09.84 及以后安装的设备为17.11.83
A.529(13) 导航仪精度标准	货船；客船	货船；客船	17.11.83
A.538(13) 海上移动装置上人员的航海安全培训	移动式近海钻井装置	1995年STCW会议的决议10	17.11.83
A.539(13) 船长在24米及以上的渔船船长和负责航行值班驾驶员的证书	渔船	STCW-F公约 reg. Ⅱ/1 和 2	17.11.83
A.561(14) 证书上文字的翻译(参考MSC/Circ.704)	货船；客船		20.11.85
A.568(14) 全球卫星搜救系统低极轨卫星 EPIRB 系统的使用	货船；客船	SOLAS公约第Ⅳ章	20.11.85
A.576(14) 船长在24米及以上的渔船船长和负责航行值班驾驶员在非限制水域和限制水域中的作业标准	渔船	SOLAS公约 reg. Ⅴ/13；FAO/ILO/IMO 关于渔船船员培训和发证指南的文件	20.11.85
A.600(15) IMO 关于船舶识别号方案	货船；客船	SOLAS公约 reg. Ⅰ/12，Ⅰ/13 和 Ⅺ/3	01.01.96
A.601(15) 船上操纵信息的规定和陈列	货船；客船	SOLAS公约 reg. Ⅱ-1/28；STCW公约规则/1	19.11.87
A.606(15) GMDSS审核和评估	货船；客船	SOLAS公约 reg.Ⅳ	19.11.87
A.609(15) 具有语音通信和数字选择性呼叫的船舶 VHF 无线电设备的性能标准〔参考 res. A.803(19)〕	货船；客船	SOLAS公约 reg. Ⅴ/14.1	23.11.96（对于1987年11月19日之前安装的设备）
A.610(15) 具有语音通信和数字选择性呼叫的船舶 MF 无线电设备的性能标准〔参考 res. A.804(19)〕	货船；客船	SOLAS公约 reg. Ⅴ/14.1	23.11.96（对于1987年11月19日之前安装的设备）
A.612(15) 自浮式 VHF EPIRBs 设备的性能标准〔参考res.A.805(19)〕	货船；客船	SOLAS公约 reg. Ⅴ/14.1	23.11.96（对于1987年11月19日之前安装的设备）

Name of the instrument	Ship types to which the requirements are applicable	Reference to relevant regulations in Conventions, as appropriate	Application date
A.613(15) Performance standards for shipborne MF/HF radio installations capable of voice communication, narrow-band direct-printing and digital selective calling (refer to res. A.806(19))	Cargo ships; passenger ships	SOLAS reg. V/14.1	19.11.87 for equipment installed before 23.11.96
A.622(15) Basic principles to be observed in keeping an engineering watch on board fishing vessels	Fishing vessels	FAO/ILO/IMO Document for Guidance on Fishermen's Training and Certification	19.11.87
A.623(15) Minimum requirements for certification of chief engineer officers and second engineer officers of fishing vessels powered by main propulsion machinery of 750 kW propulsion power or more	Fishing vessels	STCW-F reg. /5	19.11.87
A.657(16) Instructions for action in survival craft (revokes res. A.181(VI) and A.216(VII))	Cargo ships constructed before 01.07.98; passenger ships Cargo ships constructed on or after 01.07.98; passenger ships	SOLAS regs.III/38.5.1.22, 38.5.1.23, 41.8.4 and 51.15 SOLAS regs. III/3.5.15; LSA Code paragraphs 4.1.22, 4.1.23 and 4.4.4	19.10.89
A.661(16) Performance standards for float-free satellite EPIRBs operating through the geostationary INMARSAT satellite system on 1.6 GHz (refer to res. A.812(19))	Cargo ships; passenger ships	SOLAS reg.IV/14.1	19.10.89 for equipment installed before 23.11.96
A.662(16) Performance standards for float-free release and activation arrangements for emergency radio equipment	Cargo ships; passenger ships	SOLAS reg.IV/14.1	19.10.89
A.663(16) Performance standards for INMARSAT standards ship earth stations capable of transmitting and receiving direct-printing communications (refer to res. A.807(19))	Cargo ships; passenger ships	SOLAS reg.IV/14.1	19.10.89 for equipment installed before 23.11.96
A.664(16) Performance standards for enhanced group call equipment	Cargo ships; passenger ships	SOLAS reg.IV/14.1	19.10.89
A.665(16) Performance standards for radio direction-finding arrangements	Cargo ships; passenger ships	SOLAS reg.IV/14.1	19.10.89
A.694(17) General requirements for shipborne radio equipment forming part of the GMDSS and for electronic navigational aids (revokes res. A.569(14) and A.574(14))	Cargo ships; passenger ships	SOLAS reg.IV/14.1 and V/12(r)	06.11.91

文件名称	适用规定要求的船舶类型	涉及的有关公约规则	实施日期
A.613(15) 具备声音通信和数字选择性呼叫功能的船用MF/HF无线电设备的性能标准〔参考res.A.806(19)〕	货船;客船	SOLAS公约reg.Ⅴ/14.1	19.11.87(对于1996年11月23日之前安装的设备)
A.622(15) 渔船轮机值班应遵守的基本原则	渔船	FAO/ILO/IMO有关渔民培训和发证的指导文件	19.11.87
A.623(15) 主推进器功率750 kW及以上渔船轮机长和大管轮的发证最低要求	渔船	STCW-F公约reg./5	19.11.87
A.657(16) 救生艇操作说明〔撤销res.A.181(Ⅵ)和A.216(Ⅶ)〕	建造于1998年7月1日之前货船;客船	SOLAS公约reg.Ⅲ/38.5.1.22, 38.5.1.23, 41.8.4和51.15	19.10.89
	建造于1998年7月1日或之后的货船;客船	SOLAS公约reg.Ⅲ/3.5.15;LSA规则第4.1.22, 4.1.23和4.4.4款	
A.661(16) 以1.6 GHz通过INMARSAT同步卫星工作的自浮式卫星EPIRBs的性能标准〔参考res.A.812(19)〕	货船;客船	SOLAS公约reg.Ⅳ/14.1	19.10.89(对于1996年11月23日之前安装的设备)
A.662(16) 应急无线电设备自浮释放和触发式装置的性能标准	货船;客船	SOLAS公约reg.Ⅳ/14.1	19.10.89
A.663(16) 具备发射和接收直接打印信息功能的INMARSAT标准船舶地面站的性能标准〔参考res.A.807(19)〕	货船;客船	SOLAS公约reg.Ⅳ/14.1	19.10.89(对于1996年11月23日之前安装的设备)
A.664(16) 加强的群呼设备性能标准	货船;客船	SOLAS公约reg.Ⅳ/14.1	19.10.89
A.665(16) 无线电测向设备的性能标准	货船;客船	SOLAS公约reg.Ⅳ/14.1	19.10.89
A.694(17) 构成GMDSS组成部分的船用无线电设备和电子导航设备的一般要求〔撤销res.A.569(14)和A.574(14)〕	货船;客船	SOLAS公约reg.Ⅳ/14.1和Ⅴ/12(r)	06.11.91

Name of the instrument	Ship types to which the requirements are applicable	Reference to relevant regulations in Conventions, as appropriate	Application date
A.698(17) Performance standards for earth stations capable of two-way communications (revokes res. A.608(15)) (refer to res. A.808(19))	Cargo ships; passenger ships	SOLAS reg.IV/14.1	06.11.91 for equipment installed before 23.11.96
A.700(17) Performance standards for narrow-band direct-printing telegraph equipment for the reception of navigational and meteorological warnings and urgent information to ships (MS) by HF (refer to res. A.420(XI), A.525(13) and A.613(15))	Cargo ships; passenger ships	SOLAS reg. IV/14.1	06.11.91
A.701(17) Carriage of INMARSAT EGC SafetyNET receivers under the GMDSS	Cargo ships; passenger ships	SOLAS reg.IV/14.1 and V/20	06.11.91
A.702(17) Radio maintenance guidelines for the GMDSS related to sea areas A3 and A4	Cargo ships; passenger ships	SOLAS reg.IV/15.7	06.11.91
A.712(17) Recommended Standards of specialized training, qualification and certification of key personnel assigned responsibility for essential marine functions on mobile offshore units (MOU) Radio maintenance guidelines for the GMDSS related to sea areas A3 and A4	MOUs	1995 STCW Conference resolution 10	06.11.91
A.741(18) International Management Code for the Safe Operation of Ships and for Pollution Prevention (International Safety Management (ISM) Code)	Cargo ships; passenger ships	SOLAS ch. IX	04.11.93
A.762(18) Performance standards for survival craft two-way VHF radiotelephone apparatus (refer to res.A.809(19))	Cargo ships; passenger ships	SOLAS reg.III/6.2.1	04.11.93 for equipment installed before 23.11.96
A.763(18) Performance standards for float-free satellite EPIRBs operating on 406 MHz (revokes res, A.695(17)) (refer to res. A.810(19))	Cargo ships; passenger ships	SOLAS reg. IV/14.1	04.11.94 for equipment installed before 04.11.94 or before 23.11.96, where applicable
A.788(19) Guidelines on implementation of the ISM Code by Administrations	Cargo ships; passenger ships	SOLAS ch. IX	23.11.95
A.802(19) Performance standards for survival craft radar transponders for use in search and rescue operations (revokes res. A.697(17)) (refer to res. A.694(17))	Cargo ships; passenger ships	SOLAS reg. III/6.2.2 and IV/7.13	23.11.95

文件名称	适用规定要求的船舶类型	涉及的有关公约规则	实施日期
A.698(17) 能够进行双向通信的地面站的性能标准〔撤销 res.A608(15)〕〔参考 res.A.808(19)〕	货船；客船	SOLAS 公约 reg.Ⅳ/14.1	6.11.91（对于 1996 年 11 月 23 日之前安装的设备）
A.700(17) 用高频接收航海和气象警告以及船舶紧急信息(MS)的窄带直接印字电报设备的性能标准〔参考决议 A.420(Ⅺ), A.525(13) 和 A.613(15)〕	货船；客船	SOLAS 公约 reg.Ⅳ/14.1	06.11.91
A701(17) 配备 GMDSS 系统 INMARSAT EGC 安全网络接收机	货船；客船	SOLAS 公约 reg.Ⅳ/14.1 和 Ⅴ/20	06.11.91
A.702(17) A3 和 A4 海区 GMDSS 无线电维修指南	货船；客船	SOLAS 公约 reg.Ⅳ/15.7	06.11.91
A.712(17) 根据 A3 和 A4 海区 GMDSS 无线电维修指南指定负责移动式近海装置主要海上职能的关键人员的特殊培训、资格和发证的推荐标准	移动式近海装置	1995 年 STCW 大会决议 10	06.11.91
A.741(18) 国际船舶安全营运和防污管理规则〔国际安全管理(ISM)规则〕	货船；客船	SOLAS 公约第Ⅸ章	04.11.93
A.762(18) 救生筏双向 VHF 无线电话设备性能标准〔参考 res.A.809(19)〕	货船；客船	SOLAS 公约 reg.Ⅲ/6.2.1	04.11.93（对于 1996 年 11 月 23 日之前安装的设备）
A.763(18) 406 MHz 工作频率的自浮式卫星 EPIRBs 的性能标准〔撤销 res.A.695(17)〕〔参考 A.810(19)〕	货船；客船	SOLAS 公约 reg.Ⅳ/14.1	04.11.94(对于在 1996 年 11 月 23 日之前，可行的话在 1996 年 11 月 23 日之前安装的设备）
A.788(19) 主管机关实施 ISM 规则的指导原则	货船；客船	SOLAS 公约第Ⅸ章	23.11.95
A.802(19) 用于搜救作业的救生艇雷达应答标性能标准〔撤销 res.A.697(17)〕〔参考 res.A.694(17)〕	货船；客船	SOLAS 公约 regs. Ⅱ/6.2.2 和 Ⅳ/7.13	23.11.95

Name of the instrument	Ship types to which the requirements are applicable	Reference to relevant regulations in Conventions, as appropriate	Application date
A.803(19) Performance standards for shipborne VHF radio installations capable of voice communication and digital selective calling (refer to res. A.609(15) and A.694(17))	Cargo ships; passenger ships	SOLAS reg. IV/14.1	23.11.95 for equipment installed on or after 23.11.96
A.805(19) Performance standards for float-free VHF EPIRBs (refer to res. A.612(15) and A.694(17))	Cargo ships; passenger ships	SOLAS reg. IV/14.1	23.11.95 for equipment installed on or after 23.11.96
A.806(19) Performance standards for shipborne MF/HF radio installations capable of voice communication, narrow-band direct-printing and digital selective calling (refer to res. A.613(15) and A.694(17))	Cargo ships; passenger ships	SOLAS reg. IV/14.1	23.11.95 for equipment installed on or after 23.11.96
A.807(19) Performance standards for INMARSAT-C ship earth stations capable of transmitting and receiving direct-printing communications (refer to res. A.663(15) and A.694(17))	Cargo ships; passenger ships	SOLAS reg. IV/14.1	23.11.95 for equipment installed on or after 23.11.96
A.808(19) Performance standards for ship earth stations capable of two-way communications (refer to res. A.694(17) and A.698(17))	Cargo ships; passenger ships	SOLAS reg. IV/14.1	23.11.95 for equipment installed on or after 23.11.96
A.809(19) Performance standards for survival craft two-way VHF radiotelephone apparatus (refer to res. A.694(17) and A.762(18))	Cargo ships; passenger ships	SOLAS reg.III/6.2.1	23.11.95 for equipment installed on or after 23.11.96
A.810(19) Performance standards for float-free satellite EPIRBs operating on 406 MHz (refer to res. A.694(17) and A.763(18))	Cargo ships; passenger ships	SOLAS reg.IV/7.1.6 and 14.1	23.11.95 for equipment installed on or after 23.11.96
A.811(19) Performance standards for a shipborne integrated radiocommunication system (IRCS) when used in the GMDSS (refer to res. A.694(17))	Cargo ships; passenger ships	SOLAS reg.IV/4, 6 and 14	23.11.95
A.812(19) Performance standards for float-free satellite EPIRBs operating through the geostationary INMARSAT satellite system on 1.6 GHz (refer to res. A.661(16), A.662(16) and A.694(17))	Cargo ships; passenger ships	SOLAS reg.IV/7.1.6 and 14.1	23.11.95 for equipment installed on or after 23.11.96

文件名称	适用规定要求的船舶类型	涉及的有关公约规则	实施日期
A.803(19) 具备声音通信和数字选择性呼叫功能的船用VHF无线电设备的性能标准〔参考res.A.609(15)和A.694(17)〕	货船；客船	SOLAS公约reg.Ⅳ/14.1	23.11.95(对于在1996年11月23日或之后安装的设备)
A.805(19) 自浮式VHF EPIRB的性能标准〔参考res.A.612(15)和A.694(17)〕	货船；客船	SOLAS公约reg.Ⅳ/14.1	23.11.95(对于在1996年11月23日或之后安装的设备)
A.806(19) 具备声音通信、窄带直接印字电报和数字选择性呼叫功能的船用MF/HF无线电设备的性能标准〔参考res.A.613(15)和A.694(17)〕	货船；客船	SOLAS公约reg.Ⅳ/14.1	23.11.95(对于在1996年11月23日或之后安装的设备)
A.807(19) 具备发射和接收直接打印信息功能的INMARSAT-C船舶地球站的性能标准〔参考res.A.663(15)和A.694(17)〕	货船；客船	SOLAS公约reg.Ⅳ/14.1	23.11.95(对于在1996年11月23日或之后安装的设备)
A.808(19) 具备进行双向通信功能的船舶地球站的性能标准〔参考res.A.694(17)和A.698(17)〕	货船；客船	SOLAS公约reg.Ⅳ/14.1	23.11.95(对于在1996年11月23日或之后安装的设备)
A.809(19) 救生艇双向VHF无线电话设备的性能标准〔参考res.A.694(17)和A.762(18)〕	货船；客船	SOLAS公约reg.Ⅲ/6.2 1	23.11.95(对于在1996年11月23日或之后安装的设备)
A.810(19) 406 MHz工作频率的自浮式卫星EPIRBs的性能标准〔参考res.A.694(17)和A.763(18)〕	货船；客船	SOLAS公约reg.Ⅳ/7.1 6和14.1	23.11.95(对于在1996年11月23日或之后安装的设备)
A.811(19) 用于GMDSS时船用综合无线电通信系统(IRCS)的性能标准〔参考res.A.694(17)〕	货船；客船	SOLAS公约reg.Ⅳ/4,6和14	23.11.95
A.812(19) 通过INMARSAT同步卫星以1.6 GHz频率工作的自浮式卫星EPIRBs的性能标准〔参考res.A.661(16)，A.662(16)和A.694(17)〕	货船；客船	SOLAS公约reg.Ⅳ/7.1.6和14.1	23.11.95(对于在1996年11月23日或之后安装的设备)

Name of the instrument	Ship types to which the requirements are applicable	Reference to relevant regulations in Conventions, as appropriate	Application date
A.816(19) Performance standards for shipborne DECCA navigator receivers	Cargo ships; passenger ships	SOLAS ch.V	23.11.95
A.817(19) Performance standards for electronic chart display and information systems (ECDIS)	Cargo ships; passenger ships	SOLAS reg. V/20	23.11.95
A.818(19) Performance standards for shipborne LORAN-C and CHAYKA receivers	Cargo ships; passenger ships	SOLAS ch.V	23.11.95
A.819(19) Performance standards for shipborne GPS receiver equipment	Cargo ships; passenger ships	SOLAS ch.V	23.11.95
A.820(19) Performance standards for navigational equipment for high-speed craft	High-speed craft	SOLAS reg.X/3; HSC Code	23.11.95
A.821(19) Performance standards for gyro-compass for high-speed craft (refer to res. A.694(17))	High-speed craft	SOLAS reg.X/3; HSC Code	23.11.95
A.822(19) Performance standards for automatic steering aids (automatic pilots) for high-speed craft (refer to res. A.694(17))	High-speed craft	SOLAS reg. X/3; HSC Code	23.11.95
A.823(19) Performance standards for automatic radar plotting aids (ARPAs) (refer to res. A.422(XI), A.477(XII) and A.694(17))	Cargo ships; passenger ships	SOLAS reg. V/12	23.11.95 for equipment installed on or after 01.01.97
A.824(19) Performance standards for devices to indicate speed and distance (refer to res. A.478(XII), A694(17))	Cargo ships; passenger ships	SOLAS reg. V/12	23.11.95 for equipment installed on or after 01.01.97
A.828(19) Recommendations on maritime safety and emergency preparedness training for all personnel working on Mobile Offshore Units (MOUs)	MOUs	1995 STCW Conference resolution 10	23.11.95
A.848(20) Implementation of the ISM Code	Passenger ships including passenger high-speed craft, oil tankers, chemical tankers, gas tankers, bulk carriers and cargo high-speed craft, regardless of their date of construction	UNCLOS art.217; SOLAS ch. IX	01.07.98
	Other general cargo ships and mobile offshore drilling units	UNCLOS art.217; SOLAS ch. IX	01.07.2002

文件名称	适用规定要求的船舶类型	涉及的有关公约规则	实施日期
A.816(19) 船用 DECCA 导航仪接收器的性能标准	货船；客船	SOLAS 公约第 V 章	23.11.95
A.817(19) 电子海图显示与信息系统性能标准(ECDIS)	货船；客船	SOLAS 公约 reg. V/2C	23.11.95
A.818(19) 船用 LORAN-C 和 CHAYKA 接收器的性能标准	货船；客船	SOLAS 公约第 V 章	23.11.95
A.819(19) 船用 GPS 接收机设备的性能标准	货船；客船	SOLAS 公约第 V 章	23.11.95
A.820(19) 高速艇导航设备的性能标准	高速艇	SOLAS 公约 reg. X/3；HSC 规则	23.11.95
A.821(19) 高速艇陀螺罗经的性能标准〔参考 res. A.694(17)〕	高速艇	SOLAS 公约 reg. X/3；HSC 规则	23.11.95
A.822(19) 高速艇自动驾驶仪(自动舵)的性能标准〔参考 res.A694(17)〕	高速艇	SOLAS 公约 reg. X/3；HSC 规则	23.11.95
A.823(19) 自动雷达标绘仪(ARPAs)的性能标准〔参考 A.422(XI)、A.477(XII)和 A.694(17)〕	货船；客船	SOLAS 公约 reg. V/12	23.11.95(对于在 1997 年 1 月 1 日或之后安装的设备)
A.824(19) 速度和距离指示装置的性能标准〔参考 res.A.478.(XII)、A.694(17)〕	货船；客船	SOLAS 公约 reg. V/12	23.11.95(对于在 1997 年 1 月 1 日或之后安装的设备)
A.828(19) 有关移动式近海装置(MOUs)的所有工作人员海上安全和应急准备培训的建议案	移动式近海装置	1995 年 STCW 大会决议 10	23.11.95
A.848(20) ISM 规则的实施	无论何时建造的客船(包括客运高速艇、油船、化学品船、气体运输船、散货船和货运高速艇)	UNCLOS 公约第 217 条；SOLAS 公约第 IX 章	01.07.98
	其他杂货船和移动式近岸钻井装置	UNCLOS 公约第 217 条；SOLAS 公约第 IX 章	01.07.2002

Name of the instrument	Ship types to which the requirements are applicable	Reference to relevant regulations in Conventions, as appropriate	Application date
A.849(20) Code for the Investigation of Marine Casualties and Incidents (revokes res. A. 173(ES.IV), A.440(XI) and A.637(16))	All ships	UNCLOS art.2 and 94; SOLAS reg.I.21; LL art.23; MARPOL art.12	27.11.97
A.861(20) Performance standards for shipborne voyage data recorders (VDRs)	Cargo ships; passenger ships	1995 SOLAS Conference resolution 12	27.11.97
A.862(20) Code of practice for the safe loading and unloading of bulk cargoes (revokes MSC/Circ.690 and DSC/Circ.3)) (refer to res. A.713(17) and A.797(19))	Ships carrying solid bulk cargoes	SOLAS reg. VI/7	27.11.97
A.865(20) Minimum training requirements for personnel nominated to assist passengers in emergency situations on passenger ships (revokes res. A770(18))	Passenger ships	SOLAS reg.III/10.2; STCW regs. VI/1, VI/2, VI/3 and VI/4; STCW 95 regs V/2 and V/3	27.11.97
A.866(20) Guidance to ships' crews and terminal personnel for bulk carrier inspections	Bulk carriers	SOLAS reg. XI/2	27.11.97

INSTRUMENTS BY JOINT MEETINGS

Name of the instrument	Ship types to which the requirements are applicable	Reference to relevant regulations in Conventions, as appropriate	Application date
FAO/ILO/IMO Code of Safety for Fishermen and Fishing vessels, Part A and B	Fishing vessels		09.68 (Part A); 02.74 (part B)
FAO/ILO/IMO Document for Guidance on Fishermen's Training and Certification	Fishing vessels		1988

MSC RESOLUTIONS[1]

Name of the instrument	Ship types to which the requirements are applicable	Reference to relevant regulations in Conventions, as appropriate	Application date
MSC.36(63) International Code of Safety for High-Speed Craft (HSC Code)	High-speed craft	SOLAS ch.X	01.01.96
MSC.37(63) Amendments to the Code of Safety for Dynamically Supported Craft (res A.373(X))	Dynamically supported craft constructed before 01.01.96		20.05.94
MSC.48(66) Adoption of the International Life-Saving Appliance (LSA) Code	Cargo ships constructed on or after 01.07.98; passenger ships;	SOLAS ch.III	01.07.98

---

1 this section does not include MSC resolutions listed in the section "Conventions" above

文件名称	适用规定要求的船舶类型	涉及的有关公约规则	实施日期
A.849(20) 海上伤亡和事故调查规则〔撤销res.A.173(ES.Ⅳ),A.440(Ⅺ)和A.637(16)〕	所有船舶	UNCLOS公约第2条和第94条;SOLAS公约reg.Ⅰ.21;LL公约第23条;MARPOL第12条	27.11.97
A.861(20) 船用航行数据记录仪(VDR)的性能标准	货船;客船	1995年SOLAS大会决议12	27.11.97
A.862(20) 散装货物安全装卸操作规则〔撤销res.A.713(17)和A.797(19)〕〔参考res.A.713(17)和A.797(19)〕	固体散货船	SOLAS公约reg.Ⅵ/7	27.11.97
A.865(20) 客船紧急状态协助乘客指定人员的最低培训要求〔撤销A.770(18)〕	客船	SOLAS公约reg.Ⅲ/10.2;STCW公约reg.Ⅵ/1, Ⅵ/2和Ⅵ/4;STCW 95公约reg.Ⅴ/2和Ⅴ/3	27.11.97
A.866(20) 船员和码头人员检查散货船指导书	散货船	SOLAS公约reg.Ⅺ/2	27.11.97

联席会议文件

文件名称	适用规定要求的船舶类型	涉及的有关公约规则	实施日期
FAO/ILO/IMO渔民和渔船安全规则,A部分和B部分	渔船		1968年9月(A部分);1974年2月(B部分)
FAO/ILO/IMO渔民培训和发证指导文件	渔船		1998年

MSC决议[1]

文件名称	适用规定要求的船舶类型	涉及的有关公约规则	实施日期
MSC.36(63) 高速艇安全国际规则(HSC规则)	高速艇	SOLAS公约第Ⅹ章	01.01.96
MSC.37(63) 动力承载艇安全规则修正案〔res.A.373(Ⅹ)〕	1996年1月1日之前建造的动力承载艇		20.05.94
MSC.48(66) 国际救生设备(LSA)规则的采用	1998年7月1日或之后建造的货船;客船	SOLAS公约第Ⅲ章	01.07.98

---

1 本节没有包括列在上面的"公约"一节的MSC决议

Name of the instrument	Ship types to which the requirements are applicable	Reference to relevant regulations in Conventions, as appropriate	Application date
MSC.68(68) Adoption of amendments to performance standards for shipborne radiocommunication equipment (amends res. A.803(19), A.804(19), A.806(19) and A.807(19))	Cargo ships; passenger ships	SOLAS reg.IV/14	01.01.2000
MSC.72(69) Adoption, designation and substitution of archipelagic sea lanes	Cargo ships; passenger ships	SOLAS reg. V/8	
MSC.77(69) Maintenance of a continuous listening watch on VHF channel 16 by SOLAS ship whilst at sea after 1 February 1999 and installation of VHF DSC facilities on non-SOLAS ships	Cargo ships; passenger ships	SOLAS reg.IV/12.3	01.12.98

MSC CIRCULARS

Name of the instrument	Ship types to which the requirements are applicable	Reference to relevant regulations in Conventions, as appropriate	Application date
MSC/Circ.443 Measures to prevent unlawful acts against passengers and crews on abroad ships (refer to res. A.584(14))	Passenger ships	SUA 1988[1]	17.09.86 06.12.96
MSC/Circ.472 Guidelines on the definition of near-coastal voyages	Cargo ships; passenger ships	STCW reg.I/1.1.13	01.05.87
MSC/Circ.566 Provisional guidelines on the conduct of trials in which the officer of the navigational watch acts as the sole look-out in periods of darkness (refer to MSC/Circ.867)Guidelines on the definition of near-coastal voyages	Cargo ships; passenger ships	STCW reg.I/5	24.05.91
MSC/Circ.619 Minimum in-service eyesight standards	Cargo ships; passenger ships	STCW reg. I/9	28.05.93
MSC/Circ.673 On-board communication phrases for passenger care	Passenger ships	SOLAS ch. IV	09.12.94
MSC/Circ.692 Clarification of SOLAS reg.III/50 regarding general/emergency alarm systems	Cargo and passenger ships constructed before 01.07.98; Cargo and passenger ships constructed on or after 01.07.98	SOLAS reg. III/50 LSA Code paragraph 7.2	17.05.95
MSC/Circ.693 Draft amendments to the International Safety Management (ISM) Code	Cargo ships; passenger ships	SOLAS ch.IX	17.05.95

1 "SUA 1988" means the Convention for the Suppression of Unlawful Acts against the Safety of Maritime Navigation, 1988

文件名称	适用规定要求的船舶类型	涉及的有关公约规则	实施日期
MSC.68(68) 船用无线电通信设备性能标准修正案的采用〔修改 res.A.803(19)，A.804(19)，A.806(19)和 A.807(19)〕	货船；客船	SOLAS 公约 reg. IV/14	01.01.2000
MSC.72(69) 群岛间海上通道的采用、指定和更换	货船；客船	SOLAS 公约 reg. V/8	
MSC.77(69) 1999年2月1日之后SOLAS船舶在海上保持连续守听VHF 16频道；非SOLAS船舶安装VHF DSC设备	货船；客船	SOLAS 公约 reg. IV/12.3	01.12.98

表 3-9　MSC 文件

文件名称	适用规定要求的船舶类型	涉及的有关公约规则	实施日期
MSC/Circ.443 防止船上乘客和船员非法行为的措施〔参考 res.A.584(14)〕	客船	SUA 1998[1]	17.09.86 06.12.96
MSC/Circ.472 有关近岸航行定义的指导原则	货船；客船	STCW 公约 reg. I/1.1.13	01.05.87
MSC/Circ.566 黑暗期间担当唯一瞭望人员的航行值班驾驶员实施试航行的临时性指导原则(参考 MSC/Circ.867)；有关近岸航行定义的指导原则	货船；客船	STCW 公约 reg. I/5	24.05.91
MSC/Circ.619 任职最低视力标准	货船；客船	STCW 公约 reg. I/9	28.05.93
MSC/Circ.673 船上乘客管理通信用语	客船	SOLAS 公约第 IV 章	09.12.94
MSC/Circ.692 有关一般/紧急警报系统的 SOLAS 公约 reg. III/50 的解释	1998年7月1日之前建造的货船和客船； 1998年7月1日或之后建造的货船和客船	SOLAS 公约 reg. III/50 LSA 规则第 7.2 款	17.05.95
MSC/Circ.693 国际安全管理(ISM)规则修正案草案	货船；客船	SOLAS 公约第 IX 章	17.05.95

1　"SUA 1988"指1988年制止影响海上航行安全非法行为的公约

Name of the instrument	Ship types to which the requirements are applicable	Reference to relevant regulations in Conventions, as appropriate	Application date
MSC/Circ.704 Listing of certificates and documents required to be carried on board ships (revise MSC/Circ.704)	Cargo ships; passenger ships	SOLAS regs. I/12, II-2/54.3, VI/9, VII/5(5), X/3, XI/2, II-1/22, V/13(b); MARPOL regs.I/5, 20, 26,13G, III/4, II/12 and 12a, II/9, 13(4); TM art.7; LL art. 16; STCW art. VI	21.09.95
MSC/Circ.710 Model agreements for the authorization of recognized organizations acting on behalf of the Administration	Cargo ships; passenger ships	SOLAS reg. XI/1	17.05.95
MSC/Circ.733 Officer of the navigational watch acting as the sole look-out in periods of darkness (refer to MSC/Circ.867)	Cargo ships; passenger ships	STCW reg. VIII/2	06.06.96
MSC/Circ.760 Guidelines for a structure of an integrated system of contingency planning for shipboard emergencies	Cargo ships; passenger ships	SOLAS ch. III and IX; MARPOL Annex I, regs.XI/1	05.06.96
MSC/Circ.762 Implementation of the ISM Code- Guidance to companies operating multi-flagged fleets and supplementary guidelines to Administrations	Cargo ships; passenger ships	SOLAS reg. XI/4.1	10.07.96
MSC/Circ.788 Authorization or recognised organizations acting on behalf of Administrations	Cargo ships; passenger ships	SOLAS reg. XI/1	06.12.96
MSC/Circ.794 IMO Standard Marine Communication Phrases (SMCPs) (refer to res. A.380 (X))	Cargo ships; passenger ships	STCW ch.II	06.06.97
MSC/Circ.795 Clarification of regulations II/1, II/2 II/3 and II/4 of the STCW-F Convention	Fishing vessels	STCW-F regs II/1, II/2, 11/3 and II/4	06.06.97
MSC/Circ.805 Guidance for the use of radio signals by ships under attack of threat of attack from pirates or armed robbers (refer to res. A.738(18))	Cargo ships; passenger ships	SUA 1988 (refer to the footnote to MSC/Circ.443)	06.06.97
MSC/Circ.853 Guidance on shipboard assessments of proficiency	Cargo ships; passenger ships	STCW reg.I/6; STCW Code Section A-I/6	20.05.98
MSC/Circ.857 Revised medical first aid guide (MFAG) (revokes MSC/Circ.333, 371,392 and 643)	Ships carrying dangerous goods	SOLAS Ch.VII	20.05.98
MSC/Circ.862 Clarification of certain requirements in IMO performance standards for GMDSS equipment	Cargo ships; passenger ships	SOLAS reg.IV/14	01.02.99
MSC/Circ.867 Officer of the navigational watch acting as the sole look-out during period of darkness (refer to MSC/Circ.566 and MSC/Circ.733)	Cargo ships; passenger ships	STCW reg.I/13	20.05.98

文件名称	适用规定要求的船舶类型	涉及的有关公约规则	实施日期
MSC/Circ.704 船舶必须携带的证书和文件列表(修正MSC/Circ.704)	货船；客船	SOLAS 公约 reg. Ⅰ/12, Ⅱ-2/54.3, Ⅵ/9, Ⅶ/5(5), Ⅹ/3, Ⅺ/2, Ⅱ-1/22, Ⅴ/13(b); MARPOL 公约 regs. Ⅰ/5, 20, 26, 13G, Ⅲ/4, Ⅱ/12 和 12a, Ⅳ/9, 13(4); TM 第 7 条；LL 第 16 条；STCW 第Ⅵ条	21.09.95
MSC/Circ.710 代表主管机关的认可组织的授权示范协议	货船；客船	SOLAS公约 reg. Ⅺ/1	17.05.95
MSC/Circ.733 在黑暗期间担当唯一瞭望人员的航行值班驾驶员（参考MSC/Circ.867）	货船；客船	STCW 公约 reg.Ⅷ/2	06.06.96
MSC/Circ.760 为船上紧急情况设计的意外事故综合处理系统结构的指导原则	货船；客船	SOLAS公约第Ⅲ和Ⅸ章；MARPOL 附件 I.公约 regs. Ⅺ/1	05.06.96
MSC/Circ.762 多国籍船队的经营公司实施ISM规则的指导及主管机关补充的指导原则	货船；客船	SOLAS 公约 reg. Ⅺ/4.1	10.07.96
MSC/Circ.788 代表主管机关的经授权或认可的组织	货船；客船	SOLAS 公约 reg.Ⅺ/1	06.12.96
MSC/Circ.794 IMO标准航海通信用语(SMCPs)〔参考 res. A.380(X)〕	货船；客船	STCW公约第Ⅱ章	06.06.97
MSC/Circ.795 STCW-F 公约规则 Ⅱ/1, Ⅱ/2, Ⅱ/3 和 Ⅱ/4 的解释	渔船	STCW-F公约 reg.Ⅱ/1, Ⅱ/2, Ⅱ/3 和 Ⅱ/4	06.06.97
MSC/Circ.805 受海盗或武装强盗攻击威胁的船舶无线电信号的使用指导〔参考res.A.738(18)〕	货船；客船	SUA 1988（参考 MSC/Circ.443 脚注）	06.06.97
MSC/Circ.853 船上熟练评估指导	货船；客船	STCW 公约 reg. Ⅰ/6; STCW 规则第 A-Ⅰ/6 节	20.05.98
MSC/Circ.857 经修订的医疗急救指南(MFAG)（撤销MSC/Circ.333, 371, 392和643）	装载危险货物的船舶	SOLAS公约第Ⅶ章	20.05.98
MSC/Circ.862 对IMO GMDSS设备性能标准的某些要求的解释	货船；客船	SOLAS公约 reg. Ⅳ/14	01.02.99
MSC/Circ.867 在黑暗期间担当唯一瞭望人员的航行值班驾驶员(参考 MSC/Circ.566 和 MSC/Circ.733)	货船；客船	STCW 公约 reg.Ⅰ/13	20.05.98

OTHER SPECIFIC CIRCULARS

Name of the instrument	Ship types to which the requirements are applicable	Reference to relevant regulations in Conventions, as appropriate	Application date
SN/Circ.92 Guide to the planning and conduct of passage	Cargo ships; passenger ships	STCW ch.VIII	23.10.78
SN/Circ. 105 IALA buoyage system	Cargo ships; passenger ships	SOLAS reg.V/8	15.06.81
SN/Circ. 107 Maritime buoyage system	Cargo ships; passenger ships	SOLAS reg.V/8	18.09.81
SN/Circ. 114 Amendments to the standard marine navigational vocabulary	Cargo ships; passenger ships	STCW ch. II	01.08.83
SN/Circ. 120 IALA Maritime Buoyage System agreement	Cargo ships; passenger ships	COLREG	08.05.84
SN/Circ.129 Amendments to the standard marine navigational vocabulary	Cargo ships; passenger ships	STCW ch.II	01.01.87
SN/Circ.200 Adoption, designation and substitution of archipelagic sea lanes (Indonesian archipelagic waters) refer to res. MSC.72(69))	Cargo ships; passenger ships	SOLAS reg. V/8	19.05.98 not in force; implement not earlier than six months after the date of designation of sea lanes by the Government of Indonesia
COM/Circ.95 Recommendation on testing of the automatic device for generating the radiotelephone alarm signal	Cargo ships; passenger ships	SOLAS Ch.IV	18.04.84
COM/Circ. 108 GMDSS operating guidance for masters of ships in distress situation	Cargo ships; passenger ships	SOLAS Ch.IV	23.01.92
COM/Circ. 124 IMO/IHO Guide to drafting radio navigational warnings for the world-wide navigational warning service	Cargo ships; passenger ships	SOLAS Ch.V	20.02.95
STCW.6/Circ.4 Guidance regarding additional training for masters and chief mates of large ships and ships with unusual manoeuvring characteristics	Large ships and ships with unusual manoeuvring characteristics	STCW Code section B-VIII/5, part 5	20.05.98
STCW.7/Circ.2 Model training record book for candidates for certification as officers in charge of a navigational watch	Cargo ships; passenger ships	STCW regs.II/1, 2 and 3	20.09.96
STCW.7/Circ.3 Model training record book for candidates for certification as officers in charge of an engineering watch or designated duty engineers	Cargo ships; passenger ships	STCW regs. III/1, 2 and 3	20.09.96
STCW.7/Circ.8 Applications of provisions of the 1978 STCW Convention to Mobile Offshore Units (MOUs) (refer to res. A.583(13), A.712(17) and A.828(19))	Self-propelled MOUs	STCW	20.05.98

其他特别文件

文件名称	适用规定要求的船舶类型	涉及的有关公约规则	实施日期
SN/Circ.92 航行计划和管理指南	货船;客船	STCW 公约第Ⅷ章	23.10.78
SN/Circ.105 IALA 浮标系统	货船;客船	SOLAS 公约 reg.Ⅴ/8	15.06.81
SN/Circ.107 海上浮标系统	货船;客船	SOLAS 公约 reg.Ⅴ/8	18.09.81
SN/Circ.114 标准航海用语修正案	货船;客船	STCW 公约第Ⅱ章	01.08.83
SN/Circ.120 IALA 海上浮标系统协议	货船;客船	COLREG 公约	08.05.84
SN/Circ.129 标准航海用语修正案	货船;客船	SOLAS 公约第Ⅱ章	01.01.87
SN/Circ.200 群岛海上通道的采用、指定和替换(印尼群岛水域)〔参考 res.MSC.72(69)〕	货船;客船	SOLAS 公约 reg.Ⅴ/8	19.05.98 尚未生效,印尼政府采用海上航道指定日期之后不早于6个月生效
COM/Circ.95 试验无线电话警报信号产生自动装置的建议案	货船;客船	SOLAS 公约第Ⅳ章	18.04.84
COM/Circ.108 遇险船船长 GMDSS 操作指导	货船;客船	SOLAS 公约第Ⅳ章	23.01.92
COM/Circ.124 IMO/IHO 关于全球航海警告发布机构起草航海警告的指南	货船;客船	SOLAS 公约第Ⅴ章	20.02.95
STCW.6/Circ.4 大型船舶和具有特殊操纵特性的船舶船长和大副的附加培训指导	大型船舶和具有不寻常操纵特性的船舶	STCW 公约第 B-Ⅷ/5 节第5部分	20.05.98
STCW.7/Circ.2 航行值班高级船员证书申请人示范培训记录簿	货船;客船	STCW 公约 reg.Ⅱ/1,2 和3	20.09.96
STCW.7/Circ.3 轮机值班或指定值班轮机员的高级船员证书申请人示范培训记录簿	货船;客船	STCW 公约 reg.Ⅲ/1,2 和3	20.09.96
STCW.7/Circ.8 对移动式近海装置(MOUs)应用1978年STCW 公约的规定〔参考 res.A.583(13)、A.712(17)和 A.828(19)〕	自推式移动式近海装置	STCW 公约	20.05.98

IBC and IGC Codes

13. The following mandatory requirements for trained personnel are incorporated into Chapter 16, "Operational Requirements", of the International Code for the Construction and Equipment of Ships Carrying Dangerous Chemicals in Bulk (IBC Code):

   16.3   Personnel training*

   16.3.1   All personnel should be adequately trained in the use of protective equipment and have basic training in the procedures appropriate to their duties, necessary under emergency conditions.

   16.3.2   Personnel involved in cargo operations should be adequately trained in handling procedures.

   16.3.3   Officers should be trained in emergency procedures to deal with conditions of leakage, spillage or fire involving the cargo, and a sufficient number of them should be instructed and trained in essential first aid for cargoes carried.

   * *Reference is made to the provisions of the Regulation V/1 of the International Convention on Standards of Training, Certification and Watchkeeping for Seafarers, 1978, as amended and in particular to Section A-V/1.15—Chemical Tanker Training Programme*

14. The following mandatory requirements for trained personnel are incorporated into Chapter 18 of the International Code for the Construction and Equipment of Ships Carrying Liquefied Gases in Bulk (IGC Code):

   18.3   Personnel training**

   18.3.1   Personnel involved in cargo operations should be adequately trained in handling procedures.

   18.3.2   All personnel should be adequately trained in the use of protective equipment provided on board and have basic training in the procedures, appropriate to their duties, necessary under emergency conditions.

   18.3.3   Officers should be trained in emergency procedures to deal with conditions of leakage, spillage or fire involving the cargo and a sufficient number of them should be instructed and trained in essential first aid for the cargoes carried.

   ** *Reference is made to the provisions of the Regulation V/1 of the International Convention on Standards of Training, Certification and Watchkeeping for Seafarers, 1978, as amended and in particular to Section A-V/1.22—Liquefied Gas Tanker Training Programme*

ILO Convention No. 53

15. The relevant extract from the text of the ILO Officers' Competency Certificates Convention, 1936, is as follows:

IBC 和 IGC 规则

13. 下列关于教员的强制性要求被编入《国际散装运输危险化学品船舶构造和设备规则》(IBC 规则)第 16 章"操作性要求"。

    16.3　人员培训*

    16.3.1　所有人员都应充分地进行防护设备使用方面的培训,并进行适合其职责和紧急状态下必需程序的基本训练。

    16.3.2　与货物作业有关的人员应参加相应的装卸程序方面的培训。

    16.3.3　高级船员应进行有关货物溢漏或火灾应急程序方面的培训,其中大部分人还应接受对应所装运货物的必要的急救知识的指导和培训。

    * 参考经修订的《1978 年海员培训、发证和值班标准国际公约》规则 V/1 的规定,尤其是参考第 A-V/1.15 节——化学品船培训程序

14. 下列关于教员的强制性要求被编入《国际散装运输液化气体船舶构造和设备规则》(IGC 规则)第 18 章。

    18.3　人员培训**

    18.3.1　与货物作业有关的人员应参加相应的装卸程序方面的培训。

    18.3.2　所有人员都应充分地进行船上防护设备使用方面的培训,并进行适合其职责和紧急状态下需要的操作程序基本训练。

    18.3.3　高级船员应进行有关货物溢漏或火灾紧急程序方面的培训,其中大部分人还应接受基本的装运货物紧急救护方面的指导和培训。

    ** 参考经修订的《1978 年海员培训、发证和值班标准国际公约》规则 V/1 的规定,尤其是参考第 A-V/1.22 节——液化气体船培训程序

ILO 公约 No.53

15. 1936 年《ILO 高级船员适任证书公约》相关条文摘录如下:

Article 3

1. No person shall be engaged to perform or shall perform on board any vessel to which this Convention applies the duties of master or skipper, navigating officer in charge of a watch, chief engineer, or engineer officer in charge of a watch, unless he holds a certificate of competency to perform such duties, issued or approved by the public authority of the territory where the vessel is registered.

2. Exceptions to the provisions of this Article may be made only in cases of *force majeure*.

Article 4

1. No person shall be granted a certificate of competency unless—

    (a) he has reached the minimum age prescribed for the issue of the certificate in question;

    (b) his professional experience has been of the minimum duration prescribed for the issue of the certificate in question; and

    (c) he has passed the examinations organised and supervised by the competent authority for the purpose of testing whether he possesses the qualifications necessary for performing the duties corresponding to the certificate for which he is a candidate.

2. National laws or regulations shall—

    (a) prescribe a minimum age to have been attained by and a minimum period of professional experience to have been completed by candidates for each grade of competency certificate;

    (b) provide for the organisation and supervision by the competent authority of one or more examinations for the purpose of testing whether candidates for competency certificates possess the qualifications necessary for performing the duties corresponding to the certificates for which they are candidates.

3. Any Member of the Organisation may, during a period of three years from the date of its ratification, issue competency certificates to persons who have not passed the examinations organised in virtue of paragraph 2(b) of this Article who—

    (a) have in fact had sufficient practical experience of the duties corresponding to the certificate in question; and

    (b) have no record of any serious technical error against them.

第 3 条

1. 除非持有船舶登记地区公共机关签发或核准的履职适任证书,任何人不得在船上履行船长、负责值班的驾驶员、轮机长或负责值班的轮机员的职责。

2. 本条规定仅在不可抗力的情况下才有例外。

第 4 条

1. 除非满足以下条件,否则任何人不得被授予适任证书——

    (a) 达到签发所述证书规定的最低年龄;

    (b) 具备签发所述证书规定的最低专业资历;及

    (c) 通过主管机关组织和监督的,旨在审验证书申请人是否拥有履行证书相应职责所需资格的考试。

2. 国内法律或规则应——

    (a) 规定证书申请人申请每一等级适任证书须达到的最小年龄和须具有的最低专业资历;

    (b) 规定主管机关须对每项旨在审验证书申请人是否拥有履行证书对应职责所需的资格的考试进行组织和监督。

3. 根据本条第 2 款 (b) 项,国际海事组织的任何成员在其批准之日起 3 年的期限内,可签发证书给考试不合格但满足下列条件者——

    (a) 事实上已具有担任证书对应职责的充分实际经历;及

    (b) 没有严重技术错误的记录。

ILO Convention No. 74

16. The relevant text of the ILO Certification of Able Seamen Convention, 1946, is as follows:

Article 1

No person shall be engaged on any vessel as an able seaman unless he is a person who by national laws or regulations is deemed to be competent to perform any duty which may be required of a member of the crew serving in the deck department (other than an officer or leading or specialist rating) and unless he holds a certificate of qualification as an able seaman granted in accordance with the provisions of the following Articles.

Article 2

1. The competent authority shall make arrangements for the holding of examinations and for the granting of certificates of qualification.

2. No person shall be granted a certificate of qualification unless—

    (a) he has reached a minimum age to be prescribed by the competent authority;

    (b) he has served at sea in the deck department for a minimum period to be prescribed by the competent authority; and

    (c) he has passed an examination of proficiency to be prescribed by the competent authority.

3. The prescribed minimum age shall not be less than eighteen years.

4. The prescribed minimum period of service at sea shall not be less than thirty-six months: Provided that the competent authority may—

    (a) permit persons with a period of actual service at sea of not less than twenty-four months who have successfully passed through a course of training in an approved training school to reckon the time spent in such training, or part thereof, as sea service; and

    (b) permit persons trained in approved sea-going training ships who have served eighteen months in such ships to be certificated as able seamen upon leaving in good standing.

5. The prescribed examination shall provide a practical test of the candidate's knowledge of seamanship and of his ability to carry ont effectively all the duties that may be required of an able seaman, including those of a lifeboatman; it shall be such as to qualify a successful candidate to hold the special lifeboatman's certificate provided for in Article 22 of the International Convention for the Safety of Life at Sea, 1929, or in the corresponding provision of any subsequent Convention revising or replacing that Convention for the time being in force for the territory concerned.

ILO 公约 No.74

16. 1946年《ILO一等水手发证公约》相关条文如下：

第1条

除非被认为具备国内法律或规则要求的履行甲板部船员(高级船员、领导或专家船员除外)职责的资格,并持有根据下列各条规定发给的一等水手资格证书,任何人在船上不得被用作一等水手。

第2条

1. 主管机关须安排考试和授予资格证书。

2. 任何人不得被授予资格证书,除非——

    (a) 达到主管机关规定的最低年龄;

    (b) 具备主管机关规定的甲板部服务的最低海上资历;及

    (c) 通过主管机关规定的熟练考试。

3. 规定的最低年龄须不低于18岁。

4. 规定的最低海上资历须不少于36个月,同时规定主管机关可以——

    (a) 允许具有不少于24个月实际海上资历并在认可的培训学校完成一门训练课程并经考试合格者,把训练时间或部分训练时间算作海上资历;及

    (b) 允许在认可的海上训练船训练并在此类船上已有8个月海上资历且表现良好者,在离船时授予一等水手证书。

5. 规定的考试须对申请人的船艺知识和有效履行一等水手(包括救生艇人员)所有职责的能力进行实操测试;以使考试合格者有资格持有由1929年《国际海上人命安全公约》第22条,或修正或取代该公约的、在有关地区生效的后续公约相应条款规定的救生艇员专项证书。

ILO Recommendation No. 137

17. The relevant text of the ILO Vocational Training (Seafarers) Recommendation, 1970, is as follows:

   III.   NATIONAL PLANNING AND ADMINISTRATION

   A.   *Organisation and Co-ordination*

   5.   (1)   The training programmes of all public and private institutions engaged in the training of seafarers should be co-ordinated and developed in each country on the basis of approved national standards.

   (2)   Such programmes should be drawn up in co-operation with government departments, educational institutions and other bodies which have an intimate knowledge of the vocational training of seafarers, and should be so designed as to meet the operational requirements of the shipping industry, as established in consultation with shipowners' and seafarers' organisations.

   6.   Bodies which draw up such programmes should, in particular—

   (a)   maintain close contacts between the training institutions and all those concerned so as to keep training in line with the needs of the industry;

   (b)   make regular visits to the training schools with which they are concerned and be fully conversant with the programmes being carried out;

   (c)   ensure that information about available training opportunities is disseminated to all those concerned;

   (d)   co-operate in setting up and operating practical maritime training schemes;

   (e)   participate in establishing the general training standards provided for in Paragraph 11;

   (f)   participate in establishing such national certification standards as are appropriate for the various grades and categories of seafarers;

   (g)   promote direct co-operation between training institutions and those responsible for recruitment and employment.

   7.   The competent authorities and bodies, in co-operation with shipowners' and seafarers' organisations, should ensure that full information on public and private training schemes for seafarers and on conditions of entry into the shipping industry is available to those providing vocational guidance and employment counselling services, to public employment services and to vocational and technical training institutions.

ILO 建议案 No.137

17. 1970年《ILO职业培训(海员)建议书》相关条文如下：

Ⅲ. 国家计划和主管机关

A. 组织和协调

5. (1) 每个国家应根据认可的国家标准对所有从事海员培训的公立和私立机构的培训计划进行协调和完善。

   (2) 培训计划应由政府部门、教育机构和其他对海员职业培训有深入了解的组织合作制订，并且也应与船东和海员组织协商以便制订的计划满足航运业的实际工作要求。

6. 制订培训计划的组织尤其应——

   (a) 保持培训机构和所有有关机构之间的密切联系，以保持培训符合行业的要求；

   (b) 定期访问与他们有关的培训学校，了解培训计划的实施情况；

   (c) 保证向所有有关人员公布现有培训机会的信息；

   (d) 合作制订和实施切实可行的海上培训计划；

   (e) 参与制定第11款规定的一般培训标准；

   (f) 参与制定适合各个等级和层次海员的国家发证标准；

   (g) 促进培训机构和招聘、雇用机构之间的直接合作。

7. 与船东和海员组织合作的主管机关和组织，应保证提供职业指导和就业咨询的机构、公立的就业机构和职业技术培训机构，能够得到公立和私立的海员培训计划的所有相关信息和有关航运业准入条件的所有信息。

8. The competent authorities and bodies should endeavour to ensure that—

   (a) the facilities of shipyards, engineering workshops, manufacturers of equipment, naval installations, etc., are utilised where available and appropriate in training both officers and ratings;

   (b) arrangements are made in order that, other things being equal, preference may be given in employment placement to persons who have received appropriate and recognised training.

C. *Training Standards*

11. Training standards should be laid down in conformity with national requirements for obtaining the various seafarers' certificates of competency. In particular, there should be laid down—

    (a) the nature of medical examinations, including chest X-rays and diabetic, hearing and sight tests, required for persons entering training schemes; the standards of such examinations, particularly of the hearing and sight tests, could differ according to the departments which the persons concerned are planning to enter, but should in no case be lower than the medical standards required for entry into employment in the shipping industry;

    (b) the level of general education required for admission to vocational training courses leading to certificates of competency;

    (c) the subjects, such as navigation, seamanship, radio, electronics, engineering, catering and human relations, that should be included in the training curricula;

    (d) the nature of any examination to be taken upon completion of training courses which are subject to examination;

    (e) a procedure whereby the authorities ensure that the teaching staff of training institutions have the requisite experience and qualifications, including adequate practical and theoretical knowledge of technical and operational developments.

IV. TRAINING PROGRAMMES

12. The various training programmes should be realistically based on the work to be performed on board ship. They should be periodically reviewed and kept up to date in order to keep abreast of technical developments. They should include the following, as appropriate:

    (a) training in navigation, seamanship, ship handling, signalling, cargo handling and storage, ship maintenance, and other matters relating to the operation of merchant ships;

8. 主管机关和组织应竭力保证——

   (a) 利用对高级船员和普通船员培训有效并相适应的船厂设施、制造车间、设备制造厂、船用设备,等等;

   (b) 那些其他方面条件相同但已接受适当的、经认可的培训的船员优先获得就业的安排。

C. 培训标准

11. 制定与取得各种海员适任证书国内要求相符的培训标准,特别是下列各项标准的制定——

    (a) 对参加培训者所要求的体格检查种类(包括胸部 X 光透视和糖尿病、听力、视力测试);这些体格检查的标准,特别是听力和视力标准,可以应服务部门不同而不同,但无论如何不应低于航运业就业所要求的健康标准;

    (b) 参加适任证书职业培训课程所要求的总体教育水平;

    (c) 培训课程应包括的科目(例如,航海学、船艺、无线电、电子学、工程学、伙食服务和人事关系);

    (d) 完成指定的培训课程时要举行的考试类型;

    (e) 主管机关用以保证培训机构教员具有的必备经历和资格(包括适当的相关技术部门和操作部门的实践知识和理论知识)的程序。

IV. 培训计划

12. 各种培训计划应当以船上实际从事的工作为基础,并应定期审核和更新,以适应技术的发展。合理的培训计划应包括下列各项:

    (a) 航海学、船艺、船舶操纵、信号、货物装卸和积载、船舶维修保养和有关商船经营有关的其他事务等内容的培训;

(b) training in the use of electronic and mechanical aids, such as radio and radar installations, radio direction-finders and compasses;

(c) theoretical and practical instruction in the use of life-saving and fire-fighting equipment, survival at sea procedures, and other aspects of the safety of life at sea;

(d) theoretical and practical instruction in the operation, maintenance and repair of main propulsion installations and auxiliary machinery, with emphasis on the types of equipment, including electronic equipment, installed in ships of the country concerned;

(e) training for the catering department as appropriate for those to be employed as stewards, cooks, waiters and galley staff, account being taken of training requirements, for different categories of ships;

(f) training in accident prevention on board ship, particularly as regards safe working practices in all departments, and including personal safety as part of training in professional subjects, training in first aid, medical care and other related matters and health and physical training, especially swimming; training in medical care and particularly special training for personnel placed in charge of medical care on board should in all cases be related to the content of medical guides compiled by competent authorities and to full utilisation of medical radio services;

(g) particularly in the case of trainees under 18 years of age, instruction in subjects of general educational value;

(h) instruction in elements of social and labour legislation related to merchant ship operations and to industrial relations, regulations concerning seafarers transportation economics, maritime insurance, maritime law, etc.;

(i) instruction in management techniques, including such subjects as personnel relations and work study.

13. Training programmes should be designed, inter alia, to prepare trainees for certificates of competency and should be directly related, where appropriate, to national certification standards. They should include adequate practical training and take account of any minimum age and minimum working experience laid down by the competent authorities in respect of the various grades of certificates. Account should also be taken of other nationally recognised certificates.

14. The duration of the various training programmes should be sufficient to enable trainees to assimilate the teaching given and should be determined with reference to such matters as—

(a) the level of training required for the shipboard occupation for which the course is designed;

(b) 使用电子和机械设备(例如,无线电和雷达设备,无线电测向仪和罗经)方面的培训;

(c) 救生和消防设备的使用、海上求生方法和海上人命安全的其他方面的理论和实践指导;

(d) 主推进器装置和辅助机械[强调有关国家的船舶安装的设备(包括电子设备)型号]的操作、保养和修理的理论和实践指导;

(e) 伙食服务部门的业务培训(考虑船舶不同层次的培训要求,适合那些受雇为管事、厨师、服务员和厨工的人员);

(f) 船上事故预防,特别是对于各部门安全工作措施的培训,包括作为专业课程一部分的个人安全、急救、医护和其他相关内容的培训以及体育训练,特别是游泳训练;医护培训,特别是对在船上负责医护的人员的特殊培训,应当包括主管机关编制的医疗指南和充分利用医疗无线电服务的内容;

(g) (特别是对18岁以下学员的)普通教育科目内容指导;

(h) 有关商船和有关海员、运输、经济、海事保险和海商法等的社会和劳动立法原理的指导;

(i) 管理技术指导,包括诸如人事关系和工作分析的科目。

13. 培训计划应使学员做好获得适任证书的准备,并且应直接与国家发证标准相联系。培训计划应包括足够的实践训练,应考虑主管机关对于不同层次的证书制定的最低年龄和最短工作经历限制,同时也应考虑国家认可的其他证书。

14. 各种培训计划的时间安排应足以使学员能够掌握讲授的课程,时间的确定应参考下列的内容——

(a) 设置课程对应的船上工作所需的培训水平;

(b) the general educational level and age required of trainees entering the course;

(c) the trainees' previous practical experience.

VI. ADVANCED TRAINING

18. (1) Retraining, refresher, familiarisation and upgrading courses should be available as required for suitable officers and ratings to enable them to increase and widen their technical skills and knowledge, to keep abreast of technological changes, in particular in the development of automated ships, and to meet the requirements of new methods of operations on board ship.

    (2) Such courses may be used, for instance, to complement general courses and provide advanced specialised training opening the way to promotion, as well as to provide advanced electronics courses for appropriate personnel.

    (3) Special attention should be given to the ability of masters, other officers and ratings to navigate and handle new types of ships safely.

19. Where training would be facilitated thereby, shipowners should release suitable seafarers employed on board their ships for training periods ashore, at appropriate schools, to enable them to improve their skills, learn to use new techniques and equipment and qualify for promotion. Persons in a supervisory position on board ship should take an active part in encouraging such training.

VII. TRAINING METHODS

20. The training methods adopted should be the most effective possible, having regard to the nature of the instruction, the trainees' experience, general education and age, and the demonstration equipment and financial resources available.

21. Practical training, requiring active participation of the trainees themselves, should be an important part of all training programmes. It may be provided by assigning seafarers to merchant ships for periods of training at sea, to engineering workshops or shipyards or to shipping company offices.

22. Training vessels used by training institutions should provide practical instruction in navigation, seamanship, machinery operation and maintenance and other nautical subjects as well as comprehensive shipboard safety education.

23. Appropriate demonstration equipment such as simulators, engines, boat models, ship equipment, life-saving equipment, navigational aids and cargo gear should be used in training schemes. Such equipment should be selected with reference to the shipboard machinery and equipment which the trainee may be called upon to use.

24. Films and other audio-visual aids should be used, where appropriate—

    (a) as a supplement to, but not a substitute for, demonstration equipment in the use of which trainees take an active part;

(b) 要求参加课程的学员达到的普通教育水平及学员的年龄；

(c) 学员以往的实际经历。

VI. 高级培训

18. (1) 适用于高级船员和普通船员的再教育、知识更新、熟悉和课程提高应按规定进行，使他们能够提高和扩展技术技能和知识水平，特别是跟上船舶自动化的技术发展，满足船上作业的新要求。

    (2) 可以使用诸如补充普通课程的内容、职务晋升高级专门培训、为相应人员安排高级电子学等课程。

    (3) 应特别注意船长、其他高级船员和普通船员的安全驾驶和操作新型船舶的能力。

19. 船东让船上受雇的相应海员离船到岸上适当的学校参加培训会更有利于他们提高技能，学习使用新技术和设备以及获得资格晋升。船上处于管理岗位的人员应当积极鼓励这种培训。

VII. 培训方法

20. 在考虑到课程的性质、学员的经历、总体教育水平和年龄、可用的演示设备和资金来源的同时，所采用的培训方法应该是最有效方法。

21. 实操训练要求学员积极参与，并应成为所有培训计划的重要部分。可以通过下列方法提供实训：指派海员到商船进行一定时期的海上实习，或指派海员到制造车间、船厂或航运公司办公室实习。

22. 培训机构应利用实习船提供航海学、船艺、机械操作与保养和其他海上科目以及广泛的船上安全教育等方面的实践教学。

23. 在培训中应使用适当的演示设备，如模拟器、主辅机、船舶模型、船舶设备、救生设备、导航设备和装卸设备等。这类设备的选择应参考学员可能用到的船上机械和设备。

24. 如果合适，可使用视频和其他视听设备——

    (a) 作为学员参与操作的演示设备的补充，但不能替代演示设备；

(b) as a primary training aid in special fields such as the teaching of languages.

25. Theoretical training and general education given as part of a training course should be related to the theoretical and practical knowledge required by seafarers.

General objectives

18. The general objectives of all international instruments dealing with the training and examination of seafarers are to develop and maintain a global minimum standard of maritime and environmental safety in merchant ship operation.

19. International shipping is highly competitive and, because of the sophistication of modern ships, their size, their speed and the hazardous nature of much of the cargo carried by them, traditional methods of on-the-job training are no longer considered satisfactory without the benefit of approved and structured training being provided in a number of key areas of safety.

20. Completion of a training course does not in itself guarantee that the knowledge, principles and skills taught have been fully assimilated by the trainee, nor that he can properly and reliably apply them in practice. Whilst on-going in-course evaluation of a trainee's progress forms an essential part of the teaching process, competency to perform shipboard duties in a safe and effective manner can only be fully and reliably gauged by observance of the trainee's subsequent on-the-job performance.

It is not feasible for an Administration charged with the responsibility of ensuring the competency of its seafarers to undertake such a process.

21. Resort must therefore be made to criterion-related testing of candidates for certificates of competency. Such tests are designed to assess the knowledge, the comprehension of principles, the ability to apply principles and the associated skills of candidates in respect of all tasks associated with the duties concerned. Such testing is made mandatory through STCW 95.

22. Since the maintenance of maritime safety and the protection of the environment are global concerns, the Authorities of States visited by ships must also be able to satisfy themselves that the ships calling at their ports are sufficiently and efficiently manned. The requirement for ships to be sufficiently and efficiently manned is embodied in regulation 13 of chapter V of the 1974 SOLAS Convention.

23. The issue of certificates bearing a globally agreed common endorsement certifying as to the competency of the holder is achieved by Article VI and by the Regulations in chapter I of the 1978 STCW Convention, as amended.

24. The intention is also that shipowners and masters can engage seafarers who are not previously known to them to fill posts of responsibility but can be reasonably reassured of their competency because they have a certificate that has been issued by or under the authority of, or which is recognized by, their Administration.

(b) 在诸如语言教学等特殊领域,作为训练的主要辅助设备。

25. 作为培训课程一部分的理论培训和概况教育应该与海员所要求的理论和实践知识相关联。

综合目标

18. 所有解决海员培训和考试有关国际文件的总体目标是制定和保持商船活动方面的海上和环境安全的全球性最低标准。

19. 国际航运的竞争十分激烈,而且由于现代化船舶的复杂化、尺寸、速度及其载运的许多货物的危险性质,也没有考虑到与船舶安全相关的许多关键领域所规定的认可和精心安排的培训的好处,因此传统在职培训方法已不再合适。

20. 完成培训课程本身并不能保证所教的知识、原理和技能完全被学员掌握,也不能保证学员在实际工作中能够正确和可靠地应用。对学员学业进步的过程评估应作为教学过程的重要部分,学员是否具备安全有效地履行船上职责的适任能力,只能通过连续观察他们在工作中的表现来充分和可靠地评价。

    但让负责确保海员适任能力职责的主管机关具体进行这一操作是不可行的。

21. 因此,必须要采取手段对适任证书申请人进行与标准有关的测评。这种测评是用以评估申请人与岗位工作有关的所有知识、对原理的理解、应用原理的能力和相关的技能。根据STCW 95公约,这种测评是强制性的。

22. 保持海上安全和保护环境是全球关心的问题,船舶到访国的主管机关也要求挂靠他们港口的船舶得到充分和有效的配员。1974年SOLAS公约第V章第13条规定了对于船舶充分和有效配员的要求。

23. 按修订的1978年STCW公约第Ⅵ条和第Ⅰ章规则进行证书的签发。所签发的证书应采用国际认可的签注方式并能证明持有者的适任能力。

24. 主管机关按公约规定的签发证书可以使船东和船长在雇用之前不了解的持证船员担任相应职务时对其适任能力有信心。

Certification of fishermen

25. The relevant texts of the ILO Fishermen's Competency Certificates Convention, 1966 may be found in Part II Certification, Articles 4-10 inclusive and in Part III Examinations Articles 11 and 12.

26. Recommendations concerning the training and certification of fishermen are contained in IMO Assembly resolutions A.539(13), Certification of skippers and officers in charge of a navigational watch on fishing vessels of 24 metres in length and over; in A.576(14), Standards for skippers and officers in charge of a navigational watch on fishing vessels of less than 24 metres in length operating in unlimited and limited waters; and in A.623 (15), Minimum requirements for certification of chief engineer officers and second engineer officers of fishing vessels powered by main propulsion machinery of 750 kW propulsion power or more.

    These provisions were drawn up by IMO in consultation with the United Nations Food and Agriculture Organization (FAO) and with ILO.

    Recommendations concerning the training and certification of fishermen are also contained in the ILO Vocational Training (Fishermen) Recommendation, 1966 (No.126).

27. Subsequently, the joint FAO/ILO/IMO Document for Guidance on Fishermen's Training and Certification was prepared and published by IMO on behalf of the three Organizations.

    The document for guidance is currently being revised. A joint FAO/ILO/IMO Ad Hoc Working Group met to undertake this work in January 1998 and January 1999 and a new version will appear in due course (probably 2000 or 2001).

    The draft revised document for guidance will be submitted to the International Maritime Organization's Maritime Safety Committee, or one it its subsidiary sub-committees, for consideration. Afterwards, it will be submitted to the appropriate FAO and ILO bodies for approval.

渔民发证

25. 1966年《ILO渔民适任证书公约》的相关条款包括在第Ⅱ部分——发证(包括第4条至第10条在内)和第Ⅲ部分——考试(第11条和第12条)。

26. 有关渔民培训和发证的建议案包含在IMO大会决议A.539(13)中;在长度24米及以上渔船上负责航行值班的船长和高级船员的发证,以及在船长少于24米、作业于无限和受限水域的渔船上负责航行值班的船长和高级船员的发证包括在A.576(14)中;750 kW推进功率及以上主推进机械提供动力的渔船的轮机长和大管轮发证的最低要求包括在A.576(15)。

    这些条款由IMO与联合国粮农组织(FAO)和ILO协商制定。

    有关渔民培训和发证的建议案也包含在1966年《ILO职业培训(渔民)建议案》(No.126)中。

27. 随后,FAO/ILO/IMO有关渔民培训和发证的联合指导文件由IMO代表这三个组织起草和出版。

    目前,该指导文件正在修订。FAO/ILO/IMO Ad Hoc联合工作组在1998年1月和1999年1月一起开展这项工作,新版本即将(可能在2000年或2001年)完成。

    修订的指导文件草案将递交国际海事组织海上安全委员会,或它的附属分委会研究。然后,递交给相应的FAO和ILO机构批准。

Part 4
Authority and Organization

Authority

1. Paragraph 2 of Article I of the revised STCW Convention, which sets out the general obligations of the Convention, provides as follows :

    (2) The Parties undertake to promulgate all laws, decrees, orders and regulations and to take all other steps which may be necessary to give the Convention full and complete effect, so as to ensure that, from the point of view of safety of life and property at sea and the protection of the marine environment, seafarers on board ships are qualified and fit for their duties.

2. Parties are thus required to give effect to the Convention by incorporating in their national legislation all powers and authority necessary to:

    .1 require ships to be provided with masters and officers who are the lawful holders of specified certificates of competency;

    .2 specify the types, grades and classes of certificates which may be issued;

    .3 specify the qualifications and other requirements which must be met by those applying for certificates;

    .4 specify the qualifications and other requirements which must be met by those responsible for the training and assessment of competence of seafarers to ensure that they are appropriately qualified for the type and level of training or assessment involved;

    .5 lay down the conditions under which the examinations are to be conducted and permit the appointment or designation of persons or boards to be responsible for the conduct of such examinations;

    .6 provide for the endorsement of certificates by the Administration in accordance with Article VI and chapter I of the Convention;

    .7 establish procedures for withdrawing, suspending and cancellation of certificates for just causes and for the prevention of fraud;

    .8 provide for the periodic revalidation of certificates at intervals not exceeding five years;

    .9 permit the issue and use of dispensations issued in accordance with Article VIII and chapter I of the Convention;

第4章
机构与组织

机构

1. 经修订的STCW公约第Ⅰ条第2款陈述公约的一般义务,它规定如下:

    (2)　缔约国承担发布所有法律、法令、命令和规则,采取所有其他可充分实施公约的必要措施,从海上人命和财产安全以及海上环境保护的角度保证船上海员能胜任和适合他们的职责。

2. 缔约国因此必须把下列各项所需的所有机构编入国内法规,使公约生效:

    .1　规定船舶配备合法持有规定适任证书的船长和高级船员;

    .2　规定可能签发证书的类型和层次;

    .3　规定证书申请者必须满足的资格和其他要求;

    .4　规定负责培训和评估海员适任能力者必须满足的资格和其他要求,以确保他们适合有关类型和层次的培训或评估;

    .5　规定实施考试和使规定(或指定)人员(或机构)负责实施这种考试的条件;

    .6　规定主管机关按照公约第Ⅵ条和第Ⅰ章对证书进行签证;

    .7　制定因适当原因和为了防止欺诈而收回、中止和注销证书的程序;

    .8　以不超过5年的时间间隔,规定证书的定期再有效;

    .9　允许发给和使用根据公约第Ⅷ条和第Ⅰ章签发的特免证明;

.10 exercise control, in accordance with Article X and chapter I of the Convention, over foreign ships while they are located in any national port;

.11 provide for the approval of training courses for the purposes of the Convention;

.12 require special training requirements for personnel on certain types of ships;

.13 endorse a certificate issued by or under the authority of another Party to a master, officer or radio officer to attest its recognition;

.14 ensure that all training, assessment of competence, certification, endorsement and revalidation activities are continuously monitored through a quality standards system to ensure achievement of defined objectives, including those concerning the qualifications and experience of instructors and assessors;

.15 establish the standards of medical fitness for seafarers;

.16 maintain a register or register(s) of all certificates and endorsements for masters and officers and, as appropriate, ratings and of dispensations issued and make available information on the status of such certificates, endorsements and dispensations to other Parties and companies;

.17 hold companies responsible for the assignment of seafarers for service in their ships in accordance with the provisions of the Convention;

.18 allow the establishment of appropriate regulations or administrative instructions in support of the foregoing; and

.19 provide suitable penalties for non-compliance with mandatory provisions;

3. In establishing legislation of the above nature, use is commonly made of enabling provisions so as to avoid encumbering main statutes, acts or laws of a legislative body with a great amount of detail. Subsidiary legislation in the form of regulations, decrees or orders is then established by the minister, official or regulatory body enabled or empowered to make the regulations or rules etc. concerned.

4. Subsidiary legislation is generally given the same force and mandatory effect as the main statutes.

PRINCIPLES OF SAFE MANNING

5. A comprehensive review of Resolution A.481(XII)—Principles of Safe Manning was conducted in 1998. The Resolution A.890(21) was presented to the IMO 21st Assembly in 1999 and supercedes Resolution A.481 (XII).

   The annexes to the Resolution are as follows:

   a. Annex 1: Principles of Safe Manning

.10 根据公约第X条和第I章对在本国港口的外国船舶行使监督；

.11 规定对本公约培训课程的审批；

.12 规定对某些类型船舶人员的特殊培训要求；

.13 签注并承认由其他缔约国签发或授权签发的船长、高级船员和无线电操作员证书；

.14 确保运用质量标准体系连续监控所有培训、适任评估、发证、签证和再有效工作，以确保达到规定目标，其中包括对于教员和评估员的资格和经历的目标；

.15 制定海员健康标准；

.16 保持船长和高级船员，若合适也包括普通船员的所有证书和签证以及签发的特免证明的记录，并使其他缔约国和船公司可以获得有关的证书、签证和特免证明状况的信息；

.17 要求船公司负责按照公约规定派遣船员到船上工作；

.18 准许制定适当规则或支持性行政指令；及

.19 规定对违反强制性规定的适当处罚。

3. 在制定上述性质的法规时，一般利用授权条款，以避免在大量的细节上妨碍立法机构的主要条例、法案和法律。因此，以规则、法令和行政指令形式发布的辅助性法规，可以由具有或被授予权限的有关部委、官方机构或管理机构制定。

4. 辅助性法规一般被认为与主要法规具有相同的约束力和强制权限。

安全配员原则

5. 在对1988年实施的安全配员原则〔决议A.481(XII)〕综合评估后，制定了新的1999年决议A.890(21)提交给IMO第21次大会决议并取代原决议。

该决议的附则如下：

a. 附则1：安全配员原则

b. Annex 2: Guidelines for the Application of Principles of Safe Manning

c. Annex 3: Guidance on Contents and Model Form of Minimum Safe Manning Document
Appendix: Model Form of Minimum Safe Manning Document

Organization

Issue of certificates

6. Paragraph (c) of Article II of the 1978 STCW Convention, as amended, defines "certificate" as follows:

   "Certificate" means a valid document by whatever name it may be known, issued by or under the authority of the Administration or recognized by the Administration authorizing the holder to serve as stated in this document or as authorized by national regulations.

   Thus, as stated in Section B of the STCW Code, which recommends guidance to assist Parties to the STCW Convention, the definition of "Certificate" provides for three possibilities:

   .1 the Administration may issue the certificate;

   .2 the Administration may have the certificate issued under its authority; or

   .3 the Administration may recognize a certificate issued by another Party as provided for in regulation I/10 (Recognition of certificates).

7. Where an Administration recognizes a certificate issued by another Party, it should communicate full details to the Secretary-General of IMO, in accordance with Regulation I/10 of STCW (Communication of information).

   Recognition of certificates is further dealt with in Part 20 of this compendium.

8. In all cases it is the responsibility of the Administration that the requirements of the Convention have been met before a certificate is issued under its authority or is recognized, see STCW Convention Regulation I/10 and STCW Code Section A-I/10: Recognition of certificates.

9. Further guidance is provided in MSC/Circ. 393 (incorporated into Section B of the new STCW Code "Guidance regarding provisions of the arlicles") in respect of the following articles of the revised STCW Convention, dealing with certification:

Conduct of examinations

10. Under the provisions of paragraph 1 of Article VI of the STCW Convention, as amended:

    1. Certificates for masters, officers or ratings shall be issued to those candidates who, to the satisfaction of the Administration, meet the requirements for service, age, medical fitness, training, qualification and examinations in accordance with the appropriate provisions of the Annex to the Convention.

b. 附则2：运用安全配员原则的指导

c. 附则3：最低安全配员文件的内容和示范格式的指导
附录：最低安全配员文件的示范格式

组织结构

证书的签发

6. 经修订的1978年STCW公约第Ⅱ条(c)款对"证书"定义如下：

"证书"系指由主管机关签发或经主管机关授权签发或被主管机关认可的一种有效文件，不论其名称如何，该文件准许其持有人担任该文件所指定的或国家法规规定的职务。

因为，正如为协助缔约国而建议指导的STCW规则B部分所述的那样，"证书"有三种可能定义：

.1 主管机关可以签发证书；

.2 主管机关可以授权签发证书；或

.3 主管机关可以按公约规则Ⅰ/10(证书的承认)的规定承认另一缔约国签发的证书。

7. 若主管机关承认其他缔约国签发的证书，则应按照STCW公约规则Ⅰ/10(资料交流)的规定把全部细节通告IMO秘书长。

证书的承认在本纲要第20章将进行更深入的阐述。

8. 主管机关有责任确保在任何情况下签发或承认的证书都满足公约的要求。有关规定参阅STCW公约规则Ⅰ/10和STCW规则第A-Ⅰ/10节：证书的承认。

9. 文件MSC/Circ.393(已编入新的STCW规则B部分"关于STCW公约条款的指导")就有关发证的经修正的STCW公约条款提供进一步的指导。

考试的实施

10. 根据经修订的STCW公约第Ⅵ条第1款的规定：

1. 根据本公约附则的相应规定，船长、高级船员或普通船员证书只能签发给主管机关认为其服务、年龄、健康、培训、资格和考试成绩满足规定要求的申请人。

11. Also, under paragraph 2 of regulations II/2 and III/2 and similar regulations which prescribe the requirements for the various certificates, the language used requires that the Administration ensures that the various requirements are met, e.g

    2. Every candidate for certification shall:

        .1 meet the requirements for certification as an officer in charge of a navigational watch on ships of 500 gross tonnage or more and have approved seagoing service in that capacity:

            .1.1 for certification as chief mate, not less than 12 months, and
            .1.2 for certification as master, not less than 36 months; however, this period may be reduced to not less than 24 months if not less than 12 months of such seagoing service has been served as chief mate; and

        .2 have completed approved education and training and meet the standard of competence specified in section A-II/2 of the STCW Code for masters and chief mates on ships of 3,000 gross tonnage or more.

12. These provisions permit Administrations either to conduct their own examinations and screening of applications for examination or to delegate these functions to an independent board or to maritime training institutions or make other suitable arrangements. No matter what arrangements may be made, the Administration of a State Party to the revised STCW Convention, remains fully responsible for the strict observance of all provisions of the Convention.

13. Examinations may therefore be "internal", i.e. conducted by the training providers: academies, colleges or schools, or they may be "external", in which case they are conducted by an outside authority such as the Administration itself or an independent board or body appointed by the Administration. The advantages and disadvantages of these two approaches are listed below.

Internal Examinations

Advantages

.1 Each academy is free to set its own standards above the level of the Convention;

.2 It is easier to ensure that the courses given by the academy adequately prepare the candidates for the examinations;

.3 It is more convenient and less disturbing to the candidates, who may take their examinations in familiar surroundings;

.4 The Administration is not burdened with the cost of running an examination service (personnel and accommodation);

.5 Fewer examinations may be held and examinations may be timed to coincide with course endings.

11. 公约规则Ⅱ/2的第2款、公约规则Ⅲ/2以及其他对应各种发证要求的相似规则,也要求主管机关保证满足其他各种要求,例如:

   2. 每个证书申请者应:

      .1 符合对500总吨或以上船舶负责航行值班的高级船员的发证要求,并具有对应该职位的认可的海上服务资历:

         .1.1 申请大副证书,不少于12个月,及

         .1.2 申请船长证书,不少于36个月;但是,如果已具有不少于12个月担任大副的海上服务资历,则此段时间可缩短为不少于24个月;及

      .2 已完成认可的教育和培训,并且达到STCW规则第A-Ⅱ/2节规定的3000总吨或以上船舶的船长和大副的适任标准。

12. 上述规定允许主管机关自己实施考试和遴选考试申请表,或授权独立机构或海上培训机构履行这些职能,或采用其他合适的做法。无论采用何种做法,经修订的STCW公约缔约国的主管机关仍然对严格遵守该公约的所有规定负全部责任。

13. 根据不同管理安排,考试可以是"内部的",例如,考试由培训提供者:培训院校、正规大学或学校实施;考试也可以是"外部的",这种考试由外部机构(例如,主管机关自己或主管机关指定的独立机构或团体)实施。这两种方法的优点和缺点列出如下:

内部考试

优点

.1 各院校可自由制定自己的高出公约水平的标准;

.2 比较容易保证院校针对开办的课程为学员进行适当的考试准备;

.3 对学员更方便,也较少受干扰,因为可在熟悉的环境参加考试;

.4 主管机关不负担主持考试的服务费用(考务人员和场所);

.5 考试场次较少,并且考试时间可与课程结束时间保持一致。

Disadvantages

.1 Lack of national uniformity in minimum standards;

.2 The links between those responsible for setting the examination and those responsible for teaching the course may influence results to a greater extent than in the case of outside examinations;

.3 The Academy may be burdened with the costs of conducting and administering the examinations;

.4 Candidates self-trained or trained elsewhere may be excluded from such examinations either as a matter of policy or by the timing and frequency of the examinations;

.5 The Administration must monitor the level and effectiveness of examinations conducted by the various bodies involved;

.6 Assessments for grant of dispensations may not be conducted by the same body of persons who assess competency for issue of certificates (Grant of dispensations cannot be delegated).

External Examinations

Advantages

.1 National uniformity in minimum standards;

.2 Expertise of the Administration is retained and kept up to date;

.3 Examination fees may offset costs of examination services in part or in whole;

.4 Greater control may be exercised by the Administration over the interpretation of the Convention;

.5 Candidates may have greater access to examinations through their being provided more frequently at more locations;

.6 Assessments for grant of dispensations may be dealt with by the same persons who conduct the examinations to assess competency for the issue of certificates.

Disadvantages

.1 Candidates who are studying at Academies may have to travel some distance to an examination centre;

.2 Administration has to bear costs of administering and conducting examinations;

缺点

.1 在最低标准上缺乏全国统一性；

.2 与外部考试的情况相比，考试命题人员和课程教学人员之间的关系可能在更大程度上影响考试结果；

.3 培训院校可能需要负担实施和管理考试的费用；

.4 自学或在其他地方培训的学员可能因政策、考试时间安排及考试频度问题而不能参加这种考试；

.5 主管机关必须对各种有关团体实施的考试的水平和有效性进行监控；

.6 特免证明的认可评估无法由签发证书时评估适任能力的相同团体和人员进行(特免证明认可不能委派)。

外部考试

优点

.1 在最低标准上具有全国统一性；

.2 保持和更新主管机关的专门评价；

.3 考试费可以部分或全部补偿考试服务费用；

.4 主管机关可以行使更大的公约解释权；

.5 通过在更多的地点提供更频繁的考试，学员可以有更多的参加考试的机会；

.6 特免证明的认可评估可由签发证书时适任能力评估的相同团体和人员进行。

缺点

.1 在院校学习的学员到考试中心可能有一定的路程；

.2 主管机关需承担管理和实施考试的费用；

.3 Interpretations of examiner and instructor on various provisions of the Convention may differ and candidates may face questions on an unexpected topic area.

A typical organization chart for an Administration which has elected to establish an external examination system is shown in figure 4-1 and that for an Administration which has elected to delegate the examining function to its maritime training academies is set out at figure 4-2.

Process to establish external examinations

14. In order to establish an external examination system, all necessary legislation must be in place as itemized in paragraph 2 of this Part. A decision has to be made on whether accommodation provided by the academies is to be used or if separate examination centres are to be set up, or if a combination of these arrangements would be best. Much depends on the scope of application of the legislation and hence the variety of certificates which are to be issued, particularly for internal waters.

15. Generally, it is more economic and convenient to conduct the examinations at the academies. They will generally have little difficulty in allocating the use of a classroom to the examiner for the period concerned. For the Administration to purchase or rent suitable accommodation involves considerable expense for space which may only be used for a small part of the time unless the number of candidates to be examined is high for a large part of the year.

16. A further point to bear in mind is that the equipment of the Academy may also be used for examination purposes (subject, of course, to their agreeing to this). Some cost-sharing arrangement may have to be entered into.

    Such measures can allow the testing of candidates on simulators where this is considered appropriate and necessary to adequately test the skills of or the application of principles by candidates.

    Such dual use of academy facilities and equipment maximizes their economic use and allows trainees to feel at ease in familiar surroundings and working with familiar equipment.

17. Limited examination facilities may still have to be provided to allow examinations to be conducted at times other than those which suit the completion of training courses at the Academy.

.3 考试官和院校教员对公约各种规定的解释可能不同,并且学员可能面临回答超出准备范围的问题。

选择采用外部考试方法的主管机关的典型组织结构如图4-1所示,而选择采用授权由海上培训机构实施考试职能的主管机关的典型组织结构如图4-2所示。

制定外部考试的方法

14. 为了制定外部考试方法,必须像本章第2节一样分条详细列出所有必要的法规。确定是否使用学校提供的场所、是否建立单独的考试中心,是否最好集中安排。这些决策确定主要取决于法规的适用范围和所签发证书的种类(尤其是对于国内水域证书)。

15. 一般情况下,在学校实施考试更经济和方便。在考试期间配置教室供考官使用,一般没有困难。而由主管机关购置或租借合适场所进行考试则牵涉到相当可观的费用,除非全年大部分时间参加考试的考生数量很大,否则考试场所一年可能只使用较少的时间。

16. 更要记住的一点是学校的设施也可用于考试(当然,要首先得到学校的同意)。有关费用分摊协议可能需要订立。

这种方法可使学员在模拟器上进行考试。对于正确评测学员的技能和对原理的运用来说,在模拟器上的考试被认为是合适和必需的。

学校的设施和设备的双重使用可以使设施和设备的经济用途最大化,并且也可使学员在熟悉的环境中减少拘束感并可以操作熟悉的设备。

17. 除了配合院校完成本身的培训课程外,可能还要不时提供有限的考试设施用于其他考试。

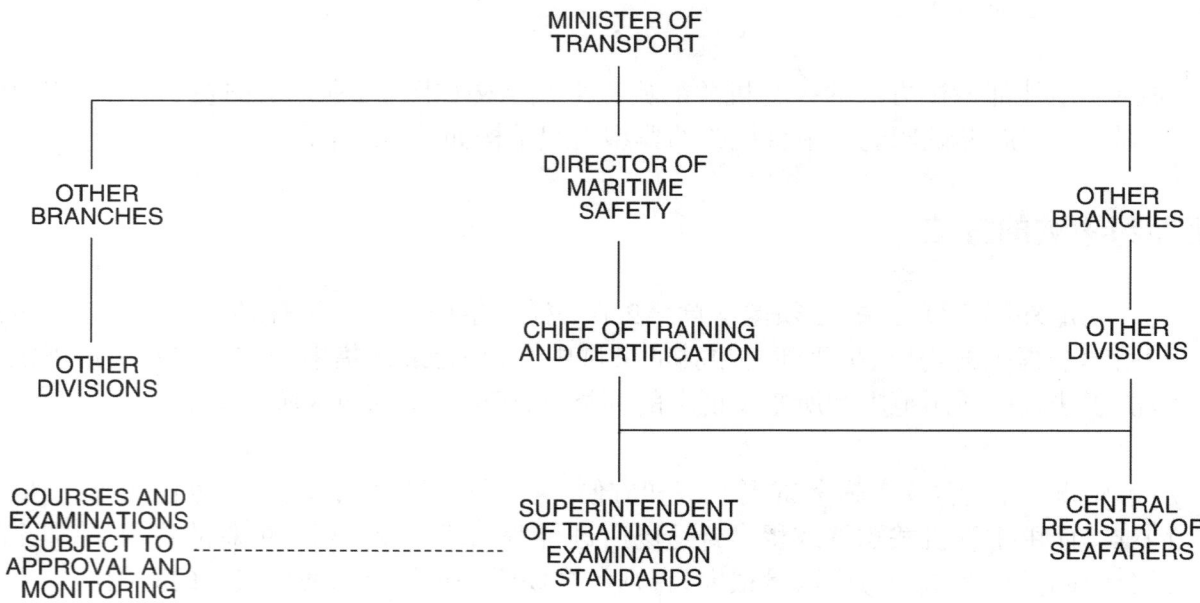

Fig. 4.1　Example of an Organization Chart of an Administration which uses an External examination system

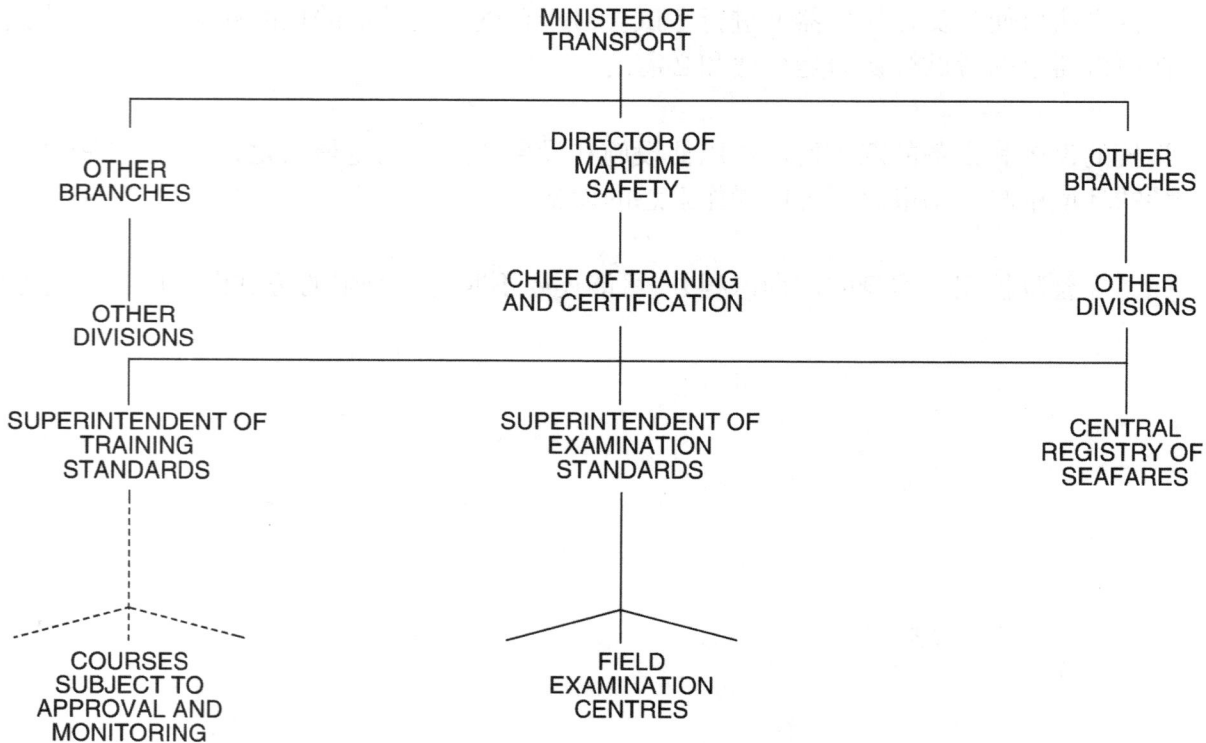

Fig. 4.2　Example of an Organization Chart of an Administration which uses an Internal examination system

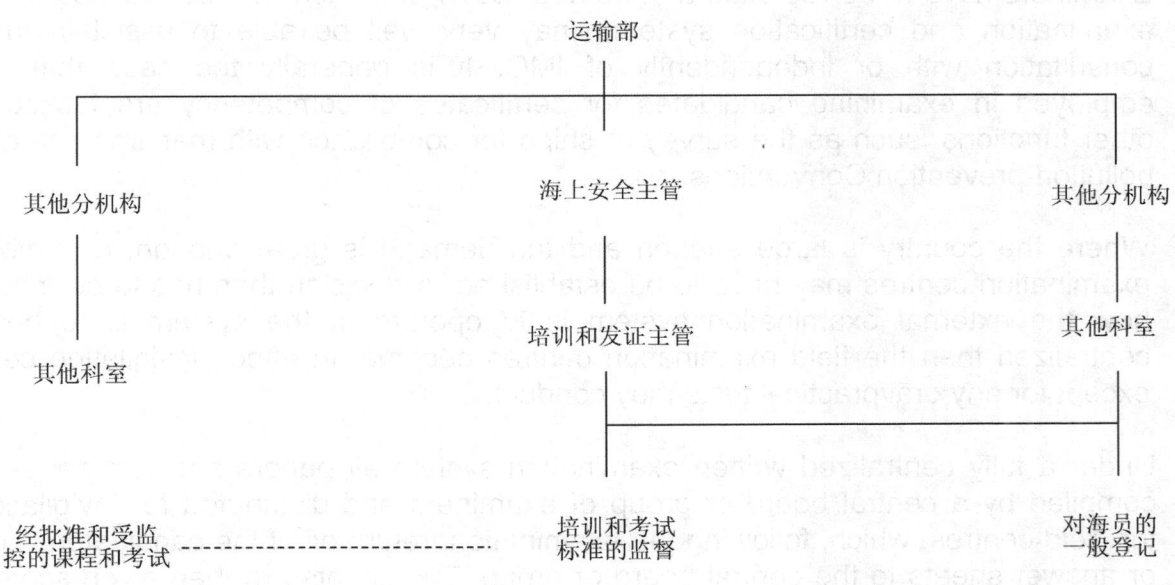

图4.1 采用外部考试方法的主管机关组织结构图

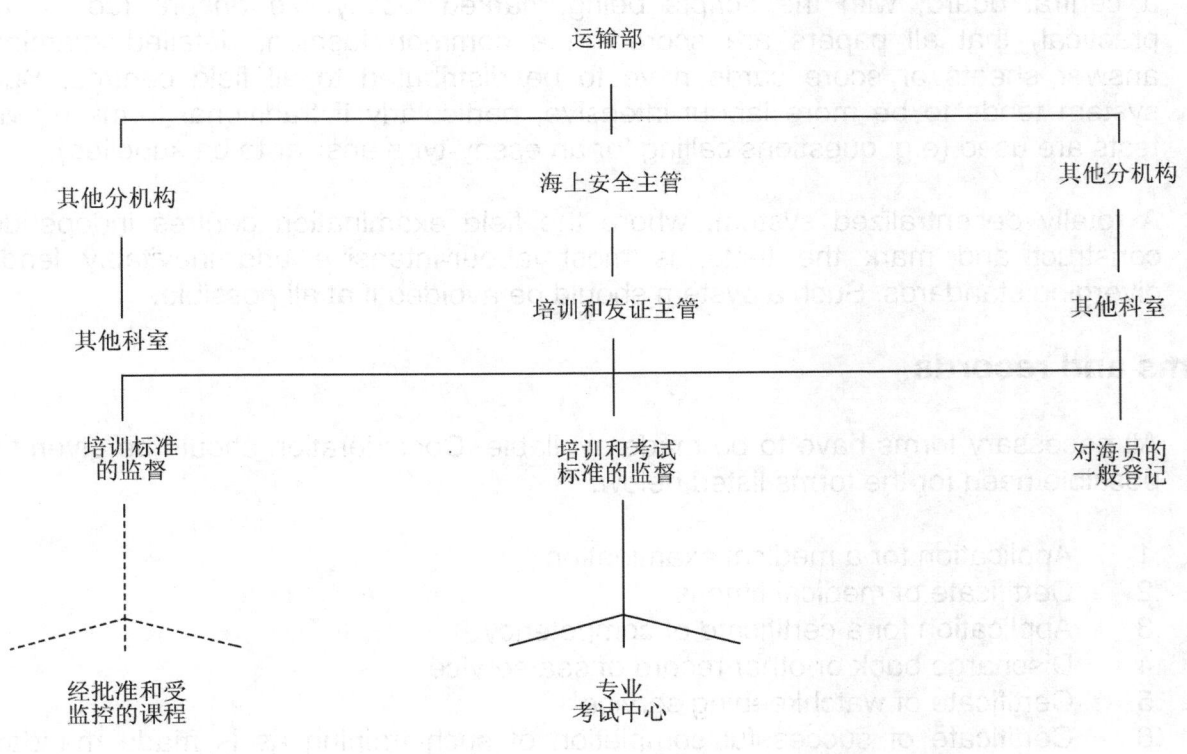

图4.2 采用内部考试方法的主管机关组织结构图

18. Examiners have to be recruited and trained. Other countries with established training, examination and certification systems may very well be able to assist in this, in consultation with or independently of IMO. It is generally the case that those employed in examining candidates for certificates of competency are tasked with other functions, such as the survey of ships for compliance with maritime safety and pollution-prevention Conventions.

19. Where the country is large enough and the demand is great enough, a number of examination centres may have to be established. A decision then has to be made on how the external examination system is to operate. If the system is to be fully centralized then the field examination centres become, in effect, invigilation centres except for any oral/practical tests they conduct.

20. Under a fully centralized written examination system all papers and test series are compiled by a central board or group of examiners and distributed for invigilation in the field centres, which, following the examination, return all of the candidates' scripts or answer sheets to the central board or group. The scripts are then given scores by this board, which advises the field centres of the results. Such a system assures a uniform quality of examination questions and a more uniform scoring of the results. It may, however, involve delays caused by postal or courier services.

21. A semi-centralized system involves the examination papers or test series being set by a central board, with the scripts being marked locally. To ensure (so far as is practical) that all papers are scored in a common fashion, detailed examination answer sheets or score cards have to be distributed to all field centres. Such a system tends to be more labour-intensive, particularly if traditional forms of written tests are used (e.g questions calling for an essay-type answer to be supplied).

22. A totally decentralized system, where the field examination centres independently construct and mark the tests, is most labour-intensive and inevitably leads to diverging standards. Such a system should be avoided if at all possible.

Forms and records

23. All necessary forms have to be made available. Consideration should be given to the possible need for the forms listed below:

    .1 Application for a medical examination
    .2 Certificate of medical fitness
    .3 Application for a certificate of competency
    .4 Discharge book or other record of sea service
    .5 Certificate of watchkeeping service[1]
    .6 Certificate of successful completion of such training as is made mandatory pursuant to or in addition to the requirements of the 1978 STCW Convention, as amended[1]
    .7 Record of partial success or failure in an examination
    .8 Record of examinations held (internal)

---

1 *This may be supplied independently by the industry or academies, as appropriate, in an agreed standard format.*

18. 必须要招聘并培训考官。已建立培训、考试和发证制度的国家可与IMO协作或独立地在这方面很好地提供帮助。这些考官通常从事不同于学员适任证书考试的其他职务的工作,例如,检查船舶是否遵守海上安全和防止污染公约。

19. 在地域大、需求也很大的国家,可能需要建立许多考试中心。这样,对于如何运作外部考试方法应做出决策。如果用完全集中的方法,则可以成立专门实施除口试/实操测试之外所有考试的地区考试中心。

20. 根据完全集中的书面考试方法,所有试卷和考试系列试题由中央机构或考官小组编写并分发给各地考试中心。考试结束后,中心把全部学员的答卷或答题纸交回中央机构或考官小组。然后,答卷由中央机构评分并由该机构把成绩通知各地区考试中心。这种方法可以保证试题质量统一和评分标准一致,然而可能因邮递或传送而产生延误。

21. 半集中方法由中央机构编写考试系列试题,答卷在各地评判。为了尽可能确保所有试卷以相同方式评分,应给所有地区中心分发详细的答题纸或记分卡。这种方法,尤其是使用传统的书面考试形式(例如:试卷有要求用短文回答的问题)时,往往需要较大的劳动强度。

22. 完全放权的方法,即地区考试中心独立组织考试和评分,这需要最大的劳动强度并不可避免地导致执行标准的分歧。如可能,应当避免使用这种方法。

表格和记录

23. 必须制作所有必需的表格,应考虑可能需要的表格如下:

    .1 健康检查申请
    .2 健康证书
    .3 适任证书申请表
    .4 离船登记簿或其他海上资历记录
    .5 值班服务证书[1]
    .6 完成诸如按照经修订的1978年STCW公约要求的或其他要求的强制性培训合格证书[1]
    .7 考试部分合格或不合格记录
    .8 举办的考试记录(内部方法)

---
1 可由相应行业或院校以认可的标准格式提供。

.9 Authority to deliver a certificate
.10 Certificates of competency of each class and grade which is to be issued
.11 Record of certificates issued (internal)
.12 Application for revalidation of a certificate
.13 Application for replacement of a certificate lost or destroyed
.14 Dispensation from the requirement to hold an appropriate certificate

24. It is important that reliable records are kept of all examinations held and their results and of the certificates issued, revalidated, replaced, suspended, revoked or cancelled. A comprehensive centralized record system is essential in order to:

— enforce administrative decisions with respect to non-admission to examinations for specified periods;

— allow verification that certificates for which a replacement or revalidation is sought have previously been issued; and

— allow verification of the certification of seafarers, so as to be able to respond to: enquiries from officers responsible for ensuring compliance with the national legislation, enquires from other Administrations as a result of port State control, and enquiries from officers conducting enquiries into marine casualties or incidents.

This may be supplied independently by the industry or academies, as appropriate, in an agreed standard format.

25. Such records should allow location of the information through the name of the seafarer and through the number of the certificate.

In those regards it must be borne in mind that certificates of competency that have been lost or stolen are occasionally altered and used by persons other than the lawful holders.

As in the case of counterfeit currency, authorities issuing certificates make them as difficult as possible to counterfeit or alter, but those who are determined to produce a fraudulent certificate use sophisticated methods, and counterfeits can be difficult to detect. Thus central records form the only reliable proof of qualification; the records should be kept secure and the information duplicated or otherwise protected from loss by fire or other cause.

Examinations for medical fitness
— **Guidelines for conducting Pre-Sea and Periodic Medical Fitness for Seafarers**

26. Provisions on medical care and health protection for seafarers are contained in a number of instruments adopted by the ILO. The Medical Examination (Seafarers) Convention (No. 73) requires that a seafarer must hold a valid medical certificate as a condition of sea service. Convention No. 73 has been widely ratified and is listed in the Appendix to the ILO Merchant Shipping (Minimum Standards) Convention No. 147. Compliance with the requirement for medical certificate is frequently checked by the flag state and also in port State Control.

.9 发证授权书
.10 拟签发的各层次和级别的适任证书
.11 签发证书的记录(内部方法)
.12 证书再有效申请表
.13 遗失或损坏证书更换申请表
.14 持有相应证书要求的特免证明

24. 可靠地对所有举行的考试及其成绩以及对证书的签发、再有效、更换、中止、吊销或注销进行记录是很重要的。出于以下的目的,全面的集中记录系统是必需的:

— 执行在规定时期不准考试的有关行政决定;

— 证明申请更换或再有效的证书确实是以前签发的;及

— 为海员证书提供证明,以便答复:国家执法官员的询问、其他港口国监督主管机关的询问,以及海上人员伤亡或事故调查官员的询问。

可由相应行业或院校以认可的标准格式提供。

25. 通过海员的名字和证书的号码,应能查到相应的记录资料。

必须注意遗失或失窃的适任证书有时候被合法持有者以外的人涂改和使用。

与假币的情况一样,虽然发证主管机关已尽可能使证书难于伪造或涂改,但是,伪证制作者使用精妙的方法使伪证很难被辨别。因此,集中记录资料构成了唯一可靠的资格证据;记录应安全可靠,资料应备份,并且也应保护资料免遭火灾或其他事故的损毁。

健康检查——海员出海前检查和定期健康检查实施指南

26. ILO通过了包括有关海员医疗保健和健康保护在内的许多文件的规定。《健康检查(海员)公约》(No.73)规定:作为海上服务的条件之一,海员必须持有有效的健康证书。公约No.73已被广泛接受并被列入《ILO商船运输(最低标准)公约》No.147附录中。船旗国和港口国监督应经常检查健康证书要求的遵守情况。

27. For many years a need has been expressed for developing international criteria for the medical fitness examination itself. This issue was also addressed in Resolution No. 9 of the revised STCW Convention.

Based on a survey of ILO and WHO Member States on the subject of medical examination of seafarers, an early draft of medical guidelines for seafarers was prepared by the ILO and WHO secretaries. The Guidelines for Conducting Pre-sea and Periodic Medical Fitness Examinations for Seafarers were developed by a Joint WHO/ILO meeting in Nov 1997. These Guidelines provide:

— overview of relevant international laws and regulations;

— description of the purpose and contents of the seafarers' medical certificates;

— guidance on the right of privacy;

— recommendations for those conducting medical fitness examinations of seafarers;

— appeals procedures for seafarers denied medical certificates;

— brief description of seafaring life relevant to the medical examination of seafarers;

— brief description of the types and frequencies of medical examinations of seafarers;

— recommended procedures for the conduct of medical examinations;

— recommendations on vaccinations;

— minimum in-service eyesight standards;

— hearing standards;

— a list of conditions which should be considered by medical examiners when deciding on whether o issue medical certificates;

— minimum medical requirements for medical examination (in the format of a medical examination form);

— medical certificate for service at sea; and

— information on the collection, processing and communication of medical data.

Process to establish internal examinations

28. The principal differences between establishing an internal and an external examination system centre on the delegation of authority to the institutions which are to administer and conduct the examinations.

27. 多年来,一直强调需要为健康检查制定国际标准。这一问题在经修订的 STCW 公约决议 No.9 中也有相关陈述。

基于 ILO 和 WHO 缔约国对海员健康检查的调查,早期起草的海员健康检查指南由 ILO 和 WHO 秘书处编写。《海员出海前检查和定期健康检查实施指南》由 1997 年 11 月 WHO/ILO 联席会议规划制定。这些指导提供:

— 相关国际法律和法规综述;

— 海员健康证书的用途和内容说明;

— 隐私权的指导;

— 海员健康检查实施人员的建议;

— 未获签发健康证书的海员的申诉程序;

— 与海员健康检查有关的航海生活简述;

— 海员健康检查的类型和频度简述;

— 健康检查实施程序的建议;

— 接种疫苗的建议;

— 任职最低视力标准;

— 听力标准;

— 决定是否签发健康证书时体检医生应考虑的条件一览表;

— 健康检查最低要求(以健康检查表格的形式表示);

— 海上服务健康证书;及

— 有关健康资料收集、处理和交流的信息。

制定内部考试的方法

28. 内部和外部考试方法制定的主要不同集中在授予考试管理和实施机构的权利上。

Guidance has to be provided as to the interpretation of the national legislation, which legislation, apart from the designation or appointment of examiners, will not differ greatly from that required where external examinations are used, if it differs at all.

29. The conditions under which the authority to conduct examination is delegated have to be established in such detail as is necessary for the Administration to be fully aware of the scope of the examinations, the methods of conducting and scoring them and the levels of competence thereby demonstrated, and to assure itself that they fully meet the minimum requirements of the 1978 STCW Convention, as amended. The academies' compliance with the conditions of such delegation should be monitored on an on-going basis.

30. The Administration may well wish to directly involve itself at the stage of the issue of certificates and must involve itself in respect of the endorsement required by Article VI, paragraph (2) of the Convention, which provides that:

    2. Certificates for masters and officers, issued in compliance with this Article, shall be endorsed by the issuing Administration in the form as prescribed in Regulation I/2 of the Annex. If the language used is not English, the endorsement shall include a translation into that language.

    Under Article II, paragraph (b) of the Convention, "Administration" means "the Government of the Party whose flag the ship is entitled to fly". Thus, endorsement of certificates is solely a function of a government, a ministry or a department, and cannot be delegated.

31. The forms that it will be necessary for the Administration to issue under the internal examination system will depend on the precise terms of the delegation of authority given to the academies. However, the information provided to and the records of the academies must be complete in respect of decisions or evaluations made by them on behalf of the Administration.

对于国家法规的解释,除指定或指派主考官外,采用内部考试与外部考试不会有太多的不同(如果有不同的话)。

29. 制定实施考试的授权条件必须足够详细,使主管机关能完全了解考试的范围、考试的实施和评分的方法以及由此反映的适任水平,并确信它们完全满足经修订的STCW公约的最低要求。主管机关应监控符合这种授权条件的机构的运作。

30. 主管机关会希望直接参与证书签发阶段的运作,并且必须直接实施按公约第Ⅵ条第2款规定的签注。公约第Ⅵ条第2款规定:

    2. 按本条规定签发给船长和高级船员的证书,应由发证的主管机关按公约规则Ⅰ/2规定的形式予以签注。如使用的文字不是英文,则该签注应包括英文译文。

    根据公约第Ⅱ条(b)款,"主管机关"系指"船舶有权悬挂其国旗的缔约国政府"。因此,证书的签注是政府、部委的职责,不能授权。

31. 根据内部考试方法,主管机关签发证书所需的形式取决于明确授予院校权利的委托条款。然而,院校代表主管机关所做的决策和评估必须提供完善的资料和院校的记录。

Part 5
Quality Standards System

Quality standards system

1. All training that is required by the revised STCW Convention must be monitored as part of a quality standards system (QSS).

   A Quality Standards System is a system that provides for, and ensures that, the most practicable standards for seafarers' competence are met.

   QSS activities would include widely differing activities like:

   a. Approval of training courses

   b. Assessment of competence

   c. Certification, endorsement and revalidation (upgrading and renewal)

   d. Approval of trainers and assessors

   e. Medical standards

   Quality Standards—Regulation I/8
   - Administration's systems for control, approval and certification
   - National MET, examination and certification systems

2. Regulation I/8 of the revised STCW Convention refers to the application of quality standards systems to all activities concerning training and assessment. Therefore, training providers: maritime training centres, simulator training centres and administrations which carry out any training and assessment activity must establish a quality standards system for the activity.

   Lecturers should note the specific requirements in Regulation I/8 Quality standards paragraph 1, 2 and 3; and in Section A-I/8 Quality standards paragraphs 1, 2, 3 and 4.

第5章
质量标准体系

质量标准体系

1. 经修订的STCW公约规定的所有培训必须受质量标准体系(QSS)监控。

    质量标准体系是用于规定和保证海员的适任能力满足最可行的适任标准体系。

    QSS活动广泛地监控不同的活动,如:

    a. 培训课程的核准

    b. 适任评估

    c. 发证、签证和再有效(晋升和更新)

    d. 培训和评估人员的核准

    e. 健康标准

质量标准——规则 I/8
- 监督、核准和发证管理制度
- 国家MET、考试和发证制度

2. 经修订的STCW公约规则 I/8涉及把质量标准体系运用于所有与培训和评估相关的事务。因此,培训提供者(海上培训中心、模拟器培训中心和参与培训与评估活动的主管机关)必须建立培训质量标准体系。

    教员应当注意公约规则 I/8质量标准第1、2和3款,以及第A-I/8节质量标准第1、2、3和4款规定的要求。

> **Quality Standards—Regulation I/8**
> - MET Institutions
> - In-service training
> - Qualification—instructor and assessor
> - Training programmes and courses

3. All Parties have to ensure that all activities which give effect to Convention requirements are *continuously monitored* through a quality standards system, whether they are carried out by other entities under its authority or carried out within a Government ministry, department or organization (see regulation I/8).

The essential steps to take to ensure the good quality of an operation are to:

.1 establish clear policies and standards governing staff quality and the conduct of the activities;

.2 adopt realistic and properly funded implementation and control measures which give practical effect to these policies and standards in order to allow the objectives to be achieved;

.3 develop and introduce procedures which allow the performance and results of these activities to be monitored and checked to ensure that the objectives (i.e. the Convention requirements) are being achieved; and

.4 ensure that staff participate fully in the development and establishment of the system and are kept fully informed at all times.

ISO-9000

History

International Organization for Standardization developed this set of quality system standards in 1987. They have been adopted as THE standard by virtually all industrial nations. The standards were updated in 1994 to strengthen preventative action requirements and further changes come in 2000.

Process

Each company must implement and document a quality System that meets the requirements of one of the Standard levels(9001, 9002, or 9003:9001 is the most difficult to implement as it includes product design and development). A third-pany registrar audits the company's quality system, documentation, and processes for compliance to the specification and issues a registration certificate. Periodic surveillance audits are perfomed by the third-party to ensure on-going compliance.

Why companies Implement ISO-9000

1. Ensures a solid quality system foundation; good basis for other quality initiatives like Total Quality Management (TQM).
2. Excellent vehicle for continuous improvement.
3. Market advantage–virtual requirement in some markets.
4. Reduces need for customer audis.
5. Cost savings inherent in improved quality.

What Does ISO-9000 Mean to a Customer?

Purchasing from a company that is certified to ISO-9000 assures you:

- The quality system is reviewed by management on a regular basis.
- Customer complaints will be addressed and resolved.
- The enterprise has a quality policy that is implemented.
- Your contract or purchase order will be reviewed and approved by appropriate individuals.
- Products are developed Under a controlled methodology that includes documented reviews and verification tests.
- All parts for your products are purchased under strict control from only approved and proven vendors and subcontractors.
- Manufacturing processes are documented and controlled to ensure product consistency.
- All product is adequately tested before Shipment and the results of these tests are kept for your inspection if required.
- All equipment used to test your products is regularly calibrated for accuracy.
- There is a formal closed-loop corrective action system in place to fix problems and prevent new ones from occurring.
- The company's packaging and handling is designed to prevent damage to your products.
- The company performs formal internal audits of all of its key processes with a focus on continuous improvement.
- All employees that are involved in the design, manufacture, test, and transportation of your product are properly trained to meet a standard.

质量标准——规则I/8

- MET机构
- 在职培训
- 资格——教员和评估员
- 培训计划和课程

3. 公约要求的质量体系无论是根据授权由其他团体执行,还是在一个政府部委、部门或组织内执行,所有缔约国必须保证公约要求的所有活动都受到质量标准体系的连续监控(参阅公约规则Ⅰ/8)。

确保体系可靠运行应采取的重要步骤为:

.1 制定控制人员素质和约束人员行为活动的具体方针和标准;

.2 采取切合实际的和有适当资金支持的执行和监督措施,这些措施能够切实执行上述方针和标准,以实现管理目标;

.3 开发和应用监控和检查这些活动运作和结果的程序,以确保目标(例如,公约要求的目标)的实现;及

.4 保证人员完全参与体系的开发和建立,并且要求他们始终保持对体系的充分了解。

ISO-9000

历史

国际标准化组织在1987年开发了这套质量体系标准。它们事实上已被所有工业国家作为标准采用。标准在1994年进行了更新以加强预防性行动要求,并于2000年进行了进一步的修订。

过程

每个公司必须实施质量体系并提供文件证明。该质量体系满足9001、9002或9003(9001因涉及产品设计和开发而最难实施)其中一个质量标准的要求。第三方注册审核员审核公司的质量体系、文件和符合规范的过程并签发登记证书。周期性评审和审核由第三方实施,以确保符合程序。

公司为什么要实施ISO-9000

1. 确保坚实的质量体系基础;为其他质量措施(如全面质量管理(TQM))提供基础。
2. 持续改进极好的途径。
3. 市场优势——某些市场的实际要求。
4. 减少顾客检查的需要。
5. 节约成本是质量提高所固有的性质。

ISO-9000对顾客来说意味着什么?

从ISO-9000认证的公司采购,保证:

- 质量体系由管理部门定期评审。
- 顾客投诉会得到反映和解决。
- 企业有可执行的质量方针。
- 合同或采购订单将由适当人员审核和批准。
- 产品按受控方法开发。该方法包括文件审核和确认检验。
- 产品的所有部件受严格控制,包括从最合适的并经核准的原卖主和中间商购买部件。
- 生产过程有文件化证明并受到控制,以确保产品合格。
- 所有产品在装运前受适当检验,检验结果保存供查(如需要)。
- 用于检验产品的所有设备定期校验精度。
- 具备有效的闭环纠正系统功能以解决问题和防止新问题出现。
- 公司包装和搬运尽力防止损害产品。
- 公司对所有的关键过程实施内部审核,并把焦点集中在持续改进方面。
- 所有参与产品设计、生产、试验和运输的人员受到适当培训以满足标准。

4. Positive support and participation of staff at all levels assures success; alienation of any staff member signals potential failure. Quality standards systems are already widely applied in the business world and increasing use is being made of them by academic institutions. Appropriate use should be made of national standards and organizations concerned with their implementation. Adjustment of a well tested system to meet an organization's particular needs is to be preferred to "reinventing the wheel". Extensive and detailed guidance is provided in section B-I/8.

5. Section B-I/8 of the STCW Convention describes a quality management system paralleling ISO 9000 guidelines (see box above on ISO 9000) in paragraphs 1 and 2. Section B of the STCW Code is recommendatory, but a quality management system will be most suited in applying the provisions of Regulation I/8 and Section A-I/8. Paragraphs 3–5 present a quality standards model for assessment of competence.

Quality Standards–Elements
- Certification requirements
- Principles for quality assurance
- Planning, development and preparation phase
- Operations phase
- Result phase

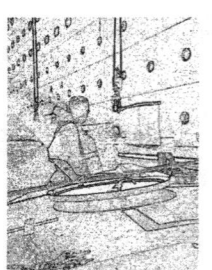

6. In the development of quality standards it is essential to determine what is considered as good practices and what to include in the standards. This is to ensure that the education and training institutions operate with acceptable quality and cover the requirements set forth in the Convention.

    The mentioned standards consist of five parts:

    a. The two first parts cover the certification requirements and the so-called "*quality assurance*" principles. These elements of quality are requirements which will be found in any quality management system.

    b. Another part of the standard covers *development activities*, i.e., development of courses, simulator exercises and curriculum plans. This should be performed in a structured way. Specific verification activities shall ensure that all courses and plans fulfil regulatory requirements.

    c. The standards also cover the *operational* part of any training activity. This could be identifying instructor and trainer needs. Necessary equipment required for any specific training shall be identified, including maintenance requirements.

4. 各层次人员对体系的积极支持和参与是成功的保证,而任何人员的消极怠工预示可能失败。质量标准体系在商界已被普遍使用,而且学术机构正加大对它的利用。应适当利用有关现有国家标准和执行机构。对经过充分检验的体系进行调整,以满足机构的特定需要,这比"重新建立新系统"更好。第B-Ⅰ/8节提供了大量和详细的指导。

5. STCW公约第B-Ⅰ/8节在第1和2款中叙述与ISO 9000指南相对应的质量管理体系(参阅下表)。STCW规则B节是建议性的,但最适用于按公约规则Ⅰ/8和第A-Ⅰ/8节的条款建立和管理的质量管理体系。第3~5款对适任评估的质量标准模型做了介绍。

6. 在制定质量标准的过程中,确定什么是良好做法和在标准中包括什么内容很重要。这将确保教育和培训机构以可接受的质量运作和适应公约提出的要求。

上述标准由5部分组成:

a. 开头两部分包括发证要求和"质量保证"原则。这些要素是任何质量体系都要求的。

b. 标准的另一部分涉及活动的开展,如课程安排、模拟器训练和课程计划。这将按既定方式进行。详细的验证活动将确保所有课程和计划满足规则要求。

c. 标准也涉及培训活动的运营。这包括确定教员和培训者需要、确定具体培训所需的必要设备以及维护要求。

d. The final part of the standards focus on the *"result phase"* of any training. This will include examination criteria to be specified and how this is to be carried out. Procedures for issuing diploma or documents of evidence must be identified. A system for ensuring that all mandatory elements are covered through tests and exams during the education must be established.

Section B-I/8 Guidance regarding quality standards paragraphs 1 to 8 inclusive provide essential guidance and although not repeated here should be referenced by the lecturer.

Independent evaluation

6. Paragraphs 6 and 7 of Section B-I/8 deals with independent evaluation of activities.

    Parties have to ensure that an independent evaluation of each quality standards system that covers the training, assessment of competency, certification or other activity that gives effect to the Convention is carried out at intervals of not more than five years and that the results and the implementation of recommendations made are reported to IMO (see regulations I/8 and I/7). An "independent evaluation" means an evaluation earned out by suitably qualified persons independent of, or external to, the unit or activity being evaluated and is defined further in section A-I/1 of the STCW Code.

7. The following charts show the structure of the standards for:

    a. maritime academies

    b. maritime training providers/centres

    c. maritime simulator centres

    d. crew manning offices

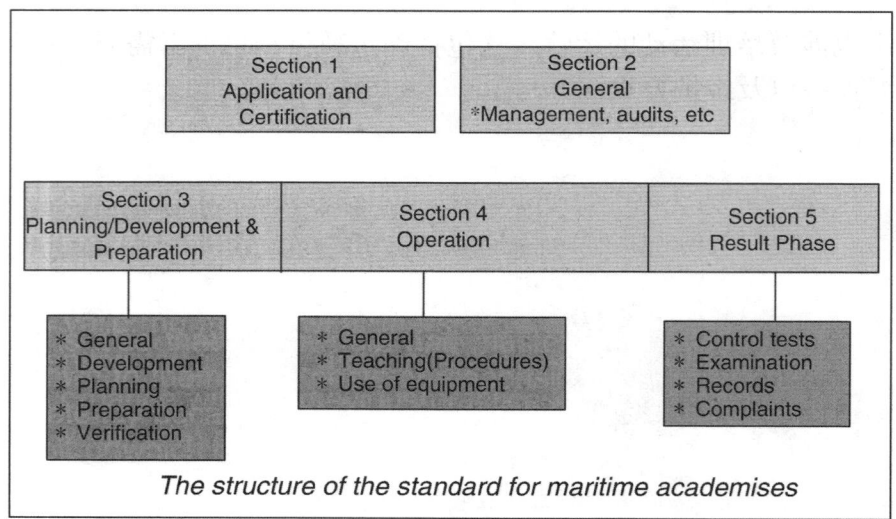

The structure of the standard for maritime academises

d. 标准的最后部分集中于培训的"成果阶段"。其包括规定考试标准和如何实施考试。必须确定签发证书或证明文件的程序，建立在培训期间通过测试和考试确保培训覆盖所有强制性要素的体系。

有关质量标准的第B-I/8节(包括第1至8款)提供了重要的指导。虽然没有在此重复，但教员应当参考。

独立评估

6. 第B-Ⅰ/8节第6和7段涉及活动的独立评估。

    各缔约国必须保证对包括：培训、适任评估、发证或实施本公约的其他活动在内的每个质量标准体系以不超过5年的间隔实施独立评估，并把结果和落实建议情况报告给IMO (参阅公约规则Ⅰ/8和Ⅰ/7)。"独立评估"系指由独立于被评估单位或活动、或由被评估单位或活动以外的有适当资格的人员实施的评估。STCW规则A-Ⅰ/1节对其做了进一步的规定。

7. 下图表示以下各种机构的质量标准结构：

    a. 海事院校

    b. 海上培训提供者/中心

    c. 海上模拟器中心

    d. 船员调配处

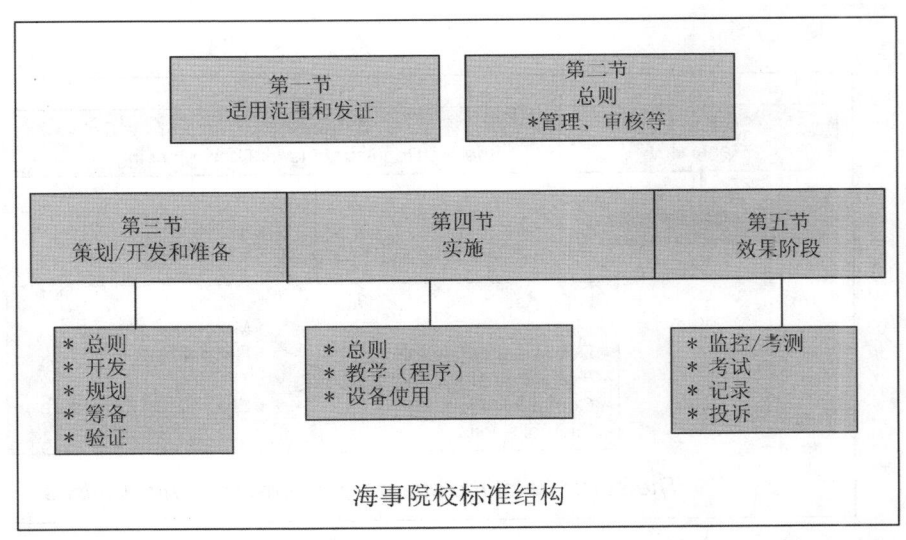

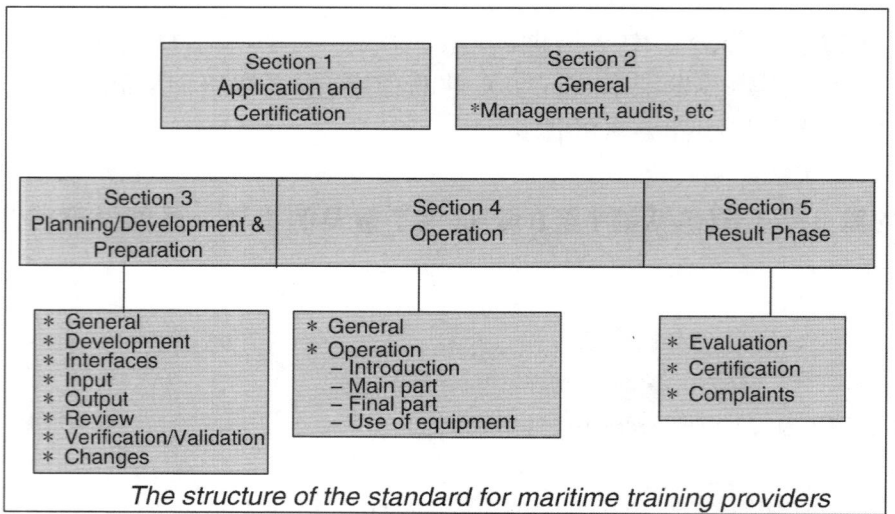

The structure of the standard for maritime training providers

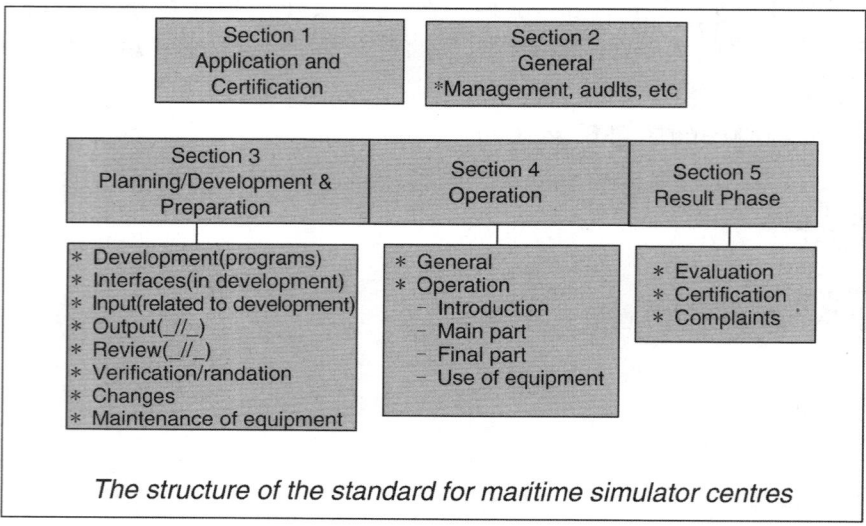

The structure of the standard for maritime simulator centres

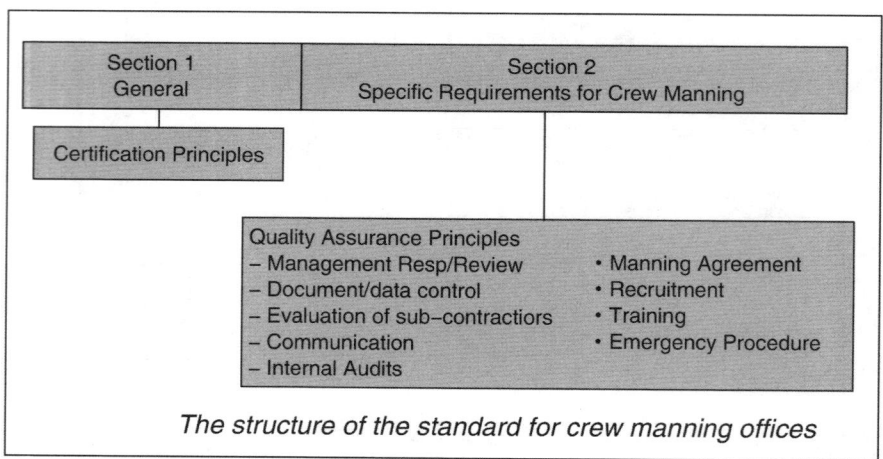

The structure of the standard for crew manning offices

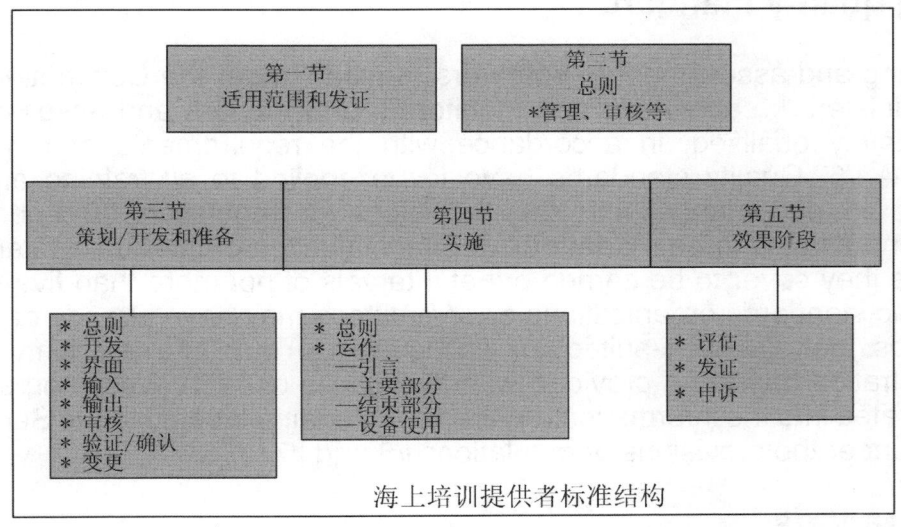

海上培训提供者标准结构

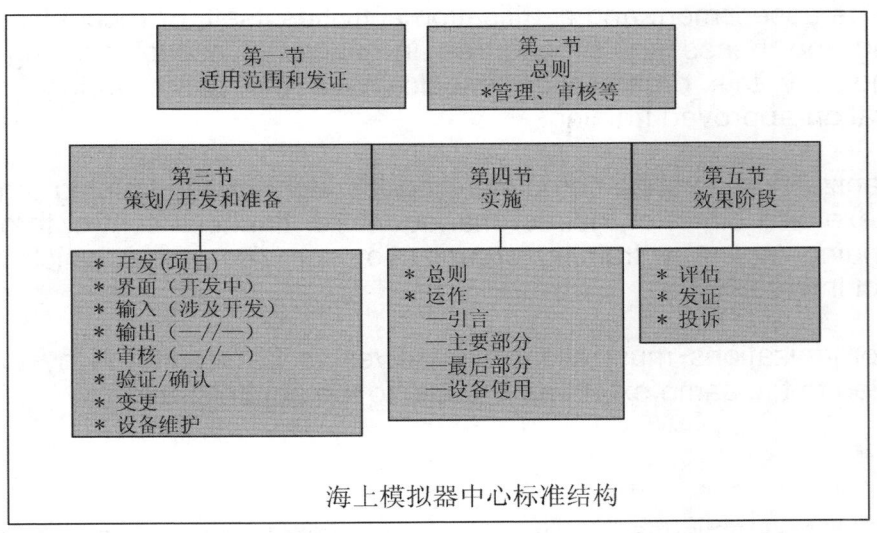

海上模拟器中心标准结构

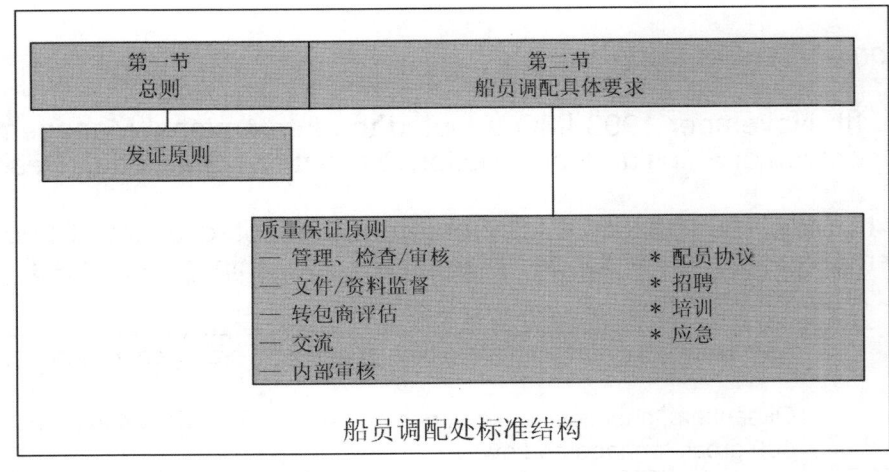

船员调配处标准结构

Maintaining quality standards

8. All training and assessment of seafarers required under the Convention is required to be administered, supervised and monitored, and trainers and assessors have to be appropriately qualified, in accordance with the requirements of regulation I/6 and section A-I/6. Quality standards have to be applied to all training and assessment activities in accordance with the provisions of regulation I/8 and section A-I/8. Provision has also to be made for external evaluation of the quality standards and the activities they cover to be carried out at intervals of not more than five years. National academic standards organizations or committees may have already developed quality standards that are well suited for application to maritime academy activities. The Administration has to be provided with the results of each evaluation so they may be incorporated into the information required to be communicated to the Secretary-General of IMO under the provisions of regulations I/8 and I/7.

QSS organizations

9. An administration could monitor, through a quality standards system, all training, competence assessment and certification activities itself, or recognize an organization as having the necessary procedures in place to accept training on its behalf. Recognition by this organization should have the same weight and bearing as administration-approved training.

 QSS organizations must be completely independent of any training organization. They may not exercise direct or indirect managerial or financial control through contract or understanding over any training organization, or *vice versa*, which may result in a "conflict of interest".

 Training organizations must allow themselves to be monitored by the chosen QSS organization to the same extent as it would to the administration.

ISM Code

10. The ISM Code establishes an international standard for management and operation of ships in relation to safety and pollution prevention. One aim should be to ensure that personnel are properly informed and equipped to fulfil their operational responsibilities safely.

Implementation of the ISM Code

10 On the 4th November 1993 IMO adopted the International Management Code for the Safe Operation of Ships and for Pollution Prevention (ISM Code), Resolution A 741(18).

 The 24th May 1994 the SOLAS Conference adopted a new Chapter IX to SOLAS which makes the ISM Code mandatory for ships, regardless of the date of construction, as follows:

1st July 1998	All passenger ships, including high speed light craft (regardless of size). Oil tankers, chemical tankers, gas carriers, bulk carriers and cargo high speed craft of 500 gross tonnage and over.
1st July 2002	Other cargo ships and mobile offshore drilling units of 500 gross tonnage and over.

保持质量标准

8. 必须对公约要求的所有海员培训和评估进行管理、监督和监控。根据公约规则Ⅰ/6和第A-Ⅰ/6节的要求,培训和评估人员必须具备适当资格。公约规则Ⅰ/8和第A-Ⅰ/8节规定必须将质量标准应用于所有培训和评估活动,也必须制订以不超过5年的间隔实施对于质量标准及其涉及的活动的外部评估规定。有些国家的学术标准机构或委员会可能已经开发了非常适合海事院校各种活动应用的质量标准。每次评估的结果必须提供给主管机关,并因此可能编入根据公约规则Ⅰ/8和Ⅰ/7规定必须传送给IMO秘书长的资料中。

QSS(质量审核)机构

9. 主管机关通过质量标准体系可以监控所有培训、适任评估和发证事务,或按必要程序认可其他机构代表主管机关开展适当的培训。该机构的培训与主管机关认可的培训应当有相同的分量和内容。

    QSS机构必须完全独立于培训机构。它们不可以通过合同或协议对培训机构进行直接或间接的经营或财务监督。反之亦然,否则会导致"利益冲突"。

    培训机构必须接受选定的QSS机构以与主管机关相同的监控程度对自己的活动进行监控。

ISM规则

10. ISM规则在安全与防止污染方面建立了船舶管理和营运国际标准。规则的一个目标应是确保人员获得适当的信息和获得适当的训练以安全地完成他们的工作任务。

ISM规则的实施

10 1993年11月4日,IMO通过了《国际船舶安全营运和防止污染管理规则》(ISM规则),决议A.741(18)。

1994年5月24日,SOLAS大会通过了SOLAS新增加的第Ⅸ章。这使ISM规则对于任何建造日期的船舶都为强制性的要求,具体规定如下:

1998年7月1日	所有客船,包括高速轻载艇(不论大小)。
	油船、化学品船、气体运输船、散货船和500总吨及以上的载货高速艇。
2002年7月1日	500总吨及以上的其他货船和移动式近海钻井装置。

ISM Code objective

11. The objective of the ISM Code is formulated as follows:

    .1 The objectives of the Code are to ensure safety at sea, prevention of human injury or loss of life, and avoidance of damage to the environment, in particular, to the marine environment, and to properly.

    .2 Safety management objectives of the Company should, *inter alia*:

    .1 provide for safe practices in ship operation and a safe working environment;

    .2 establish safeguards against all identified risks;

    .3 continuously improve safety management skills of personnel ashore and on board ships, including preparing for emergencies related both to safety and environmental protection.

    .3 The safety management system should ensure:

    .1 compliance with mandatory rules and regulations;

    .2 that applicable codes, guidelines and standards recommended by the Organisation, Administrations, classification societies and maritime industry organizations are taken into account.

    The Code does not provide detailed and prescriptive requirements, neither do the IMO Guidelines on ISM Code implementation.

    The figure below shows the ISM Code as an "umbrella" regulation, encompassing The STCW Convention, MARPOL and other standards. ISM constitutes the new chapter IX (from 1994 onwards) in SOLAS.

ISM Code and STCW QSS

12. STCW works in concert with the ISM Code. Paragraph 6.5 of the ISM Code states that "*The Company should establish and maintain procedures for identifying any training which may be required in support of the safety management system (SMS) and ensure that such training is provided for all personnel concerned*". Thus it requires the implementation of a training program as part of the ISM Code's SMS, but does not proscribe specific requirements for the training program. Therefore, a training program, simply by virtue of being under the ISM umbrella, may not necessarily meet the STCW QSS criteria. The detail required in the implementation of STCW QSS is much greater than the requirements of the ISM Code.

ISM 规则目标

11. ISM 规则的目标陈述如下：

   .1 规则的目标是确保海上安全、防止伤亡和避免对环境特别是海洋环境造成危害以及对财产造成损失。

   .2 公司的安全管理目标尤其应：

      .1 提供船舶营运的安全做法和安全工作环境；

      .2 针对已确定的所有风险制定防范措施；

      .3 不断提高岸上及船上人员的安全管理技能，包括安全及环境保护方面的应急准备。

   .3 安全管理体系应当保证：

      .1 符合强制性规定及规则；

      .2 对国际海事组织、主管机关、船级社和海运业组织所建议的适用的规则、指导和标准予以考虑。

本规则没有规定详细的、指定的要求，有关 ISM 规则实施的 IMO 指导也没有做出这样的规定。

下图表示 ISM 规则作为"伞"（包容性）规则，包含 STCW 公约、MARPOL 公约和其他公约要求的标准。ISM 规则从 1994 年起成为 SOLAS 新增的第 IX 章。

ISM 规则和 STCW 公约 QSS

12. STCW 公约的作用与 ISM 规则一致。ISM 规则第 6.5 款规定"公司应当建立和保持程序，以确定实施 SMS 可能需要的培训项目并保证向所有有关人员提供这种培训"。因此，规则要求将实施培训计划作为落实 ISM 规则的 SMS 的一部分，但没有规定对于培训计划的具体要求。所以，培训计划只是包含在 ISM 规则中，可能未必满足 STCW 公约的 QSS 标准。实施 STCW 公约的 QSS 要求的细节比 ISM 规则的要求多得多。

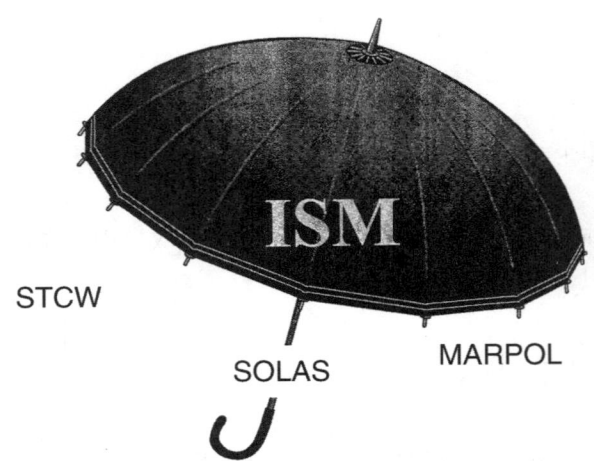

13. The ISM Code, in paragraph 6.3 *"The Company should establish procedures to ensure that new personnel and personnel transferred to new assignments related to safety and protection of the environment are given proper familiarization with their duties. Instructions which are essential to be provided prior to sailing should be identified, documented and given."*, requires newly assigned crew members to be familiarized with the vessel to which they are reporting. This ISM Code requirement is identical to the general STCW requirement in regulation I/14-para.1.4 (Responsibilities of Companies). Satisfying the ISM Code for shipboard familiarization also satisfies STCW regulation I/14-para.1.4. This training does not have to be approved by the administration.

    Regulation I/14 Responsibilities of companies

    1.4... seafarers, on being assigned to any of its ships, are familiarized with their specific duties and with all ship arrangements, installations, equipment, procedures and ship characteristics that are relevant to their routine or emergency duties;...

14. The ISM Code requirement for shipboard familiarization (paragraph 6.3 above) is not sufficiently detailed to meet the requirements for specific vessel type familiarization training in STCW regulations V/1-para.1.2 and V/2-para.5. The familiarization training in STCW regulation V/1-1.2 (Tanker familiarization) must be approved by the administration. The familiarization training in STCW regulation V/2-5 (Ro-ro familiarization) must be approved by the administration.

STCW 95 "Check List" according to ISM

15. In the following table, the requirements in STCW 95 are stated in relation to the ISM requirements. It may be used as a "check list" to ensure that all STCW 95 requirements, derived from the ISM Code, are taken care of. Note that the requirements are stated in a general (international) form, as stated in the STCW 95. Additional Flag State requirements must also be taken care of.

    The structure of the "check list" follows the chapters in the ISM Code. Note that some requirements in the STCW 95 are mentioned in several chapters. This is due to the ISM system's structure and demand for policies and procedures.

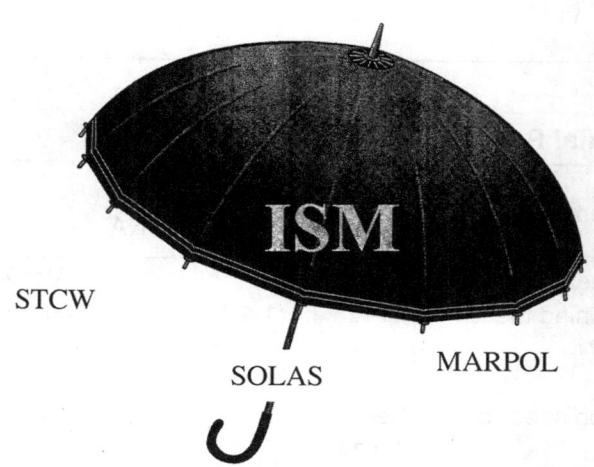

13. ISM规则,在第6.3款"公司应建立程序,以保证与安全和环境保护有关的新聘人员及调至新岗位的人员正确熟悉其任务。必要的指令应在开航前制定、形成文件并提供给有关人员"中,规定新聘船员应熟悉他们新任职的船舶。ISM规则的该要求与STCW公约规则Ⅰ/14第1.4款中的一般要求相同。船上熟悉培训满足ISM规则也满足STCW公约规则Ⅰ/14第1.4款。该培训不需经过主管机关批准。

公约规则I/14公司的责任

1.4 ……刚被指派到任何船上服务的海员应熟悉自己的具体职责以及与自己日常或应急职责有关的船舶所有布置、装置、设备、程序和船舶的特性;……

14. 与STCW公约规则Ⅴ/1第1.2款和规则Ⅴ/2第5款对于具体船舶类型的熟悉培训要求相比,ISM规则对于船上熟悉的要求(上述的第6.3款)不够详细。STCW公约规则Ⅴ/1第1.2款(液货船熟悉)的熟悉培训必须经主管机关批准,STCW公约规则Ⅴ/2-5 (滚装船熟悉)的熟悉培训也必须经主管机关批准。

依据ISM规则的STCW 95公约"检查表"

15. STCW 95公约中与ISM规则相关的要求在下表中列出。该表可以用作"检查表"以确保所有源于ISM规则的STCW 95公约要求得到落实。应注意这些要求用通用(国际)表格列出,与在STCW 95公约中所列的一样,也必须注意船旗国提出的其他要求。

"检查表"的结构依照ISM规则的章节结构编排。应注意在STCW 95公约中有些要求分别在几章中提及,这是出于ISM系统的结构及ISM方针和程序的需求。

A. General (1)				
B. Safety and Environmental Policy (2)				
STCW Requirement	STCW Ref.	ISM Ref.	Y/N/NA	Comments
1. **Training Policy:** Does the company have a training policy defining the objectives of the training?	Reg. I/14	2.1 (1.4.1)		Verification: Check policy statements in SMS.
2. Is shipboard familiarization specifically covered in the policy?	Sec. A-I/14			
3. **Fitness for duty:** Does the company meet the requirements related to the crew members fitness for duty?	Ch. VIII	2.1 (1.4.1)		Verification: Check policy statements in SMS. Please note national requirements for medical fitness (as set out in Reg. I/9)
C. Company Responsibilities and Authority (3)				
1. **In-service training:** Has the function of training supervisor/Company training officer been defined, documented and assigned?	Reg. I/6, A-I/6	3.2		Application: The requirements regarding in-service training for certification apply only when the company performs such training. The requirements are only applicable to seafarers starting their training and education after 1 August 1998.
2. Has the function of instructor and supervisor been defined, documented and assigned?				Please note that implementation of in-service training is also depending on pertinent national legislation. Note in particular that the function of assessor may be interpreted in different ways. Some countries will not delegate the assessment function to the company.
3. Has the function of assessor been defined, documented and assigned?				
D. Designated Person(s) (4)				
E. Master's Responsibility and Authority (5)				
1. **In-service training:** Has the Master's responsibility for training been defined and documented?	A-I/6	5.1.1		Application: The requirements regarding in-service training for certification apply only when the company performs such training. The requirements are only applicable to seafarers starting their training and education after 1 August 1998.

第5章 质量标准体系

A.总则(1)

B.安全和环保方针(2)

STCW要求	STCW Ref.	ISM Ref.	Y/N/NA	说明
1. **培训方针**:公司是否已制定培训方针以规定培训目标?	Reg.Ⅰ/14 Sec.A-Ⅰ/14	2.1 (1.4.1)		确认:检查安全管理体系中的方针声明。
2. 方针是否详细包括船上熟悉培训?				
3. **适于值班**:公司是否满足关于船员适于值班的要求?	Ch.Ⅷ	2.1 (1.4.1)		确认:检查安全管理体系中的方针声明。请注意国家健康要求(如规则Ⅰ/9规定)

C.公司的责任和权限(3)

1. **在职培训**:是否已规定、用文件规定和指派培训监督员/公司培训官员的责任?	Reg.Ⅰ/6, A-Ⅰ/6	3.2		适用范围:在职发证培训的要求仅在公司实施这种培训的情况下适用。要求仅对1998年之后开始参加培训和教育的海员适用。
2. 是否已规定、用文件规定和指派指导与监督人员的责任?				请注意在职培训的实施方案也取决于国家法规。应特别注意评估员的责任可能以不同方式解释。有些国家不将评估职能委托给公司。
3. 是否已规定、用文件规定和指派评估员的责任?				

D.指定人员(4)

E.船长的责任和权限(5)

1. **在职培训**:是否已规定和用文件规定船长在培训方面的责任?	A-Ⅰ/6	5.1.1		适用范围:在职发证培训的要求仅在公司实施这种培训的情况下适用。要求仅对1998年之后开始参加培训和教育的海员适用。

STCW Requirement	STCW Ref.	ISM Ref.	Y/N/NA	Comments
F. Resources and Personnel (6)				
1. **Familiarization:** Are there procedures in place to ensure that crew members and other personnel are familiarised with the ship and with their duties before being assigned to such duties? 2. Is the task of familiarization assigned to knowledgeable crew members aboard?	Reg. 1/14, A-I/14 A-I/14, para. 2.2	6.3 (3.2)		Verification: Check that the company has established procedures for shipboard familiarizations and that the familiarization of each crew member has been duly recorded. Make sure sufficient time has been allowed and that the familiarization was carried out in a language understood by the crew member. Check on the training outcome by asking questions regarding the specific equipment, procedures and arrangements with which they should be familiar.
3. **Knowledge of maritime legislation:** Does the company ensure that officers have sufficient knowledge of pertinent maritime legislation?	Table A-II/1, A-II/2, A-II/3, A-III/1, A-III/2	6.4 (1.2.3)		Verification: Check that the relevant personnel are aware of the relevant international and national legislation currently applicable, that they have knowledge of regulations pertinent to their duties, and that they are able to find those regulations.
4. **Fitness for duty:** Does the company ensure that watchkeeping personnel are fit for duty? 5. Does the Company maintain records of work hours or of rest hours? 6. Has the Company put in place safeguards against drug and alcohol abuse?	Ch. VIII B-VIII/34-36	6.2 (1.2.3)		Record of work/rest hours and safeguards against alcohol abuse implicit in Ch. VIII. Ref. B-VIII/1 and B-VIII/2, part 5. Some Flag States have issued national legislation with regard to the registration of work hours. Verification: Check that documentation on work/rest hours is properly filled out. Pending National legislation
7. Does the Company have routines for arranging training, updating, or replacement of the individual crew member as applicable?	A-I/14	6.5 (11.1)		
8. **In-service training:** Is training conducted according to an approved training programme? 9. Is training registered in an approved training record book?	A-I/6	6 (6.5) (11.1)		Application: The requirements regarding in-service training for certification apply only when the company performs such training. The requirements are only applicable to seafarers starting their training and education after 1 August 1998. See also Part C above.

第5章 质量标准体系

STCW要求	STCW Ref.	ISM Ref.	Y/N/NA	说明
F.资源和人员(6)				
1. **熟悉**:是否制定了适当程序以确保船员和其他人员在被指派担任某项工作之前熟悉船舶和他们的工作?	Reg. 1/14, A-Ⅰ/14	6.3		确认:检查公司是否已制定船上熟悉培训程序和适当记录每个船员的熟悉培训情况。确信有充足的时间和以船员理解的语言实施熟悉培训。通过询问船员应当熟悉的有关具体设备、程序和安排的问题检查培训结果。
2. 是否指派熟悉任务给船上在行的船员?	A-Ⅰ/14, para. 2.2	(3.2)		
3. **海事法规知识**:公司是否能确保高级船员有充足的有关海事法则的知识?	Table A-Ⅱ/1, A-Ⅱ/2, A-Ⅲ/3, A-Ⅲ/1, A-Ⅲ/2	6.4 (1.2.3)		确认:检查相关人员对现行的相关国际和国内法规的熟悉情况,对有关他们工作的法规的熟悉情况,以及他们能够找出这些法规。
4. **适于值班**:公司能否确保值班人员适于值班?	Ch. Ⅷ	6.2 (1.2.3)		记录包含在上述的第Ⅷ章、第B-Ⅷ/1节和第B-Ⅷ/2节第5部分的工作/休息时间和防止吸毒和酗酒的措施。一些船旗国已发布有关登记工作时间的国家法规。
5. 公司是否保持工作时间和休息时间的记录?				
6. 公司是否已采取防止吸毒和酗酒的措施?	B-Ⅷ/ 34~36			确认:检查有关工作/休息时间的文件是否正确填写。有待于国家立法。
7. 公司是否已制定正常安排船员培训、知识更新或换班的程序?	A-Ⅰ/14	6.5 (11.1)		
8. **在职培训**:培训是否按照认可的培训计划进行?	A-Ⅰ/6	6 (6.5) (11.1)		适用范围:在职发证培训的要求仅在公司实施这种培训的情况下适用。要求仅对1998年之后开始参加培训和教育的海员适用。
9. 培训是否在认可的培训记录簿上登记?				此外,参阅以上C部分。

	STCW Requirement	STCW Ref.	ISM Ref.	Y/N/NA	Comments
10.	**Special training for tankers:** Does the Company ensure that personnel have special familiarization training as required?	A-V/1	6.3 6.5		Verification: Check documents of evidence, course diplomas, or similar.
11.	Are training programmes applied as required, i.e., **oil tanker training programme** **chemical tanker training programme** **liquefied gas tanker training programme**		6.5		
12.	**Special training for ro-ro passenger ships:** Does the Company ensure that personnel have special competence as required?	A-V/2	6.5		See also STCW.7/Circ. 1, Annex 2, App. 1 Verification: Check relevant procedures, documents of evidence, course diplomas, or similar, to make sure that the required training has been carried out. 1. Crowd Management 2. Familiarisation 3. Safety training for personnel providing direct services to passengers in passenger spaces Application: The requirement for crisis management and human behaviour training may not be applicable before 1 August 1998, depending on national legislation. Please do also refer to STCW.7/Circ.1.
13.	Is the training in—**passenger safety, cargo safety and hull integrity**—and in—**crisis management and human behaviour**—approved?	A-V/2, para.1, para.5			
1.	**Common language:** Has the company decided common language for this particular crew?	Reg. I/14, para.5	6.7 (6.6)		Verification: Check that a common language has been decided. Check procedures for ensuring a common language. Ask crew members what language they use when carrying out their duties. Check with answers from other crew members.
2.	**Communication:** Are there procedures in place to ensure that designated crew members have a sufficient knowledge of English?	Table A-II/1, A-II/4, A-III/1, A-IV/2	6.7		Requirement implicit in all Tables and in A-V/2 3.1.2. Also pending National legislation

STCW要求	STCW Ref.	ISM Ref.	Y/N/NA	说明
10. **液货船特殊培训**：公司能否确保人员接受规定的特殊熟悉培训？	A-Ⅴ/1	6.3 6.5		确认：检查证明文件、课程证书或类似文件。
11. 培训计划是否按规定实施？例如，**液货船培训计划** **化学品船培训计划** **液化气体运输船培训计划**		6.5		
12. **滚装客船特殊培训**：公司能否确保人员具备规定的特殊能力？	A-Ⅴ/2	6.5		此外，参阅STCW.7/ Circ.1,附件2,附录1。
13. 在**旅客安全**、货物安全和船体完整方面以及**在危机管理和人的行为方面**的培训是否经过认可？	A-Ⅴ/2, para.1, para.5			确认：检查有关程序、证明文件、课程证书或类似文件，以确信所要求的培训已实施： 1. 密集人群管理 2. 熟悉 3. 对在客舱中直接向旅客提供服务的人员的安全培训。 适用范围：危机管理和人的行为培训的要求在1998年8月1日之前可以不执行，具体取决于国家法规。此外，请参阅STCW.7/Circ.1。
1. **通用语言**：公司是否已规定特定船员的通用语言？	Reg. Ⅰ/14, para.5	6.7 (6.6)		确认：检查对通用语言是否已做规定。检查确保使用通用语言的程序。询问船员进行工作时使用什么语言。用其他船员的回答核对。
2. **交流**：是否已制定适当的程序确保特定船员有足够的英语知识？	Table A-Ⅱ/1, A-Ⅱ/4, A-Ⅲ/1, A-Ⅳ/2	6.7		要求包含在所有表格和第A-Ⅴ/2节第3.1.2款。 此外，同样有待于国家立法。

STCW Requirement	STCW Ref.	ISM Ref.	Y/N/NA	Comments
G. Development of Plans for Shipboard Operations (7)				
1. **Crew co-ordination:** Are there procedures in place to ensure crew co-ordination in performing functions vital to safety or the prevention of pollution?	Reg. I/14, para.5	1.2.3 (7)		Verification: Check that activities vital to safety and pollution prevention have been defined, that there are procedures in place for the activities, and that there is documentary evidence that drills and exercises have been carded out. Crew co-ordination may be further verified by questions related to a particular operation, and the organisation and responsibility related to the operation. Such operations might be bunker operation, launching of life-saving appliances, fire-fighting etc. Authorities may require demonstration through drills.
H. Emergency Preparedness (8)				
1. **Crew co-ordination:** Are there programmes for drills and exercises to prepare for emergency actions?	Reg. I/14, para.5	8.2 (8.1)		Authorities may require demonstration through drills.
I. Reports and Analysis of Non-Conformities, Accidents and Hazardous Occurrences (9)				
J. Maintenance of the Ship and Equipment (10)				
K. Documentation Control (11)				
1. **Seafarer's documentation:** Are documentation and data relevant to all seafarers maintained and readily accessible aboard?	Reg. 1/2.9			The certificates and other relevant information, e.g, course diplomas, documents of evidence, CRAs, health certificates, employee agreements, etc., shall be kept in original aboard. Documentation required is also defined in national legislation.
2. **Control of certificates:** Are all certificates and documentation of competence required by STCW 95 verified for authenticity and validity?	Reg. I/14, para. 1	11.1 (6.1.1, 6.2)		Overview of required documents in IMO STCW.7/Circ. 1. Verification: Check procedures and documentary evidence that the procedures have been carried out. Please note that authorities issuing professional certificates are required to maintain records and provide information on such certificates, as set out in STCW.7/Circ. 1
I. Company Verification, Review and Evaluation (12)				
J. Certification, Verification and Control (13)				

STCW 要求	STCW Ref.	ISM Ref.	Y/N/NA	说明
G.制订船舶操作计划 (7)				
1. **船员协作**:是否已制定确保船员在执行与安全和防污关系重大的职责时的适当协作程序?	Reg. Ⅰ/14, para.5	1.2.3 (7)		确认:检查已确定与安全和防污关系重大的活动,有适当的针对该活动的程序,并且有文件证明已实施训练和演习。船员协作可通过对有关具体操作和有关作业的组织和职责情况的询问进一步证实。这类操作可以是加油作业、放救生设备下水、消防等。 主管机关可要求通过训练演示。
H.应急部署(8)				
1. **船员协作**:是否有针对应急行动而部署的训练和演习计划?	Reg. Ⅰ/14, para.5	8.2 (8.1)		主管机关可要求通过训练演示。
I.不符合项、事故和险情的报告及分析(9)				
J.船舶和设备的维护(10)				
K.文件监控(11)				
1. **海员文件**:所有与海员有关的文件和资料是否保存在船上并能迅速取到?	Reg. 1/2.9			证书和其他相关资料,例如,课程证书、文件证明、CRAs、健康证书等正本保存在船上。要求的文件在国家法规中也有相关规定。
2. **证书监控**:STCW 95 规定的所有证书和适任文件证明是否真实有效?	Reg. Ⅰ/14, para. 1	11.1 (6.1.1, 6.2)		查看IMO STCW.7/Circ.1规定的文件。 确认:检查程序和证明程序已执行的文件。请注意主管机关签发的专业证书需要有保存记录和提供诸如STCW.7/ Circ.1规定的证书资料。
I.公司确认、审核和评估(12)				
J.认证、验证及控制(13)				

Part 6
Certificate Requirements

STCW Convention requirements

1. The structure of certificates specified in the STCW Convention the master and deck department is set forth in Table 6-1 and that for the engine department is set forth in Table 6-2.

Harmonized interpretations

2. STCW.7 is a new series of STCW circular under which clarifications, recommendations, guidance and other information on clarification of the STCW Convention and Code, which are not included in amendments to these instruments, will be circulated.

STCW.7/Circ. 1 was issued on 24 Sep 96. This circular contained clarification of the regulations I/2, I/9, I/10 and I/15, we quote two examples:

I/2–Certificates and endorsements
Provides a list of certificates or documentary evidence required under the STCW Convention, which gives details of whether an endorsement is needed and records of certificates should be maintained in a register or registers.

Regulations	Certificate or documentary evidence	Endorsement required	Registration required[1]
II/1, II/2, II/3, III/1, III/2, III/3, IV/2, V/1, VII/2	Appropriate certificate for Master, officers and radio officer	Yes	Yes
II/4, III/4	Ratings duly certificated to be part of a navigational or engine room watch	No/yes[2], as appropriate	
V/1	Ratings assigned to specific duties...on tankers	No	Yes[2], as appropriate
V/2	Training requirements for personnel serving on ro-ro passenger ships	No	no
V/3	Training requirements for personnel serving on passenger ships	No	no
VI/2	A certificate of proficiency in survival craft, rescue boats...and fast rescue bloats	No	No
VI/3	Training in advanced fire fighting	No	No
VI/4	Training related to medical first aid and medical care	No	No

---

1 Records of all certificates should be maintained in accordance with regulation I/9.4.
2 The Party issuing or endorsing the certificate is responsible for maintaining a register or registers in accordance with regulation I/9.4.1. However, records may be maintained by an agency or entity acting under its authority.

第6章
发证要求

STCW 公约要求

1. STCW公约对船长和甲板部证书格式的规定列在表6-1中,对轮机部证书格式的规定列在表6-2中。

统一的解释

2. STCW.7是STCW通告的一个新系列,解释、建议、指导及其他说明STCW公约和规则的信息以及修正案未包括的内容都将通过本通告发布。

STCW.7/Circ.1于1996年9月24日发布。此通告包括对公约规则Ⅰ/2、Ⅰ/9、Ⅰ/10和Ⅰ/15的说明,我们在此引用两个例子:

Ⅰ/2——证书和签证
　　下表提供STCW要求的证书或证明文件清单,并详细说明是否要求签证及是否需要保持证书的登记记录。

公约规则	证书或证明文件	是否要求签证	是否要求登记[1]
Ⅱ/1, Ⅱ/2, Ⅱ/3, Ⅲ/1, Ⅲ/2, Ⅲ/3, Ⅳ/2, Ⅴ/1, Ⅶ/2	船长、高级船员和报务员的适当证书	是	是
Ⅱ/4, Ⅲ/4	适当发证成为航行或机舱值班部分的普通船员	如合适,否/是[2]	
Ⅴ/1	指定在液货船上担负特定职责的普通船员	否	如合适,是[2]
Ⅴ/2	对在滚装客船上服务的人员的培训要求	否	否
Ⅴ/3	对在客船上服务的人员的培训要求	否	否
Ⅵ/2	救生艇筏,救助艇……和快速救助艇熟练操作证书	否	否
Ⅵ/3	高级消防培训	否	否
Ⅵ/4	有关急救和医护的培训	否	否

1　应当按照公约规则Ⅰ/9.4保存所有证书的记录。
2　发证或签证的缔约国应当按照公约规则Ⅰ/9.4.1负责保持登记。然而记录有可能由发证或签证缔约国的代表或直属机构保存。

TABLE 6-1 MASTER AND DECK DEPARTMENT – CONVENTION GRADES AND CLASSES OF CERTIFICATES

Summary of deck certification system—STCW95 Chapter II and STCW Code A-II/1, II/2, II/3

Three × Grades:	Officer in charge of a Navigational Watch (OOW), Chief Mate, Master
Two × Voyages:	Near-Coastal Voyages (NCV), Unrestricted
Three × GT:	<500, <3000, ≥3000
Three × Standard of Competence:	Table A-II/1—OOW≥500 GT
	Table A-II/2—Chief Mate and Master≥500 GT
	Table A-II/3—OOW and Master—NCV, <500 GT

DIFFERENCES between the various grades

1 **Voyages: NCV vis-à-vis Unrestricted**
Chief Mate and Master
omit (a) celestial navigation; and
(b) those electronic systems of position fixing and navigation that do not cover the waters for which the certificate is to be valid (A-II/1.7); and
(c) such subjects (A-II/2) as are not applicable to the waters or ships concerned, bearing in mind the effect on the safety of all ships which may be operating in the same waters (A-II/2.8)

OOW
omit (a) celestial navigation; and
(b) those electronic systems of position fixing and navigation that do not cover the waters for which the certificate is to be valid (A-II/1.7).

2 **GT: <3000**
Chief Mate and Master
(a) the level of theoretical knowledge, understanding and proficiency required under the different sections in column 2 of A-II/2 may be varied according to the GT (A-II/2.5).

Unrestricted Voyages
Master
  (1) <3000 GT
  (2) ≥3000 GT

Chief Mate
  (3) <3000 GT
  (4) ≥3000 GT

OOW
  (5) <500 GT
  (6) ≥500 GT

NCV
Master
  (7) <500 GT
  (8) <3000 GT
  (9) ≥3000 GT

Chief Mate
  (10) <3000 GT
  (11) ≥3000 GT

OOW
  (12) <500 GT
  (13) ≥500 GT

表6-1 船长和甲板部——公约的证书等级一览

甲板发证体系一览——STCW95公约第Ⅱ章和STCW规则 A-Ⅱ/1, Ⅱ/2, Ⅱ/3

3×级别：负责航行值班的高级船员（OOW），大副和船长
2×航区：近岸航行（NCV） 无限航区航行
3×总吨：<500, <3000, ≥3000
3×适任标准：
表A-Ⅱ/1——负责航行值班的高级船员≥500总吨
表A-Ⅱ/2——大副和船长≥500总吨
表A-Ⅱ/3——负责航行值班的高级船员和船长——近岸航行，<500总吨

无限航区航行

船长
(1) <3000总吨
(2) ≥3000总吨

大副
(3) <3000总吨
(4) ≥3000总吨

负责航行值班的高级船员
(5) <500总吨
(6) ≥500总吨

近岸航行

船长
(7) <500总吨
(8) <3000总吨
(9) ≥3000总吨

大副
(10) <3000总吨
(11) ≥3000总吨

负责航行值班的高级船员
(12) <500总吨
(13) ≥500总吨

各种等级之间的差异

1　**航区：近岸航行相比无限航区航行**
　大副和船长
　省略　(a) 天文航海；及
　　　　(b) 不覆盖适用于当事船舶有效水域的电子定位和导航系统（A-Ⅱ/1.7）；及
　　　　(c) 不适用于当事水域或当事船舶的那些科目(A-Ⅱ/2)，但要切记对可能在同一水域航行的所有船舶安全的影响(A-Ⅱ/2.8)

　负责航行值班的高级船员
　省略　(a) 天文航海；及
　　　　(b) 不覆盖适用于当事船舶有效水域的电子定位和导航系统（A-Ⅱ/1.7）

2　**总吨位：<3000**
　大副和船长
　　　　(a) 表A-Ⅱ/2第2栏不同部分对理论水平，理解和熟练的要求根据总吨位的不同可能有所变动(A-Ⅱ/2.5)。

TABLE 6-2: SUMMARY OF STCW 95 ENGINE DEPARTMENT—Chapter III and Code A-III/1, 2, 3, 4

Four × Ranks:　　　Rating, OOW, Second Engineer Officer, Chief Engineer Officer.
Two × Voyages:　　Near-coastal, Unlimited
Four × Power:　　　$\geqslant 750$, $750 - 3000$, $\leqslant 3000$, $\geqslant 3000$ (kW).
Three × Standard of Competence : Table A-III/1, A-III/2, A-III/4

Rating

  (1) Unlimited $\geqslant 750$ kW

OOW

  (2) Near-coastal $\leqslant 3000$ kW
  (3) Unlimited $\geqslant 750$ kW

Second Engineer Officer

  (4) Near-coastal $750 - 3000$ kW
  (5) Near-coastal $\geqslant 3000$ kW
  (6) Unlimited $750 - 3000$ kW
  (7) Unlimited > 3000 kW

Chief Engineer Officer

  (8) Near-coastal $750 - 3000$ kW
  (9) Near-coastal $\geqslant 3000$ kW
  (10) Unlimited $750 - 3000$ kW
  (11) Unlimited $\leqslant 3000$ kW
  (12) Unlimited $\geqslant 3000$ kW

表6-2：STCW 95公约轮机部的汇总——第Ⅲ章和规则A-Ⅲ/1、2、3、4

4×级别： 普通船员，负责航行值班的高级船员，大管轮，轮机长
2×航区： 近岸航行，无限航区航行
4×功率： ≥750,750~3000,≤3000,≥3000（千瓦）
3×适任标准：表A-Ⅲ/1,A-Ⅲ/2,A-Ⅲ/4

普通船员

  （1） 无限航区航行 ≥750千瓦

负责航行值班的高级船员

  （2） 近岸航行 ≤3000千瓦
  （3） 无限航区航行 ≥750千瓦

大管轮

  （4） 近岸航行 750~3000千瓦
  （5） 近岸航行 ≥3000千瓦
  （6） 无限航区航行 750~3000千瓦
  （7） 无限航区航行 >3000千瓦

轮机长

  （8） 近岸航行 750~3000千瓦
  （9） 近岸航行 ≥3000千瓦
  （10） 无限航区航行 750~3000千瓦
  （11） 无限航区航行 ≤3000
  （12） 无限航区航行 ≥3000千瓦

	STCW 95 REG	RANK	VOYAGE	POWER kW	AGE YRS	SEAGOING REQUIREMENTS	STANDARD OF COMPETENCE
1	III/4	Rating	Unlimited	≥750	≥16	Completed 6 months of approved seagoing service; or 2 months of approved seagoing service with special training, either pre-sea or on board ship; or served 12 months in relevant capacity in engine dept within last 5 years preceding entry into force of Convention.	Table A-III / 4
2	III/1	OOW	Near-coastal	≤3000	≥18	The requirements of 30 months of approved education and training, including 6 months seagoing service may be varied.	Table A-III / 1
3	III/1	OOW	Unlimited	≥750	≥18	Completed 30 months of approved education and training, including 6 months of seagoing service.	Table A-III/1
4	III/3-1 III/3-2.1 III/3-2.1.1 III/3-2.2	Second Engineer Officer	Near-coastal	750–3000	≥18	The requirements of 12 months of approved seagoing service as Assistant Engineer Officer or Engineer Officer may be varied.	Table A-III/2 Column 2, level of knowledge, understanding & proficiency may be varied.
5	III/2-1 III/2-2.1 III/2-2.1.1 III/2-2.2	Second Engineer Officer	Near-coastal	≥3000	≥18	Completed 12 months of approved seagoing service as Assistant Engineer Officer or Engineer Officer.	Table A-III/2 Column 2, level of knowledge, understanding & proficiency, may be varied with power limitation as considered necessary.
6	III/3-1 III/3-2.1 III/3-2.1.1 III/3-2.2	Second Engineer Officer	Unlimited	750–3000	≥18	Completed 12 months of approved seagoing service as Assistant Engineer Officer or Engineer Officer.	Table A-III/2, Column 2, level of knowledge may be lowered.
7	III/2-1 III/2-2.1 III/2-2.1.1 III/2-2.2	Second Engineer Officer	Unlimited	≥3000	≥18	Completed 12 months of approved seagoing service as Assistant Engineer Officer or Engineer Officer.	Table A-III/2
8	III/3-1 III/3-2.1 III/3-2.1.2 III/3-2.2	Chief Engineer Officer	Near-coastal	750–3000	≥18	The requirements of 24 months of approved seagoing service of which 12 months served while qualified as Second Engineer Officer may be varied.	Table A-III/2 Column 2, level of knowledge, understanding & proficiency may be varied.

第6章 发证要求

	STCW 95 公约规则	等级	航区	功率 千瓦	年龄	海上服务要求	适任标准
1	Ⅲ/4	普通船员	无限航区航行	≥750	≥16	已完成6个月的认可的海上服务资历；或 2个月的认可的海上服务资历和上船前或船上的专门训练；或在本公约生效前的5年内有12个月在轮机部相应的职位上服务。	表A-Ⅲ/4
2	Ⅲ/1	负责航行值班的高级船员	近岸航行	≤3000	≥18	要求完成30个月的认可的教育，包括6个月的海上服务资历，可以有所变动。	表A-Ⅲ/1
3	Ⅲ/1	负责航行值班的高级船员	无限航区航行	≥750	≥18	已完成30个月的认可的教育，包括6个月的海上服务资历。	表A-Ⅲ/1
4	Ⅲ/3-1 Ⅲ/3-2.1 Ⅲ/3-2.1.1 Ⅲ/3-2.2	大管轮	近岸航行	750~3000	≥18	要求具有12个月的助理轮机员或轮机部高级船员的认可的海上服务资历，可以有所变动。	表A-Ⅲ/2 第二栏，知识、理解和熟练，可以有所变动。
5	Ⅲ/2-1 Ⅲ/2-2.1 Ⅲ/2-2.1.1 Ⅲ/2-2.2	大管轮	近岸航行	≥3000	≥18	已完成12个月的助理轮机员或轮机部高级船员的认可的海上服务资历。	表A-Ⅲ/2 知识、理解和熟练，如认为有必要，可根据功率限制有所变动。
6	Ⅲ/3-1 Ⅲ/3-2.1 Ⅲ/3-2.1.1 Ⅲ/3-2.2	大管轮	无限航区航行	750~3000	≥18	完成12个月的助理轮机员或轮机部高级船员的认可的海上服务资历。	表A-Ⅲ/2，第2栏，可能降低知识水平的要求。
7	Ⅲ/2-1 Ⅲ/2-2.1 Ⅲ/2-2.1.1 Ⅲ/2-2.2	大管轮	无限航区航行	≥3000	≥18	完成12个月的助理轮机员或轮机部高级船员的认可的海上服务资历。	表A-Ⅲ/2
8	Ⅲ/3-1 Ⅲ/3-2.1 Ⅲ/3-2.1.2 Ⅲ/3-2.2	轮机长	近岸航行	750~3000	≥18	24个月认可的海上服务资历，其中具备大管轮资格并实际担任大管轮12个月，这样的要求可以有所变动。	表A-Ⅲ/2，第2栏，知识、理解和熟练的要求，可以有所变动。

	STCW 95 REG	RANK	VOYAGE	POWER kW	AGE YRS	SEAGOING REQUIREMENTS	STANDARD OF COMPETENCE
9	III/2-1 III/2-2.1 III/2-2.1.2 III/2-2.2	Chief Engineer Officer	Near-coastal	⩾3000	⩾18	Completed 36 months of approved seagoing service of which 12 months served as Engineer Officer-in-Charge of watch while qualified to serve as Second Engineer Officer.	Table A-III / 2 Column 2, level of knowledge, understanding & proficiency, may be varied with power limitation as considered necessary.
10	III/3-1 III/3-2.1 III/3-2.1.2 III/3-2.2	Chief Engineer Officer	Unlimited	750 – 3000	⩾18	Completed 24 months of approved seagoing service of which 12 months served while qualified as Second Engineer Officer.	Table A-III / 2, Column 2, level of knowledge may be lowered.
11	III/3-3	Chief Engineer Officer	Unlimited	⩽3000	⩾18	Completed 12 months of approved seagoing service as Engineer Officer-in-Charge of watch and certificate is so endorsed.	Table A-III / 2
12	III / 2-1 III / 2-2.1 III / 2-2.1.2 III / 2-2.2	Chief Engineer Officer	Unlimited	⩾3000	⩾18	Completed 36 months of approved seagoing service of which 12 months served as Engineer Officer-in-Charge of watch while qualified as Second Engineer Officer.	Table A-III/2

I/9.4—Database for certification registration

In implementing Reg I/9.4.1 for the maintenance of a register of certificates and endorsements, a standard database is not necessary provided that all relevant information is recorded and available. The following items of information should be recorded and available either on paper or electronically in accordance with regulation I/9, as a minimum:

.1 *Status of certificates*
Valid
Suspended
Cancelled
Reported lost
Destroyed
With a record of changes to status to be kept, including dates of changes

.2 *Certificate details*
Seafarer's name
Date of birth
Nationality
Sex
Preferably a photograph
Relevant document number

	STCW 95 公约规则	等级	航区	功率 千瓦	年龄	海上服务要求	适任标准
9	Ⅲ/2-1 Ⅲ/2-2.1 Ⅲ/2-2.1.2 Ⅲ/2-2.2	轮机长	近岸航行	≥3000	≥18	完成36个月认可的海上服务资历,其中具备大管轮资格并实际担任职务负责值班12个月。	表A-Ⅲ/2,第2栏,知识、理解和熟练的要求,如认为有必要,可根据功率限制有所变动。
10	Ⅲ/3-1 Ⅲ/3-2.1 Ⅲ/3-2.1.2 Ⅲ/3-2.2	轮机长	无限航区航行	750~3000	≥18	完成24个月的助理轮机员或轮机部高级船员的认可的海上服务资历,其中12个月担任大管轮。	表A-Ⅲ/2,第2栏,可能降低知识水平的要求。
11	Ⅲ/3-3	轮机长	无限航区航行	≤3000	≥18	完成12个月认可的实际担任负责值班的轮机高级船员的资历,证书也据此签注。	表A-Ⅲ/2
12	Ⅲ/2-1 Ⅲ/2-2.1 Ⅲ/2-2.1.2 Ⅲ/2-2.2	轮机长	无限航区航行	≥3000	≥18	完成36个月认可的海上服务资历,其中具备大管轮资格并实际任职负责值班12个月。	表A-Ⅲ/2

I/9.4——发证登记数据库

在实施规则Ⅰ/9.4.1保持发证登记和签证时,如果所有的相关资料做了记录并能够取得,那么就不一定需要一个标准的数据库。但作为最低要求,应当按照公约规则Ⅰ/9取得并以书面或电子方式记录以下项目的资料:

.1 证书的状况
   有效
   中止
   注销
   报失
   损毁
   保存变动状况的记录,包括改变的日期

.2 证书的详细情况
   船员的姓名
   出生日期
   国籍
   性别
   最好附上一张相片
   相关的证书编号

Date of issue
Date of expiry
Last revalidation date
Details of dispensation(s)

.3 *Competency details*
STCW competency standards (e.g regulation II/1)
Capacity
Function
Level of responsibility
Endorsements
Limitations

.4 *Medical details*
Date of issue of latest medical certificate relating to the issue or revalidation of the appropriate certificate

Assembly resolutions and MSC circulars superseded by the adoption of the 1995 amendments to the 1978 STCW Convention

3.1 The 1995 amendments to the 1978 STCW Convention incorporated several resolutions and circulars which could be expected thereafter to be revoked.

3.2 However, before any conclusion can be reached, a fundamental matter of principle must be addressed: in view of the fact that there are many seafarers and maritime personnel (for example fishermen) who are not within the scope of the revised STCW Convention, does the fact that the contents of the Assembly resolutions and MSC circulars are fully incorporated in the revised STCW Convention make them redundant and as such, they should be revoked. The issue has yet to be resolved at IMO.

General information on certification

4. The following information is taken from materials used in seminars and workshops on the implementation of the revised Convention arranged by IMO. It has no official standing and is not an approved interpretation but it is nevertheless useful for purposes of illustration. Approved interpretation would be promulgated through STCW.7 Circulars (see paragraph above).

Chapter II
Master and deck department

The watchkeeping provisions contained in Chapter II of the 1978 STCW Convention have been transferred to a new chapter VIII and the revalidation requirements for masters and deck officers have been consolidated with those for engineer officers and radio operators in new regulation I/11.

签发日期
到期日期
上一次再有效日期
特免证明的详细情况

.3 适任的详细情况
STCW 适任标准(例如,公约规则 II/1)
能力
职能
责任级别
签注
限制

.4 详细健康情况
与证书的签发或再有效有关的最新医疗证明的签发日期。

取代大会决议和海上安全委员会(MSC)通告的1978年STCW公约1995年修正案

3.1 1978年STCW公约1995年修正案并入了几个预计以后可能被取消的决议和通告。

3.2 然而,在任何决议达成之前,我们必须提出一个最基本的原则:考虑到实际上有很多海员和海上工作者(例如渔民)并不属于修订的STCW公约的范围,如果事实上并不需要将所有的大会决议和海上安全委员会通告的内容收编到修订的STCW公约,就应当取消这些多余的内容。国际海事组织(IMO)尚未就此问题做出决定。

发证概况

4. 以下的信息摘自IMO组织的有关补充修改的公约讨论会和专题研讨会中使用的资料。该信息不具有官方立场并且不是认可的解释,但是无论如何,用于说明的目的是有作用的。认可的解释必须通过STCW.7通告予以公布(见上一款)。

第 II 章
船长和甲板部

1978年STCW公约第 II 章的值班规定已经移到新的一章,即第 VIII 章。在新公约规则 I/11 中,船长和甲板部高级船员的证书再有效要求已经与轮机部高级船员和无线电操作人员的证书再有效要求合并。

Regulation	Summary of main changes
II/1−Mandatory minimum requirements for certification of OOW on ships of ≥500 GT	Approved education and training required in all grades. Not less than 12 months approved seagoing service documented in approved training record book or 36 months seagoing service.
II/2−Mandatory minimum requirements for certification of masters and chief mates on ships of ≥500 GT	All reductions of seagoing service for special training eliminated. Minimum seagoing service for chief mate reduced to 12 months.
II/3−Mandatory minimum requirements for certification of OOW on ships of ≥500 GT	NCV—OOW required to have completed approved education and training.

.1 Regulation II/2, paragraph 2(c)

It is considered inappropriate to specify a universally applicable upper limit for the phrase "ship of limited size", which in paragraph 2(c) of this Regulation relates to ships of 1600 gross registered tons or more.

.2 Regulation II/5, paragraph 3

The special training referred to in paragraph 3 of this Regulation need not be required in respect of a master or deck officer who has the approved sea-going service in accordance with the requirements of paragraph 1(b)(i) [= Section A-I/11, para 1.1], provided he has previously undergone the special training or has been exempted from it in accordance with intentionally agreed provisions in respect of service in a relevant capacity in ships to which the special training requirements apply. However, if a master or deck officer is required to satisfy the Administration as to his professional competence in accordance with paragraph 1(b)(iii) [=Section A-I/11, para. 1.3] then he should also be required to complete successfully any special training provided for under paragraph 3.

Chapter III
Engine department
The watch keeping provisions previously contained in Chapter III have been transferred to a new chapter VIII and the revalidation requirements for engineer officers have been consolidated with those for deck officers and radio operators in new regulation I/11.

Regulation	Summary of main changes
III/1−Mandatory minimum requirements for certification of officers in charge of an engineering watch in a manned engine-room or designated duty engineers in a periodically unmanned engine-room	Not less than 6 months of seagoing service. 30 months approved education and training which includes on-board training documented in approved training record book as well as training in workshop skills
III/2−Mandatory minimum requirements for certification of chief engineer officers and second engineer officers on ships powered by main propulsion machinery of 3,000 kW propulsion power or more	Candidates to have completed approved education and training

公约规则	主要变动
Ⅱ/1—对≥500总吨船舶的负责航行值班的高级船员发证的强制性最低要求	所有级别认可的教育和培训。认可的培训记录簿中载明不低于12个月的认可的海上服务资历或36个月的认可的海上服务资历。
Ⅱ/2—对≥500总吨船舶的船长和大副发证的强制性最低要求	取消所有专门训练替代海上服务资历的缩短时间。大副最少海上服务资历缩短为12个月。
Ⅱ/3—对≥500总吨船舶的负责航行值班的高级船员发证的强制性最低要求	要求近岸航行——负责航行值班的高级船员已完成认可的教育和培训。

.1 公约规则Ⅱ/2,第2款(c)

用"船舶尺度限制"的术语来说明一个普遍适用的上限是不恰当的。该短语在有关1600总登记吨位或以上船舶这条规则的第2款(c)。

.2 公约规则Ⅱ/5,第3款

如果船长或甲板高级船员已经具有与第1款(b)(i)[=第一部分A-Ⅰ/11,第1.1款] 的要求相一致的认可的海上相关职位服务资历,并已接受了专门训练或者允许豁免专门训练,那么对本规则的第三段提到的专门训练就不做要求。但是,如果要求船长或甲板部高级船员达到主管机关的要求与第1段(b)(ⅲ)[=第一部分A-Ⅰ/11,第1.3款]相一致的职务适任能力,那么应当要求他成功完成第3款中规定的专门训练。

第Ⅲ章
轮机部

原来在第Ⅲ章的值班规定已经移到新的一章,即第Ⅷ章。在新的公约规则Ⅰ/11里,轮机部高级船员的证书再有效要求已经与甲板部高级船员和无线电操作人员的证书再有效要求合并。

公约规则	主要变动
Ⅲ/1—对有人值班机舱负责轮机值班的高级船员或周期无人值班机舱指定值班的轮机员发证的强制性最低要求	不少于6个月的海上服务资历。30个月的认可的教育和培训,其中包括在认可的培训记录簿上载明的船上训练和车间技术培训
Ⅲ/2—对主推进动力装置为3000千瓦或以上船舶轮机长和大管轮发证的强制性最低要求	申请人已完成认可教育和培训

Regulation	Summary of main changes
III/3-Mandatory minimum requirements for certification of chief engineer officers and second engineer officers on ships powered by main propulsion machinery of between 750 kW and 3,000 kW propulsion power	Candidates to have completed approved education and training

.3　Regulation III/3

To facilitate the exercise of the control provisions with regard to engineer officers holding a second engineer certificate who are permitted to serve as chief engineer officer it is advisable for a Party to issue a new certificate, or an endorsement to an existing certificate, when satisfied that the sea-going requirements under this paragraph have been met.

Chapter IV
Radiocommunications and radio personnel

The revalidation requirements for GMDSS radio personnel have been consolidated with those for deck officers and engineer officers in new regulation I/11.

Regulation	Summary of main changes
IV/1-Application	Certification of radio personnel on ships not subject to SOLAS chapter IV now included
IV/2-Mandatory minimum requirements for certification of GMDSS radio personnel	Candidates to have completed approved education and training

Chapter V
Special requirements for personnel on certain types of ships

New provisions have been added to require additional training for personnel on passenger and ro-ro passenger ships.

Regulation	Summary of main changes
V/1-Mandatory minimum requirements for the training and qualification of masters, officers and ratings	The previous 3 different types of tanker familiarization course is merged into one Tanker Familiarization Course "MSC.33(63) entered into force on 1 Jan 96) As appropriate certificate or endorsement of an existing certificate is now required
V/2-Mandatory minimum requirements for the training and qualifications of masters, officers and other personnel on ro-ro passenger ships	Additional familiarization and training required, in accordance with capacity, duties and responsibilities, in: .5　Crowd management and human behaviour*; .6　Familiarization training; .7　Safety training; .8　Passenger safety, cargo safety and hull integrity*; and .9　Crisis management and human behaviour training*(Table A-V/2) *　refresher training is required

公约规则	主要变动
Ⅲ/3—对主推进动力装置为750~3000千瓦或以上船舶轮机长和大管轮发证的强制性最低要求	申请人已完成认可教育和培训

  .3 公约规则Ⅲ/3

    为了便于实行关于允许持有大管轮证书的轮机高级船员担任轮机长的控制性规定,同时如果符合本段的海上服务资历的要求,建议缔约国签发新的证书,或者对现有的证书进行签注。

第Ⅳ章
无线电通信和无线电人员

  在新的公约规则Ⅰ/11里,全球海上遇险和安全系统(GMDSS)的无线电人员证书再有效要求已经与甲板部高级船员和轮机部高级船员的证书再有效要求合并。

公约规则	主要变动
Ⅳ/1—适用范围	现在包括了船上无线电人员的发证无须遵从SOLAS第Ⅳ章
Ⅳ/2—对GMDSS无线电人员发证的强制性最低要求	申请人已完成认可教育和培训

第Ⅴ章
特定类型船舶的船员特殊培训要求

  新规定增加了客船和滚装客船上工作人员的附加培训要求。

公约规则	主要变动
Ⅴ/1—液货船船长、高级船员和普通船员培训与资格的强制性最低要求	先前三种不同类型液货船的熟悉课程合并为一种课程〔1996年1月1日生效的MSC.33(63)〕 现在要求有相应的证书或者对现有证书进行签注
Ⅴ/2—对滚装客船的船长、高级船员和其他人员的培训与资格的强制性最低要求	根据职位、职责和责任,要求在以下几个方面增加熟悉和培训: .5 拥挤密集人群管理和人的行为*; .6 熟悉培训; .7 安全培训; .8 旅客安全、货物安全和船体完整性培训*;及 .9 危机管理和人的表现培训*(表A-Ⅴ/2) * 要求知识更新培训

Regulation	Summary of main changes
V/3–Mandatory-minimum requirements for the training and qualifications of masters, officers and other personnel on passenger ships other than ro-ro passenger ships	Additional familiarization and training required, in accordance with capacity, duties and responsibilities, in: .10 Crowd management training* ; .11 Familiarization training; .12 Safety training; .13 Passenger safety*; and .14 Crisis management and human behaviour training* (Table A-V/2) * refresher training is required

Chapter VI
Emergency, occupational safety, medical care and survival functions

New provisions have been added regarding familiarisation and basic safety training and instruction, training in fast rescue boats, training in advanced fire fighting, training in medical first aid and training in medical care on board ship.

Regulation	Summary of main changes
VI/1–Mandatory minimum requirements for familiarisation, basic safety training and instruction for all seafarers	Familiarisation training for all except passengers. The regulation required that those with safety or pollution prevention duties in the operation of the ship provide evidence that they met or retained the standard of competence in basic training within the previous five years.
VI/2–Mandatory minimum requirements for the issue of certificates of proficiency in survival craft, rescue boats and fast rescue boats	Candidates to meet the standard of competence for issue of a certificate of proficiency. Separate standard of competence established for certificate of proficiency in fast rescue boats.
VI/3–Mandatory minimum requirements for training in advanced fire fighting	Candidates to provide evidence that they met the standard of competence within the previous five years.
VI/4–Mandatory minimum requirements relating to medical first aid and medical care	Candidates to provide evidence that they met the standard of competence.

Chapter VII
Alternative certification

This new chapter will allow those Parties wishing to do so to issue appropriate certificates to those candidates who have met all requirements for certification as officer in charge of a navigational watch or as officer in charge of an engineering watch and, in addition, have been found qualified in a function or functions of another discipline. The functions are identified in the competence tables of chapters II, III and IV of the STCW Code.

In the same way, Parties wishing to do so may issue appropriate certificates to those candidates who have met all requirements for certification as master or as chief engineer officer and in addition have been duly qualified in a function or functions of the other discipline.

公约规则	主要变动
V/3 除滚装客船以外的客船船长、高级船员和其他人员的培训和资格的强制性最低要求	根据职位、职责和责任,要求在以下几个方面增加熟悉和培训: .10 密集人群管理和人的表现*; .11 熟悉培训; .12 安全培训; .13 旅客安全*;及 .14 危机管理和人的表现培训*(表A-V/2) *要求知识更新培训

第Ⅵ章
应急、职业安全、医护和救生职能

新的规定增加了关于熟悉和基本安全培训及教导,快速救助艇培训,高级消防培训,船上急救培训和医护培训。

公约规则	主要变动
Ⅵ/1—对所有海员的熟悉和基本安全培训以及训练的强制性最低要求	除旅客外,所有人员的熟悉培训。该公约规则要求那些在船舶操作中负有安全或防止污染职责的海员提供他们在近五年内已达到或保持基本培训适任标准的证据。
Ⅵ/2—签发救生艇筏、救助艇及快速救助艇熟练操作证书的强制性最低要求	申请人达到签发熟练操作证书的适任标准。建立单独的快速救助艇熟练操作证书的适任标准。
Ⅵ/3—高级消防培训的强制性最低要求	申请人提供其近五年内业已达到适任标准的证据。
Ⅵ/4—急救和医护的强制性最低要求	申请人提供其近五年内业已达到适任标准的证据。

第Ⅶ章
可选择的发证

对于那些已达到负责航行值班高级船员或负责轮机值班高级船员发证的所有要求而且在另一类训练中的一项或几项职能合格的申请人,规则新设的一章允许希望给这些申请人发证的缔约国签发合适的证书。STCW规则的第Ⅱ、Ⅲ和Ⅳ章的适任表中规定了相应职能。

同时,对于那些已达到船长或轮机长发证的所有要求而且在另一类训练中的一项或几项职能合格的申请人,规则也允许希望给这些申请人发证的缔约国签发合适的证书。

Regulation	Summary of main changes
VII/1-Issue of alternative certificates	Parties to inform IMO of relevant provisions. Same education, training and competence required as under chapters II, III and IV. Equivalent seagoing service as per STCW Code Radio certificate for navigational watchkeeping-to meets regulation I/9 and chapter VII of the STCW Code.
VII/2-Certification of seafarers	To hold an appropriate certificate to perform all functions at the operational level or above referred to in either chapters II or III
VII/3-Principles governing the issue of alternative certificates	Equivalent level of safety and pollution. Requires that chapters II, III, IV and VII certificates or endorsements be "interchangeable" and the competency of officers not to be reduced Alternative certification not to be used in itself to reduce crew size, to de-skill individual crew members or to justify the assignment of combined deck and engineering duties during any particular watch.

Alternative methods of issuing certificates (Chapter VII)

16. The revised Convention permits governments, if they so choose, to issue certificates to seafarers using alternative arrangements not based solely on conventional divisions between deck and engine departments. This additional flexibility is intended to create opportunities to devise improved forms of shipboard organisation, facilitating the redistribution of work during busy periods such as when a ship is in port, as well as to enhance possibilities for career progression at sea, permitting deviation from traditional vertical career paths within one or other of the ship's departments.

17. The option of issuing alternative forms of certificate has been facilitated by the adoption of self-contained functions, defined at different levels of responsibility, as the most logical means of grouping together the different competencies which provide the framework for the establishment of the new standards of competence in the revised Convention.

18. Provided officers are fully qualified in all of the functions that comprise either the deck or engine department at the operational level (i.e. as a junior officer or above), governments will be permitted to issue certificates qualifying them to serve in one or more of the functions in the other department. In other words, to become qualified to perform individual functions at a particular level of responsibility in a second department, it will no longer be necessary to become qualified in all of the functions that constitute that department.

For example, a junior engineer or a chief engineer may also be able to qualify in one or more additional functions in the deck department, such as cargo handling and stowage at the operational level. Similarly, a deck officer could qualify in engineering maintenance and repair in addition to the functions that form the deck department.

公约规则	主要变动
Ⅶ/1——可供选择的证书的签发	缔约国应将相关的规定通知 IMO。教育、培训和适任能力与第Ⅱ、Ⅲ和Ⅳ章要求的一样。海上服务资历与STCW规则规定的等同。航行值班无线电证书——达到公约规则Ⅰ/9及STCW规则第Ⅶ章的要求。
Ⅶ/2——海员证	持有能履行第Ⅱ章或者第Ⅲ章规定的操作级或以上的所有职能的合适证书。
Ⅶ/3——关于签发可供选择的证书的原则	安全和防污的相当等级。要求相互适用于按第Ⅱ、Ⅲ、Ⅳ和Ⅶ章规定签发的证书或签证,并且不降低对高级船员适任的要求。可供选择的发证本身并非用于减少船员人数,降低海员的技能,或证明在任何特定的值班场合、混合甲板和轮机的职责是正当的。

可供选择的签发证书的方法

16. 经修订的公约允许政府,如果他们选择这样做,在给海员签发证书时使用可选择的安排,这种安排不是仅仅基于公约对甲板部和轮机部的划分。这种额外的灵活性的目的在于创造改善船上组织形式的机会,有助于在繁忙时期(例如船舶在港时)人员的重新分工,以及加强海上职务晋升的可能性,允许改变某个船上部门内的传统的垂直式的职务路径。

17. 由于采用了独立的职能体系,规定了不同的责任等级,用最合理的方法将不同的适任能力组合到一起使可供选择的发证形式变得方便可行,为修订的公约建立了一个新的适任标准体制。

18. 如果高级船员完全合格地履行甲板部或轮机部的所有操作级职能(即作为三副/三管轮或以上职务),允许政府给他们签发在其他部门履行一项或几项职能的合格证书。换言之,具有在第二个部门履行特定等级单独职能的资格,而不再需要具备履行该部门包括的所有职能的资格。

例如,一位初级轮机员或一位轮机长也可能有能力合格履行甲板部的一项或几项其他的职能,譬如货物装卸和配载的操作级职能。同样地,一位甲板高级船员除了履行甲板部的职能外也可能合格履行轮机维护和修理的职能。

19. The revised Convention will also permit extra flexibility regarding the common elements of training in the deck and engine departments for those trainees seeking to qualify in both departments. For example, 12 months' seagoing service will be required for one candidate to qualify as both a deck and engine watchkeeper.

However, the revised Convention also establishes clear principles governing the issue of alternative certificates, including:

.1 the issue of alternative certificates shall not be used in itself:
   .1 to reduce the number of crew on board,
   .2 to lower the integrity of the profession or "de-skill" seafarers,
   .3 to justify the assignment of the combined duties of the engine and deck watchkeeping officers to a single certificate holder during any particular watch; and

.2 the person in command shall be designated as the master; and the legal position and authority of the master and others shall not be adversely affected by the implementation of any arrangement for alternative certification.

20. It is expected that only a few governments will exercise the option to issue alternative certificates in the immediate future. Moreover, seafarers qualified in self-standing functions— additional to qualifications for the department in which they are primarily qualified to serve—will not be able to perform these additional functions unless permitted to do so by the flag state, which of course may not be the state issuing the certificate.

Nevertheless, the new provisions should provide a progressive framework in which the whole concept of alternative certification can be further developed in order to accommodate the anticipated requirements of the industry in the 21st Century.

Chapter VIII
Watchkeeping

All watchkeeping provisions previously contained in chapters II and III and the basic guidelines and operational guidance relating to safety radio watchkeeping adopted by the 1978 Conference have been incorporated into this new chapter. New provisions have been added regarding hours of rest for watchkeeping personnel. Part B of the STCW Code also contains recommendations on drug and alcohol abuse.

Regulation	Summary of main changes
VIII/1–Fitness for duty	Hours of rest
VIII/2–Watchkeeping arrangements and principles to be observed	Voyage planning, watchkeeping at sea, in port.

19. 对于那些寻求在甲板部和轮机部两个部门都具备资格的学员,修订的公约也允许在处理这两个部门共同的培训内容方面具有其他的灵活性。例如,对要求同时具备甲板和轮机值班员资格的申请人仅需要有12个月的海上服务资历(而不是两项职能要求之和24个月)。

    然而,修订的公约也制定了签发可供选择的证书的明确原则,包括:

    .1 签发可供选择的证书本身并非用于:
        .1 减少船上的船员人数,
        .2 削弱专业的完整性或"降低海员的技能",
        .3 证明在任何特定的值班场合,由一名证书持有人独自承担任轮机值班和航行值班高级船员的混合职责是正当的;及

    .2 负责指挥的人应被指定为船长;船长和其他人员的法律地位和权限不应因实施可供选择的发证安排而受到不利影响。

20. 预计只有少数政府会很快实施签发可供选择的证书。此外,具备自选职能资格的船员——在他们主要服务的部门以外的额外资格——也不能履行这些额外的职能,除非得到船旗国的允许,该船旗国当然不是指签发证书的国家。

    然而,新的条款应当提供一个进步的体制,该体制使可选择性发证的整个构思得到进一步的发展,从而符合21世纪行业所期待的要求。

第Ⅷ章
值班

本章并入了原先第Ⅱ章和第Ⅲ章包括的所有值班条款以及1978年大会采纳的基本指南和有关安全无线电值班的操作指南。有关值班人员的休息时间已经加入该新条款。STCW规则B部分也包含了有关防止吸毒和酗酒的指南。

公约规则	主要变动
Ⅷ/1—适于值班	休息时间
Ⅷ/2—值班安排和应遵守的原则	航次计划,海上、在港值班

Near-coastal voyages

21. The definition and treatment of near-coastal voyages proved to be one of the most contentious points arising during the 1978 STW Conference. Fears were expressed that this relaxation, intended for the coasting trades, would be subject to abuse and if not adequately controlled by the provisions of the Convention might allow extensive voyages to be undertaken in which, theoretically at least, the vessel would remain within any distance from the shore that might be specified as being "near to the coast".

22. The principles laid down in regulation I/3 are intended to prevent such abuses and have been reinforced by Guidelines contained in MSC/Circ. 472 dated 18 May 1987 (incorporated into Section B of the new STCW Code). Lecturers should refer to *STCW Code: Section B-1/3 Guidance regarding near-coastal voyages*, paragraphs 1, 2 and 3

Approved sea-going service

23. As defined in STCW regulation I/1, Para. 1.2, "Approved" means approved by the Party in accordance with the Regulations of the Convention.

    "Approved sea-going service" is required by regulations:
    II/2, Para. 2.1 and Para. 4.1 and 4.2
    II/3, Para. 6.2
    II/3, Para. 4.2.2
    II/1 , Para. 2.2

    Code: Section
    A-I/11, Para. 1.1 and Para. 1.3.3
    II/4, Para. 2.2.1
    III/2, Para. 2.1.1 and Para. 2.1.2
    III/3, Para. 2.1.1 and Para. 2.1.2
    III/4, Para. 2.2.2
    VI/1, Para. 1.2

    The purpose of these provisions is to require Administrations to apply appropriate rules regarding the acceptance of the sea-going service of candidates. It follows from the definition of "sea-going ship" contained in Article II(g) that seagoing service may include service in ships of any size or type, engaged in any activity on voyages of any duration or length, other than those voyages which involve navigation exclusively within inland waters or in waters within or closely adjacent to sheltered waters or areas where port regulations apply.

24. The sea-going service or experience of candidates for certificates of competency should be appropriate to the size and type of ship in which they are to be authorized to carry out key functions. Under chapter V of the STCW Convention, tankers, ro-ro passenger ships and passenger ships are singled out for special treatment, all other ship types being treated on a common basis.

近岸航行

21. 近岸航行的定义和条件是1978年STW大会中产生的最具有争议性的问题之一。有缔约国担心这种为了沿岸贸易而放松的条件会被滥用,并且如果公约规定不能充分控制可能会导致,至少理论上会导致,船舶在规定的近岸距离内无限拓展他们的航程。

22. 公约规则Ⅰ/3制定原则的目的是为了防止条款被这样滥用。于1987年5月18日失效的MSC/Circ.472中包含的指南强化了这些原则(指南被并入新的STCW规则B部分)。教员应当参考STCW规则:B部分Ⅰ/3关于近岸航行的指导,第1、2、3款。

认可的海上服务资历

23. 正如STCW公约规则Ⅰ/1,1.2款定义的那样,"认可的"系指缔约国按照公约的规则认可的资历。

    要求"认可的海上服务资历"的公约规则有:
    Ⅱ/2,第2.1、4.1和4.2款
    Ⅱ/3,第6.2款
    Ⅱ/3,第4.2.2款
    Ⅱ/1,第2.2款

    规则:部分
    A-Ⅰ/11,第1.1款和第1.3.3款
    Ⅱ/4,第2.2.1款
    Ⅲ/2,第2.1.1款和第2.1.2款
    Ⅲ/3,第2.1.1款和第2.1.2款
    Ⅲ/4,第2.2.2款
    Ⅵ/1,第1.2款

    这些条款的目标是要求主管机关考虑接受申请人的海上服务资历时应用适当的规则。按照第Ⅱ条(g)中的"海船"定义,海上服务资历可以包括在任何尺寸或类型,从事任何航期或航程航行的船上的服务资历,航行在内陆水域中或者受庇护的水域或港章所适用的区域以内或与此两者相邻的水域中的除外。

24. 申请人申请适任证书的海上服务资历或经验应当适合他们即将被授权履行主要职能的船舶的尺寸或类型。按照STCW公约第Ⅴ章,对于液货船、滚装客轮和客轮有特殊的要求,对于所有其他类型的船舶则有共同的要求。

Thus service in tankers is acceptable for qualifications valid on any other type of ship but service on other types of ships is not considered sufficient, by itself, to adequately prepare a seafarer for service on board tankers of the identified types.

25. Size of ship is another obvious criterion which must be considered. The Convention provides different levels of qualification according to the gross registered tonnage in the case of deck certificates and to the power of the main propulsion machinery in the case of certificates for engineer officers.

    Whilst the criteria used in the STCW Convention for the classification of certificates may be used directly (for example, service in ships of less than 3,000 kW power for an engineer officer certificate or in ships of less than 1,600 GRT for a deck certificate may not be accepted for certificates valid in ships exceeding those criteria), sufficient flexibility should be provided to allow consideration to be given to the acceptance in part, at full or partial rate, of service performed in ships of a lesser "class". This allows for employment mobility and recognizes the arbitrary nature of the "cut off" points.

26. It must always be possible for service aboard a ship that is required to be provided with certificated personnel to be accepted in full towards the certificates appropriate to such a ship.

27. Thus the factors to be considered in respect of the acceptance of sea service are basically factors 1.1 to 1.4 and 1.6 set forth in the "Guidance regarding Near-coastal Voyages".

National certificates

28. States Parties to the 1978 STCW Convention, as amended, do not necessarily have to provide a national certificate structure which is exactly the same as that embodied in the Convention.

    For example, a Party which is an island State and has no near-coastal trade or a Party which determines that it wishes to apply the full standards of the Convention to all of its ships is not obliged to create a range of national near-coastal certificates nor to define near-coastal voyages for the purposes of the Convention.

29. Such a decision not to define near-coastal voyages means that other Parties to the Convention are obliged to similarly apply the full standards of the Convention to their ships which engage on voyages off the coast of that Party which has not defined near-coastal voyages. This is because of the provisions of STCW Regulation I/3, paragraph 2.

30. Should a Party decide to issue fewer certificates than are provided for in the Convention, it is free to do so. However, the national certificate structure must be compatible with that of the Convention. In effect this means that one or more grades or classes of STCW certificates must be combined to form the national certificate. Then the qualification, experience and knowledge requirements for such a "combined" certificate must incorporate or, if so desired, be superior to the highest requirements for qualification and for experience contained in each of the STCW certificates concerned.

因此,液货船上的服务资历对于其他类型的船舶是有效的,但是对于准备到液货船上服务的船员,他所具备的其他类型船舶上的服务资历本身并不足够。

25. 船舶的大小是另一个必须考虑的标准。公约规定了不同的资格等级:甲板部人员证书按照总登记吨位,轮机高级船员的证书则按照主推进动力装置。

    虽然我们可能直接采用STCW公约中证书分类的标准(例如,3000千瓦动力以下轮机员或1600总吨以下船舶驾驶员的服务资历不能用于超过这些标准的船舶),但是应当提供灵活的考虑方案,全部或按比例接受在较低一级船舶上履行的服务资历。这样会使雇佣具有流动性并且认可自由中断船上工作的行业特性。

26. 船舶必须总是雇用持有完全适合该船所需证书的人员。

27. 因此接受海上服务资历的基本考虑因素是"关于近岸航行的指导"中列出的要素1.1~1.4和1.6。

国内证书

28. 根据修订的1978年STCW公约,缔约国没有必要非要规定一个与公约所描述的完完全全一样的国内证书结构。

    例如,缔约国是一个岛国并且没有近岸贸易,或者缔约国决定将公约的全部标准都适用于本国的所有船舶,那么该缔约国就没有义务制定一系列国内近岸航行证书或者为实施公约而规定近岸航行体系。

29. 决定不规定近岸航行意味着本公约其他缔约国的船舶在没有规定近岸航行的缔约国的海岸附近从事近岸航行时,同样有义务将本公约的全部标准适用于他们国内的所有船舶。这是因为STCW公约规则Ⅰ/3,第2款条款做了相应规定。

30. 缔约国具有决定签发的证书类别少于公约准许类别的自由。然而,国内证书的结构必须符合公约的规定。实际上,必须将STCW的一个或以上的等级或级别合并成国内一个的证书等级或级别。那么这种"复合"证书要求的资格、经验和知识也必须是组合的,如果这样,复合证书将高于每一个对应的STCW证书对资格和经验的最高要求。

In general, such a combination would, in effect, be the same as deciding not to issue the lower of the two STCW certificates concerned.

31. Should a Party decide to sub-divide an STCW certificate into two or more classes of national certificate, the qualification, experience and knowledge requirements of each of the national certificates so created must meet or exceed those of the single STCW Convention certificate concerned.

    However, there is one case in which the establishment of more than one class of national certificate in place of a single STCW certificate may allow a differing application of the requirements of the single STCW certificate. The case is that involving certificates valid for use on board ships engaged in near-coastal voyages. Here the level of knowledge may, in appropriate circumstances, be varied as a result of differences in the extent of that part of the defined near-coastal voyages for which each certificate is to be valid.

总之,这种组合证书实际上取决于两种对应的STCW证书中签发要求较高的那种证书。

31. 如果一个缔约国决定把一种STCW规定的证书细分为两个或以上级别的国内证书,每个这样形成的国内证书要求的资格、经验和知识必须符合或超过对应的单一的STCW公约证书。

    然而,在代替单一的STCW证书而制定的多种级别的国内证书时出现的一种情况,可能会允许将单一的STCW证书相关要求分开用于不同的证书。这种情况就是涉及签发近岸航行船舶的有效证书。在这种情况下,每种证书的知识等级根据情况恰当定出与公约规定的近岸航行证书要求有所不同的范围。

Part 7
Assessing Applications

1. The information typically required for application for a certificate of competency is indicated in the following example of an application form issued by the Maritime and Port Authority of Singapore (MPA).

    The documents typically required to be submitted are also identified on the application form, together with details of the relevant requirements.

2. International conventions which provide guidance or which have to be kept in mind when assessing applications include the conventions summarised in the following paragraphs:

    .1 The ILO Seafarers' Identity Documents Convention, 1958 (No. 108) provides for the issue of an identity document to every seafarer who is engaged in any capacity on board a vessel other than a ship of war, registered in the territory of a Party and ordinarily engaged in maritime navigation.

    .2 The ILO Minimum Age (Sea) Convention, 1920 (No. 7) prohibits the employment of children under the age of 14 years on board vessels other than those upon which only members of the same family are employed or on properly supervised school ships and training ships.

    .3 A further ILO Minimum Age (Sea) Convention, 1936 (No. 58) prohibits the employment of children under the age of 15 on vessels of any nature whatsoever engaged in maritime navigation.

    .4 The ILO Minimum Age Convention, 1973 (No. 138) prohibits, in general, the employment of children under the age of completion of compulsory schooling, and in any case, under the age of 15. This Convention will replace the preceding Minimum Age (Sea) Conventions if and when it comes into force.

    .5 Guidelines for conducting Pre-Sea and Periodic Medical Fitness for Seafarers—based on a survey of ILO and WHO Member States on the subject of medical examination of seafarers, an early draft of medical guidelines for seafarers was prepared by the ILO and WHO secretaries. A Joint WHO/ILO meeting in Nov 1997 developed these guidelines. The STW Sub-Committee has set a target completion date of year 2000 for these Guidelines.

    .6 The Officers' Competency Certificates Convention, 1936 prescribes the minimum requirement of professional capacity for masters and officers on board merchant ships.

    .7 The revised STCW Convention sets out more detailed mandatory requirements concerning the training and certification of masters and officers of seagoing ships. It defines "seagoing service" as service on board a ship relevant to the issue of a certificate or other qualification—the key phrase is "relevant to the issue of".

第7章
评估申请

1. 以下的例子是一份由新加坡海事港口局(MPA)发布的申请表,说明申请适任证书通常要求的资料。

   申请表也指明了通常要求提交的各种文件,同时附上相关要求的细节。

2. 提供指导或评价申请时应记住的国际公约包括摘录如下的公约:

   .1 1958年《ILO海员证明文件公约》(第108号),其提供了签发证明文件给每位在非军舰船上担任任何职务,在缔约国领土登记的并且正常从事海上航行的船员的相关规定。

   .2 1920年《ILO最低年龄(海上)公约》(第7号),其禁止雇佣14岁以下的儿童在船上工作,但那些只雇佣同一个家庭成员的船舶或者得到恰当监管的校船和培训船除外。

   .3 1936年补充的《ILO最低年龄(海上)公约》(第58号),其禁止雇佣15岁以下的儿童在任何性质(不管是否从事海上航行)的船上工作。

   .4 1973年《ILO最低年龄公约》(第138号),其全面禁止雇佣完成强制教育年龄以下的儿童和任何情况下雇佣15岁以下的儿童。本公约一旦生效,将取代先前的最低年龄(海上)公约。

   .5 基于国际劳工组织和世界卫生组织(WHO)关于海员健康检查的指南,以及ILO和WHO秘书处为海员医疗准备了一部早期草案,其中提出了出海前和定期检查海员健康的实施指南。1997年11月WHO/ILO联合召开的会议使该指南得到进一步的发展。STW分委会已经设定2000年为该指南完成的目标日期。

   .6 1936年《高级船员适任证书公约》规定了商船上船长和高级船员专业能力的最低要求。

   .7 修订的STCW公约对海船的船长和高级船员的培训和发证提出更加详细的强制性要求。该公约规定"海上服务资历"系指与签发的证书或其他资格有关的船上服务——关键用语是"与签发……有关的"。

Radiocommunications and radio personnel

    .8   The ITU Radio Regulations prescribe mandatory minimum requirements for the personnel of ship stations and ship earth stations. Under STCW 95, the relevant regulations could be found in chapter IV.

Ratings

3.   The mandatory minimum requirements for certification of watch-keeping ratings for the deck and engine departments could be found in Reg. II/4 and III/4 respectively i.e. all watch-keeping ratings must be duly certificated.

Procedure for assessing applications

4.   Under Reg. I/9.3, candidates for certification shall provide satisfactory proof:

— Of their identity;

— That their age is not less than that prescribed in the regulation relevant to the certificate applied for;

— That they meet the standards of medical fitness and hold a valid document attesting to their medical fitness;

— Of having completed the seagoing service and any relevant compulsory training required by there regulations for the certificate applied for; and

— That they meet the standards of competence prescribed by the appropriate regulations.

5.   The burden of checking sea service is considerable even if all ships served on are registered within the territory of the Administration to which application for a certificate is being made. Where service has been performed in foreign-flag ships, verification of sea service becomes even more difficult. All entries made in the seafarer's discharge book or record of service should be checked for any sign of having been tampered with and cross checked (for dates, signatures, etc.) against any supporting watch-keeping certificates or letters of reference produced. Any document which appears to have been tampered with should not be accepted and appropriate action should be taken towards imposing a sanction, as provided by law or by administrative orders, if it is proved to have been altered in an attempt to fraudulently obtain a certificate.

Doubtful service may be verified in some cases by checking with records of sea service or with the agreements with crew that are maintained by some Administrations. In other cases it may be necessary to obtain such verification from the shipping company concerned. In all cases, the onus should be placed upon the candidate to satisfy the examiner that he has satisfactorily completed the sea service and other requirements for the certificate that is being applied for.

无线电通信和无线电人员

  .8 国际电信联盟(ITU)规定对船站和船舶地面站人员强制性的最低要求。STCW 95公约第Ⅳ章有相关的规则。

普通船员

3. 公约规则Ⅱ/4和公约规则Ⅲ/4分别规定了甲板部和轮机部值班普通船员发证强制性的最低要求,即必须给所有值班普通船员签发合适的证书。

评估申请程序

4. 按照公约规则Ⅰ/9.3,证书申请人应提供下列符合要求的证明:

— 其身份;

— 年龄不小于有关申请证书的规则中规定的年龄;

— 其符合健康标准,并持有证明其健康的有效文件;

— 已具备所申请证书规定要求的海上服务资历并完成任何有关的强制培训;及

— 达到相应规则规定的适任标准。

5. 即使管理的所有船舶是在主管机关所在国的领土内登记的,检查海上服务资历的工作量也是相当大的。而审核船员在挂外国旗船上的海上服务资历,难度就更大。应当检查船员服务簿的所有记录或服务记录内容,查看是否有擅自改动的迹象,并对任何用于支持值班的证书或介绍信的内容如日期、签名等进行交叉检查。不应认可有擅自改动过迹象的文件,并且如果有证据表明这种改动是企图以欺骗的方式获得证书的,那么应当按照法律或行政命令采取适当的强制处罚措施。

  对于存在疑点的服务资历可以检查海上服务资历记录簿或某些主管机关保存的海上服务资历记录。在某些情况下,可能有必要从有关的航运公司获取审核证明。在任何情况下,申请人有责任令检查员满意,即他圆满完成申请证书所要求的海上服务资历和其他要求。

For masters' and officers' certificates issued under Chapter II, III and IV/2, every candidate shall have completed approved education and training and meet the standard of competence specified in the appropriate sections of the STCW Code. The authenticity of the certificate attesting attendance or successful completion of the approved education should be checked and, if considered necessary, the attendance should be checked against the records of the training institute concerned.

For candidates with a lower grade Certificate, the examiner may request the issuing Authority to make available information on the status of such certificates or endorsements-provided for under Reg. I/9.4.

Equivalencies

6. Provisions regarding the acceptance of seagoing service considered equivalent to that approved may be incorporated in the national rules or administrative instructions. The virtual impossibility of producing regulations or instructions which will ensure that the result is both just and technically acceptable in all cases makes it necessary for those assessing applications to exercise their judgement in individual cases. Local conditions may, in certain circumstances, render the adoption of a reasonable technical interpretation difficult if administrative rules, directives or instructions are strictly applied. Deviation may therefore have to be considered, provided the law contained in the appropriate legislation is complied with and the deviation is just and consistent with the intent of the rules.

7. On a national basis, consideration may also be given to retaining or adopting other educational and training arrangements, including those involving seagoing service under the provisions of Article IX of the 1978 STCW Convention, as amended, provided that the level of seagoing service, knowledge and efficiency as regards navigational and technical handling of ship and cargo ensures a degree of safety at sea and has a preventive effect as regards pollution at least equivalent to the requirements of the Convention. Details of such arrangements are required to be reported as early as practicable to the Secretary-General of IMO, who circulates such particulars to all Parties.

Alternative certification

8. Chapter VII of STCW 95 allows those Parties wishing to do so to issue appropriate certificates to those candidates who have met all requirements for certification as officer in charge of a navigational watch or as officer in charge of an engineering watch and, in addition, have been found duly qualified in a function or functions of another discipline. To clarify the linkage between these alternative certification provisions and the certification provisions of chapter II, III and IV, the abilities specified in the standards of competence are grouped, as appropriate, under the following seven functions:

    .1   Navigation

    .2   Cargo handling and stowage

按照第Ⅱ、Ⅲ和Ⅳ/2章签发船长和高级船员证书，每位申请人应当完成认可的教育和培训，并且达到STCW规则相应部分所规定的适任标准。应当检查证明其参加或圆满完成认可教育的证书的可靠性。如果认为有必要，应当依据有关培训机构的记录核对其参加培训的情况。

对于具有较低级别证书的申请人，核查人可以请求发证当局提供有关这类证书或签证状况的资料，公约规则Ⅰ/9.4对此有相关规定。

等效

6. 有关接受与认可的海上服务资历相当的资历的规定可以并入国家的法规或行政指令。实际上不可能针对所有情况制定既能保证结果正确，技术上又可接受的规则和指令。因此，评估申请人条件的人员有必要对个别情况运用他们的判断能力。如果严格执行行政法规、指示或指令，在某些情况下，特定的条件会给采纳技术上的合理解释造成困难。因此在这种情况下，只要遵守适当的法规规定，偏差是恰当的并与法规的目的是一致的，可考虑与规定的偏离。

7. 可以考虑在国内保留或采纳其他教育或培训的安排，包括修订的1978年STCW公约第Ⅸ条规定的涉及海上服务资历的各种安排，但是，海上服务水平、船舶和货物的航行和操作技术方面的知识和效率，应至少相当于本公约的要求，以保证海上安全的程度和防止污染的效果。应尽早将这种安排的详情报告给世界海事组织秘书长，秘书长则应将这种详情通报所有缔约国。

可供选择的发证

8. 对于那些已达到负责航行值班的高级船员或负责轮机值班的高级船员的所有发证要求，以及以此也可以证明自己具备其他一项或几项职能资格的申请人，STCW 95公约第Ⅶ章的规定允许那些希望给这些申请人发证的缔约国签发合适的证书。为了阐明可供选择的发证规定和第Ⅱ、Ⅲ和Ⅳ章的发证规定之间的联系，适任标准规定的应具备的能力可以适当地归纳为以下7项职能：

　　.1　　航行

　　.2　　货物装卸和积载

.3 Controlling the operation of the ship and care for person on board

.4 Marine engineering

.5 Electrical, electronic and control engineering

.6 Maintenance and repair

.7 Radiocommunications

at the following levels of responsibility:

.1 Management level—means the level of responsibility associated with:

— serving as master, chief mate, chief engineer officer or second engineer officer, and

— ensuring that all functions within the designated area of responsibility are properly performed;

.2 operational level—means the level of responsibility associated with:

— serving as officer in charge of a navigational or engineering watch or as designated duty engineer for periodically unmanned machinery spaces or as radio operator ; and

— maintaining direct control over the performance of all functions within the designated area of responsibility in accordance with proper procedures and under the direction of an individual serving in the management level for that area of responsibility;

.3 Support level—means the level of responsibility associated with performing assigned duties or responsibilities under the direction of an individual serving in the operational or management level.

The principles governing the issue of alternative certificates could be summarised as:

— equivalent level of safety and pollution prevention is required;

— certificates or endorsements issued under chapter II, III, IV and VII be "interchangeable" and the competency of officers not to be reduced;

— alternative certification not to be used in itself to reduce the size of crew, to de-skill individual crew members or to justify the assignment of combined deck and engineering duties during any particular watch.

.3 船舶作业管理和人员管理

.4 船舶轮机

.5 电气、电子和控制工程

.6 维护和修理

.7 无线电通信

在以下的责任级别中：

.1 管理级——系指与下列内容有关的责任级别：

— 担任船长、大副、轮机长或大管轮，及

— 确保正确履行指定责任范围内的所有职能；

.2 操作级——系指与下列内容有关的责任级别：

— 担任负责航行或轮机值班的高级船员或被指定为周期无人机舱的值班轮机员或担任无线电操作员；及

— 在相同责任范围的管理级人员的指导下，按照正规的程序，对指定责任范围内的所有职能的履行保持直接的控制；

.3 支持级——系指在操作级或管理级人员的指导下，履行指定的职责和责任有关责任的等级。

可以将签发可供选择的证书的原则归纳为：

— 要求相当的安全和防污的级别；

— 按照第Ⅱ、Ⅲ、Ⅳ和Ⅶ章规定签发的证书或签注"互相通用"，并且不能降低高级船员的适任要求；

— 可供选择的发证本身并非用于减少船员人数、降低船员的技能或证明在任何特定的值班时间，混合安排甲板和轮机职责是正当的。

Therefore, under this chapter, a qualified officer in charge of an engineering watch who has been found duly qualified in the function "Cargo handling and stowage" may keep a cargo watch while in port. In the same way, Parties wishing to do so may issue appropriate certificates to those candidates who have met all requirements for certification as master or as chief engineer officer and in addition have been found duly qualified in a function or functions of the other discipline. One point to note is that no alternative certificates shall be issued unless the Party has communicated information to IMO in accordance with article IV and regulation I/7.

In assessing applications, sea-going service apparently performed in contravention of the above conventions is not normally accepted in those States that are Parties to them.

因此,按照本章的规定,如果负责轮机值班的合格的高级船员在"货物装卸和积载"这项职能合格,那么船舶在港时,其可以履行货物的值班。同样地,对于那些已达到船长或轮机长发证的所有要求,此外具备其他一项或几项职能资格的申请人,希望给这些申请人发证的缔约国可以给他们签发合适的证书。要强调的是,除非缔约国按照第Ⅳ条和公约规则Ⅰ/7将有关的交流资料送交国际海事组织,否则不应签发可供选择的证书。

在评估申请条件时,上述公约的缔约国一般不接受明显违反这些公约规定的海上服务资历。

Part 8
Regulation I/6: Training and Assessment

Qualifications of trainers and assessors

Each Party has to ensure that all training and assessments required for certification under the Convention are carried out by persons who themselves are appropriately qualified and experienced and have been trained or instructed as required by section A-I/6 of the Code. This means that all Parties are now **required to establish appropriate standards** for those carrying out such training or assessments on board ship or ashore. They have to also ensure that these standards are monitored and maintained by all training providers-maritime academies, colleges etc and in respect of all other training and assessments that may be produced by candidates as evidence of their having met any requirement for certification under the Convention.

Regulation I/6, Section A-I/6 and B-I/6 of the STCW Convention deal with training and assessment and lecturers should refer to these texts.

Regulation I/6 Training and assessment
Each Party shall ensure that:

.1 the training and assessment of seafarers, as required under the Convention, are administered, supervised and monitored in accordance with the provisions of section A-I/6 of the STCW Code; and

.2 those responsible for the training and assessment of competence of seafarers, as required under the Convention, are appropriately qualified in accordance with the provisions of section A-I/6 of the STCW Code for the type and level of training or assessment involved.

Section A-I/6 Training and assessment	Section B-I/6 Guidance regarding training and assessment
1 Each Party shall ensure that all training and assessment of seafarers for certification under the Convention is: .1 structured in accordance with written programmes, including such methods and media of delivery, procedures, and course material as are necessary to achieve the prescribed standard of competence; and .2 conducted, monitored, evaluated and supported by persons qualified in accordance with paragraphs 4, 5 and 6. 2 Persons conducting in-service training or assessment on board ship shall only do so when such training or assessment will not adversely affect the normal operation of the ship and they can dedicate their time and attention to training or assessment.	

第8章
公约规则I/6: 培训与评估

培训与评估人员的资格

各缔约国要保证由合格和有经验并且接受过本规则A部分-Ⅰ/6节要求的培训或指导的人员按照本公约发证要求实施所有培训和评估。也就是要求所有的缔约国为实施船上或岸上培训或评估的人员**制定适当的标准**。他们还要确保提供培训的机构如航海院校、大学等,以及所有为申请人提供证据用以证明其已达到本公约发证所要求的培训和评估的其他组织,能够监督和保持这些标准。

STCW公约规则Ⅰ/6,A部分-Ⅰ/6节和B部分-Ⅰ/6节 涉及培训和评估。教员应当参阅这些内容。

公约规则I/6 培训和评估
各缔约国应保证:

.1 按照STCW规则A部分-Ⅰ/6节规定对按公约要求进行的海员培训和评估项目进行管理、监督和检查;及

.2 按照STCW规则A部分-Ⅰ/6节规定确保负责按公约要求进行的海员培训和适任评估的人员,应具备相应的培训或评估种类和级别所要求的资格。

A部分-I/6节 培训与评估	B部分-I/6节 关于培训与评估的指导
1. 各缔约国应保证,对按公约申请发证的海员的所有培训与评估是: 　.1 按照书面计划来组织进行的,该计划应包括为达到规定的适任标准所必需的授课方法和手段、程序和教材;及 　.2 按照第4、5和6段的规定由具备资格的人员来实施、监督、评价和提供支持。 2. 在船上进行在职培训或评估的人员,仅应在培训或评估不会影响船舶的正常操作以及在他们能抽出时间和精力时进行培训或评估。	

Section A-I/6 Training and assessment	Section B-I/6 Guidance regarding training and assessment
Qualifications of instructors, supervisors and assessors 3 Each Party shall ensure that instructors, supervisors and assessors are appropriately qualified for the particular types and levels of training or assessment of competence of seafarers either on board or ashore, as required under the Convention, in accordance with the provisions of this section.	*Qualifications of instructors and assessors* 1 Each Party should ensure that instructors and assessors are appropriately qualified and experienced for the particular types and levels of training or assessment of competence of seafarers, as required under the Convention, in accordance with the guidelines in this section.
In-service training 4 Any person conducting in-service training of a seafarer, either on board or ashore, which is intended to be used in qualifying for certification under the Convention, shall: 　.1 have an appreciation of the training programme and an understanding of the specific training objectives for the particular type of training being conducted; 　.2 be qualified in the task for which training is being conducted; and 　.3 if conducting training using a simulator: 　　.3.1 have received appropriate guidance in instructional techniques involving the use of simulators, and 　　.3.2 have gained practical operational experience on the particular type of simulator being used.	*In-service training and assessment* 2 Any person on board or ashore conducting in-service training of a seafarer intended to be used in qualifying for certification under the Convention should have received appropriate guidance in instructional techniques.
5 Any person responsible for the supervision of in-service training of a seafarer intended to be used in qualifying for certification under the Convention shall have a full understanding of the training programme and the specific objectives for each type of training being conducted.	3 Any person responsible for the supervision of in-service training of a seafarer intended to be used in qualifying for certification under the Convention should have appropriate knowledge of instructional techniques and of training methods and practice.

A 部分-I/6 节 培训与评估	B 部分-I/6 节 关于培训与评估的指导
教员、监督员和评估员的资格 3. 各缔约国应按照本节的规定确保教员、监督员和评估员完全胜任公约要求的船上或岸上特定种类和级别的培训或对海员适任能力的评估。	教员和评估员的资格 1. 各缔约国须保证,教员和评估员对于公约要求的特定种类和级别的培训和海员适任能力的评估,按照本节的指南是合格并具有经验的。
在职培训 4. 在船上或岸上对海员进行旨在根据公约用于取得发证资格的在职培训的任何人员应: .1 对培训计划有正确认识并对所进行的特定种类的培训的具体目标有充分的了解; .2 胜任所进行的培训工作;及 .3 如果使用模拟器进行培训: 　.3.1 接受过有关使用模拟器的教学技术的适当指导,及 　.3.2 已获得对所使用的特定种类模拟器的实际操作经验。 5. 对海员旨在根据公约用于取得发证资格的负责在职培训监督的任何人员,应对培训计划和正在进行的各种培训的具体目标有充分的了解。	在职培训和评估 2. 任何在船上或岸上开展为按照公约获得发证资格的在职培训的海员,应接受过相应的教学技术指导。 3. 任何负责按照公约取得发证资格的海员的在职培训实施监督的人员,应具有教学技术和培训方法与实践的适当知识。

Section A-I/6 Training and assessment	Section B-I/6 Guidance regarding training and assessment
Assessment of competence 6 Any person conducting in-service assessment of competence of a seafarer, either on board or ashore, which is intended to be used in qualifying for certification under the Convention, shall: .1 have an appropriate level of knowledge and understanding of the competence to be assessed; .2 be qualified in the task for which the assessment is being made; .3 have received appropriate guidance in assessment methods and practice; .4 have gained practical assessment experience; and .5 if conducting assessment involving the use of simulators, have gained practical assessment experience on the particular type of simulator under the supervision and to the satisfaction of an experienced assessor.	4 Any person, on board or ashore, conducting an in-service assessment of the competence of a seafarer intended to be used in qualifying for certification under the Convention, should have: .1 received appropriate guidance in assessment methods and practice; and .2 gained practical assessment experience under the supervision and to the satisfaction of an experienced assessor. 5 Any person responsible for the supervision of the in-service assessment of competence of a seafarer intended to be used in qualifying for certification under the Convention, should have a full understanding of the assessment system, assessment methods and practice.
Training and assessment within an institution 7 Each Party which recognizes a course of training, a training institution, or a qualification granted by a training institution, as part of its requirements for the issue of a certificate required under the Convention, shall ensure that the qualifications and experience of instructors and assessors are covered in the application of the quality standard provisions of section A-I/8. Such qualification, experience and application of quality standards shall incorporate appropriate training in instructional techniques, and training and assessment methods and practice, and comply with all applicable requirements of paragraphs 4 to 6.	

Functions required under Regulation I/6

A training regime to be established under Regulation I/6 includes taking responsibility for functions like:

1. **Training supervisor:** a function given the responsibility for monitoring training and assessment of the individual company seafarer.

2. **Instructor:** the function of delivering in-service training and instruction.

3. **Assessor:** the function of evaluating the competence of seafarers.

A 部分-I/6 节 培训与评估	B 部分-I/6 节 关于培训与评估的指导
适任评估 6. 在船上或岸上对海员进行旨在根据公约用于取得发证资格的在职适任评估的任何人员应： .1 对所评估的适任能力的知识和理解具有适当的水平； .2 胜任实施评估的任务； .3 接受过有关评估方法和实践的适当指导； .4 已获得评估的实际经验；及 .5 如果所进行的评估涉及模拟器的使用，已获得在监督下的特定种类模拟器的实际评估经验，并能令有经验的评估员满意。	4. 任何在船上或岸上负责为按照公约取得发证资格的海员实施在职适任评估的人员需： .1 接受过有关评估方法和实践的适当指导；及 .2 在有经验的评估员的监督下已获得实际评估经验并使其满意。 5. 任何负责为按照公约取得发证资格的海员的在职适任评估实施监督的人员，需对评估制度、评估方法和实践有全面的了解。
在培训机构内开展的培训和评估 7. 将认可培训课程、培训机构或培训机构所核准的资格，作为其按公约签发证书的一部分要求的缔约国应保证，将教员和评估员的资格和经历纳入A部分-Ⅰ/8节的质量标准条款的适用范围。该资格、经历和质量标准的应用应包括适当的教学技术培训以及培训和评估方法与实践，并应符合第4至6段所有适用的要求。	

公约规则Ⅰ/6要求的职能

应按照公约规则Ⅰ/6制定培训体制，包括界定各种职能的职责如：

1. **培训监督员**：负责监督单独公司海员的培训和评估的职能。

2. **教员**：实施在职培训和指导的职能。

3. **评估员**：评估海员适任能力的职能。

4. **Training management on board:** the responsibility for organising and follow-up of cadets' onboard training.

The above are **functions** and not necessarily **positions**. (As there are no clear requirements given in STCW 95, some or all of the above functions may be covered by the same person. However, it is assumed that the same person cannot cover the function of Assessor and Instructor at the same time for the same competence element. This in order to have some degree of objectivity in the assessment.)

For a shipping company the organisation of training should preferably be developed as an integral part of the company's Safety Management System.

Training Supervisor (Company)

The Training Supervision function should be assigned by top management to a person who fulfils the requirements in STCW 95 Section A-I/6. The Training Supervisor should have thorough understanding and experience from ship operations and managerial experience. This could for example be an experienced Master.

The Training Supervisor should, together with the quality assurance manager and the personnel manager, develop the company training policy according to the requirements in ISM/STCW 95. It should, in addition to the formal requirements, include:

- Training aims

- Allocation of resources

- Company intentions for implementing training in accordance with the requirements

The Training Supervisor should decide whether the whole fleet or just a part of it should be involved in the training scheme. In any case, crew co-ordination and familiarisation training must be conducted onboard all ships covered by the convention. It is only the in-service training for professional certificates that need the formal structure as described in STCW 95 Section A-I/6. The Training Supervisor should also decide upon the structure of the training organisation.

Company Instructors and Assessors

Each individual Company has to take some initiative to find, train and motivate people considered likely to succeed in instructing and assessing seafarers competence.

A shipboard instructor and assessor must fulfil the requirements in the STCW 95 Section A-I/6. The Training Supervisor, together with the QA-manager and the personnel manager, should seek advice from the masters of each vessel (since they know their crew) and dedicate the instructor/assessor function to qualified personnel within each department onboard. It would seem natural to choose the most experienced personnel. By qualified, it is meant that the instructor/assessor shall have a valid certificate on the same (or higher) level as the training being conducted.

4. **船上培训管理**：负责组织和实施实习生的船上培训。

以上提到的是**职能**，无须设为**职位**。（因为 STCW 95 公约没有明确的要求，以上部分或所有的职能可能由同一个人担任。然而，可以肯定，对于相同的适任项目，同一个人不能同时担任评估员和教员的职能。这可以保证评估具有某种程度上的客观性。）

航运公司最好将培训的组织进一步发展成为公司内部安全管理体系的一部分。

培训监督员（公司）

应当指派一名满足 STCW 95 公约 A 部分-Ⅰ/6 节要求的高层管理人员担任培训监督职能。培训监督员应对船舶营运和管理实际情况有全面的了解和经验。譬如可以是一位有经验的船长。

培训监督员应协同质量保证部门经理和人力资源部经理，按照 ISM/STCW 95 公约的要求制定公司的培训方针。方针中除了常规要求外，还应包括：

■ 培训目标

■ 资源的分配

■ 公司按照要求实施培训的目的

培训监督员应决定整个培训方案是涉及整个船队或仅仅涉及船队的一部分。在无论何种情况下，必须在所有船上进行公约规定的船员相互协助和熟悉的培训。在各类培训中只有为了取得职业证书的在职培训需要采用 STCW 95 公约 A 部分-Ⅰ/6 节规定的正式结构。培训监督员还应决定培训组织的结构。

公司培训员和评估员

各公司必须主动发现、培训和鼓励那些被认为可能胜任进行海员适任能力培训和评估的人员。

船上培训和评估人员必须符合 STCW 95 公约 A 部分-Ⅰ/6 节规定的要求。培训监督员应协同质量保证部经理和人力资源部经理，向各船船长征询意见（因为他们了解自己的船员）并且将教员/评估员的职能托付给船上各个部门的合格人员，当然应选择最有经验的人员。合格是指教员/评估员应当持有与其指导的培训相同（或更高）级别的有效证书。

Taken into account that the STCW 95 requires the instructor/assessor to have an appreciation of the training being conducted, it is necessary to select personnel who are motivated for the task.

.1 Instructor

The Company has to establish criteria for what they believe is good basic background and qualifications for an instructor delivering training on board. The selection must be based on the requirements given in STCW 95 Reg. 1/6 and Section A-I/6. Necessary support and training needs of each individual instructor has to be analysed and provided for. This could be in the form of i.e. train the trainer courses and seminars.

In any case, the intention under STCW 95 is to appoint personnel with more experience to train crew with less experience.

Below are mentioned samples of topics to be evaluated in the selection process:

- Basic background of the potential instructor
- Seagoing experience
- Ship type experience
- Other relevant shore-based experience
- Basic qualifications of the potential instructor
- Rank, certificates
- Instructor experience (if any)
- Behaviour and attitude suitable for the purpose
- Motivation and understanding of the instructor role
- Ability to motivate trainees
- Ability to deliver training
- Support and training that the instructor needs
- Available courses (if any)
- Company support (policy, instructions to master)
- Training Supervisor support
- Shipboard support (shipboard management)
- Equipment for training and education

考虑到STCW 95公约要求教员/评估员充分了解其所指导的培训,有必要挑选那些主动承担该项任务的人员。

.1 教员

公司必须为进行船上培训的教员制定他们认为是具有良好背景基础和资格的标准。教员的挑选必须基于STCW 95公约规则Ⅰ/6和A部分-Ⅰ/6节的要求。必须分析和为各个教员提供必要的支持和培训需要。其形式可能是教员培训课程和研讨会。

无论何种情况下,STCW 95公约规定的目的是指派经验较丰富的人员培训经验较少的人员。

下列是教员挑选程序中需要评价的项目的例子:

- 有潜力教员的基本背景
- 海上服务经验
- 船舶类型经验
- 其他相关的岸上经验
- 有潜力教员的基本资格
- 级别和证书
- 教员的经验(如有)
- 为此目的合适的表现和态度
- 对教员角色的主动性和理解度
- 有激发学员的能力
- 有进行培训的能力
- 教员需要的支持和培训
- 已完成的课程(如果有)
- 公司的支持(方针、对船长的指示)
- 培训监督员的支持
- 船上的支持(船上的管理)
- 培训和教育的设备

- Training plans with learning objectives (to be provided or developed)

- Record books or forms for cadets' training progress and assessment of competence

The instructor should be the "driving force" and most importantly be able to motivate the trainees. The selection must therefore be done carefully. It is vital that the instructor is motivated, and as the STCW 95 states: "… **has an appreciation of the training program…**", meaning that he has a **positive** attitude towards training.

2. Assessor

With reference to STCW 95 Section A-I/6, the conclusion is that the Assessor must to some extent have the same qualifications as the Instructor as mentioned above. In addition, he must receive proper guidance, training and experience in assessment of competence. This training may be in the form of courses, seminars and on-job training. Some administrations might require assessors to attend certain courses/tests to ensure their ability and objectivity.

The performance of the Assessor role will tend to become more formal because the credibility and success of any training of personnel fully depend on objective assessment and proper record keeping. Many otherwise well designed training programmes fail due to poor assessment.

In addition to the instructor and assessor on board, there may be a need for instructors and assessors ashore. (Note: Some Flag Administrations may require that the assessor function is cared for outside the company.) Eventually, the Administrations will have to come forward with more guidance on the qualification requirements for Instructors and Assessors.

.3 Training Responsibilities on board

When delegating this task to personnel onboard, one should consider the following;

Is the person:

- Qualified according to the STCW 95?

- Senior officer?

- Motivated for such a task?

Since training includes both training and upgrading training of ratings, cadets and officers, it is recommended to assign the responsibility for on board training to a senior officer, i.e. chief mate. The officer must have the necessary authority to implement the training programme onboard, and the necessary seniority to identify training needs within the crew.

Competences of Assessors

The competences developed by an Assessor include the ability to:

- develop the strategies needed to assess whether someone has achieved competence;

- 规定了学习目标的培训计划(提供或发展)

- 实习生培训过程和适任评估的记录簿或表格

教员应当是训练的"促进力量",而且其最重要工作是能够激发学员。因此对教员的挑选必须相当谨慎。教员具有主动性是很重要的,正如STCW 95公约所述:"……**对培训计划有正确的认识**……",含义是对于培训具有**积极**的态度。

2. 评估员

参照STCW 95公约A部分-Ⅰ/6节,得出的结论是评估员必须在某种程度上与以上提及的教员有相同的资格。此外,他还必须接受适任评估正确的指导、培训和实践。这种培训有可能是以课程、研讨会和在职培训的形式完成。一些主管机关或许会要求评估员参加某种课程/测验来确保他们的能力和公正性。

评估员工作应更加规范,因为任何人员培训的可靠性和成功完全是由客观的评估和正确记录保证的。许多其他精心策划的培训计划的失败就是因为评估没做好。

除了船上的教员和评估员,也可能需要岸上的教员和评估员。(注:一些船旗主管机关可能会要求评估员的职能由船公司以外的人员完成。),主管机关最终将出台更多有关教员和评估员资格要求的指导。

.3 船上的培训责任

委托此项任务给船上的人员时,应当考虑如下因素:

此人:

- 根据STCW 95公约是否合格?

- 是否是高级船员?

- 是否主动承担此项任务?

既然培训同时包括普通船员、实习生以及高级船员的职务晋升培训和其他培训,那么建议指派一名资深高级船员即大副负责船上的培训。此资深高级船员必须拥有必要的权限来完成船上的培训计划,并且有必要的工作经验以确定船员的培训需求。

评估员的适任能力

评估员适任能力包括有能力:

- 制定用于评估某人是否具备适任能力的方案;

- collect evidence and make judgements;
- plan and organise assessment activities;
- assessment techniques, and
- give feedback.

Assessor's role

The assessor's role is to:

- work closely with the candidate to identify opportunities for gathering evidence, including evidence from prior learning.
- agree assessment plans with the candidate
- assess the evidence against the standards
- make judgements about the candidate's competence
- keep assessment records
- provide feedback to the candidate on outcomes
- liaise with the candidate's lecturers or trainers, mentor and with the external verifier

This may be undertaken individually or in conjunction with other assessors. When a training institution has no suitably qualified assessors at a particular site where candidates are located, it may be convenient to make arrangements for assessors from other sites to visit in order to provide assessment opportunities for candidates.

The assessor will:

- Assess evidence submitted by candidates against the evidence specification, performance criteria and range for particular elements within the qualification.
- Ensure that the evidence is sufficient, valid and demonstrates competence for the appropriate standard.
- Ensure that evidence presented by the candidate is bona-fide e.g is endorsed by line manager etc.
- Ensure that prescribed performance evidence of products, processes and knowledge evidence of theories, principles and methods and facts and data is presented in accordance with the evidence specification.

- 收集证据并且做出评断；

- 计划和组织评估活动；

- 应用评估技巧，及

- 提供反馈信息。

评估员的作用

评估员的作用是：

- 与申请人密切合作寻找收集证据的机会，包括先前参加学习的证明。

- 与申请人就评估计划达成一致意见

- 按照标准评估适任证据

- 对申请人的适任能力做出评判

- 保存评估记录

- 给申请人提供关于评估成绩的反馈信息

- 联络申请人的授课者或培训员、导师和外部的审核人

这项任务可能由个人或与其他评估员一同完成。如果某个培训机构在安排申请人评估的特定地点没有适当的合格评估员，那么为了给申请人提供评估机会，方便的做法是安排其他地点的评估员到该地进行评估。

评估员应：

- 对照证据的详细内容、作业标准和资格范围内需要的特定要素评估申请人提交的证据。

- 确保证据是充分的、有效的并且表明具备适当标准要求的适任能力。

- 确保申请人提供的证据是真实的，例如是部门负责人签署的，等等。

- 确保规定的客观证据的产生，收集过程和知识证据的理论、原则、方法、事实和数据是依据证据收集的相关规定进行的。

Assess evidence by:

- reviewing portfolios of documentation

- observation of actual work or simulated work activities (or verifying that testimonial evidence from others who have observed the candidate is satisfactory and valid)

- interviewing candidates to establish authenticity of evidence

Training and experience of assessors

Assessors must be competent, both at assessment and in the technical area and at the level at which the candidates are to be assessed. The technical competence, in this context, is likely to be met by having substantial experience and qualifications in the appropriate discipline. Competence in assessment is proved by being accredited against standards which have been developed by the national administration.

Typical Assessor Competences

Assess Candidates Performance

- for assessors who are mainly involved in observing candidates performing activities or in examining things they produce and in checking their underpinning knowledge.

Assess Candidates Using Differing Sources of Evidence

- for assessors who need to draw upon a wider range of sources of evidence in making an assessment decision, such as assignments, reports from other assessors and candidate's previous outside experience.

USCG Instructor Qualifications

Instructors of approved courses are largely responsible for the successful completion of course objectives. Hence, they possess the necessary qualifications. To be effective, an instructor must have specific experience, knowledge and skills, and the ability to communicate them. Knowledge that cannot be communicated is worthless, and a good communicator lacking the experience, knowledge or skills, has little to communicate. Consequently, when reviewing an instructor's credentials, the following criteria must be applied:

1. An instructor must hold a license and/or merchant marine's document and any endorsements appropriate to the content of the course. These certifications serve as an initial indication of the individual's professional qualifications. A person without a license or holding a license below the level of the course may have significant experience, knowledge and skills and be very capable of teaching the course. In these situations, evidence must be presented to verify an equivalent level of experience, skills and knowledge.

证据评估：

- 审阅证据文件

- 考察实际工作或模拟操作中的作业（或审核来自他人，能说明经其考察申请人是令人满意和胜任的证据）

- 与申请人约谈来确定证据的真实性

评估员的培训和经验

评估员必须同时在评估和技术领域以及在申请人被评估的职务级别具备适任能力。文中提到的技术适任能力一般要求有足够的经验和资格以满足规定要求，并按照国家主管机关制定的标准认定是否具备适任评估员的能力。

评估员标准的适任能力

评估申请人表现的评估员

- 指主要从事考察申请人的表现或检验他们提供的证据及检查他们的知识基础的评估员。

用不同来源的证据评估申请人的评估员

- 指需要采用更多来源的证据以做出评估决定，例如考察分派的任务，分析来自其他评估员的报告和申请人以前在别处的经验。

美国海岸警卫队（USCG）的教员资格

规定课程的教员全面负责课程目标的成功完成。所以，他们应具有必要的资格。为了达到预期效果，教员必须具备专门的经验、知识和技能并且具有传授能力。不能够被传授的知识是毫无价值的，而优秀的授课者缺乏经验、知识和技能也就没有东西可传授。因此，审核教员的证明书时，必须应用下列准则：

1. 教员必须持有证书和/或商船海员的文件和任何适用于课程内容的证明。这些证明文件是个人专业资格的基本证明。没有证书或持有低于课程水平证书的人也可能有重要的经验、知识和技能并且非常有能力担任此课程的教学。在此情况下，必须提供证据证实他具有相当水平的经验、技能和知识。

2. An instructor should have experience in teaching (or training), and a knowledge of instructional techniques. A prospective instructor's teaching ability is to be demonstrated before the OCMI or the OCMI's representative during the conduct of a course. If this is not possible, the individual will be interviewed to review his or her background in teaching and to evaluate his or her communication skills. A working knowledge of teaching techniques is desirable; however, if an individual has good communication skills, teaching techniques can be acquired.

3. When recommending a person for acceptance as an instructor, the manager must compare the person's background to the list of relevant experience, knowledge and skills, and explain why the person is qualified. This process should be followed in establishing a new course or replacing instructors in existing approved courses.

Evaluating potential instructors

The instructors in any type of educational program are an important part of the training package, therefore, reviewers must ensure they have the appropriate qualifications. To assist in evaluating potential instructors, the training facility must include a list of the experience, knowledge and skills the course instructors must possess to effectively teach the courses offered. There are several factors that must be considered.

1. *Experience.* The individual should have a valid Coast Guard license, document, or certificate appropriate to the content of the course. If the person does not hold a valid license, evidence must be presented that demonstrates an equivalent level of maritime (industry/field) experience, knowledge, and skill. For example, an instructor for an unlimited radar observer course should have at least a license as master of near coastal steam or motor vessels of not more than 500 gross tons with an unlimited radar observer endorsement, or other equivalent watchkeeping experience appropriate to the course.

2. *Skills.* An instructor must have a high level of understanding of the knowledge and skills taught in the course in addition to having experience in their practical application. A license does not always mean the individual has experience with, or a thorough understanding of, all topics covered by the license examination. On the other hand, a person without a license may have the appropriate experience, knowledge, and skills necessary to teach the course. In either case, the following items must be verified.

    1. Instructor credentials—a background or experience in teaching or instructional techniques.

    2. Subject knowledge—a high level of understanding of the particular subject area.

    3. Instructor skills—the ability to use appropriate training techniques to accomplish the objectives of the training.

2. 教员应具有教学(或培训)经验和指导技巧的知识。预选教员需向 OCMI 或其代表展示其实施课程教学的能力。如果不能这样做,那么应通过约谈复查其教学背景和评估其授课技能。虽然期望教员具有实际教学技巧方面的知识;然而,如果某人具有良好的沟通能力,他也能获得教学技巧。

3. 推荐某人作为教员时,主管必须把此人的背景资料与规定的相关经验、知识和技能相比较,并且解释为什么此人是合格的。这是认可开设新课程或替换现行课程的教员的程序。

评价有潜质的教员

在任何类型的教育计划里,教员是整个培训重要的一部分,因此审核员必须确保他们有适当的资格。为了协助评价有潜质的教员,培训条件必须包括为了有效教授所开设的课程,教员必须具备的一系列的经验、知识和技能。这里有几个必须考虑的因素。

1. 经验。教员应当具有有效的海岸警卫队证书、文件,或适用于课程内容的证明。如果此人没有有效的证书,必须出示表明其具有与航海(行业/领域)经验、知识和技能相当的证据。例如,作为无限航区雷达观测员课程的教员至少应当具有近岸 500 总吨以下蒸汽机船或内燃机船船长证书和无限航区雷达观测员的签注,或者其他相当的适合此课程的值班经验。

2. 技巧。教员除了必须对课程教授的知识和技能有高水平的理解,还必须具有实际应用它们的经验。持有证书并不一定表明教员具有相应的经验,或对证书考试涉及的所有项目完全了解。另一方面,没有证书的人可能具有教授课程所必需的适当经验、知识和技能。在任何一种情况下,必须审核以下的项目。

   1. 教员证件——具有教学的或指导性技术的背景或经验。

   2. 学科知识——具有对特定学科领域高水平的理解。

   3. 教员技能——具有使用适当的培训技术实现培训目标的能力。

3. *Teaching Ability.* A prospective instructor should have experience in teaching or training and/or knowledge of instructional techniques. An instructor must be able to communicate his/her experience, knowledge, and skills to the students. A highly knowledgeable person will not add to the course if he or she is unable to communicate that knowledge effectively. A prospective instructor's teaching ability may be determined by observation. If this is not possible, the individual should be interviewed to assess the candidate's background and communication skills. If an individual has good communication skills teaching techniques can be learned. Additionally, student's course critiques should provide beneficial feedback to the training institution concerning an instructor's effectiveness.

Courses for Instructors and Assessors

Assessor course

A typical training course for assessors would include the following topics:

- The background and methodology of the new STCW 95

- The framework for assessment

- The role of the assessor

- Sufficiency, validity, currency and reliability of evidence

- Collecting and assessing evidence

- The accreditation of prior achievement

- Giving constructive feedback

- Completing the assessment documentation

- Candidate Information Pack and Evidence Portfolio (training record book)

Instructor Course

Instructors who provide competency-based training should attend a course which develop competences listed below.

The competences developed by this course include the ability to:

- collect, analyse and organise information;

- communicate ideas and information;

- plan and organise activities;

- work with others and in teams;

3. 教学能力。预选教员应当拥有教学经验或培训和/或指导技巧的知识。教员应当具备将其经验、知识和技能传授给学员的能力。如果具有丰富知识的人不能够有效地传授这些知识,那么也不得参与该课程。可以通过考察来决定一名预选教员的教学能力。如果不能这样做,则通过约谈申请人以评估其背景资料和授课技能。如果他具有良好的沟通能力,他就能够学到教学技术。此外,学员的课程评价应给培训机构提供有利于确定教员教学效果的有关反馈信息。

为教员和评估员开设的课程

评估员课程

为评估员开设的典型培训课程包括以下主题:

- 新的STCW 95公约的背景资料和原理

- 评估的体制

- 评估员的作用

- 证据的充分性、有效性、现实性和可靠性

- 证据的收集和评估

- 认可原先的成绩

- 提供有助益的反馈信息

- 完成评估文件

- 申请人的数据库和证明文件(培训记录簿)

教员课程

提供适任培训的教员应当参加下列培养适任能力的课程。

本课程培养的适任能力包括:

- 收集、分析和组织资料;

- 沟通理念和信息;

- 计划和组织活动;

- 与他人一起工作及团队工作;

- solve problems; and
- use technology.

Example I: USCG Train the Trainer Course

Qualified Instructor Training with Designated Examiner Training

4 days, 32 training hours

Description

This course has been developed in cooperation with the Cadwalder Behavioral Programs and Training Institute and is a classroom based Train the Trainer course. The curriculum has been specifically designed for the maritime community and meets the STCW Regulations for Instructor, Supervisor and Assessor (Designated Examiner) training pursuant to STCW Regulation I/6, STCW Code Section A-I/6 and Section A-I/8. The course is based on IMO Model Course 6.09 (Training Course for Instructors) and is intended to meet the guidance of US Coast Guard NVIC 6-97, and 46 CFR Parts 10 and 12. This training is required of all mariners under the STCW who provide original license, basic safety training, other instruction and assessment for STCW upgrade and competencies. This training is highly recommended for staff captains, security officers, safety officers, training officers and, in general, anyone who will provide training and assessment under the STCW, or training in a general marine environment. This course includes a student manual, classroom instruction, practical exercises, written assessment and course certificate. Successful completion of this course will allow the mariner to instruct and assess other mariners to meet STCW requirements.

Topics

Course Design Development

- Clarifying Basic Concepts
- Identifying Critical Training Parameters

Learning System Development

- Identifying Training/Learner Needs

Instructional Strategy Development

- Plan Content
- Instructional Methods and Selection Criteria

Learning System Evaluation

- Assessment and Evaluation Strategy Development

- 解决问题；及

- 应用技术。

例Ⅰ：美国海岸警卫队教员培训课程

有指定主考官参与的资深教员培训

4天，32个培训小时

介绍

本课程采用卡德沃尔德行为方案(Cadwalder Behavioral Programs)和培训院校的教学形式开展，是一门培训教员的课堂教学课程。本课程特别为航海界设计，符合STCW规定并遵循STCW公约规则Ⅰ/6、STCW规则A部分-Ⅰ/6节和A部分-Ⅰ/8节关于的教员、监督员和评估员指派的考官的培训要求。本课程以IMO示范课程6.09（对教员的培训课程）为基础，也力求符合美国海岸警卫队指南NVIC6-97，和46 CFR第10和12部分的要求。按照STCW的要求，所有开展基本证书、基本安全培训，以及进行针对STCW升级和适任的其他指导与评估的航海人员都要参加本培训。特别向下列人士推荐本课程：船长、保安官员、安全官员、培训官员，以及任何按照STCW公约提供培训和评估，或提供航海环境下常规培训的人员。本课程包括学员手册、课堂指导、实践练习、书面评估和课程证书。圆满完成本课程的航海人员可以根据STCW公约的要求指导和评估其他船员。

科目

课程设计开发

- 阐明基本概念

- 明确重要的培训要素

学习体系制定

- 明确培训/学员的需要

指导策略制定

- 计划内容

- 指导方法和选择标准

学习体系评价

- 评估和评价策略制定

Planning, Organizing and Conducting a Course

Example II: DNV Courses

Training Supervision Course

This is one day course is aimed for ship owners and ship managers and their personnel involved in seafarers' training ashore and onboard.

The purpose of the course is to give an introduction to a systematic approach for the management of crew competence. It also provides increased awareness of new and enforced responsibilities according to STCW 95 concerning education, qualification and performance of seafarers in ship operations.

Train the Trainer Course

This two-day course is aimed at personnel who are responsible for training and instruction. The course focuses on communication and planning aspects, and instructional means and methods.

The participants will improve practical skills as trainers and increase their awareness through feedback on their own instruction skills. A spin-off result of the course is increased consciousness and self-confidence when instructing individuals or groups of people.

Assessor Course

This is another one-day course designed to enable senior officers to perform competence assessment as required by STCW 95. It includes instruction, dialogue and interactive methods such as group work and role-play. The topics covered include:

- Knowledge of relevant clauses in the STCW 95 regarding assessment

- Understanding of the purpose of the standard competence tables

- General understanding of the Assessor function in relation to the Instructor, Training Responsible and Training Supervisor functions.

- Basic understanding of planning and evaluating learning processes

- Use of a Training Record Book

The role of the external verifier

The national administration is responsible for verifying that assessment, in its approved centres, has been carried out systematically, validly and to the required STCW standards. This is achieved through external verifiers. The external verifier requires access the training provider's documentation and records. Part of the external verifier's role is to provide feedback and support to the centre. By helping to develop internal quality systems, the external verifier assists the centre in gaining approval and in its continuous improvement.

策划、组织和指导一门课程

例子Ⅱ：DNV课程

<u>培训监督课程</u>

本课程为期一天，对象是船东、船舶管理人及其参与海员岸上和船上培训的人员。

本课程的目的是介绍船员适任管理的系统方法。本课程也为学员提供根据STCW 95公约要求公司在海员教育、资格和操作船舶表现方面新的和强化了的责任的理解。

<u>教员课程培训</u>

本课程为期两天，对象是负责培训和指导的人员。本课程重点在沟通和计划方面，以及指导的方式和方法。

参加者作为教员的实际技能将会得到提高，并且通过针对他们自己的指导技能的反馈信息来加强理解。本课程的连带效果是加强了在对个人和团体进行指导时的意识和自信。

<u>评估员课程</u>

这是另外一门为期一天的课程，设置的目的是使高级船员能够按照STCW 95公约的要求实施适任评估。本课程包括指导、对话以及互动性的方法如分组活动和角色扮演。涉及的主题包括：

- 了解STCW 95公约关于评估的相关条款

- 理解适任标准表的目的

- 总体理解评估员在职能方面与教员、培训职责及培训监督员职能间关系

- 基本理解计划和评价学习进程

- 使用培训记录簿

外部审核员的作用

国家主管机关负责审核在其批准的评估中心评估工作是否已经系统、有效以及按照STCW的标准开展。这类审核通过外部审核员进行。外部审核员须评估培训机构的文件和记录。给评估中心提供反馈和支持信息也是外部审核员工作的部分内容。通过帮助开发内部质量体系，外部审核员可以起到协助评估中心通过审验，以及协助其不断提高的作用。

1. Verifiers will visit centres, normally at least twice per year to review progress, procedures and documentation.

   Formally the verifiers will:

   a. Check that agreed procedures have been carried out and where this has not, record and constructively comment on any deviations.

   b. Record and comment on the assessment methods and their suitability for achieving relevance, consistency and reliability. Particular note should be made of innovative ideas for assessment of competence.

   c. Examine samples of assessment evidence (both acceptable and unacceptable) and comment on the appropriateness of assessment decisions.

   d. Take note of and where appropriate, advise on any problems encountered by centres

2. The external verifier will judge a centre's effectiveness against the criteria laid down for approval and the centre's agreed action plan.

3. Approved assessment centres must appoint an internal verifier. External verifiers are not expected to moderate assessments during any sampling process- this quality control role is that of the internal verifier.

Role of the Internal Verifier

The internal verifier has the following main roles:

- provide advice and support to assessors including:
    — ensuring assessors possess necessary documents, records and guidelines
    — identifying assessors' training needs and making provision to satisfy them
    — providing prompt advice on additional evidence
    — assisting assessors with arrangements for special needs candidates
    — clearly allocating duties to their assessors

- maintain and submit assessment documentation including ensuring that:
    — candidate records are complete, legible and accurate
    — security and confidentiality are maintained.

- undertake internal verification including ensuring that:
    — assessors are suitably qualified
    — assessment practice is monitored and constructive feedback is provided
    — assessments conform to national standards
    — documentation is complete and up to date
    — disputes and appeals are referred to appropriate authority
    — recommendations for external action to maintain quality of assessment are accurately communicated to the external verifier.

1. 审核员一般至少每年两次到评估中心检查运行、程序和文件情况。

    在形式上,审核员应:

    a. 检查批准的程序是否已经得到实施,如有问题,则记录下任何不符合项以及提供有益的建议。

    b. 记录和评价评估方法以及这些方法在取得评估的相关性、一致性和可靠性方面是否合适。应当特别注意记录在适任评估方面的创新想法。

    c. 抽样检验评估证据(包括可接受的和不被接受的),并且评价评估结论的正确性。

    d. 记录评估中心遇到的任何问题,如果合适,提出相应建议。

2. 外部审核员将按照规定的审核标准和预先确定的活动计划来评定中心的有效性。

3. 认可的评估中心必须指派一名内部审核员。因为不能期望外部审核员完成所有的评估抽查工作——这种质量控制职责是由内部审核员担当的。

内部审核员的作用

内部审核员有以下几个主要的作用:

- 为评估员提供建议和支持,包括:
    — 确保评估员有必要的文件、记录和指南
    — 明确评估员的培训需要以及提供培训条件
    — 对额外的证据提供正确建议
    — 协助评估员安排有特殊需要的申请人
    — 清楚地给评估员分配工作

- 保存和提交评估文件包括确保:
    — 申请人的记录是完整的、可以看懂的和准确的
    — 保持安全性和机密性

- 担任内部审核工作包括确保:
    — 评估员的资格合适
    — 评估活动受到监控,并且正确提供有益的反馈信息
    — 评估符合国家的标准
    — 证明文件是完整的并且是最新的
    — 争议和上诉提交适当的部门处理
    — 对于为保持评估质量而采取的外部措施的建议,应当准确无误地传达给外部审核员。

In addition responsibilities of the internal verifier include:

- carrying out sampling of the assessment process as required in the centre's & agreed action plan

- liaison with the external verifier and gathering information required for administration verification visits

- keeping up to date with developments in competence assessment education and training

Assessor/Verifier training and experience

Internal verifiers need the following qualifications and experience:

- familiarity with the new STCW framework

- familiarity with the training approval procedures used by the national administration

- familiarity with the competence standards being assessed at the centre and the means of assessing competence

Verifiers and assessors must be competent, both at assessment and in the technical area and at the level at which the candidates are to be assessed. The technical competence, in this context, is likely to be met by having substantial experience and qualifications in the appropriate discipline.

Vocational qualifications and experience

Internal verifiers will be appropriately experienced and qualified in the field covered by the qualification. Their experience should be recent and up to date.

An example of approval of training schools with approved courses may be found in the USCG Title 46 regulations that are reproduced below.

TITLE 46—SHIPPING
CHAPTER I—COAST GUARD, DEPARTMENT OF TRANSPORTATION
PART 10—LICENSING OF MARITIME PERSONNEL—Table of Contents

Subpart C—Training Schools with Approved Courses
Sec. 10.302 **Course approval.**

1. The Coast Guard only approves courses satisfying regulatory requirements. The owner or operator of a training school desiring to have a course approved by the Coast Guard shall submit a written request through the appropriate Officer in Charge, Marine Inspection to the Director, National Maritime Center, NMC-4B, 4200 Wilson Boulevard, Suite 510, Arlington, VA 22203-1804, that contains:

此外,内部审核员的责任包括:

- 按照评估中心的要求和预先确定的活动计划随机抽查评估过程

- 联系外部审核员以及收集主管机关审核要求的资料

- 了解最新的适任评估教育和培训发展

评估员/审核员的培训和经验

内部审核员需要有以下的资格和经验:

- 熟悉新的STCW公约的状况

- 熟悉国家主管机关使用的培训的批准程序

- 熟悉评估中心的评估适任标准以及评估的方式

审核员和评估员必须具备与申请人要评估的级别相对应的评估和技术领域方面的能力。对于技术适任能力的要求是指达到对应学科所要求的充分的经验和资格。

职业资格和经验

内部审核员应在要求的范围内具有适当的经验并且具备资格。而且,他们的经验应当是新近的。

批准开设认可课程的培训学校的例子可以参照以下介绍的美国海岸警卫队卷46的规则。

书目46——航运
第I章——海岸警卫队,运输部
第10部分——航运人员的证书——内容目录

第C子部分——有认可课程的培训学校
10.302节 课程认可

1. 海岸警卫队仅批准满足规则要求的课程。希望某课程得到海岸警卫队认可的培训学校,其所有人或经营者应当通过负责海上检查的适当官员提交一份书面申请给国家海事中心的负责人。地址(略),申请内容包括:

a. A list of the curriculum including a description of and the number of classroom hours required in each subject;

b. A description of the facility and equipment;

c. A list of instructors including the experience, background, and the qualifications of each; and

d. Specify the Coast Guard training requirements the course is intended to satisfy.

2. The Coast Guard notifies each applicant in writing whether or not an approval is granted. If a request for approval is denied, the Coast Guard informs the applicant the reasons for the denial and describes what corrections are required for an approval.

3. Unless sooner surrendered, suspended or revoked, an approval for a course at a training school that meets Coast Guard standards expires 24 months after the month in which it is issued, or on the date of any change in the ownership of the school for which it was issued, whichever occurs first.

4. If the owner or operator of a training school desires to have a course approval renewed, they shall submit a written request to the address listed in paragraph (a) of this section. For the request to be approved, the Coast Guard must be satisfied that the content and quality of instruction remain satisfactory. Unless sooner surrendered, suspended or revoked, a renewal of the approval expires 60 months after the month it is issued, or on the date of any change in ownership of the school for which it is issued, whichever occurs first.

GUIDELINES FOR SITE ACCEPTANCE FOR COAST GUARD APPROVED COURSES

46 CFR 10.303 requires each school with an approved course to have a well maintained facility that accommodates the students in a safe and comfortable environment conducive to learning. To prevent classroom overcrowding the following guidelines apply to all classroom facilities at primary and alternate, or satellite, locations.

- The maximum number of students allowed at a training facility will be limited to the number permitted in the original Coast Guard course approval, and may be further limited by the physical size of the training facility or classroom.

- To assist in the determination of suitability of training facilities, the OCMI should obtain a site plan for each training site or facility location. The site plan must show the arrangement of student's desks, instructor's area, training aids placement, aisles, doors and fire exits. If the classes are to be held in a local alternate training site or facility not indicated in the original Course Approval, the site plan should be accompanied by marketing brochures or other reliable information, such as signed copies of contracts, to support the information set forth in the site plan.

a. 课程目录,包括每个科目的说明和所要求的课时数量;

b. 设施和设备的说明;

c. 教员名单,包括每位教员的经验、背景和资格;及

d. 载明此课程所要达到的海岸警卫队的培训要求。

2. 海岸警卫队书面通知申请人申请是否获得批准。如果未获批准,海岸警卫队应告知申请人未获批准的原因以及说明为获批准要求改正的内容。

3. 除非即将放弃、终止或撤销,符合海岸警卫队标准的培训学校课程的认可有效期为24个月,有效期自签发日期第2个月,或者自学校所有权的变动获得认可之日算起,以较早的日期为准。

4. 如果一所培训学校的所有人或管理人想要更新其课程批准,他们需要向本节(a)段中所列的地址提交书面申请。为获得申请,其教育内容和质量必须始终令海岸警卫队满意。除非即将放弃、终止或撤销,更新的批准会在批准后下一个月,或者自学校所有权的变动获得认可之日算起到第60个月过期,以较早的日期为准。

海岸警卫队认可课程培训点的指南

46 CFR 10.303要求获得认可课程的每所学校具备维护良好的设施,从而有助于学生在安全和舒适的环境中学习。为了避免教室过于拥挤,所有主要的、供替换的或附属的场所的教室设施应满足以下指南。

■ 培训设施可容纳的最多学员人数受海岸警卫队最初批准数量的限制,并可能还受培训设施或教室的限制。

■ 为有助于确定培训设施的合适性,OCMI应当向每个培训点或设施所在地索取一份场地平面图。场地平面图必须展示学员课桌的安排、教员的位置、培训设备安放的位置、过道、门和消防通道。如果在当地的备用培训场地或不在原始批准课程指定的设施开展培训课程,场地平面图应附上说明或其他可靠资料,比如签署合同的复印件等支持材料。

■ The following guidelines for determining the maximum number of students permitted for any classroom or training facility where crowding of students is a concern are based, in part, on existing DOD guidelines for classroom space requirements.

— AREA. A minimum area of 36ft^2 per student is required after deducting the minimum area of 72ft^2 for the instructor.

EXAMPLE: A request is made to conduct training in a local hotel conference room measuring 900 square feet.

The site plan area is:	900 ft^2
deduct (instructor area)	−72 ft^2
usable student area	828 ft^2

Dividing the student area of 828 ft^2 by 36 ft^2/student, the maximum number of students permitted in the class would be 23 students.

— TABLES. In courses incorporating practical work, such as nautical chart work, each student must have sufficient table space to use the equipment, publications and/or charts without folding or overlapping another student's chart or publications. An acceptable chart table should be five feet by two and one half feet as a minimum (folding tables are acceptable).

Unless superseded by local code, the set up of tables and chairs should include aisle space between rows of desks of no less then 2.5 feet. Perimeter aisles should be no less than 3 feet wide.

■ Schools requesting approval to conduct approved training at an alternate site or facility must request, in writing, approval from the OCMI in the zone in which the alternate site is located. Schools making requests for alternate site approval should include in the letter of request:

a. The names and starting dates of the courses to be offered;

b. Class schedules for the classes to be offered;

c. A list of the instructors who will be teaching the classes; and,

d. The address and telephone number of the central location where student records are kept and where the validity of an individual student and/or instructor's certification can be validated.

■ 下列指南给出任何教室或设备允许容纳的最大学员数,主要根据现有的DOD指南中教室空间要求考虑学员的拥挤程度。

— 面积。要求每个学员最小面积为36 ft²,在减去的基础上教员最小面积72 ft²。

例子:要求在当地宾馆一间面积为900 ft²的会议厅进行培训。

场地平面图面积：   900 ft²

减去(教员位置)   -72 ft²

可用学员面积   828 ft²

用学员总面积828 ft²除以36 ft²/学员,得出此班级最大允许学员数为23名。

— 桌子。对于需要进行实操作业的课程,比如海图作业,每个学员必须有足够桌子面积来使用工具、出版物和/或海图,而不会折叠或者覆盖其他学员的海图或出版物。允许的海图桌最小尺寸应当为5英尺长、2.5英尺宽(允许使用折叠桌)。

除非当地法规另有规定,桌子和椅子的布置应当包括每排桌子的行距,不小于2.5英尺。周围的过道应当不小于3英尺。

■ 请求获准在一个备用场所或设施进行认可培训的学校必须以书面申请备用场地所在区域的OCMI的批准。学校请求批准使用备用场所的申请书里应当包括:

a. 开设课程的名称和开课日期;

b. 开课班级的课程安排表;

c. 教授课程的教员名单;及

d. 保存学员记录和可以确认学员和/或教员的证书有效性的监管中心的地址和电话号码。

Table of Competence for Assessors

column 1 competence	column 2 knowledge, understanding and proficiency
1 Identify and recognise the purpose of competence assessment according to STCW 95.	Understanding of the purpose of in-service training outlined in STCW 95. Knowledge of the requirements in STCW 95 Regulation 1/6. Understanding the Assessor function. Proficiency in using the STCW 95 standard of competence tables. Understanding the meaning of competence in the context of job performance.
2 Adapt, schedule and maintain plans for in-service assessment.	Proficiency in the development and usage of checklists. Proficiency in sharing information with instructors and supervisors regarding trainee progress and improvements of training/assessment processes. Understanding the usage of assessment criteria's as input for training purposes. Understanding the importance of a uniform system where objective evidence can be obtained. Knowledge and understanding of additional requirements from a Company training policy.
3 Identify, observe and maintain high grade of objectivity.	Understanding the necessity to create a good relation to the trainee without being patronizing. Proficiency in respect of individuals, with focus on support and encouragement of the trainee's professional progress. Proficiency of handling comradeship in a ship's complement. Proficiency in performing assessment with pride and professionalism.
4 Plan and conduct processes for job performance assessment using appropriate methods.	Understanding the necessity of explaining the purpose of the assessment to the trainee. Knowledge of basic interview technique. Understanding the importance of constructive feedback. Proficiency in setting general conditions, assessment criteria and time limits for an assessment. Understanding the phases before and after an assessment. Proficiency in using, but not limited to, all of the following methods: ■ observation of work activities ■ skills/proficiency/competency tests ■ projects and assignments ■ written questioning techniques ■ oral questioning techniques ■ computer-based questioning techniques

评估员职能表

第1栏	第2栏
适任	知识、理解和熟练
1. 按照STCW 95公约的要求明确和了解适任评估的目的。	对STCW 95公约规定的在职培训目的的理解。 STCW 95公约规则Ⅰ/6要求的知识。 理解评估员的职能。 熟练使用STCW 95公约适任标准表。 理解在履行工作时适任的含义。
2. 为在职评估编制、预设和维护计划。	熟练制作和使用核查表。 熟练与教员和监督员共享有关学员进步和培训/评估过程改善的资料。 理解如何将评估标准纳入培训目标。 理解能够获得客观证据的统一系统的重要性。 公司培训方针额外要求的知识和理解。
3. 确定、观察和保持高度客观性。	理解与学员创造良好平等关系的必要性。 熟悉学员个人的情况,同时关注对学员专业进步的支持和鼓励。 熟练处理船上同事之间的关系。 自信和专业地熟练履行评估工作。
4. 应用适当的方法策划和指导针对工作表现的评估过程。	理解向学员解释评估目的的必要性。 面试技巧的基本知识。 理解有益反馈的重要性。 熟练为评估设定的整体条件、评估标准和时间限制。 理解评估前后使用的措辞。 熟练应用,但并不仅限于下列所有的方法: ■ 工作表现的考察 ■ 技能/熟练/适任测试 ■ 计划和分配 ■ 书面提问技巧 ■ 口头提问技巧 ■ 运用电脑的提问技巧

column 1	column 2
competence	knowledge, understanding and proficiency
5 Recognise and use constructive feedback.	Proficiency in how to encourage the trainee's progress. Understanding of how differences in culture/nationality can affect the trainee's views of assessment and perception of feedback. Proficiency in giving positive and negative criticism in a constructive way.
6 Collect and document sufficient, valid and reliable evidence.	Proficiency in usage of various Training Record Books or similar documentation. Proficiency in documenting sufficient notes supporting evaluation results. Proficiency in judgement of unsuccessful or unacceptable performance and handling thereof.

第1栏	第2栏
适任	知识、理解和熟练
5. 判断和使用有益的反馈信息。	熟练如何鼓励学员进步。 理解文化/国际差异是如何影响学员对评估工作的看法和对反馈信息的理解。 熟练采用有益的方式提供正反面的评价。
6. 收集和证实充分的、有效的和可靠的证据。	熟练使用各种培训记录簿或类似的文件。 熟练使用充分的记录来证明评价成绩。 熟练判断失败的或不可接受的表现和决定随后的恰当处理。

Part 9
Approved Training

Specification of standards

1. The information typically required for application for approval of courses and training providers is discussed in the paragraphs that follow.

2. By issuing a certificate of competency or other qualification required by national or international requirements, the Administration is certifying that the holder has, amongst other things, met the requirements for training and examination. It is, therefore, necessary to have a procedure for monitoring training courses, particularly where the training establishment also conducts the assessments to determine whether a trainee has satisfied the requirements or not.

3. A further consideration is the need to define the minimum acceptable standard of training for all trainees. In the absence of well-defined guidelines, a training provider may fall short of the minimum acceptable standards because it has nothing against which to judge its performance.

4. To promote uniform national standards of training at all locations, specifications of standards should be produced for training courses leading to, or forming part of, required international or national qualifications. The items to be covered by the specification will depend, to some extent, upon the nature of the training but would normally include some or all of the following:

    .1 facilities related to the intended number of trainees;

    .2 equipment;

    .3 staff qualifications and experience;

    .4 entry standards of the trainees;

    .5 course programme and syllabus; and

    .6 minimum performance standards for the issue of a document attesting successful completion.

第9章
认可的培训

标准说明

1. 以下段落讨论的是申请认可课程和培训机构时要求的一般资料。

2. 主管机关通过按国家或国际的要求签发适任证书或其他资格证书以证明持有者达到培训和考试的要求。因此有必要为培训课程制定一个监督程序,特别是在培训机构也实施评估以决定学员是否已经达到发证要求的情况下更应如此。

3. 需要进一步考虑的是确定所有学员的可接受最低培训标准。在没有清晰指南的情况下,培训机构可能达不到可接受的最低标准,因为没有可以用于判断的对照标准。

4. 为促使各地采用统一的国家培训标准,应当就完全或部分针对国际或国家资格的培训课程的标准制定详细说明。详细说明涉及的内容,在某种程度上取决于培训的性质,但通常包括以下列出的一些或全部内容:

   .1 与计划学员人数有关的设施;

   .2 设备;

   .3 人员的资格和经验;

   .4 学员的入学标准;

   .5 课程计划和大纲;及

   .6 签发完成课程证明文件要求的最低操作标准。

5. Specifications of equipment should be stated in terms of the required performance, not by the make of equipment. Where international or national performance standards exist, it may be sufficient to stipulate that equipment can perform in accordance with those standards, although some modification may be necessary or acceptable in the case of simulators. When specifications are drawn up or revised, account should be taken of the latest equipment in use on board ships, so that establishments buying equipment for the first time, or replacing old equipment, will be up to date. Because of the high capital expenditure involved in the provision of simulators, machinery and electronic apparatus, training establishments find it difficult to justify the replacement of a piece of equipment while it is still in good working order. When specifications are revised, consideration should be given to continuing the approval of existing equipment until such time as replacement would normally be expected. The existence of specifications can be of considerable help to a training establishment when negotiating with its funding authority for replacement of old equipment.

6. When the use of equipment or special facilities forms a major part of the course, trainee intake limitations should be stipulated to ensure that each trainee has sufficient hands-on experience to meet the objectives of the course. The number of trainees per instructor may also need to be taken into account in courses such as fire fighting, where close supervision is essential for safety reasons.

7. All instructors should be suitably qualified and experienced to teach their subjects. More detailed requirements may be included in the specification for certain courses; for example, personal survival, where the instructor may be required to have undergone special training before taking charge of a course.

8. Entry standards will normally be stipulated to meet the mandatory requirements regarding age, medical fitness, seagoing experience and prior qualifications which all trainees must satisfy. Other non-mandatory standards may also be included where they are considered necessary if trainees are to benefit fully from the course. Minimum educational standards, both general and in specific subjects, may be stated for new entrants to the profession intending to enter courses leading to the issue of a certificate of competency, or a minimum period of seagoing service may be required before taking certain simulator courses. Provision to allow the admission of trainees who do not fully meet such entry requirements, on condition that they undergo extra initial training, can be included in the specifications.

9. A general indication of the course programme and syllabus should be provided, including any specific requirements, such as the minimum number of hours to be spent on particular aspects of the training or topics which must be covered in practical exercises.

The specification could simply state that training should meet the requirements of the relevant section of the 1978 STCW Convention, as amended, or the recommendations in an IMO Assembly resolution, leaving the training provider to develop the details of the course programme and syllabus. Alternatively, a more detailed syllabus could be included in the specifications, possibly by making use of an appropriate IMO model course.

5. 设备规范应涉及性能要求而不是设备本身。如果有国际的或国家的性能标准,则完全可以要求按照这些标准操作设备,但有时在使用模拟器的情况下,对性能标准的修改可能是必要的或可接受的。制定或修改规范时,应当考虑船上使用的最新设备,因此,培训部门首次购买的或用以代替旧设备的设备应是最先进的。由于购买模拟器、机器和电子仪器涉及巨大的费用支出,培训部门会觉得很难提供正当的理由替换运行状态良好的设备。因此,修改规范时,要考虑对现有设备的继续认可直到到达预计的正常替换时间。规范的存在对于培训机构与资助当局协商替换旧的设备有相当大的帮助。

6. 如果设备或特殊仪器的使用是课程的主要部分,应当规定招收学员的名额限制,从而确保每位学员有足够的实践机会以达到课程的目标。对于某些课程,还需要考虑每位教员指导的学员人数,如消防课程出于安全原因必须得到密切监督。

7. 所有的教员应当有适当的资格和经验来教授相应的科目。在某些课程的说明里包括了更加详细的要求;例如,人员救生,要求教员在担任此课程之前必须接受过专门的培训。

8. 通常应当规定入学标准,从而符合有关所有学员必须满足的年龄、健康、海上服务资历和先前资格的强制性要求。如果有必要,可以包括其他非强制性的标准,目的是使学员能学好课程。总体或具体科目的最低的教育标准,或参加某种模拟器课程前可能要求的海上服务资历的最短时间,都可以向为获得适任证书而打算参加此课程的新进学员说明。课程说明可以包括这样的规定:允许接收尚未完全符合入学要求的学员,条件是他们需参加额外的学前培训。

9. 应当提供一份课程计划和大纲的综合说明,包括所有具体的要求,例如,培训的某个特定方面需要的最少时间或实际练习必须包含的内容。

   课程说明可以只是简要说明培训应当符合修订的1978年STCW公约相关部分或IMO大会决议建议的要求,课程计划和大纲的详细内容由培训机构制定。另一方面,课程说明可以包括一份更加详细的大纲,如合适,可以采用一门适当的IMO示范课程作为大纲。

10. If trainees are to be internally assessed or examined, the number and form of examinations or other assessments should be laid down together with guidance on the criteria for successful completion. This guidance may be provided by including specimen papers in the specifications, with an indication of the acceptable minimum performance in each paper and in the examination as a whole. It may also be necessary to specify conditions for the reassessment of trainees who fail all or part of the examinations. Such conditions might include the treatment of partial passes, any requirements for the repetition of course work or the imposition of a minimum interval before re-examination and the circumstances in which referral in a single test may be permitted.

11. The form of certificate or other document to be issued by a training provider, attesting successful completion of a course, must be laid down. The certificate can either be provided by the Administration or, in an agreed form, by the training provider. Procedures for notifying the Administration of the issue of certificates and the requirements for records to be kept by the training provider will need to be drawn up so that verification of qualifications and replacement of lost or destroyed certificates can be dealt with.

Evaluation against standards

12. Training establishments should be required to make formal written application for approval or re-approval of courses leading to required international or national qualifications or which are to be considered equivalent to seagoing service. The application should contain a sufficiently detailed description of facilities, of equipment, of staff and of how the course will be conducted to enable an initial evaluation against specifications to be made. The application should include a detailed syllabus (unless one is laid down in the specifications), the course curriculum and an outline timetable showing the hours allotted to the main topic areas. The names, qualifications and experience of the instructors who will teach each topic area should also be shown.

13. The question of whether there is a need for the course, in the light of the existing provision of similar courses, may arise. That is primarily a matter for the funding authority of the academy or school making the application. Since an academy is unlikely to be able to run a course satisfactorily without support from its funding authority, assurance should be sought that such support exists before considering an application.

14. The need to prepare a detailed written application ensures that a training provider has fully considered all aspects of the implementation of the course, has identified possible difficulties and has dealt with them, and will be ready to run the course if approval is granted. On occasions, an academy may ask for approval of a new course for which no specifications have been published. A similarly detailed application should be submitted to enable the Administration to consider the request.

10. 如果对学员进行内部评估或测验,应当规定测验或其他评估的次数和形式,以及圆满完成课程的标准指南。课程说明应提供包括模拟考题的指南,指明每一模拟题和总体测验可接受的最低操作。有必要载明对于未通过全部或部分考试的学员重新评估的条件。这样的条件可能包括部分内容及格的处理方式、重修课程的所有要求或强制规定的补考最短间隔期,以及允许安排单独测试的条件。

11. 必须编制由培训机构签发的证明圆满完成课程的证书或其他文件的格式。可以由主管机构或由培训机构提供经过批准的证书格式。必须制定对于主管机构的证书签发通知程序和培训机构记录保存的要求,以便用于资格审核和在替换遗失或损坏的证书时查阅。

评价标准

12. 应当要求培训机构提出正式的书面申请,以获得课程的认可或再认可,参加这些课程可取得要求的国际或国内的或被认为等同于海上服务资历的资格。申请书应当包含对设施、设备、人员以及如何实施该课程的充分而详细的说明,从而能据此对将制定的课程说明做出初步评价。申请书应当包括一份详细的课程大纲(除非在课程说明中已包含)、课程表和一个说明主要课程时间分配的概况表。也应当写明教授每门课程的教员的名字、资格和经验。

13. 根据类似课程的现有规定,可能出现是否有必要开设该课程的问题。这对于院校的资助机构或提出申请的学校是一个主要的问题。因为没有院校资助机构的支持院校不可能顺利地开设课程。在考虑申请之前,应当确保得到这样的支持。

14. 需要准备一份详细的书面申请以确保培训机构对课程的实施已经过全面充分的考虑,已经认识到可能遇到的困难并且已经着手处理这些困难,以及一旦申请获得批准即能准备好开课。有时候,院校可能会为未出版课程说明的新课程申请认可,在这种情况下应提交一份相似的详细申请书供主管机关参考。

15. If the application appears satisfactory, a representative of the Administration should arrange to visit the training establishment to inspect the facilities and equipment to ensure that they are adequate for the proposed number of trainees and the particular training to be undertaken. The inspection should determine the number and size of classrooms, laboratories and other facilities for practical training which will be available for the proposed course. Where a course is dependent upon a particular piece of equipment, such as simulator, it should be seen to be working satisfactorily. The arrangements for its maintenance and repair should also be explored.

16. During the visit, discussions should be held with the course organizer and with the instructors involved in teaching the course. This affords an opportunity to question the training provider about any matters in the application which need to be clarified and to make sure that the requirements and expectations of the Administration are known and understood by those who will be involved in the teaching.

    The discussion also permits an evaluation of the preparedness of the staff for implementation of the course. Informal talks with some of the current trainees can be useful in judging the effectiveness of training when dealing with re-approval of an existing course.

17. For major courses which are to be examined by the academy, such as those for certificates of competency, a set of specimen examination papers with model answers and marking schemes should be prepared and agreed between the Administration and the academy. These specimens will serve as a reference against which to compare future papers and marking, so as to maintain a consistent standard of examination despite changes in teaching and examining staff. When external moderators are appointed, copies of the specimen papers and marking schemes should form part of their briefing. The specimen papers may also be published for the information of trainees on the type and level of assessment to expect.

18. Approval for a new course or for a course at a new training provider not previously known to the Administration should be conditional on the successful completion of the first course. This procedure allows for modifications to be made if problems are encountered and for renegotiations with the training provider before extending the approval. The course should be closely monitored by a representative from the training and certification division of the Administration.

Maintenance of standards

19. Recognition of courses is often subject to periodical re-approval, a five-yearly interval being typical. There are several advantages of such a system over an indefinite approval time. An academy knows that it will be accountable to the Administration for its performance through a review of the running of the course since the previous approval. It is convenient to incorporate any major changes (whether in the syllabus or in methods of training needed, as a result of experience with the course or as a result of developments in technology) as part of the process of re-approval. In addition, those changes which have been made since the previous approval can be consolidated.

15. 如果申请书看起来令人满意,应当安排一名主管机关的代表到培训机构检查设施和设备,以确保它们满足计划的学员人数和即将进行的特定培训。这种检查应当确定计划课程的实际培训所需要的教室、实验室和其他设施的数量和规模。如果课程需要特别的设备如模拟器,应保证这些设备能正常运行。同时也应考虑设备的保养和维修。

16. 在考察过程中,应当与课程组织者和课程所涉及的教员进行讨论。这将提供一个向培训机构询问有关申请书中需要澄清的任何问题的机会,以及确保涉及任教的人员知道和理解主管机关的要求和期望。

    这种讨论也提供了评估员为实施课程所做的准备工作的机会。在处理现有课程的再认可时,与正在学习的一些学员进行非正式的谈话,可能对评定培训的有效性有帮助。

17. 对于由院校测试的主要课程,例如那些申请适任证书的课程,应当准备一套得到主管机构和院校的同意的、有示范答案的试卷和评分方案的样本。这些样本将作为将来试卷和评分的参考,以便保持考试具有一个统一的标准,不会因为更换教员和考试人员而受到影响。当指派外部考试监督员时,试卷样本和评分方案应作为给他们的简报材料的组成内容。也可以出版试卷样本,作为不同评估类型和等级学员的资料。

18. 主管机关对新课程或先前不了解的新的培训机构的认可,应当在其圆满完成其首次教学过程或首门课程后再决定。这样的批准程序留有如果遇到问题可以做出修改的余地,并且允许在批准展期之前与培训机构再协商。应当由主管机关的培训和发证部门的代表密切监督课程开展的情况。

标准的维护

19. 应意识到课程通常需要接受定期再认可,定期再认可的间隔期一般为5年。与不定期的认可相比,这样的体系有几方面的优势。院校知道有义务通过审查向主管机关说明课程自上次认可以来的运行情况。将所有的主要改变(根据课程的实践或技术的发展做出的不论是大纲还是培训需要方法方面的改变)作为再认可依据的一部分是合适的。此外,上一次认可以来所做的其他改变也应考虑在内。

20. Course approvals should require notification of changes in essential equipment or of instructors. If changes in the curriculum are proposed, the prior agreement of the Administration should be obtained.

21. The Administration should reserve the right to monitor all or any part of a course without notice. However, it is usual to check with an academy before making a visit to inspect a course in progress, if only to avoid arriving to find that trainees are sitting an assessment or away on a field trip. Members of the Administration sometimes attend short courses as trainees to widen their experience; that provides an excellent opportunity to evaluate the course at the same time.

22. One of the most effective ways to maintain standards in internally assessed courses is through a system of moderation of assessments and examinations. An added advantage is that moderators' reports provide independent evidence of the performance of trainees. Moderators can be drawn from the training and certification division of the Administration or they may be independently appointed persons with suitable qualifications and experience, preferably including some involvement with examining. Their terms of reference and duties should be clearly defined.

    Drafts of all examination papers, marking schemes and other arrangements for assessment should be sent to moderators sufficiently far in advance for changes to be made, if required. They will check the draft papers to see that the content is valid and comprehensive, that questions are unambiguous and that the marking schemes are fair and consistent with general guidelines on marking. Although moderators are usually given the right to substitute a question or questions of their own, they would normally, in the first instance, request the originator of the examination to make changes in questions, or in the allocation of marks, in line with their suggestions. Marked scripts are scrutinized as a check on completeness and consistency of marking and adjustments are made if necessary.

    After each examination, moderators should submit a report to the Administration, commenting on the standards of the papers and the performance of examinees, including any areas of general weakness shown by them. Recommendations regarding future assessments may also be included.

23. Administrations may inspect examination scripts on an occasional basis or as a matter of routine. An inspection of scripts discloses whether the passing grade satisfactorily discriminates between performances which demonstrate competency and those that do not. Failure to discriminate suggests that changes may have taken place in the standard of questions or in the application of marking schemes in subjective tests. The matter should be taken up with the academy concerned. Where a large number of examinees is involved, the scripts chosen for inspection may be confined to the two highest and the two lowest marked papers and marginal cases, such as those within 5% below and above the pass mark, for example.

24. Where the Administration conducts an oral test as part of the overall assessment that is otherwise conducted by the academy, the performance of trainees in the various areas covered by the test will give a good indication of the strengths and weaknesses of the training they have received. The academy should be informed of any area in which weakness is shown generally by trainees presenting themselves for oral tests and be invited to make proposals for strengthening the training in those areas.

20. 课程认可应当要求通报主要设备或教员的变化。如果计划要改变课程体系,应当事先取得主管机关的同意。

21. 主管机关应当保留随时突击检查所有课程或某课程任何部分的权力。然而,为了避免到达现场后才发现学员正在接受评估或出外实习,在去检查正在开课的课程之前通常应与院校联系。主管机关的成员有时可以作为学员参加短期的课程培训以获得更多的体验;这种做法同时为评价课程提供非常好的机会。

22. 保持内部评估标准最有效的方法之一是建立一个评估和考试的监督系统。这样做的附带好处是考试监督员的报告可以提供学员实操的独立证据。可以从主管机关的培训和考试部门选派考试监督员,或单独指派具有合适资格和经验的人员,最好包括参加过监考的人员,并应清楚地说明他们的任期和职责。

应当尽早将为评估准备的所有考卷、评分方案和其他安排的副本送交考试监督员,以便如果要求做出更改可以有足够的时间。考试监督员将检查试卷副本确保内容是有效的和全面的,考题是明晰的,评分方案是公平的,并且与评分总体指南一致。尽管通常授予考试监督员用自己的一个或多个考题替换原来考卷中的考题的权利,但他们一般会首先要求出题者根据他们的建议对考题或分数的分配做出更改。应详细审阅已评分的试卷,对评分的完整性和一致性进行检查,并在有必要时做出调整。

每一门考试结束后,考试监督员应当向主管机关提交一份报告,评价试卷的标准和考生的实操,包括他们在任何方面的总体薄弱环节,也应当包括有关今后评估的建议。

23. 主管机关可以随时或例行检查学员的试题答卷。对试题答卷的检查可以了解及格分数线是否能很好地区分适任或不适任。若不能区分,则认为主观测试中的考题标准或应用的评分方案可能需要改变。这个问题应当引起有关院校的关注。如果涉及的考生人数很多,可选择两份最高分和两份最低分的答卷以及处于临界分数段(例如那些分数在及格线上下5%范围内)的试卷进行检查。

24. 在由主管机关而不是由院校实施的作为整个评估的一部分的口试中,学员在测试中各个方面的表现能很好地表明他们所接受的培训的强度和薄弱环节。主管机关应当将其学员在口试中表现出的总体薄弱环节通告相关院校,并且要求院校做出加强这些方面培训的方案。

25. An explanation should be sought for an unusually high or low pass rate compared with previous years. It is unlikely that training standards will change greatly from one course to the next; although a change in the ability of the particular intake cannot be ruled out, a likely cause of the change in pass rate is a variation of the standard of assessment.

Uniform standards of competence

26. One of the significant features of the 1995 amendments to the STCW Convention is that for the first time precise standards of competence are established relating to the actual ability of seafarers to perform their tasks safely and effectively.

    This is a major advance upon the 1978 Convention which stipulated knowledge requirements, leaving standards of competence largely to be determined by governments.

    If fully implemented these standards will be measurable and so more readily enforced internationally. They should reduce the degree to which governments (and industry) can apply different interpretations to STCW requirements and thus increase the reliance that can be placed on STCW certificates.

Training "Outcomes"

27. The revised Convention places much more emphasis on the outcome of training, i.e. the ability of qualified seafarers to perform their duties competently, irrespective of the content or the length of the training required. This principle is reflected in the newly adopted education, training and seagoing service requirements and the stress that is given to the importance of on board training in particular.

Seagoing service

28. The STCW Convention of 1978 required a long period of seagoing service without setting standards regarding its quality, but permits reductions in the duration of time spent at sea if evidence is provided that a structured on board training programme is being followed.

    The revised Convention, however, establishes an irreducible minimum length of seagoing service that must satisfy certain standards.

29. In addition to meeting the required standards of competence explained below, candidates for certification as navigational watchkeepers will require a minimum of 12 months' seagoing service, including 6 months' supervised bridge watchkeeping, provided that they follow a programme of structured in-service training approved by their government: in other words, a programme approved by the government to ensure that trainees actually practise and demonstrate their competence to perform the particular tasks and duties that will be required of them when they are qualified.

    If, however, a structured on board training programme is not followed then 3 years' seagoing service will be required.

25. 如果与往年的通过率相比较时发现有异常的高或低的情况,应当对此做出解释。一门课程从一次培训到下一次培训的标准不太可能发生巨大的改变;尽管不能排除学员的能力会有变化,然而通过率改变的最可能原因是评估标准的改变。

适任标准的统一

26. STCW公约1995年修正案最有意义的特征之一是,首次制定了关于海员安全和有效地履行自己工作的实际能力的详细适任标准。

    与主要由各国政府规定知识要求及适任标准的1978年公约相比,此举是一大的进步。

    如果得到完全贯彻,这些标准将是可评测的并更具有国际有效性。这些标准应使政府(和行业)能够对STCW公约要求应用不同的解释的程度降低,从而增强对STCW证书的信任。

培训"效果"

27. 修订的公约更加强调培训的效果,如不管培训要求的内容或时间如何安排,合格海员必须具备履行职责的能力。新通过的对教育、培训和海上服务资历的要求体现了这一原则,对船上培训的要求特别强调了这一原则。

海上服务资历

28. 1978年STCW公约要求长时间的海上服务资历而没有制定关于海上服务资历质量的标准,但是,只要提供证据证明参加了有组织的船上培训计划则允许减少海上服务时间。

    然而,修订的公约规定了不可减少的最低的必须符合某些标准的海上服务资历。

29. 除须符合下列解释中要求的适任标准以外,要求航行值班员的证书申请人具有最低12个月的海上服务资历,包括6个月的驾驶台值班管理,前提是他们参加过一个经过他们的政府认可的有组织的在职培训的计划:即经过政府认可的确保学员确实能够在特定工作和职责中实际运用和展示他们有能力履行适任要求的计划。

    然而,如果没有参加过有组织的船上培训计划则要求具有3年的海上服务资历。

30. For engineer watchkeepers six months' seagoing service in the engine department will be required, although as part of 30 months' education and training approved by the government, which must include workshop skills.

31. The revised Convention stipulates that approved seagoing service for deck officers and engineer officers will have to be recorded in a training record book approved by the government. The footnotes to the amended text refer to the ISF Training Record Books for deck and engine cadets as a model for such documentation.

Approach adopted for Development of Standards of Competence

32. The approach adopted to develop precise standards of competence relevant to all of the safety and pollution prevention tasks that must be performed on board a ship comprises the following elements:

"Competences"

33. All of the individual tasks and skills required to operate a ship have been identified and grouped together as "competences" which represent small practical units of ability that can be readily assessed.

    For example, the competence of being able "to plan and conduct a voyage and determine position" comprises tasks and skills using:

    1. celestial navigation

        — terrestrial and coastal navigation

        — electronic position fixing systems

        — echo sounders

        — compasses

        — steering control systems

        — meteorological information.

"Functions"

34. Competences for all of the tasks, duties and responsibilities that need to be performed on board have been grouped together to form self-contained shipboard functions.

    For example, the function of "Navigation at the operational level" comprises the competences necessary to:

    — plan and conduct a passage and determine a position

    — maintain a safe navigational watch

30. 要求轮机值班员具有在机舱 6 个月的海上服务资历,尽管这种资历可以是政府认可的 30 个月的教育和培训的一部分,但其中必须包括车间工作技能训练。

31. 修订的公约规定必须将甲板高级船员和轮机高级船员认可的海上服务资历记录在政府认可的培训记录簿里。对修订内容的脚注参阅国际航运联合会(ISF)甲板和轮机实习生培训记录簿,其作为这种证明文件的范本。

制定适任标准的方法

32. 制定详细的有关船上必须履行的所有安全和防污工作的适任标准采用的步骤包括以下的要素:

"适任"

33. 将操作船舶所要求的所有个人的任务和技能明确归纳为"适任","适任"用能力的最小实际单位体现,并随时可以接受评估。

    例如,"计划并进行航行和定位"的适任能力包括执行和运用下列的任务和技能:

    1. 天文航海

        — 地文航海和沿海航行

        — 电子定位系统

        — 回声测深仪

        — 罗经

        — 操舵控制系统

        — 气象资料

"职能"

34. 已经将船上需要履行的任务、职责和责任的适任归纳组成为独立的船上职能。

    例如,"航行(操作级)"的职能包括的必要适任:

    — 计划并进行航行和定位

    — 保持安全的航行值班

- use radar and ARPA

- respond to emergencies

- respond to distress signals

- use English language

- transmit and receive information by signalling

- manoeuvre the ship

35. Functions identify more distinct groups of skills, abilities and responsibilities than those established by conventional departmental divisions which form the basis of standards in the present Convention. In total, the revised Convention defines standards of competence for seven functions:

   - Navigation

   - Cargo handling and stowage

   - Controlling the operation of the ship and care for persons on board

   - Marine engineering

   - Electrical, electronic and control engineering

   - Maintenance and repair

   - Radiocommunications

36. The standards of competence that need to be achieved for each of these functions are defined at three levels of responsibility, which are explained in the new Convention in Section A-I/1 paragraph 1.2, 1.3 and 1.4.

   The management level thus corresponds with senior officers, the operational level with junior officers and the support level with ratings.

Specification of Standards of Competence

37. The standards of competence specified in the revised Convention relate to the outcome of training, in addition to the content of the training itself. These standards are presented in detailed Competency Tables throughout Part A of the STCW Code. The standards relating to specified competences are grouped together to form functions at different levels of responsibility as described above.

   An extract from one of these STCW Competency Tables is shown below as an example. It specifies part of one of the minimum standards of competence for the function of "Navigation at the operational level". The competence specified is "Plan and conduct a passage and determine position".

— 使用雷达和自动雷达标绘仪

— 应急反应

— 对遇险信号的反应

— 使用英语

— 用视觉信号发出和接收信息

— 操纵船舶

35. 在目前公约标准的基础上确定的技能、能力和责任的职能组别要比传统管理部门确定的更明确。修订的公约将所有适任标准归纳为七个职能：

— 航行

— 货物装卸和积载

— 船上作业管理和人员管理

— 船舶轮机

— 电气、电子和控制工程

— 维护和修理

— 无线电通信

36. 对于上述每个职能需要达到的适任标准，新公约A部分-I/1节第1.2、1.3和1.4段分别对三个责任级别进行了解释。

因此，管理级对应高职高级船员，操作级对应低职高级船员，支持级对应普通船员。

适任标准的说明

37. 修订的公约规定的适任标准与培训的效果和培训的内容有关。STCW规则整个A部分用详细的适任表列明了这些标准，并将与规定的适任能力有关的标准归纳为上述的不同的责任级别的职能。

以下的例子摘自STCW适任表。它列明了"航行（操作级）"职能的一部分最低适任标准。规定的适任项目是"计划并进行航行和定位"。

Unlike the present Convention, which only specifies knowledge required by candidates for certification, the new Competency Tables specify detailed criteria for each element of competence to be achieved. Referring to the Table below, these criteria include:

1. knowledge, understanding and proficiency (column 2)

— methods for demonstrating that competence has been achieved (column 3)

— criteria for evaluating the competence (column 4)

The format of the Competency Tables used for all of the other functions, as well as for special competence requirements such as advanced fire fighting or medical care, is consistent throughout the STCW Code.

Table A-II/1 [extract]

Specification of minimum standard of competence for officers in charge of a navigational watch on ships of 500 gross tonnage or more

Function: Navigation at the operational level

Column 1	Column 2	Column 3	Column 4
COMPETENCE	KNOWLEDGE, UNDERSTANDING AND PROFICIENCY	METHODS FOR DEMONSTRATING COMPETENCE	CRITERIA FOR EVALUATING COMPETENCE
Plan and conduct a passage and determine position	*Celestial Navigation* Ability to use celestial bodies to determine the ship's position *Terrestrial and Coastal Navigation* Ability to determine the ship's position by use of: .1 landmarks .2 aids to navigation, including lighthouses, beacons and buoys .3 dead reckoning, taking into account winds, tides, currents and estimated speed Thorough knowledge of and ability to use navigational charts and publications, such as sailing directions, tide tables, notices to mariners, radio navigational warnings and ships' routeing information. NOTE: ECDIS systems are considered to be included under the term "charts".	Examination and assessment of evidence obtained from one or more of the following: .1 approved in-service experience .2 approved training ship experience .3 approved simulator training, where appropriate .4 approved laboratory equipment training. using: chart catalogues, charts, navigational publications, radio navigational warnings, sextant, azimuth mirror, electronic navigation equipment, echo sounding equipment, compass	The information obtained from navigational charts and publications is relevant, interpreted correctly and properly applied. All potential navigational hazards are accurately identified. The primary method of fixing the ship's position is the most appropriate to the prevailing circumstances and conditions. The position is determined within the limits of acceptable instrument/system errors. The reliability of the information obtained from the primary method of position fixing is checked at appropriate intervals. Calculations and measurements of navigational information are accurate. The charts selected are the largest scale suitable for the area of navigation and charts and publications are corrected in accordance with the latest information available.

以前的公约只规定了证书申请人具备的知识要求,与之不同的是,新的适任表列明达到每个适任要素详细的标准。参照下列的表格,这些标准包括:

1. 知识、理解和熟练(第2栏)

— 表明已经满足适任的方法(第3栏)

— 评价适任的标准(第4栏)

STCW规则始终用统一格式的适任表说明所有的职能以及特殊的适任如高级消防或医护的适任要求。

表A-Ⅱ/1(节选)

500总吨或以上船舶负责航行值班的
高级船员的最低适任标准说明

职能:航行操作级

第1栏	第2栏	第3栏	第4栏
适任	知识、理解和熟练	表明适任的方法	评价适任的标准
计划并进行航行和定位	天文航海 能利用天体确定船位 地文航海和沿海航行 能利用下列条件确定船位: .1 陆标 .2 灯塔、立标和浮标等助航标志 .3 考虑风、潮汐、水流和估计航速下的航迹推算 使用诸如航路指南、潮汐表、航海通告、无线电航行警告和船舶定线资料等的全面知识和能力。 注:ECDIS系统被认为包括在"海图"一词中。	从下列一项或数项获取的考试和评估证据: .1 认可的工作经历 .2 认可的实习船经历 .3 如合适,认可的模拟器培训 .4 认可的实验室设备培训 使用:海图目录、海图、航海出版物、无线电航行警告、六分仪、方位镜、电子导航设备、回声测深仪、罗经	从海图和航海出版物获取的信息是恰当的,并能正确地解释和正确地应用这些信息,准确识别所有潜在的航行危险。 主要定位方法最适合于当时环境和条件。 确定的船位在认可的仪器/系统误差限度内。 以适当的时间间隔核查从基本定位方法获得的资料的可信性。 航海信息的计算和测量是精确的。 所选的海图是适合于航行区域的最大比例尺的,并且海图和航海图书是根据船上可用的最新资料进行了改正的。

Criteria for defining Competence

38. As explained above, the detailed criteria for defining competence are:

    Knowledge, understanding and proficiency

    Although the Competency Tables in the STCW Code will place greater emphasis on proficiency and the actual ability of seafarers to perform their tasks satisfactorily, the need for the acquisition of necessary academic knowledge is not eliminated.

    In general, the basic knowledge and skills expected of seafarers under the revised Convention are not fundamentally changed. However, the knowledge that underpins most maritime skills is now clearly allied to the practical skills necessary to carry out tasks safely and efficiently.

Methods for demonstrating competence

39. Depending on the particular competence, the methods specified for its demonstration will vary, but in addition to using specific, relevant reference materials—for example nautical charts to demonstrate the ability to plan a passage—demonstration methods frequently include examination and/or assessment of evidence obtained from approved in-service training and simulator training.

In-service training and assessment

40. In addition to the requirements mentioned above, which attach special importance to the need for on board training to be documented in a training record book, the revised Convention contains new provisions regarding the qualifications of instructors and assessors, including a requirement that they are qualified for the specific task for which the training or assessment is being conducted.

    Training providers, in particular, will need to anticipate the implications of these requirements concerning the qualifications of instructors. These provisions will also be relevant to personnel on board such as junior officers with responsibility for supervising the completion of cadets' training record books.

Simulator training

41. The revised Convention contains extensive mandatory requirements and guidance concerning performance standards for simulators, although equipment in use before 1 February 2002 may be exempted from such standards.

    The use of radar and ARPA simulators in training and as a method of demonstrating competence will be a mandatory requirement for watchkeepers in the deck department.

定义适任的标准

38. 如上述说明,适任的详细标准的定义是:

知识、理解和熟练

尽管STCW规则的适任表更为强调熟练和海员按要求履行任务的实际能力,但不能因此减少获得必要的理论知识的需要。

修订的公约对海员的基本知识和技能的总体要求基本上没有改变。然而,现在明确地加强了将大部分海上技术知识与安全和有效地履行任务所必需的实际技能相结合。

表明适任的方法

39. 表明适任的方法根据不同的特定适任内容而变化,但是,除了使用专门的、相关的参考资料(例如,使用海图表明航线设计的能力)表明适任的方法,通常还包括来自认可的在职培训和模拟器培训考试和/或评估的证据。

在职培训和评估

40. 除了以上提及的、需要存档于记录簿的、与船上培训有特别重要关系的要求,修订的公约还包含了关于教员和评估员资格的新条款,包括要求他们具备实施特定培训或评估任务的资格。

培训机构尤其需要预先理解涉及教员资格的这些要求的含义。这些条款也与船上人员,如负责监督实习生培训记录簿填写的较低职别的高级船员有关。

模拟器培训

41. 修订的公约包含大量关于指导模拟器的强制性要求和性能标准,然而2002年1月前已经使用的设备可以不受该标准的限制。

在培训中使用雷达和ARPA模拟器以及将其作为展示适任的设备对于甲板部的值班员来说是强制性的要求之一。

Assessment criteria

42. The criteria specified in the competence tables of part A of the STCW Code have to be used in the assessment of all competences listed in column 1 of those tables. No competence table is provided in respect of the special training requirements for personnel on tankers and on ro-ro passenger ships.

Examinations

43. The examinations required under the Convention have to assess the knowledge, understanding and proficiency of each candidate against those specified in the competence table and have to clearly demonstrate or confirm that the candidate has the abilities, skills and competence required.

On-board assessment

44. Any assessment of competency required under the Convention that is performed on board ship has to be carried out under the immediate supervision of an assessor duly qualified as required by regulation I/6, recorded as required by the provisions of regulation I/14 and entered in the seafarer's training record book or similar document as may be appropriate.

Practical test

45. Any practical test required under the Convention is required to be carried out under the immediate supervision of an assessor duly qualified as required by regulation I/6, recorded as required by the provisions of regulation I/14 and entered in the seafarer's training record book or similar document as may be appropriate.

Evaluating competence

46. The competency tables in the STCW Code contain specific criteria for evaluating competence which relate to the actual ability required by a seafarer to perform his or her job effectively.

   For example, in addition to absorbing knowledge concerning the theories and factors affecting trim and stability, a candidate seeking to qualify in the function of "Controlling the operation of the ship and care of the persons on board" will be required, according to the evaluation criteria, to demonstrate an ability to maintain stability and stress conditions within safety limits at all times.

Criteria for evaluating competence

47. Criteria for evaluating competence are provided in respect of each competence item identified in the competence tables of STCW Code chapters II, III, IV and VI. At present these criteria are qualitative and should be interpreted on the basis of established good practice. The continuing application of new and improved technology to shipping requires frequent review and adjustment of current practices so as to take advantage of any resulting improvement in accuracy or safety margins. Assessors should therefore make an effort to keep their own knowledge of current good practice up to date.

评估标准

42. STCW规则A部分适任表规定的标准必须应用于适任表第1栏列出的所有适任评估。对于液货船和滚装客船上人员的特殊培训要求没有提供适任表。

考试

43. 公约要求的考试必须依照适任表中规定的知识、理解和熟练要求评估每位申请人，并且必须清楚地表明或证实考生具有所要求的能力、技能和资格。

船上评估

44. 公约要求的针对船上适任的任何评估，必须在具备公约规则Ⅰ/6要求的合适资格的评估员的直接监督下实施，必须按照公约规则Ⅰ/14规定的要求记录，并在海员培训记录簿或类似的适当文件中登记。

实操考试

45. 公约要求的所有实操考试，必须在具备公约规则Ⅰ/6要求的合适资格的评估员的直接监督下实施，必须按照公约规则Ⅰ/14规定的要求记录，并在海员培训记录簿或类似的适当文件中登记。

适任评价

46. STCW规则的适任表包含了评价船员有效履行其工作所要求的实际能力的具体标准。

    例如，除了学习关于影响纵倾和稳性的理论和因素的知识以外，还要求希望取得"船舶作业管理和人员管理"职能履行资格的申请人，按照评价标准展示始终在安全界限内保持船舶稳性和强度状况的能力。

适任评价的标准

47. STCW规则第Ⅱ、Ⅲ、Ⅳ和Ⅵ章的适任表规定了各个适任项目的相应适任评价标准。目前，这些标准是定性的并且应当在良好的习惯做法的基础上进行解释。新的和改进的技术在航运中的不断应用要求经常对当前的实际操作进行核查和调整，从而可以利用任何精良或安全的技术进步成果。因此，评估员应当努力使他们自己在良好的习惯做法方面保持最新的知识。

Knowledge, understanding and proficiency

With some exceptions,* such as workshop training for engineer officers and radar simulator training for deck officers, the "knowledge, understanding and proficiency" set out in column 2 of the tables of competence for deck and engineering certificates of competency is in each case a restatement of the syllabus contained in the appendices to the relevant regulations of chapter II or III as adopted in 1978. In other words, the knowledge required for certificates as master, officer, or rating forming part of a watch has not been significantly increased. However, the competence that knowledge is expected to provide is now more clearly defined and the candidate's overall competence is to be focused on when determining fitness to hold the certificate applied for.

Use of automatic radar plotting aids (ARPA) also has been introduced for masters and chief mates and officers in charge of a navigational watch, if the certificate is to be valid for service in ships so equipped. The application of constant rate of turn techniques in navigation and pilotage has also been added.

知识、理解和熟练

除了某些例外情况*，譬如，对轮机高级船员的车间培训和对甲板高级船员的模拟器培训，适任表第2栏中规定的甲板和轮机适任证书的"知识、理解和熟练"，是对1978年公约的第Ⅱ章或第Ⅲ章相关规定的附录中的大纲内容的重新表述。换言之，对于船长、高级船员，或参与值班的普通船员，证书要求的知识并没有显著地增加，然而，现在对适任所需要的知识做出了更加明确的解释，并且在确定持有的申请证书是否恰当时，要强调申请人总体的适任能力。

*公约纳入了在装备有ARPA的船上服务的船长、大副和负责航行值班的高级船员，其证书的有效性应满足ARPA的使用方面的要求，也增加了在航行和引航中应用航行和转向技术的要求。

Part 10
Training and Assessment

Assessment criteria

As mentioned previously, the criteria specified in the competence tables of part A of the STCW Code have to be used in the assessment of all competences listed in column 1 of those tables. No competence table is provided in respect of the special training requirements for personnel on tankers and on ro-ro passenger ships.

The criteria used in evaluating the understanding of tanker personnel of the additional theoretical and practical knowledge required by regulation V/1 should be that all tanker operations involving application of the knowledge concerned are conducted within acceptable limits of safety.

The criteria used in evaluating the ability of ro-ro passenger ship personnel to safely perform the duties and responsibilities specified in section A-V/2 should be that the procedures followed are appropriate and all tasks concerned are correctly performed with due regard to safety and the requirements of table A-V/2.

Where additional training is provided for masters or chief mates of large ships or ships with unusual manoeuvring characteristics, the criteria used should be those applicable to evaluation of the competence to manoeuvre and handle a ship in all conditions set out in table A-II/2.

Where additional training is provided for officers and ratings responsible for cargo handling on ships carrying dangerous and hazardous substances in solid form in bulk or in packaged form, the criteria used should be those applicable to evaluation of competence in the function of cargo handling and stowage at the operational level in table A-II/1 and for the carriage of dangerous cargoes set out in table A-II/2.

Examinations

The examinations required under the Convention have to assess the knowledge, understanding and proficiency of each candidate against those specified in the competence table and have to clearly demonstrate or confirm that the candidate has the abilities, skills and competence required.

The form of examination used should be that best suited to evaluate the competence concerned and may involve the written, oral or practical demonstration of knowledge, understanding, skill or ability. Written examinations may be of the precis type or be in one or more of the so-called objective formats. Objective formats include short-answer, true/false, multiple-choice and coded multiple-choice types. Each format and type of examination has its own strengths and weaknesses. A careful choice should therefore be made from the types and formats of examination that are available. Whatever type of examination system is adopted, strict attention has to be paid to the security of the examination which will not be compromised in any way.

第10章
培训与评估

评估标准

正如前面提到的，STCW规则A部分适任表规定的标准必须在这些适任表第1栏列出的所有适任评估中使用。对于液货船和滚装客船上人员的特殊培训要求没有提供适任表。

评价液货船人员对公约规则 V/1 要求的附加理论和实践知识的标准是：应用所有涉及的有关知识进行的液货船操作，应当在可接受的安全界限内。

评价滚装客船人员安全履行A部分-V/2规定的职责和责任的能力标准是：应当遵循的程序是适当的并且适当地考虑安全和表A-V/2的要求正确地履行所有有关的任务。

如果规定大型船舶或具有特殊操作特性船舶的船长或大副参加附加的培训，使用的标准应当是那些适用于表A-II/2规定的，在所有条件下操纵和操作船舶的适任评估标准的内容。

如果规定高级船员和负责在运载危险和有害固体，散装或包装物质的船上装卸货物的普通船员参加附加的培训，使用的标准应当是适用于表A-II/1中货物装卸和积载（操作级）的职能，以及表A-II/2规定的危险货物运载的适任评估内容。

考试

公约要求的考试必须按照适任表规定的标准评估每位申请人的知识、理解和熟练状况，并且必须能够清楚地展示或证实申请人具有所要求的能力、技能和适任。

使用的考试形式应当最适合评价有关的适任，并且能够以反映知识、理解和技能或能力的书面、口头或实际操作展示。书面考试可以是纲要形式的或者采用一种或多种通常所说的客观题形式。客观题形式包括简答、正确/错误选择、多项选择和编码多项选择等类型。每种考试的形式和类型各有其优点和缺点。因此，要仔细选择这些考试类型和形式。不论采纳何种考试系统，必须严格注意试卷的保密，确保不会出现任何方式的泄密。

In setting pass marks or levels of acceptable performance, the potential impact that errors made may have on safety of life, property and the environment has to be taken into account and the score value of questions and responses weighted accordingly. Allowance should also be made for candidates guessing the best responses to multiple-choice questions by increasing the pass levels required or by deducting marks for wrong responses.

The assessment, test or examination results of those candidates who marginally achieve or marginally fail to achieve the required standard should be carefully reviewed and a second opinion obtained in case of doubt. The governing concern in all cases has to be the safety of life, property and the environment.

Familiarization training

The purpose of the familiarization training required by regulation VI/1 is to ensure that all persons on board other than passengers are able to react to an emergency in a calm, orderly and reasonably informed way so that they can make their way to muster stations or emergency assembly areas without assistance. This requirement applies to all on board, including, for example, hairdressers, manicurists and entertainers. No exception is permitted other than that set out in section A-VI/1, paragraph 3. The objective is to allow those members of the ship's complement designated to perform safety or pollution-prevention duties in the operation of the ship to concentrate on safeguarding the lives and well-being of passengers and protecting the safety of the ship, property and the environment.

On-board assessment

Assessment of competency for certification that is performed on board ship has to be carried out under the immediate supervision of an assessor duly qualified as required by regulation I/6, recorded as required by the provisions of regulation I/14 and entered in a training record book or similar document as may be appropriate.

Practical test

Any practical test required under the Convention is required to be carried out under the immediate supervision of an assessor duly qualified as required by regulation I/6, recorded as required by the provisions of regulation I/14 and entered in the seafarer's training record book or similar document.

Qualifications of trainers and assessors

Each Party has to ensure that all training and assessments required for certification under the Convention are carried out by persons who themselves are appropriately qualified and experienced and have been trained or instructed as required by section A-I/6 of the Code. This means that all Parties are now required to establish appropriate standards for those carrying out such training or assessments on board ship or ashore. They have to also ensure that these standards are monitored and maintained by all training providers—maritime academies, colleges and in respect of all other training and assessments that may be produced by candidates as evidence of their having met any requirement for certification under the Convention.

在确定及格分数或可接受的实操时,必须考虑操作失误可能对生命安全、财产和环境造成的潜在影响,以及试题的分值和相应的权重。也应当通过提高及格水平的要求或采用答错扣分的措施,允许申请人猜测多项选择的最佳答案。

对于那些勉强达到或达不到要求标准的申请人,应当谨慎复核他们的评估、测验或考试的成绩,若有疑问,应再次评定。在所有情况下,监督过程必须关注生命安全、财产和环境的问题。

熟悉培训

公约规则Ⅵ/1 所要求的熟悉培训的目的是确保除旅客之外的所有船上人员能够对紧急情况做出冷静、有条不紊和合理判断的反应,从而使他们可以无须协助独自到达集合站或应急集合区。这些要求适用于所有船上人员包括例如,理发师、指甲美化师和演艺人员。除了A部分-Ⅵ/1节第3段所述的情况外,不允许有例外情况。该条款的目的是允许船上补充指派的履行安全或防污职责的人员,能专心保护旅客的生命和健康,并且保护船舶、财产和环境的安全。

船上评估

在船上进行的适任证书的评估,必须在符合公约规则Ⅰ/6要求的资格的评估员的直接监督下实施,必须按照公约规则Ⅰ/14规定的要求记录,并在海员培训记录簿或类似的适当文件中登记。

实操测试

公约要求的任何实操测试,必须在符合公约规则Ⅰ/6要求的资格的评估员的直接监督下实施,必须按照公约规则Ⅰ/14规定的要求记录,以及登记在海员培训记录簿或类似的适当文件中。

培训和评估人员的资格

各缔约国要保证由那些具备资格的和有经验的并且接受过本规则A部分-Ⅰ/6节要求的培训或指导的人员按照本公约发证要求实施所有培训和评估。也就是要求所有的缔约国为那些实施船上或岸上培训或评估的人员制定适当的标准。他们还要确保培训举办方如航海教育机构、院校以及所有其他机构为申请人提供的用来证明其已达到本公约发证所有要求的培训和评估项目满足公约要求的标准。

Part 10-1
Introduction to competence-based training

Introduction

The purpose of this chapter is to describe, from a practical viewpoint, some of the concepts underlying a competence-based approach to education and training, as applied to vocational qualifications in the UK and the Merchant Navy in particular.

In one sense, competence-based training is not new. Certificates of competency have been a feature of employment at sea for many years. Excellent education and training programmes have been built around the requirements for the various grades of certificate, which include practical experience at sea and the skills, knowledge and understanding that underpin satisfactory performance of shipboard duties. This does not change in a competency based system. What does change is the way those requirements are defined, in terms of outcomes to be achieved rather than examination syllabuses, and how achievement of the specified outcome is measured or assessed.

The objective is to establish a clearly defined single set of standards of competence recognised by all concerned. Achievement of those standards signals a successful outcome of training.

Why Have Standards?

Competence standards enable:

- an industry to define its competence requirements and training can then be based on these requirements

- training to be responsive to industry needs

- establishment of benchmarks for delivery of training, certification and recognition of individual skills (no matter how through what learning experiences competences are achieved)

What Do Competence Standards Look Like?

The format of a typical set of standards taking those of Australia as an example consist of:

1. Unit title: The title of a general area of competence. (=Function)

2. Unit Descriptor: Optional, assists with clarifying the unit title.

3. Elements: Describe outcomes which contribute to a unit. (=Competence)

4. Performance Criteria: Specify the required level of performance. (=Criteria for evaluating competence)

第10-1章
适任培训介绍

介绍

本章的目的是从实用的观点描述一些关于适任教育和培训方法的理念,这些方法在英国尤其是在其商船队的职业资格教育培训中使用。

在某种意义上,适任培训并不是新举措。适任证书成为海上职业的一个特征已经有很长时间。根据证书不同等级的要求,已经制订了非常好的教育和培训计划,计划也包括提供履行船上职责所需的海上实践经验、技能、知识和理解方面的训练。适任系统的要求并没有改变,改变的是确定这些要求的方法,即根据取得的效果而不是考试大纲来确定是否达到要求,以及如何衡量或评估具体的效果。

目标是制定单独一套定义清楚的、所有相关方面都认可的适任标准。而满足这些标准也就标志着获得成功的培训结果。

为什么要有标准?

适任标准能使:

- 一个行业确定它的适任要求和基于这些要求的培训

- 培训可以反映行业需要

- 制定培训传授、发证和个人能力认可的基准(不管是通过什么学习经历获得的适任)

适任标准的形式是怎样的?

一套选自澳大利亚的适任标准的典型格式包括:

1. 项目名称:适任的整体范围的名称。(=职能)

2. 项目描述:可选择、帮助阐释项目名称。

3. 要素:描述构成项目的各项成绩。(=适任)

4. 表现标准:规定表现的等级。(=评估适任的标准)

5. Range Statement: Range of contexts and conditions to which the performance criteria apply. (not found in Tables of Competences)

6. Evidence Guide: Optional, assists with interpretation and assessment of unit.

COMPETENCY-BASED TRAINING IN AUSTRALIA
Competency-based training (CBT) is concerned with what a person can do as a result of training rather than time spent in training. It focuses on the skills and knowledge an individual has, rather than on how attained them. CBT gives individuals, businesses and industries greater choice and diversity in what, where and how they learn. Whether training is undertaken in a classroom college, workshop, in the workplace or a combination of any or all of these. It can result in a qualification which is recognizable, portable and consistent across the country. What an individual already knows is also taken into account, irrespective of how the knowledge and skills were gained. A CBT system is primarily concerned with ensuring workers are equipped with the skills needed by industry.

WHAT IS COMPETENCY?
The concept of competency focuses on workplace expectations rather than on the actual learning process. It refers to skills and knowledge that can be transferred and applied to new situations and environments.

WHY WAS A CBT SYSTEM INTRODUCED?
During the 1980's there was a growing realisation that the existing vocational education and training system in Australia was not adequately meeting the needs of industry or individuals. The traditional approach to learning, based on the completion of a course after a fixed time and not on actual workplace requirements, was becoming increasingly viewed as too strict and rigid to adequately meet industry and individual needs. As a result, Ministers first endorsed a competency-based approach to training in April 1989. They believed this would be more flexible and give industry a much greater role in identifying and determining the standards and outcomes of training.

In May 1989 a Competency-Based Training Working Party was established to produce an options paper and provide advice on policies for the implementation of CBT and to assist with pilot testing of CBT initiatives. The Working Party produced its final report in August 1993. The report outlines achievements in the implementation of a competency-based system of training.

KEY FEATURES OF A CBT APPROACH
The key features of such a system are that it:
- ▶ is based directly on the skills and abilities required to do a job;
- ▶ takes account of learners' existing level of competency, irrespective of how it was acquired;
- ▶ allows learners to enter and exit training programs at various stages;
- ▶ suits the learner's pace and style of learning;
- ▶ allows training to take place in a variety of settings including workplaces, simulated work environments, and training rooms;
- ▶ allows learners to be assessed when they are ready; and
- ▶ provides learners with a record of the competencies they have achieved.

CBT PROCESSES
A CBT system is made up of a series of linked processes including:
- ▶ the development of competency standards, based on industry and enterprise standards;
- ▶ training package development and endorsement;
- ▶ training delivery;
- ▶ assessment; and
- ▶ certification.

Achievement of competency by meeting the relevant standards, irrespective of how they have been acquired, results in a credential, or statement of attainment.

5. 综合说明:应用表现标准的背景和条件。(在适任表中没有给出)

6. 证据指导:可选择、帮助解释和评估该项目。

澳大利亚的适任培训

适任培训(CBT)关注的是一个人经过培训后能够做什么,而不是花费在培训中的时间。它强调个人具有的技能和知识,而不是如何获得这些技能和知识。CBT给个人、职业和行业在学习什么、在哪里学习、如何学习提供更多的选择和变化。无论培训是在学校的教室、车间、工作现场或任何场所或在所有的场所结合开展,都能够获得全国公认的、便利的和一致的资格。也考虑了被评估人已经具备的,不论用什么方法获得的知识和技能。CBT系统主要关注的是保证工作人员具备行业需要的技能。

何谓适任?

适任的概念关注的是工作实际的要求,而不是学习的过程。它是指可以转换和应用于新形式和环境的技能和知识。

为什么介绍CBT系统?

1980年代,人们逐渐意识到澳大利亚当时的职业教育和培训系统无法满足行业和个人的需要。传统的学习方法以在固定的时间内完成课程为基础,而不是以工作的要求为基础。这种方法越来越被认为太局限和太刻板,以至于不能满足行业和个人的需要。结果部长们于1989年4月首先认可了基于适任的培训方法。他们相信该方法将更加灵活,并且使行业在明确和决定标准和培训效果的方面发挥更大的作用。

1989年5月成立的适任培训工作组负责拟定一份可选择的草稿和提供实施CBT方针的建议,以及协助CBT最初的试验性测验。工作组于1993年8月拟定出它的总结报告。报告概述实施适任培训系统所取得的成绩。

CBT方法的主要特点

该系统主要的特点是:
- 直接以做某项工作所需要的技能和能力为基础;
- 考虑学员所具备的适任级别,而不论其如何获得;
- 允许学员在各种阶段加入或退出培训;
- 适合学员的学习速度和模式;
- 允许在各种场合包括工作场地、模拟工作环境和培训室进行培训;
- 允许学员充分准备后才对其进行评估;及
- 给学员提供他们所获得的适任记录。

CBT过程

CBT系统由互相联系的一系列过程组成:
- 适任标准的制定以行业和公司的标准为基础;
- 培训方案制定和认可;
- 培训实施;
- 评估;及
- 发证。

通过达到相关的标准取得的适任资格,不论其如何获得,结果都应用证明书或成绩报告书说明。

Competence

Despite familiarity with the system of statutory certificates of competency which have been required for employment at sea for many years, little attention has been given until fairly recently to exactly what competence means. Most people have their own ideas of what it involves and would almost certainly claim to be able to pass subjective judgment on the ability or performance of others as being of an acceptable standard or not. A typical dictionary definition of competence is the condition of being capable; ability; and of competent is having sufficient skill, knowledge etc., capable / suitable or sufficient for the purpose. This is a good starting point. But the notion of sufficiency and fit for purpose might be interpreted as implying a minimalist or narrow approach when applied to qualifications for work. Capability gives a broader meaning but it is important, when considering qualifications that attest to competence, to encompass all aspects of what has been termed occupational competence.

Occupational competence

At the heart of vocational qualifications is the concept of occupational competence:

> *the ability to perform to the standards required in employment across a range of circumstances and to meet changing demands.*

Occupational competence is the bringing together of all the diverse skills, knowledge and abilities needed to ensure that individuals are capable of fulfilling the roles expected of them in the way and to the standards expected in employment. Precise definition is difficult but the main components are:

- Skills, knowledge and understanding that are specific to an occupation.

- More general skills and knowledge.

- Personal effectiveness.

The precise definition is not important. What is important is that a broad or holistic view of competence is fostered. This will help to ensure that individuals are assessed to a high standard.

Competence-based qualifications in the UK

Competence-based qualifications are now widely available in all parts of the United Kingdom. Known as National Vocational Qualifications (NVQs) and Scottish Vocational Qualifications (SVQs), they were introduced in 1987 following a major review of qualifications in England and Wales, building on a competence-based system that had previously been launched in Scotland.

适任

　　尽管对于海上工作需要具备法定的适任证书已实施多年，适任的真正含义是什么却很少得到关注。大多数人认为适任就是经过他人对能力表现的主观判定认为已达到认可的标准。一部权威词典指出适任的定义是：具有资格；能力；以及适任是指具有完成任务的适合和充足的技能和知识等。这是定义适任的一个好的开端。但是，充足和适合的概念可能在针对工作资格时被解释得过于局限和狭隘。能力是一个广泛而重要的概念，在考虑证明适任资格时应将职业适任的所有方面包含进去。

职业适任

　　职业资格的核心是职业适任的概念：

　　　　在职业领域的不同环境中以及符合职业变化需要的按要求的标准操作的能力。

　　职业适任是所有各种不同的，确保个人能完成预期工作，以及达到职业标准所需要的技能、知识和能力的总和。很难做出精确的定义，但其主要构成是：

- 相应职业的技能、知识和理解

- 更多的普通技术和知识

- 个人工作效率

　　精确的定义并不重要。重要的是制定一个广阔的或整体的适任概念。这将有助于确保以高标准评估每个人。

英国的适任资格认证

　　现在，在英国各地都能广泛地获得适任资格认证，这种认证称为国家职业资格（NVQ）认证和苏格兰职业资格（SVQ）认证，该体系是在对原先的英格兰和威尔士资格认证体系进行大量研究之后，于1987年引入并在苏格兰早前提出的基于适任体系上建立的。

The review noted the many strengths of the then existing arrangements. These included the high regard in which the standards set by many of the examining and validating bodies and the reliability of their assessment arrangements were held nationally and internationally. But, despite this, the review concluded that there was no effective national system for vocational qualifications. In particular, it was felt that many qualifications did not, at that time, adequately assess or indicate competence. Mostly there was either an assessment of knowledge relating to occupational skills and understanding, with performance taken to mean performance in a written examination, or performance in stated skills was assessed. Neither form of assessment necessarily indicated competence, by which was meant the ability to work effectively in an occupation or range of occupational tasks, and most qualifications failed to give recognition to work-based learning.

Competency specifications

1. Competences are based on an analysis of the professional role(s) and/or a theoretical formulation of professional responsibilities.

2. Competency statements describe outcomes expected from the performance of professionally related functions, or knowledge, skills and attitudes thought to be essential to the performance of those functions.

3. Competency statements facilitate criterion-referenced assessment.

4. Competences are treated as tentative predictors of professional effectiveness and are subjected to continual validation procedures.

5. Competences are specified and made public prior to instruction.

6. Learners completing the CBET programme demonstrate a wide range of competency profiles.

Assessment

13. Competency measures are validly related to competency statements.

14. Competency measures are specific, realistic and sensitive to nuance.

15. Competency measures discriminate on the basis of standards set for competency demonstration.

16. Data provided by competency measures are manageable and useful in decision-making.

17. Competency measures and standards are specified and made public prior to instruction.

Source Bourke et al. (1975)

Figure 10.1 *Competency-based education and education (CBET) criteria for describing and assessing competence-based programmes*

To address these shortcomings, it was stated that vocational qualifications should be structured as true statements of competence, which incorporate assessment of three key components:

研究注意到原体系的优点,包括高度关注由许多考试和认证部门设定的标准,以及它们在国内和国际进行评估安排的可靠性。但尽管如此,研究得出英国没有有效的职业资格认证国家系统的结论。特别是当时的许多资格认证评估或适任表现评判缺乏充分的手段。大部分评估,或者用书面考试表现来评价有关职业技能和理解的知识,或者仅对少量指定技能的表现进行评价,没有形成对于职业或职业工作整体范围内有效工作所要求的适任能力进行评估的体系,而且,大多数资格认证缺乏对基于工作的学习的重视。

适任要求

1. 适任以专业工作分析和/或专业责任理论规划为基础。

2. 适任要求描述了履行职业职能预期的效果,或履行这些职能所必要的知识、技能和态度。

3. 适任规范适用于涉及标准的评估。

4. 适任可作为职业工作效率的假定预测因素,并且受持续有效的程序监控。

5. 适任应先于相关指导规定和公布。

6. 完成 CBET 计划的学员应显示有广阔的适任能力。

评估

13. 适任判定方法应与适任要求有效地联系。

14. 适任判定方法对于细微差异应是具体的、现实的和敏感的。

15. 应根据为表明适任而规定的标准来确定判定适任的方法。

16. 适任判定方法提供的证据应可用于做出是否适任的决定。

17. 适任判定方法和标准应先于指导规定和公布。

资料来源于 Bourke 等(1975)

图 10.1 为描述和评估适任程序的适任教育和教育(CBET)规则

针对这些缺点,研究报告认为,职业资格应按适任的真实情况确定,并在评估中包含三个主要成分:

- Skills to defined standards.

- Relevant knowledge and understanding.

- The ability to use skills and to apply knowledge and understanding to the performance of relevant tasks.

Guidance published by the National Council for Vocational Qualifications (NCVQ) and the Scottish Qualifications Authority (SQA) includes the following, to emphasise the broad approach that competence-based qualifications must reflect:

- The qualification, as a statement of competence, concentrates on the ability to perform effectively. However, effective performance depends on the individual having an appropriate body of knowledge, theory, principles and cognitive skill on which to draw. While the ultimate focus of qualifications must be effective performance, much of the contributory learning and assessment will deal with knowledge, understanding and skills.

- Vocational qualifications are first and foremost about what people can do. This must go beyond the technical skills and knowledge to include planning, problem solving, dealing with unexpected occurrences, working with other people and applying the knowledge and understanding that underpins overall competence.

- Jobs are seldom performed in isolation and are rarely simply procedural. People need to be able to communicate effectively with colleagues, organize and prioritize their work activities, respond to contingencies, make decisions, solve problems, apply ethical judgments, work safely and so on. It is the ability to integrate these demands when performing in the work environment that defines the competent individual.

This breadth of competence cannot be over-emphasized. Without it, there would be a risk that a competence-based system would concentrate on technical abilities and skills at the expense of other skills that encompass knowing what to do, how to do it and when and how it should be done- including the ability to cope with emergencies and allowing for all contingencies that might arise.

Structure of the UK NVQ standards and awards

National Vocational Qualifications (NVQs) are qualifications awarded for demonstrating competence in the workplace. Employers organisations or "Lead Bodies" have worked together with traditional Awarding Bodies to devise the measurement of competence and to identify the tasks which are common to people doing similar work in a variety of environments.

N/SVQs are designed to improve individual skills. They focus on the particular, job-related skills and knowledge needed in employment. In effect they serve as a guarantee that someone can do the job, to the standards required by employers and regulatory bodies.

- 与标准对应的技能。

- 相关的知识和理解。

- 在履行相关任务中使用技能和应用知识与理解的能力。

由国家职业资格认证理事会（NCVQ）和苏格兰资格认证局（SQA）出版的指南包括下列内容，以强调适任资格认证必须体现的基本方法：

- 资格认定的适任要求，应侧重于描述有效履行职务的能力。然而，有效的履行能力取决于个人所具备的适当的知识、理论、原理和认知技能。虽然，资格最终的焦点必定是有效的履行职务，但大部分学习和评估的促进措施都涉及知识、理解和技能。

- 职业资格认证首先并最关心的是人们能做什么。这不仅包括技术能力和知识，还必须包括策划、解决问题、处理突发事件、与他人一起工作的能力，以及应用所有支持适任的知识和理解。

- 很少工作是孤立开展的，也只有极少工作的程序是简单的。因而，人们需要能够有效地与同事交流，组织和按先后次序安排活动，应付突发事件，做出决定，解决问题，应用合乎道德的判断，安全地工作等。某个人有能力在实际工作环境中满足组合的各种需求即可确认其适任。

不能过分地强调适任的广泛性。否则会使适任的系统侧重技术能力和技能而忽略其他的适任内容，包括知道要做什么，如何做和对工作完成时间和质量的判断的技能，也包括处理紧急情况和所有突发事件的能力。

英国 NVQ 标准和职业资格授予结构

国家职业资格（NVQ）是显示岗位工作适任的一种资格。雇主组织或"行业领导机构"与传统的资格授予机构合作制定适任的认定方法以及确定在不同环境中人们做类似工作的共同任务。

N/SVQ 的目标是提高个人的技能。他们关注特定的、与工作相关的技能和职业中需要的知识。实际上，这些知识可以作为相关的个人能够按照雇主和管理团体要求的标准工作的保证。

They are designed to:

- equip an individual to do a particular job, whilst providing some transferable skills which are relevant to many occupations

- respond to the current and future needs of business and industry

- be available to people of all ages and at all stages in their career

- be built up gradually over time

- encourage people to progress to further qualifications

It is important to note that N/SVQs are not training programmes. They do not specify the kind of training needed in order to achieve this standard. Indeed, some people who are very experienced in their jobs may need minimal training before being assessed. In these times of rapid change, many more are likely to need some kind of training programme before they can be successfully assessed for the qualifications.

Competency standards are written in a format and conform to agreed levels which fit the requirements of the national qualifications framework.

Each standard consist of a number of units of competence (function). Each unit (function) describes a particular function required at work. By achieving each unit of competence (function) over a period of time, individuals can build up to the achievement of a full N/SVQ qualification at a pace which suits them.

Each unit (function) is, in turn, made up of a number of elements (competences) which describe the activities that an individual has to perform. Each element (competence) consists of the following:

- performance criteria—these specify the standards to which the activities, described in the unit element (competence), have to be performed

- range statement—this specifies the range of contexts in which the activities have to be performed and for which evidence must be gathered

For each element (competence), additional information is provided in the form of:

- knowledge specification—this outlines the knowledge and understanding required to do the job and can be useful to refer to when deciding what training is required

- evidence requirements—these describe the evidence that must be gathered to demonstrate that the individual has met the standards of performance required for all the contexts covered in the range statement

设计 N/SVQ 的目的是：

- 训练个人具备从事一份特定工作的能力，同时提供一些与很多职业相关的可转化的技能

- 反映业务和行业的当前和未来需要

- 处于所有年龄和所有职业阶段的人都可获得认证

- 随着时代而逐渐进步

- 鼓励人们提高资格等级

特别要注意的是 N/SVQ 体系并不是培训计划。它们没有规定为获得这些标准所需要的培训种类。实际上，许多在工作中非常有经验的人在评估前可能只需要最少的培训。在变化迅速的时代，更多的人需要在成功地通过评估获得资格之前参加某种培训安排。

适任标准制作成书面形式并与相应的国家资格要求水平一致。

每个标准由几个适任项目（职能）组成。每个项目（职能）描述了工作要求的特定职能。通过分时段分别完成各适任项目（职能），个人能够按适合他们的进度逐步获得 N/SVQ 的完整资格。

每个项目（职能）由一些个人必须表现的规定的活动要素（适任）组成。每个要素由下列内容构成：

- 表现标准——规定项目要素（适任）要求进行的活动的表现标准

- 综合说明——规定必须进行的活动和收集证据的内容

各要素（适任）提供下列形式的附加资料：

- 知识说明——概述从事该工作所要求的知识和理解，以便在决定培训需求时参考

- 证据要求——描述必须收集的证据，用于显示被评估人已经达到规定要求的全部表现标准

NVQ structure	Revised STCW Convention
NVQ(5 levels)	Deck or Engine Certificates (3 levels)
Standard: group of modules/units	(Occupation/Role)
Unit (of competence): group of elements	Function
Element	Competence

NVQ Units of Competence relate to distinct aspects of the standards of competence required.

For example, the standards for NVQ Management at level 4 are divided into nine units:

- maintaining and improving services and product operations;
- contributing to the implementation of change in services, products and systems;
- recommend, monitor and control the use of resources;
- contribute to the recruitment and selection of personnel;
- develop teams, individuals and self to enhance performance;
- plan, allocate and evaluate work carried out by teams, individuals and self;
- create, maintain and enhance effective working relationships;
- seek, evaluate and organize information for action; and
- exchange information to solve problems and make decisions.

Alternative Certification

Some of the Units in the NVQ framework are applicable to more that one NVQ and employment sector. Often these common units relate to core skills-personal attributes that are fundamental to successful practice in many occupations. The common and core units, where they exist, greatly assist transfer from one area of competence to another and re-training. Once attained they are applicable to any other occupation to which they are relevant.

A similar situation exists for seafarers, whereby, for example, the function *Controlling the operation of the ship and care for persons onboard at operational level* is common to both the "occupations" of "officer in charge of a navigational watch" and "officer in charge of an engineering watch". This flexibility has lead to the new Chapter VII *Alternative Certification*.

Assessment

The candidate must satisfy an assessor that they are competent in performing the task in line with the performance criteria. They must show that they have sufficient depth of knowledge, and that they realise how different circumstances may affect their methods. They must adopt a planned approach to collecting evidence, and make a claim to competence-based on the evidence they have produced.

NVQ 结构	修订的 STCW 公约
NVQ（5 个级别）	甲板或轮机证书（3 个级别）
标准:模块/项目组	（职业/岗位）
项目（适任的）:要素组	职能
要素	适任

NVQ 适任项目涉及不同的适任标准要求。

例如，NVQ 管理 4 个级别的标准分为 9 个项目：

- 保持和提高服务及产品管理；
- 有助于实现服务、产品和系统改变；
- 建议、监督和控制资源的使用；
- 有助于人员的招募和挑选；
- 发展小组、个人和本人以提高表现；
- 计划、分配和评价小组、个人和本人的工作；
- 创造、保持和提高有效的工作关系；
- 寻找、评价和组织活动资料；及
- 为解决问题和做出决策交换资料。

可供选择的发证

NVQ 方案的一些项目可以适用于一个以上的职业资格和雇佣部门。通常，这些共同的项目与共有的核心技能有关，如成功从事许多职业必须具备的个人工作态度。这些共同的核心能力，对于转换适任领域和再培训极有帮助。一旦获得，它们就可以适用于相关的任何其他职业。

海员也存在类似的情况，例如，操作级的船舶管理和人员管理的职能对于"负责航行值班的高级船员"和"负责轮机值班的高级船员"的工作是一样的。这种灵活性导致新的第 7 章——可供选择的发证的制定。

评估

申请人必须使评估员对他们有能力按照实操标准履行任务感到满意。他们必须展示他们有足够的知识深度，并且能够意识到不同的环境会如何影响他们的操作。申请人必须接受预先计划好的证据收集方法，并要求他们提交的证据必须以适任为基础。

Standards

Traditionally, maritime qualification and training arrangements have been based on the twin assumptions that:

- Adequate experience could be gained, and the acquisition and demonstration of skills needed for sea-going employment be achieved, simply by requiring candidates for certificates of competency to serve specified periods of time at sea.

- Knowledge and understanding of subjects relevant to the work involved could be tested adequately through written examinations.

These arrangements have worked well over the years. Certainly no criticism is intended or implied of the quality of performance of the holders of certificates awarded on this basis. It is questionable, though, whether reliance can continue to be placed on this approach to determining competence in the circumstances of today's shipping industry. For instance, the quality of the mandatory periods of sea experience can vary widely. Although training record books are used extensively to guide trainees in the tasks and skills in which they need to become proficient, there is no clear definition of the standard required. That is left to the professional judgment of those supervising training. Other factors include the increasing specialisation of types of ships, reductions in crew numbers made possible by developments in technology and the emergence of new labour supply countries which do not have the long, historical seafaring traditions on which the cascade of skill from experienced to new seafarer depends.

To a large extent, the standards for seafarers are already established in the requirements for existing statutory certificates of competency. But the standards are set by the examination system rather than by reference to the desired outcomes of the education and training process. Moreover the passage of time, in the form of mandatory minimum sea service, is not in itself a valid indicator of competence.

Standards of competence

Against this background, the development of competence-based qualifications has presented an opportunity to re-examine the way in which seafarers achieve and prove their competence. it involves:

- Making the desired outcomes of training explicit, in terms of standards of competence.

- Ensuring that assessment incorporates the ability to perform to the defined standards and to apply relevant skills and knowledge in practice.

- Ensuring that a range of learning opportunities is open to individuals, which facilitate access to new qualifications and assist career development and progression.

The standards therefore represent the outcomes, which must be attained at the end of any period of learning for a certificate to be awarded.

标准

传统上，海上资格和培训安排基于以下考虑：

- 能获得足够的经验，并获得和显示海上职业需要的技能，要求适任证书申请人具有规定的海上服务时间。

- 通过书面考试充分测验对应工作的有关科目知识和理解。

这些安排已经良好运作多年。当然，没有理由对在此基础上得到证书的持有人工作的质量提出批评。尽管不能确定继续依靠这样的方法来确定当今的海运业环境的资格的可靠性。例如，强制规定的海上经历的时间质量会有很大的差别。尽管广泛使用培训记录簿被用来规范学员需熟练掌握的工作和技能，但是没有对标准做出明确定义，这就只能依赖监管培训的人员的专业判断。其他因素包括船舶类型专业化程度的增加、科技发展使船员人数减少成为可能，以及新的劳动力输出国的出现，这些国家没有历史悠久的航海传统和新船员所依赖的大量技术经验沉淀。所有这些，都使传统的适任评价方法受到挑战。

现有的法定适任证书的要求已经在很大程度上确立了海员的标准。但是这些标准是由考试系统而不是参照教育和培训过程所期望获得的效果设定的。此外，以强制的最低海上服务时间表示的资历本身并不是一个适任的有效指标。

适任标准

在此背景下，适任资格体系的发展已经提供了重新审核船员适任资格的获取和认可方式的机会。它涉及：

- 按照适任标准，明确培训的期望效果。

- 确保评估内容包含按规定标准操作的能力，以及在实际中应用相关技能和知识的能力。

- 确保给个人提供大量的学习机会，以便取得新的资格，协助个人的事业的发展和进步。

因此，标准体现了在与发证相关的各种学习阶段结束时必须达到的效果。

Standards of competence are now specified in STCW 95. As noted earlier the standards are grouped within a framework of seven functions at three levels of responsibility. They are incorporated into the chapters of the convention that specify the requirements for the issue of the various certificates of competency. Functions and levels are identified by sub-title in tables of standards of competence. The scope of the function at the level of responsibility stated in the title is defined according to abilities for a number of topics listed in the first column of each table. The knowledge, understanding and proficiency, the methods for demonstrating competence and criteria for evaluating competence are listed alongside each topic.

At national level the STCW standards can be incorporated within a national system of qualifications, such as that developed in the UK. The starting point is a systematic analysis of all the functions that need to be performed aboard ship. The analysis continues within each functional area to a sufficient level of detail to enable performance criteria to be written to describe the critical aspects of competent performance of each task. This establishes the standard, which describes competence performance of a task and the range of circumstances over which the task may have to be performed. It also indicates what evidence should be collected for the purposes of assessment.

The UK framework covers occupations at five levels of competence, from the most humble to the professional. Qualifications for seafarers have been developed at three of these levels, which correspond to the levels of responsibility in the STCW convention, and a higher level qualification for masters and chief engineers is under development (see below).

Most occupations in the UK have competence-based qualifications included in the framework. It therefore provides a basis for identifying relationships between them where there are common competences or requirements, thus facilitating transfer and progression through the various levels. The higher the level of qualification, the more of the following characteristics it is likely to require:

- Breadth and range of competence.

- Depth and breadth of knowledge and understanding.

- Capability in dealing with complexity and difficulty.

- Specialised capabilities.

- Ability to transfer competence from one context or work area to another.

- Ability to innovate and cope with non-routine activities.

- Ability to recognize and plan work.

- Ability to supervise others.

Some functions may be performed at different levels so, in setting national standards, the descriptions of the task and performance required have to take the above characteristics into account. The amount of detail is important and largely a matter of judgement. Too much detail makes the task of gathering and assessing evidence of competence unworkable—too little and the definition of competence will be too broad to be meaningful.

目前的 STCW 95 公约对适任标准做了规定。正如前文提到的,公约将标准归纳为 3 个责任级别、7 个职能结构。有关标准被纳入对签发各种适任证书要求做出规定的章节。可以通过适任标准表的副标题识别职能和级别。与标题对应的责任级别的适任内容根据与表格第 1 栏列出的主题相对应的各项能力确定。在每个主题旁边列出知识、理解和熟练,表明适任的方法和评价适任的标准。

在国家层面,可以将 STCW 公约标准纳入国家的资格认定系统,英国制定的标准就是如此。工作的起点是对在船上需履行的所有职能进行系统的分析。应进一步对各职能范围进行充分详细的分析,直到能够以文字表达的履行标准来规定针对各项任务的关键适任表现。这样就确定了规范某项任务的适任表现和履行任务的环境的标准,同时也规定了评估应当收集的证据。

英国认证系统覆盖职业的 5 个适任级别,从最低级别的到最专业的级别。海员资格被分为这些级别中的 3 个级别,分别与 STCW 公约的责任级别相对应,对应船长和轮机长的更高级别资格正在制定当中(见下文)。

英国大部分需要适任资格的职业都包括在上述系统中,因而为确定这些职业之间的共同适任标准或要求的联系打下了基础,从而使各种级别之间的转换和职务晋升更加容易。资格级别越高,越有可能要求具备更多的以下特性:

- 适任的广度和范围。

- 知识和理解的深度和广度。

- 处理复杂和困难情况的能力。

- 专业能力。

- 将适任从一种环境或工作转换到另一环境或工作的能力。

- 改革和处理非常规活动的能力。

- 了解工作和制订计划的能力。

- 监管他人的能力。

某些职能可能适用于不同级别,因此,在规定国家的标准时,对任务和履行要求的规定必须考虑以上的特性。标准内容的详尽性很重要,尤其在需要就是否符合标准做出判断时。内容太详细会使收集和评估适任证据的工作难于进行;内容不够详细,则适任的定义将会太广泛而变得毫无意义。

Levels of competences

Competence-based standards and qualification are provided in the NVQ framework at the following five levels. The corresponding levels of qualifications of seafarers are tabulated for comparision.

Level	NVQ Framework	Revised STCW Convention	Rank
1	Competence in the performance of a range of varied work activities, most of that may be routine and predictable.	NIL	
2	Competence in a significant range of varied work activities, performed in a variety of contexts. Some of the activities are complex or non-routine, and there is some individual responsibility or autonomy. Collaboration with others, perhaps through membership of a work group or team, may often be a requirement.	Competence relating to the job roles of all qualified ratings, on deck, in the engine room or elsewhere. This means that the person has to exercise some individual responsibility and autonomy, though collaboration with others through membership of a work group or team is sometimes required.	Ratings（Deck cadets）(Junior engineers)
3	Competence in a broad range of varied activities performed in a variety of contexts and most which are complex and non-routine. There is considerable responsibility and autonomy, and control or guidance of others is often required.	Competence relating to the job role of a junior watchkeeping officer. This means that the person must apply knowledge in a broad range of varied work activities performed in a wide variety of contexts, many of which are non-routine. There is considerable personal responsibility and control or guidance of others is often required.	3rd/2nd deck officers 4th/3rd engineers
4	Competence in a broad range of complex, technical or professional work activities performed in a wide variety of contexts and with a substantial degree or personal responsibility and autonomy. Responsibility for the work of others and the allocation of resources is often present.	Competence relating to the job role of a senior officer. This means that the person must apply knowledge in a broad range of varied and complex work activities, performed in a wide variety of contexts and with a substantial degree of personal responsibility and autonomy. Responsibility for the work of others and the allocation of resources is often present.	chief officer Second Engineer
5	Competence, which involves the application of a significant range of fundamental principles and complex techniques across a wide and often unpredictable variety of contexts. Very substantial personal autonomy and often-significant responsibility resources feature strongly, as do personal accounting for analysis and diagnosis, design, planning, execution and evaluation.	(Competence relating to the job roles of master or chief engineer. This means that the person must apply a significant range of fundamental principles across a wide and often unpredictable variety of contexts. Very substantial personal autonomy and often significant responsibility for the work of others and for the allocation of substantial resources feature strongly, as does personal accountability for analysis and diagnosis, planning, execution and evaluation.)	Master Chief Engineer

适任的等级

在 NVQ 框架中,以下 5 个等级的适任标准和资格被提供,与海员资格的相应等级列表做比较。

级别	NVQ 框架	修订的 STCW 公约	职位
1	适任广泛的不同工作活动,其中大部分活动可以是常规的和普通的。	无	
2	适任较大范围的工作活动,其中某些活动是复杂的或非常规的,并负有个人的责任或自主权限。可能要求经常与他人合作,开展群体或团队活动。	与在甲板、机舱或其他部门的所有合格的普通船员的岗位工作相关的适任。这意味着这部分人负有个人的职责或自主权限,有时也通过群体或团队关系与他人合作。	普通船员（甲板实习生）（初级轮机员）
3	适任广泛范围的工作活动,活动大部分是复杂的和非常规的。负有一定的责任和自主权限,通常要求监督或指导他人。	与初级的值班高级船员的工作角色相关的适任。这意味着这部分人必须应用知识开展广泛范围的工作活动,其中,很多是非常规活动。有一定的责任和自主权限,通常要求监督或指导他人。	三副/二副 三管轮/二管轮
4	适任广泛范围的复杂的、技术的或职业的工作活动并具有相当程度的个人责任和自主权限。对他人的工作负责并通常需要分配资源。	与高级船员的岗位工作相关的适任。这意味着这部分人必须应用知识从事广泛范围复杂的、技术的或职业的工作活动并具有相当程度的个人责任和自主权限。对他人的工作负责并通常需要分配资源。	大副 大管轮
5	适任广泛而经常是不可预料的各种情况下应用一些重要的基本原则和复杂技术的工作。相当大的个人自主权限并有对他人的工作和实际资源的分配负有重要责任,个人对分析、判断、设计、履行和评价负责。	（与船长或轮机长的工作角色相关的适任。这意味着这部分人必须在一个广泛并经常是不可预料的各种情况下应用一些重要的基本原则。具有相当大的个人自主权限并对他人的工作和实际资源的分配负重要责任,个人对分析、判断、设计、履行和评价负责。）	船长 轮机长

Assessment

Assessment is the process of obtaining and comparing evidence of competence with the standards.

The aim is to ensure that sufficient, reliable and verifiable evidence is available to enable an assessor to be satisfied that a candidate has the ability to work in accordance with the standards required in employment.

Performance aboard ship can be a valuable source of evidence of competence alongside some of the more familiar and traditional methods of evaluating competence. But whether sufficient evidence can be obtained this way is another matter.

评估

评估是获得适任证据并把适任证据与标准比较的过程。

评估目标是确保可以获得足够的、可靠的和可审核的证据，保证评估员对申请人在具备职务标准要求的工作能力方面感到满意。

在某些较熟悉的和传统的适任评价方法中，船上工作可以作为适任证据的有价值的来源，但却不一定能从中获得足够的证据。

Glossary of NVQ Terms

APA Advisor

(also known as facilitator, mentor, guide, counsellor, APA tutor).

A person trained and competent in assisting a candidate in determining the evidence of their prior achievements which will meet the assessment requirements of elements and units of competence.

Approved Centre

An organisation which has been evaluated and formally approved in writing by an awarding body to deliver and assess a named qualification and from which the awarding body will accept candidate claims for certification.

Assessor

A person with relevant experience in the occupational sector who is responsible for looking at evidence/performance and judging whether the candidate has achieved the required standards.

Authentic

Relating to a particular candidate's own efforts and achievements rather than someone else's work or the combined work of a group.

Candidate

A person preparing to be assessed or examined for a qualification or award.

Competence

The ability to perform the activities within an occupation or function to the standards expected in employment.

Credit Accumulation

The process of allowing candidates to collect units of certification, either within a single award or qualification or across more than one. Once the unit is achieved, there is no need for further assessment for it to count towards another qualification or award of which it is part.

Current/Currency

Relating to a competence which, although it may have been originally demonstrated some time ago, can be demonstrated to still be possessed by a candidate to the full requirement of the present standards.

Element of Competence

A description of a single action, behaviour or outcome required to be demonstrated separately, in satisfying the requirements of the full set of competences in the industry standards for an occupation.

Endorsed Statement

A statement written and signed by an independent witness that the work product to be used as evidence by the candidate is the authentic work of the candidate.

Evidence

Information which supports judgements about achievements. It can be drawn from a range of activities and be in a variety of forms, but it must always relate directly to the element of competence being assessed.

NVQ 术语

APA 顾问

（也称为 facilitator、mentor、guide、counselor、APA tutor）

经过专门培训并且有能力协助申请人确定他们早先已获得的符合适任评估要求的要素和项目的证据的人员。

认可的中心

一个经过授予机构审核和正式书面认可的，实施和评估指定的资格并且使授予机构接受其申请人发证请求的组织。

评估员

具有本职业范围相关的经验，负责检查经验/表现和判定申请人是否已达到要求的标准的人员。

可信度

获得的结果仅与特定的申请人的个人努力和成绩有关，而不是靠其他人的工作或小组的联合工作达到。

申请人

一个为获得资格或得到授权准备接受评估或考试的人。

适任

按照职业所期望的标准履行某项工作或职能的能力。

资格条件积累

允许申请人积累聚齐单项或多项授权或资格的各项资格要求。一旦完成所有项目，没有必要再对其另做评估，可以直接认可资格。

现有水平

对于某些适任要求，尽管申请人过去已经满足，仍然可以要求申请人按照目前标准显示能够满足全部要求。

适任要素

对要求单独表明的，满足某项工作的职业标准的全部适任要求的单个行动、表现或效果的描述。

签发证明

一份由独立证人书写和签名的证明，证明申请人用来作为证据的工作成果是真实的。

证据

对成绩做出判断的支持资料。可以取自一系列的活动以及用各种形式表示，但必须总是与评估的适任要素有直接的关系。

External Verifier

A person appointed by the Awarding Body, who will check the Approved Centre's own internal quality assurance systems and procedures relating to the delivery and assessment of the qualifications, thereby ensuring the maintenance of the national standards through consistent judgements in all Centres.

Internal Verifier

The person within an approved Centre charged with monitoring the Centre's provision of a named group of qualifications and who is responsible to the awarding body for internally verifying the assessment process by advising and supporting assessors, maintaining and monitoring arrangements for processing assessment information and verifying assessment practice.

Knowledge

The underpinning knowledge and understanding listed within the standards which is essential in order for the candidate to be able to demonstrate competent performance.

Level (of qualification)

All NVQs are placed at one of five levels which denote the degree of supervisory/ management responsibility, or technical expertise required. The higher the level the more complex or responsible the job.

Open Access

Available to as many potential candidates as possible, without any artificial barriers, such as prescription of particular courses, modes of learning or time constraints being imposed on candidates wishing to present themselves for assessment.

Performance Criteria

Statements of required outcomes of competent performance, by means of which an assessor can judge the evidence that an individual can perform the activity specified in a competence, to a level acceptable in employment.

Portfolio (of Evidence)

A collection of materials providing detailed evidence for claims of competence which is cross referenced against the Performance Criteria and Range contained within the elements and units of competence.

Range Statements

A description of the different contexts or circumstances in which a person should be able to demonstrate achievements of an element of competence.

Reliability

The consistency with which an assessment can distinguish between those who have achieved competence and those who have not.

Standards

A list of competences expected of an individual performing a particular occupational role, expressed in terms of outcomes of work activity.

Sufficiency (of evidence)

The evidence which has been collected being enough in both quantity and quality to convince an assessor that competence has been achieved and that the candidate will continue to work at or above this level.

外部审核员

受授权机构指派检查各认可中心的与资格教学和评估活动相关的内部质量保证体系和程序,从而令所有中心都能保证维持国家的资格认定统一标准的人员。

内部审核员

在认可的中心负责对质量规定的履行情况进行内部监督,以及按授权机构要求通过向评估员提出建议和支持意见,保持和监督评估资料管理以及监督实际评估等手段,对评估过程进行内部审核的人员。

知识

指申请人显示适任必须表现的,列于适任标准中的基础知识和理解。

(资格的)级别

将所有的NVQ分为5个级别,分别表示不同的监督/管理级别或要求的技术专业知识。级别越高,工作越复杂或其责任越大。

开放的途径

采用开放的获得资格的途径以便尽可能多的有潜力的申请人可以参与,不设置任何人为的障碍,如对希望接受评估的申请人规定特殊的课程、学习模式或时间限制。

表现标准

指对适任表现要求的效果的说明,评估员可以根据标准对被评估人履行适任规定的活动的证据是否满足职业要求进行评价。

(证据的)形式

指为申请适任资格而提供的,与适任要素和项目所要求的表现标准和范围相关的详细证据资料的总和。

范围说明

指适用于申请人显示获得适任要素的不同背景环境和条件的说明。

可靠性

指评估在区分已适任和尚未适任的申请人方面的标准一致性。

标准

指期望被评估人在履行特定工作中应达到的适任项目列表,表内的适任项目用工作效果表达。

(证据的)充分性

收集的证据在数量上和质量上是充分的,可以使评估员确信申请人已经适任并且能够始终在与此相当或以上的水平工作。

Transferable

The ability for a competence to be applied in a different environment or used under circumstances differing from those under which it was first assessed.

Unit of (competence)

A group of elements of competence making up a recognisable separate function within an occupation, which makes sense to employers as worthy of separate certification. The smallest grouping of competences which is recognised by NCVQ for separate certification and credit accumulation.

Validity

An assessment can be said to be valid if it measures what it is intended to measure (expressed in terms of the element of competence).

可转换的

应用适任于不同环境或与原先评估不同的环境的能力。

(适任)的项目

指一种职业职能内可明确划分的,对于雇主是值得单独发证的一组适任要素。也是NCVQ认可的最小发证和资格积累的适任单元。

有效性

如果评估对所有要求评价的内容(通过适任要素表达)进行了评定,那么可以说该评估是有效的。

Part 10-2
Competence-based assessment

Introduction: The NVQ assessment model

Assessment of NVQs and SVQs is based on the concept of sufficiency where the candidate shows sufficient evidence to satisfy a specified set of criteria; these being the "Performance Criteria". This approach to measuring ability is referred to as **criterion referencing**. This is in contrast to the second method termed **norm referencing**.

Criterion-referenced assessment

Criterion-referenced assessment, also known as standards-based assessment, is designed to provide a measure of a candidate's performance in relation to a clearly defined standard. It is not the intention, in this form of assessment, to compare the performance of one candidate with another. Instead, what the candidate does or knows is compared with the standard of performance defined by the outcomes and associated performance criteria, and a decision is made as to whether the candidate has achieved those outcomes or not. In a criterion-referenced assessment system therefore there is no arbitrarily set pass mark or ranking of candidates in order of ability. All those who have achieved the standard for a unit receive the same certificate.

Example. The driving test is an everyday example of a criterion-referenced assessment. The standards of the test are set out in advance and are known to both the assessor and the candidate. During the test, the assessor sets the candidate a series of tasks (outcomes) and assesses his or her driving ability against the preset conditions of performance laid down by the Department of Transport (performance criteria).If the candidate measures up to these conditions, a pass is awarded. There is no mark attached to this pass.

Norm-referenced assessment

In contrast to criterion-referenced assessment, some assessment is designed to allow candidates to be compared with each other. This kind of assessment is known as norm-referenced assessment and is based on the assumption that the abilities of different candidates vary widely and that the function of assessment is to highlight these differences by interpreting a candidate's performance in relation to the performance of others. Candidates are therefore ranked in an ascending scale of marks from, for example, zero to 100. At a predetermined point on the scale, usually just above 49, a line is drawn and the candidates below the line are deemed to have failed, while the candidates on or above the line are deemed to have passed. The candidate who achieves the highest score is judged to be the best.

Example. An everyday example of a norm-referenced assessment system is an athletics event such as the Olympic 100 metres race. Here, the gold medal goes to the athlete who runs fastest, not to those who run the distance in a given time. However, both types of assessment are often used together. Taking our example further, some athletics events, such as qualifying races and trials, are criterion-referenced in the early stages when the athletes aim to complete the race within a particular time and all those who achieve that time are selected either for the final or for the next round.

第10-2章
适任评估

介绍：NVQ评估模式

NVQ和SVQ的评估是以申请人出示的满足规定标准的证据的充分性概念为基础的；是一种"表现标准"。这种评测能力的方法称为**参照标准法**。这与另一种称为**参照常模**的方法相反。

参照标准的评估

参照标准的评估也称为基于标准的评估，评估提供了一种与明确规定的标准相关的评价申请人表现的方法。这种评估形式的目的不是将申请人的表现与他人做比较，而是把申请人的工作情况或所知道的知识与表现标准以及表现要求做比较，并做出申请人是否达到这些标准的判断。因此，在参照标准的评估系统中，没有人为地设置几个分数等级或按照能力排列申请人的等级。达到一个科目标准的所有人获得相同的证书。

例子。汽车驾驶员考试是一个参照标准的评估的日常例子。考试的标准事先设定，并为评估员和申请人所共知。考试过程中，评估员给申请人设置一系列的任务，并根据由交通部门指定的事先设定的表现标准评估申请人的驾驶能力。如果申请人被判定达到这些规则，则获得通过。没有附带的通过分数。

参照常模的评估

与参照标准的评估不同，某些评估方式允许将申请人与他人相互比较。这种评估称为参照常模的评估，是以假设不同申请人之间的能力差别很大为基础，并且评估的职能是通过以一个申请人与其他申请人的有关表现进行比较和解释来强调这些差别。因此，申请人以从低分到高分分段定级，例如从0到100。在一个事先设定好的分数点（通常是49分以上）划定一条及格线，在此分数线下的申请人被认为不合格，而在分数线或以上的申请人则为合格，获得最高分的申请人被认为是最好的。

例子。参照常模评估系统的一个日常例子是奥林匹克的运动项目。如100米比赛。在这里，谁跑得最快就获得金牌，而不是那些在给定时间内跑完全程的人。当然，两种评估方法通常一起使用。在这里举另外一个例子，一些运动项目，比如资格赛和测验，在最初阶段，运动员的目标是在规定的时间完成比赛，那些达到时间规定的运动员将被挑选参加决赛或下一轮的比赛。

Competence-based systems

The competence-based movement has been in existence for some time. There was research into what makes people effective and what constitutes a competent worker. Consequently, several different models of competence are in use. The one which the Tables of Competence in the STCW Code most closely resembles is the UK competency system.

The UK competency system

We have already dealt with the development of the UK competency system in Part 10-1. In this system, competence-based standards reflect the *expectations of workplace performance*. These are therefore *occupational competences* and are *criterion-referenced*, meaning that competences are developed and agreed by industry or by an organization.

A Comparison of Assessment Principles and Practice

The key differences between competence-based assessment and more traditional forms of occupation-related assessment (in qualification-driven systems) are noted in Table 10B-1 .*

Table 10B-1 Traditional vs competence-based assessment (qualification-driven systems)

	Traditional (course-based)	Competence-based (workplace)
Concept	Assessment of learning ability or achievement	Assessment is independent of any learning programme
Foundation	Curricula, defined centrally by teaching staff/ divisional boards	Explicit standards of required performance defined by industry (UK)
Assessment requirements	Assessment is an integral part of learning programmes	Assessment of actual performance in a work role
Evidence	Assessment evidence drawn from course assignments/exams	Assessment evidence collected from actual workplace performance supplemented by other methods
	Types of evidence predetermined by course syllabus	Types of evidence governed only by rules for quality of evidence
	Assessment is norm-referenced	Assessment is criterion-referenced (UK)

* Sections of the text of parts 10-2 to 10-8 and figures 10B-1, 10B-2, 10B-3, 10D-1, 10D-2, 10D-3, 10D-4, 10F-1, 10F-2, 10F-3, 10G-1, 10G-2 and 10G-3 have been taken from *Competence-based Assessment Techniques*, © Shirley Fletcher, 1997, Kogan Page.

The key features of the UK competence-based system are as follows:

- Standards of performance (competences) developed and agreed by industry (national) or by the organization (company-specific)

- Assessment of workplace performance

基于适任的系统

基于适任的运作模式已经存在一段时间。对于是什么令人们有效地工作和由什么要素构成一个工作者的适任资格已经进行过研究。因此,现有几种不同的适任模式。STCW规则中的适任表使用的模式与英国的适任系统最为相似。

英国的适任系统

我们已经在第10-1部分中论及英国建立的适任系统。在该系统中,适任标准反映了期望的岗位表现,也因此就是职业的适任和参照的标准,其含义是由行业或组织制定和认同的适任资格。

评估的原则和实践的比较

适任评估与其他有关职业传统形式的评估之间的主要区别见表10B-1。*

表10B-1 传统评估与适任评估的区别

	传统的(基于课程)	基于适任的(岗位工作)
概念	学习能力或成绩的评估	学习能力或成绩的评估
基本原则	主要由教员/部门委员会规定的课程	行业(英国)规定的要求表现的明确标准
评估要求	评估是学习计划的必要部分	评估独立于学习计划
证据	从课程作业/考试中获得评估证据	从实际的工作表现收集评估证据由其他方式补充
	证据类型由课程大纲预先决定	证据的类型只由证据质量规则规定
	评估是参照常模法	评估采用参照标准法(英国)

* 第10-2至10-8部分和图10B-1、10B-3、10D-1、10D-2、10D-3、10D-4、10F-1、10F-2、10F-3、10G-1、10G-2和10G-3的内容章节取自《基于适任评估方法》,雪莉弗莱切,1997, Kogan Page.

英国基于适任的系统的主要特点如下:

- 职业(国家的)或组织(具体公司)制定和认同的表现(适任)标准
- 岗位工作的表现标准

- Competence = expectations of employment

- Standards outcome-based (criterion-referenced)

- Standards of occupational competence (actual performance at work)

- Agreed benchmark of competent performance

- Product—hard competences

The following checklist allows one to judge whether an assessment system is truly competence-based:

Is the proposed system:

- based on the use of explicit statements of performance?

- focused on the assessment of outputs or outcomes of performance?

- independent of any specified learning programme?

- based on a requirement in which evidence of performance is collected from observation and questioning of actual performance as the main assessment method?

- one which provides individualized assessment?

- one which contains clear guidance to assessors regarding the quality of evidence to be collected?

- one which contains clear guidelines and procedures for quality assurance?

Planning Competence-Based Assessment

Key questions in the planning of competence-based assessments are:

1. What do we want to assess?

    (a) Technical competence

    (b) Occupational competence

    (c) Behaviours

    (d) Individual performance

    (e) Group/team performance

- 适任=职业期望
- 基于效果的标准(参照标准)
- 职业适任标准(工作的实际表现)
- 认同的适任表现基准
- 产品——严格的适任

以下的核对表可用于判断某个评估系统是否真的以适任为基础：

设置的系统是否：

- 以明确规定所需表现为基础？
- 将评估表现成绩或效果作为重点？
- 独立于所有规定的学习计划？
- 用以反映要求的表现证据取自于实际考察并以针对实际表现进行的提问作为主要的评估方法？
- 是一个提供个体化评估的系统？
- 是一个包含对评估员收集的证据质量提供清晰指导的系统？
- 是一个包含质量保证的清晰指南和程序的系统？

规划适任评估

规划适任评估时主要考虑的是：

1. 评估什么？

    (a) 技术适任

    (b) 职业适任

    (c) 行为

    (d) 个人表现

    (e) 团队/小组表现

(f) Ability to learn

(g) Learning achievements

2. Why do we want to assess?

(a) To measure individual contribution to business objectives

(b) To measure group/team contribution to business objectives

(c) To certificate competence to nationally agreed standards

(d) To confirm competence against company specific standards

(e) To identify potential for further development

(f) To confirm outcomes of learning

All Forms of Assessment Have a Common Factor

Assessment is about the *collection of evidence*. All forms of assessment can be included in this description—from everyday activities to the most complex statistical systems.

For example, when shopping for clothes you assess the suitability of various items by matching the qualities of those items to the set of *requirements* you have established for yourself Your requirements may relate to price, size, colour, style and fit. You will therefore seek *evidence* from price tags and from examination and fitting of the items to help you make a judgement and final choice. Your final choice may allow for some compromise if you cannot find an item which meets *all* your requirements—that is, you will make a decision based on the best match of requirements and evidence.

Similarly, if you were taking a course of learning within a traditional vocational education and training system, you would be assessed by a tutor and/or examiner who would seek *evidence* that you had acquired the required *learning*. This evidence would be in the form of course assignments and probably a final examination, and would be matched against course *learning objectives*. The final decision would be influenced by a "norm-referenced" process, in other words, your results will be compared with those of other people. You would need to achieve an agreed percentage in order to pass the assessment (or indeed gain a "credit" or "distinction").

There are many instances in which we are either assessing or being assessed. In each instance, the assessment concerns the *collection of evidence*. This is, therefore, the common factor within all forms and all types of assessment. So why are there so many types?

（f） 学习能力

（g） 学习成绩

2. 评估目标是什么？

  （a） 评判个人对业务目标的贡献

  （b） 评判团队/小组对业务目标的贡献

  （c） 证明达到国家认可的适任标准

  （d） 确定达到公司规定的适任标准

  （e） 确定进一步发展的潜力

  （f） 确定学习的成绩

所有形式的评估有一个共同的要素

评估就是进行证据的收集。从日常活动到最复杂的统计系统，所有形式的评估都可以包括在该描述中。

例如，买衣服时，你通过将各种衣服的质量与你为自己设定的一套要求进行比对，评估各种衣服的适合性。你的要求可能与价格、尺寸、颜色、款式和舒适有关。因此，你会通过价格标签、检查和试衣寻找证据，从而帮助你做出判断和最终的选择。如果你不能够找到完全符合你所有要求的衣服，你最终可能会在自己的选择上做出让步，也就是在要求和证据最佳匹配的基础上做出决定。

同样地，如果你参加传统职业教育和系统的课程学习，一名辅导员和/或测试员会寻找你已经达到学习要求的证据，从而对你进行评估。证据可能是课程作业的形式，也可能是考试，并且与课程学习的目标相符。最终的决定将受"参考常模"程序的影响，换言之，会将你的成绩与其他人的成绩做比较。为了通过评估（或获得一个"学分"或获得"优秀成绩"的评价），你需要达到一个认可的百分点。

评估或被评估有多种不同的程序。无论采用什么程序，评估都涉及证据的收集。因此，这是所有评估形式和类型的共同要素。那么，为什么存在这么多的评估类型？

Although all forms of assessment concern the use of evidence, each form of assessment may have a different purpose. It is the purpose of assessment which will define the nature and process of the assessment system.

The Purpose of Assessment

The purpose of assessment when buying clothes is to collect sufficient evidence to enable you to buy the right clothes at the right price, or the closest possible match between your requirements and what is available.

The purpose of assessment within a programme of learning is to collect sufficient evidence to demonstrate that you have *learned* at least the required minimum percentage of the syllabus. If the programme of learning is also linked to an award system, a further purpose may be the achievement of formal recognition that learning has been acquired. This usually takes the form of a certificate or diploma.

In a competence-based assessment system, the purpose of assessment is to collect sufficient evidence that individuals *can perform or behave to the specified standards in a specific role*. If this assessment is also linked to an award system, a further purpose is formal recognition of successful performance.

The Assessment Process

A process is a "series of actions or events", or a "sequence of operations". We could say that all forms of assessment involve the following sequence of operations:

- defining requirements or objectives of assessment;

- collecting evidence;

- matching evidence to requirements or objectives; and

- making judgements based on this matching activity.

A programme of learning assessment is shown in Figure 10B-1.

From the figure, we can see how the purpose of assessment affects the assessment process and the assessment outcome.

尽管所有评估形式都涉及证据的采用,但每种评估形式可能有不同的目的。正是评估目的决定了评估系统的性质和程序。

评估目的

买衣服时,评估的目的是收集足够的证据,从而使你能够以适当的价格或在现有的商品中选择购买尽可能匹配你的要求的合适衣服。

在学习计划中,评估的目的是收集足够的证据以显示你已经学到大纲要求的最低百分比的知识或技能。如果,学习计划也与资格认证系统相联系,进一步的目的会是获得对已完成学习内容的正式认可。这种认可通常采用证书或文凭的形式。

在适任评估体系中,评估的目的是收集足够的证据,证明被评估人能够在特定岗位上按照规定的标准工作和表现。如果该评估也与资格认证系统相联系,进一步的目的是对成功表现的正式认定。

评估过程

过程是"一系列的行动或事件",或"操作流程"。可以说所有的评估形式都涉及以下的操作顺序:

- 规定评估要求或目标;
- 收集证据;
- 将证据与要求或目标进行比对;及
- 在比对的基础上做出评价。

图10B-1展示了一个学习评估的计划:

从图中,我们可以看出评估目的是如何影响评估过程和评估成绩的。

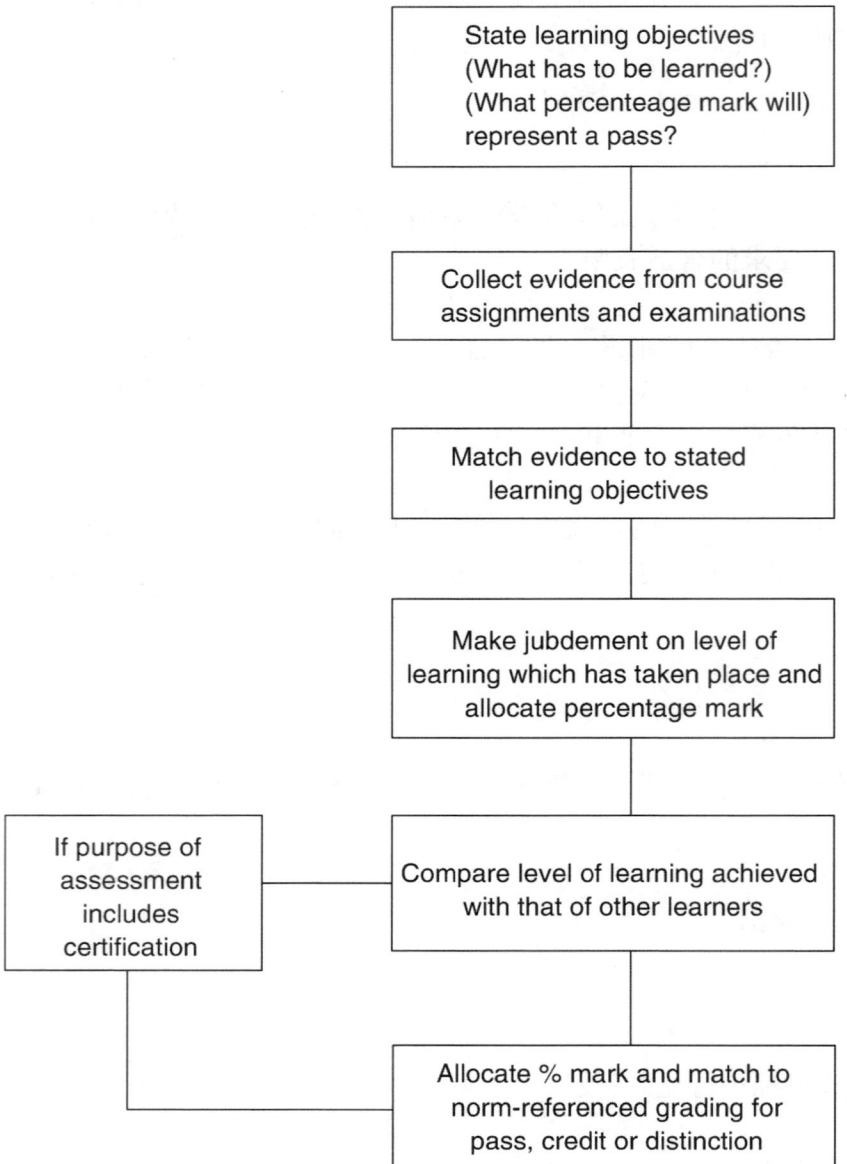

Figure 10B-1   Assessment process—programme of learning

In the above example, the basic process of stating objectives, collecting and matching evidence and making a judgement is consistent with all forms of assessment as noted at the beginning of this section. However, at this point, different sequences of actions are put into operation because the final purpose of assessment differs for each assessment event.

The assessment events move along a *comparison* route; by comparing the results of the assessment with the results of other, similar assessments in order to *decide what final grading to apply.*

This type of assessment process follows a comparative approach—it involves some form of comparison of assessment results or "norm-referencing", where an *average* achievement grade has been calculated and all *individual* achievements are judged against the average. Norm-referencing is the basis of most traditional assessment systems.

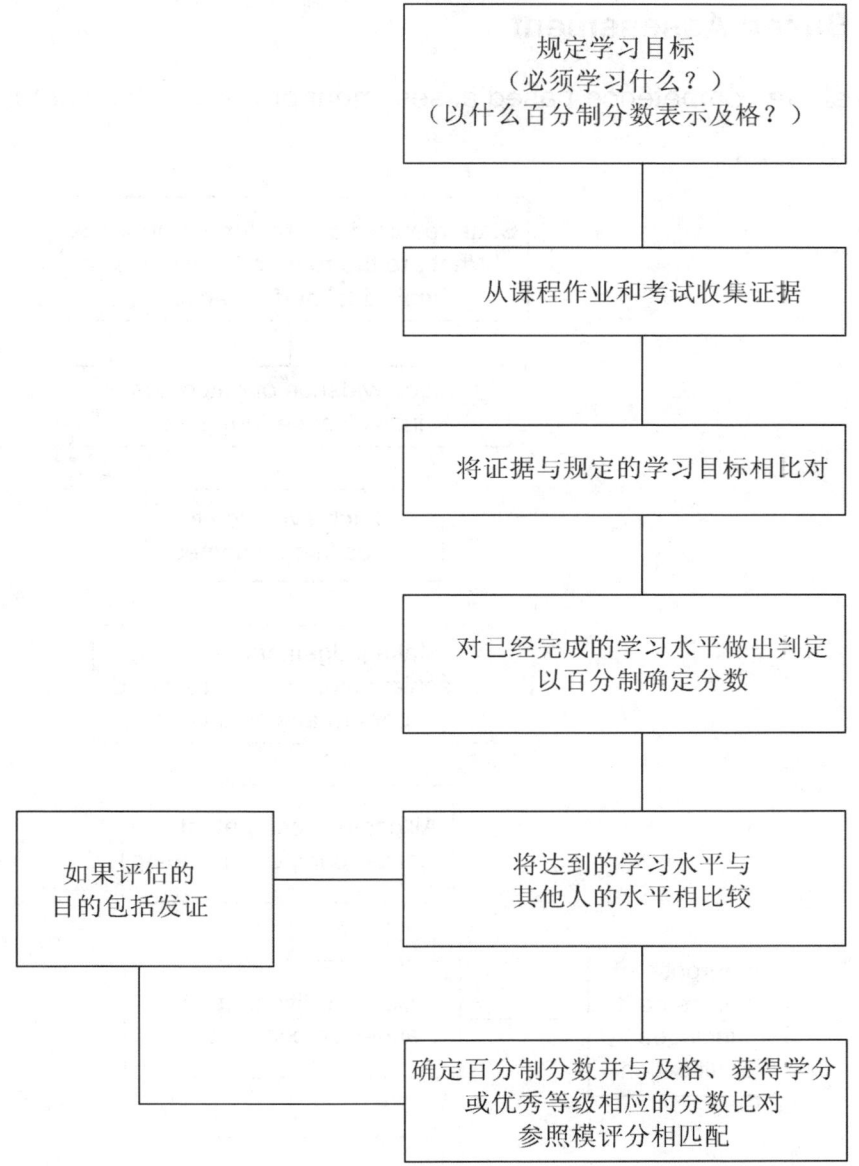

图 10B-1　评估过程——学习计划

在以上的例子中,正如本章的开始部分所说明的,规定目标、收集证据和比对证据以及做出评价的基本过程对于所有评估的形式都是一致的。然而,此时在操作中采用不同的运作顺序,因为对于不同的评估,其最终目的有所不同。

评估是采用比较的原理;通过将评估的成绩与类似评估的其他的成绩相比较,从而,决定应该采用怎样的最终评价标准。

这种类型的评估过程采用的比较方法涉及评估成绩之间的比较或采用所谓的"参照常模"形式,具体方法是先计算出平均成绩分数,然后参照平均分数评定所有被评估人的成绩。参照常模法是大部分传统评估系统的基础。

Competence-Based Assessment

Fig. 10B-2 looks at the competence-based assessment process in the same way.

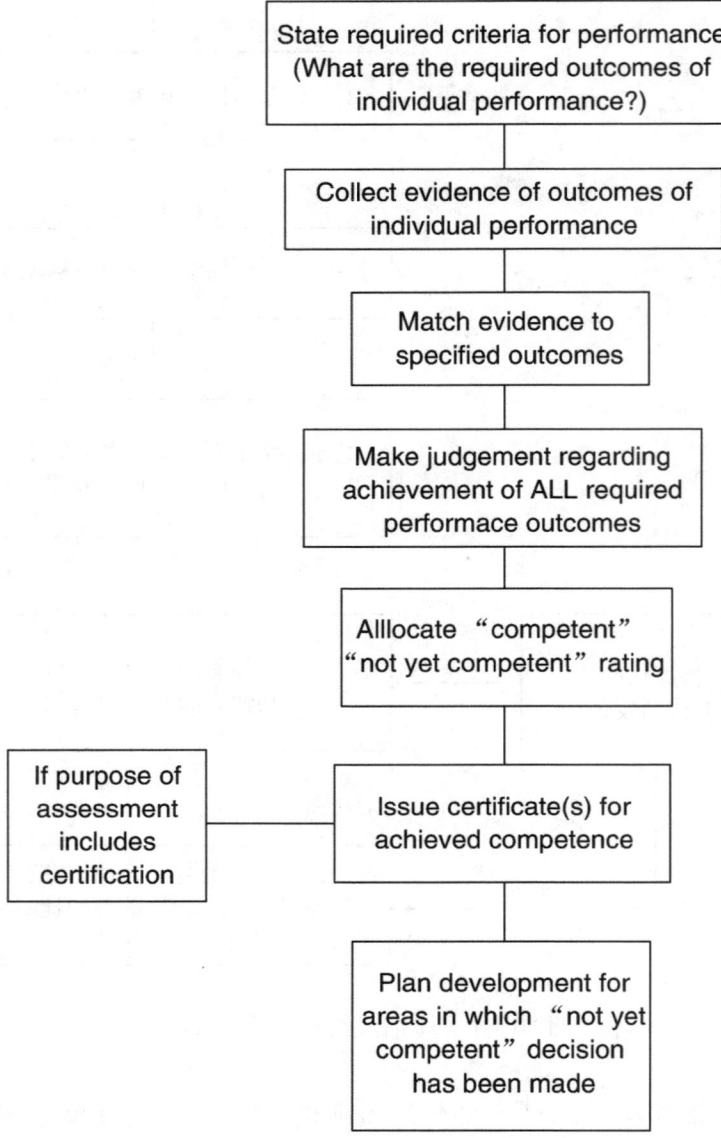

Fig. 10B-2 Assessment process—competence-based assessment

You may notice some key differences in the competence-based assessment approach:

- focus on "outcomes";
- individualized assessment;
- no percentage rating;
- no comparison with other individuals' results;

适任评估

图 10B-2 以相同的方式研究适任评估的过程。

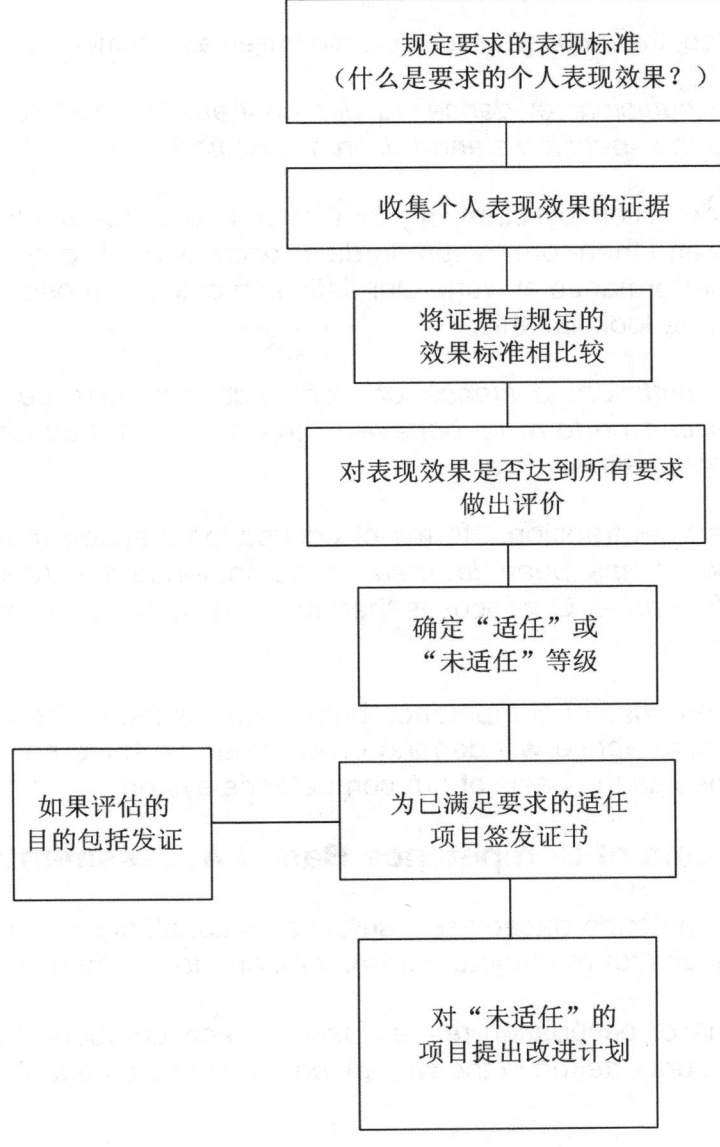

图 10B-2 评估过程——适任评估

你可能注意到基于适任评估的方法的一些主要不同点：

- 侧重"效果"；

- 个体化的评估；

- 没有百分制等级；

- 不与其他被评估人的成绩相比较；

- all standards (requirements) must be met;
- on-going process (leads to further development and assessment);
- only "competent" or "not yet competent" judgements made.

As we have already noted, the *purpose* of competence-based assessment is:

> *To collect sufficient evidence to demonstrate that individuals can* **perform or behave** *to the specified standards in a specified role.*

We can add to this definition by clarifying that in competence-based assessment we are referring to *work roles* and therefore to standards of *occupational competence*. Occupational competence reflects performance at work. Our definition of the purpose of competence-based assessment will therefore look like this:

> *To collect sufficient evidence of workplace performance to demonstrate that individuals can perform or behave to the specified standards required within a specified occupational role.*

This differs drastically from traditional forms of occupational assessment in which evidence collected relates to what has been *learned*. In competence-based assessment, our key concern is *actual performance*. Our focus is therefore, on *what individuals* can do rather than what individuals know.

This outlines the *key purpose* of competence-based assessment. The issue of "perform" vs "behave" in the definition above will depend on whether we have set vocational outcomes or behavioural outcomes as the basis of our competence system.

Practical Implications of Competence-Based Assessment

The introduction of competence-based assessment at national, organizational or departmental level has wide implications for managers, for trainers, and for those being assessed.

Unlike traditional forms of occupation-related assessment, competence-based assessment can be, and should be, undertaken in the workplace, and should be individualized.

Who Assesses?

The first question then is if assessment is to be undertaken in the workplace, who are the assessors?

The most obvious choice is the supervisor or line manager. This arrangement raises a number of questions:

- Do supervisors and managers have time to undertake formal assessment?
- What if the supervisor or assessor doesn't like, or has a poor relationship with the person being assessed?
- What skills will assessors need?

- 必须符合所有标准（要求）；

- 跟进程序（引导进一步的发展和评估）；

- 只做出"适任"或"未适任"的评定；

正如我们前面已经说明的，适任评估的目的是：

> 收集足够的证据，证明被评估人能够在具体岗位上按照规定的标准**工作和表现**。

我们可以将此定义增加到岗位工作适任评估的规定和职业适任的标准中。职业适任反映了个人在工作中的表现。适任评估的目的的定义将因此是：

> 收集在岗位工作方面表现的足够的证据，以证明被评估人能够在特定的职业岗位上按照规定的标准工作和表现。

这与仅收集有关完成学习的证据的传统形式的职业评估有很大的不同。在适任评估中，我们主要关心的是实际表现。因此，我们所关注的是被评估人能做什么而不是被评估人知道什么。

在这里我们概述了适任评估的主要目的。上述定义中的"工作"及"表现"的确定取决于我们设定作为适任系统基础的工作或表现效果标准。

适任评估的实际问题

在国家、组织或部门层面引进适任评估，对于主管、培训人员和接受评估的人都具有广泛的意义。

与传统的职业评估形式不同，适任评估可以并且应当在工作岗位上进行，以及应当针对被评估人安排。

由谁评估？

如果评估在工作岗位上进行，那么首要的问题是：由谁担任评估员？

最显然的选择是管理人或部门主管。但这种安排会造成一些问题：

- 管理人或部门主管是否有时间承担正式的评估工作？

- 如果管理人或评估员不喜欢接受评估的人或与其关系甚差，会出现什么情况？

- 评估员需要什么技能？

What about quality?

The second implication concerns the movement of assessment to a local rather than a central basis:

- How can quality of assessment be assured if it is undertaken locally by line managers?
- Who trains assessors?
- Who ensures that quality of assessment is maintained?
- Who pays for this?

Training

Last but not least is the issue of linking competence-based assessment to training. As the assessment system operates on a continuous—rather than one-off-basis, and is operated within the workplace environment, training needs are identified at individual level. Questions here include:

- What systems do we need to ensure that identified training needs are communicated to those who can take relevant action?
- In what way do we need to reorganize our training resources to provide training which meets those needs?

For educational institutions and for business organizations, the issues of resourcing, reorganization and administration are paramount.

Assessment for Certification

In a competence-based system, assessment leading to certification refers to "certification of competent performance", not to certification of ability to learn or to completion of a learning programme.

Think this through carefully. There is a huge difference between the various purposes of certification: consider some of the certificates you have seen at various times. What do these certificates actually tell you about the certificate holder? That the certificate holder:

- has *attended* a course of study or learning?
- has *completed* a course of study or learning?
- has demonstrated the *ability to learn to a particular level*?
- has demonstrated that specified theories/facts *have been learned*?
- has achieved a specified percentage grade in a *written exam*?
- has achieved a specified percentage grade in a *practical test*?

质量如何？

第二个问题关注的是分散开展而不是集中的评估活动：

- 如果评估分散地由行业主管负责，如何确保评估的质量？
- 由谁培训评估员？
- 由谁保证评估质量得到保持？
- 由谁支付这些费用？

培训

最后一个但也是相当重要的问题是如何将适任评估与培训结合起来。因为评估系统是在一个持续的，而不是一次性活动的基础上运作的，并且是在工作岗位环境下运作的，因此培训需要因人而异。问题包括：

- 需要怎样的系统来确保将已经确定的培训需求告知采取相关行动的人？
- 需要用什么方法来重组我们的培训资源，从而提供符合需要的培训？

对于培训机构和行业组织，提供资源并进行重新组织和管理是最重要的。

发证评估

在适任评估体系中，发证的评估指"对适任表现发证"，而不是对学习能力或完成学习的项目发证。

应仔细考虑不同发证的目的之间有很大的不同：研究你在不同时间看见过的证书实际上证明相关持有人的什么情况？即证书持有人：

- 是否已经参加了课程研究或学习？
- 是否已经完成了课程研究或学习？
- 是否已经显示了达到特定水平的学习能力？
- 是否已经显示了学习过规定的理论/实际？
- 是否已经达到笔试中规定的百分制评分的成绩？
- 是否已经达到实践测试中规定的按百分制评分的成绩？

In a competence-based assessment and certification system, individuals achieve a certificate when they can *demonstrate performance which meets all the required standards*. Remember, there is no percentage grading, no norm-referencing, no pass or fail—only competent or not yet competent.

Figure 10B-3 illustrates these differences between the traditional and competence-based systems.

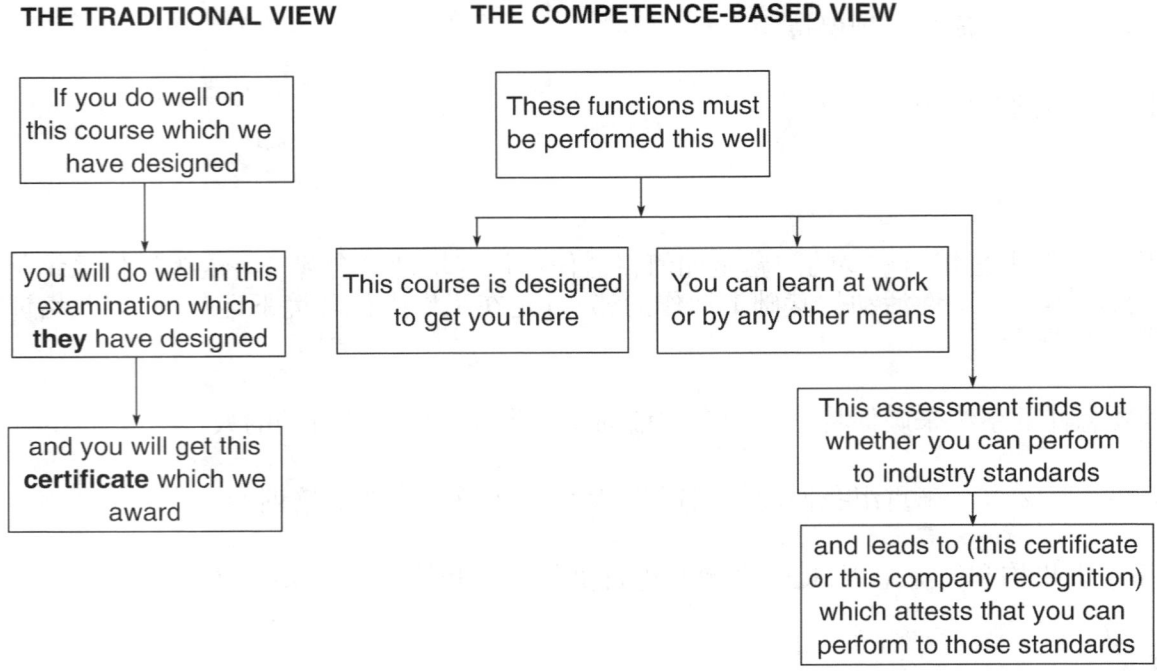

Figure 10B-3 Key differences between the traditional and competence-based systems

Other Uses of Competence-based Assessment

1. Performance Appraisal

Many organizations have performance appraisal systems. These usually operate on an annual basis and involve an interview with a line manager and use of a pre-interview question sheet.

Most criticisms of this system stem from the use of measures which are very difficult to assess and of rating scales which generally lead to assessors taking the "middle road" as an easy option.

Competence-based assessment as the basis of performance appraisal provides a more specific measure of performance.

To use the full potential of competence-based assessment within performance appraisal often requires a complete rethinking of the existing process and a broader view of appraisal as one part of a wider performance management system.

在适任评估和发证的系统中,如果被评估人能够显示符合所有要求的标准时,则可获得证书。记住,不按百分制评分、不参照常模(不与其他人的成绩进行比较)、不分及格或不及格——只有适任或未适任。

图 10 B-3 说明传统的观点与基于适任系统之间的差别。

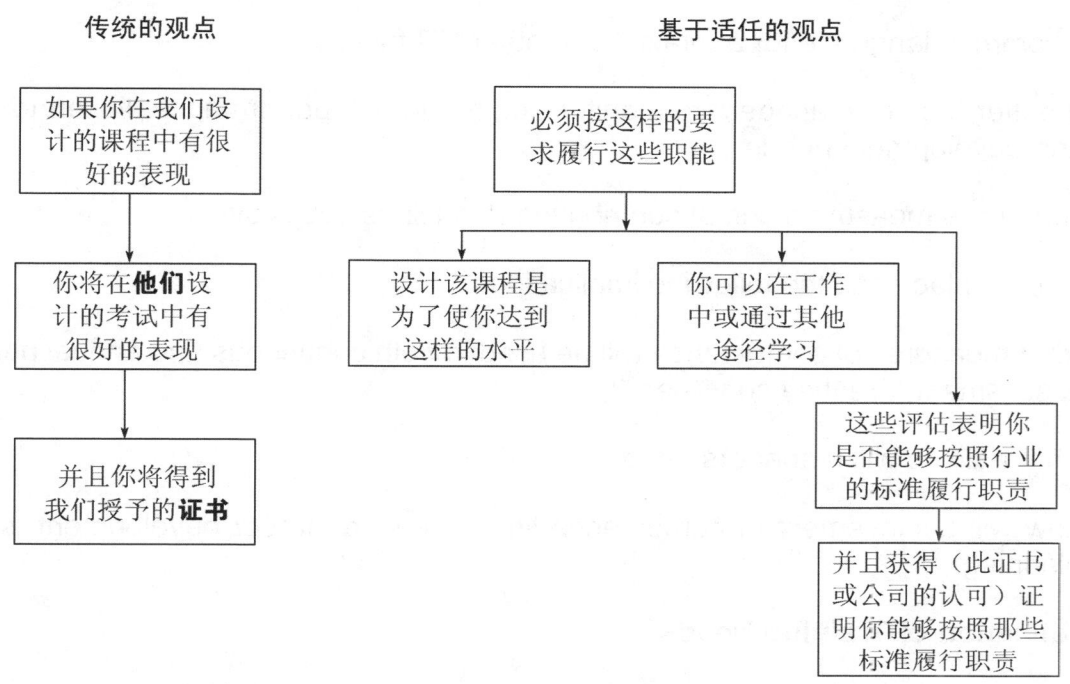

图 10 B-3　传统的与基于适任系统方法之间的主要区别

适任评估的其他用途

1. 工作表现评价

许多组织有工作表现评价系统。评价通常以年度为基础并且包括部门主管约谈和在约谈前的进行问卷调查。

对该系统形式的大部分批评是因为其使用的方法很难进行评价,导致评估员一般采取较易选择的"中庸路线"来评定等级。

以适任评估作为表现评价系统的基础可以提供更专业化的评价。

要在工作表现评价中充分发挥适任评估的潜力,通常要求对现有过程全面进行重新考虑,引进更开阔的评价观念以建立一个更加广泛的工作表现管理系统。

Implications and benefits

A competence-based performance appraisal system could provide the following benefits:

- integration of continuous performance management with annual/ biannual review and objective setting;
- a common language for appraisal and other HR functions;
- a better tool for managers to monitor and feed-back performance, linked to objectives and development needs;
- appraisals measuring actual contribution to business objectives.

Putting this in place has the following implications:

- what measures of competence will be used in both continuous and annual performance assessment (are they consistent?);
- what training will managers need;
- how will achievement of competence link to reward, career development, succession planning.

2. Identification of Training Needs

Competence-based assessment offers an opportunity, through continuous measuring and managing of performance, for managers to identify training needs at individual level.

If such a system is introduced at organization level, the ability to identify these needs, and thus to provide training which is targeted to specific needs, is greatly improved.

Implications and benefits

Operation of a competence-based system for the identification of training needs requires that managers are skilled in identifying real, rather than perceived, needs, in providing feedback, and in identifying those needs which can be dealt with by on job development. A further added value aspect of competence-based systems therefore is that managers are encouraged to take more of a development role. However, managers will need appropriate skills to achieve this effectively. Key questions in this context are:

- What training will our managers need in

  — identifying training needs?
  — coaching?
  — mentoring?
  — opportunity training?

- What communication structure needs to be in place to ensure that training needs are collated?

问题和效益

基于适任的工作表现评估系统能够提供下列的效益：

- 通过每年/每两年进行的审核和目标设定工作来保持连续完整的工作表现管理；
- 为评估和其他人力资源管理职能提供共同的管理语言；
- 是主管人员对与目标和发展需要相关的工作表现进行监督和反馈的更好的工具；
- 是衡量对业务目标实际贡献的评价。

使用该系统应恰当考虑下列问题：

- 持续的和年度的工作表现评估应当使用什么样的适任措施（它们是否统一？）；
- 需要对主管进行什么培训；
- 如何将适任与奖赏、个人事业发展和随后的计划相联系。

2.确定培训需要

适任评估通过连续评价和管理雇员的工作表现，为主管提供了确定适合被评估人水平的培训需要的机会。

如果在机构层面引进这样的系统，则可大大地提高确定这类需要和针对性地提供以需要为目标的培训的能力。

问题和效益

为了确认培训需要，基于适任的系统的运作要求主管能够确认真正而不是感觉上的培训需要，确认可以在工作中获得提高的培训需要并向雇员反馈。因此，基于适任的系统的另一个价值是鼓励主管对于雇员的事业发展发挥更大的作用。然而，主管需要具备适当的技能以便有效地达到这个目的。主要的问题是：

- 我们需要对主管进行以下哪方面的培训：

  —确认培训需求？
  —技术指导？
  —职业顾问？
  —培训机会？

- 需要怎样适当的交流结构以确保对培训需求进行审核？

■ What changes do we need to make to our training delivery function to provide modular development programmes?

This last question is often missed. If needs are identified more accurately, there is no longer a need for individuals to attend a "standard" course—they need only attend courses where on-job development is not available or appropriate, and the course is modular in format and targeted to their specific needs.

At strategic level, identification of training needs as part of a skills audit, using a competence-based system, can assist with the development of corporate training strategies and plans, or indeed with manpower planning activities.

3. Skills Audit

All organizations would probably find it valuable to be able to take stock of their workforce skills. A competence-based system of assessment allows for this to take place either as an initial, introductory process or as the result of collated data from an on-going assessment process.

You may consider introducing a computerized assessment recording system. This is particularly useful in organizations which need to put together project teams, each member having specialist skills or expertise.

As an initial assessment, the competency measures can be used to assess current levels of performance (and identify training needs). As continuous assessment, the competence-based system allows for regular monitoring and updating of workforce skill levels.

For example, by providing individuals and their line managers with a copy of the standards which are relevant to their work role, and with guidance on their use, initial assessment will provide an analysis of current skills levels and training needs. As the assessment requires that evidence of competent performance is provided, and this evidence is generated from normal workplace activity, the individual can prove competence through the provision of relevant evidence.

Similarly, in a continuous assessment process, the level of competent performance, and training needs, continue to be identified.

In essence, a competence-based assessment system should make explicit what effective line managers do on a daily basis—*measure and manage performance*. Competence-based assessment should become an integral part of everyday management activity and involve line managers and those being assessed in a continuous process of development and improvement.

Implications and benefits

Again, the measures must be in place before you start, so you may need to invest in this development.

The term "skills audit" has unfortunate connotations. Any introduction in a strong union environment may therefore need careful planning and negotiation. The purpose of the skills audit must be clear if it is to be used as a positive motivator for improvement of performance.

■ 需要做出怎样的改变使我们的培训教学职能以便提供模块化的发展计划？

最后一个问题经常被遗忘。这就是——如果能更加精确地确定需求，被评估人则不再需要参加"传统的"课程——他们只需要参加在职学习中缺少的或不适于开展的课程，并且此类课程应以模块化形式以及以特定的需求为目标开设。

在决策层面上，利用基于适任的系统来确认技能培训需求，有助于开发公司的培训策略和计划，也有助于人力资源规划活动。

3.技能审查

所有的机构都可能会发现，能对他们的劳动技能做出评估是有价值的。在基于评估系统的适任能力体系，无论在初始介绍过程中，还是在持续评估过程整理数据结果中，这样做都是可行的。

您可以考虑引进电脑评估记录系统。这对需要集中项目团队、有专业技能或专业知识各成员国组织特别有用。

作为初始评估，可以运用的适任性手段，以评估现行操作水平（和确定培训需求）。经过不断的评估，基于能力的系统允许定期监督和提高员工技能水平。

例如，与工作角色相关的标准的复印件及其使用指南提供给个人和他们的一线管理者，则初始评估将给出对现有技能水平和培训需求的分析。因为评估要求提供的适任资格证明，并从正常的工作场所活动形成这方面的证据，所以个人可以通过提供相关证据证明适任能力。

同样，在连续的评估过程中，可以继续确定其适任能力水平和培训需求。

从本质上说，基于评估系统的适任性应该明确有效的一线管理者每日所做的——措施和管理能力。基于评估的适任性应该成为日常管理事务完整部分，并涉及一线管理者和那些在不断发展和改进过程中被评估的人员

意义与效益

再次，在你开始之前必须要准备好这些措施，所以你可能需要投资于这一发展。

"技能审核"这个术语有着不幸的含义。因此，在一个强大的联盟环境中的任何采用，可能需要仔细的规划和谈判。如果要作为一个能力改善的积极促进因素使用，技能审计的目的必须要明确。

4. Accreditation of Prior Learning (APL)

The APL process provides a useful tool in three areas:

- introducing competence-based assessment;

- taking a skills audit;

- as a staff development process.

APL is an integral part of competency-based assessment, not a separate process. It is one which allows for evidence from past achievements to be included in the total of evidence collected during assessment. There are particular rules of evidence which apply in this context, but there is no reason why APL cannot be as reliable and effective as continuous assessment of performance-as long as quality rules are applied.

Implications and benefits

APL is a useful tool for motivating staff and for introducing competence-based assessment. It requires trained assessors and probably advisers. It can be a very cost-effective process for skills audit. Check carefully about costs-per-head quotations when seeking advice from external sources.

5. Selection and Recruitment

Again, the issue of having measures developed arises: you cannot assess competence unless you have a clear measure of competence to begin with. However, once you have the measures they can be used for a wide range of purposes.

Competence-based measures of performance focus on outcomes. If you know what outcomes you require, you can design your recruitment and selection processes around them.

Using the competence measures as a starting point, your recruitment material and interview schedules can be designed to elicit information which directly relates to required performance. (Note the use of the term "schedules" for interviews—the implication is that questions are pre-determined and follow an agreed format and presentation. This will enable interviews to be conducted in a fair and effective way.)

Implications and benefits

Recruitment and selection processes can be defined with more clarity using a competence-based system. The standards used as a basis for the design of these processes are common across all activities within the organization; there is therefore less chance of a mismatch between staff recruited and staff required. To implement such a system, time must be devoted to the development of interview schedules and training of interviewers. (Again, use of competence-based assessment leads to identification of training needs and requires that training is more systematic and directed to real needs.)

4.事先学习的认可 (APL)

　　APL 过程在下面三个领域提供有用工具：

■　　引入基于能力的评估；

■　　举行技能审核；

■　　作为员工的发展过程。

　　APL 是基于评估的适任能力的完整部分，而不是一个独立的过程。这是一个允许从过去的成就包括在评估过程中收集证据的证据。在这方面证据运用有具体规定，但没有理由在持续的能力评估中 APL 不能作为可靠和有效的证据——只要质量规则适用。

意义与效益

　　APL 是激励员工的一个有用的工具，也是采用基于适任评估的有用工具。它需要训练有素的评估员和可能顾问。对审计员来说，它能作为一个非常具有成本效益的过程。在征求外部意见时，仔细检查每头报价的成本。

5.选拔和招聘

　　同样，制定措施的问题出现了：只有以明确的适任性措施作为开始，才能评估适任性。但是，一旦你有措施，这些措施就可以用于多种用途。

　　基于操作措施的适任性聚焦于结果。如果你明了你所要求的结果，那就可以围绕结果设计你的招聘与选拔方法。

　　使用适任性措施作为一个起点，就能设计出你的招聘材料和面试时间表，以便得出与所要求的操作直接有关的信息。(注意面试要使用"时间表"这个术语——其含义是，问题是预先定好的，并按照约定的格式和内容进行。这将使面试以公平而有效地方式进行。)

意义与效益

　　运用适任性体系可以更清楚地确定招聘和选拔的过程。设计这些过程所运用的标准在本机构所有事务中是常见的；因此，招聘来的人员与所要求的人员之间不匹配的机会少了，要实施这样一个体系，必须花时间来制定面试时间表和对面试官的培训。(还有，运用基于评估的适任性，有助于确定培训需求，并要求培训更加系统性以满足实际需求。)

6. Evaluating Training

This is an area which has caused considerable concern but least remedial effort in many organizations. As long as employers see training as a cost rather than an investment, little action will be taken to evaluate the effectiveness of training programmes. When training becomes an investment issue, the question of gaining the best possible return on that investment becomes important.

With competence-based assessment systems, the measures of competent performance are available for a before-and-after picture to be taken. If measures are used, as they should be, on a continuous basis to measure and manage performance and to identify training needs, then the measurement required to check on the effectiveness of training is already in place.

Training is too often an activity in which individuals are allocated to programmes on a "grade-related" basis, or are sent to the most appropriate programme on the company's "menu". Far too few training consultancies actually make training applicable to the working context. So-called evaluation of programmes is in practice often no more than an enquiry as to the food, accommodation and whether participants liked the trainer.

If an organization needs to evaluate the effectiveness of training and perhaps the effectiveness of managers' identification of real training needs—then a competence-based assessment system provides a framework in which this can be operated.

Implementation and benefits

The key costs are in development—development of the competence measures and the associated assessment framework. Operational costs are minimal once competence measures are established they are available for use in the full range of business activities. In effect, their use for training evaluation is a spin-off or added-value aspect of the implementation process.

6.评估培训

这是一个在许多机构中引起了相当大的关注，但补救努力却最少的领域。只要用人单位看到培训作为一种成本，而不是一种投资，则很少采取行动来评估培训计划的有效性。当培训成为投资问题时，获得这种投资的最佳回报问题就变得很重要。

运用基于能力的评估系统，适任性作业措施可以采纳一个之前和之后的情景。如果运用一个持续的基础上的措施来衡量和管理绩效，并确定培训需求，然后用来检查培训效果所需的措施就已经到位。

培训是一个十分平常的教育活动，以相关等级为基础来分派人员训练，或者被派到公司"菜单"中最适合的训练。太少的培训咨询公司实际上使得培训适用于工作坏境。所谓的培训评估实际上还不及关于食物、住宿和参加者是否喜欢培训员的一个咨询。

如果一个机构需要评估培训的有效性，也或许评估管理者确定真实培训需求的有效性——那么基于评估的适任性体系就可提供能运作的工作框架。

补充与效益

主要的成本在于制定——制定适任性措施和相关的评估框架。营运成本是最少的。一旦适任性措施得以确立，这些措施就广泛地使用于事务活动。实际上，在培训评估中这些措施的运用只是在实施过程的次要用途或者说是附加增值部分。

Part 10-3
Methodologies in standards development

Preparing the ground for industry participation

The starting point in the development of competence standards is the familiarization and education of the different stakeholders. Examples of this preparation work included:

- systematic market research and needs analysis to identify priority areas and concerns.

- newsletters explaining in user-friendly language different aspects of national training reform, the purposes of standards development as well as the processes and benefits.

- developing clear industry focused frameworks for the standards development process, showing the clear links between standards, business objectives and individual career path progression.

- ensuring equity balance and expertise on reference groups established.

- briefing workshops for reference groups as well as workplaces to familiarise them with the purpose, process, terminology and tools of standards development.

- pilot projects to gain support and establish credibility at broad industry level.

- establishing a clear tri-partite approach to standards development by enlisting the active support of unions and key employers.

Representation

As well as equity representation and input at decision making levels, representation of all sectors of the industry is critical at developmental stages to enhance the quality and inclusiveness of the competency standards and training arrangements.

The inclusion of equity expertise is necessary to ensure the inclusiveness and validity of the outcomes.

Holistic approach

The advantages of a holistic approach to standards and skills development have been widely discussed and accepted in recent years. From industry's perspective, holistic approaches to standards and learning have been recognised as vital if they are to the raise quality, speed and flexibility of their products and services. It is generally recognised that given similar levels of technology across the world, the only competitive edge an enterprise has resides in its human resource base: its people, their skills, knowledge and ability to work together.

第10-3章
制定标准的方法

建立行业合作的基础

制定适任标准的起点是了解和教育各个利益相关方。准备工作包括：

- 系统的市场调查和需求分析，以确认优先区域和利害关系。

- 通过简报使用友善的语言解释国家培训改革的各个方面，制定标准的目的、过程和好处。

- 应为标准的开发过程建立明确的关注行业的体系，清楚显示标准、业务目标和个人事业途径发展之间的联系。

- 保证成立公正、平衡和内行的鉴定小组。

- 召开鉴定小组简报会介绍情况，并召开研讨会使他们熟悉标准制定的目的、过程、术语和工具。

- 在广泛的行业阶层获得支持和建立信任的引导计划。

- 通过获得工会或主要雇主的积极支持，为标准建立一个清晰的三方方案。

代表性

除了合理代表和采纳决策层次的要求，很有必要在方案制定阶段就使其具备对于行业所有部门的代表性，以便提高适任标准和培训安排的质量和包容性。

有必要采纳公正的专家意见以保证定出的标准的包容性和有效性。

整体方案

近几年，在标准和技能开发中采用整体方案的优点已得到广泛讨论和接受。从行业的角度，要提高他们的产品和服务的质量、速度和可靠性，采用对于标准和学习的整体方案被认为是非常重要的。大家公认，在全球技术水平相当的情况下，行业竞争的唯一优势在于它的人力资源：在于它的员工，员工的技能、知识和工作协作能力。

From an equity perspective, it has also been generally accepted that the adoption of a holistic rather than a narrow approach to skills identification and development allows for the recognition of previously taken for granted, assumed competencies, such as conceptual and human competencies (interpersonal skills, resourcefulness and organisational ability, etc) in addition to mechanical and technical competencies.

Adopting a holistic approach to standards development requires a complex set of skills from standards developers, and is to a great extent dependent on the prevailing work culture in the industry, and the support provided for re-conceptualising work beyond a checklist of observable tasks.

The skills of standards developers

In many ways, standards developers are the linchpin to the quality and inclusiveness of standards. Consultations indicated their critical role in brokering between the different stakeholders and probing for good practice rather than just settling for minimalist consensus. Almost invariably, standards developers are consultants contracted for a specific standards development project. Their own levels of awareness and expertise vary greatly, and in the absence of clearer process and content guidance to assist them in their task, the outcomes will continue to be of varied quality:

"Consultants are pivotal to the quality of product, but unfortunately, the quality of the consultant is often left to chance, with no training." (Vocational Education Training (VET) consultant)

Some of the critical underlying competencies identified for effective consultants included:

- VET and industry knowledge—the ability to massage workshop results to accord with national policies and trends, knowledge of industry and VET best practice, to propose flexible structures for standards

- facilitation and negotiation, skills—the ability to challenge the status quo, to present future work scenarios, deal with power relationships, and industry factions, enhance participation from equity groups

- realism and political know how in terms of what can be achieved

- expertise in equity, language and literacy, document design, or the ability to draw on resources in these areas

- open mindedness and responsiveness to feedback, the ability to critically reflect on one's own work and assumptions.

Structure of standards

The ways that standards are structured have considerable implications for equity. The flexible design of units, for example, can maximise career path opportunities and cross-industry transferability.

从公正的角度,也普遍采纳整体方案而不是局限的方法来识别和发展技能,允许认可先前已认可的和可能已具备的适任能力,例如理性和人类的能力(交际的技能、资源积累和组织的能力等),以及体能和技术的能力。

采纳标准开发的整体方案要求标准开发者具备综合的技能,并且从很大程度上取决于行业现行的工作文化,以及支持对没有被列入核查表的其他任务的必要考虑。

标准开发者的技巧

在许多方面,标准制定者是标准的质量和包容性的关键。咨询意见显示他们作为中间人在不同利益方之间和调查良好惯例方面可以起到重要的作用,而不仅仅是取得最低的统一意见。在绝大多数情况下,标准开发者是为开发特定的标准项目而签约的顾问。他们的学识和专业水平会有很大的差异,并且缺乏比较清晰的过程和内容指导以协助他们的工作,工作成果的质量并不稳定:

"顾问对于产品的质量是非常重要的,但不幸的是没有经过培训的顾问的素质常常是不稳定的。"〔摘自职业教育培训(VET)顾问〕

得力的顾问的重要基本能力包括:

- 职业教育培训和行业知识——将工作结果与国家的政策和趋势、行业知识和职业教育培训最好的惯例进行协调,从而制定结构灵活的标准

- 促进和协商的能力及技巧——挑战现状、呈现将来工作状况、处理权力关系及行业摩擦、加强公正机构参与的能力

- 对现实主义和如何实现的政治了解

- 是公平理念、语言和读写能力、文件设计方面的专家,或利用这些领域资源的能力

- 对反馈有开阔的思路和快速的反应,对自己的工作和设想的批判式反省能力

标准的结构

制定标准结构的方法对能否确保公正具有相当大的意义。例如,项目的灵活设计能够扩大就业途径、机会和跨行业就业的转换能力。

Ways of enhancing equity through attention to the structure of standards included:

- Maximising flexibility based on an industry framework emphasising the commonalities across related sectors. As well as providing flexibility of career path opportunities, such an approach also allows for particular competencies to be recognised and developed.

- Structuring units to break down traditional rigidities and demarcations. In the case of the following enterprise standards for example, the standards were deliberately designed to facilitate the access of women to less traditional work roles:

"Our competency profile has broken down some of barriers with areas like fork lift driving, and maintenance. They've just become part of the work, and more women are involved in those areas as a result." (Training and Development Manager)

- Ensuring a systematic progression from lower classification levels to more highly skilled work. Rather than relying on entry-level being solely based on a higher qualification, providing a work-based career path option is a real way of creating more opportunities for those at work.

Language and terminology used in standards

As previous work in skills analysis has pointed out, the naming of skills is crucial in giving due recognition to skills and maximising career path opportunities. For example, in the Clerical/Administrative competencies, "technology" is the term used to refer to the operation of office equipment such as computers, rather than more reductionist terms such as "word-processing".

With standards being used as the sole benchmark for skills recognition and development, there is a major equity issue with the current levels of abstraction and complexity of language used in standards documents. Draft competency descriptions are often rewritten after a standards development workshop to make them more concise, consistent and authoritative. The requirement to "report problems with work" for example, can find itself translated as "variations and constraints affecting work requirements are identified and reported to nominated person so that appropriate corrective action can be taken".

As with this fictitious illustration, the majority of standards use jargon, dense phrases and the passive voice to supposedly express performance criteria in an outcome focused way. This inevitably makes them more opaque and less accessible to direct users, such as trainees, trainers and assessors. More significantly perhaps, such linguistic mystification sends a clear but erroneous message to workers that the texts are not intended for their use. Yet, more than ever, employees and trainees need to be thoroughly familiar with the format and content of the standards relevant to their work. There is therefore, a greater imperative for them to be in jargon free and transparent language.

Assessment Systems and Processes

While assessment systems and processes are not strictly part of standards development, they are mentioned briefly here. As a result of these reforms, evidence guides have in many cases, needed to be reviewed and considerably expanded to specify the context for assessment, and the underpinning knowledge and skills.

通过考虑标准的结构加强公平性的方法包括：

- 强调跨部门的共同标准使行业体系具有最大灵活性，以及提供就业机会的灵活性，这种措施也允许认可和发展特定领域的适任。

- 打破传统的定式和界限。例如，在下列企业标准中，经过仔细地设定以便加快妇女加入非传统的工作。

  "能力结构的变化已经使一些领域的就业障碍被打破，如在叉车驾驶和维护领域，已有部分工作由妇女完成，结果将导致更多的妇女加入这些领域。"（摘自《培训和发展管理者》）

- 确保从较低级别水平到更高技能的工作有一个系统的过程，而不是仅仅依靠以较高的入门水平为资格基准。提供一个以工作为基础的事业道路选择是给正在工作的人们创造更多机会的真正方法。

标准中使用的语言和术语

正如先前对技能分析所指出的，技能的命名对于正确认可技能和扩大事业机会相当重要。例如，对于人员的/管理的能力，采用"技术"这样一个针对办公室设备（如电脑）操作的术语，而不采用更约简的术语如"文字处理"。

由于标准是技能认可和发展的唯一基准，目前的缩写水平和标准文件中语言的复杂性存在较大的公平性问题。用于说明适任能力的初步方案通常需要通过标准开发研讨会研讨并重新修改，以使它们更加简洁、统一和具有权威性。例如对于"报告工作中的问题"的要求，可以诠释为"确定并向上级报告影响工作需要的变化和限制，从而可以做出适当的改正措施"。

出于误解，大部分的标准采用行话、大量短语和被动语态，意图采取针对结果的方式表达表现标准。这无可避免地使标准更加难理解以及与直接使用者如学员、培训和评估人员拉开距离。也许更加重要的是，这样的语言困惑给操作人员传送一个清楚的信息，即这东西不是给他们使用的。然而，现在比以往更加需要雇员和学员完全熟悉与他们工作有关的标准的格式和内容。因此，更加有必要采用通用的和明晰的语言。

评估系统和过程

评估系统和过程严格说来并不是标准开发的一部分，因此在这里只是简要提及。由于评估系统和过程的改革，在很多情况下需要对证据管理进行研究以及扩展指定的评估、基础知识和技能范围。

In specifying the context, many standards developers reported a preference for locating assessment on the job, as closely linked as possible with normal working activity. In terms of equity, there are several advantages of such an approach. Firstly, there would be potentially greater access to assessment, because of the increased convenience. Secondly, extra requirements, such as competence in language and literacy, or formal test methods would be minimal. Competence would be established on the basis of work performance on real tasks, rather than artificial ones. Trainees would also presumably feel more confident in their daily work situation, and therefore potentially be able to perform at their optimum.

The greater detailing of knowledge and skills, it was argued, will enable trainees to self assess, and better prepare for their assessment.

Potential Benefits of Standards development in Training

1. A greater integration of theory and practice, with increased emphasis on workplace based learning

The focus is shifting much more to the enterprise level, with training becoming more directly linked to competency standards, and workplace applications rather than formal, off the job, structured training.

In the same way, the new arrangements envisage that largely institutionally based assessment will, over time, give way to assessment models which will allow learners to demonstrate competence in real work situations, often, as part of their daily work routines, rather than undergoing artificial or double assessments in a training institution.

2. Greater flexibility in training provision

Under the new arrangements, learners are able to access the same outcomes through different means that best suit their particular situations.

3. Greater mechanisms for recognition and access to further training

With assessment being directly referenced to competency standards, rather than accredited courses, and conducted in the workplace, there is a greater likelihood of individuals having their prior learning and current competency recognised. This shift will also potentially allow for incremental recognition and partial access to qualifications, as trainees acquire different units of competence.

The introduction of a uniform, recognised qualification will also provide greater consistency across different training arrangements in different countries.

Potential pitfalls of Standards development in Training

1. The increasing importance of competency standards at the expense of curriculum

Standards have now become much more than a descriptive exercise, they are the benchmark for skill development, recognition and credentialling. While the focus on standards provides greater flexibility in terms of skill development and recognition, there are a number of concerns about the concurrent "deregulation" of curriculum. As a number of training providers consulted commented, accredited competency based curriculum provided a "catch up" for standards that had inadequately captured the skill and knowledge requirements of the work.

在指定范围时,许多标准开发者都会优先考虑对与正常工作紧密联系的活动采用在职评估。根据公平性原则,这样的方法有几个优点。首先,由于实施方便,可以评估更多的项目。其次,可以将完成评估需要的但又与所评估的技能不相关的要求(如语言和文字能力,或正式考试的技巧)降到最低程度。可以采用真实而不是虚拟的任务的工作表现开发适任。学员可能也会在日常工作的环境中感到更加自信,因此,可能可以表现最佳状态。

已经证明,将知识和技能更细节化可以便于学员自我评价并更好地准备他们的评估。

制定培训标准的潜在好处

1.理论和实践的广泛结合越来越重视以岗位工作为基础的学习

焦点更多地集中于企业层面,培训与适任标准及岗位工作应用的联系更加直接,而正规的离职培训将会减少。

同样地,新的安排预示大量的传统评估将被新的评估模式代替,新评估模式允许学员在真正的通常作为他们日常工作事务一部分的工作环境中展示能力,而不是在培训院校里接受虚拟的或虚拟加上现实的双重评估。

2.培训规定方面更大的灵活性

按照新的安排,学员可以通过不同的、最适合他们具体情况的方式取得相同的效果。

3.更多地认可和达到进一步培训的机制

由于评估直接对照适任标准而不是参照认可的课程,并且在工作现场进行,被评估人的先前学习结果和现有能力很可能被认可。这种变化也使学员为获得不同的适任项目在资格的分步积累和认可成为可能。

统一的、经认可的资格体系的引入也将为不同国家的不同培训安排提供更高的一致性。

培训标准制定的潜在误区

1.强调适任标准的重要性但削弱培训课程质量的问题

现在标准已经变得不仅仅用于说明所需要开展的训练,它们已成为技能发展、认可和证明的基准。虽然标准在注重提供技能发展和认可方面允许有更大的灵活性,但仍应密切关注同时存在于的课程"不规范问题"。因为一些课程培训机构批评认可的适任课程提供的针对标准的"速成"教学没有充分满足工作的技能和知识要求。

This is particularly crucial in industry sectors that are relatively inexperienced in standards development, and are developing standards within training packages for the first time. If the benchmark fails to accurately reflect present and future skill requirements and work patterns, inequities are likely to be more strongly entrenched rather than addressed. Attention to process quality in standards development has consequently become all the more critical to enhance the validity and usefulness of the outcomes.

2. Customisation of Training Packages

Context customisation is an important feature of the new reforms, and will allow industry and enterprises flexibility to tailor endorsed competency standards to meet specific training requirements. Customisation is based on three broad principles: that industry skill requirements are adequately addressed, that industry portability requirements are incorporated and that the integrity of the competency standards system is ensured. However, without more explicit regulatory mechanisms, such flexibility may well result in equity considerations being "customised" out in a purely business-led system.

"Flexibilities" in standards can lead to inconsistencies, for example in the size of units of competence.

3. The shift from training processes and products to assessed competencies

Under the new system, quality assurance in training will be output focused. Training organisations will be registered on the basis of their ability to assist and assess individuals' development of competence, rather than on their ability to provide structured learning opportunities and programs. With the demise of teaching curriculum, there is less attention to the means of making the links between the competency standards on the one hand, and the assessment of achieved competence on the other. One of the main concerns with this change is the likely predominance of assessment over learning and development of competence.

With the move to locate the development and assessment of competence firmly in the workplace, vocational institutional pathways to competence and recognition may disappear. For prospective learners not in a work or training contract, their access to these pathways may be blocked.

4. Workplace based training, learning and assessment

With workplace based learning and assessment, there will inevitably be greater reliance on workplace trainers and assessors to instruct and assess in an inclusive way. While there are clearly a number of advantages for both the learner and the workplace in moving the focus of learning to real workplace applications, there are also a number of concerns relating to the increased "blurring" of boundaries between learning and working. Flexible, on the job learning arrangements can, in a pressured, often under-resourced workplace, easily lead to trainees being exploited, or left to be totally "self-directed" learners.

以下问题对于不大熟悉标准制定的,并且第一次为其培训计划制定标准的行业部门特别重要。如果标准不能够精确地反映目前和将来的技能要求和工作模式,那么可能不仅是表达上显露出不公平性而是会使不公平性牢固地确立在标准中。标准制定过程的工作质量最终会成为提高结果的有效性和有用性的关键。

2.培训计划的制订

培训内容专门化是新改革一个重要的特点,它允许行业和企业在制定认可的适任标准时具有灵活性,以符合具体的培训要求。培训内容专门化以三个主要的原则为基础:充分提出行业技能要求,结合行业技能的可转换性要求,保证适任标准系统的完整性。然而,如果没有更明确的调节机制,这样的灵活性可能会导致公平因素在一个完全职业导向的系统中被"狭隘化"。

标准的"灵活性"可能导致某些方面(例如,在适任项目的范围方面)的不统一。

3.评估适任培训过程和效果的变化

在新的系统中,保证培训质量主要针对培训的效果。培训组织获得认可的基础是他们协助个人发展和达到适任标准的能力,而不是他们提供规范化的学习机会和项目的能力。由于教学大纲的变化,满足适任标准与获得适任能力之间的关系较少得到关注。对于这一状况的主要的忧虑之一是评估可能变得比学习和提高适任能力更重要。

由于这种转变将适任能力的提高和评估与工作环境牢固地联系在一起,通过职业培训机构取得适任及认可的途径可能会消失。对于没有工作或培训合约的未来学员,他们想通过这种途径获得适任的机会可能不复存在。

4.基于工作环境的培训、学习和评估

由于在实际工作环境中开展的学习和评估,将不可避免地更加依赖工作现场的培训和评估人员的全方位指导和评估。虽然将学习的焦点转移到实际工作应用方面对于学员和工作有不少的优点,但也应该关注在学习和实际工作之间的界限"模糊性"的增加。通常,由于是来自实际工作的压力,在职学习安排中的灵活性容易导致放任学员的自我发挥或变成一种完全靠"自我监督"的学习。

Part 10-4
Setting criteria for required performance

The key aspects to be borne in mind when considering the specific requirements of performance to be used within a competence-based assessment system were addressed in Part 10-2. Your two key questions at this point are *Why am I assessing?* and *What is to be assessed?*

Why Am I Assessing?

Competence-based assessment was defined as follows:

> *To collect sufficient evidence of workplace performance to demonstrate that individuals can perform or behave to specified standards.*

What is to be Assessed?

If we are focusing on performance in the workplace, then what you want to assess is that *performance*. But is it the *process of performing* or the *outcome of performance* that you want to assess? Do you want a one-off demonstration of that performance, or do you want to know that people can perform to a specified standard over a period of time? Are you going to assess on an individual or a group basis? Will you need to assess simply what people do or also how well it is done?

In a competence-based system, as our key features list in Part 10-2 shows, the focus is on *outcomes* of performance and assessment of *individuals* over a *continuous period*.

A further key point is whether you are assessing competence or excellence. Do you want to set common standards of performance which you can use as a benchmark for competent performers? Do you wish to add a further benchmark of "excellence"? What are the implications of doing this? If everyone has to meet "excellent" standards will you be raising the level of performance or risking losing good workers? Will you have a reward system attached to these standards and will excellence gain a higher reward than competence? Is this system to be linked to certification? Is this certification to include national recognition by an external body, or is it to be company certification only?

In a competence-based assessment system, there is no grading of results, only a simple judgement of "yes, you have met the standards" or "no, you have not met the standards yet".

Establishing Criteria for Performance

In the UK, national standards of occupational competence for all sectors of industry are being published at all levels. These standards, defined by industry, provide an agreed benchmark of competent performance for occupational roles within each sector.

第10-4章
设定实操的评判标准

在考虑适任评估体系对于的工作特殊要求时,应注意的重要方面在第10-2章中进行了说明。其中两个关键的问题是"为什么要评估?"和"要评估什么?"。

为什么要评估?

适任评估的定义如下:

收集足够的岗位工作表现证据以表明被评估人能够履行规定标准或按规定标准工作。

要评估什么?

如果我们关注的是工作表现,那么你所要评估的就是表现。但你是否要评估工作的过程和工作的成绩?你是要评估人们的阶段表现还是想知道他们持续按规定标准进行工作的情况?你是要对个体还是群体进行评估?你需要仅仅评估人们做了什么还是也想知道他们做得好不好?

适任评估的关键特性在第10-2章中已列明,评估目标集中在工作效果和个体的持续表现的评估。

进一步的评估重点是被评估者的表现是适任还是优秀。你是否准备设定共同的工作标准以便给负责评估的人员用作参考基准?你是否想为参考基准增加一个"优秀"等级?这样做的意义是什么?如果每个人都达到"优秀"标准,你是否会提高对工作表现水平的要求而甘冒解雇好工人的风险?你是否设立了附带的奖励系统使优秀者得到比一般适任者更高的报酬?这个系统是否与证书颁发相联系?这种证书包括了国内的外部机构认可,还是仅为公司的内部证书?

在适任评估体系中,成绩不分等级,只做出"是,你已达到标准"或"不,你还没达到标准"的判断。

制定表现标准

在英国,各种行业的职业资格不同等级的国家标准都已经出版。这些标准由行业进行确认,在每种行业中,为职业岗位提供一套对于适任表现的公认标准。

In the UK, they are also incorporated into National Vocational Qualifications (NVQs). In the USA, similar standards are available as the basis of competency-development programmes.

These standards will provide you with a sound starting point on which to make your decisions about the standards or criteria for performance which you need to set. They are outcome-based, reflecting expectations of workplace performance, and have been agreed through consultation with role holders.

They do, however, reflect an agreed benchmark of competence (UK) or "excellent performers" (USA) .If you are seeking to establish company-specific standards of excellence and/or to incorporate your company's mission statement and objective into the final standards, then further work will be needed. Should you not wish to make use of national or other available standards, but to develop your own, then you may use a range of methods. Current standards development methodology uses *functional analysis*.

Of key importance is the list of features of a competence-based system provided in Part 10-2. When you set your "requirements" or "standards" of performance for use in a competence-based system, these key features must form a central part of your development process. You may need consultancy support to achieve this.

Two examples of outcome-based standards of performance follow, taken from the UK system. Competence-based standards can be defined for all occupations, as these examples illustrate.

You will notice that in Figure 10D-2, the example has "range indicators" rather than "range statements". This is because the management field is "generic"—that is, managers work in all occupational areas. Range indicators therefore serve as a guide for users in all occupations and can be made into more specific range statements by detailing the range to match the occupational context.

In the UK, the use of functional analysis has led to standards which are very explicit in terms of the required outcomes of actual workplace performance.

Some believe that the UK system focuses too much on the performance of work activities and not enough on the personal effectiveness of individuals. The UK system does have a set of "personal competences"—illustrated at Figure 10D-3 in the following section.

Using Standards of Competence

Standards of occupational competence provide guidance to the assessor on three key aspects of competent performance:

1. What has to be achieved (Element)

2. How well it must be achieved (Performance criteria)

3. In what context/conditions (Range Statement)

在英国,表现标准也被纳入国家职业资格(NVQ)。在美国,也有相似的标准作为拟定资格方案的基础。

这些标准提供了一个正确的起点,使你能够对需要规定的工作标准或要求做出决定。表现标准基于效果建立,反映了工作的期望值,并经过协商获得岗位提供者的认同。

无论如何表达,标准确实体现了公认的适任基准(联合王国用语)或"出色的履行者(的标准)"(美国用语)。如果想要建立公司特有的优秀标准和/或把公司自己的任务要求和目标纳入最终的标准,则需要做进一步的工作。如果不想采用国家的或其他现成的标准,那么你可以使用许多方法自行开发标准。目前的标准制定使用的方法是职能分析法。

关键的重点是第10-2章中提供的基于适任系统的要素表。在使用基于适任的系统开发你的工作"要求"或"标准"时,这些关键要素必须成为开发过程中的核心。一般需要聘用顾问以支持完成这项工作。

以下是来自联合王国系统的两个基于效果的表现标准的例子。用这些例子所采用的方法可以定义所有职业的适任标准。

你会注意到在图10D-2中,例子采用"范围指标"而非"综合说明"。这是因为管理领域是"通用的",也就是说,管理工作存在于所有的职业领域。因此,采用的范围指标可以作为所有职业的使用者的指导并可以据此做出更加具体的综合说明使之与职业背景相符。

在联合王国,应用工作分析得出的标准,非常明显地表达了实际岗位工作要求表现的效果。

一些人认为联合王国系统过于注重对于工作活动的适任,而不够关注个人的效率。但联合王国系统实际上有一系列相应的"个人的适任"(在后面章节的图10D-3列出)。

适任标准的使用

职业适任标准给评估员提供适任表现的三个主要方面的指南:

1. 必须满足什么(要素)

2. 必须完成得多好(表现标准)

3. 在什么背景/条件下(综合说明)

Within this system, assessors will assess the elements of competence, performance criteria and range statements. A number of elements grouped together form the first level of certification within a vocational award.

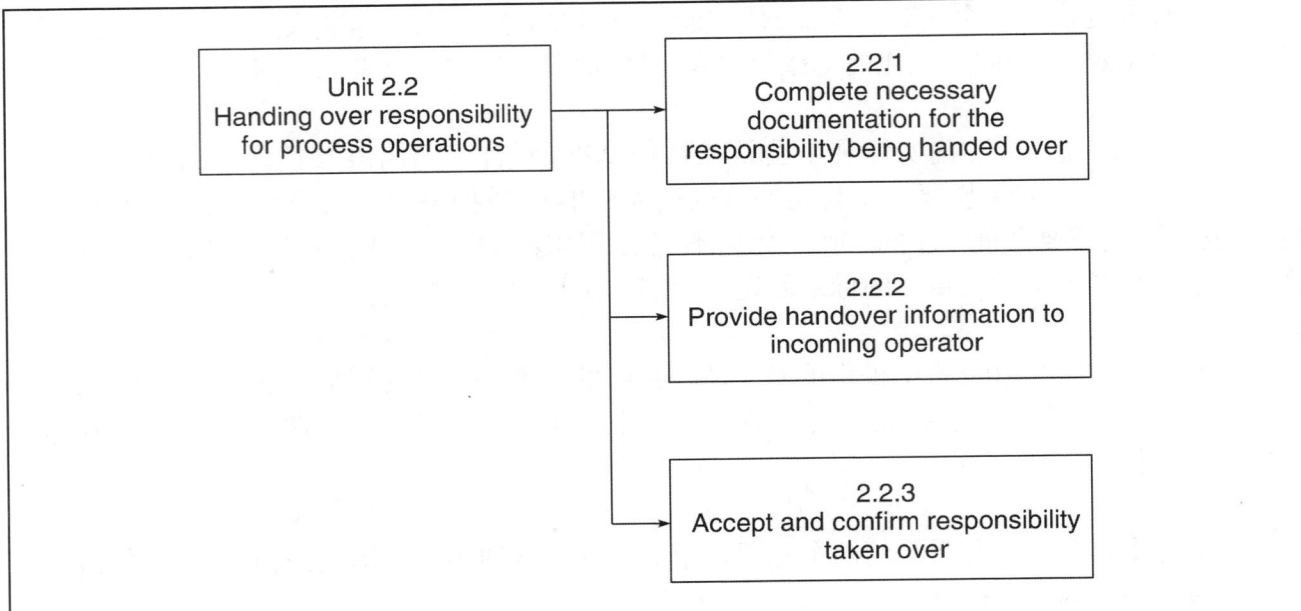

Element 2.2.1: Complete necessary documentation for the responsibility being handed over

Performance criteria
(a) All documentation required by procedures and/or necessary for the incoming operator is completed accurately and legibly.
(b) Documentation is assembled and passed to the incoming operator as specified in procedures.
(c) Any missing or incomplete documentation which would prevent the handover being carried out fully is brought to the attention of the appropriate authority.

Range
Handover situations: During a shift at the appropriate point in an operating cycle, at the end of a shift. Oral and written information

Operations: Moderately complex process operations and related tasks, involving several different unit operations and some problem solving

Plant/equipment: Moderately complex plant and equipment, with some control instrumentation, several interactions between items of equipment and people, and with a number of parameters within the operator's control

Evidence requirements

The candidate should:

— demonstrate completing documentation for at least one handover

For all activities specified in the range the candidate should:

— explain the consequences of not keeping accurate and up-to-date records for this activity,

— describe the correct procedure to follow in the event of documentation being missing or incomplete

Figure 10D-1 Example of competence-based standards(UK)—Process Operatiens(CIA)

在该系统内,评估员按适任要素、表现标准和综合说明开展评估。一组要素对应于一个级别的职业证书。

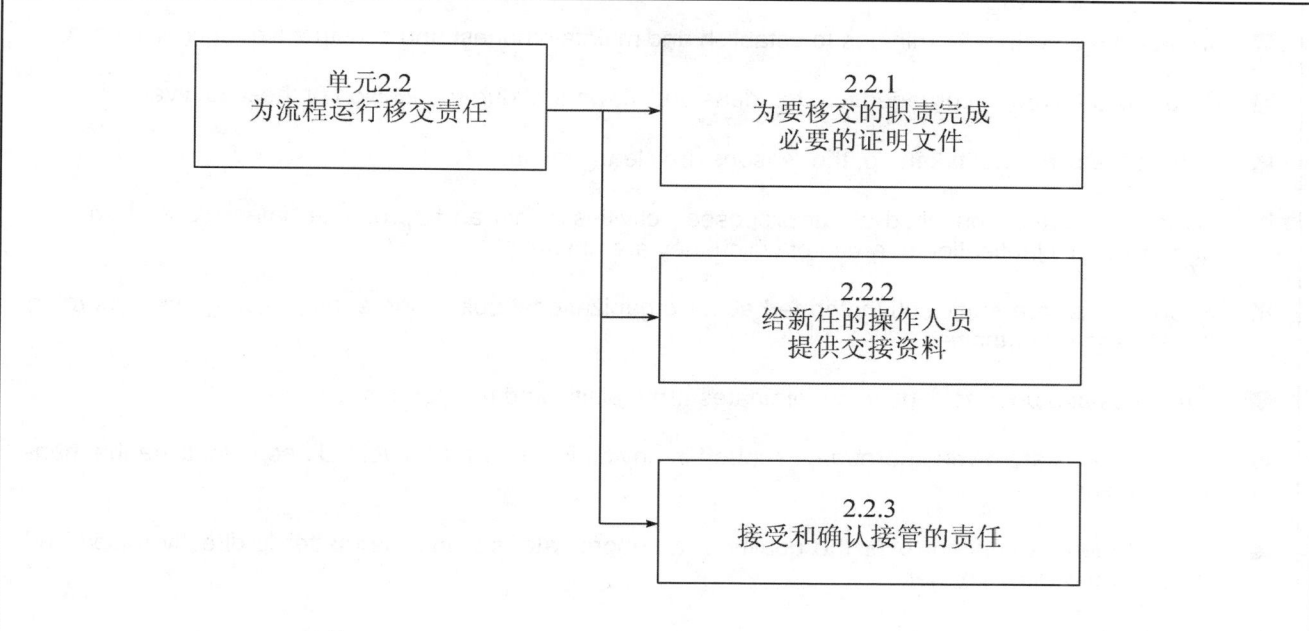

要素2.2.1:填写移交职责的必要证明文件

实操标准

(a) 精确和明了地填写程序要求的和/或新任的操作人员需要的所有证明文件。

(b) 按程序规定汇集证明文件并交给新任操作人员。

(c) 由于证明文件遗失或不完整导致移交工作不能够完整进行的任何情况应提请上级注意。

内容

移交环境: 运作循环中适当的换班时间,一个班次结束时。口头或书面的资料。

操作: 中等复杂程度的程序操作和相关的任务,涉及几个不同项目的操作并解决一些问题。

机器/设备: 中等复杂程度的机器和设备,配有一些控制仪器、需要操作一些在设备与人之间有相互作用的项目以及一些需要操作人工控制的参数。

证据要求

申请人应当:

— 至少展示一次移交证明文件的填写操作

对于规定内容的所有活动,申请人应当:

— 说明没有为此活动保持精确和最新的记录会造成的后果

— 描述证明文件遗失或不完整的情况下应遵循的正确程序

图10D-1 适任标准范例1(联合王国)——流程运作(CIA)

Element 7.1: Establish and maintain the trust and support of one's subordinates

Performance criteria

- Time is taken with subordinates to establish and maintain honest and constructive relationships
- Subordinates are encouraged to offer ideas and views and due recognition of these is given
- Where ideas are not taken up, the reasons are clearly given
- Subordinates are consulted about proposed activities within an appropriate timescale and encouraged to seek clarification of areas of which they are unsure
- Subordinates are sufficiently informed about organizational policy and strategy, progress, emerging threats and opportunities
- Promises and undertakings to subordinates are realistic and are honoured
- Subordinates are given appropriate support in any situations which involved people outside the manager's team
- Where there is concern over the quality of a subordinate's work, the matter is directly raised and discussed with him or her

Range indicators

Subordinates are all those within the manager's direct line responsibility

Subordinates include—staff (permanent, temporary, full/part-time); subcontractors; trainees/students placed with the manager's team

Communication may be instigated by—the manager; the subordinate

Information giving and consultation takes place both—formally; informally

Information giving and consultation is through the means of—team meetings; one-to-one

discussions; telephone conversations; written communication

UNIT: Create, maintain and enhance effective working relationships

ELEMENTS:
1. Establish and maintain the trust and support of one's subordinates
2. ...
3. ...

Figure 10D-2 Example of competence-based standards (UK)—management (Management Charter Initiative, 1991)

Individuals must demonstrate evidence which can be matched to all specified standards, across the full specified range of activities. This is because a "competent individual" is someone who can perform:

- to the specified standards;
- consistently;
- over a range of contexts or conditions.

Examples of the structure of standards of competence are given in Figure 10D-3 which illustrates the UK personal competence model.

要素7.1：建立和保持对某人下属的信任和支持

表现标准

- 花时间与下属建立和保持诚实和有益的关系

- 鼓励下属提出主意和观点，并且适当给予的认可

- 如果不采纳他们的主意，应当清楚解释原因

- 在适当时间向下属咨询计划的活动情况，鼓励他们弄清不确定的地方

- 充分通知下属有关组织政策和策略、进程、出现的危险和机会的信息

- 对下属的承诺和保证是真实的和可承兑的

- 给予管理人员以外的所有下属适当的支持

- 如果关注到下属的工作质量问题，立即提出并且与他或她讨论。

范围指标

下属指所有那些在主管直接管理下的人员

下属包括——职员（永久的、临时的、全职/兼职）；分包人；与管理人员一起工作的受训者/学员

交流可能由——主管；下属——促成

提供资料和进行咨询——正式地；非正式地

资料的提供和咨询的进行方式通过——小组会议；一对一；讨论；电话交谈；书面交流

  项目：创造、保持和提高有效的工作关系
  要素：1. 建立和保持对下属的信任和支持
     2. ……
     3. ……

图10D-2 （联合王国）适任标准范例——管理（《管理宪章创新》,1991）

  个人必须在规定的所有活动范围内显示符合所有标准的证据。这是因为一个"适任人员"是能够：

- 按照规定的标准；

- 始终如一地；

- 在一定环境和条件范围内。

  下图提供了联合王国的个人适任标准体系模型的例子。

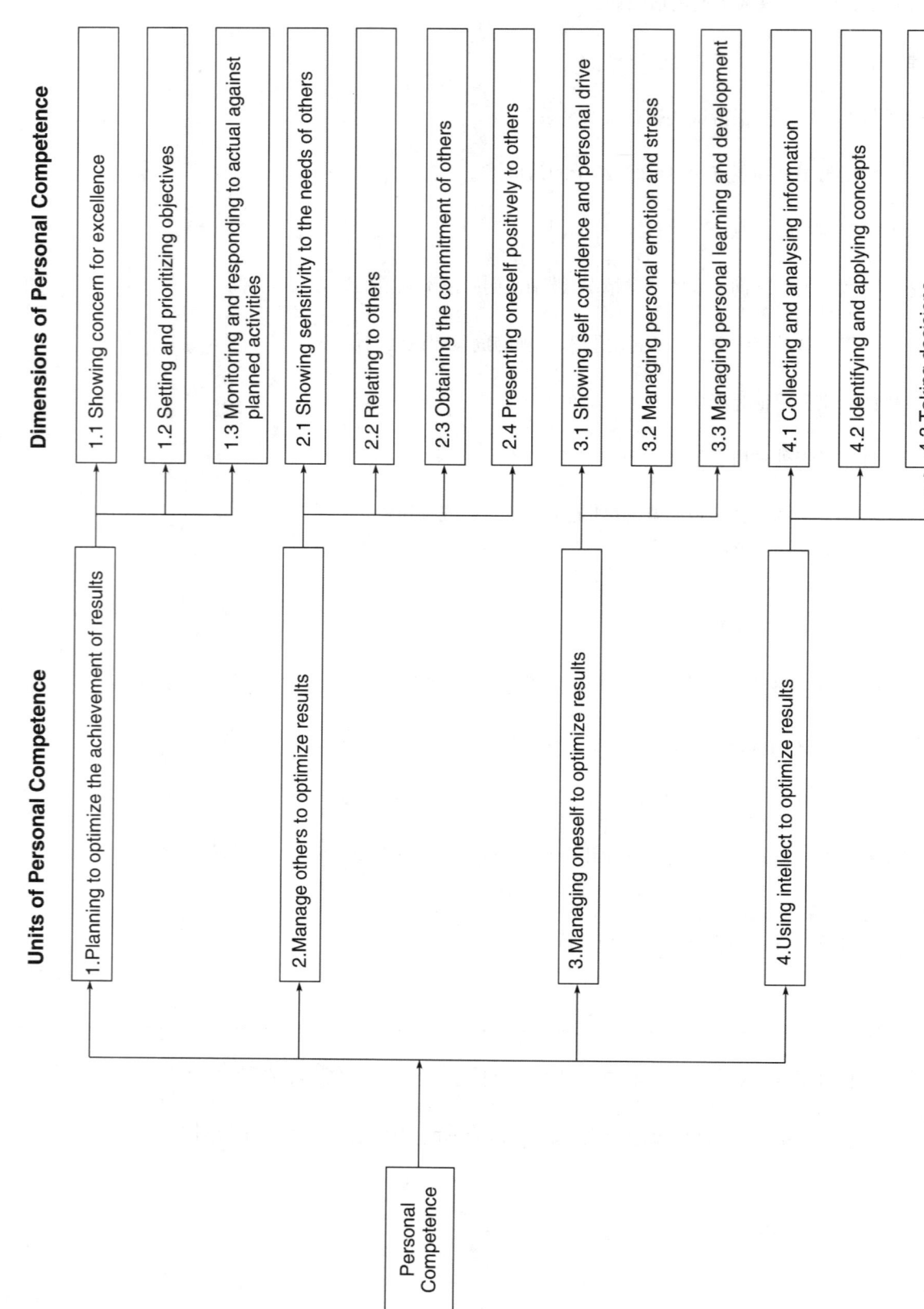

Figure 10D-3 Structure of personal competences (UK) (Management Charter Initiative 1991)

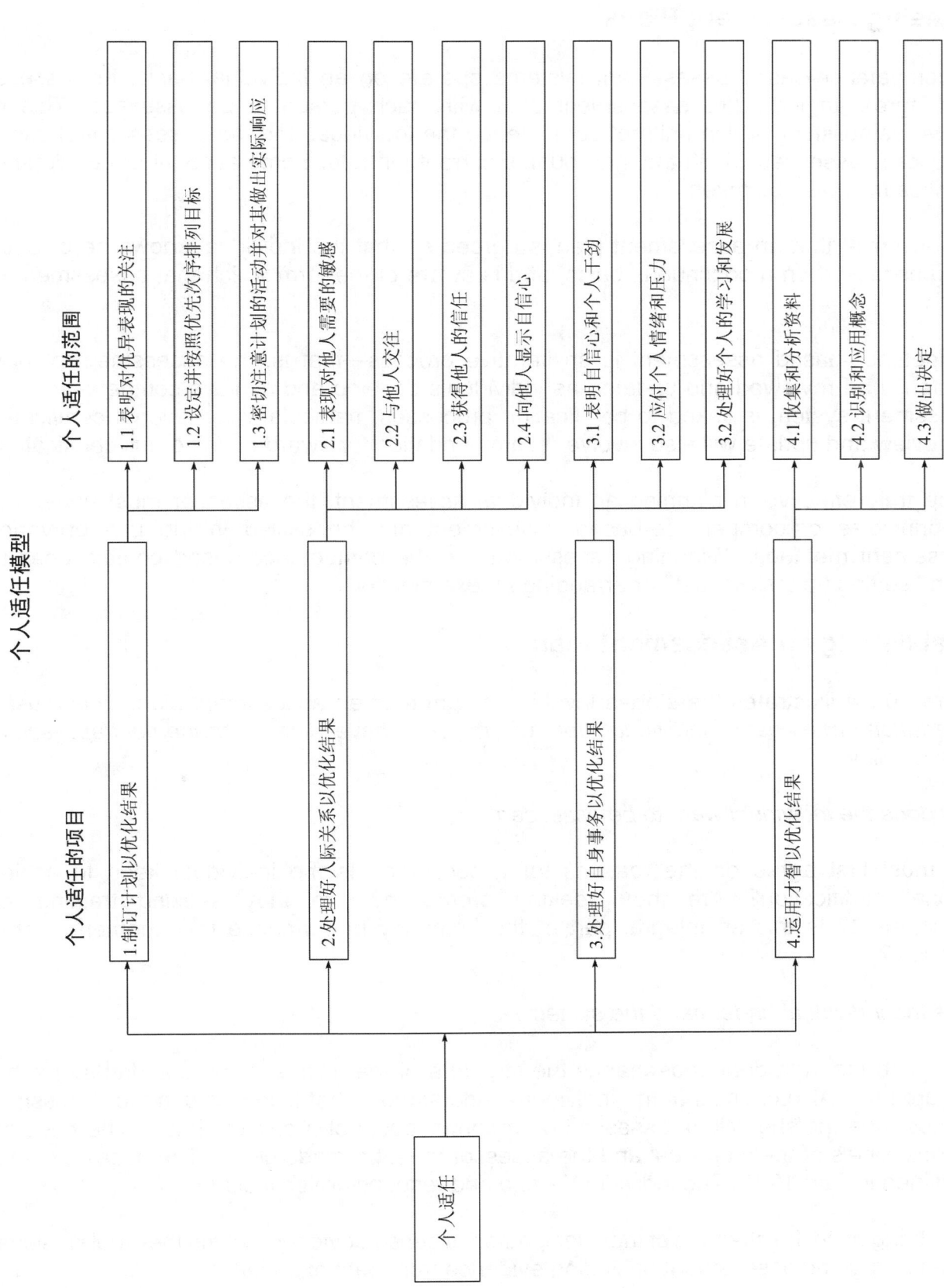

图10D-3 基于适任标准的范例(联合王国)——管理(管理宪章初步,1991年)

Agreeing Assessment Plans

As competence-based assessment systems operate on an individual basis, the assessor must agree an individual assessment plan with each person to be assessed. This will involve establishing which units of competence the individual and the assessor feel can be realistically assessed within the individual's current job role. Some account of development activities may also be taken.

It is essential that an assessment plan is agreed so that the individual knows he or she is being assessed on a continuous basis, and is aware of the form which that assessment will take.

Competence-based assessment is an iterative process—that is, the assessment plan will constantly be reviewed and updated as individuals develop and achieve competence. If the assessment system is linked to certification processes, particularly to national certification, this review and update will also involve recommendation for award of unit or full certificates.

To be truly effective in planning an individual assessment, the assessor must understand the principles of competence-based assessment and be skilled in the use of various assessment methods. "Planning assessment" in the competence-based context does not mean "setting up a skills test" or arranging an examination.

Establishing an Assessment Plan

Figure 10D-4 illustrates the stages involved in agreeing an assessment plan. *This must be undertaken with each individual for whom you have line management/assessment responsibility.*

Why does the individual want to be assessed?

You must first agree on the reasons for assessment. Is the individual keen to achieve national certification? Are they seeking promotion? Are they seeking training and development? Is this an integral part of the company performance management system/appraisal?

Does the individual understand the system?

Make sure the individual understands the structure of the units and the standards on which they are built. Also check that the individual understands what is involved in the assessment process—that he/she will be assessed on a continuous, not a one-off, basis. The roles and responsibilities of the individual and the assessor must be made clear. (The assessor's role is outlined in Part 10-5.) The individual's role and responsibilities include:

- bringing to the attention of their designated assessor, evidence which they feel is relevant to on-going assessment (including evidence from past experience);

- agreeing an assessment plan with the line manager.

评估计划的认可

由于适任评估体系是针对个人操作的,评估员必须与每位被评估人就个人评估计划达成一致意见。这涉及确定哪些是被评估人和评估员都认为可以在当前的工作环境真实地进行评估的项目,可能也涉及个人发展的考虑。

评估计划得到认同是最重要的,被评估人因此知道评估是持续进行的,并且了解评估将要采取的形式。

适任评估是一个反复进行的过程——即随着个人适任能力的发展和获得,会经常地研究和更新评估计划。如果该评估系统与发证程序特别是与国家的发证程序相联系,这种研究和更新也会涉及颁发单项或完整证书的建议。

为了真正有效地策划一项个人评估,评估员必须理解适任评估的原则,以及熟练使用各种评估手段。"策划评估"在基于适任的环境中并不仅仅是指"设定一次技能测验"或安排一场考试。

制订一个评估计划

图10D-4说明了认同一项评估计划所包括的步骤,必须与你直接负责管理/评估的每个人商定评估计划。

个人为什么想要接受评估?

首先,你必须确定评估的理由。个人是否渴望获得国家证书?是否试图职务晋升?是否寻求培训和发展?评估是否是公司工作表现管理系统/评价必要的一部分?

被评估人是否了解评估系统?

确保被评估人了解每个评估项目的体系和相应标准。也要核查被评估人对评估过程的了解——他/她将接受连续的,而不是一次性的评估。必须明确被评估人和评估员的义务和责任。(第10-5章概述了评估员的义务)被评估人的义务和责任包括:

- 引起指定的评估员对他们认为与进行的评估有关的证据的注意(包括源自以往经历的证据);

- 与直接主管就评估计划达成一致意见。

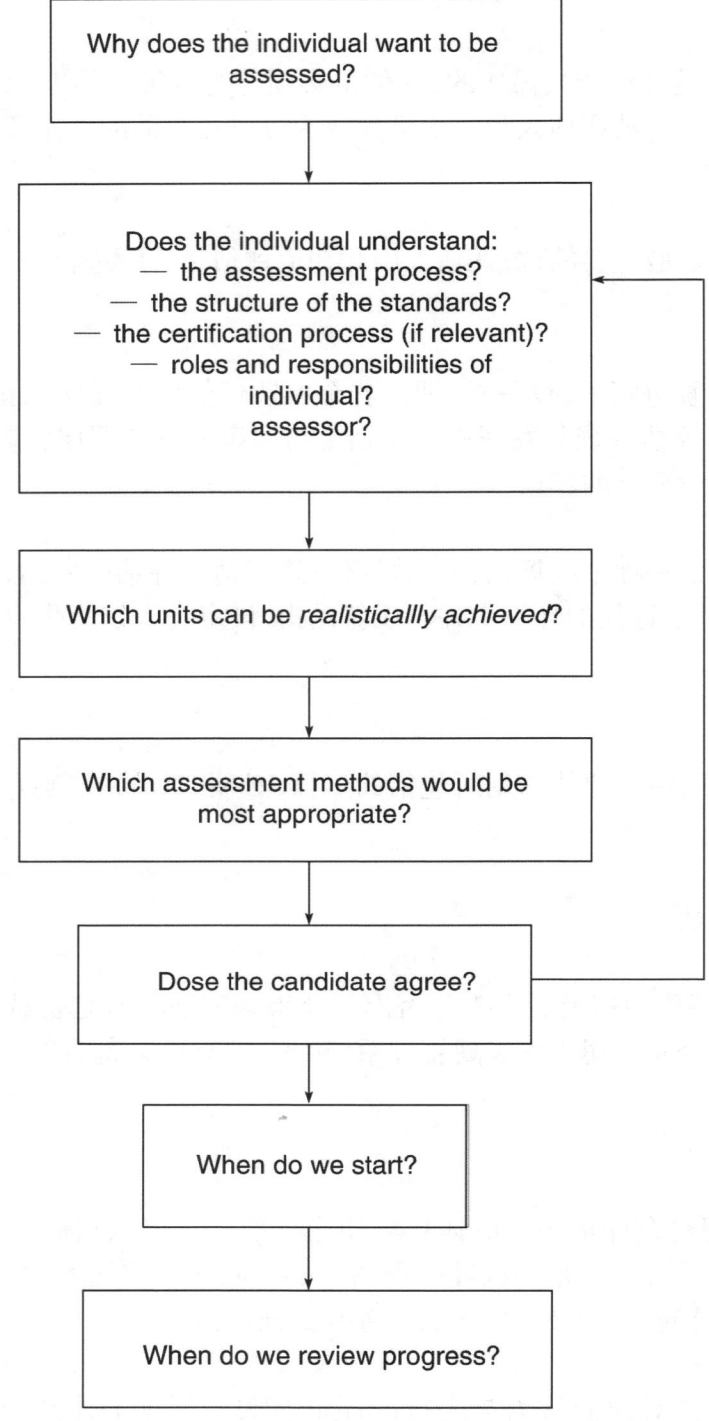

Figure 10D-4 *Establishing an assessment plan*

Which units can the individual realistically achieve?

You must negotiate with the candidate the number of units which realistically reflects their current work role. You may also work with them to identify units which relate to their training or future development needs, but you must keep in mind that the individual must be in a position, or have the opportunity, to provide actual evidence of performance.

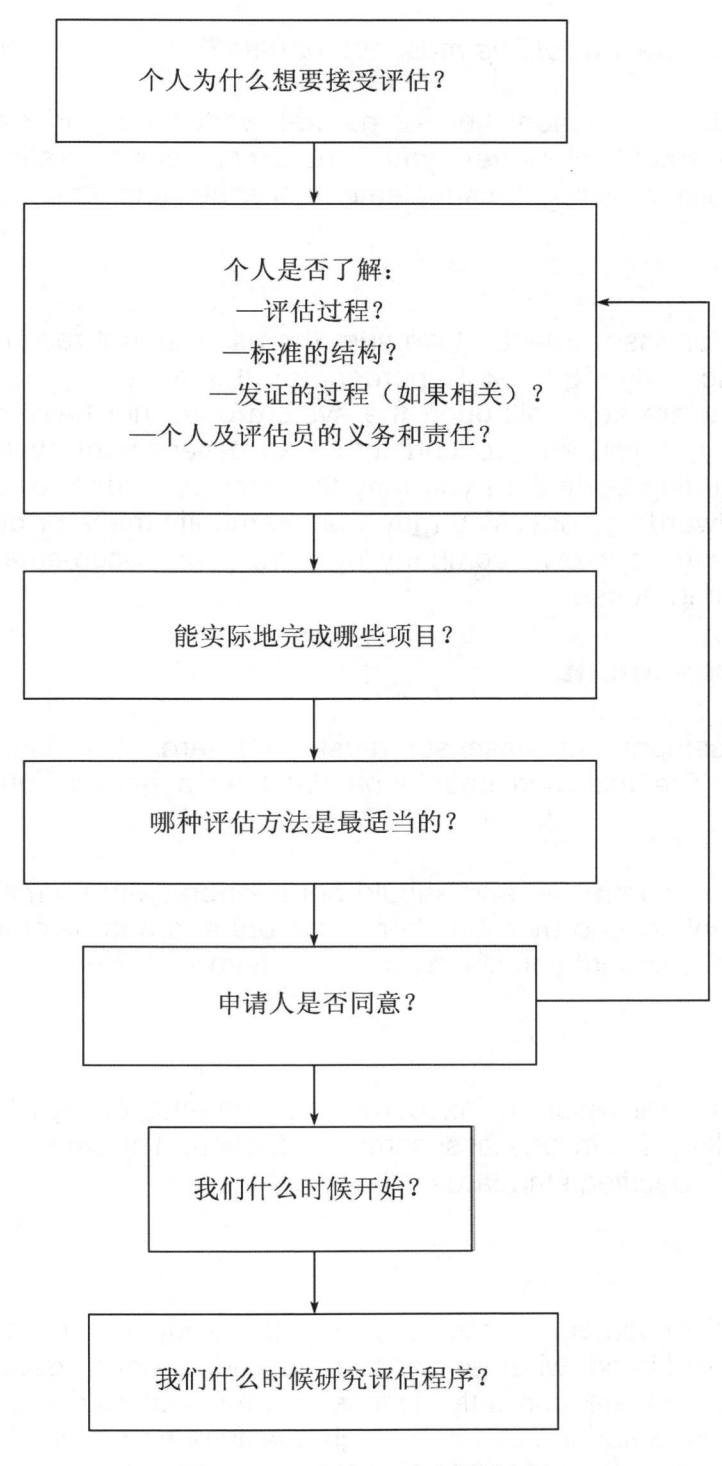

图10D-4　制订一个评估计划

被评估人实际能完成哪些项目？

　　必须与被评估人协商可以实际地反映他们目前岗位工作的评估项目数量，也可以协助他们确定与他们有关的培训或未来发展需要的项目，但必须记住，被评估人必须在对应的或有机会担任的工作岗位提供工作表现的实际证据。

What methods of assessment would be most appropriate?

As we have noted already, observation of natural workplace performance must be the primary form of assessment. However, you should consider operational constraints and identify those areas which may require supplementary assessment methods.

When do we start?

Set a clear start date for assessment. Make sure the assessment records are ready for use (including the awarding body log book if appropriate). It is essential that clear and accurate records of assessment are kept, although the system does not have to be elaborate and should be user-friendly. If you are working within an assessment system linked to formal recognition by an awarding body then you may find that pro forma for assessment records are provided by that awarding body. You may wish to modify these or develop your own. Of course, if you are using your own company system, your documentation will have been devised and developed in-house.

Influences on Assessment

When planning assessment, the assessor must be aware of various influences on the assessment process. The following should be used as a general guidance note in this respect.

Assessment should be unobtrusive and should not interfere with normal workplace activity. All assessors can be influenced by a number of factors and it is helpful to be aware of the most common influences so that you can try to avoid them.

A sense of direction

Unplanned assessment will result in inaccurate judgements. Always be clear about what evidence you are looking for in any assessment situation. This means being familiar with and understanding the specified standards.

An illusion of validity

It is very easy to observe someone or to review written evidence and conclude that "this is good". The issue at hand is not whether or not an individual does "good work"; the issue is whether the evidence you are currently assessing provides valid proof that the required standards are being met. Evidence can be of high quality but have nothing whatsoever to do with the particular area of competence which you are assessing!

Stereotyping

Stereotyping is never useful in an assessment situation. Your concern as an assessor is to collect and evaluate relevant evidence of actual performance. This has nothing to do with categorizing people.

什么是最适当的评估方法？

正如我们已经提到的，评估的主要形式必须是考察在实际岗位上工作的表现。然而，也应该考虑操作的限制和确定那些可能需要采用补充评估方法的内容。

什么时候开始评估？

为评估确定一个明确的开始日期。确保评估记录已经备妥待用（如可行应采用授权机构的评估日志）。尽管评估系统应该便于操作而没有必要设计成过分复杂的，但保持清楚和精确的评估记录仍是重要的。如果是在一个由授权机构正式认可的评估系统内运作，那么正式的评估记录格式是由授权机构提供的。你或许希望修改这些记录方式或开发自己的记录方式。当然，如果你是采用公司自己的系统，相应文件会由公司内部进行设计和开发。

评估的影响因素

在做评估计划时，评估员必须了解影响评估过程的不同因素。以下内容可以作为这方面注意事项的一般性指导。

评估应谨慎开展并且不应干扰正常的工作活动。所有的评估员都可能会受到一些因素的影响，了解这些最普遍的影响因素有助于尽量避免它们产生的影响。

方向感

未经计划的评估将导致不准确的评价。因此应该始终清楚地了解你在任何评估情况下需要寻找的证据。这就意味着需要熟悉和理解具体的标准。

证据有效性的假象

考察某人或研究其书面证据并且总结出"这是好的"这样的结论是非常容易的。但我们要解决的问题不是判断某人"工作是否做得好"；而是你获得的评估的证据是否能够有效地证明其符合要求标准的。证据本身可能具有高质量，但是与你正在评估的适任的特定内容毫无关系！

常规评估模式

在适任评估过程中不要援用常规的评估模式。作为一名评估员，你关注的应该是收集和评估相关的实际工作表现的证据，而不要试图去评价个人。

Halo and Horns Effects

A very common source of inaccurate judgement is due to preconceived ideas about a person's performance. These ideas may be based on the fact that you actually like the person concerned (they have a halo), or that you don't like them (they have horns) — or that they usually do good or excellent work. The reverse works as well: maybe they do or don't like you! None of these considerations should affect your judgement. Your concern is the actual evidence presented.

Hawthorne effect

People act differently when they know they are being assessed. Competence-based assessment is continuous and should therefore be carried out under normal working conditions on an everyday basis. We have already noted that assessment should also be unobtrusive.

Contrast effects

Competence-based assessment is individualized assessment. It is concerned with individual performance, not a comparison or contrast with how other people perform. You should be careful to avoid comparing and contrasting the group of candidates for whom you are responsible.

光环和犄角效应

一种非常普遍的影响精确评价的因素出于对某个人工作表现的成见。这种成见可能基于这样的事实,即你确实喜欢某人(他们头上有光环)——或者通常他们的是工作良好或优秀的;或你不喜欢某人(他们头上长犄角)。或者是相反:他们可能喜欢或不喜欢你!所有这些因素都不应当影响你的评定。你关注的是实际呈现的证据。

霍索恩效应

当人们知道自己正在被评估,他们的表现就会与平常不同。适任评估是连续的并因此应以日常工作为基础并在正常的工作条件下进行。我们前面也提到评估应该不是经过特别安排的。

对比效应

适任评估是纯个体化的评估。它只涉及个人的实操,不应与他人的实操进行对比或比较。你应谨慎避免对你所负责的那组考生进行相互对比和比较。

Part 10-5
Collecting evidence of competence

Assessment is about making judgements. A skilled assessor, in any context, is one who is able to review evidence which has been presented and make a confident decision of "competent" or "not yet competent" based on that review.

Assessors must be able to establish and agree a clear assessment plan with individuals. They must also be aware of *influences on assessment*. These issues were dealt with in Part 10-4.

All of this also requires, however, that assessors are skilled in the choice of *methods* of assessment and that they understand the strengths and weaknesses of each method. They must also be aware of the *sources* of evidence.

In this Part, we look at the who, when, where and how of competence-based assessment. We explore the roles of assessors and methods of assessment together with the strengths and weaknesses of each.

Who Assesses?

An assessor's role is to review individual candidates' evidence of performance and to make a decision, based on that evidence, regarding the competence of each individual in his or her work role. This is an important and responsible position in which to operate. To be effective, assessors need answers to questions such as:

- How do I know what competent means?

- Where does the evidence come from?

- How do I choose the right assessment methods?

There are no magic answers. The quality of assessment however, lies in the skills of the assessors and in their understanding of the concepts and principles of competence-based assessment. A skilled assessor is able to adopt new and creative approaches to assessment based on this clear understanding. Competence-based assessment is *individualized* assessment—each individual may produce different or unique collections of evidence of performance, thus providing a different or unique challenge to the assessor. The assessor must therefore adopt a flexible and creative approach to this challenge.

If competence-based assessment is *individualized* and *focused on performance* then the best person to assess is a first-line manager or supervisor.

> *An assessor within a competence-based system should be someone who is in regular contact with the individual and therefore has the opportunity to observe and monitor actual performance in a realistic working environment.*

第10-5章
适任证据的收集

评估就是做出评判。一个熟练的评估员,无论从哪方面定义,都是能够根据审核提供的证据,自信地判断出被评估人是"适任"还是"未能适任"。

评估员必须有能力制订清晰的评估计划,并与被评估人达成一致。他们也必须了解影响评估的各种因素。第10-4章讨论过这些问题。

此外,还要求评估员能熟练选择评估方法,并且了解每种方法的利弊。他们还必须了解证据来源。

在这一部分里,我们讨论适任评估的人员、时间、地点和方式。我们也会探讨评估员的作用和评估方法以及每种方法的优缺点。

由谁评估?

评估员的职责是审核每个申请人工作表现方面的证据,以及在这些证据的基础上,对被评估人是否适任其岗位做出判定。这一职位很重要,并且需要很强的责任心。为了有效工作,评估员需要解答一些问题,如:

- 如何理解适任的含义?

- 证据出自何处?

- 如何选择恰当的评估方法?

当然,这些问题没有标准答案。然而,评估的质量取决于评估员的技能和他们对适任评估的概念、原则的理解。在此基础上,一名熟练的评估员能够采纳新的和有创造性的评估方法。适任评估是个体化的评估,即每个人提供的其工作表现证据群就可能不同。因此,评估员就要面对不同的难题。对此,评估员必须运用灵活、有创造性的方法来应对。

如果适任评估是个体化的并且强调工作表现,那么最适合做评估员的就是一线主管或监管人员。

基于适任系统的评估员应当是经常与被评估人接触的,因为他有机会考察和监督被评估人在实际工作环境中的真实工作表现。

The role of a workplace assessor can be summarized as follows:

- A workplace assessor is usually a line manager—because a line manager is the best person to observe natural workplace performance.

- The workplace assessor is responsible for judging *evidence of performance* and ensuring that this evidence is of the correct *type* and *quality* to ensure that a confident decision about the sufficiency of evidence to meet required standards is achieved.

- The workplace assessor may use a range of assessment methods but the primary form of assessment must always be *observation of performance*. *Feedback* should be given to individuals on a regular basis and *training needs* will be identified during the course of assessment.

- The workplace assessor is also responsible for *recording assessment*. Details of evidence and of judgements made must be entered on an assessment record.

This creates a new perspective in many organizations. In a competence based system, the workplace assessor will be a line manager; all line managers must therefore be trained in the skills and application of competence-based assessment. This has considerable long-term benefits: managers become more effective at measuring and managing performance and operate on a more people-oriented basis. A learning culture also develops. However, achievement of these outcomes requires an initial investment in the training of line managers.

Multiple assessors

When we talk of a workplace assessor, we usually refer to a "designated" assessor. Within a competence-based assessment system, each individual should have a designated assessor responsible for recording evidence and "signing off" satisfactory achievement of competence within a particular area (usually a unit) of competence.

However, as we shall see when we look at sources of evidence (see Part 10-6) a number of assessors can (and often should) be involved in the assessment process. Many people may observe an individual's performance—senior managers, peers, trainers and tutors; all have relevant evidence. An assessor may use these other people as sources of evidence, or they may take a more formal role in supplying evidence on a regular basis. As a rule of thumb, one should remember that the use of multiple assessors can increase the reliability of assessment. However, to keep communication lines clear, only one assessor should have the responsibility for formally recording achievement. (Note also the use of the term "achievement" rather than "completion"—this helps to keep your mind focused on *outcomes* rather than training or learning *inputs*.)

How does the assessor know what "competent" means?

The assessor in a competence-based system is guided in the assessment process by the specified standards of performance. These were outlined in Part 10-4.

岗位工作的现场评估员其作用可以归纳为如下几个方面：

- 岗位工作的现场评估员通常是部门主管，因为他是考察被评估人实际岗位工作表现的最佳人选。

- 岗位工作的现场评估员负责评定工作表现证据，以及确保这些证据的类型和内容适合评估，确保有足够的证据满足标准要求进而做出可靠的判定。

- 岗位工作的现场评估员可以使用各种各样的评估方法，但是最主要的评估形式必须始终是对工作表现的考察。应当定期给被评估人反馈评估情况，并且在评估过程中确认其是否需要培训。

- 岗位工作的现场评估员也要负责记录评估情况。在评估记录簿中记录证据和评定的详细情况。

这为许多机构创造了一个新的评估前景。在适任评估体系中，工作现场的评估员将是部门主管；因此，所有的部门主管都要进行适任评估技能和应用的培训。这具有很大的长期效益：主管可以更有效地评价和管理下属的工作，并且实行以人为本的管理。同时也发展了学习的文化。然而，要想取得这样的效果，首先要对部门主管进行培训。

多样的评估员

当我们谈到岗位工作的现场评估员时，我们通常是指"指定的"评估员。在适任评估体系中，每个被评估者应当由有一名指定的评估员来负责记录特定适任范围内（通常是一个项目）的证据并且签署达到满意适任能力的成绩。

然而，当涉及证据的来源时（见第10-6章），正如我们从前面内容已经了解的，许多评估员可以（而且通常应当）参与评估过程。很多人可以考察到被评估人的工作表现，包括他的高级主管、同事、培训员和辅导员；所有这些人都可以提供相关的评估证据。评估员可以将这些人作为证据的来源，也可以让他们担任更加正规的角色定期提供证据。根据经验证实，使用多方面的评估员可以提高评估的可信度。但是，为了保证沟通方式清晰，只由一名评估员负责正式记录成绩。（还要注意使用"获得"这个词，而不用"完成"——这有助于你关注"效果"而不是培训或灌输学习。）

评估员如何了解"适任"的含义？

详尽的适任标准可以指导适任系统中的评估员进行评估。第10-4章对此提供了概要说明。

Key issues for assessors

Assessment is about *generating* and *judging* evidence. Different methods of assessment can be used, at different times, to produce evidence of different types.

There are many assessment methods. For example:

- observation of performance;
- skills test;
- simulation exercise;
- project or assignment;
- oral questioning;
- written examination;
- multiple-choice question paper.

Some of these methods provide evidence of *performance*, some provide evidence of *knowledge* and/or *application of knowledge and understanding*.

Assessors may use all or only a few of these. Decisions on which methods to use and on how and when to use them will be influenced by four key components:

- what is to be assessed (the standards);
- the assessment framework (the units or clusters);
- the context of assessment (operational constraints);
- skills of the assessor.

The first component—what is to be assessed—was explored in Part 10-4. Competence-based assessment must always start with matching what people actually do to the specified standards of performance. If you are not using nationally agreed standards, then your own must be in a format which clearly indicates the *outcomes* which individuals must achieve.

The second component—the assessment framework—again depends upon the system you are using. In the UK certification system of National Vocational Qualifications, the framework consists of *units of competence*. If you are using a different model, your framework may be *clusters of behaviour* or competencies as behavioural measures. Whatever your system, it should be in usable chunks—each chunk representing an area of activity which has real meaning in the workplace. This is essential if you are linking your assessment to certification and reward systems.

评估员面对的主要问题

评估涉及证据的产生和评价,可以在不同时间使用不同的评估方法产生不同形式的证据。

评估方法有多种,例如:

- 考察工作表现;
- 技能测试;
- 模拟演习;
- 设计或作业;
- 口头提问;
- 笔试;
- 多项选择问卷。

上述方法中有一些提供的是工作表现证据,一些提供所掌握知识证据和/或对知识的应用和理解。

可以全部或部分使用这些评估方法。使用哪种方法、怎样使用以及何时使用会受下列四个关键因素的影响:

- 要评估什么(标准);
- 评估体系(项目或项目群);
- 评估的范围(操作限制条件);
- 评估员的技能。

第一个要素——要评估什么——在第10-4章中讨论。适任评估必须从一开始就将人们的实际工作情况与规定的标准进行比对。如果你没有使用国家的认可标准而是使用自己的标准,那么你自己的标准形式必须能够清楚说明被评估人应该达到的效果。

第二个要素——评估体系——仍然取决于你正在使用怎样的系统。在英国的国家职业资格发证系统中,体系由适任项目组成。如果你正在使用一种不同的模式,你的体系可能以多项表现或者适任组合作为表现的度量单位。不管采用什么系统,都应该模块化,每个模块代表岗位工作中有实际意义的一个活动领域。如果你把评估与发证和薪酬系统联系起来的话,就必须这样做。

The third component—the context of assessment—is crucial to the successful operation of your assessment scheme. In an ideal situation, each individual to be assessed will have a line manager as a designated assessor. Each designated assessor will be monitored by a verifier or quality assurance assessor (see Part 10-8), and each verifier will in turn be monitored by an external verifier if your system is part of a National Vocational Qualification. However, ideal situations do not often exist!

Your particular operational constraints must be taken into account and issues such as lines of communication and accountability must be paramount in these considerations. But these are not the only issues: operational constraints affect the choice of assessment methods, and assessors will need to tailor the choice of assessment method to the operational context.

The skills of the assessor—the fourth component—are therefore of utmost importance, which is why assessors will need training and development (see Part 10-8). Assessors need skills in the selection and use of assessment methods, and they need an understanding of the strengths and weaknesses of each method. They also need to make the best use of various sources of evidence in addition to being fully aware of the many influences on assessment. The remainder of this Part deals with these issues.

Sources of Evidence

In order to select the most appropriate and effective assessment methods, an assessor must have a clear understanding of the various sources of evidence. This section reviews the following key sources of evidence of performance:

- multiple assessors;
- performance at work;
- specially set tasks/projects/assignments;
- questioning;
- historical evidence.

1. Multiple assessors

Earlier in this Part, we briefly reviewed the idea of multiple assessors a variety of people who have contact with the individual being assessed and who therefore can provide evidence of that individual's performance. One source of evidence, therefore, is other people who have this contact.

If we are to make best use of this source, however, we need to have clear lines of communication. People need to know that they have a role in providing evidence.

第三个要素——评估的范围——这是评估计划成功运作的关键。在理想的情况下，每个接受评估的人都会有一个指定的部门主管作为评估员。每个指定的评估员要由一个核审员或质量保证评估员（见第10-8章）监督，而且，如果你的系统是国家职业资格系统的一部分，每个核审员都要接受外审员的监督。然而，现实情况并不总是处于理想状态。

特殊的操作限制规定和其他极为重要的问题，如沟通方式和责任划分，也必须加以考虑。考虑的因素还包括其他方面：影响评估方法选择的操作限制条件；评估员需要使评估方法的选择满足操作范围的要求。

评估员的技能——第四个要素——是最重要的，这也说明为什么评估员需要培训和提高（见第10-8章）。评估员应具备选择和使用评估方法的技能，需要了解每种方沄的优缺点。他们也需要充分利用不同的证据资源并充分考虑到影响评估的多方面因素。本章的余下部分将讨论这些问题。

证据的来源

为了选择最适当、有效的评估方法，评估员必须清楚知道证据的各种来源。这部分讨论以下几个表现证据的重要来源：

- 多来源的评估员；
- 工作中的表现；
- 特别制订的任务/设计/作业；
- 提问；
- 历史证据。

1.多种来源的评估员

在这部分的开头，我们简要地讨论评估员的多来源的观点，各种各样的评估员与被评估人进行接触并据此提供其表现证据。因此，证据的来源之一是与被评估人接触的其他评估员。

然而，如果我们想要充分利用这一资源，就需要有清晰的沟通方式，使他们意识到有提供证据的义务。

In your own context, consider who these people might be. For example:

- senior managers;
- tutors and trainers;
- peers and co-workers;
- customers;
- contacts in other divisions/departments.

Basically, anyone with whom an individual has contact within their normal working activity can be a source of evidence. But take care—your approach to each source will need to be planned. You will also need to make sure that the evidence you receive reflects the performance of the particular individual, and is not clouded by that person's involvement in team activities. All sources must be carefully considered in terms of the quality of evidence provided. (The issue of quality is dealt with in the next Part.)

2. Performance at work

The best evidence comes from actual workplace performance. Remember, competence-based standards reflect outcomes of performance; where better to collect evidence of achievement of these outcomes than in the realistic, everyday working environment:

> *Observation of actual workplace performance should always be an assessor's* **primary** *form of evidence collection.*

3. Performance on specially set tasks

Where observation of normal workplace activity is not possible, special tasks or assignments can be set to *generate* the required evidence. Because it is produced in a "false" or "simulated" setting, evidence provided by this route will not be of the same high quality as that generated by normal workplace activity. However, evidence produced by simulated methods will *contribute* to continuous assessment and help the assessor make decisions about the individual's competence across the specified range of activities.

There are times when a simulation or skills test or project will be an essential means of generating evidence. For example, an assessor cannot set fire to a building, or shut down equipment and machinery to assess whether an individual knows how to deal with such an emergency. Similarly, where licensing is required, such as with fork lift truck drivers, health and safety requirements would prohibit assessment in real working situations until the licence had been obtained.

Other issues also come into play. Competence-based assessment requires that individuals are assessed across the full range of activities specified within the standards. Individuals do not always have the opportunity to demonstrate their competence on all types of equipment or machinery. For example, a welder may need to demonstrate competence in the use of MIG, TIG and arc welding, but may not have an opportunity to do so for some time if the particular work in hand requires only two out of the three methods. In this type of circumstance, use of specially set tasks, projects, assignments and tests can generate the evidence required.

从你自己的角度讲,考虑这些评估员可能由谁担任。例如:

- 高级经理人;

- 教员和培训员;

- 同辈和同事;

- 顾客;

- 其他部门相关人员。

基本上,在正常工作活动中与被评估人接触的任何人都可以提供证据、但要注意:每一处理来源的方法需做好计划,也需要确保你所收集的证据能够反映被评估人的个人表现,不能与其参加的集体活动的行为混为一谈。为保障证据的质量,所有证据来源都必须经过仔细研究。(质量问题在下一章处理。)

2.工作表现

最好的证据来自实际工作岗位的表现。应记住:适任标准反映了工作表现的效果;只有在实际的日常工作中才能获得工作效果的证据。

对实际岗位工作表现的考察往往是评估员收集证据的**最主要**方式。

3.特别设置任务中的表现

如果不可能考察正常的工作活动,可以设置特别的任务或工作来获取要求的证据。由于证据是在一个"非真实的"或"模拟的"环境中产生的,因此,通过这种途径提供的证据其质量将不如正常工作活动中产生的证据质量高。然而,通过模拟方式产生的证据会对连续评估有所帮助,并且可以协助评估员通过考察被评估人在规定的活动中的表现来做出是否适任的判断。

有时候,模拟或技能测验或项目都会成为产生证据的最主要方式。例如,评估员不能通过点火烧一幢楼或关闭设备和机器来评估被评估人是否懂得如何处理这样的紧急情况。同样地,如果叉车驾驶员要考取证书,在获得证书之前,出于健康和安全考虑会禁止进行正式工作环境中的评估。

其他的问题也会出现。适任评估要求在标准规定的所有活动范围内进行,但被评估人不总是有机会在所有的设备或机器上展示他们的能力。例如,焊工可能需要展示他们在使用MIG(金属焊条惰性气体保护焊)、TIG(钨极惰性气体保护焊)以及弧焊的能力,但评估可能没有机会在一段规定的时间内完成,因为他在岗位中可能只用到上述三种方法中的两种。在这种情况下,采用特别设置任务/专题/作业的方法就能够产生所需要的证据。

4. Questioning

It is often the case that observation of normal activity and specially set tasks do not provide sufficient evidence. For example, if an individual needs to be assessed across a wide range of contexts or conditions, or in the use of a wide range of equipment or machinery, the assessor may have to spend years waiting for, or trying to create, the right opportunity!

In assessing competence, the assessor is attempting to collect evidence that demonstrates an individual's performance to required standards. This includes *application* of knowledge and understanding it is not "knowing" itself that is important in competent performance, but what individuals do with that knowledge.

If you want to know that an individual is able to drive a car on a clear day, with little traffic about, you might observe their performance by sitting in the car with them. However, if you also want to know that they can drive the same car, or different cars, in rain, snow, sleet, hail, high winds, thunderstorms, in light and heavy traffic, and on motorways, main roads and dirt tracks, you might take years to assess them this way!

Your basic aim as an assessor in this context, and in all other competence-based assessments, is to collect sufficient evidence to make a confident judgement that the individual can perform to the required standards across the full range of specified activities.

One very simple way of finding out what you need to know is to ask. In the assessment context, your questions need to be carefully framed to elicit the *evidence* you are seeking. You might ask "What if..." to elicit evidence of performance across the range of activity. You might set a series of open, written questions to assess that an individual is able to apply relevant knowledge and understanding to activities which require decision-making, or problem-solving. For example, assessing a doctor's performance across the full range of diagnoses, medicines and medical tests applied to patients could take forever unless a written form of evidence collection was used!

5. Historical evidence

The term "historical evidence" has been used to refer to evidence of past achievements and often occurs in literature and guidance on the accreditation of prior learning (APL).

Evidence from past achievements can be valuable in competence-based assessment and often forms part of the on-going assessment process.

Again, the *quality* of evidence is of paramount importance and the "rules of evidence" must apply (see Part 10-6).

In a sense, we might say that all evidence is historical, since once it has been produced it is immediately in the past! However, this source of evidence can, when used effectively, help to fill the gaps when an assessor is attempting to collect evidence across the full range of an activity.

4.提问

经常会出现这样的情况：仅靠考察正常的活动和特别设置的任务不能充分提供证据。例如，如果要完成对被评估人的评估，就要包括以下内容：对多种内容或不同状态下的评估，对使用各种各样的设备或机器的技能评估，评估员可能要花上几年时间去等待或尝试创造适当的评估机会。

在评估适任时，评估员要收集能够体现被评估人满足标准要求的表现证据。这包括对知识的应用和理解，在适任表现中被评估人运用知识比了解知识更重要。

如果你想知道一个人在天气晴朗、车辆稀少的环境下的驾驶情况，你可以坐在他们的车里观察他们的表现。然而，如果你还想知道他们驾驶同一款式或不同款式的车，在雨中、雪里、雨雪中、冰雹里、大风里、雷雨中，在晴天和交通繁忙时，以及在高速公路、大路和泥泞小道上的驾驶情况，那你可能要花上几年的时间对他们进行这样的评估。

在本章和所有其他适任评估中，评估员的目标是收集足够的证据，从而按照要求的标准对被评估人在全部规定的活动中表现的状况做出可靠的判断。

如果想得到你所需要了解的事情，提问是最简单的方法。在评估中，你需要仔细地设计问题以便得出你寻求的证据。你可以这样问"如果…… 会怎样……"通过各种活动获取表现的证据。你可以设计一系列开放的书面问题，去评估某人按规定要求，应用和理解相关知识做出决定或解决问题的能力。例如，评估医生的适任能力，只有书面证据可以是用过的，其他证据可以通过观察医生给病人做出的各种诊断、药物和医疗测试的这些表现来获得。

5.历史证据

"历史证据"这个术语通常用来指过去成绩的证据，以及经常在文献和指南中出现的：先前学习的合格鉴定（APL）。

在适任评估中过去成绩的证据很有价值并且通常是评估过程的一部分。

同样，证据的质量是最重要的，并且必须应用"证据准则"（见第10-6章）。

从某一角度，我们可以说所有的证据都是历史的，因为证据一旦产生就立刻成为过去！但是，当评估员试图收集所有的各种活动的证据时，如果能有效地利用这种证据来源，有助于填补空白。

Choosing the Right Assessment Methods

Assessment methods include:

- observation of performance;
- skills tests;
- simulation exercises;
- project or assignment;
- oral questioning;
- written examination;
- multiple-choice question paper.

We noted earlier that some of these methods provide evidence of *performance* and some provide evidence of *knowledge* and *understanding*. You will also recall that it is *application* of knowledge and understanding that is of key interest in a competence-based assessment system.

When considering the use of various assessment methods, an assessor must keep these questions in mind:

- What evidence do I need?
- How much evidence do I need?
- Which methods will provide quality evidence?

The following pages provide guidance on the use of each of the assessment methods listed above, with these key questions in mind. This guidance refers to the selection of assessment methods; guidance on quality of evidence follows in Part 10-6.

选择正确的评估方法

评估方法包括：

- 考察工作表现；
- 技能测试；
- 模拟练习；
- 专题/作业；
- 口头提问；
- 笔试；
- 多项选择问卷。

在前面我们已提到这些方法中有一些提供工作表现的证据，而另一些提供掌握知识和理解能力的证据。同时也提到在适任评估体系中，主要注重的是对知识的应用和理解。

在考虑采用不同的评估方法时，评估员应谨记这些问题：

- 我需要什么证据？
- 我需要多少证据？
- 用什么方法能得到合格的证据？

针对这些关键的问题，下面几页的表格对上述的每种评估方法的使用提供了指引。该指引是关于评估方法选择的，在第10-6章提到的为证据质量相关指引。

The various strengths and weaknesses of each method is given in the following table:

Method	Strengths	Weaknesses	Key issues
Observation of performance	▶ Provides high quality evidence of competence. ▶ Is undertaken (or should be) as usual part of line manager's responsibility. ▶ Individuals become accustomed to on-going assessment. ▶ Provides continuous assessment basis. ▶ Evidence is produced regardless of whether it is used for assessment.	▶ Opportunities to demonstrate competence across full range of activities may be limited. ▶ Interference of "local" standards/procedures may affect time allocated to workplace assessment. ▶ Assessor/assessee relationship.	▶ Need for trained assessors. ▶ Use of multiple assessors. ▶ Need for clear lines of communication and quality-assurance measures.
Specially set tasks: skills tests, simulations, projects, assignments	▶ A useful tool for generating evidence where opportunities for assessment across the full range are limited or prohibited by health and safety regulations. ▶ Can be off-site and therefore avoid noisy or disruptive environments. ▶ Test conditions can be standardized for skills tests. ▶ Time for testing can be effectively allocated.	▶ Removed from realistic working conditions. ▶ Individuals react differently in a test situation. ▶ Structure of assignments and projects often very loose. ▶ Difficulties in predicting Exactly what type of evidence will be generated.	▶ Need for planning and structure.
Oral questioning	▶ Valuable tool for collecting evidence across full range of activities (ie, providing supplementary evidence). ▶ Valuable tool for collecting evidence of underpinning knowledge and understanding and its application in the workplace. ▶ Can be rigorous, and standardized with planning and structure.	▶ Assessors can often answer their own questions! ▶ Evidence collected by this method alone would not be sufficient to assign competence. ▶ Least likely to reflect or represent real working conditions.	▶ Need for trained assessors with effective questioning techniques. ▶ Requires largest inferential jump to assigning competence.

下表给出每种方法的优点和缺点：

方法	优点	缺点	主要问题
考察工作表现	▶ 提供的工作表现证据质量高。 ▶ 作为（应当作为）部门主管的部分职责。 ▶ 被评估人习惯于在工作中进行评估。 ▶ 提供连续评估的基础。 ▶ 不管是否用于评估都会产生证据。	▶ 不能展示所有各种活动能力。 ▶ "分散的"标准/程序可能影响现场评估的时间分配。 ▶ 评估员/被评估人的牵连关系。	▶ 评估员需要接受训练。 ▶ 运用多来源的评估员。 ▶ 需要清晰的沟通渠道和质量保证的措施。
特别设置的任务：技能测试模拟、专题、作业	▶ 当评估范围受到限制或由于健康和安全规则受到禁止时，它是产生证据的有效方法。 ▶ 可以离开工作现场可以因此避免噪声或环境的干扰。 ▶ 技能测试的测试条件可以标准化。 ▶ 测试时间可以有效地分配。	▶ 不同于实际的工作环境。 ▶ 在测试下被评估人会有反应差异。 ▶ 专题和作业的体系通常是松散的。 ▶ 很难确切预计将产生什么形式的证据。	▶ 需要计划和组织。
口头提问	▶ 是收集覆盖所有领域的活动证据的重要的方法（如，提供补充的证据）。 ▶ 收集被评估人对知识掌握和理解以及在岗位工作中应用知识这些证据的重要方法。 ▶ 经过计划和组织，可以是严密而且标准化的。	▶ 评估员通常可以回答自己的问题。 ▶ 仅靠这种方法收集证据不足以确定工作表现。 ▶ 最不可能反映或代表真实的工作情况。	▶ 受过训练的评估员需要具备有效提问技巧。 ▶ 要求对选定的适任问题做出最快速的推论性判断。

Method	Strengths	Weaknesses	Key issues
Written examination	▶ Valuable tool for assessment in areas where knowledge forms a key component of competent performance (eg, information providers). ▶ Can be well structured to elicit key areas of knowledge and understanding.	▶ Also assesses ability to write and construct written material. ▶ Needs skilled assessors to judge responses. ▶ Time away from workplace required to complete the examination. ▶ Time for assessors to review and mark responses.	▶ Danger of assumption that "knowing" means "able to do". ▶ Often unstructured or unplanned. ▶ Supplies supplementary evidence of actual performance.
Multiple-choice question papers*	▶ Well-designed questions can be standardized. ▶ Elicits key knowledge/ understanding in short timescale.	▶ Always a 25 per cent possibility of correct answer being chosen at random (where four possible answers are given). ▶ Needs skilled designer to prepare item bank and question paper. ▶ Time away from work to complete test needed.	▶ Time and skills needed for design, delivery and marking. ▶ Supplementary evidence only-not direct evidence of actual performance.

*   Multiple-choice question papers provide a useful tool for assessing knowledge of a particular topic. They need careful construction and are usually put together by subject experts who are also skilled in the use of this form of assessment. The basic model of a multiple-choice question paper is, as its name implies, a question followed by several possible answers for the candidates to choose between.

When and Where should Assessment Take Place?

In planning competence-based assessment, one of the key aims should be to make it flexible so that candidates can be assessed in a variety of ways. An assessor should also take into account any operational constraints.

Wherever possible, assessment should take place in the workplace with *observation of normal workplace activity*. This may not always be possible, either because the opportunity to assess across the full range of activity is limited, or because the noise within the working environment makes questioning or discussion difficult.

Competence-based assessment may, therefore, take place in the workplace or off the job. It should be continuous, making the best use of naturally occurring evidence (from normal work activity). Assessors will need to be able to set up and manage other forms of assessment, however, in order to ensure that high-quality and sufficient evidence is generated, collected and recorded before competence can be assigned to an individual.

方法	优点	缺点	主要问题
笔试	▶ 对于掌握知识是适任表现的一个主要组成部分的那些领域（如资料提供者），这种评估方法是有用的工具。 ▶ 可以组成良好的评估体系以获得主要领域的知识和理解方面的证据。	▶ 同时要评估写作和编写书面材料的能力。 ▶ 需要熟练的评估员评判答卷。 ▶ 离开岗位完成考试要耗用工作时间。 ▶ 评估员审核答卷和评分需耗用时间。	▶ 将"知道"错误的推断为"有能力完成"。 ▶ 通常没有组织或计划。 ▶ 需提供实际工作表现的补充证据。
多项选择问卷	▶ 设计良好的问题可以标准化。 ▶ 在短时间内得到关键的知识和理解的证据。	▶ 随机选择都可以有25%的可能性答对题（如果给出四个选择答案）。 ▶ 需要熟练的设计人员准备题目组和试卷。 ▶ 需要离开岗位一段时间来完成测试。	▶ 设计、递送、评分需要时间和技巧。 ▶ 仅仅是补充证据，但不是实际工作表现的直接证据。

* 多项选择问卷能够很好地评估对特定主题所规定的知识的掌握。它们需要认真组织并且通常是由熟练这种评估方式的学科专家负责组题。如其名，多项选择问卷的基本模式是一个问题配有几个答案供考生选择作答。

评估进行的时间、地点

在计划适任评估时，关键的目标之一应该是它的灵活性，这样能通过不同的途径对考生进行评估。当然，评估员也应该考虑到任何操作的局限性。

只要有可能，评估过程都应该是观察考生在工作场地的正常的现场活动。这种情形有时候实现不了，不是因为无法覆盖评估所涉及的所有领域的活动，就是因为工作环境中的噪声使提问或讨论无法顺利进行。

因此，适任评估可能发生在工作现场也可以在工作之外进行。它应是不间断的、最大限度地使用自然发生的证据（来自正常的工作活动的证据）。无论如何，在确定被评估人具备适任能力之前，为了保证产生、收集、记录足够的高质量的证据，评估员需要有能力创立并管理其他评估形式。

Assessors must first understand the basis on which a competence-based assessment system operates. They must be clear about the principles of assessment and the requirements for high-quality evidence of performance. They must be aware of and develop skill in the use of various assessment methods and be able to use any combination of methods to meet the operational constraints in which they operate. Only when assessors have been trained in these skills can the assessment system operate effectively.

评估员必须首先了解适任评估体系操作的基本要求。他们必须清楚评估的原则和高质量演示的要求。他们必须了解和拓展各种评估方法的使用技能,并能够兼用几种方法来克服操作中的限制。只有在评估员接受训练掌握这些技能,才能保证评估体系有效地运作。

Part 10-6
Matching evidence to standards

Introduction

The quality of a competence-based assessment system depends, as we have noted earlier, on the skills of the assessor. A key assessor skill concerns making judgements about the quality of evidence collected. In Part 10-5 we explored various assessment methods, together with the strengths and weaknesses of each. Now, we look at the quality of evidence which is generated from these various assessment methods.

As a general rule, evidence generated from normal workplace activity will be of the highest quality. We can then move down a scale of quality as illustrated in Figure 10F-1.

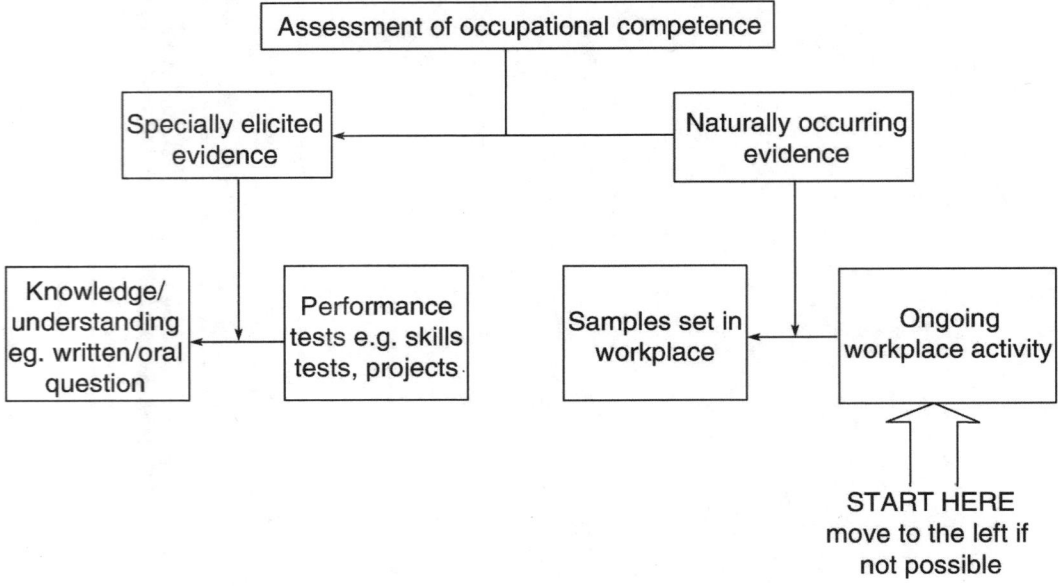

Figure 10 F-1 Quality of Evidence of Occupational Competence

Another area of general confusion for those new to competence-based systems occurs when discussions about types of evidence takes place. Once again, a variety of terms tends to be used interchangeably, often including:

- performance evidence;

- knowledge evidence;

- direct evidence; primary evidence;

- indirect evidence;

- supporting evidence;

- supplementary evidence;

第10-6章
证据与标准的匹配

介绍

正如我们之前提到的,适任评估体系的质量依赖于评估员的技能。评估员的一个主要技能是对已收集的证据对其质量做出评价。在第10-5章中,我们探讨了各种评估方法及其各自的优缺点。现在,我们要讨论从不同的评估方法中产生的证据的质量。

按照一般的规律,在正常现场活动中产生的证据的质量是最高的。图10F-1表明了质量等级。

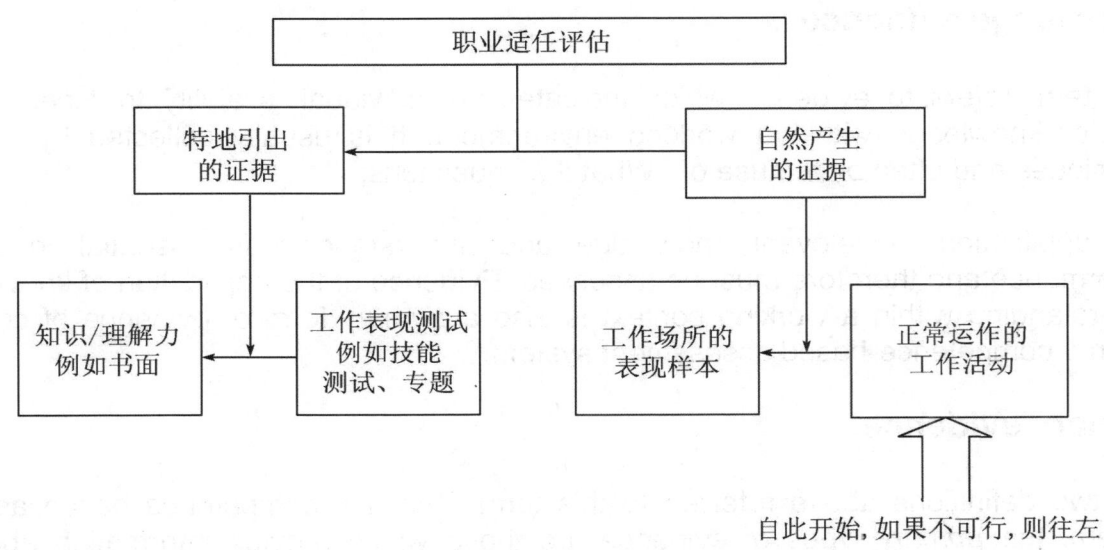

图10F-1 职业适任的证据质量

对于那些不熟悉适任系统的人,对于产生证据的形式会有其他的困惑。同样地,对于这方面,也有一些术语可以交替使用,通常包括:

■ 表现证据;

■ 知识证据;

■ 直接证据;主要证据;

■ 间接证据;

■ 支持证据;

■ 补充证据;

- historical evidence.

In this initial section, these terms will be defined so that further exploration of rules of evidence can be undertaken without the added clutter of confusing terminology.

Performance evidence

This term has been used in earlier chapters and refers specifically to evidence of an individual *actually doing something*. For example, performance evidence of an individual undertaking a selection interview would be actual observation, or a video recording of that interview. Similarly, performance evidence of an individual completing a regular or requested maintenance check would be observation of that check being undertaken. Performance evidence is one form of direct evidence. It is also one of the required primary forms of evidence within a competence-based assessment system (see below).

Knowledge evidence

This term refers to evidence which indicates an individual's ability to recall, apply and transfer knowledge within a working environment. It is usually collected by questioning techniques and often by the use of "What if..." questions.

The application of relevant knowledge and understanding is essential to competent performance and therefore must be assessed. Evidence of the application of knowledge and understanding within a working context is also a *primary* form of evidence of competence within a competence-based assessment system.

Primary evidence

The two definitions above referred to this term. Within a competence based assessment system, the *primary* types of evidence are those which provide information about actual performance or the *application* of knowledge and understanding within *realistic* (normal) workplace activity.

Direct evidence

This is evidence which gives clear information about the candidate's performance. It will take the following forms:

- actual products of performance;

- results of observation of performance;

- results of questioning by the assessor.

These three forms of evidence also represent *primary* evidence (see above).

Direct evidence about some aspects of performance can also be obtained from skills tests, projects and assignments. However, such evidence is usually referred to as *supporting* or *supplementary* evidence (see below).

- 历史证据。

本部分的开头将对这些术语进行阐释，以便可以顺利地对证据规则进行进一步探讨，而不会由于使用术语造成混乱。

表现证据

先前的章节已经使用过该术语，它特指被评估人实际做某事的证据。例如，被评估人参加选拔面试的表现证据将是对面试的实际观察，或录像记录。同样地，被评估人完成一项常规或要求的维护检查的表现证据将考察他的检查工作过程。表现证据是直接证据的一种形式。它也是适任评估体系中要求的主要证据之一（见以下内容）。

知识证据

该术语指用以表明被评估人在工作环境中具有回忆、应用和转换知识的能力方面的证据。它的收集一般通过提问的方法并通常使用"如果……（会/应该）怎么样"这样的问题。

对相关知识的应用和理解对于适任是很重要的，因此必须评估的内容。在某个工作环境中对相关知识的应用和理解证据也是适任评估体系中要求的一个主要证据。

主要证据

以上两个证据就是主要证据。在适任评估体系中，原始的证据是指那些可以提供实际表现或真实（正常）工作活动中应用知识和理解知识的证据。

直接证据

直接证据指能够提供关于申请人表现的真实明了的信息证据。它以下列的形式出现：

- 表现的实际效果；

- 表现的考察成绩；

- 评估员提问的成绩。

这三种形式的证据也是主要证据（见前面内容）。

从表现的某些方面获得的证据可以通过技能测验、专题和作业获得。然而，这种证据通常作为支持或补充证据（见以下内容）。

This is the simplest form of evidence for an assessor to use in matching to standards, but is often the most difficult to collect because of the time required to observe or question the individual or to examine finished products.

Indirect evidence

Indirect evidence provides the assessor with information about the individual and may take the form of:

- references or letters of validation;*

- photographs of completed work;

- audio tapes;

- trophies or awards;

- letters from customers/colleagues;

- production records;

- training records.

Many other forms of evidence may come into this category. It is important to remember that in a competence-based system, an assessor is dealing with *individualized* assessment. This means that the types of evidence presented, particularly where historical evidence is included (see below), will be unpredictable. Assessors must become used to dealing with unfamiliar and new forms of evidence. In this context, confidence in use of the rules of evidence, discussed later in this chapter, is critical to success.

Supporting or supplementary evidence

As the terms imply, supporting or supplementary evidence is that which adds to the main (or direct) forms. There is, therefore, some comparison between indirect and supporting and supplementary evidence. These terms are often used interchangeably.

Evidence from skills tests, projects and assignments is often termed supporting or supplementary; this leads to considerable confusion since this type of evidence can also be referred to as "direct" (see above).

* *A letter of validation is a form of reference, but one which provides specific information relating to the standards of performance. This form of reference is often provided by individuals as part of an accreditation of pirior learning process (see "historical evidence").*

直接证据是评估员为与标准保持一直而采用的最简单的证据形式,但它通常是最难收集的,因为要花时间去观察或提问被评估人或去检查最终产品。

间接证据

间接证据可以用以下形式为评估员提供被评估人的有关资料:

- 参考资料或有效的书信;*

- 已完成作(产)品的照片;

- 录音磁带;

- 奖品或奖状;

- 顾客或同事的来信;

- 生产记录;

- 培训记录。

很多其他的证据形式可归入这一类。要谨记的是,在适任评估体系中评估员处理的是对个人的评估。这就意味着提供的这类证据,特别是包括历史证据,都将是不能预测的。评估员必须习惯处理新的和不常见的证据形式。在这种情况下,准确地使用这些证据的准则对成功至关重要,这一问题将在本章稍后讨论。

支持或补充的证据

正如术语本身所示,支持或补充的证据就是主要(或直接)的证据给予补充。因此,就需要在间接、支持以及补充证据之间进行比较。这类术语通常交替使用。

通过技能测验、专题和作业获得的证据通常称之为支持或补充证据,这就容易出现混淆,因为这种证据类型有时也被认为是"直接"证据(见前面内容)。

* 有效的书信是参考资料的一种形式,但也是提供表现标准的一种具体资料。这种形式的资料可作为认定先前学习过程参考,通常由被评估人本人提供(参阅"历史证据")。

Use of these terms, as in many contexts, depends upon the perspective being adopted. If the discussion concerns the direct/indirect dimensions, then evidence from skills tests, projects and assignments will be direct because the evidence collected in this way directly reflects *part of* the required performance. However, if the discussion concerns primary versus supporting/supplementary evidence (see above), then skills tests, projects and assignments will be viewed as supporting/supplementary evidence. This is because these test situations are simulated and do not fully reflect realistic workplace activity as it would be undertaken on a normal day-to-day basis.

Historical evidence

Historical evidence is that which provides the assessor with information about an individual's past achievements. It may take any form and include those listed under the primary, supporting, direct and indirect headings above. Historical evidence therefore can be the most difficult to assess, but it can also provide one of the most valuable sources of evidence.

Assessors will need skill and confidence if the credibility and quality of the assessment system is to be maintained.

Methods and Quality

Two sets of rules are applied within a competence-based system. The first refers to the *methods* of assessment and the second to the *quality* of evidence collected.

You might consider these two sets of rules as similar to rules applying to the legal profession.

In a court case, it is possible that *sufficient* evidence has been collected in order for a jury to make a confident judgement about guilt or innocence. However, technicalities relating to *how* the evidence was collected can make the sufficiency issue irrelevant.

The same rules apply in your workplace assessment. You may have sufficient evidence, but if the methods of collecting that evidence were invalid, the quality of evidence is affected.

So how can you ensure quality and sufficiency and thus make confident judgements in your assessment role?

Six key concepts must be kept in mind. These concepts relate both to quality of assessment method used and quality of evidence assessed. They are outlined below in more detail.

Rules of assessment

Transparency
Validity
Reliability

Rules of evidence

Validity
Authenticity
Currency
Sufficiency

Key concepts of methods and quality

由于在很多情况下,这些术语的使用取决于应用范畴。如果是讨论涉及直接/间接的范畴,那么通过技能测验、项目和作业获得的证据将是直接证据,因为通过这种途径收集到的证据直接反映了部分工作表现。然而,如果讨论涉及主要证据的支持/补充的证据(见前面内容),那么通过技能测验、项目和作业获得的证据将被认为是支持/补充的证据。这是因为这种测试状态是模拟的,并且不能完全反映每天正常进行的实际岗位工作中的活动。

历史证据

历史证据为评估员提供了有关个人过去取得成绩的资料。它可以以任何的形式出现,包括上述主要的、支持的、直接的和间接的方式列出的那些证据。因此,历史证据是最难评估的,但它也是可以提供最有价值的证据来源之一。

如果要保证评估系统的可靠性和质量,评估员需要具备相应技能和自信心。

方法和质量

在适任系统中要用到两套准则。第一套针对评估方法,第二套针对已收集的证据的质量。

你可以将这两套准则当作类似于法律行业中应用的准则。

在一个法庭案件中,可能要收集充分的证据使陪审团来准确做出有罪或无罪的判断。然而,收集证据的技术方法可能使充分的证据成为无关证据。

同样的事情也会发生在工作现场的评估过程中。你可以有足够的证据,但是如果收集这些证据的方法无效,那么证据的质量就会受到影响。

那么,如何保证证据的质量和充足性,从而在评估时做出准确的判断呢?

必须牢记六个主要的概念。这些概念不仅关系到评估方法的质量,还关系到评估证据的质量。以下对这些概念做更详细的叙述。

```
评估准则
透明度
有效性
可靠性
```

```
证据准则
有效性
真实性
通用性
充分性
```

方法和质量的主要概念

Rules for Assessment Methods

Transparency

If something is transparent, it is open and clear to anyone who takes time to look at, or through it. A competence-based assessment system should be clear to all involved. If standards are accessible, easily understood and have real meaning to the users, and if the assessment plans and methods are well thought out then roles and responsibilities are more easily conducted.

Validity

A well planned assessment is one in which the assessor and the individual being assessed are clear on *what* is to be assessed and *what* evidence will be generated. In addition, the types and forms of evidence will provide realistic proof of the specified standards. A common example of invalid assessment (and invalid evidence) would be a written test of practical skill. A *valid* assessment would be observation of reactions to a fire alarm (particularly when the time for testing of the alarm was not known in advance by the individuals).

As an assessor, think firstly of your objectives in assessment. Ask yourself what you need to find out (what evidence you need) about this person's performance. Then ask whether this assessment method will provide that evidence.

Reliability

An assessment system is only of real value if assessors in different locations would make the same judgement about the same candidate based on the same evidence. A well-designed assessment system builds-in tests of reliability through quality control and monitoring of assessment. A company assessment scheme will only be reliable if two different assessors provided with the same collection of evidence reach the same conclusion about the competence of the individual to whom the evidence refers. This type of testing activity should form part of assessor training.

Rules of Evidence

Validity

The same issue—assessing what is supposed to be assessed—arises when considering evidence. The key question for assessors to ask about each piece of evidence is "What does this evidence tell me?" It may tell you something about the specified standards or it may tell you about some other related activity.

For example, if you were assessing maintenance engineers, you might receive documentation referring to completed work. What does this documentation tell you? Does it tell you that the work was completed to the correct safety standards? Does it tell you that the work completed was as requested by the customer? Does it tell you that the work was completed using the correct parts and that they were all fitted correctly? Does it tell you if the customer was satisfied?

评估方法的准则

透明度

如果某事是透明的,则对于任何花时间考虑和研究它的人来说,它是公开、明了的。一个适任评估体系对所有涉及其中的人员都应当是清晰的。如果评估标准是可获得的、易懂的,并且具有真实意义的,而且如果评估计划和方法也是经过精心策划的,则评估的作用更加容易发挥,承当的责任也更加容易履行。

有效性

计划良好的评估是指评估员和正在接受评估的被评估人清楚地知道评估内容和证据内容。此外,证据的种类和形式将为规定的标准提供真实证明。一个常见的无效评估(无效证据)例子是对实践技能进行书面测验。一个有效的评估是观察评估人对火警的反应(特别是在被评估人预先不知道有警报测验的情况下)。

作为一名评估员,应首先考虑评估的目标。问一问自己需要从此人的表现中发现什么(需要什么证据)。然后,问一问这种评估方法是否能获取这种证据。

可靠性

在一个评估系统中,如果不同地方的评估员在相同证据的基础上对相同的申请人做出相同的评定,这个评估系统才具有真实价值。一个设计良好的评估系统可以通过质量控制和监督评估来进行系统内部的可靠性测试。同样,在一个公司的计划方案中,如果得到相同证据的两个不同的评估员对被评估人的适任状况得出一样的结论,该设计方案才是可靠的。这样的测试活动应当成为评估员培训的一部分。

证据的准则

有效性

在评判证据时,同样的问题出现了,即需要知道评估内容。对于每个证据,评估员需了解的主要问题是"这个证据能告诉我什么?",它可能提供与规定标准相关的内容,也可能只是提供一些其他相关活动的内容。

例如,如果你正在评估维护工程师,你可能收到其已完成工作的有关证明文件。该证明文件能告诉你什么?它是否说明此项工作是按照正确的安全标准完成的?它是否说明已按顾客要求完成工作?它说明完成工作中是否使用了合适的零配件?它是否说明顾客的满意程度?

In fact, the documentation may only tell you that the engineer is able (or not, as the case may be) to complete paperwork correctly, neatly and in accordance with company procedures!

*Remember, the issue of **validity** is critical. Ask, "What does this piece of evidence actually tell me about this individual's performance?"*

Authenticity

How do you know that the evidence presented to you was actually produced by the named individual? Was it produced by the individual alone, or as part of a team? These questions are particularly relevant when assessors are dealing with "historical" evidence, but still have to be kept in mind when current evidence is being considered.

If an assessor is to attribute competence to an individual based on the evidence presented, then the issue of authenticity must be addressed.

Currency

Once again, this is of particular relevance to evidence from prior achievement (historical evidence) but should not be ignored in on-going workplace assessment. The key here is to focus on the standards as your starting point.

It is very easy for assessors to fall into the trap of making assumptions about evidence. This can be due to the many influences on assessment (see Part 10-4), or due to lack of planning of assessment or due to lack of application of rules of assessment (see above). Most often, however, falling into the "assumption trap" is caused by assessors failing to refer (and to re-refer) to the specified standards as their starting point.

Evidence is only current if the information it provides the assessor matches that specified within the standards.

Sufficiency

Once assessors have managed the collection of evidence and the application of rules of validity, authenticity and currency, one question remains: Do you have enough evidence of the right *quality* to make a *confident* judgement about competence?

This question of sufficiency has caused considerable difficulties for new assessors who frequently ask how to decide what is enough.

Here we come back to the key principles of competence-based assessment and to the format which standards of occupational competence take. A basic rule for competence-based assessment is that *all of the standards must be assessed*. This means that evidence must be collected to demonstrate that an individual has performed the element and its associated performance criteria across the full specified range of activity before that *element* can be "signed off". In addition, this signing-off activity for each element must be completed before the unit of competence can similarly be signed off and a certificate issued for that unit.

实际上，证明文件有可能只告诉了你工程师能够（或不能够）正确地、熟练地按照公司的程序完成书面工作！

记住，**有效性**是关键。应了解"这个证据在个人表现方面实际上能告诉我什么？"

真实性

你如何知道提供给你证据的人就是完成工作的人？是由被评估人自己完成的还是小组工作的一部分？当评估员处理"历史的"证据时，这些问题需要特别关注。当然，在研究当前的证据时也要记住这些问题。

如果评估员以提供的证据为基础判定被评估人是否适任，那么必须关注证据的真实性。

可用性

同样地，可用性与源自过去的成绩证据（历史证据）是相关的，但是在当前进行的现场评估中不应忽略这个问题。关键是关注作为评估起点的标准。

评估员很容易陷入这样的误区：妄自推测证据。这可能是由于评估中的各种影响因素（见第10-4章）或由于缺少评估计划或由于没有应用评估原则（见前面内容）。但是，陷进"推测误区"的通常是由于评估员没有把规定的评估标准作为评估起点。

提供给评估员的资料只有符合规定标准的证据才是可用的。

充分性

一旦评估员完成证据的收集以及应用有效性、真实性和可用性原则进行分析，还剩下一个问题：你是否有足够的、质量合适的证据来对适任做出可靠判断？

正确判断证据的充分性对新的评估员来讲是比较困难的，他们经常会问如何才知道证据是足够的。

在这里我们重申一下适任评估的关键原则和职业适任标准所采用的形式。适任标准的基本原则是必须对所有的标准进行评估。这就意味着在签发评估证明之前，必须收集证据以表明被评估人已经在规定的所有活动范围内显示他已经符合该评估要素的相应表现标准。此外，在结束适任项目评估和为此签发证书之前，必须先对项目的各要素完成签发证明。

The issue of providing evidence for all performance criterion and across the full range sounds like a horrendous task for assessors. If this task is approached on the basis that one piece of evidence is required for each criterion and for each aspect of the range then this would be true. However, contrary to general belief, this is not the case. The issue of matching evidence and making judgements about competence is explained in the next section on matching evidence and judging competence.

This section ends with a checklist which is very useful for new assessors.

Applying rules of evidence: checklist for assessment

- All of the standards must be assessed.

- Evidence should relate clearly and directly to specified standards.

- There should be sufficient evidence to cover the full range of contexts or contingencies specified within the standards.

- There should be no comparison or contrast between candidates—evidence relates directly to individual assessment.

- Evidence should be traceable to its source (effective record keeping is important).

- Evidence should be generated in realistic conditions using valid assessment methods.

- The assessment process should put no additional pressure on candidates or assessor.

Matching Evidence and Judging Competence

The checklist in the previous section forms a useful guide for assessors in the matching and judging stages of competence-based assessment. The following text provides more detail to help assessors use the checklist and thus to develop and maintain confidence in their assessment role.

All of the standards must be assessed

Only two judgements are possible in competence-based assessment—"competent" or "not yet competent". Because the performance criteria relate to critical aspects of performance, this means that all criteria must be met. Because true competence entails transferability of skills and knowledge, evidence of performance across the specified range must also be collected.

The evidence should relate clearly to the standards

There are a number of issues relating to rules of evidence. These include validity, currency, authenticity and sufficiency and are discussed earlier in this chapter.

为所有符合表现标准以及所有规定范围的活动提供证据,对于评估员似乎是一件艰巨的任务。如果任务的实施基于每个标准和范围的每个方面都必须有一个证据,那么工作量真是非常大。然而,与普遍的观念不同,实际操作并不是这样的。下一章将会解释与适任相对应的证据和判断是否适任等有关问题。

本章的结尾提供了一个对新评估员非常有用的核对表。

应用证据准则:评估核查表

- 必须评估所有的标准。

- 证据应当清晰和直接地与规定标准对应。

- 应有覆盖所有范围或符合规定标准的足够证据。

- 不应进行考生间的比较或对比——证据应直接与个人的评估相关。

- 证据应可查到来源(保持有效的记录是重要的)。

- 证据应采用有效的评估方法在实际的状况下产生。

- 评估过程不能对申请人或评估员施加额外的压力。

核查证据,判断是否适任

上述核对表为评估员对照检查和确定适任评估的步骤提供了有用的指导。下面将提供更加详细的内容帮助评估员使用该核对表,从而培养和保持他们在评估岗位中的自信心。

必须评估所有的标准

在适任评估中,只应做两种判断,即"适任的"或"不能适任的"。因为表现的标准与表现的必须性有关,意思是必须符合所有的标准。因为真正的适任必须具有技能和知识的转换能力,也必须收集规定范围内的表现证据。

证据应当清楚地与标准有关

在证据准则方面要考虑一些问题,包括有效性、可用性、真实性和充足性,本章前面部分已提到。

Sufficient evidence must be generated in realistic conditions

Competence-based assessment assesses workplace activity. Assessment should therefore take place in a realistic working environment and relate to normal working practice.

The assessment process should be individualized, but should not put additional pressures on the candidate

As an assessor, you need to assess each individual in their normal working practice. Assessment should be unobtrusive and should relate only to the specified standards.

The assessment process should not put additional pressures on the assessor

Assessors in competence-based systems are usually line managers. Competence-based standards are designed to make explicit what people do in their normal working roles. They should therefore provide assistance to managers in their supervisory role and not increase their workload to an unmanageable degree.

How much evidence?

We come back to the question of sufficiency of evidence and to a concept which assessors invariably find difficult at first. As noted previously, one misconception which causes problems on the "sufficiency" front is that one piece of evidence must be found for each performance criterion (Figure 10 F-2).

In fact, one "package" of evidence will provide valid information for all performance criteria. It may even provide valid information about performance criteria in different elements, or different units. Figure 10 F-3 illustrates this.

Assessors have expressed initial concerns that competence-based assessment will generate mountains of paperwork, that each individual will need to collect piles of evidence which has to be stored somewhere and judged on a one-to-one basis with each performance criterion. As Figure 10F-3 illustrates, this is not the case. Assessors will only develop the confidence to make such judgements, however, through practice. It becomes clear, therefore, that building such practice into assessor training can help develop this confidence.

充分的证据必须在真实的条件中产生

适任评估是对岗位工作活动进行评估。因此,评估应当在真实的工作环境中进行,并且与正常工作结合。

评估过程应当个体化,但不应当给申请人施加额外的压力

作为一名评估员,你需要在被评估人的正常工作时进行评估。评估不能随意,应当只评估与规定的标准有关内容。

评估过程不应当给评估员额外的压力

适任系统的评估员通常是部门主管。制定适任标准的目的是明确人们在正常工作岗位中要做的事情,而不是将他们的工作量增加到令他们无法应付的程度。

需要多少证据?

我们回到证据的充分性问题,这向来是评估员最先感到困难的概念。正如前面阐述的,造成关于充分性问题的一个错误观念是必须为每个表现标准寻找一个证据(见图10F-2)。

实际上,一个证据"包"可以为所有表现标准提供有效的信息。它甚至可以为不同环节或不同项目的有关表现标准提供有效资料。图10F-3举例说明这一问题。

评估员最早对适任评估将产生的担心是繁重的文件工作,也就是对每个人都需要收集大批的证据存放在某个地方,并根据表现标准一一进行判断。但如图10F-3举例说明的,实际情况并不是这样。评估员只能通过实践才能提高做出这种判断的信心。因此,把针对这方面内容的实践添加到评估员培训中就可以帮助培养这一信心。

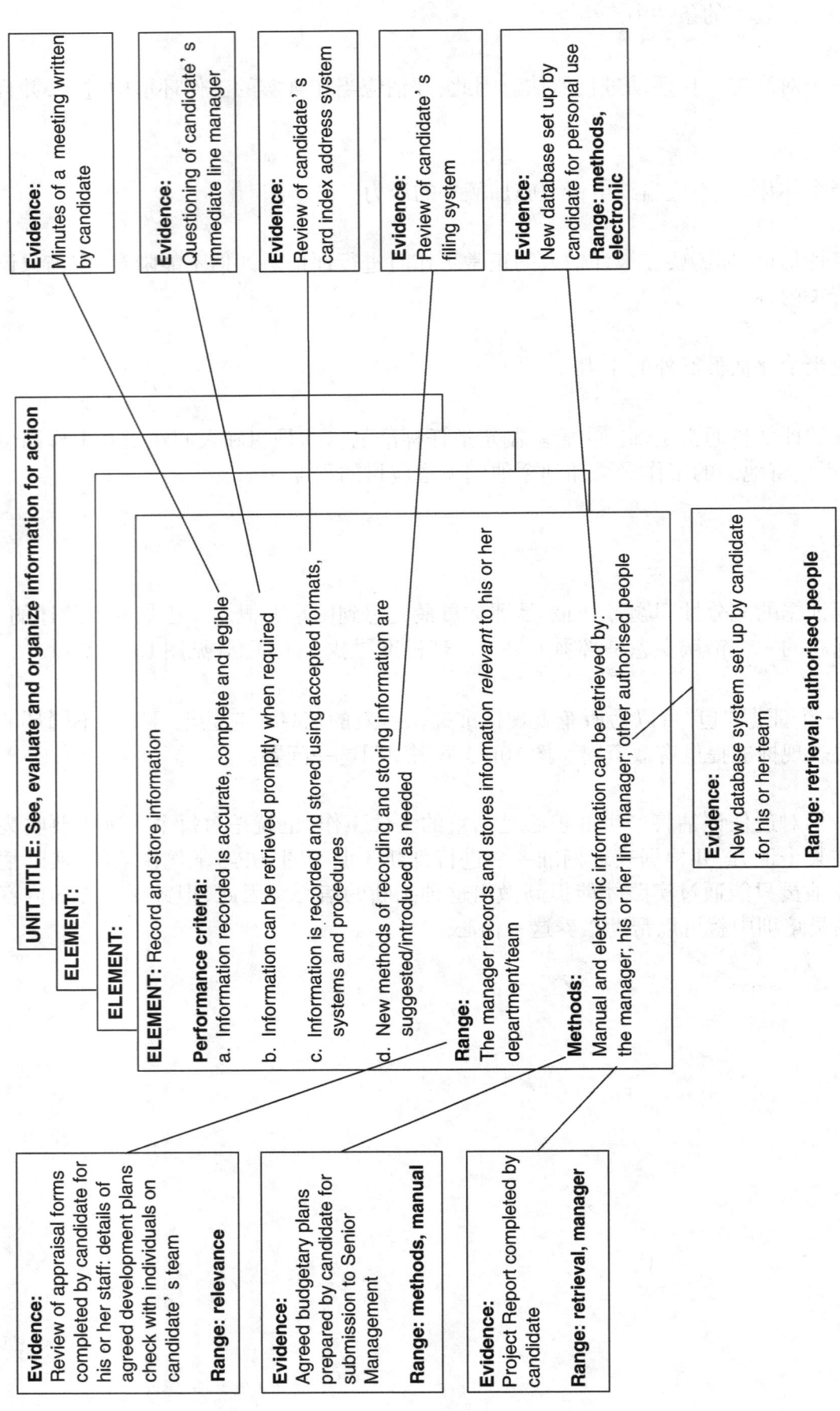

Figure 10F-2 Incorrect approach—one piece of evidence for each performance criterion

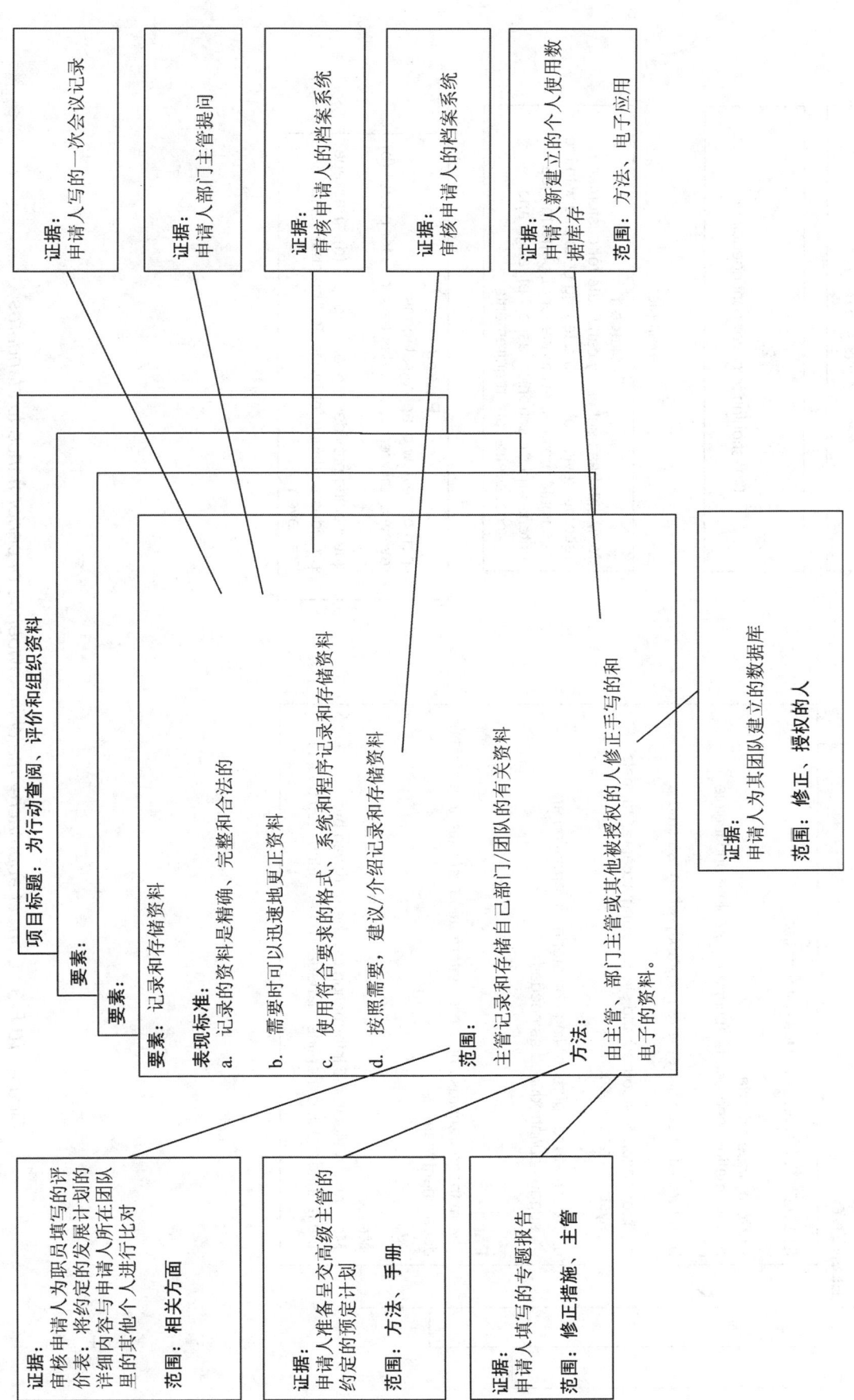

图 10 F-2 不正确的方法——为每一个表现标准提供一个证据

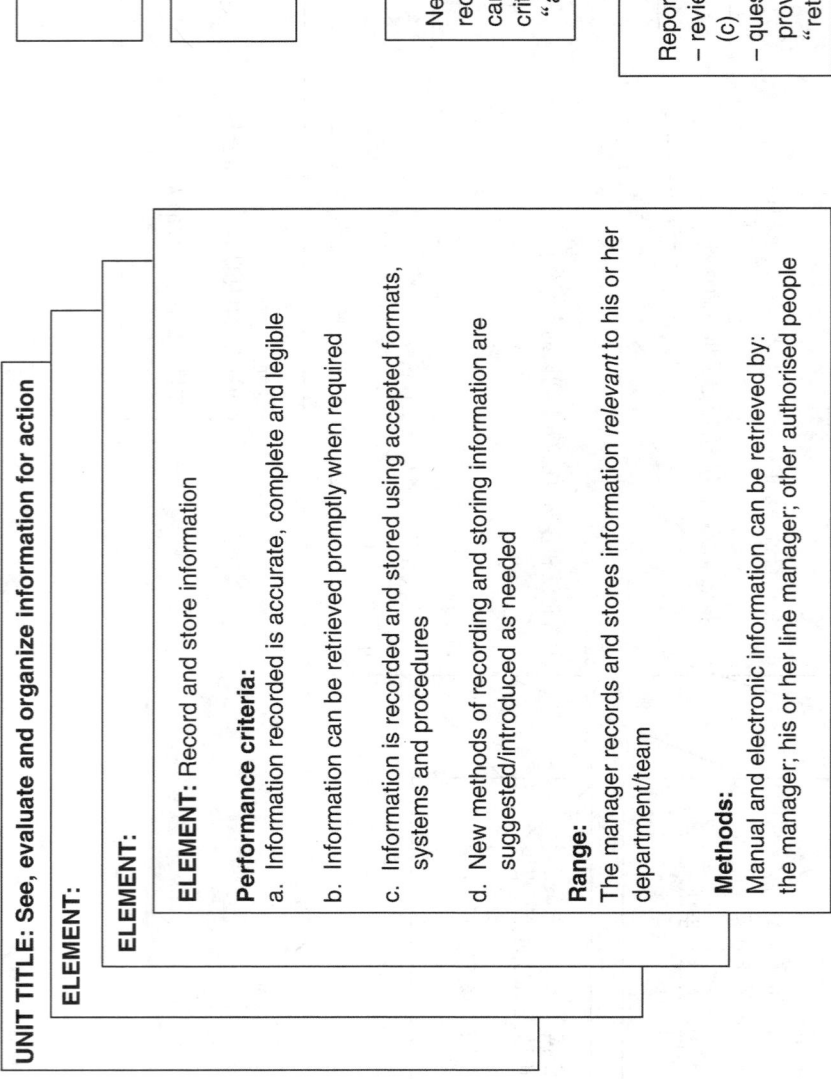

Figure 10 F-3 Correct approach—matching evidence of performance to standards

项目标题：为行动查阅、评价和组织资料

要素：

要素：记录和存储资料

表现标准：
a. 记录的资料是精确、完整和合法的
b. 需要时可以迅速地更正资料
c. 使用符合要求的格式、系统和程序记录和存储资料
d. 按照需要、建议/介绍记录和存储资料

范围：
主管记录和存储自己部门/团队的有关资料

方法：
由主管、部门主管或其他被授权的人修正手写的和电子的资料

1
符合所有相关表现标准 (p.c.) 和范围的证据 "包"

2
涉及附带内容的提问

证据包1
申请人为顾客记录建立的新数据库的使用情况，提供对应所有的表现标准和测试数据库的"方面内容以及"存取/修正"要求方面的"电子应用"方面内容的证据

证据包2
评价表的审核报告：
— 审核报告为对应表现标准 (a) (b) (c) 提供了证据
— 提问提供的对应表现标准 (d) 的证据包中的内容包括"手动"和"修正"

图 10 F-3　正确的方法——将表现的证据与标准对应

Part 10-7
Review and follow-up

Identifying Training Needs

In conducting on-going assessment of performance, an assessor will automatically identify training and development needs. When collecting evidence of performance, "gaps" in this evidence will emerge. These may be due to lack of opportunity to demonstrate competence. They may also be due, however, to lack of experience, skills or knowledge.

The competence-based assessment system therefore provides a working model for the identification of training needs—as long as the assessor is skilled in recognizing which gaps are due to training needs and which to lack of opportunity!

Such is the "knock-on effect" of introducing competence-based assessment within an organization. Once supervisors and line managers start to use the assessment system, their skills (or the need to develop them) also receive highlighted attention. Line managers need to develop skills in providing feedback and in recognition of training needs, to name but two.

In addition, the organization's procedures get some attention. It is only when assessors attempt to find quality evidence, and when they begin to ask key questions such as "What does this evidence actually tell me about Joe Bloggs's performance?" that possible improvements in the procedural and administrative systems start to emerge.

For example, in the last Part, we considered documentation which might be completed by an engineer and asked what it actually told us about the work completed by the individual engineer. Questions like this can lead us to the conclusion that our recording system is perhaps not all it should be—or that our engineers have not been trained in its use!

When we think *about identifying training* needs therefore, we are considering both assessor and assessee. Through the collection of evidence, the assessor will identify the needs of the assessee. However, the process of collecting and judging evidence will in itself highlight the assessor's own training needs!

Recording Assessment

If your organization is going to go to all the trouble of perhaps developing its own competence-based standards and assessment system, or introducing a nationally devised one, then it would be a shame if the whole system was found not to work because the records were inadequate.

The system for recording assessment needs to be both simple and efficient. Assessors need space to record what evidence they have judged, when they judged it, and the method of assessment used. There also needs to be space for the assessor to record that the element has been achieved (when sufficient, high-quality evidence has been collected and matched to the specified standards).

第10-7章
复查与跟踪

明确培训的需求

在实施现场审核的过程中,评估员会自动地确定被评估人所需要的培训和提高的内容。但在收集表现证据时,证据显现出被评估者的一些不足。这可能是由于缺少表现能力的机会,但是,也可能是由于缺少经验、技能或知识。

因此,适任评估体系提供了一套确定培训需要的工作模式——其前提是评估员能熟练地确定哪些不足需要通过进一步的培训来弥补,而哪些是由于缺少表现机会产生的!

这就是在一个机构中面对适任评估会引发的"冲击效应"。一旦主管和部门管理人员开始使用评估系统,他们的相应技能(或需要拓展的技能)也同时受到特别的关注。部门主管需要拓展在提供反馈和确定培训需要方面的辨识技能,以满足这两方面的需求。

另外,组织程序也应得到关注。只有当评估员想去寻找合格的证据并开始寻求"这个证据实际上提供了某人的哪方面表现?"这种关键问题的答案时,程序和管理系统才开始出现改进的可能。

例如,在上一章,我们已经对"某个工程师可能完成哪些文件"以及"该工程师完成的工作实际上能说明什么"这些问题进行了讨论。研究这些问题可能会使我们得出"我们的记录系统也许根本不符合要求"或是"我们的工程师没有接受过相应的培训"这样的结论。

因此,在考虑明确的培训需要时,我们应考虑评估员和被评估者。通过收集证据,评估员将发现被评估者的需要。然而,收集和判断证据的过程在本质上也在强调评估员自身的培训需要。

评估记录

如果你的机构准备开发自己的适任标准和评估系统,或者引用一个经过修订的国家系统,一旦发现由于记录不足使整个系统不能运行将是很尴尬的。

评估的记录系统需要简单有效。评估员需要有地方记录他们已经鉴定的证据、鉴定的时间以及使用的评估方法,也需要留出地方给评估员记录已经完成的项目(当已经收集了足够的、高质量的证据并且符合规定的标准时)。

These records may be used, within a national, organizational or professional vocational qualification system, as the basis for recommendation for award. It is essential, therefore, that the records used provide a solid basis on which a quality-assurance system can operate.

Recording Achievement

The assessor only needs to record positive evidence (achievement) in a record book. Evidence which indicates a training need can be passed on to the relevant personnel, or may lead to the assessor providing on job development.

Here again, the question of procedures arises. Does your organization have procedures which allow supervisors and line managers to pass on identified training needs? Do these procedures actually lead to action being taken to meet those needs?

It may be that the introduction of competence-based assessment leads to a review of your procedures in connection with the identification of training needs and the provision of required training.

Providing/Arranging Follow-up Training

As noted above, assessors will need to be skilled in the identification of training needs. However, they will also probably require skills in coaching and on job development. One might argue that these are skills that supervisors and line managers should have anyway—but in reality, few do. Managers, particularly in the UK, do not have key "people skills" which help them to make the most of their human resource.

A second issue relates to the procedural question already raised. What procedures does your organization have for:

- passing up information on identified training need? providing training and development on a modular basis?

- developing training programmes on a modular basis?

- designing and developing programmes based on explicit standards of performance?

Again, the knock-on effect of introducing competence-based assessment begins to become clear.

If the assessment system is to be used to the full, then supporting systems of training and development for all staff, including those who take on an assessor role, must be put in place. A competence-based assessment system provides a valuable foundation on which to measure, manage and maintain high-quality performance within an organization.

However, this can only happen if the implications of introducing the system are carefully considered and plans for peripheral activities are put into action at an early stage.

The final issue to be addressed is that of quality assurance. Part 10-8 explains the key issues and provides general guidance on this matter.

在一个国家的、组织的或行业的职业资格系统中，可以使用这些记录证据作为推荐其获得资格的基础。因此，记录工作是很重要的，它为质量保证体系的运行提供了坚实的基础。

成绩记录

评估员只需要在记录簿中记录实际(成绩)的证据。反映培训需要的证据可以交给相关人员处理，否则可能影响评估员的工作进展。

在这方面也同样会出现程序方面的问题。即你的机构是否制定了在主管和部门负责人之间传递培训需要的程序？这些程序是否能真正达成采取符合要求的行动？

引入适任评估可能需要对确定培训需要和规定培训要求的相关程序进行研究。

提供和安排跟踪培训

就如上面提到的，评估员需要能够熟练地识别被评估者的培训需要。当然，也可能要求他们具备提供培训和促进被评估者工作发展的能力。可能有人认为，这些是主管和部门主管的本应有的技能，但在实际中这些人却很少具备这些能力。管理人员，特别是英国的管理人员，没有具备一些"个人技能"，而这些技能恰恰有助于他们充分利用人力资源。

有关程序的第二个问题已经产生，那就是机构是否已：

- 建立确定培训需要的资料；提供模块化的培训和发展机会？

- 制订模块化的培训计划？

- 设计和开发符合明确的工作表现标准的程序？

再次，引入适任评估的"冲击效应"开始变得清晰。

如果全面使用评估系统，那么必须建立为所有员工(包括那些担任评估员角色的员工)提供培训和发展支持的系统。适任评估系统为机构内部表现评定、管理和保持的高质量提供了基础。

但是，只有在早期阶段就充分地研究所引进的系统实质，并且开始实施辅助活动的计划，才能达到上述效果。

最后的问题是关于质量的保证。第10-8章讨论了这一问题的主要方面并且提供了总体指导。

Part 10-8
Quality assurance

Introduction

There is little point in developing and introducing a competence-based assessment system unless an effective quality assurance model is put in place to ensure that standards, and the credibility of the system are maintained.

There are several aspects to quality assurance within competence-based assessment systems. These vary depending upon whether your organization introduces a nationally approved system, such as that relating to National Vocational Qualifications (NVQs) in the UK, or whether you operate your own in-house system.

However, whether your system operates in-house, and with or without certification, key issues to be addressed in the design and/or establishment of a quality assurance system will be:

- selection of assessors;
- training of assessors;
- monitoring of assessors.

If your system is also linked to certification, either in-house or national, other issues will need to be addressed, such as approval of assessment sites, and procedures for certification.

All these issues are dealt with in the following sections.

Selection of Assessors

Assessors are key personnel within a competence-based assessment system. You will wish to consider the main characteristics/technical requirements for assessors within your organization. If you operate within a national certification system, you may well find that the selection criteria are already established; nevertheless, these criteria will include the following:

- experience in the occupational role;
- experience in supervision/line management;
- willingness to undertake assessment.

第10-8章
质量保证

介绍

如果没有制定有效的质量保证体系以确保标准的质量,并且使系统的可靠性得到保持,开发和引进适任的评估系统是无意义的。

适任的评估系统内的质量保证涉及几个方面。质量保证体系根据你所在的机构是采用国家认可系统〔如关于联合王国的国家职业资格(NVQ)〕,还是采用自己的内部系统而有所不同。

然而,无论是否采用内部系统,是否涉及发证,设计和/或建立质量保证体系涉及的主要问题都会是:

- 评估员的遴选;

- 评估员的培训;

- 评估员的监督。

如果你的系统与内部或国家的发证有关联,则还需要考虑其他的问题,如评估点的认可和发证的程序。

以下的章节将讨论所有的这些问题。

评估员的遴选

评估员是适任评估体系内的关键人物。你当然希望根据自己的机构的需要来考虑评估员的主要特点和技术要求。但如果是在一个国家的发证系统内运作,你会很快发现用以挑选的标准已经存在;总之,标准会包括下列内容:

- 职业岗位的经验;

- 担任主管/部门主管的经验;

- 有意愿承担评估工作。

The last may seem strange, but it is essential. If line managers are not willing to undertake assessment, then they will not undertake the assessment thoroughly, and you will have created a situation in which the credibility of the system is threatened. You will need to know why line managers are unwilling: do they feel threatened themselves by the new system? (Remember, it highlights their skills, or lack of them.) Do they see it as extra workload? (They will need initial briefing to overcome this, as well as detailed training and development.)

You will need to explore and overcome these initial barriers to effective operation of your assessment system.

You may try a pilot programme to begin with. In this way you can choose your pilot group and make use of those people with the commitment and drive to help you make the system work. People usually feel less threatened, and put up fewer barriers, when they see a system actually operating, and operating well. Plan your pilot carefully and make sure everyone knows what is going on.

Training of Assessors

This is vital. Assessors are no different from anyone else. Would you take on new operatives, or new managers without providing training?

Everyone needs to learn what the expectations of a role are. They need to understand the importance of the role activity and the procedures which need to be followed. Assessors need to understand several aspects of the competence-based system:

- principles of competence-based assessment;
- what makes it different from other forms of assessment;
- using standards of competence;
- rules of assessment;
- rules of evidence;
- methods of assessment;
- room for flexibility and creativity;
- roles of assessors and individuals;
- the quality-assurance structure in which the assessment system operates;
- benefits of the assessment system.

You should ensure that a training programme is provided for assessors immediately before the system is put into operation. Selected assessors should be briefed prior to the formal training, so that they can prepare their staff and deal with any concerns which may arise.

最后一项看似寻常,但却很重要。如果部门主管不愿意承担评估工作,那么他们将不会很好地实施评估工作,因而会威胁系统的可靠性。需要了解为什么部门主管不愿意承担评估工作:他们是否感觉到自己受到新的系统的威胁(记住,新的系统注重他们是否具备相关技能)?他们是否把新的系统看作是额外的工作负担?需要对他们进行系统介绍以及通过详细培训和提高来克服这些顾虑。

需要探讨和克服这些首先出现的障碍,从而有效地运行评估系统。

可以首先开展一个试点计划。这样可以选择试验小组,并利用这些人的支持和努力协助运作该系统。当人们看到系统能够实际运行并且运行良好,他们通常会觉得较有安全感,并且表现出较少的抵触。要谨慎策划试点工作并确保每个人都知道到底会发生什么事。

评估员的培训

这项工作很重要。评估员与其他人相比并没有什么特殊的地方,你愿意招聘一些未经过培训的新的操作人员或新的主管吗?

每个人都应当了解对应岗位所期望的表现。他们应当理解岗位活动的重要性和应遵循的程序。评估员应当了解适任系统的以下几个方面:

- 适任原则;
- 什么使它与其他的评估形式不同;
- 使用适任标准;
- 评估准则;
- 证据的准则;
- 评估的方法;
- 灵活性和创造性范围;
- 评估员和被评估人的角色;
- 评估系统运作的质量保证体系;
- 评估系统的效益。

应当保证在系统运作之前给评估员提供培训。正式培训前应当给经过挑选的评估员通报培训安排,让他们可以对自己的工作进行人事安排以处理任何可能发生的问题。

Assessors will also need follow-up support. You should consider establishing "assessor networks"—opportunities for assessors to meet and discuss concerns, difficulties and successes. All of this activity contributes to the quality of the assessment system and encourages commitment and involvement. The network activity also provides an opportunity for assessors to discuss and identify any common training needs which may arise, such as feedback skills, coaching, further training in assessment methods, interpersonal skills and so on.

Monitoring of Assessors

The process of monitoring assessment is usually called verification. Your competence-based assessment system should operate within a verification framework. The extent of this framework will depend upon the extent of your system. For example, an in-house system leading to company certification of individual performance might have a three-tier system, whereas one linked to national certification would have as many as seven tiers. Figure 10G-1 illustrates a basic verification framework for a nationally certificated competence scheme. A model for an in-company system is illustrated in Figure 10G-2.

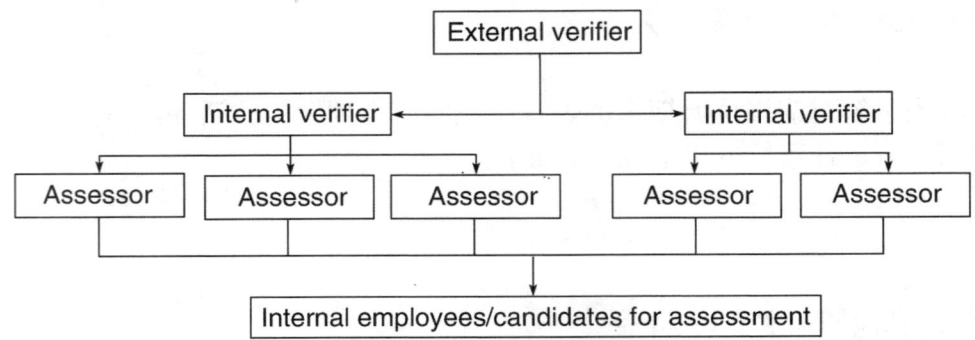

Figure 10G-1   Basic verification framework—national certification

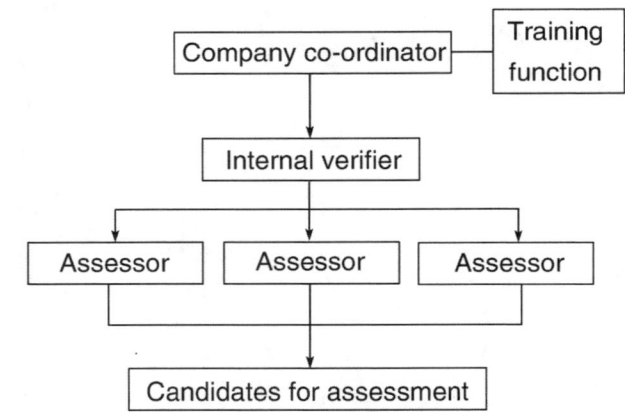

Figure 10G-2   Verification framework for in-company model of competence-based assessment

Each assessor needs to be monitored to ensure reliability of assessment—that is, that the same judgement would be reached by more than one assessor when the same collection of evidence of competence is assessed.

评估员需要跟进支持。应当考虑建立"评估员联系网络"——给评估员提供会面和讨论关注的事情、困惑和成功等问题的机会。所有的这类活动都有益于评估系统的质量,以及鼓励更多的支持与参与。网络活动平台还为评估员提供机会讨论和确定任何可能产生的、普遍的培训需要,如反馈技能、辅导技巧、有关评估方法的深入培训、讲授技能,等等。

评估员的监督

监督评估的过程通常称为审核。适任评估体系应当在一个审核体系内运行。体系的内容依据系统的内容设定。例如,一个针对个人表现发证的公司内部系统可能有三个层次,而与国家发证有关联的系统则有多达七个层次。图 10G-1 说明了国家发证的适任系统的基本审核体系。图 10G-2 提供了公司内部系统的一个范例。

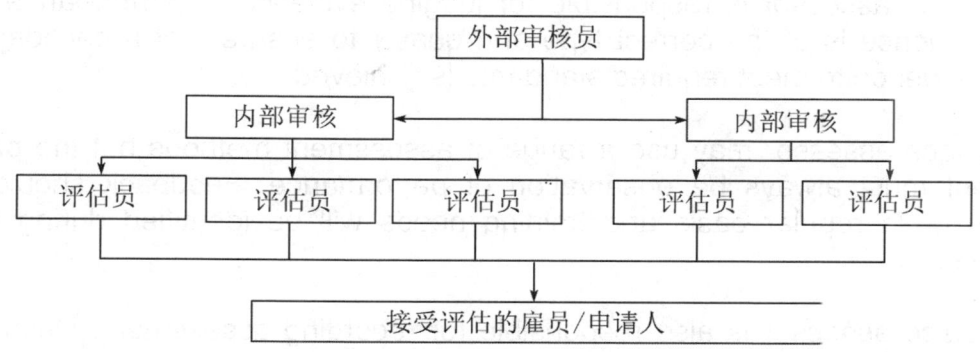

图 10G-1　基本审核体系——国家发证

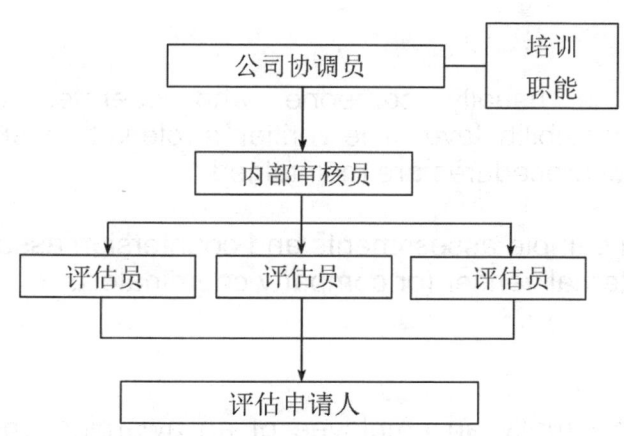

图 10G-2　公司内部的适任评估体系审核体系范例

要对每位评估员进行监督,以保证评估的可靠性——即是在评估同一适任证据时,应当多位评估员做出相同的评定。

To achieve this, you will need someone who monitors the assessors (an internal verifier) and a central coordinator.

The remainder of this chapter outlines the responsibilities of these key roles and other quality-assurance procedures which can be applied at national and at corporate or departmental level.

Verification Frameworks: Roles and Responsibilities

Workplace assessor

A workplace assessor is usually a line manager, since a line manager is the best person to observe natural workplace performance.

The workplace assessor is responsible for judging evidence of performance and ensuring that this evidence is of the correct type and quality to ensure that a confident decision on sufficient evidence to meet required standards is achieved.

The workplace assessor may use a range of assessment methods but the primary form of assessment must always be observation of performance. Feedback should be given to individuals on a regular basis and training needs will be identified during the course of assessment.

The workplace assessor is also responsible for recording assessment. Details of evidence must be entered on an assessment record.

The workplace assessor will be monitored by an internal verifier.

Internal verifier

An internal verifier is usually someone who operates in-company at the next line-management responsibility level. The verifier's role is to oversee assessment and make sure that quality-control procedures are maintained.

An internal verifier will sample assessments and countersign assessment records. He or she is monitored by an external verifier (or company coordinator).

External verifier

An external verifier is usually an employee of an awarding body or institution and visits approved assessment sites on a regular basis. You would have an external verifier if you operate a UK National Vocational Qualification (NVQ).

The external verifier will wish to see individuals' records of assessment and may also sample evidence collected. He or she will check that quality control systems are fully operational and will report back to the awarding body or institution on any difficulties encountered.

为了达到此目的,你需要配备人员(一名内部审核员)来监督评估员并且配备一位中心协调员。

本章的剩余部分概述这些主要人员的职责,以及其他适用于在国家、公司或部门级别应用的质量保证程序。

审核体系:角色和职责

现场评估员

现场评估员通常由部门主管担当,因为部门主管是观察现场行为表现的最佳人选。

现场评估员负责评判工作表现证据以及确保证据形式的正确性和高质量,从而保证证据充分性的基础上,按照要求的标准做出可靠的判断。

现场的评估员可以使用各种评估手段,但主要的评估形式必须始终是对工作表现的考察。应当定期给被评估人反馈并在评估过程中确定被评估人的培训需要。

现场评估员还负责评估记录,必须在评估记录簿记录证据的详细内容。

现场评估员的工作由内部审核员监督。

内部审核员

内部审核员通常是位于部门管理责任级别的上一级,进行公司内部运作的人员。审核员的职责是监督评估员和确保质量控制程序得到保持。

内部审核员应抽样调查评估和联合签署评估记录,并受到外部审核员(或公司协调员)的监督。

外部审核员

外部审核员通常是发证机关或机构的雇员,并经常造访认可的评估点。如果实施英国的国家资格体系,就需要一个外部审核员。

外部审核员会查看被评估人的评估记录并抽样调查收集的证据,检查质量控制体系的整体运作情况,并且向发证机关或机构报告遇到的任何困难。

The external verifier, appointed by the national awarding body (or the company coordinator in an in-company system), has responsibility for monitoring the overall assessment process and for passing on recommendations for certification to the awarding-body management structure. This is where a possible seven-tier system comes into play (see Figure 10G-3).

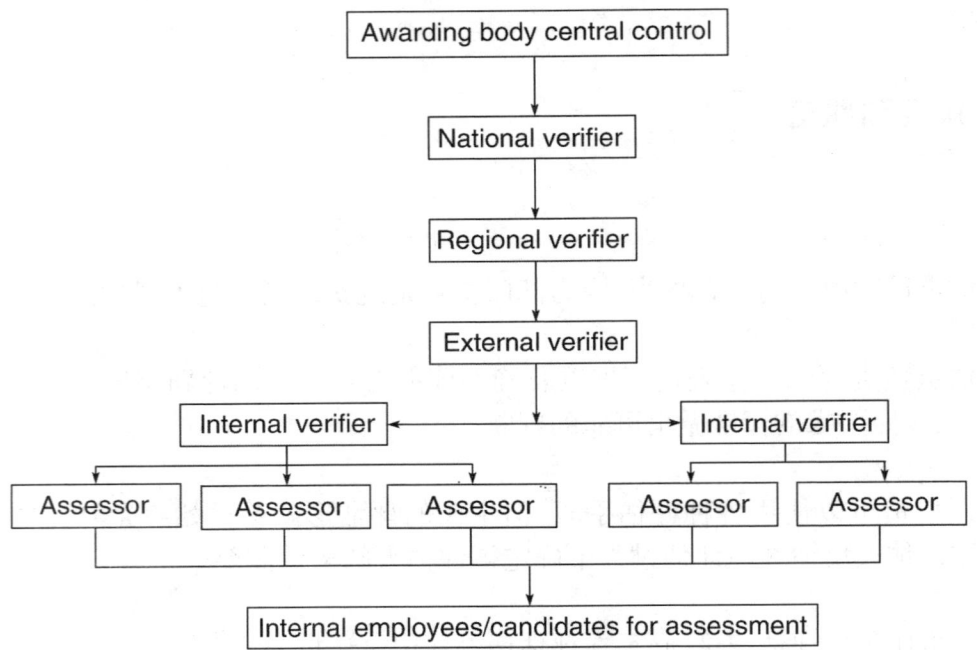

Figure 10G-3   Extended verification framework

Approval of Assessment Sites

If your organization operates within a national assessment system, it is likely that you will be required to go through an approval process for each site at which you wish to operate assessment.

If you operate your own in-company system, you will still want to ensure that a common system operates at all locations or in all subsidiaries. The following guidelines on the approval and monitoring processes which operate within the UK system at national level can therefore be applied at corporate level by substituting "corporate body" for "awarding body" and "subsidiary" for "assessment centre".

The approval process usually requires the payment of a registration fee after certain aspects relating to operation of the assessment have been checked against criteria set by the awarding body. These include:

■   trained assessors;

■   use of approved recording systems;

■   internal monitoring (verification).

由国家发证机关（或公司内部系统的协调员）指派的外部审核员有责任监督整个评估过程并向发证机关的管理部门递交发证相关的建议。这就使系统的七个层次得以运行（见图10G-3）。

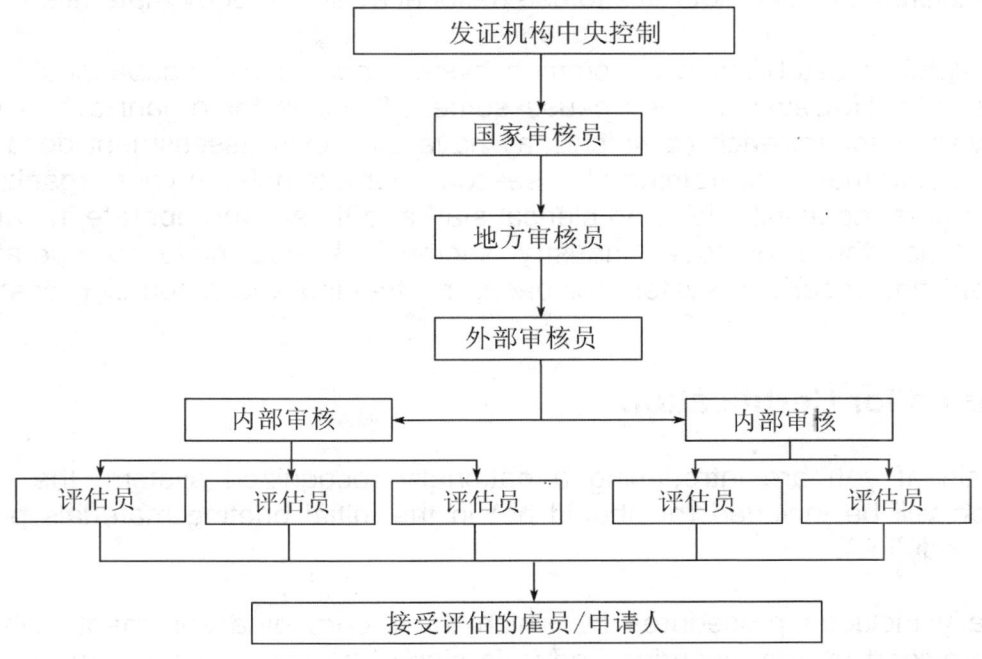

图10G-3　扩展的审核框架

评估地点的认可

如果适任评估是在国家的评估系统内运作，那么主管机关很可能要求你为将要开展评估的具体地点办理认可手续。

如果适任评估是在你自己的内部系统内运作，你也会希望在所有的地点或附属机构实施一个共同的体系。以下是关于英国国家级系统的认可和监督程序指南。它可以应用在公司级别，只要用"公司组织"替代"发证机关"以及用"附属机构"替代"评估中心"即可运行。

认可的手续通常要求支付注册费用，费用是在发证机关参照规定的标准，就有关评估操作的某些方面进行审核之后收取。审核项目包括：

■　受过培训的评估员；

■　使用认可的记录系统；

■　内部监督（审核）。

As the awarding bodies in the UK have to recoup their own quality-monitoring costs, they make a charge for registration of assessment centres and for materials, the latter being centrally devised. (You do not have to use national awarding body materials.)

This is helpful in establishing a common system across all occupational roles within an industry sector. However, it does cause some difficulties for organizations which operate within several sectors, each of which may have their own assessment documentation and their own requirements for training of assessors. For example, in your organization you may have managers, administration and clerical staff and those who operate in various technical roles—at least three or four "industry sectors". If you have to operate a different assessment and recording system for each, the training and resourcing costs start to look ominous!

Procedures for Certification

Once again, if you are introducing a nationally recognized system, the procedures for certification will be included (or should be) in the initial briefing materials provided by the awarding body(ies).

This usually includes procedures by which the record of assessment—which may be a logbook provided by the awarding body—is signed by the assessor and countersigned by the internal verifier once sufficient evidence of competence has been collected. The record will then continue through the quality-assurance framework to the external verifier and thence to the central office of the awarding body where computer records will be updated and certificates issued.

Certificates can be issued on a unit-by-unit basis as well as a full qualification (de, a required number of units). In a company certification scheme, where the corporate body would be the awarding body, a similar set of procedures would need to be established. A computerized database to store records of achievement and issue of certificates would be essential where large numbers of unit-based certificates were awarded.

由于英国的发证机关必须补偿他们所支付的质量监督费用,所以他们对评估中心的注册和资料收费,资料会集中分配。(当然你不一定非要使用国家发证机关的材料。)

评估地点的认可制度有助于在一个行业系统内对所有的职业岗位制定一个共同的系统。然而,对于跨行业运作体系的机构的确会造成一些困难。因为,各个部门可能有自己的评估文件和他们自己对评估员培训的要求。例如,在你的机构内会有主管、行政和办公人员以及那些在各种技术岗位(至少涉及三或四个"行业部门")操作的人员。如果你必须为每个部门实施不同的评估和记录系统,那么,培训资源和费用方面会出现麻烦!

发证的程序

同样,如果你引入一个国家认可的系统,发证机关提供的基本简介材料中会(或应当)包括发证的程序。

发证的程序通常包括收集足够的评估证据,然后就由评估员签署并由内部审核员连署评估记录(可能是发证机关提供的日志簿)。接着,记录将通过质量保证体系递交给外部审核员,然后上报发证机关的中心办公室,在此,将会更新电脑的记录,签发证书。

证书可以按单项或全部资格(即按要求数量项目组)签发。在一个公司的发证方案中,如果法人组织是发证机关,也应当制定类似的程序。如果要颁发大量的单项证书,那么保存成绩记录和签发证书的计算机化的数据库非常重要。

Annex 10-1
Development of standards: an example (Australia)

Maritime—Seagoing Functions Operational/Catering

1. BACKGROUND

1.1 Personnel Involved in the Project Development

During October 1992, the National Maritime Industry Training Council (NMITC) successfully applied to the Commonwealth for funding to develop national competency standards for the Maritime Industry.

A Working Group within the NMITC's Skills Based Training Sub-Committee was appointed by the Council to oversee the development project.

The Working Group consisted of: Mr. Mike Saint Executive Officer NMITC, Mr. John Morris ASP Ship Management, Mr. Ian Matthews Australian Institute of Marine and Power Engineers, Mr. Bert Dunsford Howard Smith Industries Pty. Ltd, Mr. Wal Leslie BHP Transport, Mr. Peter Curwell Australian Maritime Officers Union, Mr. Paddy Crumlin Maritime Union of Australia.

Training Strategies, part of the Department of Employment, Education and Training, was constructed to assist the Working Group in development of the competency standards. Mr. Jack Aaron and Mr. John McCaffrey were responsible for drafting the standards, with Mr. Aaron providing addition inputs to the consultation process and submission of the draft standards for NTB endorsement.

1.2 Project Objectives

The project was conducted in four stages:

- Stage 1   Analysis of the project scope in collaboration with the Australian Maritime College
- Stage 2   Development of draft standards
- Stage 3   Verification of the standards (Consultation Process)
- Stage 4   Finalisation of the standards, including preparation of NTB submission documentation.

The objectives of the project were to develop:

- develop competency standards for the Maritime Industry, being defined as parties covered by the:

附件 10-1
标准的制定：范例（澳大利亚）

海事—航海的职责实施/提供

1.背景

1.1 项目开发有关人员

1992年10月,国家海上职业培训委员会(NMITC)成功地向国家申请到用于为海上职业制定国家适任标准的经费。

委员会指定一个NMITC技能基础培训分委会的工作小组来监督该开发项目。

工作小组组成：NMITC 执行官 Mike Saint 先生、ASP 船舶管理公司 John Morris 先生、澳大利亚船舶和电力工程师学会 Ian Matthews 先生、Howard Smith 工业集团 Bert Dunsford 先生、BHP 运输事业部 Wal Lesile 先生、澳大利亚高级船员工会 Peter Curwell 先生、澳大利亚海员工会 Paddy Crumlin 先生。

编制培训战略,雇佣部门、教育和培训方面内容,用以协助工作小组制定适任标准。Jack Aaron 先生和 John McCaffrey 先生负责起草这个标准,同时,Aaron 先生为标准草案提供有关的补充咨询内容并呈报国家贸易部 NTB 签署。

1.2 项目的目标

项目计划分为四个阶段：

第一阶段：与澳大利亚海运学院合作分析项目范围

第二阶段：拟定标准草案

第三阶段：审核标准（咨询过程）

第四阶段：最后确定标准,包括准备向 NTB 提交文件。

计划的目标是开发：

- 为海上职业制定的适任标准,确定要覆盖的内容包括：

- Maritime Industry Seagoing Award

- Maritime Industry Modern Ships Award

- Tugboat Industry Award

- Maritime Industry Research Vessels Award

- Maritime Industry Offshore Oil and Gas Operators Award

■ competency standards subject to the statutory requirements of the Navigation Act and STCW;

■ competency standards subject to the principles laid down by the Maritime Industry Development Committee's Shipping Industry Reform Authority,

and may be subject to any further principles as initiated by the industry parties during the period of the project; and

■ a Maritime Industry Classification Structure related to the Australian Standards Framework.

1.3 Project Scope

The project was aimed at developing competency standards for all seagoing personnel. The personnel functions on board ship may be divided into the following fundamental areas:

■ operational functions

■ catering functions

Operational functions may be further divided into:

■ the Deck Department covering navigational and cargo operations

■ the Engineroom Department covering ship propulsion and machinery maintenance.

Ship personnel are categorised as:

■ Master: the overall ship manager

■ Mates: working in the Deck Department

■ Chief Engineer: overall propulsion and maintenance manager

■ Engineers: working in the Engine-room Department

■ Chief Integrated Rating: supervisor of integrated ratings

■ Integrated Ratings: working in both Deck and Engine-room Departments

— 海上职业航海人员的发证

— 海上职业现代船舶的发证

— 拖船的发证

— 海上职业研究船舶的发证

— 海上工业海底石油和天然气经营者的发证

- 适任标准符合航海法律和STCW公约法定的要求；

- 适任标准符合由海上职业发展委员会的海运改革局制定的原则，并符合在项目过程中该行业进一步创立的原则；及

- 海上职业分级体系应与澳大利亚标准体系相联系。

1.3 项目的范围

项目的目标是为所有的海上人员制定适任标准。船上人员的职能可以分为下列几个基本部分：

- 操作职能

- 供给职能

操作职能可以细分为：

- 甲板部，包括航行和货物操作

- 轮机部，包括船舶动力和机器保养。

船上人员分类如下：

- 船长：管理全船的人

- 驾驶员：在甲板部工作

- 轮机长：管理所有船舶动力和保养工作

- 轮机员：在轮机部工作

- 普通船员的主管：监管全体普通船员的工作

- 普通船员：在甲板部和轮机部工作

- Chief Steward: catering supervisor

- Chief Cook: working in the Catering Department

- Second Cook: working in the Catering Department

- Catering Attendant: working in the Catering Department.

1.4 Maritime Industry Career Paths

The project took into account the Industry's career path structures.

1.5 The Competency Standards Body

The NMITC is the recognised Competency Standards Body (CSB) for the Australian Merchant Navy, covering interstate and overseas shipping, the offshore oil and gas sector and the towage sector of the industry.

The CSB is comprised of representatives from:

Australian Maritime Employers Association, BHP Transport, ASP Ship Management, Howard Smith Industries Pty. Ltd, Commonwealth Steamship Owners' Association, Australian National Maritime Association, Australian Offshore Services, Western Australia Coastal Shipping Commission, Australian Maritime Safety Authority (AMSA), Australian Maritime Officers Union, Maritime Union of Australia, Australian Institute of Marine and Power Engineers, Australian Maritime College, Royal Melbourne Institute of Technology, Sydney University of Technology, Department of Employment, Education and Training, and NMITC.

1.6 Establishment of the Competency Standards Body

NMITC was recognised by the National Training Board as the Competency Standards Body for the trading, offshore and towage sectors of the Maritime Industry on 30 August 1991.

NMITC sought this recognition, being the Industry's peak council on training and human resource development matters.

2. DEVELOPMENT OF THE STANDARDS

2.1 Methodology/Research Used

The identification of Competency Unit Titles was initiated during a visit by Mr. Aaron to the Australian Maritime College (AMC), Launceston, on 9 and 10 December, 1992. A modified functional analysis of the maritime occupational areas was conducted using inputs from a team of four Departmental Heads and a Master Mariner.

The team identified eight streams (major functional areas) of work carried out within the Maritime Industry. Each stream was divided into the following sub-functions:

- 管事：服务管理者

- 大厨：在服务部工作

- 二厨：在服务部工作

- 服务生：在服务部工作。

1.4 海上职业的入职途径

本计划考虑海上职业的入职途径体系。

1.5 适任标准组织

NMITC是澳大利亚商船包括国内和远洋船舶、海上职业的海底石油和天然气部门和拖船部门公认的适任标准组织（CSB）。

CSB由下列代表组成：

澳大利亚雇主协会，BHP运输事业部，ASP船舶管理公司，Howard Smith公司，国家船东协会，澳大利亚国家海事协会，澳大利亚近海服务队，西澳大利亚沿海航运委员会，澳大利亚海事安全局（AMSA），澳大利亚高级船员工会，澳大利亚海员工会，澳大利亚船舶和动力工程师学会，澳大利亚海员学院，皇家墨尔本技术学院，悉尼技术大学，就业、教育和培训部，以及NMITC。

1.6 适任标准组织的设立

1991年8月30日，国家培训部认可NMITC作为海上职业的航行、近海工业和拖船部门的适任标准组织。

NMITC获得认可成为在培训和人力资源发展事务方面的行业内最高机构。

2.标准的制定

2.1 研究/使用的方法

最初确定的适任的项目标题是Aaron先生在1992年11月9—10日造访朗塞斯顿澳大利亚海运学院期间提出的，随后利用来自四个部门的主管和一个船长组成的小组收集的资料对海事职业领域的职能分析内容进行了改进。

该小组确定了海上工业需完成的八个类别（主要职能范围的）的工作。每个类别分为下列的子职能：

1. Navigation
- Berth/Unberth
- Plan
- Ship Handling
- Position Finding
- Watch Keeping

2. Cargo Handling
- Plan Cargo Operations
- Prepare Cargo Operations
- Transfer Cargo
- Stow and Secure Cargo

3. Communications
- Receive and Transmit Information

4. Emergency Response
- Fire
- Collision
- Abandon Ship
- Medical
- Security

5. Operate and Maintain Equipment
- Operate Plant
- Monitor Plant
- Test and Inspect Plant
- Assess Maintenance Requirements
- Maintain Plant

6. Catering and Accommodation
- Food
- Hygiene
- Consumables
- Linen

7. Administration (Plant Management)
- Finance
- Physical Resources
- Records and Documents

8. Human Resource Management
- Supervision
- Training and Development
- Employees Relations
- Planning and Change Management

1.航行
- 靠泊/离泊
- 计划
- 船舶操纵
- 定位
- 瞭望值班

2.货物装卸
- 货物计划操作
- 货物准备操作
- 货物搬运
- 货物积载和系固

3.通信
- 接收和发送信息

4.应急反应
- 火灾
- 碰撞
- 弃船
- 医疗
- 安保

5.操作和保养设备
- 操作设备
- 监管设备
- 测试和检查设备
- 评估保养要求
- 保养设备

6.服务和供应
- 食物
- 卫生
- 消耗品
- 被服

7.行政管理(设备管理)
- 财政
- 自然资源
- 记录和文件

8.人力资源管理
- 监督
- 培训和培养
- 雇员关系
- 人员计划和更换管理

The above information was recorded on a card system and displayed on a large wall area. An analysis of each of the sub-functions resulted in the development of a further set of cards representing the units of work (the initial Competency Unit Titles) carried out by the seagoing personnel previously identified in Section 1.3.

The data recorded on the cards was transcribed onto a matrix and forwarded to the AMC for comment.

Development of the draft Standards commenced on 15 December 1992. The content of the Elements of Competency and the Range of Variables Statements was obtained from a number of sources including:

- standards developed in the United Kingdom for the Merchant Navy Training Board

- desk research of relevant references, e.g Marine Orders, Navigation Act, International Convention for the Safety of Life at Sea, etc.

- endorsed National Competency Standards for the:
    — Metals Industry
    — Hospitality and Tourism Industry
    — Australian Fire Services
    — Assessor and Workplace Trainer

Progressive feedback on the content of the draft Standards was gained from the NTB Maritime Industry representative and members of the Working Group. The first draft was disseminated to Maritime Industry representatives on 18 March 1993, seeking their comment on the content and the proposed alignment of Australian Standards Framework (ASF) to the Units of Competency.

Following the initial validation of the Standards by the Maritime Industry, the Working Group met in Melbourne on 6 to 7 September 1993 to review the amended content and structure of the draft. A number of changes were made to the structure of the documentation and the matrix at Appendix C to clarify the role of individuals, and to facilitate the alignment of the Standards against the ASF levels. NTB feedback was obtained at this stage of the development before the Standards were submitted to the Consultation Process on 1 November 1993.

2.2 Alignment of Standards to the ASF

Following input from the Consultation Process, the proposed alignment of seagoing occupations to ASF levels is:

ASF Level 2. Catering Attendant
ASF Level 3. Integrated Rating . Second Cook
ASF Level 4. Chief Integrated Rating . Chief Cook
ASF Level 5. Deck Watchkeeper. Engineer Watchkeeper . Chief Caterer
ASF Level 6. Chief Mate . Senior Engineer
ASF Level 7. Master . Chief Engineer

上述资料记录在一系列卡片上并在大幕墙上展示。对每个子职能进行分析并开发出一套新卡片,这套卡片说明了在1.3部分提出的船员需承担的工作项目(基本适任的项目标题)。

整理记录在卡片上的资料并提交 AMC 评议。

标准草案的正式开发工作从1992年12月15日开始进行。适任要素的内容和各种说明内容从若干途径获得,包括:

■ 英国商船培训管理局制定的标准

■ 对相关参考资料,如海运规则、航海法规、《国际海上人命安全公约》的文件的研究

■ 已签署的国家标准:
—— 五金工业
—— 医院和旅游行业
—— 澳大利亚消防部门
—— 评估员和现场培训员

开发过程中不断获得 NTB 海上职业代表和工作小组的成员对于标准草案内容的反馈意见。首份草案在1993年3月18日发给各类海上职业的代表,寻求他们对澳大利亚标准体系(ASF)与适任项目内容和目的的评议意见。

在标准初步得到行业确认有效后,工作小组于1993年9月6—7日在墨尔本会商审核草案的修改内容和结构。对文件的结构和在附录 C 解释的个人义务的主要文本中做出若干修改,并促进标准按 ASF 等级调整。在1993年11月1日标准进入咨询程序之前获得 NTB 的反馈意见。

2.2 标准与 ASF 的结合

从协商过程得出的结果建议船上职业与 ASF 等级的对应是:

ASF 等级2. 服务员
ASF 等级3. 普通船员、二厨
ASF 等级4. 普通船员的领导、大厨
ASF 等级5. 甲板值班员、轮机值班员、管事
ASF 等级6. 大副、高级轮机员
ASF 等级7. 船长、轮机长

2.3 Description of the Standards

The Standards have been written in generic form. References to specific plant/equipment items, products, services and work organisation have been omitted due to the diversity in ship types, technology and operations performed within the Maritime Industry. Wherever possible, the Range of Variables Statements have been used to specify/categorise information.

The Standards are based on current functions and technology in the Maritime Industry and will need to be revised and updated as work practices and technology change. Further reforms initiated by the Shipping Industry Reform Authority or internationally through the review of the International Maritime Organisation's Standards of Training Certification and Watchkeeping Convention may also call for revision of the Standards.

In addition to the units categorised under the eight streams, another stream of core units has been included to address a range of common competencies required by the majority of seafaring personnel within the Industry.

3. CONSULTATION PROCESS

3.1 Organisations included in the Consultation Process

The Standards have been developed following wide circulation within the Maritime Industry, including all employer groups, maritime unions, AMSA and AMC. Consensus was sought with other CSB's on content sourced from their competency standards. The Standards were also circulated to all the State Training Authorities.

3.2 Summary of Outcomes

<u>3.2.1 Maritime Industry</u>

The Standards have been generally accepted by all parties within the Industry, subject to their further review in light of potential developments within the Shipping Industry Reform Authority (SIRA) and the review of STCW currently being undertaken by the IMO.

<u>3.2.2 Competency Standards Bodies and State Training Authorities</u>

On 9 November 1993 the draft Standards were circulated to all State Training Authorities and the following CSB's:

. National Fishing ITC
. Assessor and Workplace Trainer CSB
. National Fire Industry Training and Development Project
. National Tourism ITC
. National Metal and Engineering Training Board

In the light of nil responses from the above, there were no objections to the draft Standards.

2.3 标准的解释

标准以普通格式书写。由于船舶类型、技术和海上职业内实际操作的多样性,因此不参照特殊的机械/设备、产品、服务和工作组织的资料。如可能,对特定的/分类的资料使用不同的内容说明。

该标准以目前海上职业的功能和技术为基础并随着工作实际和技术的改变而做相应的修订和更新。由船舶工业改革机构开始的进一步改革或国际上对IMO的STCW公约的重新审查也可能要求修订标准。

除了八个主要的项目类别,核心项目的另一个主要方面,即处理行业内大部分海上人员所要求的各种共同的适任,已经包括在标准内。

3. 咨询程序

3.1 涉及咨询程序的组织

标准按照海上工业内部广泛流行的惯例开发,咨询对象包括所有的雇主团体、海员工会、AMSA和AMC,同时也与其他的标准组织协作,寻求与他们的适任标准在内容方面的一致性。另外,也向所有的国家培训当局发布此标准。

3.2 效果概述

3.2.1 海上职业

该标准在行业内的所有部门已被广泛接受,标准将根据航运改革局(SIRA)和IMO的STCW公约的规则变化而不断改善。

3.2.2 适任标准组织(CBS)和国家培训机构

1993年11月9日,标准草案发给所有的国家培训机构和下列CBS:

- 国家渔业ITC
- 评估员和现场培训员CBS
- 国家消防行业培训和发展计划
- 国家旅游ITC
- 国家五金和工程培训管理局

上述单位没有对标准草案提出反对意见。

4. TRAINING AND ASSESSMENT IMPLEMENTATION

The Standards as currently developed reflect the industry's position following major structural reforms introduced under the Maritime Industry Development Committee and Shipping Industry Reform Authority (SIRA).

These Standards will be applied to training programs as they come up for reaccreditation, including methods of assessment.

In the meantime, NMITC will liaise closely with SIRA and the AMSA on further national and international developments which will require review of the Standards.

5. VOCATIONAL APPLICATION OF THE STANDARDS

The Industry's Industrial Relations organisations were party to development of the Standards (see paragraph 1.5 above).The Standards are in complete accordance with relevant industrial awards.

6. REVIEW OF THE STANDARDS

The Standards will be reviewed as required following any future developments within SIRA or the review of the international convention STCW 78.

DRAFT NATIONAL MARITIME COMPETENCY STANDARDS

The new Australian Vocational Education and Training System is promoting the adoption of competency based training in the workplace. The training is to be based on National Competency Based Standards developed by each industry. These standards are broad based functions that integrate a series of skills which will apply in a variety of contexts.

The concept of competency focuses on what is expected of an employee in the workplace rather than on the learning process, and embodies the ability to transfer and apply skills and knowledge to new situations and environments. The attached draft standards are centred around the notion of competency.

The requirements of the National Training Board (NTB) can be met by writing statements within a defined format. This format has the following components:

<u>UNIT TITLE</u>

This is a title that refers to a general area of competence. It provides a clear statement of what is required of a person in a particular function. Its key feature is that it should define a major skill area of an industry and be related to realistic workplace activities.

<u>ELEMENTS OF COMPETENCY</u>

These define the skills associated with the broad competence of a unit. An element of competency is the basic building block of the system and its role is to provide further information on what is intended by the unit titles.

4. 培训和评估的实施

该标准反映了行业的目前发展，并遵循海上职业委员会和航运业改革局(SIRA)的改革方案制定。

当各种培训项目提出重新审核时(包括采用的评估方法)将应用这些新标准。

同时，NMITC将按国内和国际标准的新要求重新研究标准需改善的方面与SIRA和AMSA紧密协作。

5. 行业内标准的运用

行业相关组织参与了标准的制定(见前面的1.5段内容)。该标准是完全按照相关行业的发证规定制定的。

6. 标准的复审

标准将按照SIRA的任何未来发展或STCW 78国际公约的审核要求进行复审。

草拟国家海事适任标准

新建立的澳大利亚职业教育和培训体系鼓励采用岗位工作的适任培训。培训应以各行业制定的国家适任基本标准为基础。这些标准综合了一系列适用于不同技能范围的主要基本功能。

适任的概念针对的是雇员在工作中的表现而不是学习过程，并强调转换和应用技术的能力以及应对新情况、新环境的知识掌握。所附的草拟标准以适任概念为中心。

可以用一种规定的格式说明国家培训部(NTB)的要求。这种格式有下列这些组成部分：

项目标题

项目标题指适任的一般范围。它清楚描述了对某个人在一项特别职能中的要求。它的关键特性是定义行业的主要技能范围和相关的实际工作活动。

适任的细目

适任的细目是定义与主要的项目适任相关的技能。适任的细目是该系统的基本标准模块，它的作用是为项目标题提供更进一步的信息。

PERFORMANCE CRITERIA

These are statements which specify the required level of performance expected in the workplace. They guide an assessor in judging the quality of a performance.

RANGE STATEMENTS

These are statements which place a defined competency in the context in which it will be applied. Range statements give more information about the circumstances in which a competency will be applied.

When described in this format, competency standards will clearly describe a broad competency commonly required by an industry, the types of skills which underlie the competence and the outcomes that need to be achieved to meet that competence. Therefore, the competency standards have been written in generic form with reference to specific plant/equipment items, products, services and work organisation omitted due to the diversity in ship types, technology and operations carried out.

表现标准

说明要求在岗位工作中达到的适任水平。它们用于指导评估员判定适任的等级。

综合说明

综合说明是将规定的适任置于其应用背景下。它提供了更多有关适任技能应用条件的信息。

用这种格式描述的适任标准清楚地说明了行业公认的主要适任要求和为符合标准应当获得的适任技能类型和能力。适任标准以通用的格式拟定,同时由于船舶类型、技术和操作的不同而省略了特殊的装置/设备、产品、服务和工作组织的内容。

Part 11
Developing Written Tests

Examination methodology

1. The ultimate objective of an Administration is to ensure that all candidates for certificates of competency have the ability to perform safely and efficiently the tasks associated with the posts they are to be authorized to fill. Complete and certain assessment of this ability can only be carried out by "on-the-job" evaluation over a period of time, which is impracticable. The Administration must therefore satisfy itself as to the candidate's future competency by evaluating his experience and physical suitability and by assessing his achievement of immediate objectives so as to determine systematically the extent to which defined levels of knowledge and comprehension and degrees of skill and performance are met.

2. The first problem which must therefore be faced by any authority establishing a certification scheme for seafarers is to determine the standards of experience and medical fitness and the nature and levels of knowledge, comprehension, skill and behaviour (e.g safety consciousness) which are necessary to competently perform the tasks involved.

3. These criteria can most accurately be determined by a systematic task analysis, from which may be derived an interlinked series of general training objectives (see figure 7.3-1). Such task analysis and general training objectives should then be validated with the industry. This validation process should involve consultation with those currently employed in the jobs concerned and who are generally regarded as being efficient and reliable employees.

4. Having established the general training objectives, detailed learning objectives or learning outcomes should be developed, the achievement of which, when taken as a whole, would indicate that the general objective has been attained.

5. The syllabuses contained in the 1978 STCW Convention ("knowledge, understanding and proficiency" in the revised Convention) are essentially examination syllabuses and provide general training objectives which have been expanded to form teaching syllabuses through the development of IMO model training courses in learning objective format.

    They outline the training considered appropriate for those who are to apply for certificates issued under regulations II/1, II/2, III/1 and III/2 of STCW 95. Additional IMO model courses cover the requirements of chapters V and VI of the STCW Convention.

    These model courses are based on a minimal interpretation of the provisions of the Convention consistent with all aspects of maritime safety and environmental protection.

第11章
笔试设计

考试方法

1. 主管机关的最终目标是保证所有适任证书的申请人具有能力来安全有效地完成他将担任的职务所要求的任务。这种能力的完整确切的评价只能通过一段时间的"工作中"的评估完成，在实际操作中这很难做到。因此，主管机关必须通过对申请人的经验和身体适应性进行评价，以及通过对他在较短时间内取得的成绩的评价来系统地判定其知识水平、理解能力和操作技能水平，从而确定他将来是否适任。

2. 因此，主管机关在建立海员发证系统的过程中遇到的首要问题是确定衡量标准来评价海员完成相关的任务必要经验、健康情况以及知识水平、理解力、技能、行为（例如安全意识）等。

3. 通过系统的任务分析，可以最准确地确定这些标准，从这些标准中可以得到一系列相互联系的总体培训目标（见图7.3-1）。这些任务分析结果和总体训练目标应该由行业来证明是正确的。证明过程应该包括向那些目前正从事相关工作的人员咨询以及咨询普遍被认为是能干和可靠的雇员。

4. 已经设定的总体培训目标、详细的学习目标或者学习效果应该得到进一步完善，上述方面的整体成绩可以表明总体的目标是否已经达到。

5. STCW 1978公约中的大纲（修正案中的知识、理解和熟练）是最基本的考试大纲，它提供了总体的培训目标，通过按学习目标开发IMO示范课程，培训目标的范围已得到扩展并形成相应教学大纲。

    这些大纲适用于根据STCW 95公约中的规则Ⅱ/1、Ⅱ/2、Ⅲ/1和Ⅲ/2申请发证的人员。附加的IMO示范课程覆盖了STCW公约第五章和第六章的要求。

    这些示范课程是基于对公约中与海上安全和环境保护相关条款的最低要求的诠释。

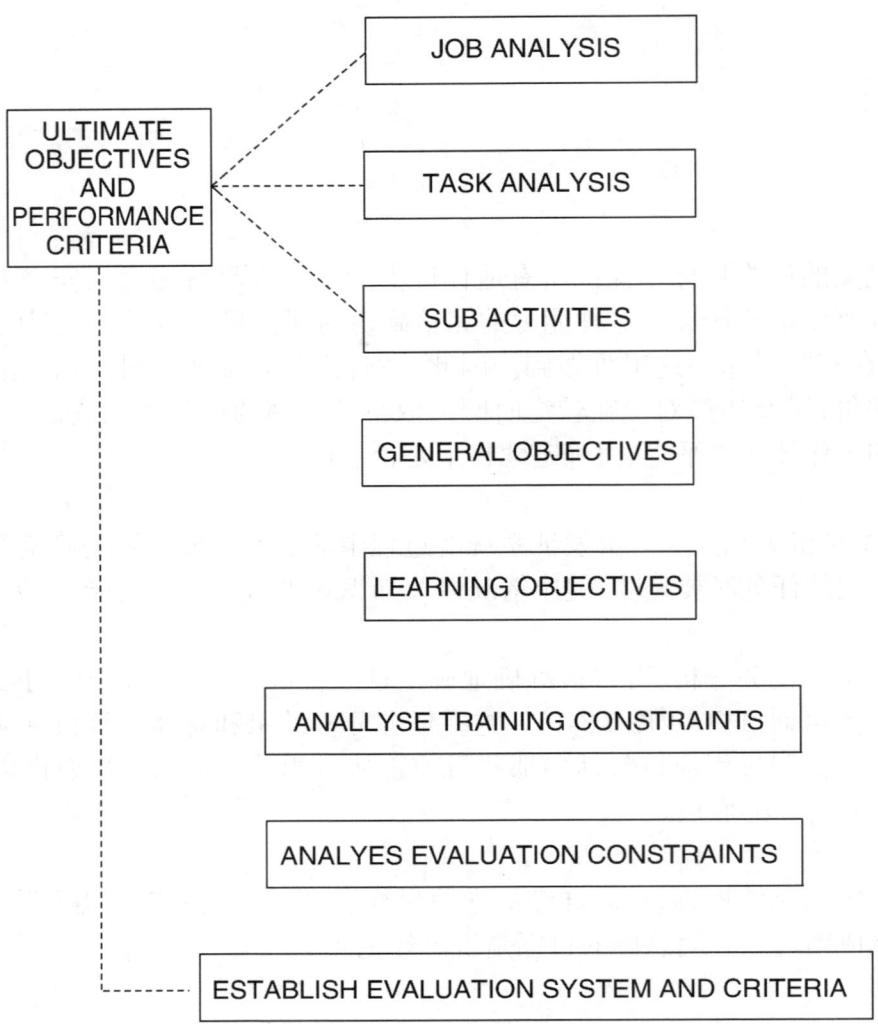

Figure 7.3-1 Matching training and evaluation to performance criteria

In certain instances, additional training that is not specified in the Convention has been included but is identified within the course as being supplementary to the provisions of the STCW Convention.

All of these syllabuses have been validated through the IMO Sub-Committee on Standards of Training and Watchkeeping and its Validation Group (on which the seafarers, shipowners and Administrations are represented) for use by technical advisers, consultants and experts for the training and certification of seafarers so that the minimum standards implemented may be as uniform as possible. "Validation", in the context of these courses, means that the Sub-Committee has found no grounds to object to their content. The Sub-Committee has not granted its approval to the courses, as it considers that they must not be regarded as official interpretations of the Convention.

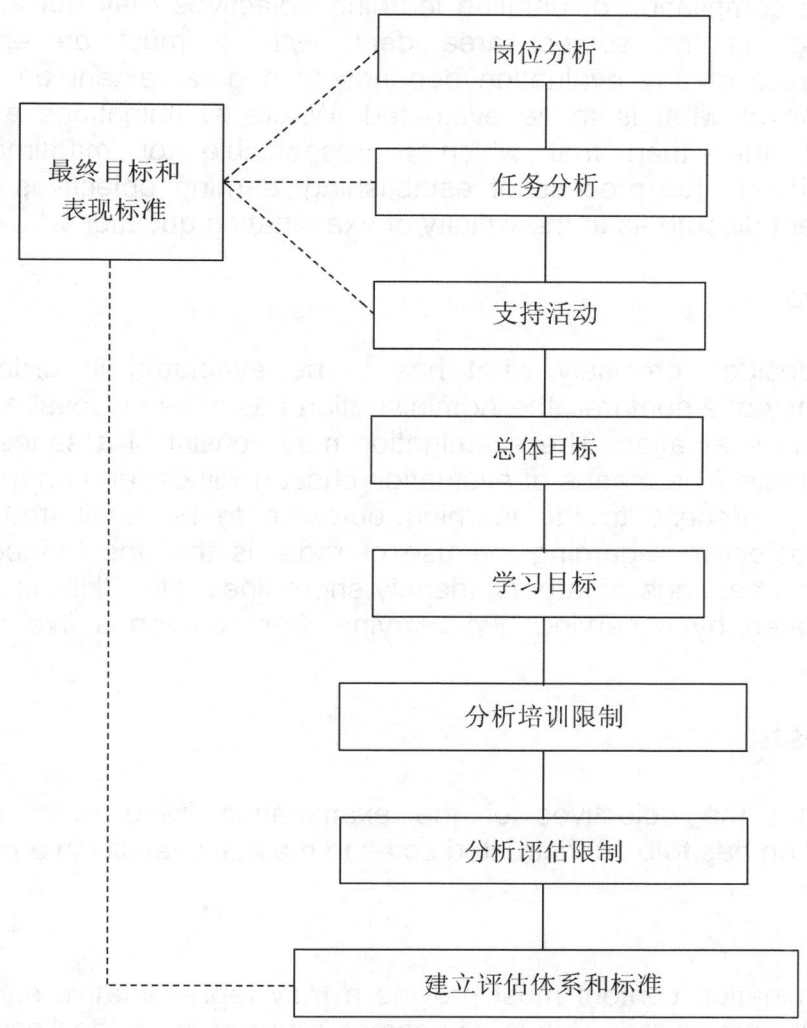

图 7.3-1　将培训和评估与表现标准比较

在某些情况下,课程大纲包括了公约中没有详细说明的附加培训,但这类附加培训仍可认为是在STCW公约补充条款规定的课程范围之内。

所有这些课程大纲已通过了IMO培训和值班分委会的认可,其认可小组(代表海员、船东和管理部门)由海员培训和发证方面的实施人员、顾问及专家组成,以便使实施的最低标准尽可能一致。在这些课程内容中出现的"认可"是指目前未发现对它内容有任何异议的部分。但是,不能认为这是公约的官方解释。

6. While the compilation of detailed learning objectives may not always be necessary, depending on the subject area dealt with, it must be emphasized that the effectiveness of any evaluation depends to a great extent on the precision of the description of what is to be evaluated. Where examinations are conducted by an authority other than that which is responsible for maritime training (external examinations), this process of establishing learning objectives also helps to avoid subsequent dispute as to the validity of examination questions.

Means of testing

7. Having decided precisely what has to be evaluated in order to determine the competency of a seafarer, the Administration has at its disposal a number of means of testing and evaluation. The examination may consist of a series of written, oral and practical tests. The means of evaluation chosen will depend on the appropriateness of the testing process to the learning outcome to be evaluated. For example, one ultimate objective regarding the use of radar is that the trainee can correctly take ranges and bearings of targets, identify shore-lines, etc. Skills in these tasks can best be evaluated by observing him carrying them out on a live radar or on a radar simulator.

Quality of tests

8. Given that the objectives of the examination have been clearly defined, the examination has to be constructed so as to maintain validity in a number of respects.

Content validity

9. The examination content must provide a truly representative sample of the range of tasks to be measured. This is sometimes referred to as the "content balance" of the examination. Not only must there be a reasonable balance with regard to the subject topics dealt with but also there must be a balance in the testing of knowing, comprehending and applying concepts. Depending on the topic and the subject concerned, a different treatment may be required of the same topic (e.g the treatment of deviation in chartwork versus the treatment of deviation in compass adjustment). Use should be made of a table of specifications for the subject, examples of which are given in tables 7.9-1 and 7.9-2. A commonly used method of drawing up a test specification is first to assign percentages of the test to be allotted to each category of objective (the bottom row of the table) and then the percentages for each subject area (the right-hand column).

Finally, the percentages are allotted to each cell within the table. In the case of objective tests, the number of test items can be used instead of percentages. Unless such a table is used, there is a danger that the examination may give undue weight to some portion of the syllabus or may unduly concentrate on basic facts and principles when skill in their application is more relevant to the ultimate objective and should be emphasized.

6. 没有必要总是将详细的学习目标汇编在一起,可以将目标分散编入各科目的内容中,需要强调的是任何评估的效果都很大程度上依赖于对评估对象描述的准确性。由主管机关管理的考试不同于海上培训(外部考试),建立学习目标程序也有助于避免日后在考试题目的有效性方面产生争议。

测试的方法

7. 已经明确地规定海员必须接受评估以确定其适任性,主管机关提供了大量的测试和评估方法。考试可以包括一系列的笔试、口试和实操测试。评估方法的选择取决于测试程序是否适于对学习效果进行评价。例如,某项与雷达用途有关的最终目标是令培训者能够正确地获取目标的距离和方位、分辨出海岸线,等等。对于这一目标,可以通过观察被评估人在真实雷达上或在雷达模拟器上完成任务的情况对其能力给出最恰当的评价。

测试的质量

8. 如果考试目标已经清楚确定,必须认真设定考试,以便保证多方面的有效性。

内容的有效性

9. 考试的内容必须能够真正反映需要评测的任务范围。有时还需要考虑到考试内容的"平衡性",不仅要在涉及的科目主题上合理平衡,而且要保持测试知识的掌握、理解能力和概念运用方面的平衡。对于所涉及的主题和科目而言,同一个主题可以有不同的处理方法(例如,海图作业中的自差处理与校正罗经中的自差处理相对应)。应该充分利用每一科目的详细说明表,实例详见表7.9-1和表7.9-2。制作测试说明表的大体方法首先是给每个指定的目标类别分配(按百分比的)分数(表格的最后一行),然后是给每一科目分配分数(表格右栏)。

最后,给表格内的每项内容分配分数。如果是进行目标测试,测试项目数可以代替分数。使用这样的表格可以防止出现大纲中某些部分的考试分数分配不恰当,比如在应用技能与最终目标更加相关而必须重视时,试题却不适当地集中在基础知识和基本原理方面。

Criterion-related validity

10. The examination must reliably estimate the current and future performance of the candidates in the field concerned when measured against other criteria, such as known performance when under training and, more particularly, their later performance on board ship. It is difficult to establish reliable criteria of success against which to judge the examination process. This is because all available criteria tend to be relative; for example, accident rate and degree of commercial success of a fleet are both influenced by a variety of factors, and we end up comparing our own fleet's record vis-a-vis others.

    Considering the possible improvements which could be made in the selection, training and competence testing of seafarers, it would seem worthwhile to follow the careers of our young seafarers so as to have better feedback on their performance in their chosen careers. A system to provide improved feedback can also benefit shipping companies and the seafarers themselves, since the information could quite obviously formulate the basis for the company's own training and development plan. Continuing education for seafarers is today essential if they are to competently man the ships of the future.

Item validity

11. The validity of individual questions must be constantly borne in mind. Poorly constructed or badly phrased questions and those which may be misleading to the candidates must be avoided. Those responsible for setting examinations should be constantly on their guard to prevent such questions from slipping through; they should also guard against setting questions at an inappropriate level of difficulty or testing a learning outcome which is inappropriate to the level of competence under assessment. It is easy for the person setting an examination to fall into the trap of expecting a candidate for a lower grade of certificate to have a level of knowledge and skill which approaches his own.

Reliability

12. To be reliable, an examination must produce reasonably consistent results. The results should be basically the same whether the candidate is faced with any one of the sets of papers or test items which are in use. Consistency of results should also prevail no matter which examiner scores the papers.

    In order to achieve reliability, an examination must be sufficiently comprehensive to cover the fields of knowledge, comprehension and skill adequately. Reliability cannot be achieved by limiting the scope of the examination to certain fields on one occasion and to others on subsequent occasions, on a "rotational" basis. The time allotted for the examination must therefore be sufficient to allow it to be comprehensive.

Discrimination power of test items

13. The discrimination power of a test item is a measure of its ability to discriminate between those who are knowledgeable in the subject area of the test and those who are not. This is measured relatively by establishing the number of passing candidates who correctly answer the item and the number of failing candidates who correctly answer it. This is further explained below.

标准的有效性

10. 当评测其他标准时,考试必须确切地估计当前和今后申请人在相关领域的工作能力,例如在接受培训时的已知能力,特别是以后在船上的工作能力。很难建立一个可靠的考试过程的成功标准,这是因为所有可用的标准都相互关联;例如,事故发生率和船队营利大小均受到各种各样因素的影响,不能用自己船队的记录与其他公司的船队一一比较。

    为改善海员的选择、培训和适任考试,应跟踪了解年青海员的工作情况,以便在他们所选择的职业工作表现方面获取较多的反馈信息。改善反馈信息的系统同样有益于船公司和海员自己,因为很明显这些信息将成为公司自身培训和发展计划的基础。为了胜任未来船舶上的工作,目前进行的对海员的继续教育是十分必要的。

试题的有效性

11. 应始终关注试题的有效性。必须避免拙劣的构题或者语言表达方式以及提出可能误导申请人的问题。负责考试设计的人应该认真负责以防出现此类问题;他们也负有责任避免把测试学习效果的题目设置在不适当的难度之上或者低于适任评估要求的水平。设置考试的人员很容易受到一些想法的诱惑,比如他们期望申请人获得低于设置者本人所具备的等级证书的水平。

可靠性

12. 为使考试更可靠,必须提供适当的符合要求的答案。无论申请人面对哪一套试题或者正在使用哪些测试项目,答案应该大体上相同。无论试卷是由哪一位考官评分,成绩也应该是普遍一致的。

    要达到应有的可靠性,考试必须充分广泛地包括知识、理解和熟练几个方面。把一次考试限制在某一领域内,把另一次考试又限制在另外一个领域,这种"交替"的考试方式不可能达到应有的可靠性。分配给考试的时间也因此必须充分。

测试题的区分度

13. 区分度是测试题区分应试者对已掌握和未掌握的测试科目知识的能力。通过确定在正确答题考试中及格的人数和不及格的人数可以对区分度进行相对判断。关于这一点在下面将做进一步解释。

Table 7.9-1 Table of specifications—elementary meteorology

Content	Objectives						Total number of Items
	Knows	Understands	Interprets		Skill in		
	symbols and terms	specific facts	influence of each factor on weather formation	weather maps	use of measuring devices	constructing weather maps	
Air pressure	2	3	3	3	Observe pupils using measuring devices (rating scale)	Evaluate maps constructed by pupils (checklist)	11
Wind	4	2	8	2			16
Temperature	2	2	2	2			8
Humidity and percipitation	2	1	2	5			10
Clouds	2	2	1				5
Total number of Items	12	10	16	12			50
Per cent of evaluation	12%	10%	16%	12%	25%	25%	100%

With acknowledgements to "Measurement and Evaluation in Teaching" by N.E. Gronlund

Table 7.9-2 Table of specifications—thermodynamics

Content	Objectives						% of evaluation
	Knows	Understands	Interprets		Skill in		
	symbols, terms and specific facts	how facts relate to behaviour of gases and vapours	uses tables and diagrams	solves problems	use of instruments and apparatus	constructing diagrams	
Properties	5	2	2	–	–	3	12
Systems	2	1	3	5	–	–	11
Heat transfer	3	2	2	5	10	3	25
Vapours	4	3	1	–	5	–	13
Ideal gases	2	3	3	5	–	1	14
Processes	4	4	4	5	–	8	25
Per cent of evaluation	20%	15%	15%	20%	15%	15%	100%

表 7.9-1　气象要素评估说明表

内容	目标						项目总数
	熟悉	理解	解释		熟练		
	符号和术语	具体的因素	每种因素对天气构成的影响	天气图	测量仪器的使用	天气图的绘制	
气压	2	3	3	3	观察学生使用的测量仪器（以额定值判断）	评价学生绘制的天气图（用检查表核对）	11
风	4	2	8	2			16
气温	2	2	2	2			8
湿度和降雨量	2	1	2	5			10
云	2	2	1				5
项目总数	12	10	16	12			50
评价的百分比	12%	10%	16%	12%	25%	25%	100%

由罗曼·格劳伦德提出的"教学测量和评估系统"

表 7.9-2　热力学评估说明表

内容	目标						评估百分比（%）
	熟悉	理解	解释		熟练		
	符号、名词和具体因素	各因素与气体和蒸汽状态之间的关系	使用表格和图解	解决问题	工具和器械的使用	绘制图表	
特性	5	2	2	-	-	3	12
系统	2	1	3	5	-	-	11
热量转换	3	2	2	5	10	3	25
蒸汽	4	3	1	-	5	-	13
理想气体	2	3	3	5	-	1	14
过程	4	4	4	5	-	8	25
评价的百分比	20%	15%	15%	20%	15%	15%	100%

Discrimination power of examination or test series

14. To serve as a useful tool in grading the performance of candidates, an examination or test series should ideally provide a well spread distribution of results or scores between the good and the poor candidates. The level of difficulty of the examination as a whole must therefore be appropriate and the level of difficulty of the individual questions making up the examination should vary from the relatively easy to the relatively difficult.

    A graph of the candidates' scores should form a bell curve with little skewness. In other words, the test should present an average overall level of difficulty to those candidates considered to be competent so that the resultant scores are not bunched towards the lower or upper ends of the percentage scale (see figure 7.14-1). The discrimination power of an examination depends in part on the clarity and appropriateness of its test items, its security from compromise and the clarity and simplicity of the test procedures and instructions.

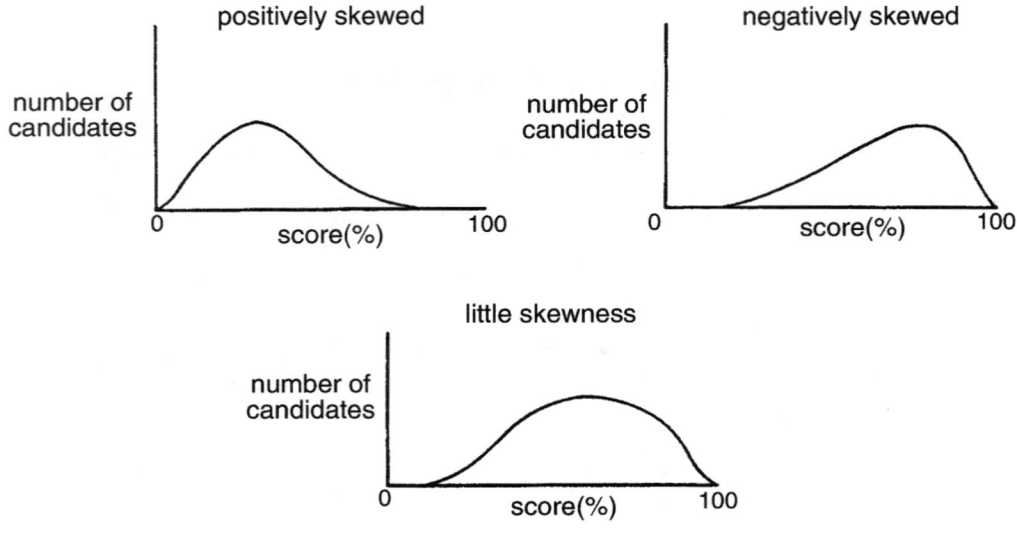

Figure 7.14-1   Distributions of candidates' scores

Usability

15. The tests should be easy and economic to administer and should be capable of being scored or marked with the minimum of delay and labour.

Types of written tests

16. A wide variety of types of written tests is available, each with its own strengths and weaknesses. These are well described in chapter 5, The Essay and Supply-type Test Items, and chapter 6, Selection-type Test Items, of "Testing and Evaluation: An Introduction" by C.M. Lindvall, published in 1961 by Harcourt, Brace & World, Inc., New York and Burlingame.

考试或系列测试的区分度

14. 作为划分申请人表现等级的有效工具,考试或者系列测试应该使优秀的申请人和较差的申请人在考试成绩和分数分布上比较合理。从总体上看,考试难度等级必须适当,构成考试的每个单独问题的难度等级应该从相对较容易到相对较难之间变化。

   申请人分数分布曲线图应该是不对称的漏斗形曲线。换言之,对于那些被认为是有能力的申请人来说,测试应该显示出总体的平均难度,使综合分数不会集中在百分比标尺的下端或上端(见图7.14-1)。考试的区分度在某种程度上取决于测试题的明晰度和适当性,并通过测试程序和考题指示的折中考虑、明晰度及简明性来保证。

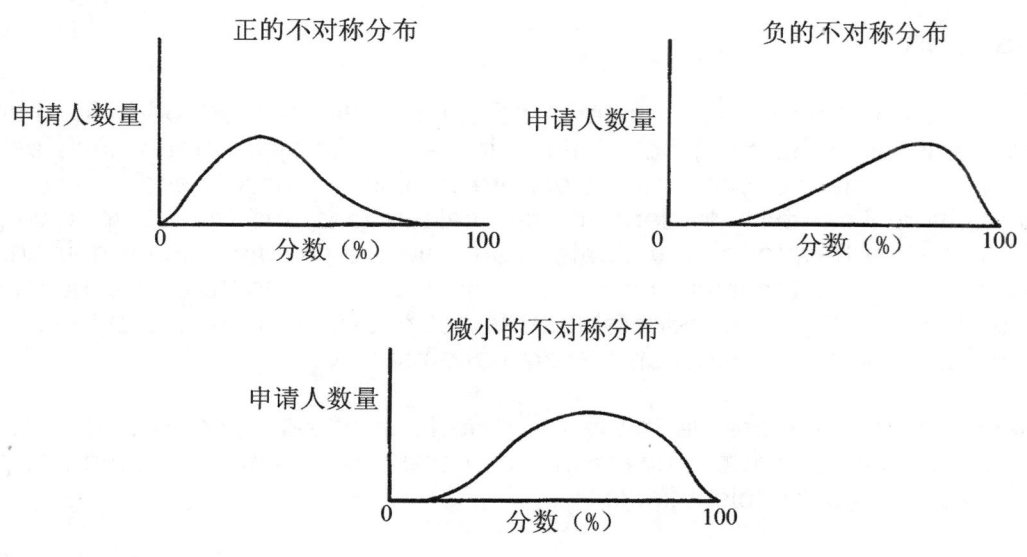

图7.14-1　申请人分数的分布

可用性

15. 对管理者来说,测试应该易于实施和经济,并且应该以最短的时间、最小的劳动量就能完成评分或者评卷。

笔试的类型

16. 笔试有广泛和多种的类型,每一种都各有优缺点。课程的第5章比较详细地描述了论述和填充类型测试题,而在第6章讨论了测试题的类型选择,参考《考试和评估导论》一书(C.M. Lindvall编著,由Harcourt, Brace & World公司于1961年在纽约和伯林盖姆出版)。

17. Guidance on the construction of multiple-choice test items is contained in chapter 7, Constructing Objective Test Items: Multiple-Choice Form, of "Measurement and Evaluation in Teaching" by Norman E. Gronlund, fifth edition, published by Macmillan in 1985.

18. The United States Coast Guard Servicewide Examination Development Manual, in its chapter on Item-Writing Principles, provides further useful guidance and examples of the construction of multiple-choice test items.

19. It is important to note that no single one of these methods can satisfactorily measure knowledge and skill over the entire spectrum of matters to be tested for the assessment of competence. Care should therefore be taken to select the method most appropriate to the particular aspect of competence to be tested, bearing in mind the need to frame questions which relate as realistically as possible to the requirements of the officer's job at sea.

Calculations

20. To carry out their duties, masters and ships' officers must be able to solve technical problems by performing calculations in various subject areas such as marine plant operation, thermodynamics, electrotechnology, cargo work, ship stability and navigation. The ability to perform such calculations and to resolve such problems can be tested by having the candidates carry out the calculations in their entirety. Since a large variety of technical calculations is involved and the time necessary for their complete solution is considerable, it is not possible to completely test the abilities of candidates within a reasonable examination time.

    Resort must therefore be made to some form of sampling technique, as is the case with the assessment of knowledge, comprehension and application of principles and concepts in other subject fields.

    In examinations conducted on a traditional essay-type basis, the sampling technique that is applied in respect of calculation requirements is to attempt to cover as much of the subject area as possible within the examination time available. This is frequently done by using questions involving shorter calculations and testing in depth on one or two topics by requiring the completion of more complex calculations. The employment of this "gross sampling" technique reduces the reliability of the examination as compared with what can be achieved with a more detailed sampling technique.

21. A greater breadth of sampling can be achieved by breaking down calculations into the various computational steps involved in their solution. This technique can only be applied to calculations in which the methodology is standardized. Fortunately, most calculations follow a standard format; where alternative methods of solution exist, the examination can be developed so as to allow candidates an appropriate freedom of choice. Such freedom of choice must be a feature of examinations of all types, in any event.

22. In order to develop a series of "step test items", covering an entire calculation, it is necessary to identify each intermediate step in each calculation involved by all methods which are accepted as being correct in principle. These questions, after they have been reviewed for clarity and conciseness, form the standard "step test items" in that calculation topic.

17. 第七章包括了多项选择测试题的设计指南,参考《教学的评测和评估》第五版的"设计客观测试题:多项选择的形式"相关内容, Norman E. Gronlund 著, Macmillan 公司 1985 年出版。

18. 在美国海岸警卫队考试开发服务指南中的"书面测试题的原理"这一章中,提供了更加实用的多项选择测试题的设计指南和实例。

19. 在评测知识和能力方面,没有哪一种方法能比系统完整的适任评估方法更令人满意,意识到这一点很重要。因此,要注意选择最适当的方法对特定的适任能力进行测试,应该尽可能设计能真实反映高级船员船上的工作能力的试题。

计算

20. 为了履行其职责,船长和驾驶员必须能够运用各种科目范围的计算来解决技术上的问题,例如航海设备的操作、热动力学、电工学、货物处理、船舶稳性和导航。可以通过检查申请人完成全部计算的情况来测试其计算能力和解决这些问题的能力。由于涉及大量的各种工程计算而给申请人解题所需的时间是有限的,因此不可能在考试时间之内测试申请人的全部能力。

    因此,在评价其他科目内容的知识、原理和概念时必须借助于经常运用的抽样技术。

    在传统的论述类型考试中,满足计算要求的抽样技术应该在规定的考试时间内尽可能地覆盖整个科目范围。通常用一定数量的较简短的计算题加上用较完整和复杂的计算题对一个或两个主题进行综合测试达到上述要求。采用这种所谓的"总体样本抽样"的方法比采用更细化的抽样方法考试的可靠性要低。

21. 把一个较大的计算问题分解为各种与其结果相关的分步计算,可以获得较为广泛的样本。但只有在采用的方法已标准化时,这种技术才能应用于计算。幸运的是,大部分计算都采用标准化的格式;提供可供选择的解决方案,可以促进考试的发展,以便允许申请人相应地自由选择。这种自由选择的方式必然成为各种类型考试的一个特征。

22. 为了开发一系列的覆盖整体计算内容的"分步测试题",必须为所有理论上正确的计算方法确定相应的中间计算步骤。经过对问题的清晰度和可理解性方面的检查后,这些问题就构成了该计算主题的标准"分步测试题"。

23. This approach allows questions to be posed which sample the candidate's knowledge and ability to perform parts of various calculations, which process takes up less time than having him perform entire calculations. The assumption is made that if the candidate can or cannot correctly complete a calculation step leading to the solution, then he can or cannot successfully carry out the entire calculation. Such detailed sampling allows a larger number of questions to be answered by the candidate within the time allotted for the examination, thus allowing a broader sampling of the candidate's knowledge and abilities, thereby increasing the reliability of the examination.

    It must be pointed out that because of the greater number of test items used, more time will be spent by candidates in reading the questions and in appreciating the precise step which each question involves.

24. However, the ability to answer correctly questions that are based on each intermediate step leading to the solution does not necessarily indicate competence in the application of the calculation methodology nor in the interpretation of the intermediate or final results. Further questions must therefore be developed which are of a "procedural" and principle nature.

25. Such "step test" and "procedural" items may be drawn up as "essay-type" items, supply-type items or multiple-choice items. Marking or scoring is easier if multiple-choice test items are used, but in some cases difficulties may arise in creating plausible distracters.

26. Detailed sampling can allow immediate identification of errors of principle and those of a clerical nature. It must be emphasized that this holds true, in general, only if the test item is based on a single step in the overall calculation. Multiple-choice items involving more than one step may, in some cases, have to be resoried to in order to allow the creation of a sufficient number of plausible distracters, but care must be exercised to ensure that distracters are not plausible for more than one reason if the nature of the error made (and hence the distracter chosen) is to affect the scoring of the test item.

Compiling tests

27. Whilst each examining authority establishes its own rules, the length of time which can be devoted to assessing the competence of candidates for certificates of competency is limited by practical, economic and sociological restraints. Therefore a prime objective of those responsible for the organization and administration of the examination system is to find the most efficient, effective and economical method of assessing the competency of candidates. An examination system should effectively test the breadth of a candidate's knowledge of the subject areas pertinent to the tasks he is expected to undertake. It is not possible to examine candidates fully in all areas, so in effect the examination samples a candidate's knowledge by covering as wide a scope as is possible within the time constraints and testing his depth of knowledge in selected areas.

23. 这种方法引出了这样的问题：哪种样本可以使申请人凭自身的知识和能力完成各种不同计算的时间比完成整体计算所花的时间更短。可以这样设想，如果申请人能/不能正确地完成分步计算并得出结果，那么他就能/不能成功地完成整个计算。这种细化的样本使得申请人在规定的考试时间之内可以回答大量的问题，因此允许在较广泛的样本范围内测试申请人的知识和能力，这样也就增加了考试的可靠性。

    必须指出的是，因为使用了较多的测试题，所以申请人需要花更多的时间来阅读题目和判别涉及每一个题目的准确步骤。

24. 然而，正确回答问题的能力取决于每一个能引出结果的中间步骤，既不需要表明运用计算方法的能力，也不需要对中间或最后结果进行解释。因此，必须研究"过程性的"和原理性的更深入的问题。

25. 这种"分步测试"和"过程性"试题可以用"论述型"、填充型或多项选择型试题的形式命题。如果使用多项选择测试题，记分或评分相对较容易，但在某些情况下可能会难以提供足够的非正确选择项。

26. 用细化的样本还可以立即鉴别出原理上的错误和笔误。必须强调的是，一般说来，只要测试题的每一步计算都决定整体计算中的结果，那么它绝对是真实的。在某些情况下，一道多项选择题需要一个以上的运算步骤才能得到答案，所以要提供试题所需的足够多的非正确选择项，但必须注意如果误选答案会对测试题的评分造成影响，那么非正确选择项应谨慎选择。

试题组卷

27. 每一个考试主管机关建立自己的规则时，用于评估参加适任证书考试的申请人其适任能力的时间长短，会受现实、经济和社会等因素的局限。因此，负责考试系统的组织和管理部门的首要目标是寻找评估申请人适任能力的最科学、有效和经济的方法。考试系统应能有效地测试申请人掌握与他将要承担的任务有关的科目知识的广度。然而，要全面检查申请人在所有领域对知识和技能的掌握状况是不可能的。所以，实际上考试只能在规定的时间内抽样测试尽可能广泛的知识范围，并且在选定范围内测试申请人对知识掌握的深度。

The examination as a whole should assess each candidates comprehension of principles, concepts and methodology; his ability to apply principles, concepts and methodology; his ability to organize facts, ideas and arguments and his abilities and skills in carrying out those tasks he will be called upon to perform in the duties he is to be certificated to undertake.

All evaluation and testing techniques have their advantages and disadvantages. An examining authority should carefully analyse precisely what it should be testing and can test. A careful selection of test and evaluation methods should then be made to ensure that the best of the variety of techniques available today is used. Each test shall be that best suited to the learning outcome or ability to be tested.

The assembly of selection-type test items to form an examination is also discussed in chapter 6 of the book by Lindvall.

Quality of test items

28. No matter which type of test is used, it is essential that all questions or test items used should be as brief as possible, since the time taken to read the questions themselves lengthens the examination. Questions must also be clear and complete. To ensure this, it is necessary that they be reviewed by a person other than the originator. No extraneous information should be incorporated into questions; such inclusions can waste the time of the knowledgeable candidates and tend to be regarded as "trick questions". In all cases, the questions should be checked to ensure that they measure an objective which is essential to the job concerned. Review of test material is more extensively discussed in Part 13 of this compendium.

Answer-response patterns

29. The numbers of A's, B's, C's and D's used as correct response choices should be nearly (but not exactly) equal throughout an exam, but the sequence of correct responses must not form a recognizable pattern on an answer sheet. The U.S. Coast Guard Servicewide Examination Development Manual provides examples of response patterns which should be avoided: these are shown in figure 7.29-1.

Data banks of test items

30. A great deal of work goes into the preparation of examination questions or test items. This is particularly so in the case of multiple-choice-type test items. However, it is also true of subjective test material, particularly if marking or scoring is conducted on a decentralized basis, which necessitates the provision of detailed answer sheets to all examination centres. Well constructed examination questions of the essay type can be re-used periodically on a random basis and the large number of test items which can be included in an objective-type examination lends itself to the re-use of these questions so long as the precise content of the examination remains unknown to the candidates.

总体而言,考试应该评定每一位申请人对原理、概念和方法的理解;运用原理、概念和方法的能力;组织行动、计划和辩论的能力;以及履行认可适任证书中规定的职责时完成任务的能力和技能。

所有的评估和测试技术有其优点和缺点。考试机构应该仔细地选择考试和评估方法,确保利用目前可以提供的各种最先进的技术。每一种测试均应达到检查学习的效果和能力的目的。

Lindvall的著作第6章也讨论到选择题考试的组题问题。

测试题的质量

28. 无论采用哪一种测试方式,最基本的要求是所有被采用的问题或测试题都应尽可能简短,因为花在阅读题目上的时间会使考试延长。题目本身也必须含义明确和完整。为了确保做到这一点,有必要通过另外的人而不是原作者对这些题目进行复查。无关的资料不应该并入这些题目中去;这种掺杂可能会浪费内行的申请人的考试时间,并且会被看作是"欺骗性的问题"。在任何情况下,都应该检查考试题目,以确保它所评测的目标基本上与所涉及的工作有关。有关测试内容的复查在第13章会做进一步详细讨论。

答案-答题的方式

29. 在整份试题中,A、B、C、D分别作为正确的选择项的数量应大致(但不完全)相等,但在答题纸上,正确答案选项不应该排列成一种可以识别的模式。美国海岸警卫队考试发展服务指南中提供了应该避免的正确答案排列方式:见图7.29-1。

考试题库

30. 准备试题特别是多项选择试题需要做大量的工作。然而,在主观测试中,特别是如果记分或评分是分散进行时,必须向所有考试中心提供详细的答题纸。设计好的论述类考试题目也可在随机状态下周期性地反复使用,在客观类型的考试中包含了大量的试题,只要保证不让申请人知道具体的考试内容,就可以反复长久地使用这些题目。

For the above reasons it is common practice to retain questions and test items for periodic selection and use. Data banks of questions or test items may be retained on cards, which allows their arrangement to form "papers" suitable for photocopying or reproduction by other appropriate means. Data concerning the test item and its use can then be entered on the backs of these cards.

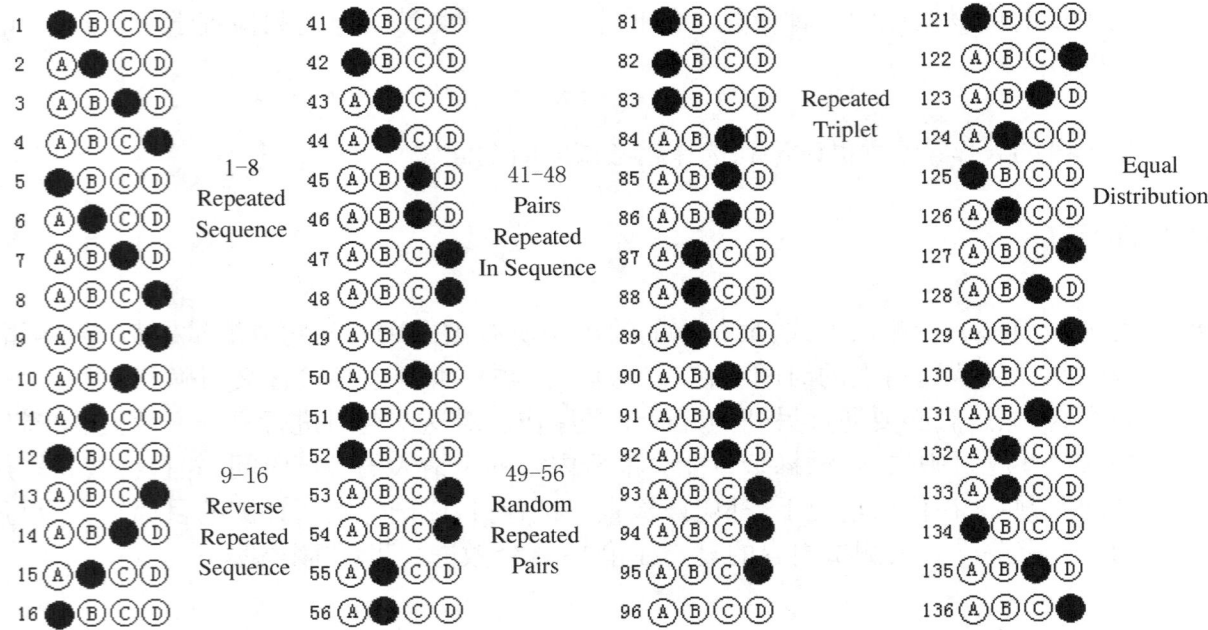

Figure 7.29-1   Examples of patterns of correct responses that must be avoided

Alternatively, a computerized data base may be established, with each item being labelled with information concerning it and its usage.

Such a data bank may also be maintained in the form of the examination papers or booklets. The usefulness of a data bank depends entirely on the amount of work and thought put into its compilation. This topic is dealt with further in Part 19, dealing with the maintenance of examination standards.

Scoring answer sheets for multiple-choice tests

31. The scoring of answer sheets for multiple-choice tests may be done manually or by electronic scanning equipment. In the former case, use can be made of plastic templates which fit over the top of the answer sheet and have been punched to indicate the "correct" or "best" response. The person scoring answer sheets in this way needs no skill or knowledge of the subject to accurately mark such sheets.

If the data bank of test items is computerized, scoring should be carried out by means of electronic scanning. This will allow the subsequent analysis of the test results, which topic is dealt with in Part 19.

基于上述原因,保存试题供循环选用是普遍的做法。试题数据库可以保存在卡片上,以便通过适当的方法制作成试卷的印刷胶版或复制底版。与试题相关的数据及其使用方法可以印在这些卡片的背面。

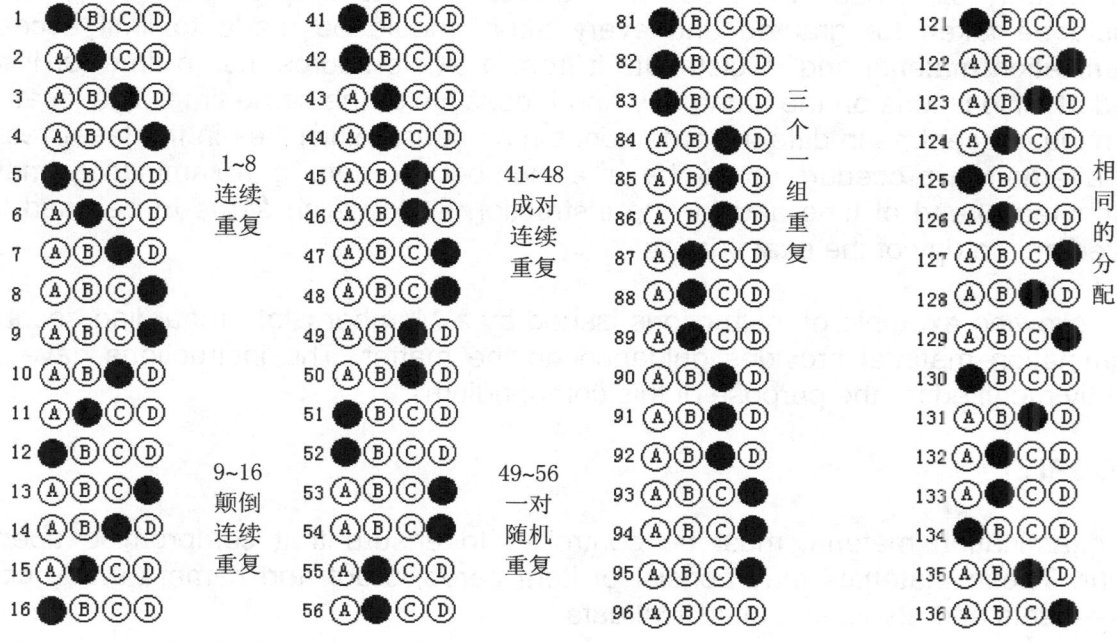

图 7.29-1 正确答案排列方式必须避免的情况

另外,也可以选择建立计算机数据库,每一个项目都标上与其相关的资料及用法。

这样的数据库也可以采用试卷或小册子的形式保存。数据库的可用性完全取决于其题量和组题方案。有关考试标准的维护问题将在第19章做深入讨论。

多项选择题答题卡的评分

31. 多项选择题答题卡的评分可以通过人工或电子扫描仪器进行。在前一种情况下,可以利用能盖过答题纸顶部的塑料膜,该塑料膜预先被刺孔以表明"正确"或"最佳"答案。在这种方法里,人工评分不需要有与考试科目相关的技能和知识就可以准确地完成答题纸的评分工作。

如果测试题数据库由计算机处理,那么评分工作应该使用扫描仪器来进行。用计算机处理评分工作便于随后对考试成绩进行分析,这方面问题在第19章讨论。

Security

32. The security exercised in respect of examination material should be strict. Nothing should be taken for granted and every effort should be made to limit access to examination material and to distribute it from a single source just in time for it to be used at all locations on the same day and if possible at the same time. The location of examination centres in differing time zones may cause difficulties in the latter respect. An alternative procedure is to have a number of sets of examination material distributed ahead of time and for the instruction as to which set is to be used to be issued on the day of the examination.

The following example of instructions issued by a Member State regarding security of examination material provides guidance on the matter. The instructions have been slightly modified for the purpose of this compendium:

SECURITY

All examination material must be controlled to ensure that compromise does not occur. These materials may consist of item cards, proof and camera-ready copies, worksheets and notes, and statistical data.

Examination materials must be kept in a locked container when the office is vacant or the materials are not being used. Access to testing material must be limited to authorized persons (those with the proper clearance and with a need to know). Under no circumstances should individuals have access to an examination in which they may participate.

Each individual who is authorized to have access to the material must ensure that access is limited to authorized persons.

When material is transported outside the examination centres and offices or transferred or mailed, great care should be taken to avoid the possibility of compromise.

All work material used in the development of test items which may compromise any item should be disposed of by shredding or equivalent secure means.

安全性

32. 应该严格注意考试内容的安全保密。不能有任何疏忽,应该尽可能限制可以接触考试内容的人员范围,应该在当天甚至如果可能应该在当时及时把试题从某一中心分发到需要使用的地方。有些地区距离考试中心太远,这样做可能会有困难。折中做法是考试之前可以先向各考试中心分发若干套试题,到了考试当天再发出采用其中某一套试题的通知。

以下是由某缔约国发出的指令实例,可以在试题的安全性方面提供指导。考虑到本纲要的目的,已对该通知稍做修改:

安全性

所有的试题都必须受到控制,以保证不会泄密。需保密的考试资料包括题卡、样题和影印件、工作单和说明以及统计数据。

当办公室无人或试题不再使用时,必须保存在上锁的容器内。必须限制接触考题的管理人员范围(指那些被授权允许阅卷的人和有必要知道的人)。尽管这些人可以参与这方面的工作,但在任何情况下都不应独自一人接触试题。

被授权接触材料的每一个人必须确定。

当试题从考试中心和办公室往外运送、转移或邮寄时,都必须十分注意,以防泄密。

所有用于试题开发的材料都可能造成泄密,任何相关材料都应该通过切碎或与其相当的可靠方法处理掉。

Part 12
Invigilation of Tests

Written tests

1. Typical guidance and instructions to invigilators of examinations are contained in Merchant Marine Personnel Examination Guidance for Regional Test Centers, issued by the Republic of Liberia.

2. An examinations officer should be designated to take charge of all administrative matters for each examination, including the provision and briefing of invigilators, the security of examination papers and supply of materials, the preparation of rooms, the conduct of examinations, the collection of completed scripts and their distribution to markers and notifying candidates of examination arrangements and issuing them with documents authorizing admission to the examination. In the case of examinations conducted by a training establishment, the examinations officer would act as the liaison between the Administration and the training establishment in all matters connected with examinations. Other duties would include drawing up a timetable for the production of draft papers, communicating with moderators and preparing question papers. The actual invigilation will probably be delegated to other members of the staff of the test contra or academy.

3. Invigilators should be provided with written instructions on the general conduct of examinations and the requirements of the particular tests they will be supervising. Relevant extracts of those instructions should also be provided to examinees, usually with the admission authorization, together with any special instructions regarding instruments, publications or other materials which may or must be brought to a particular test by the examinees.

4. Means of positive identification of candidates are essential to prevent the possibility of impersonation. In the case of internal examinations held in a training establishment, examinees are known to the teaching staff and a look around the room would immediately pick out the presence of a stranger. At an external test centre, examinees will not be known to the staff and more elaborate precautions must be taken. Commonly, a photograph of the applicant, signed on the back, is required as part of the application. The photographs are forwarded to the test centre, where the invigilator checks those presenting themselves against the photographs. Alternatively, or in addition, seamen's identity document numbers are supplied to the invigilator, who checks each arrival against the photograph in the identity document. A similar system is necessary where external candidates are admitted to examinations in a training academy. The absence of a candidate should be recorded on the invigilator's list of candidates which will accompany the worked scripts when they are sent for marking.

第12章
监考

笔试

1. 对监考人员典型的指导和培训载于由利比里亚共和国出版的《区域性考试中心的商船船员考试指南》中。

2. 应当指定考试官员负责管理每次考试的所有事务,包括监考人员的准备和对其进行考试简要介绍,试卷的安全和资料的供应,试室的准备,考试的指导,稿纸的收集并分配给记分员,把考试的安排情况通知申请人,并以文件的形式批准考试。如果考试是由培训机构管理的,那么对于所有与考试相关的事务,监考人员都应该在主管机关与培训机构之间进行传递。其他方面的职责包括制定时间表,与主考官的联系以及准备答题纸。实际上,也有可能委派考试中心或院校的其他工作人员监考。

3. 应该以书面的形式向监考人员提供一般性的考试指导以及说明监考中的一些特殊要求,也应该适当地选取一些说明提供给参加考试的考生。通常,在允许的情况下,有关的用具、出版物或者其他因特殊测试而必须具备的东西可以由考生带进考场内。

4. 对申请人身份的正确识别是防止替考的最基本方法。如果考试是在培训机构的内部进行,教学工作人员认识考生,只要环顾一下试室就可以马上把陌生者辨认出来。在考试中心外进行的考试,工作人员不认识考生,更应想方设法提防替考。在申请时通常要求使用照片并在背后签名。照片要转交到考试中心,在那里,监考人员依靠照片对报来的考生名单进行核查。也可选择提供海员身份证号码给监考人员,监考人员依靠身份证上提供的照片对每位到场的考生进行核查。在培训院校允许校外的申请人参加考试时,有必要采用相类似的系统。应该把缺席考生的名字记录在监考单上,监考单将与答卷一起送去评卷。

5. Invigilators should be given instructions regarding the security of all examination material. In particular, the procedures for passing test papers to them and collecting answer sheets and scripts from them should be clearly laid down. Answer sheets and other examination stationery should never be left in an unattended examination room; they could be used for introducing unauthorized notes into an examination.

6. Some examination authorities do not allow the admission of late arrivals because of the disturbance caused to those already working; others permit them to be admitted for a limited period after the start, with the proviso that no additional time will be allowed at the end of the test. Candidates are normally allowed to withdraw from an examination after handing in answer sheets and examination materials but should not be allowed to do so until after the latest time at which late arrivals would be admitted.

   As a general rule, no examines is permitted to return to an examination room after having left. However, it is not uncommon for a candidate to feel ill, through nervousness, in the early stages of an examination. At the invigilator's discretion, such a candidate may be allowed a few minutes to recover if accompanied by an invigilator.

7. Rough working or cancelled answers should be attached to the examinees' answer papers. Candidates should not be allowed to remove them or any other stationery from the room.

8. Examination rules normally provide that a candidate found giving or receiving help, making use of unauthorized material or discovered in any other form of misconduct will be immediately excluded from the remainder of the examination. The invigilator must make a full report of the circumstances and attach the candidate's papers and any material evidence of the misconduct. Candidates guilty of such misconduct are usually debarred from re-taking the examination for a period laid down in the rules.

9. Invigilators should know how to contact the examiner in case of queries about the paper or other difficulties which they are unable to deal with. In internal examinations it is helpful if the examiner attends the start of the test until candidates have had an opportunity to read the instructions and look through the paper.

10. There should be a minimum of two Invigilators per examination room so that one is free to seek assistance, if necessary, without leaving the room unattended. While causing as little distraction as possible, they should periodically patrol the room to look at the work on candidates' desks. Invigilators should remain alert and not undertake other tasks, such as marking, during an examination.

11. Desks should be arranged in straight rows with sufficient distance between the rows to make it difficult to read papers on an adjacent desk without it being obvious. Where more than one examination is held at the same time, the two sets of candidates should be arranged in alternate rows, as far as possible. Seating is arranged by placing cards with candidates' names or identification numbers on the desks in a convenient order for the collection of completed answer papers.

5. 应该就所有考试资料的安全性向监考人员提供指导。尤其应明确制定把试卷交给他们和从他们处收回答题纸和稿纸的程序。绝对不应该把答题纸和其他考试文卷遗留在一个无人看管的房间内；它们可能被夹带进考场。

6. 一些考试主管机关不允许迟到的考生进入考场，因为这样会打扰正在考试的考生；别的考试主管机关则在开始考试后的规定期间内允许他们进入考场，但条件是在考试的最后不会补加时间。通常申请人在递交了答题纸和试卷后允许退出考试，但在迟到者可以进入考场的最后时限之前是不允许这样做的。

   作为一般原则，任何已离开试室的考生不允许再返回试室。然而，很多时候离开考场是因为有些考生在考试的早期阶段感觉不舒服、始终神经紧张。如果有一名监考人员陪伴，并且得到监考人员的同意，则允许这样的考生有几分钟的恢复时间。

7. 答题草稿或者作废的答卷应该与考生的答卷黏附在一起。不允许考生把这些东西或者其他文卷从试室中拿走。

8. 考试规则通常提供了申请人寻求帮助或接受帮助的规定，使用未经批准的资料或以任何其他方式作弊将会被立即取消考试资格。监考人员必须写出详细的情况报告，附上该申请人的试卷和任何作弊的证明材料。规则中规定，申请人这种不正当的过失常常导致在一段时间内禁止再次参加考试。

9. 如对试题有疑问或者遇到他们不能解决的困难时，监考人员应该知道怎样与巡考员联系。在内部考试中，如果从考试刚开始一直到考生有机会阅读考试指南并且从头看完整份试卷，全过程都有巡考员在场，这样是很有益的。

10. 每个试室应该至少配备两名监考人员，以便需要时其中一人可以离开以寻求帮助，而不会令试室无人看管。在尽可能少地分散注意力的前提下，监考人员应该定期地巡视试室，查看考生书桌上的考卷。在考试期间，监考人员应该保持警觉，不要干别的事情，例如改卷评分等。

11. 书桌应该排成直行，行与行之间应有足够的距离，使考生很难看到邻桌上的试卷。在同一时间进行一门以上考试的考场，两类考生的座位应交替安排在不同行上，而且尽可能相隔远一点。通过在书桌上放置带有考生名字的卡片或者身份证号码的方法安排考生座位，合理的次序和座位安排便于收取已完成的答题纸。

A clock should be provided at the front of the room and the starting and finishing times of the test should be displayed on a blackboard or flip-chart so as to be visible throughout the room. It is also common practice to announce when there are ten or fifteen minutes remaining.

Publications and equipment

12. Part of an examinations officer's duties is to see that the necessary publications and equipment are provided in the examinations room. For the majority of tests the requirements will be standard; nautical tables, tide tables, drawing boards and T-squares or tables and graphs of data, according to the test. It is sufficient to see that there are enough in stock for the number of candidates to be examined and that the appropriate items are placed on each desk before a-test. When additional items are required, the examinations officer should be warned well in advance so that sufficient stock can be obtained. For the benefit of invigilators and candidates, a list of the items to be provided should be placed under the instructions at the head of test papers.

13. The published examination rules should contain information on what personal publications or equipment must be provided by the examines and what will be permitted. It is usual to require candidates to equip themselves with their own drawing instruments, when needed, and to permit the use of non-programmable calculators in most examinations. Where the use of calculators has been taken into account in the preparation of a paper containing a considerable quantity of calculation, candidates should be warned if they will have difficulty in completing the paper in the required time without the use of calculators. If personal publications and equipment are permitted they should be checked by an invigilator for unauthorized additions, in the form of notes or formulae in the margins of books or in instrument cases.

14. Damage to or defacement of examination property is commonly dealt with by having provision in the examination rules for withholding the qualification sought until the damaged item has been repaired or replaced by the candidate. A warning not to write or make marks on test papers which are to be used again should be given at the start of a test. Care should be taken to collect all such papers before dismissing candidates at the end of the test.

Communications

15. Communication of any sort between candidates should be prohibited. They should be told that, if they have any queries about the examination, they should raise a hand to attract an invigilator's attention and remain seated; the invigilator will come to them.

    On no account should candidates be allowed to share publications or equipment since information can easily be exchanged by this practice. A candidate whose calculator fails during an examination will have to complete it with the mathematical tables provided.

应该在试室的前面放置一个计时钟,并在黑板上或活动挂图上写明考试开始和结束的时间,以便整个试室都可看到。通常在考试还剩下最后十分钟或十五分钟时,应该提醒考生。

出版物和用具

12. 为试室提供的出版物和用具是考官职责的一部分。大多数测试要求是标准化的;根据测试需要可配备航海表、潮汐表、绘图板、直角尺以及数据表和曲线图。应注意为参加考试的申请人储备充足的用具,并且于考试前把相应的用具放在每一张书桌上。如有额外的要求,应该预先提醒考官以便获得充足的储备。为方便监考人员和申请人,提供的用具应列在试卷上方的说明栏下方。

13. 出版的考试规则应包括由考生个人提供并经允许携带的出版物或用具方面的资料。通常要求考生自行准备绘图用具,如有必要,大部分考试都允许使用非程序式计算器。允许使用计算器的考试在准备阶段已经充分考虑到试题包含了相当数量的计算,应当提醒考生注意的是,如果他们不使用计算器,那么在规定时间内完成答题是有困难的。如果允许个人携带出版物和用具,那么监考人应该检查用具的状态,特别是在书本的空白处是否用符号或公式的形式写了未经批准的附加内容。

14. 对考试财产的损害或毁坏一般都会受到处理,这点在考试规则中要做出规定,直到由考生把损坏部分修复了或更换了才承认其考试资格。告诫考生不要在试卷上做标记,因为通常考卷要反复使用。考试末期,在让考生离开之前应该仔细收集这类试卷。

交流

15. 应该禁止考生之间以任何形式进行交流。应该告诉他们,如果有任何关于考试方面的疑问,应该举手示意监考人员并且不能离开座位,然后监考人员过来解决。

    绝对不允许考生共用出版物或用具,因为他们很容易通过这种方法进行信息交流。在考试期间,如果考生的计算器损坏,则只能利用提供的数学用表来完成计算。

Part 13
Scoring Tests

Scoring subjective tests

1. The assessment of seafarers is concerned with judging whether they are competent, in terms of meeting sufficient specified learning objectives, to perform the tasks required by the qualification they are seeking. That is, they should be tested against predetermined criteria rather than against the performance of other examinees or the norm for the group as a whole, as is the case in many examinations.

   To achieve that end in subjective tests, an analytical scoring scheme should be drawn up in which a complete model answer, which would attract full marks, is produced for each question. The model answer is then analysed for the definitions, facts, explanations, formulae, calculations, etc., contained in it and marks are allocated to each item, the aim being to make the scoring as objective as possible. A subjective element will still exist in the original allocation of marks to the various sections and, to some extent, in the scoring of incomplete or partially correct sections.

2. Either credit scoring or deductive scoring may be used. In credit scoring, marks are awarded, in accordance with the scoring scheme, for each correctly completed part of the answer, no marks being credited for incorrect parts or omissions. With deductive scoring, marks are deducted for errors and omissions from the total mark for the question or part question (where a question has been divided into two or more sections). When applied to essay questions, the two methods should produce virtually the same score. Deductive scoring is usually confined to the marking of calculations.

3. Deductive scoring can be weighted to take account of the relative seriousness of different types of error. Errors are commonly classed and weighted as follows:

   .1 errors of principle; for example, using the formula for righting moment in a calculation of list; deduct 50% of the mark for the question or part question;

   .2 major errors; for example, extracting data for the wrong day or time from the Nautical Almanac; deduct 30% of the mark for the question or part question; and

   .3 clerical errors; for example, transposition of numbers from tables or question paper, careless arithmetic; deduct 10% of the mark for the question or part question for each error.

   In the case of clerical errors, only one deduction for a single error should be made. No deductions are made for incorrect answers which follow through from the original error.

   If deductions exceed the total mark for a question or part question it is given a zero score; negative scores are not carried over to other parts.

第13章
考试评分

考试主观题的评分

1. 对海员的评估是判断他们在完成职责所需资格的学习目标方面是否达到适任要求。也就是说,对他们测试依照的是预定标准而不是多数考试中采用的参考标准,即参考其他考生的表现或者测试整体表现。

    在主观考试中要达到这一目标,应该制定一个可分析的评分方案,其中包含完整的为每个题目设计的可获满分的标准答案。标准答案对定义、事实、解释、公式、计算等进行分析,把这些项目包括进去并且给每个项目分配分数,目的是尽可能达到客观评分。给不同部分指定的原始分数依然受主观因素的影响,在某种程度上说是不完全正确或者部分正确的评分。

2. 得分或扣分式的评分方案均可采用。在得分评分式方案里,根据评分方案,对于每一个能正确完成的部分都给出相应的分数,做得不正确或遗漏的部分则不给分。在扣分评分方案里,对于一个问题或问题中的一部分来说(在这里一个问题已被分为两个或多个部分),由于错答和漏题则可能从总分中扣分。在论述题中,两种方案应该都得到相同的分数。扣分式评分方案常常限于对计算题的评分。

3. 考虑到不同错误类型的相对严重性,扣分式评分可采用加权的方法。错误一般可按如下方法进行分类和加权:

    .1 概念错误,例如,在计算横倾时使用了矫正力矩公式,扣除该题目或部分题目50%的分数;

    .2 主要错误,例如,从航海天文历中用错误的日期和时间提取数据,扣除该题目或部分题目30%的分数;及

    .3 笔误,例如,从表上或答题纸上互换号码,粗心的计算;每一错误从题目或部分题目中扣除10%的分数。

    如果是笔误,只有单个错误被扣分。由原始错误造成的错误答案不会被扣分。

    如果所扣分数超出一个题目或部分题目的总分,则给零分;负分不会带到其他题目。

4. The different types of error can be taken into account in credit scoring schemes by suitably weighting the marks allocated to method, to the extraction of data and to clerical accuracy at each step of the calculation. The steps need to be smaller and more detailed than the division into parts used in deductive marking. As a result, the marks lost for errors of principle tend to be smaller in credit scoring than in deductive scoring.

5. A small percentage of the total mark, to be credited only for the correct final answer, is sometimes included in a credit scaring scheme. The answer must lie within stated accuracy limits to qualify for that credit. In deductive schemes, an answer that has otherwise been correctly calculated but which falls outside the accuracy limits is treated as a clerical error.

6. Where tests are to be marked locally at more than one test centre, a well-defined scoring scheme, which will give the same score when applied to the same paper by different markers, is essential for the uniform and fair treatment of candidates. To aid in any subsequent review of marks, possibly resulting from an appeal, the marker should make brief marginal notes on the paper to indicate the reasons for deductions.

7. Guidance on the treatment of answers produced by pocket calculators is needed. Examination rules usually warn candidates that all working must be shown to gain full marks for a question. The marks to deduct when insufficient working is shown but a correct answer is produced, or when all working is correctly shown but the answer is wrong, need to be known by the marker.

8. For essay questions, a scoring scheme would consist of a model answer, for which full marks would be awarded, showing the division of marks between the various definitions, facts, explanations and reasoning contained in it. Alternatively, a listing of the essential contents, with the allocation of marks to each item, could be used.

   When marking subjective papers it is recommended to mark them question by question, that is to say, to mark the same question on all papers before moving to the next; this procedure tends to produce more consistent marking. On completing the marking of a question, the first few papers marked should be looked at again, particularly if, by chance, they were all good or all poor ones, to check that the marking of those is consistent with the others.

   In the case of doubtful responses where the answer could possibly be correct, it is usual to allow the candidate the benefit of the doubt.

9. In papers in which all questions are to be answered, the marks may be weighted to reflect the importance or difficulty of individual questions or the length of time which will be needed to answer them. When this is done, it is usual to indicate the mark for each question on the question paper. Optional questions should all be of similar standard and carry equal marks, so that the standard of the complete test is the same regardless of the questions chosen

   Use can be made of a compulsory and an optional section in the same paper. Questions on which it is felt that all candidates should be tested can be placed in the compulsory section and suitably weighted, while the remainder of the paper offers a choice of questions each of similar standard.

4. 在得分式评分方案里,要考虑各种不同类型的错误,这点可通过在每一步的计算中对计算方法、数据提取及精度等方面适当地分配权值来实现。与扣分式评分中的每部分的分数分配相比,得分式评分分得更小、更细。因此,得分式评分与扣分式评分相比,因原理错误造成的失分较少。

5. 在使用得分式评分方案时,有时最终的正确答案只占总得分的较小比例。因为对于得分式评分,答案必须在限定的范围内。在扣分式评分方案里,对于已用的不同方法进行正确计算,但准确范围以外的答案会被当作笔误而扣较少的分。

6. 当多个考试中心进行就地评分时,设计一个良好的评分方案,这样即使不同的评卷人评阅同一份试卷也会得出一样的分数,一致和公平地对待考生很重要。为了便于以后因考生请求而可能进行的查分,评卷人应该在试卷的页边做简单的批注,以表明扣分理由。

7. 必须在如何对待用袖珍计算器得出答案这方面提供指导。考试规则通常警告考生,题目要拿到满分必须展示整个答题过程。评分人必须注意到,当答题过程不充分,但答案正确,或者答题整个过程都正确但答案却错误时,必须扣分。

8. 对于论述型题目来说,评分方案必须包括给满分的标准答案,必须在答案中说明各类定义、事实、解释和理由方面的分数划分,也可使用列表说明每一项目分数分配的基本内容。

   当评判主观性试卷时,建议用逐题评分的方案,也就是说,在评改下一个题目之前,应该对所有试卷的同一题目进行评分;这种评分程序得出的分数更加趋向一致。在完成一个题目的评分时,应该对最先评改的几份卷复查一遍,特别是如果恰巧它们的得分全部良好或者全部都差,这样检查的目的主要是使之与其他试卷的评分相一致。

   在对答案的正确性有怀疑时,通常应从有利于考生的方面考虑。

9. 在所有题目都是必答题的试卷中,分配到每个题目的分数反映了它的重要性或者难易程度或者做这些题目所需时间的长短。这时,通常要给答卷上的每一题目标示分数。所有选择题应该有相似的评分标准并占有相同的分数,以便不管选择什么题目作为考题,考试的整体标准是一致的。

   在同一份试卷里,可以使用必答题和选答题。所有申请人都需要完成的问题被安排在必答题部分并且适当地加权计分,同时,试卷的剩余部分提供了难度标准相似的题目供选择。

A problem that arises with optional papers is how to deal with cases where more than the required number of questions is answered. Various solutions are adopted by different examining boards. Many mark all questions and discard the lowest marked question or questions, although that fact is not generally advertised as it may encourage candidates to attempt extra questions. Others take the requisite number of answers in the order in which they are on the question paper and ignore the remainder. A similar problem arises in papers in which candidates are required to answer a given number of questions and including at least some stated number from each of several sections.

10. The pass mark should be set at the lowest score for which sufficient skills and knowledge are demonstrated for competency in each subject. In practice, that score is difficult to determine exactly for an individual paper and could vary slightly from one examination to another. Such an arrangement would be difficult to administer and would be considered unfair by candidates, so the pass mark is fixed and published in the examination regulations. It is, therefore, essential when preparing papers to maintain as constant a standard as possible, such that the pass mark is an appropriate measure of competency.

11. The following instructions are typical of those produced for guidance of examiners on the marking of examinations:

In order to achieve uniformity in marking between the Examiners in various centres and to facilitate the review of papers, the following guidelines are to be used at all centres:

.1 When several candidates write the same examination, papers, other than multiple choice, should be marked question by question, that is to say, question 1 of paper 1 should be marked for all applicants before proceeding to question 2, etc. This gives more uniform marking.

.2 All questions should be marked even if it becomes apparent that the candidate cannot achieve the pass mark.

.3 Neatness and Orderly Layout of Work:

Where work is not properly laid out or is not neat, marks should be deducted without regard to correctness of the answer. The number of marks deducted should vary according to the quality of the work up to a maximum of 10% where the correct answer is obtained.

.4 Important Nautical and Technical Terms:

Where, in general calculations or general questions, an incorrect term is used and such a term is incidental to the work, the Examiner should exercise his judgment as to whether or not marks should be deducted, but in any case, a deduction should not exceed 10% of the allotted marks. This does not apply to direct answers involving definitions or in answers involving the naming of parts.

有选答题的试卷引发的问题是怎样处理完成的试题数目比要求的多这种情况。不同的考试部门采用不同的解决办法。很多时候都是给所有完成的题目打分,舍弃得分最低的一个或多个题目,虽然不值得大肆宣扬这种做法,但这样可以鼓励考生尽量去做附加题。另外的做法是完成需要回答的题目数并按答题卡顺序选用,剩下的答题不予考虑。类似的问题也会出现在要求考生回答给定数量题目的试卷中,其中包括在一些规定回答特定题号题目的考试中。

10. 应当把能充分表明每一科目的适任技能和知识的最低分数设定为及格分数。实际上,很难准确地确定每一份试卷的及格分数,不同的试卷也可能有轻微的变化。对管理者来说这样的处理是很困难的,而考生也认为是不公平的,因此及格分数要在考试规则中规定和公布。所以基本做法是在准备考卷时应尽可能保持标准的不变,这样,及格分数就是衡量适任性的合适尺度。

11. 以下是为监考人员考试评分提供的典型指南:

    为了使不同考试中心的监考员达到评分标准的统一以及便于试卷的复查,以下的指南适用于所有考试中心:

    .1 当少数考生参加同一类考试,答同一类试题时,除了多项选择外,应该逐个题目地评分,也就是说应把所有申请者试卷1的第一道题全部改完后,才着手批改试卷1的第二道题,等等。这样给出的评分会更加一致。

    .2 应该给所有题目评分,即使考生明显达不到及格分数。

    .3 整齐有序的答题形式:

    答题位置不当或不整洁的地方,不论答案正确与否,一概扣分。所扣分数的多少根据答题质量而定,最多可达正确答题所得分数的10%。

    .4 重要的航海技术术语:

    在一般计算或一般问题中,可能会使用不正确的名词,在答题中这样的名词是难免的,评卷人应根据自己的经验来确定是否扣分。但在任何情况下,所扣分数不应该超过指定分数的10%。这点不适用于对定义做直接解释或者有关词类命名的解答。

.5 Types of Errors:

Errors can be divided in to 3 types:

(a) P—error in principle; 50% of marks allotted for the whole or part of the question should be deducted.

(b) C—clerical error; 10% of the marks allocated should be deducted for each such error.

(c) M—major error, 30% of the marks allotted for the question or part of the question should be deducted.

NOTE: Large mark questions should be considered in their main sections and percentages of the sections deducted. Candidates should be given the benefit of any doubt which may exist.

.6 Drawings:

Too much importance should not be attached to elaborate drawings. Often a simple sketch with captions is very explanatory and indicative of a good understanding.

.7 Incomplete Answers:

Where a problem or distinct section of a large problem is only partly worked and a step of principle remains to be made, marks allotted should not exceed 50% of the total marks or the split marks allotted as the case may be.

MARKING PAPERS:

.8 When marking papers, Examiners should enter appropriate marginal notes in brief showing why marks have been deducted, using abbreviations in Paragraph 5. The actual error should be ringed and marked with a brief statement of the reason for the error, e.g, "wrong day". A paper should be so marked that any reviewing Examiner can see at a glance just what happened, including a marginal note to indicate award of a "benefit of doubt".

Accuracy:

The following is a general rule to Examiners of the degree of accuracy expected:

(a) in calculating a ship's position, ±0.5 minutes of arc and to the nearest second of time;

(b) for a position line, to within 0.5 of a mile of the true result;

(c) in calculating compass errors, bearings and courses, ±0.5 of a degree;

(d) distances within 0.5 of a mile and times of meridian passage, to the nearest minute;

.5 错误种类

错误可以分为三种：

(a) P——概念错误；应该扣除全部或部分题目分数的50%。

(b) C——笔误；每一错误扣除所分配分数的10%。

(c) M——严重错误；应该扣除分配到该题或其中某一部分分数的30%。

注意：分数较多的题目应该考虑其主要部分以及错误部分所扣分数的百分比。如果存在任何疑问，考虑考生的利益优先。

.6 绘图：

不要过于看重作图的精细性。通常一个带有说明的草图是很容易解释并易于理解的。

.7 未完成的答题：

一道大题中的一个小问题或规定的内容只完成了一部分，并且还有主要部分未作答，所给分数不应超过总分的50%，或者看情况决定如何分摊分数。

试卷评分：

.8 进行试卷评分时，评阅人应该在试卷边缘用第五段说明的缩写做简短的注释，表明为什么要扣分。实际错误应该用表明错误原因的简短说明，例如圈上"错误的日期"并做标注。试卷的评分应该能叫复查员一目了然，包括可以在页边标明"怀疑作弊"这样的注释。

精确度：

以下是表明评阅人期望的精确度的一般规则：
(a) 在计算船位时，±0.5弧分(位置)和最接近的秒(时间)；

(b) 对于位置线，与实际结果相差0.5海里范围之内；

(c) 在计算罗经差、方位和航向时，±0.5度；

(d) 距离在0.5海里之内，中天时间在最接近的1分钟之内；

(e) tidal prediction, to ±15 cm.

.9 In the case of marginal failure, the paper concerned should be carefully reviewed.

This review is not to be regarded as having the purpose of passing the candidate, it is to ensure that the foregoing marking standards have been correctly applied and are consistent with those of other responses to the same examination. It may result in either an increase or a decrease in marks assigned. This review having been completed, the examiner should issue a fail result if it is still below the pass mark.

.10 Use of Calculators:

When a pocket, non-programmable calculator is used by a candidate in an examination, all necessary formulae and transpositions must be shown for full marks to be allotted. In the case of a correctly set out answer, or partial answer, which has an incorrect final result, 30% of the whole or part should be deducted on the major error rule.

12. The following is an example of a marking scheme for an engineering drawing examination:

Basically the candidate is being asked to produce a working drawing together with scaled view or views of a piece of machinery. This involves engineering knowledge skills in drafting, but most of all the assembled drawing MUST be technically feasible as well as functional.

Of the 100 marks assigned to the drawing the marks should be allotted as:

(i) Engineering knowledge, correct assembly — 50 marks

The assembled machinery must be able to perform the intended function with respect to size, shape and material employed. Parts shown must be capable of being removed. Proper clearances, valve lifts, etc. duly allowed for.

(ii) Proper use of paper — 5 marks

Choice of suitable scale and view positions so as to make optimum use of the paper.

(iii) Proper use of types of lines — 10 marks

Thickness and types of lines to indicate:

— visible outlines
— dimension, projection, extension, hatching and leader lines
— lines showing hidden details, portions to be removed
— centre lines, pitch circles
— cutting or viewing planes lines
— lines showing irregular boundaries, short breaks
— long break lines

(e) 潮汐预测，±15厘米之内。

.9 万一出现不及格的临界分数,要仔细复查相关试卷。

这种复查不能以让考生通过为目的,应该保证已经正确地运用上述的评分标准,并且保证与同一考试的其他答卷标准一致。复查可能造成评分的增加,也可能会减少。复查完成之后,如果仍然在及格分数以下,评阅人应该发布不及格的成绩。

.10 计算器的使用：

在考试中,当考生使用袖珍的、非程序化的计算器时,必须在卷面上显示所有必要的运算公式和变换才可以得满分。万一开始答题或部分的答题是正确的,但最后结果却不正确,那么根据严重错误规则,应该从总分中或从该部分扣除30%的分数。

12. 以下是工程制图考试评分方案的实例：

要求考生制作基本的附有比例视图或机器部件视图的工作图纸。这涉及制图方面的工程知识技能,但大部分的组合制图必须是技术上可行的和可操作的。

制图中的100分应当这样分配：

（i）工程知识,正确装配　　　　　　　　　　　　　　　　　　—50分

装配的机器必须在大小、形状和材料使用方面达到预期的功能。图示的零件必须能够移除。应该充分地考虑到适当的间距、阀门升程,等等。

（ii）图纸的正确使用　　　　　　　　　　　　　　　　　　　—5分

适当选择比例尺和视图位置,以便可以最佳地利用图纸。

（iii）图形和线条的正确使用　　　　　　　　　　　　　　　—10分

线的粗细和种类的简要说明：

— 可见轮廓
— 尺度、投影、范围、阴影和引出线
— 线的显示隐藏的细节,可移除的部分
— 中心线、节距圆
— 切割或检视平面线
— 不规则的边界线,短折点
— 长折线

(iv)	Printing of major and functional dimensions	— 10 marks

        Valve lift, working clearances or other relevant functional dimensions, neat figures and prints readable without having to turn the finished drawing.

(v)	Views or view projection	— 10 marks

        Views drawn as instructed and completed — 5 marks
        Relative position of views, first and third angle projection — 5 marks

(vi)	Drawing correct according to information	— 15 marks

        Scale used and stated — 5 marks
        Sectioning as required — 5 marks
        Materials — 5 marks

Using the foregoing guidelines an examiner will arrive at a final assessment of the exam by the process of deducting penalty marks from the maximum possible.

Before finalizing this assessment, time should be taken to review the candidate's work from the point of view of what proportion of the total has been done correctly. In this way, an examiner can balance the correct work against the incorrect and assure himself that his final assessment is fair.

Scoring objective tests

13. Simple credit scoring is usually employed for objective tests. One mark is awarded for each correct response and zero for all other responses. Schemes are sometimes used in which penalty marks are deducted for some or all of nil response, a multiple response and a wrong response.

14. Deduction for a wrong response is intended to reduce the effects of guesswork in multiple-choice and true/false tests. Taking as an example a test consisting of 40 true/false items, a candidate who knows the answers to 20 items and guesses the remainder can expect to guess about 10 more correct and 10 wrong, giving a total of 30 correct and 10 wrong responses. If one mark is deducted for each wrong answer, the score is reduced to 20, which is the number actually known. In multiple-choice questions the probability of guessing a correct answer is one divided by the number of choices per question, so, in a test with four choices, the probability of a correct guess is 0.25 and of a wrong one 0.75. There will, on average, be three wrongly guessed answers to each correct one, so the penalty mark should be one-third of the mark credited for a correct answer. Considering a test consisting of 50 multiple-choice questions with four choices, a candidate scoring 35 correct and 15 wrong responses would have 5 marks deducted, giving a corrected score of 30.

(iv) 主要的功能尺度的印刷 　　　　　　　　　　　　　　　—10分

　　阀门升程、工作间距或者其他相关的功能尺度,图形的整洁以及符号的倒置可读性。

(v) 视图或投影图 　　　　　　　　　　　　　　　　　　　—10分

　　按指示要求绘制并且完成制图 　　　　　　　　　　　—5分
　　视图的相对位置,一维和三维投影图 　　　　　　　　—5分

(vi) 根据资料正确制图 　　　　　　　　　　　　　　　　—15分

　　比例尺的使用和说明 　　　　　　　　　　　　　　　—5分
　　按要求作截面图 　　　　　　　　　　　　　　　　　—5分
　　制图资料 　　　　　　　　　　　　　　　　　　　　—5分

利用以上指南,通过扣除最多的可能罚分,评阅人可以最终达到评卷的目的。

在完成评卷之前,应该花时间复核考生做对的项目在整道题中所占的比例。这样,评阅人可以权衡正确项与不正确项,以保证自己最后的评估是公平的。

客观考试评分

13. 通常在客观考试中采用简单的得分型评分。答对每题给1分,其他回答给0分。有时采用扣分方案,题目部分或全部不作答、多答或错答都扣分。

14. 只要答错就扣分是为了减少在多项选择题和是非题考试中猜答案的影响。假设考试由40道是非题组成,知道20道题的正确答案的考生,猜测剩余的题目,期望可以猜对10道以上,猜错10道题,加起来是总共答对30道题,答错10道题。如果做错一道题扣1分,分数减少到20分,实际上这就是已经知道的正确答案的分数。在多项选择题中,猜对正确答案的概率是1除以每个题目的选择项数目,因此,在有四个选择项的考试里,猜对答案的概率是0.25,猜错答案的概率是0.75。就平均来说,每一正确答案将有三个错误的答案要猜,所以惩罚性罚分应该是每一个题应得分数的三分之一。如果一次考试由50道多项选择题组成,每道题有四个选择项,一名考生回答正确的题是35分,错误的15分,要扣的分数就是5分,最终给他的分数是30分。

The shortcoming of this method is that is assumes that all wrong responses are the result of guessing. In fact, many or all of them in a well-designed test, with good distracters, could be the result of a deliberate choice by the candidate. The same penalty is imposed for being wrong as for guessing, and the corrected score is not necessarily a better indicator of how many questions the candidate could answer correctly. A further complication is the probability distribution of the number of correct guesses. The probability of guessing exactly 5 correct out of 20, as assumed in the example above, is only 0.20.

15. Multiple responses should be treated as wrong responses even when one of them is the correct response.

    Deductions for nil responses serve to encourage guessing and should not be used unless deductions for wrong responses are also being made. Again, this penalizes the candidate for not knowing an answer, in addition to the mark not being credited, and the resulting corrected score would not truly indicate the number of questions to which the candidate knew the answers.

16. An objective test may consist of several sections, each using a different type of question; for example, sections of true/false, matching and multiple-choice. To reflect the amount of knowledge or understanding required to answer the different types of questions, correct answer scores can be given a different weighting in each section.

17. As mentioned in paragraph 14, some marks are likely to be gained by chance as a result of guesswork. The significance of chance marks in multiple-choice tests is reduced by increasing the number of choices per question. Most multiple-choice tests use four choices as a compromise between reducing chance marks and the difficulty of finding satisfactory additional distracters. The element of chance is also reduced by increasing the number of questions in the test. The probability of correctly guessing a given percentage of a large number of answers is less than the probability of correctly guessing the same percentage of a smaller number.

    The element of chance in true/false tests is very high. Even in a test consisting of 100 such questions, the probability of achieving a score of 50 or more purely by chance is 0.54, falling to about 1 in 100 for a score of 62 or more.

18. The pass mark for a multiple-choice test should be set at the number of objectives which it is necessary for the examines to satisfy to demonstrate competence in the subject of the test. Because of the element of chance, it is not possible to determine the exact number of objectives which the candidate could satisfy, either by simple credit scoring or in schemes with penalty deductions. All that is known is the number of correct responses to the test questions and that a few of them will be the result of chance. Probably, the best solution is to set a pass mark which, from experience and comparison with other tests, produces a satisfactory division between passing and failing with respect to the candidates' abilities.

这种方法的缺点是假定所有错误回答都是猜题所致。事实上，在已经预先设计好的考题里，它们中的绝大部分或者全部正确答案已经合理地分散，答题结果是经考生深思熟虑后做出的选择。但和猜测错误同样要被强制扣分，因此，这样修正过的分数不能确切地表示考生能够正确回答的题目数量。更复杂的是猜对数量的概率分布并不是相同的，正确猜对的概率是20个中有5个即0.25，当相对于上面的例子时仅为0.20。

15. 应该像对待错误回答一样对待多项选择的回答，即使它们之中有一个回答是正确的。

    不做的题扣分将会鼓励考生猜答案，除非对于答错也扣分，否则不应该这样做。另外，像这样由于不知道答案而罚分，再加上有些题未得分，这样修正过的分数不能真正地反映考生知道答案的题目数量。

16. 客观测试可以由几部分组成，每部分采用不同类型的题目；例如，是非题、比对题和多项选择题这几种。为了反映回答不同类型题目所需要的知识和理解能力，每一部分正确答案的分数应给予不同的加权值。

17. 正如第14段中提到的，可以通过猜测碰巧获得一些分数。在多项选择测试里，偶然（猜测）分的影响可以通过增加每个题目的选择项来减小。大部分的多项选择测试使用四个选择项，这是在减少偶然分数和合理的查找分散度之间采取的折中方法，也可以通过在测试中增加题量来减少偶然因素的影响。正确猜对答案的概率在题量较多时比题量较少时小。

    在是非题考试里，偶然因素是非常高的。即使是在由100道是非题组成的测试里，纯粹由碰巧获得50分或者更高分的概率是0.54，对于62分或者更高分的情况来说，概率分别下降1%。

18. 多项选择考试的及格分数应该设置在客观的数值上，在科目考试里，这一数值必须能够较好地表明适任。因为偶然的因素，靠简单地确定合格分数或者根据评分方案惩罚性扣分，不可能确定考生能够准确答题的数量。能够知道的只是正确回答题目的数量，而其中的一部分是偶然（猜测）的结果。或许，最好的解决办法是根据经验和与其他考试进行比较来确定及格分数，以较好地区分考生的能力是及格还是不及格。

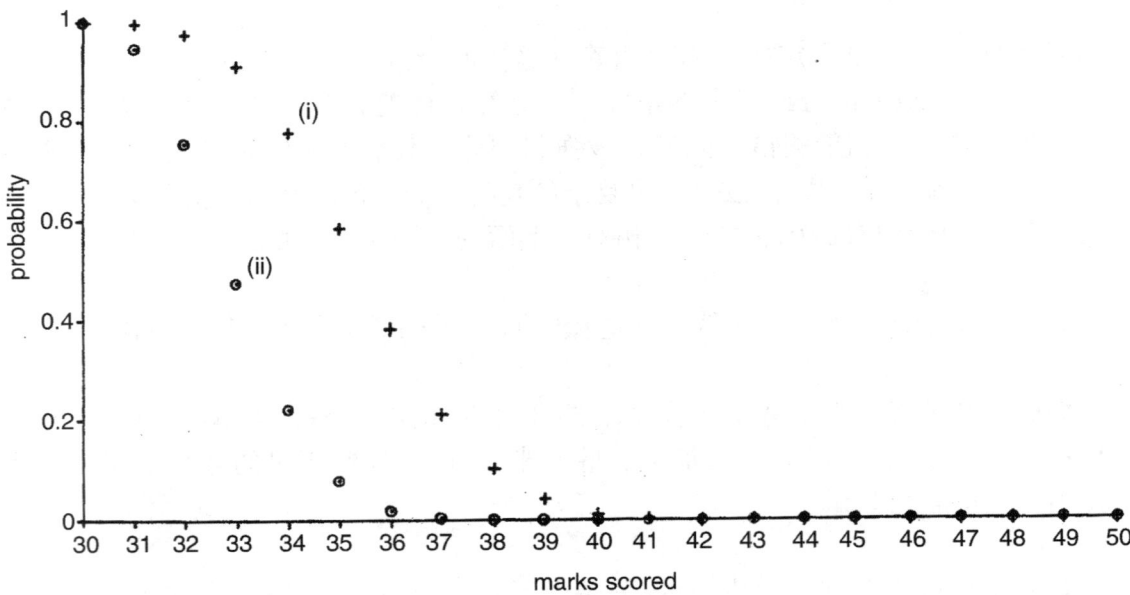

Figure 9.18-1   Probabilities of scoring marks in a test: for explanation, see text

Figure 9.18-1 shows the probability of obtaining the mark shown or more in a 50-question multiple-choice test, with four choices per question, for:

(i) a candidate who knows the correct response to 30 questions and guesses the remaining 20; and, probably more realistically,

(ii) a candidate who answers 40 questions, 30 correctly and 10 wrongly, and guesses the remaining 10.

Reviewing marginal cases

19. Those papers with scores falling within a previously decided band either side of the pass mark, typically from about 5% below to 5% above the pass mark, should be reviewed. A check would be made to see that nothing has been accidentally left unmarked and that the score has been correctly recorded. With objective tests, the score is accepted (after it has been checked) and the candidate is awarded a pass or is failed according to the score.

In the case of subjective tests, the paper should be marked independently by a second person to check that the marking scheme has been correctly followed and that its application is consistent with that of other papers. When the score, after review, is agreed, the review panel must decide whether to pass or fail the candidate on the evidence of the paper and any other knowledge of his ability which they may have. After the result has been decided it is common to re-mark the paper more or less strictly, depending upon the result, so as to shift the final mark awarded out of the marginal region, thus making the examiners' decision clear to any appeal body.

Where internal examinations are subject to moderation, it is usual for the moderator to undertake the review of marginal cases and to adjust the marks in a similar way.

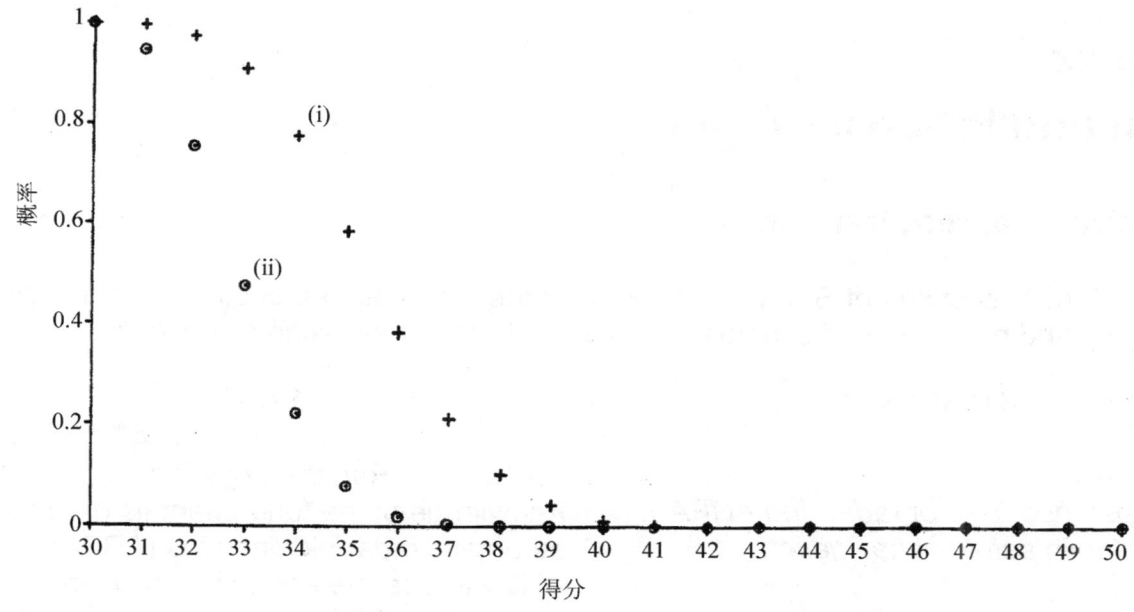

图9.18-1 考试中评卷分数的概率分布:具体说明参见正文

图9.18-1是有50道多项选择题,每题四个选择项的考试得分概率分布,说明如下:

(ⅰ)考生知道正确答案的有30题,其余20题是猜测的(可能更加可靠)的情况;

(ⅱ)考生做了40道题,30道题是正确的,10道题是错误的,剩余10道题是猜测的。

复查临界个案

19. 应该对分数落在原先确定的及格分数线上下一定范围内的试卷进行复查,这一分数的典型范围是及格分数上下5%。通过复查或许可以发现偶然遗漏的未批改的题目从而正确地记录分数。在客观考试中,根据经复查并认可之后得出的分数可以确定考生考试及格还是不及格。

如果是主观考试,试卷应该独立地由初评者以外的另一个人复查并根据评分方案正确评分。当原来的分数与复查后的分数一致时,复查小组必须根据试卷情况以及考生其他方面能证明其必备能力的知识,决定这名考生及格或者不及格。得出上述结论以后,通常做法是更严或稍松地对试卷再评分,将分数更改到临界范围外。因此应该把考官的裁决清楚标在试卷上,以便向任何请求查分的考生说明。

当内部考试成绩需要调节时,通常由主考官负责临界个案的复查以及用相似的方法校对分数。

Part 14
Oral and Practical Tests

International requirements

1. Certain sections of STCW 1995, call for the practical demonstration of the competency and proficiency of candidates; these include the following provisions:

STCW Code	Provision
Table A-II/2 *Competence: Use of radar and ARPA to maintain safety of navigation*	*Proficiency: Radar navigation* Knowledge of the fundamentals of radar and automatic radar plotting aids (ARPA) Ability to operate and to interpret and analyse information obtained from radar, including the following... Performance:... Use:... Principal types of ARPA, their display characteristics, performance standards and the dangers of over-reliance on ARPA
Table A-II/2 *Competence: Plan and conduct a passage and determine position*	*Proficiency: Compass—magnetic and gyro* Knowledge of the principles of magnetic and gyro-compasses Ability to determine errors of the magnetic and gyro-compasses, using celestial and terrestrial means, and to allow for such errors
Table A-II/2 *Competence: Maintain sea-worthiness of the ship*	*Proficiency: Ship stability* Working knowledge and application of stability, trim and stress tables, diagrams and stress-calculating equipment
Table A-II/2 *Competence: Transmit and receive information by visual signalling*	*Proficiency: Visual signalling* Ability to transmit and receive signals by Morse lights Ability to use the International Code of Signals
Table A-II/2 *Competence: Plan and conduct a passage and determine position*	*Method of demonstrating competence* Examination and assessment of evidence obtained from one or more of the following: .1 approved in-service experience .2 approved training ship experience .3 approved simulator training .4 approved laboratory equipment training

第14章
口试和实操考试

国际公约的要求

1. STCW 1995公约的某些章节,要求表明申请人实际操作方面的适任和熟练;这些包括以下规定:

STCW规则	规定
表A-Ⅱ/2 适任:使用雷达和自动雷达标绘仪保持安全航行	熟练:航海雷达 雷达和自动雷达标绘仪(ARPA)的基本知识 操作、解释和分析由雷达获得的信息的能力,包括下列各项…… 性能方面包括…… 使用方面包括…… 自动雷达标绘仪的主要类型,其显示特点、性能指标和过分依赖雷达标绘仪的危险性
表A-Ⅱ/2 适任:计划并引导航行和定位	熟练:磁罗经和陀螺罗经 磁罗经和陀螺罗经原理的知识 采用天文和地文方法确定磁罗经和陀螺罗经的误差的能力以及修正这种误差的能力
表A-Ⅱ/2 适任:保持船舶的适航性	熟练:船舶稳性 稳性、纵倾、强度图表和强度计算仪器的实际知识和应用
表A-Ⅱ/2 适任:视觉信号发出和接收信息	熟练:视觉信号通信 用莫尔斯号灯收发信号的能力 使用《国际信号规则》的能力
表A-Ⅱ/2 适任:计划并引导航行和定位	表明适任的方法 考试并评估从下列一项或数项获取的证据: .1 认可的工作经历 .2 认可的培训船经历 .3 认可的模拟器培训 .4 认可的实验室设备培训

STCW Code	Provision
Table A-II/2 *Competence: Maintain a safe navigational watch*	*Method of demonstrating competence* Examination and assessment of evidence obtained from one or more of the following: .1 approved in-service experience .2 approved training ship experience .3 approved simulator training .4 approved laboratory equipment training
Table A-II/2 *Competence: Use of radar and ARPA to maintain safety of navigation*	*Method of demonstrating competence* Assessment of evidence obtained from approved radar simulator and ARPA simulator training plus in-service experience
Table A-II2 *Competence: Prevent, control and fight fires on board*	*Method of demonstrating competence* Assessment of evidence obtained from approved fire-fighting training and experience as set out in section A-VI/3
Table A-II/2 *Competence: Transmit and receive information by visual signalling*	*Method of demonstrating competence* Assessment of evidence obtained from practical instruction
Table A-II/2 *Competence: Operate life-saving appliances*	*Method of demonstrating competence* Assessment of evidence obtained from approved training and experience as set out in section A-VI/2, paragraphs 1 to 4
Table A-II/2 *Competence: Plan and conduct a passage and determine position*	*Proficiency: Electronic systems of position fixing and navigation* Ability to determine the ship's position by use of electronic navigational aids
Table A-II/2 *Competence: Plan and conduct a passage and determine position*	*Proficiency: Echo-sounders* Ability to operate the equipment and apply the information correctly
Table A-II/2 *Competence: Use the Standard Marine Navigational Vocabulary*	*Proficiency: English language* Adequate knowledge of the English language enabling the officer to use charts and other nautical publications, to understand meteorological information and messages concerning ship's safety and operation, to communicate with other ships and coast stations and to perform the officer's duties also with a multilingual crew, including the ability to use and understand the Standard Marine Navigational Vocabulary.

STCW 规则	规定
表 A-Ⅱ/2 适任:保持安全航行值班	表明适任的方法 考试并评估从下列一项或数项获取的证据: .1 认可的工作经历 .2 认可的培训船经历 .3 认可的模拟器培训 .4 认可的实验室设置培训
表 A-Ⅱ/2 适任:使用雷达和自动雷达标绘仪保持安全航行	表明适任的方法 评估从认可的雷达模拟器和自动雷达标绘仪模拟器培训加上从工作经历中获得的证据
表 A-Ⅱ/2 适任:船上防火、控制火灾和灭火	表明适任的方法 评估从第 A-Ⅵ/3 节规定的认可的消防培训和实践经验中获取的证据
表 A-Ⅱ/2 适任:用视觉信号发出和接收信息	表明适任的方法 评估从实际训练中获取的证据
表 A-Ⅱ/2 适任:操作救生设备	表明适任的方法 评估从 A-Ⅵ/2 节第 1 至第 4 段规定的认可的培训和实践经验中获取的证据
表 A-Ⅱ/2 适任:计划并引导航行和定位	熟练:电子定位和导航系统 使用电子导航仪器确定船位的能力
表 A-Ⅱ/2 适任:计划并引导航行和定位	熟练:回声测深仪 正确操作该设备和应用所得信息的能力
表 A-Ⅱ/2 适任:使用标准航海用语	熟练:英语 足够的英语知识,能使高级船员使用海图和其他航海出版物,了解气象资料和有关船舶安全和操作的信息,并能在和他船或岸台通信以及与使用多种语言的船员沟通以履行高级船员职责时清楚地表达意思,其中包括使用并理解标准航海用语的能力。

STCW Code	Provision
Table A-II/2 *Competence: Apply medical first aid on board ship*	*Proficiency: Medical aid* Practical application of medical guides and advice by radio, including the ability to take effective action based on such knowledge in the case of accidents or illnesses that are likely to occur on board ship
Section A-VI/2 *Proficiency in survival craft and rescue boats other than fast rescue boats*	4. Every candidate for certification shall be required to provide evidence of having achieved the required standard of competence within the previous five years through: 　.1 demonstration of competence...table A-VI/2-1 (assessment of evidence obtained from practical demonstration of ability to...) 　.2 examination or continuous assessment as part of an approved training programme covering the material set out in column 2 of table A-VI

2. Administrations may thus require an oral and a practical test on topics that are essential to safety as part of the examinations for certificates of competency. However, in some cases they may wish to delegate these particular functions, in part or in whole, to suitably staffed and equipped training providers.

Advantages and disadvantages of oral and practical tests

3. It is generally considered advisable that candidates for certificates of competency should be examined orally. Some aspects of competency can only be properly judged by having the candidate demonstrate his ability to perform specific tasks in a safe and efficient manner. The safety of the ship and the protection of the marine environment are heavily dependent on the human element. The ability of candidates to react in an organized, systematic and prudent way can be more easily and reliably judged through an oral/practical test incorporating the use of models or simulators than by any other form of test.

4. One disadvantage of oral/practical tests is that they can be time-consuming. Each test may take up about 1 to 2 hours if it is to comprehensively cover the topics concerned. Equipment must also be available in accordance with the abilities that are to be tested. Some items of equipment can economically be dedicated solely for use in examinations. Examples of such items are manoeuvring boards, ship models, models of ships' equipment, models of COLREG lights and shapes, deviascopes, sextants, binnacle and compass, etc.

　　However, items such as radar simulators, ship simulators, engine-room simulators, cargo loading simulators, etc. involve investment and may not be seen as economic if they are dedicated to examinations alone unless they can be in almost continuous use for that purpose.

STCW 规则	规定
表 A-Ⅱ/2 适任:在船上应用医疗急救	熟练:医护 医疗指南和无线电咨询的实际应用,包括根据这种知识对船上易于发生的事故和疾病采取有效行动的能力
第 A-Ⅵ/2 节 熟练操作除快速救助艇以外的救生艇筏和救助艇	4. 每个证书申请人应通过下列方法提供其近 5 年内已达到所要求的适任标准的证据: 　.1　表明适任……表 A-Ⅵ/2-1(评估从实际表明能力……中获取的证据) 　.2　考试或连续的评估,作为认可培训计划的一部分,覆盖了表 A-Ⅵ/第 2 栏所列的材料

2. 主管机关因此可以在适任证书考试中的基本安全方面采用口试和实操考试。然而,在某些情况下,他们希望把这些职责部分或全部委托给配备合适人员和设备的培训机构。

口试和实操考试的优缺点

3. 一般认为,要求适任证书申请人接受口试考核是明智的。而另一方面,适任性的某些方面仅能通过申请人的展示,对其采用安全有效的方法完成具体任务的能力进行正确判断。船舶的安全和海洋环境的保护主要依赖于人为因素。申请人以有组织的、系统的和稳健的方法行动的能力可以通过口试/实操考试进行判断,利用模型或模拟器混合的方法比其他任何形式的方法更容易、更可靠。

4. 口试/实操考试的一个缺点是可能会耗费大量的时间。如果要全面覆盖相关的内容,每次考试可能要花 1~2 小时。同时,还必须提供与要测试的能力相对应的设备,配备某些专门用于考试的设备可能是经济的。例如,驾驶图解卡、船模、船舶设备模型、《国际海上避碰规则》中的号灯号型、自差观测核、六分仪、罗经柜和罗经,等等。

然而,像雷达模拟器、船舶模拟器、机舱模拟器、货物积载模拟器等设备均需大量的投资,如果它们仅仅用于考试,则被认为不够经济,除非它们可以几乎连续地用于考试。

5. For these reasons, it can be better to delegate the practical testing of candidates to properly equipped and staffed training providers or to make arrangements for the examiners to conduct such tests, using the provider's equipment.

Conduct of oral and practical tests

6. The following administrative instructions regarding the conduct of oral examinations are typical in the case of external examinations for certificates for masters, chief mates and officers in charge of a navigational watch:

    ### General remarks on oral examination procedures

    In order to put a candidate at ease, orals should be commenced by questioning about ships served in and trade in which experience was gained. A great deal can be learned by this means of the candidate's interest in the work, powers of observation and general intelligence.

    The examiner should subdivide the oral syllabus into appropriate small sections and allocate marks or otherwise as the orals progress. Where safety of life or ship is involved, the marking should be strict.

    Orals should not be cut short because of failure, the full extent of knowledge should be determined in ALL aspects of the syllabus and an additional period of sea service or study imposed if warranted. On conclusion of each oral examination, brief notes on the weaknesses shown by the candidate should be recorded by the examiner in an oral record book which should be kept at each examination centre.

    A knowledge of the International Regulations for Preventing Collisions at Sea and local special rules is vitally important. Although these are covered by multiple-choice examinations, examiners should in conducting the oral examination further assess the candidate's knowledge if the results of the written tests show a misunderstanding or lack of knowledge of the application of any rules.

    From time to time, complaints have been received about the length of some oral examinations. This instruction should in no way be taken as a directive to shorten examinations, but a candidate who has not demonstrated sufficient knowledge within two hours is usually not ready for the qualification applied for. Whenever possible, examiners should avoid bringing a candidate back after a lunch or night break.

    There is no objection to an examiner using his discretion and interrupting any examination, other than a written examination, because of excessive nervousness on the part of the candidate or other cause.

7. The following is an example of administrative instructions regarding the oral examination of candidates for engineer officer, second engineer officer and officers in charge of an engineering watch certificates:

5. 由于这些原因,更应该把申请人的实操考试委托给配备合适人员和设备的培训机构,或者使用培训机构的设备并安排主考人指导这样的考试。

口试和实操考试的指导

6. 如果是针对船长、大副以及负责航行值班的高级船员所参加的适任证书外部考试,那么以下的行政指令可以看作是对口试的典型指导:

   口试程序的一般说明

   为使申请人放松,口试应该从他们熟悉的有关船舶操作和贸易方面的提问开始。这种方法可以大量了解申请人的工作兴趣、观察问题的能力以及一般智力等方面有关情况。

   检查员应该把口试大纲细分成相应的小部分并且分配分数或者用不同的方法表示口试成绩。涉及人命和船舶安全方面的评分应该是严格的。

   口试不应该因为申请人在某个问题上不能或错误作答而缩减,应该根据大纲的所有方面以及附加的海上服务资历或者认可的强制性学习等各方面确定申请人的全面知识。在每次口试的结尾,对申请人表现出来的弱点应由主考人在口试记录本上做简短的记录,该记录本应保存在各考试中心。

   《国际海上避碰规则》和地方特殊规则的知识是极其重要的。虽然多项选择题考试包含了这些内容,但如果笔试的成绩表现出对规则的不理解或缺乏运用规则的相关知识,则主考人应该通过口试以进一步评价申请人的知识。

   有时,会收到某些有关口试时长方面的投诉。这绝不应该被看作是缩短考试时间的指令,但若在两小时之内不能表明申请人具备足够的知识通常被认为不具备所申请的资格。只要可能,在同一轮考试里,主考人应该避免给申请人两次相同的考试机会。

   主考人因为考生的极度神经过敏或其他原因,可根据自己的判断无可争议地中断除笔试外的考试。

7. 以下的实例是针对轮机长、大管轮以及负责轮机值班的高级船员证书申请人口试的行政指令。

Oral Examination

A candidate shall undergo an oral examination to test his practical knowledge of the appropriate subjects as laid down in the examination regulations. Such oral examination should include references to the candidate's answers in the written work (wherever applicable), besides being based on the oral examination syllabus.

Oral examinations should be conducted as follows:

.1 Where a candidate elects to take a Combined Certificate, an oral examination should be conducted after he has passed the written examination in all three engineering knowledge subjects.

.2 Where a candidate elects to be examined in one specialized subject, the oral should be conducted after he has passed in both engineering knowledge written papers.

.3 Where a candidate wishes to be examined for an endorsement to his certificate or to convert his certificate to a Combined Certificate, a further oral examination should be conducted after he has passed the written examinations.

The foregoing should not prevent the examiner from interviewing a candidate after any written examination if he wishes to clarify the candidate's written answers or if he considers he should advise the candidate of weaknesses demonstrated in the written paper and how they should be corrected.

Coverage of syllabus and assessment

8. With the exception of points which the examiner may wish to raise concerning wrong or incomplete answers in the candidate's written work, a standardized detailed Syllabus should be used so that the questions posed may systematically cover the main topics of concern. With such a syllabus suitably subdivided into main topics, marking or grading of the candidates' knowledge and ability in each area can be noted as the examination proceeds. Without such a process the overall assessment of the examiner at the conclusion of the test is less reliable than it should be, particularly where several candidates are examined orally in the course of a day.

Screening tests

9. In order to alleviate the workload of those responsible for the conduct of oral and practical examinations, screening tests may be used. Such screening tests generally take the form of objective-type tests since they can be quickly marked.

The examiner is then immediately aware of the areas of strength and weakness in the candidate's knowledge, thereby allowing him to arrive at a pass/fail decision with the minimum of delay. In certain cases, for example in assessing practical knowledge of the International Regulations for Preventing Collisions at Sea, the "screening test" may be established as a supplementary written test, success in which is a prerequisite for admission to the oral/practical test.

口试

申请人应经过口试来测试其对考试规则中规定的相应科目中实际知识的掌握情况。除了根据口试大纲，(若可行)这样的口试还应该参考申请人在笔试中的答题情况。

以下情况应该进行口试：

.1 申请人选择持有组合证书，在已通过全部三门工程知识科目的笔试后应该进行口试。

.2 申请人选择一门特殊科目考试，在已通过两门工程知识科目的笔试后应该进行口试。

.3 申请人希望通过考试使其证书得到认可或者把其证书改为组合证书的情况，在已通过笔试后应该进行更深入的口试。

如果主考人希望弄清申请人在笔试中的表现，或者，如果他认为应该建议申请人说明其在笔试中的弱点以及应该怎样改正这些弱点，那么以上规定不应妨碍主考人在笔试完成以后对申请人进行面试。

大纲的覆盖范围和评估

8. 除非是针对申请人答卷上的错误或者未做完的题目而由主考人增加的相应口试，其他的口试应该都用标准化的大纲细则，以便所提出的问题能系统性地覆盖相关主题。将大纲适当地细分成若干个主题，在测试过程中对申请人在每个领域的知识及能力进行评分和定级。不按这一程序，主考人对考试的总体评价结论就不够可靠，特别是在一天时间内对多位申请人进行口试，情况便如此。

筛选考题

9. 为了减轻负责口试和实操考试的工作人员的负担，可以采用筛选考试。筛选考试一般采用可以进行快速评分的客观题型。

于是，主考人可以立即知道申请人知识掌握得很好的方面和薄弱的环节，因而可以马上决定申请人及格/不及格。在某些情况下，例如，"筛选考试"可以作为笔试的补充来评估《国际海上避碰规则》实际知识，只有通过了这种考试才允许参加口试/实操考试。

Communications examinations

10. In the case of deck certificates, practical testing is required to assess the candidate's ability to communicate by means of the International Code of Signals, by radiotelephony and in English, using the IMO Standard Marine Navigational Vocabulary. The following is an example of administrative instructions dealing with the examination in signalling:

General

1. The signalling examination consists of three sections:

    .1 reading Morse Code signals flashed at a speed of 4 words per minute;

    .2 a multiple choice test described in paragraph 6;

    .3 satisfying the examiner as to ability to send Morse by flashing light.

Morse flashing light test

2. This section of the examination may be satisfied in one of two ways:
    .1 by the taped block test held at examination centres which is described in paragraph 3; or

    .2 by a statement issued by an approved training provider as described in paragraph 4, and a "write in" type of examination as described in paragraph 6.

Examination centre Morse test

3. There are six "blocks" in the tapes, each block consisting of 20 groups and each group consisting of one to three mixed letters and numerals. There are a total of 40 letters/numerals in the blocks.

    The sequence on the tapes is as follows:

Numeral 1	Sent 3 times, this is for the examiner's information when setting up the equipment. It indicates that block 1 follows and should not be sent to the candidates.
Call Sign AA	Sent 3 times, the examination commences at this point and candidates should be warned to expect the call sign before the block.
Block Number 1	After 5 seconds.
Ending Sign AR	At the end of the block. After 10 seconds.

通信考试

10. 对于驾驶证书,要求用实操考试来评估申请人使用国际信号码语进行无线电话通信的能力,采用的语言是英语并使用IMO标准海事通信用语。以下是有关信号考试官方说明的一个实例:

通则

1. 通信考试包括三个部分:

    .1 接收莫尔斯信号码语,闪光速度为每分钟4个词;

    .2 多项选择题考试在第6节说明;

    .3 令主考人满意的用闪光灯发送莫尔斯信号的能力。

莫尔斯闪光灯考试

2. 这部分的考试可以采用如下两种方法中较为适用的一种方法:

    .1 在考试中心用磁带进行的填空考试,这种考试在第3节说明;或

    .2 按第4部分说明的经认可的培训机构签发的证明,以及按第6节说明的"抄报"类型进行考试。

考试中心的莫尔斯考试

3. 磁带中有6个"模块",每个模块包括20组,每组由1~3个字母和数字组合而成。模块中共有40个字母组/数字组。

    磁带中的顺序如下:

数字组1	发3次,当设备设置好时,可以向主考人提供信息,它表示字组1将随后发送,此组信号不向考生发送。
呼叫符号AA	发3次,考试从此处开始,在发送字组之前应提醒考生注意呼叫符号。
模块1	过5秒钟后发送。
结束符号AR	在模块的最后。过10秒钟后发送。

Numeral 2   Sent 3 times, this indicates the start of the same sequence for block 2 and the same procedure is followed for all blocks.

Spacing in Morse transmissions is as given in section 3 of chapter 3 of the International Code of Signals 1969 and candidates will be required to show groups on their answer card exactly as sent and as shown on the Test Message answer cards.

When marking flashing light answers, one mark is to be allotted to each correct letter or numeral. The passing percentage is 90% and the pass mark 36. No allowance is to be made for "phonetic errors" since candidates are expected to make use of the phonetic letter-spelling table and the figure-spelling table of the International Code of Signals.

Statement from a training provider

4. A statement from an approved training provider that they are satisfied that a student can read all letters and numerals sent by Morse flashing light at a speed of not less than 4 wpm, combined with a "write in" examination as described in paragraph 6, may be substituted for the Morse test at an examination centre.

5. When a training provider wishes to take advantage of the arrangement permitted in paragraph 2(b), examiners shall be satisfied that adequate arrangements and facilities exist. The following criteria shall be used as a basis for this assessment:

    .1 Morse flashing instruction shall be regularly scheduled, in an aggregate of not less than 2 ½ hours per week, and the instruction shall be under the charge of a member of staff of the academy or college.

    .2 The equipment used shall be capable of sending, at a speed of not less than 4 wpm, well formed Morse symbols the spacing and duration of which shall comply with the International Code of Signals 1969.

    .3 Facilities shall include a room for the students, where the flashing light may be read without undue outside noise or interference, darkened if necessary and, if the Morse signals are keyed, where the noise of the key cannot be heard.

    .4 The statement required by paragraph 4 of this instruction shall be signed by a member of the staff of the academy or college and the examiner may stipulate which staff member or members may sign. The statement shall only be made after the student has satisfactorily read at least one test made on the academy or college equipment by correctly identifying 36 out of 40 characters, randomly arranged. i.e. 90%.

    .5 The statement shall be dated by the academy or college and shall be valid for the same period as a pass in the communications examination.

6. *Written Morse test (To be used when sending and receiving is done by a training provider)*

　　　　数字组2　　　　　发三次,显示模块2同样的开始程序,随后所有模块采用相同的通信程序。

　　莫尔斯符号的发送间隔在《1969年国际信号规则》第3章第3节有相关规定,要求考生按照通信考试答题卡的说明在答题卡上正确显示每一组内容。

　　给闪光灯考试评分时,每一个正确字母或数字给1分。及格百分比是90%,及格分数是36分。不考虑"语音上的错误",因为预期考生能利用《国际信号规则》中的字母拼读表和数字拼读表正确发音。

由培训机构签发的证明

4.　由认可的培训机构签发证明,其满足条件是学生应能看懂以每分钟不少于4个单词的莫尔斯闪光灯发出的字母和数字。在考试中心,可以使用如第6节说明的与"抄报"考试结合的方法来代替莫尔斯考试。

5.　当培训机构希望利用第2节第2点中允许的配置,主考人应该对现有的足够的装置和器材感到满意。以下的标准将作为这种评价的基础。

　　.1　莫尔斯灯闪光训练将定期进行,每周共计不低于2.5小时,训练应该在培训学校或正规院校的工作人员指导下进行。

　　.2　使用的设备应能以每分钟不少于4个单词的速度发送信号,同样,组成莫尔斯符号的间隔和持续时间应遵守《1969年国际信号规则》的规定。

　　.3　设施包括学生用的教室一间,在里面闪光灯信号的接收不受外界不正常噪声或其他干扰的影响,如果需要,教室应提前遮暗。如果莫尔斯信号是键控式的,则不应该听到由电键发出的噪声。

　　.4　第4段要求的训练证明应该由培训学校或正规院校的工作人员签发,主考人应该规定由哪些工作人员或成员签字。仅当学生至少有一次在培训学校或正规院校的设备上考试时能从随意安排的40个字符中较满意地正确读出36个即总数的90%以后才能签发这样的证明。

　　.5　证明应当由培训学校或正规院校注上日期,作为同一时期的通信考试及格的有效证明。

6.　莫尔斯抄收考试(当发送和接收考试均由培训机构进行的时候使用)

.1 This test consists of 20 questions and is in two parts. The first part requires the candidate to write in the Morse symbol for the given letter or numeral, the second part requires him to write in the letter or numeral for a given Morse symbol.

.2 The pass mark in this test is 20 and 15 minutes are allowed for its completion.

.3 Four different test papers are provided for this test, any of which may be used at the examiner's discretion.

7. Multiple choice test

.1 There are 6 communications test, numbered Comm. 1-6, each comprising two booklets Part I and Part II. Comm. 6, both parts, is supplied as a specimen but there is no objection to it being used from time to time as an examination.

.2 Part I consists of 20 questions on coding, general knowledge and procedures for Morse, flag and voice communications. For this part of the examination the following publications are provided:

> International Code of Signals 1969
> Radio Aids to Marine Navigation
> Notices to Mariners Annual Edition.

.3 Part II consists of 25 questions on distress, lifesaving, safety and single flag signals. No publications are permitted in this part. There are no failing questions in this part.

Multiple choice test procedure

.4 Candidates should first be given Part I of the selected test and the publications listed in paragraph 7.2. One hour should be allowed for this test, the booklet and publications then being collected and Part II of the same selected test is then issued. Again, one hour is allowed for Part II.

.5 Parts I and II are to be answered on the same response sheet, but are to be treated separately for assessment. In Part I, 14 correct answers (70%) are required in order to pass and in Part 11, 17 correct answers (68%). A candidate who gains a lower score in either Part fails the multiple choice test.

8. Answer keys are provided separately for Parts I and II.

9. The order of taking the three parts of the signalling examination is as listed in paragraph 1, and the test booklets to be used in the multiple choice test are left to the examiner's discretion A failure in any part of the examination constitutes a failure in the whole.

.1 这种考试由20题组成，分两部分。第一部分要求考生写出给定字母或数字的莫尔斯符号，第二部分要求考生写出给定莫尔斯符号的字母或数字。

.2 这种考试的及格分数是20，限于15分钟内完成。

.3 每一次考试提供四份不同的考卷，由主考人判断用其中哪一份。

7. 多项选择题考试

.1 有六组通信考试，编号为通信1~6，每组包含了两份小册子，即第一部分和第二部分。其中，第6类通信考试的两个部分是作为样本的，但也经常用于考试。

.2 第一部分有20道题，主要是编码、一般知识以及莫尔斯通信、旗号通信和语音通信程序。这部分考试可以参考以下的出版物：

《1969年国际信号规则》
《航海无线电设备》
《航海通告年度摘要》

.3 第二部分有25道题，主要是遇险、救生、安全和单字母信号旗。这部分不允许使用任何出版物。但是，这部分不能出现误导性的问题。

多项选择题考试的程序

.4 申请人首先应该进行的是选择题考试的第一部分，出版物列于第7.2段。这种考试的时间是一小时，然后收起小册子和出版物，并发下选择题考试的第二部分。第二部分也是一个小时的作答时间。

.5 第一部分和第二部分应该在同一份答题纸上作答，但要分别进行评估。第一部分，要通过考试需要答对14题（即70%），而第二部分需要答对17题（即68%）。两部分中的任何一部分所得分数低于及格分，申请人不能通过多项选择题考试。

8. 第一部分和第二部分的答案要单独提供。

9. 信号考试三个部分的顺序在第1节列出，多项选择题考试使用的目录单由主考人自行决定。考试的任何一部分不及格，则整个考试就不及格。

Communications

11. In assessing ability to use the radiotelephone, an assessment should also be made of the candidate's ability to express himself clearly in communications in English respecting meteorological information and messages concerning the ship's safety and operation as well as his understanding and use of the IMO Standard Marine Navigational Vocabulary.

Assessment of ability using simulators

12. The use of simulators to assess the abilities of candidates in performing practical tasks and using shipboard equipment is not mandatory, but is a method which is being used increasingly. Simulators offer the best method of both developing practical skills and assessing practical abilities.

    The revised Convention contains extensive mandatory requirements and guidance concerning performance standards for simulators, although equipment in use before 1 February 2002 may be exempted from such standards.

    The use of radar and ARPA simulators in training and as a method of demonstrating competence is a mandatory requirement for watchkeepers in the deck department (see STCW 95 Section A-I/12).

Deck personnel

13. The abilities of deck personnel in using electronic navigational aids and loading instruments and their practical management of ballast and cargo operations are now commonly tested on simulators, and increasing use of ship manoeuvring simulators is being made to develop and assess skills in ship-handling.

14. The following guidelines are typical of those developed for the purposes of assessing the abilities of deck department personnel in external or internal examinations:

    Examination Evaluation Guidelines

    Watchkeeping level

    1. For qualification at the watchkeeping level, any of the following will lead to automatic failure:

        .1 Having a collision or running aground
        .2 Failure to produce the required plot
        .3 Ending the exercise without being instructed to do so.

    2. The allotment of marks for the evaluation of sections and the overall examination will be as tabulated hereunder:

通信

11. 在评估使用无线电话的能力时,也应该评估申请人在下列通信中用英语清楚地表达自己的能力,例如关于气象资料,关系到船舶安全和操作的信息,同时也要评估申请人对IMO标准海事通信用语的理解和运用。

评估使用模拟器的能力

12. 运用模拟器评估申请人完成实际工作和使用船上设备的能力不是强制的,但这种方法的使用却越来越普遍。模拟器在发展实际技能和评估实际操作能力两个方面提供了最好的方法。

    在有关模拟器的性能标准方面,修正的公约包含了广泛的强制性要求。对于正在使用的设备在2002年2月1日之前可免除这些标准。

    在培训中使用雷达和ARPA模拟器并将其作为表明适任的方法对于甲板部值班人员是强制性要求(见STCW 95公约第A-Ⅰ/12节)。

甲板部人员

13. 甲板部人员使用电子助航仪器、进行货物积载以及实际管理压载和货物操作的能力现在通常都借助模拟器进行测试,船舶操纵中更多使用模拟器,可以在船舶操纵方面发展和评价甲板部人员的技能。

14. 以下典型指南是为在外部或内部考试中评估甲板部人员的能力而开发的:

    ### 考试评估指南

    值班等级

    1. 对于各值班等级的资格,发生下面任何一项失误都将自动导致评估失败:

        .1 发生了碰撞或搁浅
        .2 未按要求进行标绘
        .3 未经同意就终止练习。

    2. 可通过以下的表格说明各部分评估时的分数分配和考试的总体情况:

Manual plotting is to be allotted 35% of marks
Manoeuvring is to be allotted 30% of marks
Navigation is to be allotted 15% of marks
Use of electronic aids is to be allotted 10% of marks
Miscellaneous is to be allotted 10% of marks

The candidate is required to obtain 70% to pass.

Item	Data	Marks to be awarded
PLOTTING		
Principles	Correct construction of vector diagrams	17 or 0
Report	CPA yes/no	1 or 0
	TCPA yes/no	1 or 0
	Course yes/no	1 or 0
	Speed yes/no	1 or 0
	Aspect yes/no	1 or 0
Precision	*Target No. 1*	
	CPA within 5% of range	1 or 0
	TCPA within 3 minutes	1 or 0
	Course within 5°	1 or 0
	Speed within 2 knots	1 or 0
	Target No. 2	
	(As No. 1)	4, 3, 2, 1 or 0
Labelling of plot	Symbols on vectors	1 or 0
	Times	1 or 0
	Use of standardized labels	1 or 0
Verification	Continued plotting of targets	2 or 0
MANOEUVRING		
Manoeuvring according to COLREG	Appropriateness of manoeuvre	10 or 0
Effect of manoeuvre with respect to dangerous targets	Achieved CPA within 5% of radar range	4 or 0
Verify the effect of the manoeuvre with respect to 2nd target	yes/no	5 or 0
Verify the effect of the manoeuvre with respect to preplanned path	yes/no	5 or 0
Manoeuvre to resume original course, speed and track	yes/no	5 or 0
NAVIGATION		
Charted course		3 or 0
Chartwork practices		3 or 0
Subsequent position fixing		3 or 0
Initial position	5% of range to nearest hazard	3 or 0

人工标绘分配总分的35%

操纵分配总分的30%

航行分配总分的15%

电子助航仪器的使用分配总分的10%

杂项分配总分的10%

要求申请人获得70%的分数才算及格。

项目	内容	得分
标绘		
原理	正确作出矢量图	17分或0分
报告	CPA　　　　对/错	1分或0分
	TCPA　　　对/错	1分或0分
	航向　　　　对/错	1分或0分
	航速　　　　对/错	1分或0分
	目标舷角　　对/错	1分或0分
精确度	一号目标	
	CPA　　　　量程的5%之内	1分或0分
	TCPA　　　3分钟之内	1分或0分
	航向　　　　5°之内	1分或0分
	航速　　　　2节之内	1分或0分
	二号目标（与一号目标相同）	4,3,2,1或0分
标绘符号	矢量符号	1分或0分
	时间	1分或0分
	标准符号的使用	1分或0分
验证	对目标继续标绘	2分或0分
操纵		
根据《国际海上避碰规则》操纵	操纵的正确性	10分或0分
有关的危险目标对操纵的影响	得到的CPA在雷达量程的5%范围内	4分或0分
证明2号目标对操纵的影响	是/否	5分或0分
证明预先计划航线对操纵的影响	是/否	5分或0分
恢复原来航向、航速和航迹的操纵	是/否	5分或0分
航行		
标示航向		3分或0分
海图作业练习		3分或0分
连续定位		3分或0分
初始位置	最接近危险距离的5%	3分或0分

Item	Data	Marks to be awarded
Precision of position fixing	5% of range to nearest hazard	3 or 0
ELECTRONIC NAVIGATIONAL AIDS		
VHF procedure		3 or 0
Initial set up of radar		5 or 0
Set up of other electronic instruments		3 or 0
MISCELLANEOUS		
Master's orders	Comply with	5 or 0
Logs, publications	Use appropriately	5 or 0

Command level

3. For qualification at the command level the examination will be evaluated in accordance with the following guidelines.

   .1 A total of 100 marks is allotted, 70 marks being required to obtain a pass.

Item	Marks to be awarded
Planning	0 to 20
Execution	0 to 20
Interpretation of Collision Regulations	0 to 20
Use of available information	0 to 20
Overall comprehension of global problems posed by the exercise	0 to 20

Engineering personnel

15. The availability of engine-room simulators also offers the opportunity of testing the abilities of candidates for engineer officer certificates.

The following guidelines are typical of those for the purposes of assessing the abilities of engineer officers in external or internal examinations. The example relates to a large bulk carrier whose main propulsion machinery is a single-acting long-stroke supercharged diesel engine which uses marine diesel oil for manoeuvring and heavy fuel oil (380 cSt) when running at sea:

Examination Evaluation Guidelines

Watchkeeping level

1. Exercise scenario

The exercise is carried out in conjunction with a simulator which is representative of a modem merchant vessel propulsion plant.

Improper procedures, or non-observance of safe working practices, will result in a penalty of negative arks, and in extreme cases will mean automatic failure.

项目	内容	得分
定位精度	最接近危险距离的5%	3分或0分
电子导航设备		
VHF通信程序		3分或0分
雷达的初始安装		5分或0分
其他电子设备的安装		3分或0分
杂项		
船长命令	服从	5分或0分
航海日志、出版物	正确地使用	5分或0分

指挥水平

3. 为了评价指挥水平,考试应该根据以下的指南进行评估。

   .1 总分是100分,要求获得70分才算及格:

项目	得分
计划	0到20分
执行	0到20分
避碰规则的解释	0到20分
资料的有效利用	0到20分
训练中综合疑难问题的全面理解	0到20分

轮机员

15. 机舱模拟器的有效使用也可提供测试轮机员证书申请人能力的机会。

在评估轮机员能力的外部或内部考试中,可应用以下典型的指南。这一例子适用于大型散货船,它的主机是单作用、长冲程、增压式柴油机,操纵时使用柴油,而在海上航行时则使用重质燃油(380 cSt)。

考试评估指南

值班等级

1. 训练方案

训练是借助一些能代表现代商船推进设备的模拟器进行的。

不标准的程序或者不遵守安全有效训练,将被处罚扣分。在极端情况下将会被自动视为不及格。

The scenario will have four main elements:

.1 Preparation of the propulsion plant and other auxiliary and ancillary systems necessary for manoeuvring and making a sea voyage

.2 With the ship at sea and making its voyage, the procedures for taking over and accepting an engine-room watch

.3 Watchkeeping routines and duties

.4 With the main engine controls at normal service speed:
  .i obtain indicator diagrams
  .ii using the diagrams, evaluate the power output

2. Allocation of marks

   .1 Preparation of plant, manoeuvring and setting sea voyage conditions 25% of marks

   .2 Procedures for taking over and accepting an engine-room watch 25% of marks

   .3 Watchkeeping routines and duties 30% of marks

   .4 Obtaining indicator diagrams and evaluating power output 20% of marks

   The candidate is required to obtain 70% to pass.

3. Evaluation programme

   .1 Preparation of plant, manoeuvring and setting sea voyage conditions

Item	Data	Marks to be awarded
Use of Checklists	observing that the listed fluids are circulating properly at the required temperature and pressure: — seawater — fresh water — lubricating oil — fuel oil	0–5
Use of Checklists	— engine turning gear withdrawn — concerning that bridge/engine-room — communications are operative — consuming that cylinder lubrication is functioning — concerning that starting air is available — turns the engine one revolution on air with indicator cocks open	0–8

训练方案有四个主要方面：

    .1   推进器、其他辅助设备、操纵和海上航行辅助系统的准备

    .2   船舶在海上航行并完成整个航程，采用的程序和承担的机舱值班

    .3   值班规则和职责

    .4   在标准运营速度下主机的控制：
        .i   获取指示器图表
        .ii   利用图表，评估功率输出

2.   分数的分配

    .1   设备的准备、操纵及设置海上航行环境，占总分的25%

    .2   采用的程序和承担机舱值班，占总分的25%

    .3   值班规则和职责，占总分的30%

    .4   获取指示器图表及评估功率输出，占总分的20%

要求申请人获得总分的70%才算及格。

3.   评估计划

    .1   设备的准备、操纵及设置海上航行环境

项目	内容	得分
检查表的使用	观察列出的流体，在要求的湿度和压力下正常循环： — 海水 — 淡水 — 润滑油 — 燃油	0~5分
检查表的使用	— 机器旋转装置退出 — 注意驾驶台/机舱通信的有效性 — 确保汽缸润滑作用正常 — 注意起动气体的供应正常 — 机器示功器旋塞打开并在空气中旋转一周	0~8分

Item	Data	Marks to be awarded
Applies starting procedures	— confirms that all indicator cocks are closed — confirms fuel is circulating — confirms to bridge, "engine available" — starts engine when order is received from bridge — continues to manoeuvre, in accordance with bridge orders	0–6
Establishes normal running mode for making sea voyage	checks and establishes normal operating temperatures and pressures of: — lubricating oil — seawater — fresh water — heavy fuel oil — exhaust gas — turbocharger conditions	0–6

.2 Procedures for taking over and accepting an engine-room watch

Item	Data	Marks to be awarded
Inspection	enters engine-room 15 minutes before the watch is to change: — inspects all operational units, noting conditions and any deviation from normal — checks water level in steam boiler (if a boiler is part of the plant) — inspects bilge and underfloor spaces — inspects steering gear (this is usually outside the engine-room, and can be inspected en route to engine-room)	0–8
Observing and noting	observes, notes and, where necessary, checks: — telegraph instruction from bridge — engine control position and engine rpm — engine-room log — quantities in service tanks (fuel, water, lube. oil)	0–6
Report	receives report from engineer officer in charge of watch for period now being completed	0–5
Recording	records in the engine-room log any observations regarding operating conditions noted during inspection and worthy of comment	0–3
Responsibility	if satisfied, accepts responsibility and takes over engine-room watch	0–3

项目	内容	得分
起动程序的应用	— 确信所有示功器旋塞关闭 — 确信燃油正在循环 — 通知驾驶台机器已可用 — 当收到从驾驶台发出的命令时起动机器 — 根据驾驶台的命令继续操纵	0~6分
为海上航行设置标准的运行模式	检查并设置标准操作温度和压力： — 润滑油 — 海水 — 淡水 — 重燃油 — 排出气体 — 涡轮增压器的状态	0~6分

.2 接班的程序和担任机舱值班

项目	内容	得分
检查	换班前15分钟进入机舱 — 检查所有运转部件,记下状态以及与正常状态的任何偏差 — 检查蒸汽锅炉里的水位(如果锅炉是设备的一部分) — 检查舱底污水和底层舱 — 检查操舵装置(通常在机舱外面,可以在去机舱途中检查)	0~8分
观察和记录	观察、记录、必要时检查 — 从驾驶台传令钟发出的指令 — 主机控制位置和主机转速(r/min) — 轮机日志 — 日用舱内贮存量(燃油、水、润滑油)	0~6分
报告	接收负责机舱值班的轮机员有关值班期间进行的尚未完成的工作报告	0~5分
记录	把任何检查期间观察到的有关机器的运行状态和有价值的意见记录在轮机日志上	0~3分
职责	如果达到令人满意的标准,承担职责并履行机舱值班	0~3分

.3   Watchkeeping routines and duties

Item	Data	Marks to be awarded
Inspection	at regular internals, inspects all operational machinery units in and outside the engine-room (i.e. including steering gear and bilge spaces, tunnel recess etc.), correcting any deviation from normal operating mode	0-10
Operation	— operates centrifuges as necessary (complying with anti-pollution requirements) to maintain service tank levels — operates bilge pump as necessary — transfers fuel, fresh water, etc.	0-10
Checking and noting	— checks all temperatures and pressures and notes them as necessary in the engine-room log, — checks periodically the water level in the steam boiler and adds extra feed if necessary, — checks: 　— main engine cylinder lubrication 　— electrical plant and system board 　— compressed air system 　— all engine-room service tanks, topping up as necessary	0-10

.4   Obtaining indicator diagrams and evaluating power output

Item	Data	Marks to be awarded
Setting up equipment	— checks indicator and related equipment, springs, supply of "cards", actuating mechanism, etc. — checks indicator cocks are clear by opening by a small amount (on the simulator this may not be possible, but can be checked by Q & A session)	0-5
Operating instrument	checking that engine controls are correctly set, the indicator is operated on each cylinder in turn, obtaining a set of diagrams. (in practice about 3 sets would be obtained)	0-5
Calculation	Using a planimeter, the area enclosed by the diagram is measured. The method is to make four measurements and take the average value. Divide this by the length of the diagram and the mean height is obtained. Using the spring constant for the indicator, this will derive the mean effective pressure, from which the power can be calculated. (NOTE: The simulator will probably provide a diagram where top centre is at mid length, so that fuel injection can be studied)	0-10

.3 值班规则和职责

项目	内容	得分
检查	定期对机舱内外所有的运行机器部件进行检查(包括操舵装置、污水舱、螺旋桨轴隧槽,等等),修正与正常运行方式的偏差	0~10分
操作	— 如需要(符合防污的要求),操作离心泵保持日用水舱的水位 — 如需要,操作污水泵 — 转移燃油、淡水等	0~10分
检查和记录	— 检查所有温度和压力数据,必要时记录在轮机日志上 — 定期检查蒸汽锅炉里的水位,必要时加水 — 检查: — 主机汽缸润滑油 — 电气设备和系统配电盘 — 压缩空气系统 — 所有机舱日用油柜,必要时加满	0~10分

.4 获取指示器图表及评估功率输出数据

项目	内容	得分
设置设备	— 检查指示器及相关的设备、弹簧、各种供给"图"、传动机械等 — 将示功器旋塞打开一点,检查是否无阻塞(在模拟器上不可能做到这一点,但可以通过问答的方式进行检查)	0~5分
操作设备	检查主机控制器是否正确设置,指示器交替显示每个汽缸的情况并获得一组图(在实际中大约可获得三组图)	0~5分
计算	利用求积仪,可以量取由曲线围成的面积。这种方法可得出四种测量结果,然后求平均值。把测量的面积除以曲线图的长度就可求出平均高度。利用指示器的弹簧常数,可得出平均有效压力,据此可以计算出功率。 (注:模拟器可能提供一张曲线图,图的中心位于长度的中点处,据此可以研究燃料的注入情况)	0~10分

Part 15
Shipboard Assessment System

Development of Shipboard Assessment System

An introductory briefing should contain a description of the "learning style" of the course, by emphasizing its "participative" and "interactive" nature. In this connection, the extensive use of group work and exercises should be introduced, together with a summary of work management in groups keeping in mind that both group work and interactive training will be dealt with in detail later.

First, it is important to distinguish "education" from "training". Education usually means the preparation for careers and for life in general, which involves the learning concepts, principles, problem-solving methods etc., whereas training rather means the preparation for a specific job or set of tasks. The content of a training course is therefore more specialized than an educational programme. Some training courses contain supportive elements which many would describe as educational. This often applies to long courses.

The basic premise is that training involves LEARNING which is designed to change the PERFORMANCE of PEOPLE doing JOBS.

The four capitalized words in the definition—learning, performance, people, jobs—embraces quite a lot about training. The relationship between the terms becomes even more involved.

Training courses are often said to be aimed at skill development implying that they are not knowledge-based, however training often requires the learning of knowledge.

It is worthwhile to take each component of the definition of training and examine it more thoroughly, beginning with the last word in the definition—JOBS. By doing this it is possible to emphasize the importance of the jobs to the design of learning. Further, as will be seen later, the trainer should begin the process of planning a training programme with some ideas and information about the work which has to be done.

Jobs

Jobs are made up of a number of specific tasks that people do. The number of tasks, their complexity and difficulty, and the relationship between them vary widely from job to job. The knowledge, skills and attitudes required for job performance vary. Also there is often a range of acceptable differences in the way individuals do the same job. Nevertheless, there is usually a core of tasks and skills which are the same for a given type of job. If training is to improve job performance, the job itself must be fully understood.

People

When dealing with adults doing jobs, one must take account of the fact that the trainee brings to the training situation existing knowledge, skills and attitudes regarding that job, as well as ways of learning. This necessitates paying attention not only to the aims of training, but also to the aims—and existing skills, knowledge and attitudes of the LEARNER.

第15章
船上评估体系

船上评估体系的开发

导言中的简介部分已包含了对课程"学习方式"的说明,强调其"共享性"和"交互性"。在这种结合中,广泛采用分组作业和练习。分组管理工作纲要、分组作业和交互性培训将在稍后详细讨论。

首先,最重要的是区别"教育"与"培训"。教育通常是指为日后的职业和生活做准备,涉及学习概念、原理、解决问题的方法等方面,而培训却是为具体的工作或任务所做准备。因此,培训课程的内容比教育课程更加专业化。一些培训课程包括了很多从教育角度上讨论过的、对培训有所帮助的内容。这通常适用于时间较长的培训课程。

培训包含了为改变"人们工作表现"而设计的"学习"的基本内容。

"学习""表现""人们""工作"四个词在定义上大部分都与培训有关。这些术语之间的关系在培训中变得更加密切。

培训课程通常被认为是以技能开发为目的,这意味着它们不是以学习知识为目标,然而培训中通常要求对知识进行学习。

了解"培训"这一定义中的每个成分是很有价值的,并且通常是以最后一个词"工作"开始对它们进行更全面的研究。通过这样做,可以强调工作对于学习设计的重要性。而且,正如后面将要看到的,教练员的整个培训过程应该从设计附有对工作的建议和相关资料的培训计划开始。

工作

工作由人们承担的若干具体任务组成。任务的数量、复杂和困难程度以及两者之间的关系随着工作的不同会有很大的变化。完成工作需要的知识、技能和态度也有所不同。做同样的工作,不同的人在可接受的范围内,采用的方法也常常存在差异。不过,对于给定种类的工作,其中心任务和技能通常是相同的。如果要使培训能改善工作表现,则必须充分理解工作本身。

人员

在涉及工作中的人员的问题时,必须考虑到这样的事实,即学员已具备的与工作相关的现有知识、技能和态度以及学习的方法。不仅要注意培训目的,而且应注意"学习者"目前的技能、知识和态度。

	Training	Assessment
Traditional	What providers believe is "good" for trainees to know	Trainee performance is assessed relative to performance of other trainees

What is Competence-based Training and Assessment?

Performance

The performance of people doing jobs means how well they carry out the tasks that make up their job.

When job performance is judged and found to be below standard, training may change job performance. This approach to training is based on the need to change job performance, not on the other often used reasons for training, such as informing, motivating or rewarding. Generally, there is a need to change job performance when:

- the employee does not know how to do all or part of his/her current job

- the employee is given new tasks requiring new knowledge, skills or attitudes

- the employee is given an entirely new job requiring new knowledge, skills or attitudes.

Each of these may require a different training policy or strategy, or they may require no training at all, as we will see later.

Generally, training is needed when discrepancies exist between what an employee is expected to do and what he/she actually does, and only then if these discrepancies can be reduced through learning. It is important to recognize the difference between the symptoms, e.g poor performance, and the causes.

Learning

The world "learning" generally refers to a change of some kind in the learner. Such changes are often classified as:

- Psycho-motor—physical and manipulative skills such as those required to operate equipment, a machine or an instrument.

- Cognitive—the ability to recall learned materials, and the development of thinking skills.

- Affective—attitudes, values and interests.

	基于适任的培训和评估是什么？	
	培训	评估
传统的方法	对培训者而言想了解什么样的培训机构是"好的"	对受培训者的表现进行评估与其他受培训者的表现有关

实操

人们工作的表现指他们对其工作任务的完成情况。

当判断并发现他们的工作表现低于标准时，通过培训可以改变其工作表现。培训是基于改变工作表现的需要，并不是其他常见的原因，例如增长见闻、追求理想或者报酬。通常在发生如下情况时，有必要改进工作表现：

- 雇员不知道怎样做所有/或部分的手头工作

- 分配给雇员的新任务需要新的知识、技能或态度

- 指派雇员做一份全新的工作，需要新的知识、技能或态度。

上述每种情况都需要不同的培训方针或策略，或者像我们以后看到的那样，他们根本就不需要再培训。

通常，只有在期望雇员去做与其实际能力之间有差距的工作，并且这些差距可以通过学习减少时才需要接受培训。认识各种表现（例如拙劣的表现）的差异和原因是很重要的。

学习

"学习"一词通常是指学习者某些方面的改变。这些改变通常按如下分类：

- 心理—运动的——体能和手工操作的技能，例如要求操作设备、机器或仪器。

- 认知的——回忆已学知识的能力，以及思考能力的发展。

- 情绪上的——态度、生活理想和兴趣。

Testing

Testing is a procedure used to measure a sample of behaviour in order to discover how well a student performs, usually in comparison with others, or compared with identified performance criteria. In this context it is important that the test, in whatever form it is being used, yields consistent results by being valid, reliable and practical. Whilst we can only take a sample of a person's knowledge or comprehension about a topic in this way, testing methods do provide a more reliable estimate of performance than most other observational techniques; unsystematic or irregular observation being too unreliable.

With measurement, we are concerned with getting a statement of performance, i.e. how much?, against some established scale or rule, usually expressed in a quantitative form although it may be non-numerical. During this process information and data is being gathered but it must be systematic, valid and reliable.

Assessment

Assessment can be considered as placing an interpretation on measurement information and is usually concerned with assigning a score, mark, grade or ranking. Assessment procedures (e.g norm-referenced assessment, criteria-referenced assessment and goal-based assessment) may be used to make judgements and decisions about students, lecturers, courses, resources or curricula. Judgements about the value of such data are properly the role of evaluation. Evaluation depends upon both measurement and assessment and is concerned with the assignment of worth or merit to particular performances, behaviours, or processes.

Purpose of assessment

Students are assessed with a view to finding out the extent of their knowledge, understanding and skill, and how well they have learned. In general there are several recognised main purposes for assessment, namely motivating students, grading for advancement (further studies, career, etc.), standards setting and providing feedback to students and teachers. Their impact on the assessment process can be varied however and the lecturer setting the assignment, test or examination must be clear about the objectives of such assessment if it is to achieve its purpose.

Assessment is only one inter-linked part of the teaching process model (objectives, syllabus and assessment) and may be permitted to dominate it if care is not exercised. It is a fact of life that if marks are not an outcome in some form or other, students will not be motivated to put in their best effort. If practical work is not assessed or does not contribute to assessment, then students will ignore it. The lecturer faces the challenge of selecting and creating the most effective and relevant assessment method.

Methods of assessment

In considering the methods to be used, it is worth bearing in mind some of the factors which can contribute to a student's score:

测试

测试是用于衡量行为表现的一种途径,目的是发现学生表现得好/差程度,常常通过与其他学生比较或者与认可的行为标准比较进行。在本纲要中的测试都很重要,无论使用什么形式,都应产生有效的、可靠的、符合实际的成绩。有时我们用这种方法获得的可能仅是个人某一方面的知识和理解能力,但与大多数其他考察技术相比,测试方法提供了一种比其他不系统或不规则的考察更加可靠的评估表现的方法。

对于考试手段,我们关心的是其能在多大程度上判定表现得好/差程度。依靠某些已经建立的尺度和规则,即使评测结果可能是非数值的,通常仍然可以用定量的形式表示。在这一过程中,可以收集资料和数据,但必须是系统性的、有依据的并且是可靠的。

评估

评估被认为是对评价信息的解释,常常涉及分数的分配、评分、分级或者等级评定。评估程序(例如参照常模的评估、参照标准的评估、基于目标的评估)可用于对学生、训导员、课程、资源或全部课程进行判断和决定。评估的作用是对这些数据的价值进行正常地判断。评估依赖于评测和评价两方面,并且涉及财物的分配或者对特殊表现、行为或方法进行奖励。

评估目的

通过对学生进行检查、评估,可以发现他们的知识、理解和技能的范围以及他们学习的情况。通常有几种公认的主要评估目的,即激发学生、对晋升(进一步的学习、职务等)进行分级、设定标准以及向学生和老师提供反馈信息。然而,评估目标对过程是会发生影响的,因此,负责设定、分配测试或考试的讲师必须对评价目标十分清楚,以达到评估目的。

评估仅仅是教学过程(包括目标、课程大纲和评估)的一个内部环节,如果无须考虑别的因素,则可以充分应用其功能。但实际上,如果评估分数不能作为某种形式的学习成果,则不能激发学生尽自己的最大努力参与。如果评估与实际工作不相关,那么学生也会忽视它。因此,讲师面临的挑战是选择和建立最有效、最恰当的评估方法。

评估方法

在考虑评估方法时,应注意对学生成绩有影响的一些因素:

- General level of intelligence.

- Knowledge, skills and ability in the tested area.

- Ability to understand instructions.

- Skill and experience in sitting for examinations and in answering the type of question used.

- "Luck" in choosing questions and guessing answers.

- Student health, fatigue, motivation, stress, memory fluctuation.

- Combining of examination results.

- Unreliability of marking.

The chance or uncertainty element in the above can be reduced by:

- Keeping instructions clear and simple.

- Avoiding difficult vocabulary or irrelevant special knowledge.

- Providing students with pre-assessment experience and adequate motivation.

- Controlling assessment conditions.

Development of Competence-based Assessment

Up to the present time, most Certificate of Competency examinations conducted ashore have tested KNOWLEDGE rather than SKILLS. Both knowledge and skills are needed and it is on board ship that real competence must be demonstrated.

Knowledge-based assessments are usually in the form of written and oral examinations.

Skill-based assessments are usually in the form of observation of the candidate's practical knowledge.

Competence-based assessment incorporates the assessment of:

- skills to specified standards

- relevant knowledge and understanding

- ability to use skills and apply knowledge and understanding to the performance of relevant task

- 综合智力水平。

- 测试范围内的知识、技巧和能力。

- 对指令的理解能力。

- 参加考试和回答常用种类题目的技巧和经验。

- 在挑选题目和猜测答案方面的"运气"。

- 学生的健康、疲劳、积极性、压力、记忆波动状况。

- 考试成绩的组合状况。

- 评分的不可靠性。

可以通过以下方法减少以上因素中的偶然性或不确定性因素：

- 保持指令的清楚和简单。

- 避免使用困难的词汇或不相关的特殊知识。

- 提供学生预评估的练习以及足够的激励。

- 控制评估环境。

适任评估的开发

到目前为止，大部分在岸上进行的适任证书考试是对"知识"而不是"技能"的测试。知识和技能两者都是必要的，申请人必须表明对于船上工作的真正适任。

基于知识的评估通常采用笔试和口试的形式。

基于技能的评估通常采用考察申请人的实际知识形式。

适任评估结合了以下的评估：

- 规定标准的技能

- 相关的知识和理解

- 使用技巧和运用知识的能力以及对完成相关任务的理解

Assessment is about the collection of evidence. All forms of assessment can be included in this description—from everyday activities to the most complex statistical system.

The choice of assessment methods for a particular task should take into considerations factors that may influence it such as:

- assessment objectives
- qualifications of candidates
- the comparative effectiveness of different assessment methods
- constraints of time
- availability of facilities
- cost
- hazards

The purpose of assessment within a programme of learning is to collect sufficient evidence to demonstrate that trainees have learned at least the required minimum percentage of the syllabus. If the programme of learning is also linked to an award system, a further purpose may be the achievement of formal recognition that learning has been acquired. This usually takes the form of a certificate or diploma.

In a competence-based assessment system, the purpose of assessment is to collect sufficient evidence that individuals can perform or behave to the specified standards in a specific role. If this assessment is also linked to an award system, a further purpose is formal recognition of successful performance.

These facts were recognised when the STCW Convention was revised. The revised Convention aims to ensure that seafarers in the future will be fully competent. It is necessary to ensure that formal assessment is properly organised, carried out and recorded. It will be necessary to ensure that the evidence gathered is acceptable to national authorities responsible for issuing certificates of competency.

It should also be remembered that there are specified requirements for continued professional competence and revalidation of certificates, and refresher and updating training.

The Assessment Process

A process is a "series of actions or events", or a "sequence of operations". We could say that all forms of assessment involve the following sequence of operations:

- defining requirements or objectives of assessment;
- collecting evidence;

评估就是证据的收集。所有形式的评估都可以这样描述——从日常活动到最复杂的统计系统的评价。

对特殊任务的评估方法的选择应该考虑可能对其产生影响的因素，例如：

- 评估目标

- 申请人资格

- 不同评估方法的比较效果

- 对时间的限定

- 设备的利用率

- 费用

- 危险性

学习计划内的评估目的是收集足够证据来表明学员至少已经学完大纲所要求的最低比例的内容。如果学习计划也与评价系统相关联，更具体的目标可能是对已经学到知识的正式认可。这样通常会取得某种类型的证书或者文凭。

在适任评估体系中，评估的目的是收集足够证据，证明被评估人在具体任务中能够按规定标准执行或表现。更具体的目的是对成功表现的正式认可。

STCW公约修改时也对以上方面做了考虑。修正案的目标是确保海员将来能完全地适任。有必要确保正式评估恰当地组织、开展和记录，也必须确保收集的证据是负责适任证书颁发的国家机构可以接受的。

也要记住在继续具备适任能力、证书的再有效以及知识更新培训方面都规定了具体的要求。

评估过程

过程是指"一系列行为或事件"，或者"一连串操作"。我们可以说所有形式的评估都涉及以下一连串的操作：

- 确定评估的要求和目标；

- 收集证据；

- matching evidence to requirements or objectives;
- making judgements based on this matching activity.

Competence-Based Assessment

You may notice some key features in the competence-based assessment approach:

- focus on "outcomes";
- individualized assessment;
- no percentage rating;
- no comparison with other individuals' results;
- all standards (requirements) must be met;
- on-going process (leads to further development and assessment);
- only "competent" or "not yet competent" judgements made.

As we have already noted, the purpose of competence-based assessment is:

To collect sufficient evidence to demonstrate that individuals can perform or behave to the specified standards in a specified role.

We can add to this definition by clarifying that in competence-based assessment we are referring to work roles and therefore to standards of occupational competence. Occupational competence reflects performance at work. Our definition of the purpose of competence-based assessment will therefore look like this:

To collect sufficient evidence of workplace performance to demonstrate that individuals can perform or behave to the specified standards required within a specified occupational role.

This differs drastically from traditional forms of occupational assessment in which evidence collected relates to what has been learned. In competence-based assessment, our key concern is actual performance. Our focus is therefore, on what individuals can do rather than what individuals know.

This outlines the key purpose of competence-based assessment. The issue of "perform" vs "behave" in the definition above will depend on whether we have set vocational outcomes or behavioural outcomes as the basis of our competence system.

- 把证据与要求或目标比对；
- 根据比对情况做出判断。

适任评估

你可能已经注意到在适任评估方法中的某些关键特征：

- 焦点集中在"成绩"；
- 个体化地进行评估；
- 不用百分制分数表示评估结果；
- 不与他人的成绩进行比较；
- 必须满足所有标准；
- 评估是持续性的（导向进一步的职业发展和进一步的评估）；
- 只做出"适任"或"不适任"的结论。

我们也已经知道，适任评估的目的是：

收集充分的可以表明申请人能够按规定标准履行某项职务的证据。

这一定义可以进一步加以清楚解释，适任评估是针对岗位工作和职业适任标准的评估。职业适任反映了工作中的表现。因此，适任评估的目的可以用以下内容定义：

收集充分的岗位工作表现证据以证明申请人能够在职业岗位上按要求的规定标准履行职责和工作。

以上定义与传统的职业评估有很大区别，后者主要收集的是所学知识的证据。在适任评估中，关键的证据是实际工作表现。因此，我们关注的是申请人能够干什么而不是知道什么。

由于适任评估的关键目的是评价表现证据，因此，上述的"履行"和"工作"是否胜任的判定将取决于是否已经确定了合适的职业成绩标准，还取决于这些成绩标准能否作为适任系统的基础。

Practical Implications of Competence-Based Assessment

The introduction of competence-based assessment at national, organizational or departmental level has wide implications for managers, for trainers, and for those being assessed.

Unlike traditional forms of occupation-related assessment, competence-based assessment can be, and should be, undertaken in the workplace, and should be individualized.

Who Assesses?

The first question then is if assessment is to be undertaken in the workplace, who are the assessors?

The most obvious choice is the person who has the necessary knowledge and competence in the particular task to be assessed. This arrangement raises a number of questions:

- Do shipboard officers have time to undertake formal assessment?
- What if the officers or assessor doesn't like or has a poor relationship with the person being assessed?
- What skills will assessors need?
- What about quality?

The second implication concerns the movement of assessment to a local rather than a central basis:

- How can quality of assessment be assured if it is undertaken locally by shipboard officers?
- Who trains assessors?
- Who ensures that quality of assessment is maintained?
- Who pays for this?

The IMO competence-based assessment system is introduced for certification of seafarers in the revision to the STCW Convention.

We also need to consider what other purposes competence-based assessment can be put to within shipboard organization, and what resources we will need.

适任评估的内涵

国家级、企业(组织)级和部门级几类不同级别的适任评估对于管理人员、培训人员和被评估人员有着不同的内涵。

所有形式的职业评估、适任评估可以并且应该在工作现场评估,而且也应该是个体化的。

由谁担任评估员?

由于评估是在工作现场进行,那么,谁可以担任评估员?

正确选择的评估员是具备岗位的必要知识和适任相应工作的人员,这就产生了一些问题:

- 船上的高级船员是否有时间进行正规的评估工作?

- 如果高级船员或评估员不愿意做评估工作或者与被评估员的关系不好又怎么办?

- 评估员需要什么技能?

- 评估质量如何保证?

第二方面的问题涉及分散的而非集中的评估活动:

- 如果评估是由船上的高级船员承担,怎样才能保证评估的质量?

- 由谁培训评估员?

- 由谁来确保评估质量能够保持?

- 由谁来支付评估费用?

在 STCW 公约修正案中对海员发证的 IMO 适任评估体系做了相应规定。

我们也需要考虑有什么其他的适任评估目标也可以在船上组织,以及需要什么资源。

What about training?

Last but not least is the issue of linking competence-based assessment to training. As the assessment system operates on a continuous—rather than one-off—basis, and is operated within the workplace environment, training needs are identified at individual level. Questions here include:

- What systems do we need to ensure that identified training needs are communicated to those who can take relevant action?

- In what way do we need to reorganize our training resources to provide training which meets those needs?

For maritime training institutions and for shipping companies, the issues of resourcing, reorganization and administration are paramount.

Qualifications of Trainers and Assessors

All ships' officers are normally expected to play their part in training junior officers, cadets and crew members, passing on their knowledge and experience in their own specialist disciplines. They are also expected to evaluate the performance of trainees and provide evidence to be used as part of the certification process.

Those who are appointed with a specific and formal training or assessment role will need to pay attention to the more detailed provisions of the Standards of Training, Certification and Watchkeeping (STCW) Convention as follows. The mandatory Part A of the STCW Code requires that "each party shall ensure that instructors, supervisors and assessors are appropriately qualified for the particular types and levels of training or assessment of competence of seafarers either on board or ashore, as required under the convention ..." Part B of the code contains further guidance to assist in interpreting the requirements.

The STCW Code defines in-service training requirements. The main provisions affecting ships' officers are as follows:

1) Any person conducting in-service training of a seafarer... on board... which is intended to be used in qualifying for certification under the Convention shall:

   a. Have an appreciation of the training programme and an understanding of the specific training objectives for the particular type of training being conducted;

   b. Be qualified in the task for which training is being conducted; and...

2) Any person responsible for the supervision of in-service training of a seafarer intended to be used in qualifying for certification under the Convention shall have a full understanding of the training programme and the specific objectives for each type of training being conducted.

如何培训？

最后一个较重要的问题是与培训相关联的适任评估的发证问题。因为评估系统是在连续不断的而非断断续续的基础上运行的，并且是在工作现场的环境下运行，所以培训必须根据个人水平确定。问题包括：

- 必须采用什么系统来保证正确鉴别培训的需要并传达给采取相关行动的人？

- 必须采用什么方法来确定所提供的培训资源能满足这些需要？

对于航海培训机构和船公司来说，解决资源、重组及管理方面的问题是最重要的。

教员和评估员的资格

一般预期所有船上的高级船员可以发挥作用向培训初级干部船员、学生及普通船员传授自己在专业训练方面的知识和经验。他们也将评估学员的表现和提供证据，以作为认证过程的部分。

那些被指派负责具体、正规培训和评估的人员必须注意以下提供的培训、发证和值班公约（STCW公约）中更为详细的规定。STCW规则A部分强制性规定要求"各缔约国应确保教员、监督人员和评估人员完全胜任公约要求的船上或岸上特定种类和级别的培训或对海员适任能力的评估……"规则B部分包含了有助于解释这一要求的进一步指导。

STCW规则规定了在职培训的要求。对高级船员有影响的主要条款如下：

1) 在船上或岸上对海员进行培训时，旨在根据公约用于取得发证资格的在职培训的任何人员应：

   a. 对培训计划有正确认识并充分了解所进行的特定种类培训的具体目标；

   b. 胜任所进行的培训工作；及……

2) 针对海员旨在根据公约用于取得发证资格的在职培训负责监督的任何人员，应对培训计划和正在进行的各种培训的具体目标有充分了解。

3) Any person conducting in-service assessment of competence of a seafarer ... on board... which is intended to be used in qualifying for certification under the Convention shall:

   a. Have an appropriate level of knowledge and understanding of the competence to be assessed;

   b. Be qualified in the task for which assessment is being made:

   c. Have received appropriate guidance in assessment methods and practice;

   d. Have gained practical assessment experience.

Don't be put off by the jargon. It is not a new system. It is formalising a system which we have used for years, in which the real judges of competence are the senior staff who are responsible for the development of their juniors.

Further guidance on ship board assessment may be found in the MSC Circular—Circ.853: Guidance on On-board Assessment of 22 May 1998.

3) 在船上对海员进行旨在根据公约用于取得发证资格的在职适任评估的任何人员应：

  a. 对所评估的适任能力的知识和理解具有适当的水平；

  b. 胜任执行评估的任务；

  c. 接受过有关评估方法和实践的适当指导；

  d. 已获得评估的实际经验。

  不要被专用术语困扰。适任评估不是一个新的系统。它是正在定型的系统，这个系统我们已经用了多年，其中对是否适任的真正判定是由一些从资历浅发展到资深人员的人做出的。

  船上培训的更进一步指导可以在海上安全委员会1998年5月22日853号通告《船上评估指南》中找到。

Part 16
Performance Criteria for Shipboard Assessment

Identify of Performance Objectives

The main aim is to identify the performances, or non-performances, which lead to dire consequences if not properly carried out. Candidates should be briefed on the resource materials available to identify these performances. It should be pointed out that, all too often failure to perform or omission to perform certain critical step(s) in a given task results in unfavourable events leading to material/environmental/human sufferings. This will make the assessment more meaningful as it underscores the importance of ensuring that candidates acquire the competences required.

Select Performance Objectives for Shipboard Assessment

On-the-job assessment is undoubtably the better option than off-the-job assessment. It provides actual condition of work where the competences are needed, thus injecting realism. However, not all performances can be appropriately assessed on board the ship.

There are competences that seafarers need to attain prior to being assigned any shipboard duties, and these have to be assessed. For example, they need to receive basic safety training.

There are also constraints, such as the safety implications and the prevailing shipboard operating conditions, which make assessment on board a less suitable alternative for some performances.

The selection of the performance objectives for each individual candidate for shipboard assessment will therefore be based on three criteria. These are the candidate's current skill level, the safety consideration, and whether adequate controls can be established for the assessment period.

Determine Performance Measures and Standards

In the lecture the instructors should emphasize that the assessor must first establish the performance standards for the performances to be assessed, taking into consideration the function level of the competence required. Both performance criteria and assessment criteria should be clearly and explicitly identified, and be conveyed to the candidate.

Methods of measuring the performances should be selected based on objectivity in obtaining the measurement. These may include observation which is verifiable, recording of values from instruments, and time-clocking. The intention is to minimise the use of subjective judgements, so that the assessment outcome can be approached with discreet evidence.

第16章
船上评估的实操标准

实操目标的确定

主要目标是确定评估对象具备或者不具备规定的能力（后者指不能正确操作并会导致严重后果）。应该向申请人简要地介绍用于确定表现的资源。应该指出的是，在给定任务中，某些关键步骤频繁地出现错误操作或者疏忽导致物质/环境/人员损害的不愉快事件发生。这会令评估本身就像确保申请人获得所要求具备的能力一样具有重要意义。

船上实操评估目标的选择

在工作中评估无疑比离职评估要好，它提供了适任岗位的实际工作条件，因而很真实。然而，并非所有的项目都可以在船上进行相应的评估。

在被指派担任任何船上职责之前，海员必须具备某些能力，并且必须接受评估。例如，他们必须接受基本的安全培训。

船上评估也有一定局限性，例如安全性和船上的操作环境问题，这使得某些项目并不太适于在船上作评估。

因此对于每位申请人，船上实操现评估和实操目标的选择可基于三个标准。这三个标准分别是：申请人目前的技术水平、安全性考虑以及评估期间能否建立适当的监督。

确定实操评估方法及标准

在讲课中，教员应该强调：评估员必须首先参考要求适任的功能等级为被评估的项目设定表现标准。应该清楚明确表现标准和评估标准两方面，并传达给申请人。

评价表现的方法选择应该基于能够进行客观评价。这可能包括可证实的观测值、从仪器上记录的以及计时器的数值。目的是最低限度地采用主观判断，以便评估结果可以最完整地反映证据状况。

Assessment of competence

a. Reasons for assessment

A good assessment system should be used to measure trainees skills and knowledge at entry and as their training progresses. It should save time and minimize costs by allowing training to start at the correct point, avoid gaps and repetition and have seafarers skills recognized and recorded as evidence of competency for certification purposes.

b. Assessment at entry

The International Safety Management Code requires that each ship is manned with properly qualified seafarers. The company must identify the needs of all personnel on board, for training in support of the Safety Management System (SMS) and make proper provision for that training. It helps senior sea staff and trainers in planning shipboard training, if necessary checks and assessments are made before seafarers join the ship. Training needs can be assessed by interviews, by verifying certificates and checking documented evidence of earlier experience. To save time and ensure consistency, some companies and crewing agencies use computer-based tests related to the requirements of their ships and trades. One such system is the Videotel Seafarers Evaluation and Training System (SETS).

c. Informal assessment as part of a training programme

Senior staff and trainees do not have unlimited time for training and retraining, so it is important that whatever is done, is done quickly and done well. Assessment is the key. Formal assessments as part of the certification process will be dealt with in more detail later. With collective exercises like boat drills or fire drills, the assessment of effectiveness may consist of debriefing participants after an exercise.

Every individual or group training programme should contain some form of assessment at three points:

1. At the start to see what each trainee already knows.

2. As the training proceeds to make sure the lessons are being learned and that time is not being wasted.

3. At the end of training to make sure that the message has been received and/or the skills have been mastered.

In traditional training this usually takes the form of person-to-person conversations between the supervisor and trainee(s). To start any training programme such a face-to-face meeting is nearly always essential.

During training, it may not be easy to find time or arrange schedules for people to meet. Many training programmes are now based upon self-study principles, with self-testing routines built in. The trainee is then able to make the best use of his or her time, measure personal progress and deficiencies, repeat earlier exercises as necessary, and finally know when to come forward for formal testing.

适任评估

a. 评估背景

应该用良好的评估体系来评测受培训人的入门技能、知识以及培训进展。应该从正确的起点开始培训，以节省时间并使费用减到最小，避免知识断层和重复。同时应正确认定和记录海员技能，以作为适任证书的客观证据。

b. 岗前评估

《国际安全管理规则》要求为每条船舶配备合格的船员。公司必须确定船上全体船员的需要，为安全管理系统(SMS)的培训提供支持以及对培训做出适当的安排。这样做可以帮助高级船员和教练员制订船上培训计划。如有必要，在海员上船之前进行检查和评估。培训需求可以通过面试、核实证书以及检查以往训练的文件化证据得到确定。为了节省时间和保证统一性，一些公司和船员机构采用与他们的船舶和业务需要有关的计算机化测试。海员评估和培训电视电话系统(SETS)就是一个类似的系统。

c. 培训计划中的非正式评估

高级职员和普通学员的培训和再培训会受到时间限制，所以无论做什么，最重要的是做得快、做得好。要做到这点，评估计划的合理性是关键。作为发证过程的一部分，正规评估将在后面详细讨论。对于像救生艇操作和灭火训练这样的集体练习，其效果的评估可以包括练习之后对参加者的点评。

单独或分组的培训计划应该包含以下三方面评估：

1. 培训开始时查看每一位学员已了解什么。

2. 培训进行中确认课程有效以及不会浪费时间。

3. 培训结束时确认信息已被接受和/或技能已经掌握。

在传统的培训中，通常采用培训主管与学员之间直接对话的形式来了解上述内容。这种面对面接触的方式对于开展任何培训计划几乎都是最基本的。

在培训期间要确定时间或日期安排所有学员集会并不容易。目前很多培训计划都是基于自我学习的原理，并且建立常规的自我测试。因此，学员能充分利用自己的时间，评测自己的进步和不足，必要时重复以往的练习，最后要决定什么时候参加正式测试。

Self-study systems are harder to set up, but pay dividends in freeing the trainer's time and keeping unsuccessful assessment attempts to a minimum.

The sort of topics which are particularly relevant for self-study, are those which involve learning a lot of facts or figures, such as the Rule of the Road at Sea, learning communications procedures etc.

Important Note: STCW Section A-I/6 paragraph 2 states "Persons conducting in-service training or assessment on board shall only do so when such training or assessment will not adversely affect the normal operation of the ship and they can dedicate their time and attention to training or assessment".

d. Formal assessment for certificate of competency

Up to the present time, most Certificate of Competency examinations. conducted ashore have tested KNOWLEDGE rather than practical SKILLS. Both knowledge and skills are needed and it is on board ship that real competence must be demonstrated. These facts were recognized when the STCW Convention was revised. The revised Convention aims to ensure that seafarers in the future will be fully competent. It is necessary to ensure that formal assessments are properly organized, carried out and recorded. It will be necessary to ensure that the evidence gathered is acceptable to national authorities responsible for issuing certificates of competency.

It should also be remembered that there are specific requirements for continued professional competence and revalidation of certificates, and refresher and updating training.

Competence

A Statement of Competence incorporates the assessment of:

- skills to specified standards

- relevant knowledge and understanding

- ability to use skills and apply knowledge and understanding to the performance of relevant tasks.

In ships, as in aircraft, there are certain circumstances, where real life testing of emergency scenarios may be very costly or hazardous. However, there is real potential for part of the testing to be "in the workplace". The skills which can be tested on board are normally associated with the STCW support or operational levels corresponding approximately to seaman/petty officer and watchkeeper qualifications respectively. It is more difficult to test the STCW management level skills for master or chief engineer, which include high-level decision making (such as search and rescue organization, major engine failures etc.).

If a good ASSESSMENT SYSTEM is used, training can be made more cost-effective. By starting the training at the right point, monitoring effective delivery and ensuring satisfactory completion, training times can be minimized and the necessary standards of competence assured.

自我学习系统是较难建立的,但可以节省教练员的时间,而且使评估的不成功率保持在最低限度。

涉及实例或数字的学习内容是与自我学习关系特别密切的一类内容,例如《国际海上避碰规则》、学习通信程序等。

重要注释:STCW规则A-Ⅰ/6节第2段规定:"在船上进行在职培训或评估的人员,仅应在该培训或评估不会影响船舶正常操作以及在他们能抽出时间和精力时进行培训或评估。"

d. 适任证书的正式评估

到目前为止,大部分在岸上进行的适任证书考试,测试的是"知识"而不是实际"技能"。知识和技能两者都是必要的,而且必须表明在船上真正适任的能力。修订STCW公约时已经认识到上述事实,修正案的目标是确保海员将来能够完全适任。有必要确保正式评估适当地组织、开展和记录,也必须确保收集的证据是负责适任证书颁发的国家机构可以接受的。

也应该记住公约对持续的适任标准和证书的再有效以及知识更新培训都有特殊的要求。

适任

对适任的表述应结合以下评估内容:

- 规定标准的技能

- 相关的知识和理解

- 运用技艺和知识的能力以及对完成相关任务的理解

船上像飞机上一样有特殊的环境,因此在船上进行应急事件处理的能力这样的真实测试,费用可能是昂贵的或者具有危险性。然而,部分"在工作现场"进行的测试具有真正的可信度。可以在船上测试的通常是STCW公约的支持级技能,或者是大致对应于操作级的船员/二、三副/二、三管轮及值班船员资格的技能。测试STCW公约要求的船长或轮机长的管理级技能,包括高级别的决策(例如组织搜寻和救助、处理主机故障等)则更为困难。

如果采用好的"评估体系",培训会更加经济有效。从正确的起点开始,有效地进行监督以及确保满意地完成培训。这样,培训时间可以减到最少,而且能保证达到所要求的适任标准。

Assessment

In its simplest form, an "assessor" would see a candidate demonstrating competent performance in the workplace, but it will normally be necessary to assess pre-requisite and complementary knowledge by methods other than simple observation. Appropriate means need to be selected and assessment material developed.

Assessment methods

In Section B of the STCW Code there are five examples of types of evidence about candidates' competence given:

1. Direct observation of work activities (including seagoing service);

2. Skills/proficiency/competency tests;

3. Projects and assignments;

4. Evidence from previous experience; and

5. Written, oral or computer-based questioning techniques.

Many assessment methods are used in shore-based and sea training, including:

- practical examination (demonstration of skills "on the job")
- project work (assessments of results and records)
- oral examination
- simulation, full
- simulation, simple including part tasks
- written examination, closed book type
- written examination, open book type
- written, with multi-choice options

There are also new methods which could be used on board, in particular:

- video-based assessment with written support material
- computer-based assessment
- interactive video incorporating assessment
- audio tapes, photographs, slides etc. with written support material.

评估

评估员在现场考察申请人表现出的适任能力是最简便的评估形式,但通常必须通过简单观察以外的方法去评估必备的及补充的知识。必须选择合适的方法并且开发评估资料。

评估方法

在STCW规则的B部分,给出了申请人适任证据五种类型的实例:

1. 对工作活动(包括海上资历)的直接考察;

2. 技能/熟练/适任测试;

3. 专题和作业;

4. 取自以前经历的证据;及

5. 书面的、口头的或基于计算机的考试技术。

岸上和海上培训采用很多评估方法,包括:

- 实操考试(表明"工作中"的技能)

- 专题作业(评价结果和记录)

- 口试

- 模拟,包含完整项目

- 模拟,仅包括部分任务

- 笔试,闭卷考试

- 笔试,开卷考试

- 笔试,多项选择形式

一些新的方法也可以用于船上评估,特别是:

- 有书面材料支持的基于录像的评估

- 基于计算机的评估

- 交互式录像辅助评估

- 有书面材料支持的录音带、照片、幻灯片等的评估。

Not all methods are suitable for use in assessing practical performance on board and some of the more complex skill areas may require more than one method to be used.

Ideally, the assessment methods which are chosen should be capable of being used not only for new entrants but also for mature and experienced persons wishing to up-grade or broaden their vocational qualifications.

The assessment methods should be efficient, not only in setting the correct standards and performance criteria, but also in terms of availability, time taken and costs.

Assessment: Example

Example 1:

The following are extracts from the first part of STCW Table A-III/4:

- Specification of minimum standard of competence for ratings forming part of an engineering watch

- Function: Marine engineering at the support level

NOTE: the following example contains two of the four competencies listed for this function.

Competence:

Carry out a watch routine appropriate to the duties of a rating forming part of an engine-room watch. Understand orders and be understood in matters relevant to watchkeeping duties.

Knowledge, understanding and proficiency:

- Terms used in machinery spaces and names of machinery and equipment.

- Engine room watchkeeping procedures.

- Safe working practices as related to engine-room operations.

- Basic environmental protection procedures.

- Use of appropriate internal communication system.

- Engine room alarm systems and ability to distinguish between the various alarms, with special reference to fire extinguishing gas alarms.

Methods for demonstrating competence: Assessment of evidence obtained from one or more of the following:

1. Approved in-service experience;

2. Approved training ship experience; or

不是所有方法都适合船上的实际表现评估,某些更为复杂的技能领域可能需要使用不只一种方法。

理想的情况是被选择的评估方法不仅适用于新船员,而且也适用于熟练和经验丰富的希望职务晋升或扩大业务能力的人员。

评估方法应该是有效的;不仅在设定正确标准和能力标准方面,而且从可用性、时间耗费和费用方面也是高效的。

评估:实例

实例1:

以下摘自STCW规则表A-Ⅲ/4的第一部分:

- 机舱值班部分:普通船员的最低适任标准

- 功能:轮机工程(支持级)

注意:以下的例子仅包含了这一功能表列的四项适任中的两项。

适任:

机舱值班部分的普通船员职责是执行日常值班任务。理解指令并能向其他人表述与值班职责有关的事宜。

知识、理解和熟练:

- 机器处所使用的术语及机器和设备的名称。

- 机舱值班程序。

- 有关机舱操作的安全工作规程。

- 基本的环境保护程序。

- 相应的船上内部通信系统的使用。

- 机舱报警系统和区别各种报警特别是关于灭火气体报警的能力。

表明适任的方法:评估从下列一项或数项获取的证据:

1. 认可的工作经历;

2. 认可的培训船经历;或者

3. Practical test.

Criteria for evaluating competence:

- Communications are clear and concise and advice or clarification is sought from the officer of the watch where watch information or instructions are not clearly understood.

- Maintenance, handover and relief of the watch is in conformity with accepted principles and procedures.

In the above case, the ASSESSMENT would need to define the range of equipment and procedures to be included, and make sure they were covered adequately and results properly recorded. It would be necessary to:

- define the machinery and equipment to be included

- define the watchkeeping procedures to be covered

- specify or provide a reference to the safe working practices

- specify or provide a reference to the basic environmental protection procedures

- define the appropriate internal communication system

- define the engine room alarm systems

For certification purposes, assessments in several ships and/or on several voyages would be needed, to make sure that the seafarer could apply the skills and knowledge in an adequate range of circumstances.

National authorities would require evidence from shipboard assessments and would normally still carry out some extra testing (for example a written and/or oral examination in a shore centre) for this and the other competences involved, before issuing a certificate of competency to the seafarer.

Example 2:

The following extracts are part of STCW Table A-II/3:

- Specification of minimum standard of competence for officers in charge of a navigational watch and for masters on ships of less than 500 gross tonnage engaged on near-coastal voyages

- Function: Navigation at the operational level

NOTE: the following example is only one of the five competencies listed for this function.

3. 实际测试。

评价适任的标准：

- 语言交流清楚简明，在未能清楚地理解值班信息或指示时，能从值班高级船员处获得咨询或澄清。

- 值班、交班和接班符合公认的原则和程序。

在以上情况下，"评估"必须对所包括的设备和程序范围进行定义，并确保它们被充分地覆盖和对成绩做适当的记录。必须进行定义的有：

- 定义所包含的机器和设备

- 定义所涉及的值班程序

- 对安全作业实践的详细说明或给出其含义

- 对基本环境保护程序的详细说明或给出其含义

- 定义相应的内部通信系统

- 定义机舱报警系统

为了达到发证目的，评估必须在几条船和/或几个航次上进行，以确保海员能够在适当的环境范围内运用技能和知识。

国家主管当局要求从船上评估中获取证据，并且在发给海员适任证书之前，仍应对评估内容及其他有关的适任进行一些额外测试（例如在岸上考试中心的笔试和/或口试）。

实例2：

以下是STCW规则表A-Ⅱ/3的部分摘录：

- 从事近岸航行未满500总吨船舶的船长和负责航行值班的高级船员的最低适任标准

- 功能：航行（操作级）

注意：以下的例子只是这一功能表列出的五项适任中的一项。

Competence:

Maintain a safe navigational watch

Knowledge, understanding and proficiency:

- Watchkeeping.

- Thorough knowledge of content, application and intent of the International Regulations for Preventing Collisions at Sea.

- Knowledge of content of the principles to be observed in keeping a navigational watch.

- Use of routeing in accordance with the General Provisions on Ships' Routeing.

Methods for demonstrating competence:

Examination and assessment of evidence obtained from one or more of the following:

1. Approved in-service experience
2. Approved training ship experience
3. Approved simulator training, where appropriate
4. Approved laboratory equipment training

Criteria for evaluating competence:

- The conduct, handover and relief of the watch conforms with accepted principles and procedures

- A proper look-out is maintained at all times and in conformity with accepted principles and procedures

- Lights, shapes and sound signals conform with the requirements contained in the International Regulations for Preventing Collisions at Sea and are correctly recognized

- The frequency and extent of monitoring of traffic, the ship and the environment conforms with accepted principles and procedures

- Action to avoid close encounters and collision with other vessels is in accordance with the International Regulations for Preventing Collisions at Sea

- Decisions to adjust course and/or speed are both timely and in accordance with accepted navigation procedures

- A proper record is maintained of movements and activities relating to the navigation of the ship

- Responsibility for safe navigation is clearly defined at all times, including periods when the master is on the bridge and when under pilotage.

适任：

    保持安全航行值班

知识、理解和熟练：

- 值班。

- 关于国际海上避碰规则的内容、应用和意图的全面知识。

- 航行值班中应遵守的基本原则的内容的知识。

- 按照船舶定线制的一般规定使用定线制。

表明适任的方法：

    考试并评估从下列一项或数项获取的证据：

1. 认可的工作经历

2. 认可的船上培训经历

3. 认可的模拟器培训，如适合

4. 认可的实验室设备培训

评价适任的标准：

- 按照公认的原则和程序进行值班、接班和交班

- 随时保持正规的瞭望，并符合公认的原则和程序

- 号灯、号型和声号符合《国际海上避碰规则》中的有关要求，并能被正确辨认

- 监测交通、船舶和环境的频率和范围符合公认的原则和程序

- 按照《国际海上避碰规则》采取行动，以避免与他船在很近距离上会遇或碰撞

- 及时地按照公认的航海程序做出调整航向和/或航速的决定

- 对有关船舶航行的运动和活动保持正规的记录

- 始终明确安全航行的责任，包括船长在驾驶台时和正在被引航时

As in the previous example, the ASSESSMENT would need to define the range of equipment and procedures to be included, and make sure they were covered adequately and results properly recorded. It would be necessary to:

- define the equipment and controls to be included (which includes steering systems, automatic pilot, unmanned machinery space controls and communications as required)

- define the procedures to be included

- define the range of knowledge required including thorough knowledge of the content and application of the International Regulations for Preventing Collisions at Sea

- in complying with the principles to be observed in keeping a navigational watch, define the range of knowledge of matters related to the ship itself, activities taking place on board, the external environment, (weather visibility, sea states etc.) other craft, fixed, submerged and floating hazards

- supervision of other crew members including helmsmen etc.

- knowledge and usage of routeing in accordance with the General Provisions on Ships' Routeing

- define the appropriate internal and external communication systems

For certification purposes, although it would be possible for properly qualified assessors to carry out full examinations on board, this is unlikely to happen in practice. The normal assessment of this competence would be:

- a thorough examination of the knowledge and understanding through a formal examination system;

- laboratory-based or simulator-based assessments and shipboard assessments to make sure that the candidate can set-up, operate, monitor and control the equipment and the ship; and

- shipboard assessments and laboratory equipment or simulator-based assessments to make sure that the candidate could apply the knowledge in a range of situations in different ships, different geographical/traffic/weather/sea and visibility conditions.

The shipboard assessments are most important, because watchkeeping skills include planning, actions, observation, awareness and time-management which cannot be adequately tested in any environment other than on watch at sea.

The national authorities are likely to require evidence from several ships and/or several voyages. That evidence must be recorded and produced in a form approved by the certifying body.

如同前一个实例一样,"评估"必须对所包括的设备和程序范围进行定义,以及确保它们被充分地覆盖和对成绩适当地记录。必须进行定义的有:

- 定义所包括的设备和控制器(其中包括操舵系统、自动驾驶仪、按所要求的无人机舱的控制和通信)

- 定义所包括的程序

- 定义所要求的知识范围,包括关于《国际海上避碰规则》的内容、应用和意图的全面知识

- 遵守保持航行值班的原则,定义与船舶本身相关事务的知识范围,在船上进行的活动,外部环境(天气、能见度、海况等),其他船舶,固定、水下和漂浮的危险物

- 对其他船员包括舵工等的监督

- 按照船舶定线制的一般规定使用定线制的知识

- 定义相应的内部和外部的通信系统

为了达到发证的目的,虽然有可能由有正式资格的评估员实施船上所有考核,但实际上未必都能这样做。这方面正常的评估可能是:

- 通过正规的考试系统进行知识和理解的全面考试;

- 基于实验室或基于模拟器的评估和船上的评估确保申请人能够安装、操作、监视、控制设备和船舶;及

- 船上评估和基于实验室设备或模拟器评估确保申请人能够在不同船舶、不同地理/交通/天气/海况及能见度条件一系列情况下运用相应的知识。

船上评估是最重要的,因为值班技能包括计划、行动、观察、意识和时间安排,所有这些在不同于海上值班的任何其他环境下不可能进行充分的测试。

国家主管当局可能从几条船和/或几个航次中获取证据。证据必须用发证机关认可的形式记录和提供。

Other evidence from assessments on simulator-based and/or laboratory equipment-based assessments and examinations ashore will need to be added to the candidate's portfolio (records).

Recommended guidance on the scope of knowledge and skills required for the "Evaluation of Competence" are given in Section A of the STCW Code. Properly applied they should help to ensure that a candidate can:

1. Work competently in different ships and across a range of circumstances;

2. Anticipate, prepare for and deal with contingencies; and

3. Adapt to new and changing requirements

National authorities would require evidence covering all the elements of all the competencies for the function before issuing a certificate of competency to the candidate.

Validation and Quality Standards

The National Administration of each country which is party to the STCW Convention must ensure that all TRAINING AND ASSESSMENT for seafarers is "structured in accordance with written programmes, including such methods and media of delivery, procedures, and course material as are necessary to achieve the required standard of competence."

There are defined QUALITY STANDARDS in the STCW Convention under which all training, assessment of competence, certification, endorsement and revalidation activities... are continuously monitored through a quality systems standard to ensure achievement of defined objectives, including those concerning the qualifications and experience of instructors and assessors ..."

It is therefore most important that systems for the ASSESSMENT OF COMPETENCE are VALIDATED by appropriate authorities:

- National Administrations (responsible for the issue of Certificates of Competency to seafarers)

- Quality Auditing bodies (responsible for Quality System Standards)

Other bodies which might advise or assist with the validation of training and assessments include:

- Professional Bodies

- Employers/Trades Union Associations

- other International Organizations

In order to qualify for valid certification, certain procedures have to be followed and standards reached.

从基于模拟器上的评估和/或基于实验室设备的评估以及岸上的考试中获得的其他证据必须添加到申请人的文件夹(记录)里。

在STCW规则A部分给出了"适任评估"所要求的知识和技能范围的推荐性指南。正确运用这些指南有助于确保申请人能够：

1. 胜任不同船舶上和环境下的工作；

2. 预见、准备和处理意外事故；及

3. 适应新的和变化的要求。

国家当局在发给申请人适任证书之前，对相应功能要求的证据能覆盖所有适任的所有要素。

标准的有效性和质量

每个STCW公约缔约国的主管机关必须确保所有针对海员的"培训和评估"是"根据书面计划安排的，教学手段、媒介、程序；以及课程资料都要达到适任标准的要求"。

在STCW公约中规定了"质量标准"，在这一"质量标准"下的所有培训、适任评估、发证、认可以及再有效活动……是"通过质量标准体系的连续监控以保证达到规定的目标，包括那些与教员和评估员资格及经历相关的目标……"

因此，对"适任评估"系统来说最重要的是要得到相应机构的"认可"：

- 国家主管机关(负责给海员颁发适任证书)

- 质量审核机关(负责质量标准体系)

其他可以向培训和评估提供建议或帮助的机构包括：

- 专业机构

- 雇主/贸易联合会

- 其他国际性组织

为了取得有效的证书，必须遵循某些程序并达到标准。

Validation Procedures/Independent Evaluation

STCW Code gives basic advice on quality standards at Section A-I/8 which is further amplified in Section B-I/8. The latter contains a detailed example of "the independent evaluation of courses" (validation) and is an important reference for those responsible for course management.

Validation procedures for education and training programmes vary, but usually include approval and auditing of some or all of the following:

- content of the training and/or assessment programme

- training and/or assessment methods

- facilities and environment for the activities (space, libraries, equipment etc.)

- entry qualifications, maturity and experience of trainees/quality and breadth of evidence produced by candidates for assessment

- qualifications and experience of trainers and assessors

- internal and external auditing processes

Validation is normally carried out by a panel of qualified professionals, and is normally subject to regular auditing and re-validation and up-dating of programmes at intervals, normally not more than five years.

Examples of validation procedures may be obtained from the Edexcel Foundation (formerly BTEC) and Scottish Vocational Education Council in the United Kingdom. There are also Circulars and an Assessors Handbook available from the Higher Education Funding Council for England.

批准程序/独立评估

STCW规则在第A-Ⅰ/8节中给出了质量标准的基本建议,而在第B-Ⅰ/8节中做了进一步详述。其后包含了一个"课程的独立评估"(批准)的详细例子,可作为负责课程管理人员的重要参考。

教育和培训计划的批准程序是变化的,但通常包括以下的部分或全部认可和审核程序:

- 培训和/或评估计划的内容

- 培训和/或评估方法

- 活动的设施和环境(空间、图书馆、设备等)

- 学员的申请资格、经验和经历以及对申请人进行评估而产生的证据质量和内容宽度

- 教练员和评估员的资格和经历

- 内部和外部审核过程

批准程序通常是由具有资格的专业人员组成的小组完成,并且要进行定期审核和重新审批,更新程序的间隔期通常不超过五年。

批准程序的实例可从"Edexcel基金会"(以前的BTEC)和联合王国的"苏格兰职业教育协会"获得,也可从"英格兰高等教育基金会"的《通告》和《评估员手册》中得到。

Part 17
The Assessment Process

Prepare Assessment Package

There are several components of an assessment package. The three necessary components are (1) the student workbook, including reference material for the candidate; (2) a guide that includes detailed instructions for conducting the assessment, and additional components such as various aids for recording observed performance (checklists, worksheets, work forms) and a summary form of documented results; (3) a scheme to ascertain the compliance or non-compliance of competence performance by the candidate.

The assessment package covers the assessment process that is eventually filed for record-keeping. It may be used as evidence, for recalling of facts to formulate training and development plans, as well as for compiling statistics to serve some other purpose.

The instructor should also emphasize that, since the process of assessment is through a quality standard system, subject to verification to ensure validity, reliability and consistency of results, prudent record-keeping is necessary.

The Assessment Process

The steps involved in conducting assessment should include:

— the preparation for the assessment

— conducting a pre-assessment briefing with the candidate

— observing the candidate's performance and recording the results

— evaluating the process and determining the assessment outcome

— conducting an assessment debrief

Preparation of the Assessment

The preparation of the assessment involved the following sub-steps:

1. Gathering of materials

2. Preparing the staging area

3. Preparing and arranging equipment

4. Conducting any necessary safety checks

5. Informing affected personnel

第17章
评估过程

评估资料的准备

评估资料由几个部分组成。三个必需的组成部分是：(1)学生工作簿，包括提供给申请人的参考资料；(2)一本包括实施评估的详细指导指南，以及附加部分例如记录观测能力的各种辅助工具(核查表、工作单、工作表格)和用以记录成绩的汇总表；(3)一份用以确定申请人符合或不符合适任要求的方案。

评估资料包包含了最终以文件形式保存的评估过程记录。它可以作为证据，既便于回忆培训过程和用于开发评估计划，又可汇编成资料用于其他目的。

教员也应该强调，由于质量评估系统贯穿整个评估过程，因此以这些证据为依据可以确保成绩的正确、可靠和一致性，谨慎保存记录是必要的。

评估过程

与实施评估有关的步骤包括：

— 评估的准备

— 召开申请人参加的评估前简介会议

— 考察申请人的表现并记录成绩

— 评价整个过程并确定评估成绩

— 召开评估情况简报会

评估的准备

评估的准备与以下的分步骤有关：

1. 收集资料

2. 准备演练区

3. 准备和安排设备

4. 实施所有必需的安全检查

5. 通知相关人员

1) *Gathering of Materials*

To ensure that shipboard assessments are successfully carried out, identifying and gathering of relevant materials for items to be assessed are essential, eg. plans, checklists, manuals, nautical publications, charts, consumable, etc.

If necessary materials are not available, it has to be procured before any assessment can be carried out.

2) *Preparing the Staging Area*

The staging area where the assessment is to be carried out has to be thoroughly checked and inspected to ensure a safe working environment. Accidents occurring during a shipboard assessment is the last thing that we want. It is important to ensure that the location of the staging area will not hinder the normal operation and functioning of the ship. Appropriate life saving and safety appliances should be readily available at the staging area if there are any risk of injury during the assessment. Staging to be provided when necessary. Also ascertain the need for appropriate attire, e.g. safety shoes, helmet, gloves, goggles, safety belt, etc.

3) *Preparing and Arranging Equipment*

The equipment that is used for the assessment has to be identified and checked to ensure that it is in good working condition. Malfunctioning equipment can be hazardous to both trainee and assessor. It is also important to ascertain that the equipment being used for the assessment will not cause disruption to the normal function and operation of the ship.

4) *Conducting Any Necessary Safety Checks*

Pre-assessment safety checks are essential to ensure that there are adequate control to avoid problems and potential hazards. Contingency plans should be available so that the assessor could regain control if any problem arises during the assessment. Determine the standard safety check list for the item to be assessed and go through the check list thoroughly. For assessment in emergency drills such as boat drill or man-overboard drill, the weather condition during the assessment has to be taken into consideration. Adverse weather condition can made above-mentioned drills hazardous and extreme care has to be exercised. When the assessment involves dangerous operations such as entry into a confined space, a permit to carry out the assessment should be obtained from the master or responsible officer and ensure that the safety check list for entry into a confined space is gone through thoroughly.

5) *Informing Affected Personnel*

Trainee and other personnel, eg. watchkeepers and department heads, affected by the assessment must be informed in advance of the date and staging area the assessment is going to be conducted. In addition a brief description of the competence to be assessed should also be given. Clarify with the affected personnel that the assessment will not interfere with the normal operation of the ship. It is also important to confirm with the trainee that he/she is ready for the assessment.

1）收集资料

为了确保船上评估的圆满完成，确定和收集评估项目相关资料，如计划、核查表、使用手册、航海出版物、海图、消耗品等很重要。

如果手头没有评估必需的资料，必须在开展评估之前设法取得相应的资料。

2）准备演练区

演练区是进行评估的场所，必须进行彻底检查以确保一个安全的工作环境。在船上评估期间发生意外是我们最不希望看见的。另一个重要的考虑是应确保演练区的位置不妨碍船舶的正常操作和活动。在演练区内应能迅速地提供相应的救生和安全设备，以便在评估期间可能出现任何伤害和危险时使用，必要时要进行设备的使用演练，也应保证提供相应的服装，例如安全鞋、头盔、手套、护目镜、安全带等。

3）设备的准备和安排

必须确定评估的设备并进行检查以确保其处在良好的工作状态。失灵的设备对学员和评估员都可能是危险的。确保评估的设备不会干扰船舶的正常功能和操作也是十分重要的。

4）实施所有必要的安全检查

评估前的安全检查对于确保有足够的监控避免出现问题和潜在危险是必要的。应该制订意外事故应变计划，以便评估员可以控制评估期间出现的问题。为每一个要评估的项目确定标准的安全检查表并根据检查表进行全面核查。对于应急训练例如操艇训练或人员落水训练的评估，必须考虑评估期间的天气状况。天气状况不良可能使上述训练变得危险，因此必须十分当心。当评估涉及危险操作例如进入一个限制性场所时，必须得到船长或负责的驾驶员同意才能进行评估，而且要确保已经根据进入限制性场所的安全检查表进行了全面核查。

5）通知相关人员

将要在演练区进行评估时，必须提前通知学员和其他人员，例如值班人员和部门负责人等相关人员。此外，也应该对要评估的适任项目做出简要说明。应该使相关人员明白：评估不会干扰船舶的正常操作。通知学员做好评估准备也很重要。

Conduct Pre-assessment Briefing

A pre-assessment briefing with the candidate should be conducted and should address the following :

    1.   The scope (what and how much)

    2.   Procedures (rules)

    3.   Standards (goal to be met)

    4.   Outcome and consequences of the assessment

1)   *The Scope (What and How Much)*

Before the assessment the trainee must be briefed on the items to be assessed. The competence being assessed should also be discussed. Lay out the framework for the assessment in detail so that the trainee is fully aware of what and how much is expected of him in this assessment. The purpose of the assessment should also be explained to the trainee.

2)   *Procedures (Rules)*

Guidelines on the competence to be assessed should be provided to the trainee. Any circumstances that may require the assessment to be postponed should be clearly stated before the assessment is started. Trainee must be thoroughly briefed on the safety precautions or safe working practices that are essential for the successful completion of the assessment. The time-frame and parameter of permissible activities must be clearly spelled out to the trainee before the commencement of any assessment. Guidelines for appeal must be available in case the assessment outcome is not in favour of the trainee.

3)   *Standards (Goal to be Met)*

The trainee must be made fully aware of the fact that the acceptable level of knowledge, understanding and proficiency, as per the STCW 95 competence tables must be met.

4)   *Outcome and Consequences of the Assessment*

Brief the trainee on the form or manner by which the outcome of the assessment will be made known to him/her and also the need to agree on the trainee's strength and weaknesses after the assessment. The expected consequences of the outcome of an assessment must be made known to the trainee, eg. if the outcome is unfavourable (not yet competent) then the candidate can expect to be re-assessed or send for further training. All the results of assessment will be entered into the trainee's Training and Assessment Record Book and also the Company's own Training Record Book.

召开评估前简介会

必须召开有申请人参加的评估前简介会,并应强调以下内容:

1. 范围(内容和深度)
2. 程序(规则)
3. 标准(达到的目标)
4. 评估成绩和后果

1)范围(内容和深度)

评估前,必须就评估项目向学员简要介绍,也应该讨论正在评估的适任。为评估设计一个详细方案以便学员完全明白在这次评估中希望他做什么和做到什么程度,同时也应该向学员解释评估目的。

2)程序(规则)

应该向学员提供适任评估方面的指导。在评估开始之前,应该清楚地阐明任何可能使评估推延的情况。必须向学员全面地简要介绍安全注意事项或安全工作规则,所有这些对成功地完成评估都很重要。在开展任何适任评估前,必须向学员清楚地说明限定的时间和允许的活动范围界限。万一对学员的评估成绩不满意,则必须向这些人提供指导。

3)标准(达到的目标)

必须使学员完全明白这样的事实:他们的知识、理解和熟练程度必须满足STCW 95公约适任表中的规定。

4)评估的成绩和后果

评估结束后,向学员做简要介绍,使学员明白评估成绩的形式或方法,同时也在学员的长处和弱点方面达成共识。必须让学员知道对应其评估成绩的预期后果。例如,如果成绩不如人意(仍未适任),那么申请人可以预期要接受再次评估或者被派去进一步培训。所有的评估成绩必须记入学员的"培训和评估记录簿"中,也必须记入公司自己的"培训记录本"中。

Observe the Candidate Performance and Record the Results

The assessment should be conducted in an environment such that the candidate should be able to perform the required task independently. Coaching and assisting the candidate in whatever manner should be avoided.

Assessors should ensure that the task assessed should be kept within the scope and guidelines of the assessment.

It is important that assessors should exercise impartiality towards candidate, taking into consideration factors/conditions beyond the candidate's control that may affect his performance.

Observations of the assessment proceedings should be kept strictly to the candidate's performance not to the candidate himself.

Strict discipline should be maintained throughout the assessment proceedings.

Any unwarranted interference that may disrupt the smooth flow of the assessment proceedings should be prevented.

Safety of the candidate should be of utmost importance. If at any time a potentially hazardous situation is deemed to exist, the assessor should be in a position to intervene.

As in any form of assessment, the allocated time should be adhere to. Fairness and firmness in determining the outcome of the assessment should be observed.

It should be noted that before the commencement of the assessment the candidate should not feel that he is deprive of some relevant information, such as criteria of assessment, time to complete the task etc.

Where appropriate and applicable, the assessment should be conducted in a realistic situation, but if this is not achievable then certain scenarios should be created to assimilate the real situation; e.g responding to emergencies, etc.

Candidate should be allowed to complete the task uninterrupted, but bearing in mind that the time allocated for each task to be performed/assessed must be abide by to prevent disruption on subsequent tasks.

Upon completion of the assessment, the evidence of the performance should be noted and be recorded in the candidate's approved Training and Assessment Record Book and/or the company's issued Training Plan and Record Book.

National authorities would require evidence covering all the elements of all the competencies for the function before issuing a certificate of competency to the candidate.

考察申请人的表现并记录成绩

评估必须在申请人能够独立地完成所要求的任务的环境下进行。应该避免在评估过程中以任何方式指导和帮助申请人。

评估员应确保被评估的任务仅限于评估指南要求的范围之内。

评估员应公平地对待每一位申请人并考虑申请人在控制能力范围之外可能有影响其行为的其他因素。

评估过程中应严格的考察申请人的表现而非申请人本身。

整个评估过程都要保持严格的纪律。

应该防止任何破坏评估过程顺利进行的不恰当干扰。

申请人的安全极为重要,在任何时候如果认为存在可能的危险情况,则评估员应进行干预。

任何形式的评估都应该遵守分配的时间。在确定评估成绩时应遵守公平和固定的原则。

应该注意,在评估开始之前申请人不应觉得被剥夺了一些相关条件,例如评估的标准、完成任务的时间等。

在适当和可行的情况下,评估应在真实的环境和情况下进行,如有实际困难,例如要评估对突发事件的反应等项目时,也应该创造与真实情况相似的环境。

应该使申请人在不中断的情况下完成任务,但必须记住,必须遵守分配到每项任务的操作/评估时间,以保证不对后续任务造成干扰。

在完成评估的基础上,应该记录操作表现证据并记载在申请人的有效"培训和评估记录簿"上和/或公司发放的"培训计划和记录簿"上。

在向申请人颁发适任证书前,国家主管当局会要求所提供的申请人的证据材料能覆盖该功能所有适任项目包含的所有因素。

Evaluate the Process and Determine the Assessment Outcome

During the proceeding of the assessment, assessors should take note of the relevant/required steps in the performance of the task. These should be based on the STCW 95 Competence Tables where the required criteria for evaluating competence is stipulated.

Mistakes made by the by candidate should be noted, so as to be of used positively during the debrief.

The outcome of the assessment should be determine as soon as possible and the results documented.

Assessment Debrief

It is important that the assessment debrief be conducted as soon as possible. Since the task performed is still fresh in the candidate's memory, it may be much easier for him to have a better understanding of the correct procedures/methods to be employed in the performance of the task.

Candidate should be credited for satisfactory performances achieved.

Avoid making statements/comments that may demoralised the candidates for mistakes made during the assessment

Candidates are to be told of the areas where improvements is needed based on the earlier observations.

Discuss ways in which candidate can improve on the performances in order to satisfy the competence requirement.

Encourage candidate to ask relevant questions for further improvements.

Assure candidate that any doubts he may have will be clarified as soon as possible or before the next assessment.

Candidates are to be informed of the assessment result without hesitation. Do not withhold the result for longer than necessary.

Always make it a point to close the assessment proceedings with any useful recommendations for the candidate's improvements. These may include but not limited to:

- more exposure to a particular task
- further or refresher training
- source of materials to gain knowledge
- need for closer supervision or coaching

评估过程评价与确定评估成绩

评估进行期间,评估员应注意完成任务的相关/要求的步骤。这些要求应该根据 STCW 95 公约适任表中为适任评估规定的标准。

应该记录申请人所犯的错误,以便在进行评估简报时作为实例使用。

应尽快确定评估的成绩并为成绩提供证明。

评估情况简报

尽快地召开评估情况简报会非常重要,由于这时申请人对于已完成的任务记忆犹新,所以可能更容易理解完成任务应采用的正确程序和方法。

对申请人达到的令人满意的表现应该给予褒扬。

在评估期间,对于申请人所犯的错误应避免发表一些意见和评论使他失去信心。

根据先前的考察,应该告诉申请人哪些地方需要改进。

讨论得出方法能改善申请人的表现以便满足适任要求。

鼓励申请人提出问题做进一步改善。

使申请人确信他们的任何疑问都会尽快或在下次评估之前得到澄清。

评估的成绩会立即通知申请人。成绩公布的时间应尽可能早。

结束评估程序前总要给出一些有益建议促进申请人改善评估。这些建议可能包括但不限于如下方面:

— 更加明确特定任务

— 进一步或更新培训

— 获取知识的资料来源

— 需要更严密的监督和辅导

If appropriate, specify minimum period before the next assessment of the failed task.

The following extract is taken from Sally Brown's 500 tips on Assessment.* It looks at some of the factors involved in developing and assessing students' competences and transferable skills. Although referring to shore-based educational systems, many of the points raised are valid for the competence-based STCW 95.

* © Sally Brown, 1996, Kogan Page.

Once it was common to write a syllabus simply as a list of the principal topics to be covered by students. Now, we are expected to provide much more detail. Increasingly syllabus content is being expressed in terms of the intended learning outcomes to be achieved by students. The National Council for Vocational Qualifications uses the definitions "elements of competence", "performance criteria", "evidence descriptors" and "range statements". Many people find this interlinked terminology confusing. We hope that the sections in this chapter will help you to unravel the jargon and design a successful competence-based assessment framework.

Writing elements of competence

The next few sets of suggestions are strongly linked. In practice, it is not sensible to identify elements of competence in full detail, then to go on to specify performance criteria, evidence descriptors and range statements. It is better to be drafting them all in parallel. We have arranged our suggestions under each heading with this in mind.

1. **Look at some examples already written.** Many education and training programmes are already expressed, with varying levels of success(!), in competence terminology. For example, General National Vocational Qualifications in England and Wales use such systems, as do various management development programmer. Much can be learned about how to go about designing competence frameworks (and about how not to!), by looking carefully at a range of existing examples.

2. **Express prerequisite competences.** Most courses or modules do not start from scratch. It is normal to express the skills and knowledge which students starting a course are reasonably expected to have developed already. However, it may not be precise enough just to refer to earlier studies they have done by course title or subject. It is better to pin down some of the principal aspects of competence and knowledge that students should have derived from these earlier courses, which will be needed as starting points for their development in the new course.

3. **Move beyond your subject, towards what students will be able to do after they have studied it.** Some of the skills and competences which students will develop will depend on subject-specific expertise they develop. However, there is also likely to be a range of general skills which students will develop alongside their subject-specific ones.

4. **Think in terms of intended learning outcomes.** Look at what students should be expected to become able to do when they have successfully completed each stage of their learning. Phrase statements of learning outcomes in terms of things that students "can do" as draft elements of competence.

如果合适,为失败的任务指定最短期限来进行下次评估。

以下内容摘自萨利·布朗的《评估的500个技巧》。*著作考虑了一些与开发和评价学生的适任能力和相应技能相关的因素。虽然引用的是岸上的教育体系,但提出的很多观点对ST-CW 95公约中的适任评估也是适用的。

(注:* Sally Brown,1966,Kogan Page。)

过去通常简单写一份提纲列上学生需学习的内容主题,但现在我们要提供更加详细的内容。大纲增加了一些内容说明学生应达到的预期学习效果。全国职业资格委员会使用的定义有:"适任要素""表现标准""证据说明"和"综合说明"。很多人发现这些相互关联的术语是混乱的。我们希望这一章的各节会帮助你了解这些专门术语,并且设计一个成功的适任方案。

编写适任要素

以下的几方面建议是密切相关的。在实际中,完全细分适任要素是不明智的,应该对能力标准、证据说明和综合说明做出规定。把它们所有都编制成类似的形式。以下在每一标题下面我们给出相关建议。

1. **参考相应的编写范例**。已有许多成功例子通过用适任术语表达各种等级的教学和培训项目。例如在英格兰和威尔士,全国职业资格委员会对各种各样的管理类教育培训开发项目采用了相应系统。通过参考一系列的现有实例,可以学到更多方法来处理怎样进行适任方案设计。

2. **强调先决的适任条件**。大部分课程或者教学模块不能草率开始。应该明白,在正规课程开始时,学生已掌握了部分技能和早期知识。然而,不一定能十分准确地了解他们已完成的早期课题或科目等全部学习内容。但最好能准确说明学生从这些早期学习中需获取适任能力和某些知识作为他们新课程学习的起点。

3. **学生学完某一科目后,在科目之外的其他方面的能力发展**。学生需要发展在特定科目中的适任能力和专门技能。然而,也会围绕特定科目发展一系列普通技能。

4. **关于预期学习效果的思考**。每当学生成功地完成一个阶段的学习,应注意他们能做什么。学习成绩应依据学生"有能力完成"的适任要素所需任务进行说明。

5   **Check that elements of competence relate to things that all successful students will be able to demonstrate.** These should be achievable targets for all students, not just goals for the most successful ones. The level to which students will demonstrate each element of competence is dealt with in the finer detail of a competence framework.

6   **Make use of syllabus aims and objectives, if already formulated.** In syllabus specifications for the Business and Technology Education Council (BTEC) in England and Wales, for example, the intended learning outcomes may well already be expressed in terms of the actions that students will be able to perform after learning each topic. It is normally a relatively simple editing task to adjust such objectives to turn them into learning outcomes in "can do" competence language.

7   **Don't forget values and ethics.** A major criticism of many existing competence frameworks is that they are entirely based on evidence which may or may not be underpinned with values. Don't be afraid to add competences requiring students to show evidence of upholding sensibly chosen values.

8   **Avoid expressing competences in terms of knowledge or understanding.** Although it may well be essential that students develop such knowledge and understanding, try to express elements of competence in terms of the things that students will be able to do to demonstrate these qualities.

9   **Beware of trivial competences.** In some contexts, there is the risk of stating the obvious when expressing competences. The obvious may still need to be stated, but it is best to do so in such a way that it is clear that the competences concerned relate to appropriate levels of student development.

10 **Think ahead to the assessment.** When identifying elements of competence remember that these are to form the foundation for measuring student achievement. Be careful not to write magnificent looking outcomes which could not possibly be measured objectively.

11 **Consult the market.** When designing a new competence framework relevant to students following particular employment directions, it is very useful to bring in employers early in the design stage, and help them to tell you exactly what sorts of things they want their future employees to be able to do.

12 **Postpone going into too much detail too early.** Elements of competence are only the first step in defining and expressing measurable competences. In most cases, the elements should remain broad and simple, with subsequent elaboration to be achieved by defining "performance criteria, evidence descriptors and range statements".

13 **Decide whether you need "core" competences and optional ones.** Sometimes it can be too narrow to restrict the agenda to things all students should do. Under such circumstances it can be useful to specify a number of optional competences, and maybe add an indication of how many of these, out of the total, students should achieve.

5. **检查适任要素与所有适任学生能够完成的任务之间的联系**。这些任务是所有学生都应该能够完成的,但对大多数成功者来说应达到更高水平。有关每一个适任要素的学生表现水平的内容在稍后的详细适任方案中再讨论。

6. **利用大纲表达目标和目的**。例如,在英格兰和威尔士的"商业和技术教育协会"的大纲详细说明中,就是采用学生学完每一主题后,能够做的工作来很好地表达预期的学习效果。用"有能力做"这种适任语言将目标调整为学习效果通常只是较简单的编辑工作。

7. **不要忽视价值观和道德准则**。对很多现有适任方案给出批评是因为它们忽视了增强价值观的证据。在对学生的适任能力要求方面,不应该害怕添加显示学生价值观的内容。

8. **避免用知识或理解来表达适任**。虽然学生掌握这些知识并理解知识是最基本的,但还是应尽量用学生实际能够做的事情表达适任要素。

9. **注意次要的适任内容**。在某些情况下,当表达适任时,仅对主要的项目做出规定会有点冒险。虽然对主要的内容必须做出规定,但最好能对学生的整体适任的相应发展水平做出要求。

10. **评估前的考虑**。确定适任要素时要记住这些要素是构成评测学生成绩的基础。注意不要采用看起来重要但不能进行客观评测的项目。

11. **市场咨询**。在设计与学生特定的职业相关的适任方案时,设计的早期让雇主参与,并协助雇主准确地提供信息告知需要将来的雇员能够做什么,这对制定方案很有益。

12. **要素不应制订得过于繁细**。在确定和表达可评测的能力时,适任要素仅仅是第一步。在大部分情况下,要素应该保持内容广泛、简单,并随后通过确定"能力标准、证据说明和综合说明"加以详细说明。

13. **决定你是否需要"核心"适任并做出相应选择**。有时由于规定的时间太短而不能要求所有学生完成所有应该做的事情。在这样的情况下,指定一些优选的适任项目并提示学生在所有项目中应选择多少项来完成是很有用的。

Working out performance criteria

As we indicated in the previous set of suggestions, it is best that all aspects of a competence framework are developed together. Here, we have tried to identify the particular factors to be thought about in the context of spelling out performance criteria.

1. **Turn each element of competence into several specific actions that successful students will become able to perform.** Look at the sorts of things they will be expected to do in their professional work after leaving university, but be careful to specify the performance criteria in terms of actions they will actually have the opportunity to perform in the context of their studies.

2. **Make sure that each performance criterion is demonstrable.** Don't include things that students may well be able to demonstrate, if there would not be any possibility of actually giving them the chance to demonstrate them during the course.

3. **Expect each element of competence to require several performance criteria to cover it.** Most competences have a number of facets. It is normal for an element of competence to take between six and twelve performance criteria to cover it in a rounded way. If you end up with more than these, you may need to consider whether the element of competence concerned needs further subdividing.

4. **Think about hybrid performance criteria.** Often, there will be performance criteria which link to several elements of competence rather than to a single element. It is important that performance criteria are not stultified by trying to tie these broader ones to single elements of competence.

5. **Think ahead to the conditions under which the performance criteria will be demonstrated.** These can include whether students will be working alone or with other people, and whether they will have access to information and data. It can often become longwinded and clumsy to express these separately alongside each performance criterion, and the detail may need to be reserved for inclusion in evidence descriptors or range statements, but it is important to have this detail in mind while phrasing the performance criteria.

6. **Think ahead to the different levels to which each performance criterion can be shown to have been achieved.** These details will be relevant to the formulation of assessment criteria differentiating (for example) between pass, merit and distinction grades, or between successive classes of degree performance. It is best, however, to keep the performance criteria general and simple, and reserve the information about levels for inclusion in evidence descriptors and range statements.

7. **Think ahead to the nature of the evidence against which the performance criteria will be assessed.** In due course, specification of this evidence will play a vital part in the assessment scheme for the demonstration of the competences. When it is not easy to be clear about the forms that evidence may take, it is usually best to make adjustments to the performance criteria.

制定操作标准

正如我们先前提出的建议一样,适任方案的所有方面最好都同步发展。在这里,我们已尽量考虑上下文中涉及的因素,并对能力标准做出详细解释。

1. **把每一项适任要素转化成几项,成功的学生能够采取的具体行动**。考虑学生离开大学后将要从事的工作种类,同时根据在其学习过程中实际上有机会采取的行动来仔细规定能力标准。

2. **确信可以表明每一项能力标准**。不要把学生本来可以很好地表明,但在课程过程中实际上又不可能给他们机会表明的此类表现标准包括在标准里面。

3. **预期每一项适任要素都需要涉及几方面的操作标准**。大部分适任有许多方面。通常对一项适任要素来说,涉及6~12个方面的能力标准才够全面。但如果你使用了更多的表现标准,你可能需要考虑相关的适任要素是否应该进一步细分。

4. **考虑混合的操作标准**。通常,有些表现标准不是与一项而是与几项适任要素相关联。重要的是不要徒劳地试图将这几项要素合并成一个适任要素。

5. **预先考虑表明能力标准的条件**。这些条件可能包括:学生是单独工作还是与其他人一起工作以及他们是否能获得资料和数据。通常,对这些条件分别进行说明会使能力标准的描述变得冗长和臃肿。因而这些细节可能需要放到证据说明和综合说明中去,但重要的是在介绍表现标准时应记住这些细节。

6. **预先考虑达到每项表现标准所对应的不同成绩等级**。这方面的细节内容与系统的评估标准所采用的分级制度相关,例如:采用及格、良好和优秀的特征等级划分法,或者采用连续分级的划分方法(如百分制)。然而,最好是保持表现标准的通用、简单,并在证据描述和综合说明中包括分级方法的资料。

7. **预先考虑评价操作标准的证据性质**。对于某些课程,证据的详细说明在适任评估计划中担当极其重要的角色。如果出现难以确定证据类型的情况,最好的方法通常是调整表现标准。

8   **Look for gaps.** Ask yourself, and other people, "are there other things that any successful student should be able to show that they can do?" If necessary, revisit the elements of competence, adding new ones to cover any important aspects that may not be there already.

9   **Look beyond the subject.** It is normal for some performance criteria to relate to personal or transferable skills. Don't assume that these will have been covered in some other module. It is best to make performance criteria comprehensive enough to address everything that is relevant to each element of competence in the context of the course or module.

10 **Don't be too ambitious.** Remember that performance criteria are going to be the basis for assessment. Every important performance criterion should be associated with some kind of assessment, otherwise students can't be credited with having demonstrated the elements of competence concerned.

Writing evidence descriptors

In competence frameworks, student performance is judged not on the basis of what they know, but on what they can show. It is therefore important to be clear about the nature, range and standard of evidence we require students to produce. The following suggestions should help you strike an appropriate balance between evidence and achievement.

1   **Decide on "mandatory evidence".** This should cover minimum levels of achievement which will be considered to be adequate proof that performance criteria have been met sufficiently for the elements of competence associated with them to have been achieved.

2   **Include varied forms of evidence.** It is important, for example, that students are not measured all the time on the basis of similar forms of evidence, such as written reports. Some students are better at producing one form of evidence than another, and we need to try to ensure that such students are not disadvantaged.

3   **Work out an agenda of alternative possibilities for evidence.** When you intend students to use their initiative and creativity regarding the nature of the evidence with which they demonstrate their achievement of a performance criterion, give examples to help them select and collect evidence.

4   **Allow for students who wish to do it their way.** Arrange for students to have the opportunity to negotiate with you alternative forms of evidence they can assemble to demonstrate their achievement of performance criteria.

5   **Accept appropriate evidence from the past.** There is little point requiring students to re-invent the wheel. Make it possible for them to bring forward evidence of other work they have already done, which links directly to performance criteria in your competence framework.

8. **找出缺陷**。问自己和他人,"还有没有合格学员能够展示他们能完成的其他方面?"如有必要,应重新审核适任要素,增加一些缺少的重要适任内容。

9. **观察科目范围之外的内容**。一些表现标准与个人能力及个人可转换技能相关是很正常的。不要假定这些内容已包含在其他的教学模块中。最好的方法是使表现标准具有充分的综合性,以便覆盖课程或教学模块中与每一个适任要素相关的所有内容。

10. **不能急于求成**。记住表现标准是评估的基础。针对每一项重要的表现标准都应该采用某些方式进行评估,否则用以表明学生已经满足这些适任要素的成绩就不可能被取信。

编写证据说明

在适任方案中,判断学生的表现并不是依据他们知道什么,而是依据他们能做什么。因此,弄清我们要求学生提出的证据的性质、范围和标准是很重要的。以下建议有助于在证据与学习成效之间找出相应的平衡。

1. **确定"强制性证据"**。强制性证据反映了对于可以充分表明适任的证据方面的最低要求,能提供这些证据表明学生已经充分满足与适任要素对应的表现标准。

2. **采用不同的证据形式**。一个重要问题是:不要总是以相似的证据形式,如书面报告,来评测学生。学生通常会擅长于提供某种形式的证据,采用不同的证据提供形式可以保证评测的公平性。

3. **制定可选择证据的操作规程**。如果想要学生主动和创造性地提供自己已经达到表现标准的证据,应该应用实例帮助他们选择和收集证据。

4. **允许学生按自己的方法操作**。安排机会使学生可以与你协商适于表明他们达到表现标准的选择性证据形式。

5. **承认以前获得的合适证据**。正像我们不会要求学生重新发明舵轮一样,在适任方案里应允许学生提供他们在过往的工作中已完成的与表现标准直接关联的证据。

6   **Be sensible about overlaps with other subjects.** In competence frameworks, there is the possibility that several performance criteria will be similar in different modules. Where possible, it is desirable to make the evidence descriptors sufficiently unique to each module, so that students completing one module can't claim that they have also achieved most of the performance criteria relating to another.

7   **Make sure that not too much evidence is required.** There is a tendency for students (and staff!) to collect too much evidence relating to a given performance criterion, when they should be aiming to collect a more diverse collection of evidence, spanning several performance criteria. It is worth specifying the intended quantities of evidences "rules of thumb", either in the evidence descriptors or in range statements, setting the parameters underpinning the collection and presentation of evidence.

8   **Develop evidence descriptors in terms of standards.** Having established evidence descriptors for the successful demonstration of performance criteria, it is possible to give details of the additional evidence quality which will relate to higher levels of competence, for example, "merit" or "distinction" rather than "pass". A similar approach can be used where Degree work is assessed using a competence approach, by specifying evidence descriptors relating to the hierarchy of pass, 2:2, 2:1 and 1st.

9   **Look again at the evidence descriptors and decide what has been missed!** It's often possible to say "anyone demonstrating competence X must somewhere have done such-and-such" only to discover that the appropriate evidence has still not been specified anywhere in the competence framework. It is usually necessary to go back in such cases and add further performance criteria relating to such evidence.

10 **Keep the evidence descriptors as understandable as possible.** Keep the language simple and straightforward. One of the problems of competence-based approaches is the tendency for curriculum developers to get wrapped up in jargon and convoluted expressions, which often mean nothing to the students themselves.

Writing range statements

In this final set of suggestions regarding competence frameworks, we present a few ideas about the role of range statements. We conclude with some overall suggestions pertaining to the whole framework.

1   **Use range statements to complete the competence framework.** The combination of elements of competence, performance criteria, and evidence descriptors should be made completely self-explanatory by the additional detail provided in range statements. These should alert students to any additional specifications regarding the nature, quality, quantity and standards of the evidence they should provide for each element of competence.

2   **Use range statements as illustrations.** Include examples of things that will provide satisfactory evidence of the achievement of the learning outcomes. These can be particularly useful to students if they are framed in a straightforward way, and relate to real life practice.

6. **判别与其他科目重叠的内容**。在适任方案里,不同的项目中有可能几项表现标准是类似的。如可能,应使证据说明充分地与每一项目相对应,这样,学生完成一个模块后就不能声称他们也达到另一个相关项目的大部分表现标准。

7. **确信不会要求过多的证据**。在学生(工作人员)中存在一种趋势——在本应该收集更广泛地涉及几方面表现标准的不同证据时却收集了过多的只与某项表现标准相关的证据。应该在证据说明,或者在综合说明中对证据的收集和提出做出相应限制性规定。

8. **根据标准制定证据说明**。为有效表明表现标准而编写的证据说明可能包含与较高的适任水平相关的额外证据质量的细节,例如,"良好"或者"优秀"而不仅是"及格"。可以使用类似的方法来评估学位,给相关的及格等级规定相应的证据说明。

9. **复查证据说明并确定是否有遗漏**!通常参照"任何人要表明在某方面适任,则必须已经能够如此做"的原则来发现在适任方案中哪些方面仍存在需要规定的证据。在这种情况下,通常有必要再次调整证据说明,以加入更多的与这些证据相关的表现标准。

10. **尽可能保持证据说明的可理解性**。应保持证据说明所用的语言简单易懂。存在于基于适任体系的一个问题是课程开发者热衷于使用难懂的语句和复杂的表述方式,而这些对于学生来说通常毫无意义。

编写综合说明

以下是关于适任方案的最后一组建议,建议中对于综合说明的作用提出几方面的想法,并且我们总结出与整体方案有关的几点综合建议。

1. **以综合说明完成适任方案**。适任要素、表现标准和证据说明的组合完全依赖综合说明中提供的附加细节来进行自我诠释。这些诠释提醒学生对每一适任要素需要提供的证据的性质、质量、数量和标准有关的附加说明保持警惕。

2. **将综合说明用作例证**。这包括给达到的学习效果提供一些例子作为其能力令人满意的证据。综合说明如果设计成结构直观并且与实际生活结合,则可能对学生特别有用。

3   **Provide guidelines rather than imperatives.** While it is useful to be specific, it is important to clarify that original, divergent and creative responses from students are also possible and credit-worthy.

4   **Use range statements to address collaborative working.** While it may be necessary for students to provide evidence that demonstrates individual achievement, it is also important that they have the opportunity to display the cooperative aspects of their work.

Some unifying points about competence frameworks...

5   **It's best to number everything!** Assign number systems to elements of competence, performance criteria, evidence descriptors and range statements, so you can refer students easily to particular components in the framework.

6   **Cross-reference everything.** For example, indicate clearly which performance indicators are to be demonstrated by each specified piece of evidence. Link evidence to the relevant elements of competence.

7   **Decide where grading is appropriate and possible.** Not all competences, performance criteria, or pieces of evidence can be graded. Some can only be used on a pass-or-fail basis.

8   **Establish priorities clearly, and link assessment to them.** For example, when an element of competence is broken down into six performance criteria, don't expect each criterion to be equally important. Use assessment details to show students which performances, and which pieces of evidence, to put their best efforts into.

9   **Use short print-runs!** After implementing the teaching and assessment of a competence framework just once, there will be a substantial number of adjustments you should expect to wish to make to it, based on experience. Don't become lumbered with large stocks of outdated documents.

10 **Don't pretend that because you have got a competence framework, assessment will be entirely objective.** Most competence frameworks simply mean that the decision-making tasks involved in assessment are smaller and more manageable, but they are still always subjective in the final analysis.

Assessing transferable skills

At a meeting, students were discussing their experiences of recent interviews. "How did it go?" asked one. "Not very well" came the reply. "They asked me if I had developed any personal transferable skills as part of my course, and I didn't know what they meant." "Of course you have—you were Treasurer of the Canoe Club and you gave a presentation about your project...". The following suggestions may help you—and your students—to address such skills.

3. **提供指导而不是强制性的**。虽然需要做出相应规定,但重要的是要阐明学生做出原始的、发散的、独创性的反应是可能和可信的。

4. **使用综合说明来强调合作**。要求学生提供能表明个人成绩的证据,同时,让学生有机会展示他们工作上的合作能力也是重要的。

关于适任体系的一些统一观点……

5. **最好是给每种文件编号**。给适任要素、表现标准、证据说明和综合说明分配号码,以便学生可以容易地从方案中查阅特定的内容。

6. **交叉参考各种文件**。例如,清楚地指明能力指标应用哪个特定的证据说明,以及将证据与相关的适任要素相联系。

7. **确定合适和可行的分等级方法**。并不是所有的适任、表现标准或者每一项证据都能划分等级。某些项目只能划分为及格或不及格。

8. **明确规定优先项目并与评估相联系**。例如,当一个适任要素被分解成六项表现标准时,各项标准不会都同等重要。应利用评估数据使学生知道应特别注意哪些项目的表现和证据。

9. **经常调整教学评估安排!** 一轮的教学和评估框架完成后,应根据实际情况做出一些调整。在调整过程中应保持不断更新文件。

10. **不能因为制定了适任方案,就认为评估是完全客观的**。大部分的适任方案只是意味着相关的评估决策工作较少并且便于处理,但最终的分析仍然是主观的。

对可转换技能的评估

在一个会议上,学员正在讨论最近的面试经历。有人问"情况怎么样?""不怎么样。"回答说。"他们问我是否已发展了作为课程的一部分的个人的可转换技能,而我不知道他们的意思是什么。""你当然已经具备可转换技能——你是独木舟俱乐部的出纳员,你已经对相关主题做了说明……"。以下的建议可以帮助你和你的学员表达这些技能。

1. **Open up a debate about what these skills are.** Different terminology abounds, from common skills, personal transferable skills, core skills and so on. The skills themselves normally include those relating to communication (written and verbal), working with others, numerary, foreign languages, presentation, leadership, and adhering to values.

2. **Select which common skills to address in the context of your students' work.** Make sure that the skills are clearly relevant to the subject and topic, and not seen as optional extras by your students.

3. **Brainstorm with students the evidence they need to produce to prove their development of each skill.** Then open up a discussion about different levels of the respective skills, and how these levels may be distinguished by the quality and nature of the evidence.

4. **Collect examples of evidence of common skills for students themselves to assess.** Such evidence may take many forms, ranging from written reports to video-recorded interviews or presentations.

5. **Think about how the chosen skills can best be developed.** Before thinking about assessing such skills it is useful to think about where their development best fits into the course or module. A grid or matrix format may work well in planning which skills relate to which parts of a course. With modular programmer, it can become more complex deciding how to plot an individual student's development of a range of skills.

6. **Ask whether the skills are involved in all years of a course.** There is a tendency, for example, to think that presentation skills should be addressed in Year 1 and can then be ticked off. It is useful to think how such skills should be developing throughout a course, and how the levels should advance appropriately.

7. **Allow students the opportunity to use a range of media to demonstrate transferable skills.** Some skills can best be demonstrated with evidence derived from leisure activities, home life or work contexts. The evidence may comprise documents, tapes, videos, or computer programs. It is often valuable for students to include testimonials and statements of competence, provided by qualified colleagues, supervisors and others, who can testify appropriately to the achievements of the candidate.

8. **Get students involved in the assessment of others' competences.** Peer assessment of each other's transferable skills is an excellent method of enabling students to develop their own skills, and also provides a high level of engagement and commitment.

9. **Help students to develop their ability to evaluate their own transferable skills.** They can do so in a variety of ways such as filling in self-assessment forms, writing reflective accounts and participating in evaluative discussions with peers and/or tutors.

10. **Refer closely to the particular requirements of your own context.** For example, BTEC and GNVQ give very clear guidance about what is expected in the assessment of such skills, and many universities have their own strategies and policies on core skills or transferable skills, to which you may relate your own assessment methods.

1. **讨论各类技能的含义与划分**。关于技能有许多不同的术语,包括:通用技能、个人的可转换技能、核心技能,等等。技能本身通常包括交流(书面和口头)、与他人一同工作、数字处理、外语、展示、组织领导等能力以及其他有价值的内容。

2. **根据学生工作内容选择通用技能**。确信这些技能与科目和主题密切相关,不要被你的学生看作是随意的附加内容。

3. **与学生就他们用来证明各项技能得到发展所需的证据开展自由讨论**。然后就技能的不同水平以及怎样依据证据的质量和特性去划分不同的水平等级开展讨论。

4. **收集学生自我评价其通用能力的证据实例**。这种证据可以有多种形式,范围从书面报告到电视录像式面试或者个人展示。

5. **考虑怎样使所选择的技能得到最好的发展**。在考虑这些技能的评价工作之前,应该先考虑哪些课程和教学模块最适于发展这些技能,这是很有价值的。网格和矩阵技术很适于应用在课程相关的技能规划方面。使用模块化程序,在决定怎样划分学生个人的一系列技能发展方面可能会比较复杂。

6. **了解技能是否涉及多年前的课程**。有这样一种趋势,例如安排某些技能在第一年展示并记录成绩以后不再进行评测。应认真考虑这些技能在课程随后的进程中如何得到发展以及应该怎样相应地提高水平。

7. **给学生提供机会可以用多种方法表明他们已具备的可转换技能**。可以从业余活动、家庭生活和工作环境中得到证据来最好地加以证明一些技能。证据可以包括文件、录音带、录像或者计算机程序。通常,对学生有价值的证明包括具备资格的同事、监督人员和其他人提供的证明和适任说明,这些人可以恰当地证明申请人的表现。

8. **让学员参与其他人的适任评估**。可转换技能的相互比较评估是能够使学生发展自己技能的一种极好方法,也给学生提供了一种高标准的参与以及承担任务的机会。

9. **帮助学员提高自我评价可转换技能的能力**。他们可以使用多种多样的方法,例如填自我评估表格、经过深思熟虑编写的报告以及与同学和/或导师一起参加关于评估的讨论来提高这方面能力。

10. **紧密结合特定内容的要求**。例如,BTEC 和 GNVQ 已经为评估这类技能提供可预期的结果方面很清楚的指导。很多大学在核心技能或可转换技能方面有着自己的策略和方针,在这点上你可以结合自己的评估方法加以应用。

Part 18
Developing Performance Improvement Plan

Introduction

The purpose of the performance improvement plan is to address areas for improvement in both the assessment process and the candidate's performance. Without it the system will not be complete, as there may be deficiencies either in the manner of conducting the assessment which will be carried forward to the next assessment, or the assessed candidate would continue to be incompetent.

The performance improvement plan may require changes in the ship's system or the assessment process itself, apart from the recommendations made to the candidate for further training. The plan can therefore only be effective if all aspects of the shipboard assessment system is reviewed.

Dealing With Poor Performers

The candidate has done something or failed to do something which adversely affects his/her work, the ability of others to do their work, or the inability to meet the performance criteria. You are faced with decisions on how to handle the incident or series of incidents. First, you must decide whether the incident involves the candidate's poor job performance or an act of misconduct or delinquency. Normally it is one or the other, but in some cases it may be both. Next, you must decide what type of management action will best deal with the incident(s).

There are many possible causes for an candidate's performance and/or conduct problem, for example, illness, disability, substance abuse, personality conflict, family problems, lack of training, and low job morale. The nature of the problem will determine the course of action to be taken. For example, the candidate could be referred to an assistance programme for drug or alcohol abuse counselling. or a fitness-for-duty medical examination may be needed to determine physical or mental capability to do the job.

If the problem is failure to meet one or more critical elements and standards, and the candidate has been advised of those elements and standards, then appropriate actions would be taken under the a Performance Management Plan. Initial steps could include performance counselling, training, and/or closer supervision. If performance continues to be unacceptable, then more severe actions could be reassignment, demotion, or removal.

There may be instances where the problems are both performance and conduct. In these cases you could take action under either program, or both simultaneously.

Purpose of Performance Reviews

1. The purpose of performance reviews:

For performance reviews to be constructive and effective, it is important that both assessor and candidate understand the various purposes for conducting reviews. Some of these purposes are:

第18章
制订操作改进计划

引言

实操改进计划的目的在于同时改善评估程序和考生的操作表现。缺少这一环节,整个体系就不算完整。因为评估方式的缺陷将被带到下一评估项目中,而操作缺陷会使考生继续不及格。

与对考生做进一步培训的建议不同的是,操作表现改进计划需要船上系统或评估程序本身做出改变。只有在对船上评估系统进行了全面的研究,本计划才是行之有效的。

对表现不良情况的处理:

如果发生被评估人的操作表现未能达到操作表现标准或给他人造成了负面影响这类情况,你将要面对如何处理这些情况的问题。首先,你要判断是否被评估人的不良工作表现或出现处理不当和失职的行为导致了这些情况的发生。通常会导致上述某个问题,但有时会同时都涉及。其次,你要决定处理这些事情的最佳方式。

影响被评估人操作表现和/或行为的可能原因会很多,例如,疾病、残疾、材料滥用、个性冲突、家庭问题、缺乏训练、组织纪律不强等。这些问题的性质将决定要采取怎样的行动,例如,对吸毒或酗酒的考生将展开帮教程序,开展适任体格检查以决定考生的身体及精神情况是否适于该项工作。

如果存在的问题导致未能符合关键的要素和标准,而已经对考生在相应要素和标准方面提出过知道的情况下,应采取"表现管理计划"规定的适当行动。最初的步骤应包括行为辅导、训练和/或严密的监督。若操作表现仍不符合标准,更严厉的行动将是重新分配工作、降级或免职。

以下是处理考生操作表现与行为的一些实例。你可参照其中的程序之一或全部采取行动。

操作考查的目的

1. 操作考查的目的:

由于操作考查是建设性的并有效的,对评估员及被评估人而言,理解考查的目的非常重要。这些目的包括:

- To provide information concerning the candidate's quality of work.

- To promote open and continued communication between the candidate and the supervisor on related job performance issues and professional growth.

- To provide feedback to the candidate on how s/he is perceived by colleagues and clients, and, if applicable, subordinates.

- To assist the candidate in accomplishing present and future job performance requirements and skills development goals.

- To serve as documentation that can help differentiate between performance that deserves merit compensation and performance that does not.

The performance review system is responsive to the candidate's right to know where he or she stands with respect to ideal job performance and the employer's need to achieve necessary organizational goals and objectives. Ideally, assessor and candidate engage in ongoing dialogue on these issues. The performance review document or feedback session should not contain any major surprises about performance weaknesses or failure to achieve stated goals. Rather, the performance review represents a formal statement. The review session can serve as an opportunity to discuss career planning.

The review should be directly tied to a current job description, along with any established personal, management group, and organizational goals and objectives. The candidate and assessor must discuss the performance review in its entirety.

A skillfully conducted performance review will allow for a partnership between candidate and assessor. Ideally, it will provide the candidate and the assessor with several desired outcomes, including:

- Setting of mutual goals and objectives that address personal and organizational needs.

- Improving understanding between the candidate and the assessor about expectations regarding job performance requirements and professional growth.

- Improving job performance, job satisfaction, and professional development.

Performance Improvement Method: A discussion Guide

A. *Develop a careful definition first if there is a problem.*
   1. State what it is. View a problem as a deviation from the standard.
   2. How do you know that it's a problem? What are the signs that indicate a problem?
   3. Determine how much the problem is costing the ship's organization in terms of:
      a. Work not being done
      b. Work not being done on time
      c. Problems being caused in other parts of the organization.

- 提供被评估人工作质量的相关信息。

- 促进被评估人及管理者在相关工作能力认证及职业发展方面的公开和连续的沟通。

- 提供被评估人的同事、客户和部属(如合适)的反馈信息。

- 帮助被评估人达到目前以致未来要求的工作能力和技能发展目标。

- 分别给表现优良和未达优良程度的被评估人提供不同的证明文件。

被评估人有权知道自己是否已达到理想的工作成绩和满足雇主的目标与成绩的需求,操作考查系统应对此做出回应。理想的情况应该是评估员及被评估人在这些问题上进行对话。操作考查文件或考查情况反馈会议不应对表现的缺陷或未能达到规定目标表示任何意外,相反地,操作考查应对此做出正式的说明。考查情况反馈会议可以提供机会讨论职业规划。

考察应直接与当前的一个工种(连同相应的工作人员、管理层和组织目标)相联系。被评估人与评估员必须充分审核全部的内容。

完善的考察应允许被评估人与评估员良好合作,在理想的情况下,应达到几个结果,包括:

- 建立个人与组织需要的共有目标。

- 改善被评估人与评估员在预期的工作能力要求及个人发展方面的相互理解。

- 改善工作能力、工作满意度及促进职业发展。

提高表现的方法:一份供探讨的指导

A. 如果存在问题,首先要明确其性质。
   1. 确定是什么问题。将问题视为与标准的偏离。
   2. 你如何确定那是一个问题?有何明显的特征?
   3. 根据以下方面确定存在的问题对船上组织造成的影响:
      a. 工作未完成
      b. 工作未及时完成
      c. 出现的其他方面问题。

B. *Try to determine the cause of the problem.*
   1. Is something preventing the work from being done?
      a. Does the candidate have the right tools to do the job?
      b. Are organizational policies/procedures hindering performance? (confusion, conflicting goals, complicated procedures, lack of money, time, etc.)

   2. Does the candidate have enough knowledge to do the work?
      a. Does he know why it should be done a certain way?
      b. Does he know how his work contributes to the work of the organization?
      c. Does the candidate possess enough knowledge about the work and how it is to be done to be able to do it?
      d. Has he ever been told that his work is not meeting acceptable standards?

   3. Try to determine if the job (task) itself has a built-in problem that leads to poor performance.
      a. Is the work too difficult for one person?
      b. Is the work so disagreeable that it is avoided?
      c. Is there no reward or sense of satisfaction in doing the particular task?

C. *Accurately record the results of the session.*
   1. Prepare a rough draft and let the candidate review it.
   2. Include all expected changes that should occur.

Suggestions for the Performance Review Process

Step 1. Starting the meeting.

Objectives :
- Relieve tension and anxiety.
- Get cooperation and participation.
- Set task-oriented climate.

Skills and techniques :
- Be cordial and open.
- Spell out purpose: to appraise performance and set stage for objective setting.
- Establish benefits gained from the performance review.
- Outline ground rules.

Step 2. Getting the candidate's view.

Objective :
- Get the candidate's candid appraisal of his own performance, along with the reasons for having accomplished (or not accomplished) their objectives.

Skills and techniques :
- Address one objective at a time.
- Focus first on achievement of the objective.

B. 尝试找出问题的起因。
   1. 是什么阻碍了工作的完成?
      a. 被评估人有没有完成工作所需的合适工具?
      b. 组织的方针或程序是否阻碍操作的完成?(组织混乱、自相矛盾的目标、复杂的程序、资金和时间的欠缺等。)

   2. 被评估人是否具备足够的知识来完成工作?
      a. 他是否懂得为什么一定要以某种方式处理某项任务?
      b. 他是否知道他的工作对于组织的作用?
      c. 他是否充分了解他的工作并具备如何完成工作以及如何开展工作的足够知识?
      d. 他是否曾被告知他的工作未能达到规范的要求?

   3. 要确定工作(任务)的本身是否存在内在问题而导致不良的表现。
      a. 对被评估人来说,工作是否太难了?
      b. 是否很厌恶以致要逃避这工作?
      c. 在完成特定的任务时没有令人感觉满意的回报?

C. 准确记录会议结果。
   1. 准备初稿并允许被评估人查看。

   2. 包括所有可预见的可能变化。

对于操作考查程序的建议

步骤一、召开会议。

目的:
- 减轻压力和忧虑。
- 获得合作与参与。
- 创建面向任务的氛围。

技巧:
- 要诚恳、开放。
- 阐明目的:评价表现并说明目标的设定步骤。
- 说明操作考查的好处。
- 略述基本的规则。

步骤二、收集被评估人的意见。

目的:
- 收集被评估人对其成绩和达到目标或未能达到目标的原因的客观评价。

技巧:
- 每次处理一个目标。
- 首先应关注目标是否达到。

- Then focus on causes for both achieved and non-achieved objectives. Determine the effects of what the staff member did, what you did, and the impact of contingencies, on the achievement on the objective.
- Throughout the meeting, probe, listen, and summarize.

Step 3. Explaining your views.

Objective :
- Give your reactions to candidate's appraisal, and then give your own appraisal.

Skills and techniques :
- First, tell candidate where you agree with his or her appraisal.
- Second, explain where you disagree.
- Finally, if necessary, present additional data about your appraisal.
- Ask for candidate's reaction.

Step 4. Resolving disagreements.

Objective :
- Mutually discuss and reach acceptable consensus on disagreements.

Skills and techniques :
- First, use reflective statements to vent any interfering emotions.
- If there are several disagreements, identify and work on only one at a time.
- Clearly state the disagreement and the positions of both parties.
- Discuss both positions, starting with the candidate's. Probe, listen, summarize.
- Reach final conclusions.
- Repeat the conclusions, to insure that both parties agree.

Step 5. Working out the final resolution.

Objectives :
- Mutually work out and agree to the final performance review.
- Write out the agreements.
- Obtain candidate's commitment to the review, and to areas for setting objectives for the following assessment.

Skills and techniques :
- Work with staff member to come up with recommendations for the final appraisal and for next assessment's objectives. Summarize those recommendations.
- Add own views, as needed.

Solving Performance Problems

Problem

Something prevents the work from being done

- 然后关注达成目标和未达成目标的原因。确定你本人和其他人员的言行及意外事件对达成目标所产生的影响。
- 在会议过程中,应善于探究、倾听和总结。

步骤三、解释你的观点。

目的:
- 对被评估人的自评做出回应,并提出你的评价意见。

技巧:
- 首先,告知被评估人,你对他的自评中哪些内容是认同的。
- 其次,解释哪些部分是你不同意的。
- 如有必要,最后提出你评价的补充数据。
- 了解被评估人的感受。

步骤四、解决分歧。

目的:
- 通过相互讨论,统一分歧的意见。

技巧:
- 首先,用经过深思熟虑的解释化解任何冲突的情绪。
- 如果有多处分歧,每次只找出一处进行处理。
- 清楚地阐明双方的分歧及观点。
- 与被评估人一起研究和讨论双方的观点,倾听意见并加以总结。
- 得出最终结论。
- 重申结论,确保双方都同意。

步骤五、做出最终结论

目的:
- 共同做出并统一最终操作考查结果。
- 写出考察结论文件。
- 取得被评估人对考察及设定的后续评估目标范围的认可。

技巧:
- 和其他人员一起工作以得出对最终评测及下一步考察目标范围的建议,并归纳这些建议。
- 必要时,加上自己的观点。

解决表现存在的问题

问题

工作因某些因素而未完成

Try:
a. Supply more or better tools
b. Change policy/procedures, if possible

Problem

Candidate doesn't have enough knowledge
Try
a. Tell him why the job should be done a certain way
b. Tell him how the job contributes to the work of the organization
c. Instruct the candidate in the skills needed. Determine a training or developmental experience that will help provide the skill needed
d. Inform the candidate about the specific shortcomings of his work

Problem

The work itself has a built-in problem
Try
a. Assign the task to more than one person
b. Rotate a disagreeable task among other candidates so one person isn't stuck with it all of the time
c. Provide an incentive for overcoming built-in problems and doing the job (Recognition, appreciation, greater variety of rewarding work, more independence, etc.)

措施:
a. 提供更多更好的工具
b. 如可能,改变策略或程序

问题

  被评估人不具备足够的知识

措施:
a. 告知被评估人为什么需要采用某种方法完成工作
b. 告知被评估人这项工作对组织的作用
c. 在必备的技能上给被评估人指导。确定一套训练与拓展练习,以提高其必备技能
d. 告知被评估人其工作的不足之处

问题:

  工作本身的内在问题

措施:
a. 将任务分配给多人去完成
b. 让其他考生轮流承担那些令人厌烦的任务以避免这类任务总是落到某一个考生头上
c. 对克服内在问题及完成对应工作的表现提供激励措施(如赞誉、表扬、提供更多种类奖励性工作及更多独立工作的机会等)

Part 19
Maintenance of Standards

Review of test material

1. In order to maintain a desired standard it is essential that all examination material should be reviewed to ensure its validity in all respects before it is put into use. It is also essential that its validity should be periodically reviewed in the light of experience gained in its use and to ensure that the item of knowledge concerned has not become outdated or in need of modification. Additionally, test material, particularly subjective test material, becomes compromised through use, and sensitive items must either be replaced or revised with sufficient frequency to prevent serious compromise.

Content review

2. As mentioned earlier, the task analysis and derived general training objectives should be validated with the industry. The content validity of new test items can be established by simple review of their texts and contemplated answers, a check being made against relevant job and task specifications, general objectives and specific learning objectives.

Criterion-related review

3. The objective of all tests for certificates of competency is to assess the ability of the candidates to perform the functions of the posts in which the certificates for which they are applying will entitle them to be employed. A close relationship should therefore be maintained with all of the sectors of the industry which employ the personnel who have been trained and certificated under the overall system.

   Over a period of time, a feedback can be obtained from the industry on the effectiveness of the system. It is therefore most advisable, if not essential, to establish some form of advisory group or committee of industry representatives.

   Unfortunately, this method of assessing the relationship between success in the examinations and proficiency on the job involves considerable delay.

4. A more immediate review of the effectiveness of an examination in assessing competency can be made by obtaining the co-operation of seagoing personnel who are actively employed in the industry and are considered to perform at a satisfactory level of competency by their employers. Such personnel may co-operate by voluntarily taking the examination which is being assessed for its criterion-related validity. The confidentiality of the results must be guaranteed, and if necessary the tests may be taken anonymously.

第 19 章
标准的维护

测试材料审核

1. 为了保持预期的标准,很有必要在投入使用前对所有测试材料进行全面的审核,以确保其有效性,而且也很必要根据实际使用情况对其进行定期的有效性审核以确保相关的知识项目不致过时或及时得到更新。另外,测试材料,特别是主观类型的测试材料,在使用中会泄漏,对敏感的题目必须频繁地重置或更新以防严重泄漏。

内容审核

2. 如前所述,任务分析与衍生的训练目标应经过行业验证。新测试题内容的有效性可通过简单的测试审核及其答案来证实。应针对相关工作和任务说明、总体目标及特定学习目标进行审核。

标准相关审核

3. 适任证书考试的目的是评估考生对所申请的职位的履职能力,据此获得的证书能使学生被雇用。因而应与负责雇用已接受系统训练并获发证书的人员的行业部门保持密切的联系。

    在获发证书人员被雇并经过一段时间工作后,可从行业部门获得其工作情况以及有关培训及评测系统有效性的反馈。因此即使不是强制的,也强烈建议培训/评测机构建立某种形式的咨询组织或产业代表委员会。

    然而不幸的是,这种评价考试是否通过与是否精通工作之间关系的方法处于严重的滞后状态。

4. 更及时地对适任评估考试效果的评价可以通过与实际受雇于公司并被雇主认为操作能力已达到满意的水平的远洋船员合作来实现。可以用认为达到相关标准效果的试题对其中某个志愿者进行测试以确定评估考试与标准相关有效性间的差别。测试结果的保密性必须得到保证,如有必要,测试可以匿名进行。

For example, those candidates who already hold a certificate and have just come ashore and are entering the maritime academy to take upgrading courses leading to a certificate of higher grade may be tested on the examination under review. The results from such tests will then give an indication of the relationship between success in the test and the competency of the candidates, as assessed by their employers.

Statistical review

5. In the case of objective test material, particularly of test items of the multiple-choice type, a further check is advisable prior to putting such items into use. The new test items may be introduced into a regular examination which is based on previously established items. In scoring such an examination, the new test items under review are not taken into account in assessing the examination results of the candidate.

   However, the new test items are scored separately and a statistical review can then be carried out to determine the relative difficulty and discrimination power of the new test items and the effectiveness of their distracters. This is done by comparing the results achieved by each candidate in the examination based on the established items with the results they achieve in the new items under review.

Level of difficulty

6. The difficulty index or *P*-value of a new test item is established by the formula:

$$P = \frac{S}{T}$$

   where P = difficulty index
   S = the number of candidates who selected the correct response in the new item
   T = the total number of candidates taking the test.

Thus a test item to which there is a correct response from 60% of those taking the test will have a difficulty index of 0.6, the range of the index value varying from 0 = very difficult to 1 = very easy.

It should be noted that this is an indicator of relative difficulty as experienced by those who have taken the test, who are often referred to as the "population".

Cumulative and composite P-values

7. Where the population taking a test is low (for example, less than 20 candidates), the reliability of any statistical review is unsatisfactory. It is therefore necessary to accumulate the results experienced when the same test is used on a number of occasions. It is important that the total content of the test, or at least of the subject section concerned, is consistent throughout. Thus the value of *S* in the above formula becomes $S_1 + S_2 + S_3$, each being the results of three individual tests using the same total material, and *T* becomes the total number of candidates who took the tests, which is the total population.

例如,可以对那些已持证并刚上岸进入航海院校进修以或获得更高级别证书的考生,用需要审核的考卷进行测试。测试的成绩将显示考生在通过考试与雇主认可的适任能力之间的关系。

统计审核

5. 建议在投入使用前对客观测试材料,特别是多项选择测试题,进行进一步的审核。可以在已预定的正规试题中添加新的试题以便对试题进行测试。在计算得分时,切记不应把这些测试项目计入考生的评估考试成绩。

   对于新的测试题可单独计分并进行统计,以确定其相应的难度与区分度以及达到的效果。可以通过比较考生分别在现行考题与新测试题中获得的成绩来确定难度。

难度

6. 新测试题的难度系数 P 由下式确定:

$$P = \frac{S}{T}$$

式中 P—— 难度系数;
S—— 新项目测试中选择正确答案的人数;
T—— 参加测试的总人数。

因而,如果参加测试的有60%的人答对,则难度系数为0.6,系数的数值范围从 0(十分困难)到 1(十分容易)。

应注意这是对已参加过测试的有经验的人群的困难度指标,这些人通常被称为"总体对象"。

P 值的累积与综合

7. 当参加测试的人员较少时(如少于20个考生),统计审核的可靠性是不能令人满意的。当相同的测试应用多次时,则需要对成绩进行累积。确保所有这些测试的全部内容至少是所有与科目相关的内容都完全一致,这样做是很必要的。在累积计算中,上式中的 S 变为 $S_1+S_2+S_3$,每一数值代表采用同一测试材料进行三次独立测试的成绩。而 T 则为参加测试的所有考生的全部数量,即对象总数。

8. It is also possible to arrive at a composite *P*-value if the new test items are included in several different established tests in the same subject area. This gives a comparison with a number of established test series already in use. Where an item is maintained in a data bank for periodic use, the composite *P*-value can be updated on each occasion it is used.

Efficiency of distracters

9. In carrying out the review to determine the *P*-value, note should also be taken of the number of times each distracter is selected by the candidates in each new test item. This allows calculation of a *P*-value for each of the alternative responses provided in a multiple-choice item. Thus the *P*-values for all alternative responses indicate the level of difficulty experienced by the candidate in selecting the correct response and the level of efficiency of each distracter.

Discriminating power or coefficient of correlation

10. The discriminating power, that is to say the ability of a test item to discriminate between high achievers and low achievers, can be determined by dividing the test population (candidates who have taken the test) into two groups, one forming the upper half of the group of candidates tested (the high achievers) and the other forming the lower half (the low achievers).

    The number of the high achievers who correctly answer each test item is then counted separately and the coefficient of correlation (the *D*-value) is obtained by the formula:

    $$D = \frac{C_H - C_L}{\frac{1}{2}T}$$

    where C_H is the number of high-achievers who answered the test item correctly
    C_L is the number of low achievers who answered the test item correctly
    T is the total population taking the test.

The *D*-value varies between +1, where all who correctly answer the item are high achievers and none are low achievers, and −1, where all who correctly answer the item are low achievers and none are high achievers.

Revision of items

11. A statistical review of the above nature assists in identifying those test items which may be poorly constructed or otherwise faulty. It must, however, be emphasized that the *P*-values and *D*-values are relative indicators, reflecting only the difficulty and discriminating power of the item relative to the population of candidates tested. Thus the same test item may be indicated as being difficult where the population is poorly trained and yet easy where the population is well trained.

12. Examinations to assess the competency of seafarers are intended to be criterion-related tests, and items having a high criterion validity will not necessarily have a high discrimination power or a *P*-value which lies within the normally acceptable range.

8. 如果新的测试题出现在同一科目范围内的几个不同的测试中,也可能获得P值的综合值。这样就可以与大量已使用的确定试题进行系列的比较。为周期性使用而保存在数据库的一道试题,其综合P值可以在每次使用后被更新。

错误选项的效率

9. 在进行测评以确定P值时,应对考生在每一新的测试题中所选择的答案号码进行记录。这样可以计算出多项选择的每一个备选答案的P值。因此,所有备选答案的P值显示了考生选出正确答案的实际难度和由选错答案反映出来的考题的错误选项的效率。

区分度、相关系数

10. 所谓区分度,就是试题区分考生对相关内容掌握得好和差的能力。要确定区分度可以将所有测试对象(已接受测试的考生)分为两组,一组为高分考生(内容掌握好的考生),另一组为低分考生(掌握不好的考生)。

单独算出能正确作答的高分考生的数量,然后可根据下式得出相关系数(D值):

$$D = \frac{C_H - C_L}{\frac{1}{2}T}$$

式中：C_H—— 能正确作答的高分考生数量；
C_L—— 能正确作答的低分考生数量；
T—— 参加测试的总人数。

D值的取值范围在+1(表示所有正确作答的都是高分考生而没有低分考生)与-1(表示所有正确作答的人都是低分考生而没有高分考生)之间。

修订试题

11. 以上的统计审核有助于识别评估题的不良结构及缺陷。然而,必须强调的是,系数P与D值只是相对的指标,仅反映题目对于总体参加考试人员的难度与区分度。因而,同一份考题对那些训练不良的人员来说可能是困难的,而对有良好训练的人员来说则是容易的。

12. 由于海员适任资格评估考试规定为标准相关考试,试题具有高度的准确性。因此,不必要处在一般考试所要求的高区分度和系数P的可接受范围之内。

13. Thus test items should not automatically be rejected or revised on the basis of these statistical indicators alone. The *P*-values and *D*-values should be used as aids in assisting those responsible for the construction of tests to improve the quality and effectiveness of the examination system. Notwithstanding this, the level of difficulty of an item in a multiple-choice test is affected principally by the plausibility of its distracters. Therefore those distracters which prove unattractive even to low achievers should be replaced if the test item is to be retained.

Table 11.4-1

Percent of candidates who pass the established test or are otherwise deemed competent	Average range of *P*-values
0	0.45–0.59
5	0.51–0.60
10	0.54–0.62
15	0.57–9.63
20	0.59–0.65
25	0.61–0.66
30	0.62–0.67
35	0.63–0.67
40	0.64–0.69
45	0.65–0.70
50	0.66–0.71
55	0.67–0.72
60	0.68–0.73
65	0.69–0.74
70	0.70–0.75
75	0.71–0.77
80	0.73–0.78
85	0.75–0.80
90	0.76–0.83
95	0.79–0.87
100	0.84–1.00

Desired P-values

14. Table 11.14-1 may be used as a general guide to the acceptability of *P*-values which have been established for new test items in accordance with the procedures set out in paragraphs 3 to 6 of this Part. The table is based on a pass mark of 70%.

Desired D-values

15. In general, the *D*-value of a correct response should be in the range +0.250 to +0.750. The *D*-values of distracters should be in the range −0.250 to −0.750, the total range of *D*-values being from −1.000 to +1.000, as explained in paragraph 8.

13 因此，测试题不应单独地根据这些统计指标自动地被拒纳或修订。系数 P 和系数 D 可用于提高测试题的结构可靠性以提高测评系统的质量与效力。尽管如此，多项选择测试题的难度主要受其似是而非的错误选项的直接影响。所以，如果保留原测试题，那些被证明是即使对低分考生也无效的选项应被替换掉。

表 11.4-1 难度系数 P 取值参考

通过现行考试或其他被认为适任的考生的百分比	系数 P 的平均值
0	0.45~0.59
5	0.51~0.60
10	0.54~0.62
15	0.57~9.63
20	0.59~0.65
25	0.61~0.66
30	0.62~0.67
35	0.63~0.67
40	0.64~0.69
45	0.65~0.70
50	0.66~0.71
55	0.67~0.72
60	0.68~0.73
65	0.69~0.74
70	0.70~0.75
75	0.71~0.77
80	0.73~0.78
85	0.75~0.80
90	0.76~0.83
95	0.79~0.87
100	0.84~1.00

系数 P 的理想取值

14. 对于根据本章 3 到 6 段列出的程序确定的新测试题，表 11.14-1 可提供系数 P 取值的一个参考。本表格基于的通过率为 70%。

系数 D 的理想取值

15. 通常，系数 D 对于考题的正确选项的取值在 0.250~0.750 之间，对错误选项的取值在 -0.250~-0.750 之间。正如第 8 段所述，总的取值范围为 -1.000~+1.000。

Test item label

16. The test item label records the historical performance of a test item in its initial and subsequent reviews together with other data which identify the particular test series and the test item itself. Test items should be classified to indicate, as a minimum, the subject topic, the ability or specification tested and the level of difficulty.

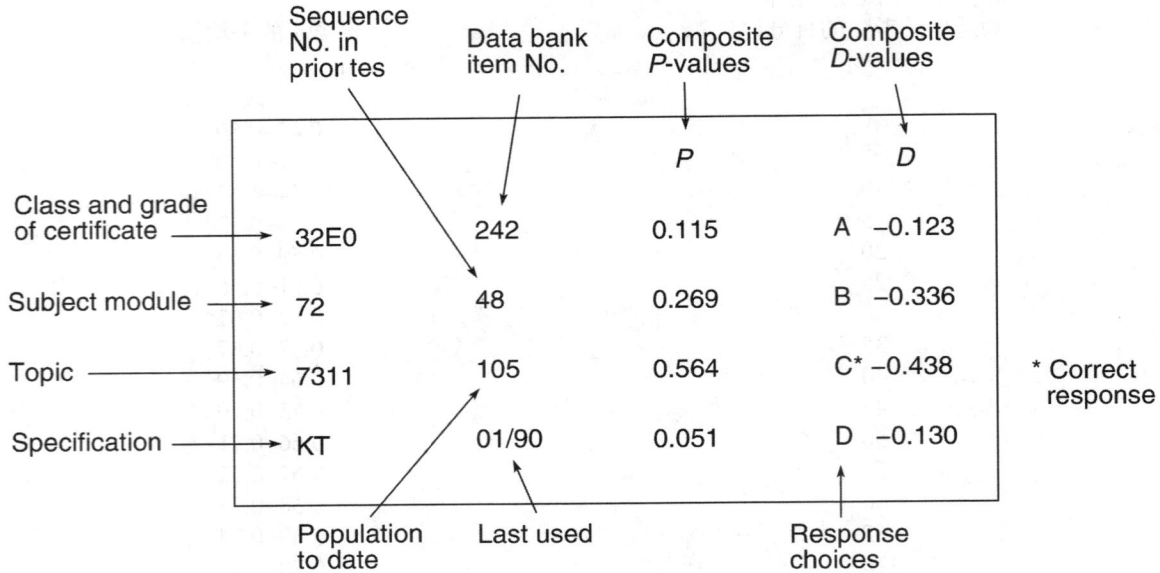

Figure 11.16-1 Example of a test item label
(Adapted from an Item Analysis Label of the U.S. Coast Guard)

A test item label to provide the optimal information on an item may be as shown in figure 11.16-1.

Use of P-values in maintaining common standards

17. The information appearing on the label of a test item should allow it to be selected from a data base on the basis of the subject topic dealt with, the ability tested and its level of difficulty.

It is then possible to compile an examination with a suitable mix of questions to cover the syllabus in a comprehensive manner, distribute the questions in accordance with the established tables of specifications (see Part 11, paragraph 9) and average out the level of difficulty of the examination to whatever level is desired.

Manual selection of test items on this basis is somewhat laborious, but the improvement in the quality of the examination that can be achieved by using such a disciplined approach makes the effort worthwhile. Computerized selection of test items allows even greater improvement.

试题标签

16. 试题标签记录了试题原始的历史表现,连同从最初到后续的审核中确定的特殊测试数据。试题应分类标识,至少应标上科目主题、测试能力或测试特点、难度等级。

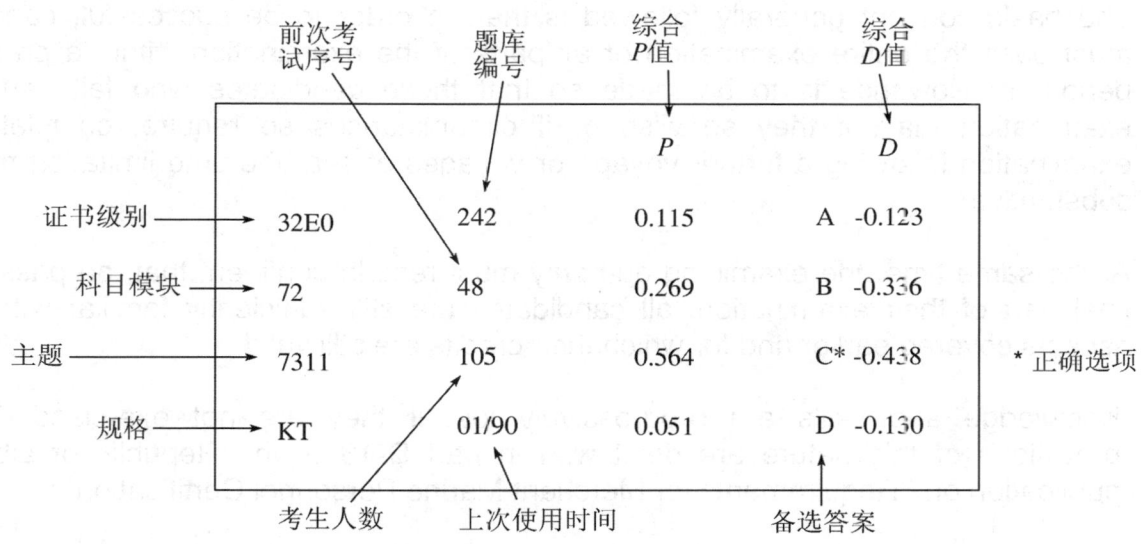

图 11.16-1　试题标签的实例
（摘自美国海岸警卫队试题分析标签）

应用 P 值保持试题的通用标准

17. 可以根据测试题目的试题标签所标示的科目主题、测试能力和难度水平的信息从数据库中选出相关考题。

然后可以在广泛覆盖大纲的范围内抽出合适的题目以编成一份试题,根据已制定的技术规格表分配这些题目(见第11章第9段),按计划的难度平衡试题。

在这些题库中人工选题有点费力,但可以通过使用这种控制方法来达到提高考试质量的目的。电脑化抽题则可以做得更好。

Failures

18. Provision should be made in the regulations or in the administrative rules concerning the re-examination of those candidates who fail to pass the whole of an examination or who fail a part or parts of an examination.

    The basic concept generally followed is that, in order to be successful, candidates must pass the entire examination or all parts of the examination within a prescribed period. If allowance is to be made so that those candidates who fail part of an examination may, if they so wish or if circumstances so require, complete their examination following a further voyage or voyages at sea, the time limitation must be substantive.

    At the same time, the examining authority must remain confident that, on passing the final part of their examination, all candidates are still sufficiently familiar with those aspects covered earlier and for which their credits are still valid.

    Knowledge and skills are progressively lost if they are not exercised. Typical provisions of this nature are dealt with in part D-13 of the Republic of Liberia's publication on "Requirements for Merchant Marine Personnel Certification":

    D-13: Re-examination upon Failure.

    1. *Waiting Period.*—A candidate who fails his examination may not be re-examined earlier than 30 days from notification of failure, and may not be re-examined more than twice in 12 months.
    2. *Reviewing Examination Papers.*—Upon request to the DCO, the score awarded to a failing candidate's examination will be reviewed. The score awarded to an examination following review shall be final.

    In other Administrations, credit is given for partial passes for a period of up to two years, on expiry of which the credits lapse.

19. The control exercised over these arrangements must generally allow for the possibility of candidates being examined at more than one examination centre, since seafarers constitute a highly mobile work force. Central control is therefore essential, whether by a computerized data bank with a computer file for each candidate or by traditional filing and recording methods. It is also necessary for the candidate himself to be provided with a record of his successes and failures, either as a manual record or as a computer print-out.

    An example of such a candidate's record of examinations is shown in figures 11.19-1 and 11.19-2.

20. The period of validity accorded each part of an examination may be varied according to the relative importance of its content and the type of skill and other factors involved. For example, success in the medical examination and sight test may be credited for a more limited period (say 12 months) than the written portions (say 24 months) and the oral/practical and communications examinations (say 6 months).

考试不及格

18. 对于未能通过考试的全部、其中一部分或几部分内容的不及格考生,应该在规则或管理规章中制定相应的重考规则。

    根据一般的基本概念,为获得成功,这些考生必须在规定的时间内通过整个考试或通过所有项目的考试。如果部分项目的考试未能通过的考生自己愿意或环境允许,可以允许他们压后到在下一个或几个航次之后再完成他们的考试。规定的时间限制必须是符合实际的。

    同时,考试机关应确保所有考生在最终通过考试时,仍能保持对于之前考过的内容的熟悉和已取得的成绩仍然有效。

    如果他们不进行练习,知识与技能会日渐遗忘。这类问题的典型处理规定可以参考以下的利比里亚共和国出版的《商船船员证书要求》D-13部分。

    D-13 不及格重考

    1. 候考期——不及格考生从收到不及格通知后30天内不得参加重考,在12个月内重考不超过两次。

    2. 试卷复查——负责官员可以要求复查不及格考生的得分,复核后的分数是最终成绩。

    一些主管机关允许部分考试成绩的有效期延至两年,到期日即信用失效。

19. 海员的工作漂泊不定,通常应允许考生可以不仅仅在一个考试中心参加考试。因此不管是采用电脑数据库进行电脑化管理还是传统的手工管理,都有必要给每一位考生提供一份是否通过考试的成绩记录。考生自己存留一份通过或不通过记录也是非常有必要的,这份记录为手工或电脑打印均可。

    这类考生考试成绩记录的范例见图11.19-1和图11.19-2。

20. 根据考试内容的相对重要性、测试的技能类型和其他相关因素,考试每一部分成绩记录的有效期可以是不同的。例如,通过体检与视力纪录的有效期(通常12个月)比书写能力成绩记录有效期(通常24个月)要短,而口语与实用通信用语的有效期通常为6个月。

Advantages of partial-pass systems

21. Initially, many of the examinations held to determine the competency of seafarers had to be passed as a whole in a single attempt. Failure in any subject meant failure in the entire examination. As the examinations become more complex, some examining authorities subdivided their examinations.

    The objective of the examinations for certificates is to assess competency. So long as the period of validity of a partial pass is sufficiently short to satisfy the examining authorities that the candidates can retain their competency in the subjects concerned, the system allows those candidates who, for one reason or another, show weakness in a particular subject, or subjects, to concentrate their further studies on their weak areas.

    It is normal, in establishing partial-pass systems, for the examining authority to require a pass mark of a uniformly high standard in all subjects rather than allowing a candidate's strength in one subject to compensate for weakness in others.

    Where a partial-pass system is in operation, the approach taken by the examining authority to marginal cases, that is those candidates whose performance in the examinations requires careful review to ensure that their competency or non-competency is properly assessed, can be made more strict, thus allowing a higher level of competency to be attained without severely crippling the overall ability of candidates to become certificated.

Disadvantages of a partial-pass system

22. A partial-pass system imposes a significant administrative burden on the examining authority since records must be available to both the authority and the candidates which clearly establish the dates of passing each particular part of an examination.

    With regard to the average standard of candidates passing the examinations, no significant difference results.

Advice to failing candidates

23. As a matter of good public relations and in the interests of providing a better service to the industry as a whole, the examining authority should be prepared to provide candidates with some general indication of their areas of weakness exhibited in an examination or test. This not only gives the candidate a better appreciation of why he failed, it also assists him in his further studies of the subjects concerned and assists in demonstrating the fairness and objectivity of the examination system as a whole.

    Where a particular weakness is demonstrated by a large number of candidates, the academy or instructors concerned should be advised so that remedial action can be taken to strengthen appropriate portions of the course.

    However, it is never advisable to show a candidate his scored or marked examination script, particularly where the questions are of the subjective type. The probability is that many candidates will, understandably, tend to argue the correctness of their answer, particularly if the omission of facts or reasoning has caused loss of marks.

分项通过考试的机制的优点

21. 过去海员需要一次性将各种考试作为一个整体通过以获得海员资格,在任何一个环节上的失败将意味着整个考试的失败。由于现在考试变得更加复杂,一些考试机关已将考试分成几个部分分别进行。

    适任证书考试的目的是评估其适任能力。只要分项考试的成绩的有效期满足考试机关的要求,就可以保持在相关科目上的适任。该机制可以让那些因各种原因在一些具体科目上表现出不足的考生在这些科目上集中精力进行进一步的学习。

    通常,在建立分项考试机制时,考试机关应对所有科目采用统一的高标准而不要允许考生以一个科目的特长来弥补其他方面的不足。

    在实施分项考试机制中,考试机关处理处于临界分数的个案的措施会更加严格,考生的成绩需要仔细复查以确保正确地对他们适任或不适任做出评价。因而,一方面考生可以获得更高的适任成绩以获得发证,同时也不会在整体技能的某方面有严重的偏废。

分科通过考试机制的局限性

22. 由于分项考试需要将成绩记录提供给主管机关及需清楚地知道考生通过每一部分考试的时间,因此增加了考试机关大量的行政负担。

    但就通过考试的考生的平均标准而言,并无明显的不同。

对不及格者的建议

23. 为达成良好的公共关系及有利于为整个航运业提供更好的服务,考试机关应对考生在考试中显示出来的弱项提出一些指导性意见。这不仅给考生提供了对于其失败原因的评价,帮助其以后在相关科目的进一步学习,同时也显示了整个考试体制的公平公正。

    当大量的考生出现了相同的弱项时,应建议航海院校及相关教师采取适当的行动加强课程相应部分的教学。

    然而,建议不要向考生展示其考卷,特别是主观题的原始得分。可以理解,很多考生都会试图争辩其答案的正确性,尤其是由于其论据或推理遗漏而引起失分的时候。

Appeals

24. An appeal procedure should be established so that those candidates who are dissatisfied with the decisions made by an examiner with respect to the acceptance of their proof of sea service, attendance at approved training courses, medical fitness, written tests or oral and practical tests may have their cases reviewed by another examiner or examiners.

The system should not be so easy as to encourage appeals being made without a reasonable basis. Advice given to failing candidates (as mentioned in paragraph 23) will more often than not satisfy a candidate who has initially been dissatisfied with the results he obtained.

On the other hand there can be room for differences of professional judgement, and an appeal system which never, or very rarely, results in a reassessment in favour of a candidate will rapidly come to be regarded as being biased.

Objectivity must be stressed in any review process; where possible, candidates should be given the benefit of any doubt.

Recognizing certificates

25. As previously noted in paragraph 6 of Part 3, the 1978 STCW Convention as amended, in its Article II(c), provides that a State Party to it may "recognize" certificates issued elsewhere. MSC/Circ. 393 further elaborates on this point, indicating that full details of certificates so recognized should be forwarded to the Secretary-General of IMO as depositary for the Convention.

Regulation I/10 (Recognition of certificates) of the revised STCW Convention further elaborate this point, see text of Regulation I/10.

It must be pointed out, however, that a knowledge of national maritime law is required for various STCW certificates. In this regard see Regulation II/2 (Table A-II/2) and Regulation III/2 (Table A-III/2).

Competence:
Monitor and control compliance with legislative requirements and measures to ensure safety of life at sea and the protection of the marine environment.

Knowledge:
Knowledge of international maritime law embodied in international agreements and conventions...national legislation for implementing international agreements and conventions.

This is a factor which must be taken into consideration when reviewing the provisions governing the issue of a certificate which is being considered for recognition.

申诉

24. 在海上服务资历和参加经核准的培训课程的学习成绩的采纳、体检情况、书面考试、口试或实操测试等方面,考生如对主考官的决定不满,应制定一个申诉程序以便可以让其他的主考官进行复查。

    如无可靠的理由,申诉机制不应鼓励轻率的申诉。应该经常地给不及格考生提供建议(23段提及),而不是试图使一个早已不满于已知成绩的考生满意。

    另一方面,应当允许专业判断存在差异,申诉机制不应或很少会导致支持考生的重新评估,如果出现上述情况,容易被认为对该考生有偏袒行为。

    在所有的考核过程中必须保证客观公正。如可能,应对考生的任何疑问提供帮助。

证书的承认

25. 我们在前面的第三章第6节提到:STCW 78公约修正案第Ⅱ条(c)允许一个国家可以"承认"其他国家签署的证书。海上安全委员会(MSC)第393号决议对这一点做了进一步的阐述,指出有关证书的"承认"的完整细节应向公约所授权的IMO秘书长报告。

    STCW修订的公约规则Ⅰ/10(证书的承认)对这一点做了做一步的阐述,见公约规则Ⅰ/10正文。

    必须指出,应具备关于各类STCW证书的相应国家海事法律的知识。具体见规则Ⅱ/2(表A-Ⅱ/2)和规则Ⅲ/2(表A-Ⅲ/2)。

    适任:
    根据立法机关的要求与措施实施监控以确保海上人命安全,保护海洋环境。

    知识:
    国际海事法律知识包括国际协议与公约等为贯彻这些协议与公约所做的国家立法。在研究关于承认发证的管理规定时,这是必须考虑的一个因素。

26. A State Party to the STCW Convention remains responsible for ensuring that all certificates recognized by it comply with the Convention. The fact that a certificate which is recognized by one State Party to the Convention is issued by another State Party to the Convention does not absolve the State recognizing that certificate from its duty to ensure that the provisions of the STCW Convention are complied with in all respects. A complete review should therefore be made of all requirements and procedures applying to the issue of the certificates which are to be recognized, the co-operation of the issuing State being sought as appropriate.

   Following the recognition of a certificate, a State Party to the Convention must inform the Secretary-General of IMO of all relevant details (Regulation I/7: Communication of information).

27. In certain cases a State Party to the 1978 STCW Convention, as amended, may wish to accord partial recognition to a certificate where it is satisfied that the appropriate requirements of the 1978 STCW Convention, as amended, have been met prior to its issue. Such partial recognition would, in effect, provide exemptions from certain of the examinations in which a pass is required by that State Party prior to the issue of its own STCW certificates.

   In some instances a State Party to the STCW Convention may decide to issue its own certificates, based wholly or partly on the certificates already held by candidates and issued by other Administrations. In these instances the same conditions of the STCW Convention apply and the State wishing to issue its own certificates on the basis of certificates of other Administrations held by candidates must ensure that all requirements of the Convention are met.

   Because of variations in national law and shipping procedures, this is an area which should receive particular attention.

Checking the validity of certificates

28. In order to fulfil the purpose and intent of the 1978 STCW Convention, as amended, each State Party to it must maintain some form of records of certificates issued. The validity of the certificates issued by other Administrations can therefore generally be checked by contacting their designated contact points, as disseminated by "National authorities responsible for issuing certificates of competency" (STW/Circ. 28 or its replacement).

29. Another point to bear in mind with respect to the recognition of certificates is the question of administrative control should it be necessary at any stage to take disciplinary action with respect to the holder of a "recognized" certificate or to require his participation in any form of investigation or hearing.

   The holder of a recognized certificate will be a national of another State and therefore not subject to the law of the State which has recognized his certificate except when he is within the territorial jurisdiction of that State.

26. STCW公约缔约国有责任确保其承认的所有证书都满足公约的要求。事实上,一个国家所承认的证书虽然是由另一缔约国所签发但并不免除承认发证国在所有方面全面满足STCW公约规定的责任。因而需要对准备承认的证书原来的所有签发技术文件及程序进行全面的审查,并寻求与发证国的适当协作。

    证书承认之后,缔约国必须将相关细节知会IMO秘书长(公约规则Ⅰ/7:资料交流)。

27. 在某些情况下,经修订的STCW 1978公约缔约国可能希望部分地承认以前签发的已满足经修订的STCW 1978公约适当要求的证书。实际上,这种部分承认,可豁免某些考试,而这些考试按照这些国家自己的STCW发证要求是必须通过的。

    在另外一些情况下,STCW公约缔约国可以基于申请人所持有的由其他国家主管机构签发的全部或部分证书来决定签发自己的证书。这种情况下,同样要满足STCW公约相同的条件,并且希望根据申请人所持有的由其他机构签发的证书来发证的国家必须保证证书满足公约所有的要求。

    因国际法律及航运程序的差异,证书的相互承认应引起特别的注意。

核查证书的有效性

28. 为了履行STCW 1978公约修正案,每一缔约国必须以某种形式保持所签发证书的记录。这样,被其他机构签发的证书的有效性可以由指定的联系点进行检查。关于联系点可查阅《负责签署适任证书的国家主管机关》(STCW/Circ. 28或其更新文件)。

29. 关于证书承认的另外一个重要问题是:主管机关在任何阶段都必须采取控制措施以便对被"承认"证书的持有人进行相应的核查或要求其接受调查或听证。

    被承认证书的持有人可能是其他国家的公民,因而并不受发证国家的法律约束,除非他处于这个国家的领土管辖之内。

Dispensations, exemptions and equivalents

Dispensations

30. While air transport has greatly reduced the delays involved in changing crew members of a ship when trading abroad, the capital investment involved in owning a ship and the daily operating costs are such that even minor delays in its operating schedule can significantly affect the profitability of a voyage. Provision has therefore been made in Article VIII of the STCW Convention, as amended, for an Administration to issue a dispensation to permit a specified seafarer in a specified ship to temporarily fill a higher post than that for which he is certificated.

31. Such dispensations can only be issued "in circumstances of exceptional necessity" and their effective period must not exceed six months. Were there to be a long-term inability on the part of a shipowner to man his ship with fully qualified personnel, the circumstances would be those of "continuing necessity" rather than "exceptional necessity".

    Furthermore, under the Convention, dispensations may only be issued to masters or to chief engineer officers in circumstances of "force majeure", that is to say an event or effect that cannot reasonably be anticipated or controlled. Sudden illness of a master or chief engineer officer preventing his sailing with the ship is a circumstance of "force majeure". However, arrangements for proper replacement of the master or chief engineer officer at the next port of call can reasonably be anticipated or controlled. The routine application for leave by seafarers also can be reasonably foreseen and controlled and is thus not a circumstance of "force majeure".

32. The ability of the chief mate to assume the responsibilities of the master and of the second engineer officer to assume the responsibilities of the chief engineer officer has been ensured by the wording of Section A-II/2 para. 3, Section A-III/2 para. 3 and Section A-III/3 para. 3 of the STCW Code. However, the practical experience of such personnel should be carefully assessed, and Administrations must assure themselves that no danger will be caused through the issue of any dispensation.

33. The assessment of the qualification and experience of persons to fill posts at such a level that the person filling the post below it is not required to be certificated under the Convention requires careful attention. Where such seafarers have not been previously examined as to their fitness and their practical and theoretical knowledge related to the duties to be performed, they will have to be tested to determine whether or not their qualifications and experience are of a clear equivalence to those required for the post.

34. Since the issue of dispensations could undermine the effectiveness of any certification scheme, strict control of these provisions is sought. Parties are required, therefore, to report on the numbers of dispensations issued each year and on the capacities involved under the provisions of Article VIII, paragraph (3) of the 1978 STCW Convention, as amended, which requires that:

特许、豁免与等效

特许

30. 虽然航空运输大大地降低了远洋船员调换的延迟时间,但船舶的庞大资本投资及每天的营运花费使得在运期表上的微小延迟都会使航次收益受到明显影响。因而,STCW公约修正案第Ⅷ条做了规定,主管机关可签发特许证明以允许在指定船舶上的特定海员可以临时性地担任比其证书更高的职位。

31. 此种特许证明只能在"必要的例外情况下"签发,且其有效期不得超过六个月。否则要负责配备全部合格船员的船东会滥用这种证明,将其演变为"必要的连续"而不是"必要的例外"情况。

    此外,根据公约,特许证明只能在"不可抗力",也就是说事件不能被适当地预见或受控的情形下签发给船长或轮机长,船长或轮机长的突然重病而无法指挥航行属于"不可抗力"的情形。然而,正常地在下一挂靠港安排轮换船长或轮机长,是可适当地预见或安排的,日常的海员休假申请也是可以预见和受控制的,因而不属于"不可抗力"的情形。

32. STCW规则A-Ⅱ/2节第3段、A-Ⅲ/2节第3段、A-Ⅲ/3节第3段,已对以大副承担船长的责任和以大管轮承担轮机长的责任的有关能力做了要求。然而,应对这些人的实践操作能力仔细评估,主管机关应确保任何特许的签发不致引起危险。

33. 根据公约,对申请在其已有职位要求水平之下职位的人员,在进行经验与资格评估时不用另外发证。但对于以前没有对其健康状况、履职相关的实践经验与理论知识进行考试的海员,必须进行测试以确定他们的资格与经验是否和他申请职位相适应。

34. 由于特许发证会损害发证体系的有效性,应对这些规定,采取严格的控制措施。因而,根据STCW 1978公约修正案第Ⅷ(3)段的规定,缔约国要报告每年签发的特许证明的数量和相关职位,具体要求是:

3. Parties shall, as soon as possible after 1 January of each year, send a report to the Secretary-General giving information of the total number of dispensations in respect of each capacity for which a certificate is required that have been issued during the year to sea-going ships, together with information as to the numbers of those ships above and below 1,600 gross register tons respectively.

35. At its fifty-fifth session the Maritime Safety Committee of IMO approved the format set forth in figure 11.35-1 for the future submission of summary reports on dispensations issued under the 1978 STCW Convention.

FORMAT OF SUMMARY REPORTS ON DISPENSATIONS ISSUED UNDER THE 1978 STCW CONVENTION

Period=1 January 1990 to 31 December 1992

PARTY	CERT	CHAPTER II—DECK DEPARTMENT			CHAPTER III—DECK DEPARTMENT			REMARKS
		MASTER	CHIEF MATE	O.I.C WATCH	CHIEF ENGINEER	SECOND ENGINEER	O.I.C. WATCH	
	GRT	1,600+ < 1,600	1,600+ < 1,600	1,600+ < 1,600	1,600+ < 1,600	1,600+ < 1,600	1,600+ < 1,600	
(Country) 1990 1991 1992								

Figure 11.35-1

36. In approving the report of the twentieth session of the IMO Sub-Committee on Standards of Training and Watchkeeping, the Maritime Safety Committee also endorsed the view that reports on dispensations are not intended for use by officers undertaking port State control procedures under the Convention, but are intended to demonstrate the degree of compliance with Convention standards. It further agreed that dispensations from requirements not included in the STCW Convention, issued by Administrations under national legislation, need not be reported to IMO.

37. Shipowners and Administrations can effectively work with educators to eliminate shortages of qualified mariners. The ultimate objective should be that the crew of each ship is sufficiently qualified to avoid dispensations if any one seafarer is prevented from sailing through unforeseeable circumstances.

38. Neither the format nor the language of the document issued by an Administration in evidence of a dispensation is prescribed by the STCW Convention. Such a document is clearly not a "certificate" since dispensations are separately mentioned, for example in Article X, paragraph (1). Hopefully, Administrations will issue such dispensations in the official language or languages of the country and, if the language used is not English, will include an English translation. If such is not done then the control procedures of the Convention would be difficult to follow.

3. 缔约国应于每年的1月1日后,尽快向秘书长送交一份报告,说明一年中间对海船所签发的关于有证书要求的每项职位的特许证明书总数,以及分别说明1 600总吨以上及以下的船舶艘数。

35. IMO海上安全委员会第55次会议批准了图11.35-1所示的依据STCW 1978公约签发特许证明的概要报告格式。

根据STCW 1978公约签发特许证明概要报告格式

期间:从1990年1月1日到1992年12月31日

缔约国		第二章 甲板部			第三章 轮机部			备注
	证书	船长	大副	其他值班驾驶员	轮机长	二管轮	其他值班轮机员	
	GRT	1 600+ < 1 600	1 600+ < 1 600	1 600+ < 1 600	1 600+ < 1 600	1 600+ < 1 600	1 600+ < 1 600	
(国家) 1990 1991 1992								

图11.35-1

36. 在批准IMO分委会第20次会议培训与值班标准的报告时,海上安全委员会指出:根据公约,特许报告不适用于按公约实施PSC检查的官员,只用以说明其符合公约标准相应的水平。它进一步指出:对于不在STCW公约管辖范围内,根据国家立法由行政主管机关所签署的特许证明,不需向IMO报告。

37. 船东和主管机关可以与教育机构开展有效的工作,去解决称职海员不足的问题。最终的目标是每一船舶的所有船员都有足够的资格而不用特许,避免任何一个海员在不可预见的环境里航行。

38. 作为特许凭证的由主管机关签署的文件所采用的格式和语言在STCW公约中没有做具体规定。既然特许证明是在发证规定之外单独提到的(如第10章第1段所示),很明显这样的文件不是一份"证书"。主管机关很可能会用某国官方语言或某国语言来签署这种特许证明,但如果不用英语,应包括一份英译本。否则,公约的约束将很难得以落实。

Exemptions and restricted certificates

39. The 1978 STCW Convention, as amended, provides that Administrations may vary the content of examinations for certain grades and classes of certificate.

    These provisions are contained in the following paragraphs of the Convention:
STCW Code	Paragraph
Section A-II/2	5
Section A-II/3	4, 7 (Master)
Section A-III/2	6
Section A-III/3	6, 8 (Near-coastal)
Section A-III/4	4

    In all cases, the variations made from the general requirements of the Convention should be based on the analysis of the tasks associated with the posts for which the certificates are intended.

    Where use is made of these provisions, the endorsements on the certificate that is issued should clearly indicate the limitations which apply to its use.

Equivalents

40. Article IX of the 1978 STCW Convention, as amended, is intended to provide flexibility so that efficient and effective alternative training measures will not be excluded. However, the level of seagoing service, knowledge and efficiency must ensure equivalent training. Thus equivalence must be established in respect of each such consideration.

    Where periods of sea service have already been reduced (as permitted in the Annex to the Convention) on the basis of special training which the Administration considers to be equivalent to the allowed reduction in sea service, it is not possible to "substitute" further special training ashore for sea service.

    Nevertheless, it may be possible to specially organize the sea service of trainees in such a way as to accelerate their exposure to the practical application of safety and pollution-prevention procedures, practical problem solving and dealing with emergencies. Shipboard simulators or training aids may play a significant role in such an accelerated training programme, but its efficiency would have to be very carefully assessed.

Revalidation of certificates

41. Regulation I/11 (and STCW Code Section A-I/11) of the STCW Convention, as amended, lay down mandatory minimum requirements to ensure the continued proficiency and updating of knowledge for master and deck officers, engineer officers and radio operators.

豁免和限定性证书

39. 修订的STCW 1978公约规定主管机关可改变某些等级的证书考试内容。
    这些规定包含在公约的以下段落中：

STCW规则	段落
第A-Ⅱ/2节	5
第A-Ⅱ/3节	4,7（船长）
第A-Ⅲ/2节	6
第A-Ⅲ/3节	6,8（近岸航行）
第A-Ⅲ/4节	4

    在任何情况下，对公约一般要求的变更应基于对证书所对应的职位进行的任务分析。

    在应用这些规定时，证书上的签注应清楚地注明限制内容。

证书的等效

40. 修订的1978年STCW公约第Ⅸ章做了灵活的规定以便可以采纳有效地替代训练方法。然而，必须确保在海上服务资历、知识与效能方面训练等效。因而必须确定这些因素的等效性。

    在主管机关已经根据可以与海上服务资历等效的特殊训练（公约附则所允许的）缩短了所需的海上服务时间的情况下，不能用更多的岸上特殊训练来在更大程度上取代海上服务资历。

    不过，可以利用岸上训练通过特别方案对学员的海上工作进行组织，以加速暴露他们在安全及防污程序的实际应用能力、实际解决问题的能力，特别是处理突发事件的能力方面的问题。船舶模拟器或船舶训练设施可在这样的加速训练程序中扮演重要的角色，但对其真实效应该审慎评价。

证书的再有效

41. 为了保证船长及驾驶员、轮机员及无线电操作员持续的适任与知识的更新，修订的STCW公约规则 Ⅰ/11（STCW规则附则A-Ⅰ/11节）添加这方面的强制性最低要求。

At periods not exceeding five years, the holders of certificates entitling them to be employed in those capacities must satisfy the Administration as to their medical fitness and continued competency.

Most seafarers will prove their continued competency by virtue of recent sea service. It should also be noted that the intention of the above provisions in the STCW Code that the holders of such certificates may demonstrate their continued competence "by having performed functions considered to be equivalent to the seagoing service required in paragraph 1.1 (approved seagoing service, performing functions appropriate to the certificate held, for a period of at least one year in total during the preceding five years)." is to allow those employed as ship surveyors, cargo superintendents, harbour masters, pilots etc. to maintain the validity of their certificates through such service.

Suspension and revocation

42. As was mentioned in paragraph 15 of Part 1 and in paragraph 2.6 of Part 3, provision must be made to allow the suspension or revocation of certificates where the holders have become incapacitated or have been found unfit to continue to perform the duties concerned. Typical of such authority is that provided in Section 18 of the Liberian Maritime Law (Suspension and Revocation Proceedings):

    Suspension and Revocation Proceedings

    The Commissioner shall have power to suspend or to revoke any licenses, certificates, permits or documents issued under the provisions of this Title, and he may from time to time make such Rules and Regulations as are deemed by him necessary and appropriate to the conduct of suspension and revocation proceedings.

    and in regulation 1.17(3) of the Liberian Maritime Regulations (Licenses and Certificates of Merchant Marine Personnel):

    (3) *Cause for Revocation*

    Any license or certificate may be suspended or revoked in accordance with published Rules upon proof of (a) incompetency; (b) physical or mental disability; (c) habitual drunkenness; (d) wilful failure to comply with the provisions of the Liberian Maritime Law or Regulations; (e) criminal conduct; or (f) other conduct incompatible with proper performance of duties and obligations in service on board a Liberian Flag vessel.

43. A further example of legislation dealing with the suspension and cancellation of certificates of officers is provided by the following extracts from the legislation of the United Kingdom.

在不超过5年的期限内,证书持有人应保证其对受雇职位在身体条件及持续的适任上能满足主管机关的要求。

大部分海员的持续适任职务能力可以用最近的海上服务表现来证明。但也应注意到,STCW规则的以上条款的意图是证书持有人能表明其持续的适任能力:"履行了等同于第1.1段要求的海上服务资历的职能(认可的海上资历,在以前的5年内有累计至少1年认可的海上服务资历履行了所持证书上相应的职能)。"受雇担任验船师、货物监督长、港务长、引航员等职业的证书持有人,可以通过这些服务保证其证书的有效。

证书的中止与作废

42. 在前面的第1章第15节及第3章第2.6节提到,当证书持有人已不逗任或不适合于继续履行相关职责,应做出规定中止或作废其证书。这种情况在《利比里亚海事法》第18节(中止与撤销程序)有典型的规定。

中止与作废程序

执行官有权中止与作废按本规定签署的任何执照、证书、特许书或文件。同时在他认为必须制定而且时间合适时可以制定中止与作废程序的实施条款和规定。

《利比里亚海事法》第1.17(3)条(船员的执照与证书):

(3)作废理由

有以下证据者其执照或证书将被作废:(a)不适任;(b)身体或智力发育不全;(c)习惯性酗酒;(d)故意不遵守《利比里亚海事法》法规;(e)犯罪行为;或(f)其他不能在利比里亚籍船舶上适当地履行其职责和服务义务的行为。

43. 以下是英国立法有关执照证书中止和作废的法律摘要。

Merchant Shipping Act 1970
(as amended)

Disqualification of Seamen, Inquiries and Investigations

52. Inquiry into fitness or conduct of officer

(1) If it appears to the Board of Trade that an officer:

    1. is unfit to discharge his duties, whether by reason of incompetence or misconduct or for any other reason; or

    2. has been seriously negligent in the discharge of his duties; or

    3. has failed to comply with the provisions of section 422 of the Merchant Shipping Act, 1894 (duty to give assistance and information after collision);

the Board of Trade may cause an inquiry to be held by one or more persons appointed by them and, if they do so, may, if they think fit, suspend, pending the outcome of the inquiry, any certificate issued to the officer in pursuance of section 43 of this Act and require the officer to deliver it to them.

(2) Where a certificate issued to an officer has been suspended under subsection (1) of this section the suspension may, on the application of the officer, be terminated by the High Court or, if the inquiry is held in Scotland, by the Court of Session, and the decision of the court on such an application shall be final.

(3) An inquiry under this section shall be conducted in accordance with rules made under section 58(1) of this Act and those rules shall require the persons holding the inquiry to hold it with the assistance of one or more assessors.

(4) The persons holding an inquiry under this section into the fitness or conduct of an officer—

    (1) may, if satisfied of any of the matters mentioned in paragraphs (a) to (c) of subsection (1) of this section, cancel or suspend any certificate issued to him under section 43 of this Act or censure him;

    (2) may make such order with regard to the costs of the inquiry as they think just; and

    (3) shall make a report on the case to the Board of Trade;

and if the certificate is cancelled or suspended the officer (unless he has delivered it to the Board of Trade in pursuance of subsection (I) of this section) shall deliver it forthwith to the persons holding the inquiry or the Board of Trade.

(5) Any costs which a person is ordered to pay under subsection (4)(b) of this section may be recovered from him by the Board of Trade.

1970年《商船航运法》
（修正案）

52. 职员健康状况或品行质询

海员不称职,质询与调查

（1） 如提交到贸易部,由一名高级船员进行:

    1. 不适合履行其职责,无论其原因是不胜任、行为不端或其他任何原因;或

    2. 履行职责时出现严重疏忽;或

    3. 已不能满足1894年《商船法》第422条之规定(碰撞后施与援助与信息的责任);

贸易部可指定一人或多人展开调查,如果调查已展开,并认为合适,可在调查期间中止根据《商船法》第43节签发给高级船员的证书并要求被调查者交回。

（2） 根据如上(1)条吊销的已签发给高级船员的证书,在个人申请下,可入禀高级法院裁定,或者,如果调查是在苏格兰进行的话,可由最高民事法庭裁定。此类判决是终审判决。

（3） 应根据《商船法》第58(1)条开展此类质询,条例规定举行此类质询要有一名或多名陪审员的协助。

（4） 根据本节规定调查高级船员的身体条件及品行的官员:

    （1） 如情形满足本节(1)款(a)到(c)条规定的,可吊销其根据法例43条签发的证书或做出谴责;

    （2） 可根据调查的费用做出裁决;及

    （3） 向贸易部提交一份案情报告;

如该证书已被吊销或中止,船员应立即将证书交回给调查官员或贸易部(除非他已依本节1款规定上交给贸易部)。

（5） 个人依本节(4)(b)款裁决支付的任何费用应由贸易部返还其本人。

56. Formal investigation into shipping casualty

(1) Where any accident has occurred, the Secretary of State may (whether or not an investigation into it has been carried out under section 33 of the Merchant Shipping Act 1988) cause a formal investigation into the accident to be held–

    (a) if in England, Wales or Northern Ireland, by a wreck commissioner, and

    (b) if in Scotland, by the sheriff;

and in this section "accident" means any accident to which regulations under that section apply or any incident or situation to which any such regulations apply by virtue of subsection (5) of that section.

(1A) A wreck commissioner or sheriff holding a formal investigation shall conduct it in accordance with rules under section 58(1) of this Act; and those rules shall the assistance of one or more assessors and, if any question as to the cancellation or suspension of an officer's certificate is likely, the assistance of not less than two assessors.

(2)...

(3)...

(4) If as a result of the investigation the wreck commissioner or sheriff is satisfied, with respect to any officer, of any of the matters mentioned in paragraphs (a) to (c) of section 52(1) of this Act and, if it is a matter mentioned in paragraph (a) or (b) of that section, is further satisfied that it caused or contributed to the accident, he may cancel or suspend any certificate issued to the officer under section 43 of this Act or censure him; and if he cancels or suspends the certificate the officer shall deliver it forthwith to him or to the Board of Trade.

(5)...

(6)...

(6A) The wreck commissioner or sheriff shall make a report on the investigation to the Secretary of State.

(7)...

56.海运事故的正规调查	（1）	当事故发生时,国务秘书可要求展开事故的正规调查(无论是否已依据1988年《商船运输法》33条做出了调查)

     （a） 若在英格兰、威尔士或北爱尔兰,由一个灾难处理专员;及

     （b） 若在苏格兰,则由州长负责;

    本节中"事故"是指适用于该节规则的事故或适用于该节第(5)款规定效力的情形的事故。

  （1A）灾难处理专员或执行全面调查的政府官员应执行法例的第58(1)节规定。规定要求有一个以上的辅佐人员协助处理,并且,如有可能涉及废止或中止高级船员证书的类似问题,辅佐人员不应少于两人。

  （2）……
  （3）……

  （4）若调查的结果令灾难处理专员或州长认为,根据法例第52(1)条第(a)～(c)款及第(a)～(b)款,是任何高级船员导致事故的,他可以吊销根据法例第43条所颁发的证书或对其做出谴责。若证书被吊销,船员应将证书上交调查员或上交给贸易部。

  （5）……
  （6）……

  （6A）难船委员会或州长应提交一份调查报告给国务秘书。

  （7）……

57. Re-hearing of and appeal from inquiries and investigations	(1)	Where an inquiry or formal investigation has been held under the preceding provisions of this Act the Board of Trade may order the whole or part of the case to be re-heard, and shall do so–
		(a) if new and important evidence which could not be produced at the inquiry or investigation has been discovered; or
		(b) if there appear to the Board to be other grounds for suspecting that a miscarriage of justice may have occurred.
	(2)...	
	(3)...	
	(4)	Where the persons holding the inquiry or investigation have decided to cancel or suspend the certificate of any person or have found any person at fault, then, if no application for an order under subsection (1) of this section has been made or such an application has been refused, that person or any other person who, having an interest in the inquiry or investigation, has appeared at the hearing and is affected by the decision or finding, may appeal to the High Court or the Court of Session, according as the inquiry or investigation was held in England, Wales or Northern Ireland or in Scotland.
59. Failure to deliver cancelled or suspended certificate		If a person fails to deliver a certificate as required under section 52 or 56 of this Act he shall be liable on summary conviction to a fine not exceeding level 3 on the standard scale; and if a person fails to deliver a certificate as required under section 53 or 54 of this Act he shall be liable on summary conviction to a fine not exceeding level 3 on the standard scale.
60. Power to restore certificate		Where a certificate has been cancelled or suspended under this Act or under section 478 of the Merchant Shipping Act 1894, the Board of Trade, if of opinion that the justice of the case requires it, may re-issue the certificate or, as the case may be, reduce the period of suspension and return the certificate, or may grant a new certificate of the same or a lower grade in place of the cancelled or suspended certificate.

57. 调查的重审和上诉	（1）	根据法例的现行规定，举行正规调查时，如有下列情况贸易部可对案件的全部或部分进行重新听证：
		（a） 已完成的质询和调查不能提供新的重要证据；或
		（b） 政府怀疑可能存在其他的不公正操作。
	（2）……	
	（3）……	
	（4）	当检查官决定吊销当事人证书或已证实有过失的人的证书时，若未根据本节（1）款的规定提出申请或申请被拒绝，出席聆讯和受到判决影响的当事人或与本案有利益关系的其他人，可根据案件审理的地点是在英格兰、威尔士或北爱尔兰还是苏格兰，分别向高级法院或最高民事法院上诉。
59.吊销或中止的证书未能上交	如果某人未能按法例第52条或第56条的规定上交证书，将被判不超过3级标准的罚金。如未能按法例第53条或第54条规定上交证书，将被判罚不超过3级标准的罚金。	
60.恢复证书的权限	根据1894年《商船法》第478条已被吊销或中止的证书，贸易部基于案件公正的原则，可重新签发证书，或依据案情，可缩短证书中止期限并返还证书，或可获签发新的同样级别或更低级别的证书以代替被吊销或中止的证书。	

Part 20
Administration

Issuing and replacing certificates

Central control and records

1. The principles regarding the issue of certificates under the 1978 STCW Convention, as amended, have already been dealt with under paragraphs 6 to 11 of Part 4.

   Whilst arrangements for the decentralized issue of certificates may be made, it is essential that some form of centralized record be kept of all certificates issued and of those replaced. Such a centralized control and record system can provide rapid and reliable information to satisfy queries made by field officers of the Administration itself and those of foreign Administrations and the shipping industry.

   Such records must be kept secure and arrangements made so as to avoid unauthorized access. They should contain at least the full name of the lawful holder of each certificate, its number, date of issue, grade and class, its endorsement and any limitations together with further particulars of the holder, including, preferably, a photograph and signature. It should also be possible to enter dates of subsequent revalidation of the certificate and other pertinent data.

2. Before any certificate is issued, the candidate's application, acceptance for examination and record of his success in the various parts of the examination should be rechecked or verified so as to prevent errors being made.

Endorsement of certificates

3. The issuing Administration is required by Article VI of the STCW Convention to endorse certificates for masters and officers in the form prescribed in Section A-I/2 of the STCW Code. This endorsement is necessary to allow officers exercising port State control to recognize and appreciate the validity and limitations of certificates held by masters and officers of ships of various flags visiting their ports.

   Guidance on the completion of the form is contained in Section B-I/2 of the STCW Code, reproduced in the following pages.

4. Limitations on a certificate's use which are to be withdrawn should not merely be deleted but instead a new endorsement should be made, showing the adjusted validity.

   STCW Code: Section B-I/2
   Guidance regarding certificates and endorsements

第20章
主管机关

发证与换证

集中监控与记录

1. 发证的规则是根据修订的STCW 78公约第4部分6~11节制定的。

   虽然可以实行分散发证的方法,但有必要实施某种形式的集中发证,以获得可以集中所有发证及换证的记录有利条件。该发证管理中心可以提供迅速可靠的信息,以供主管机关本身或其他境外机构或航运企业对证书进行查询。

   证书记录应当是安全可靠的,并可防止非官方机构非法查询。它们应至少包含合法持证人的全名、证件号码、发证日期、等级和级别;签注及任何对于持证人的限制和适用条件的细节描述;相片和签名。可能的话,它还应当记录后来持续有效的日期和相关材料。

2. 发证前,需对考证人的申请、适考情况及其已通过的各项考试记录进行复核,以防出错。

证书的签发

3. STCW公约第6章规定的发证机构应根据规则A-Ⅰ/2节规定的格式签发船长和高级船员证书以便PSC官员认可和鉴别来自不同船旗国的证书持有人证书的有效性和局限性。

   STCW规则B-Ⅰ/2节提供了完整的格式指导,我们将其复制在下文。

4. 撤销证书的某些限制项,不能仅仅在证书上删除而应重新签发,以表明其更改的有效性。

   STCW规则: B-Ⅰ/2节
   证书和签发指南

1. Where an endorsement is integrated in the format of a certificate as provided by section A-I/2, paragraph 1, the relevant information should be inserted in the certificate in the manner explained hereunder, except for the omission of the space numbered .2. Otherwise, in preparing endorsements attesting the issue of a certificate, the spaces numbered .1 to .17 in the form which follows the text hereunder should be completed as follows:

    .1 Enter the name of the issuing State.

    .2 Enter the number assigned to the certificate by the Administration.

    .3 Enter the full name of the seafarer to whom the certificate is issued. The name should be the same as that appearing in the seafarer's passport, seafarer's identity certificate and other official documents issued by the Administration.

    .4 The number or numbers of the STCW Convention regulation or regulations under which the seafarer has been found qualified should be entered here, for example:

    .4.1 II/1, if the seafarer has been found qualified to fill the capacity of officer in charge of a navigational watch,

    .4.2 III/1, if the seafarer has been found qualified to act as engineer officer in charge of a watch in a manned engine-room, or as designated duty engineer officer in a periodically unmanned engine-room,

    .4.3 IV/2, if the seafarer has been found qualified to fill the capacity of radio operator,

    .4.4 VII/1, if the certificate is a functional certificate and the seafarer has been found qualified to perform functions specified in part A of the Code, for example, the function of marine engineering at the management level, and

    .4.5 III/1 and V/1, if found qualified to act as the engineer officer in charge of a watch in a manned engine-room, or as designated duty engineer officer in a periodically unmanned engine-room in tankers. (See limitations in paragraphs .8 and .10 below)

    .5 Enter the date of expiry of the endorsement. This date should not be later than the date of expiry, if any, of the certificate in respect of which the endorsement is issued, nor later than five years after the date of issue of the endorsement.

    .6 In this column should be entered each of the functions specified in part A of the Code which the seafarer is qualified to perform Functions and their associated levels of responsibility are specified in the tables of competence set out in chapters II, III and IV of part A of the Code, and are also listed for convenient reference in the introduction to part A. When reference is made under .4 above to regulations in chapters II, III or IV it is not necessary to list specific functions.

1. STCW规则第A-Ⅰ/2节第1段提供了完整签署的证书样本。除了第二项空栏可以不填外,其他相关的内容应按以下说明的格式填写。另外,为准备签发证书,应填写以下1至17项:

   .1 填写发证机关。

   .2 填写主管机关分派给该证书的编号。

   .3 填写持证人的全名。该名字应与海员的护照、身份证及其他主管机关所发证件的名字相同。

   .4 填写STCW公约规定或确定该海员具备的相应资格证件代码,如:

      .4.1 Ⅱ/1 该海员是否具有航行驾驶值班能力,

      .4.2 Ⅲ/1 该海员是否具有人工操作机舱值班或周期性无人机舱值班的能力,

      .4.3 Ⅳ/2 是否具备无线电操作能力,

      .4.4 Ⅶ/1 证书是否为职能型证书,该海员是否具备STCW规则A部分所规定的职能,如轮机工程管理级,以及

      .4.5 Ⅲ/1和Ⅴ/1 是否具备作为一个轮机员在液货船的人工操作机舱或周期性无人机舱值班的能力。(见以下限制条款第8和10条)

   .5 填上证书有效期届满日期。该日期对于签发的任何证书,不应超过证书的有效期,也不应超过自签发之日起的5年。

   .6 该栏应填上按规则A部分规定的该海员能够胜任的职能。规则A部分Ⅱ、Ⅲ、Ⅳ章的适任表列出了适任职能及相关责任等级,并且在对A部分的介绍中列出了便于检索的条目。当该条目是上述4所述的Ⅱ、Ⅲ、Ⅳ章规定职能时,则不必详细列出该规定职能。

.7 In this column should be entered the levels of responsibility at which the seafarer is qualified to perform each of the functions entered in column .6. These levels are specified in the tables of competence set out in chapters II, III and IV of part A of the Code, and are also listed for convenient reference in the introduction to part A.

.8 A general limitation, such as the requirement to wear corrective lenses when performing duties, should be entered prominently at the top of this limitations column. Limitations applying to the functions listed in column .6 should be entered on the appropriate line against the function concerned, for example:

.8.1 "Not valid for service in tankers"—if not qualified under chapter V,

.8.2 "Not valid for service in tankers other than oil tankers"—if qualified under chapter V for service only in oil tankers,

.8.3 "Not valid for service in ships in which steam boilers form part of the ship's machinery"—if the related knowledge has been omitted in accordance with STCW Code provisions, and

.8.4 "Valid only on near-coastal voyages"—if the related knowledge has been omitted in accordance with STCW Code provisions.

Note: Tonnage and power limitations need not be shown here if they are already indicated in the title of the certificate and in the capacity entered in column .9.

.9 The capacity or capacities entered in this column should be those specified in the title to the STCW regulation or regulations concerned in the case of certificates issued under chapters II or III, or should be as specified in the applicable safe manning requirements of the Administration, as appropriate.

.10 A general limitation such as the requirement to wear corrective lenses when performing duties should be entered prominently at the top of this limitations column also. The limitations entered in column .10 should be the same as those shown in column .8 for the functions performed in each capacity entered.

.11 The number entered in this space should be that of the certificate, so that both certificate and endorsement have the same unique number for reference and for location in the register of certificates and/or endorsements, etc.

.12 The date of original issue of the endorsement should be entered here; it may be the same as, or differ from, the date of issue of the certificate, in accordance with the circumstances.

.13 The name of the official authorized to issue the endorsement should be shown here in block letters below the official's signature.

.7 该栏填入职责的等级，即第6项中所述的该海员所能胜任的职能。公约Ⅱ、Ⅲ、Ⅳ章的适任表列出了相应的职能，并在对A部分的介绍中有参考条目索引。

.8 一般限制条款，如值班时须戴上矫正眼镜，应显著地填写在限制条款项首栏。对于.6中的职能限制应填入对应的各职能栏，如：

 .8.1 "不适用于液货船"——如果不能具备第Ⅴ章要求，

 .8.2 "不适用于油船之外的液货船"——如果胜任第Ⅴ章所述的，但仅适用于油船工作，

 .8.3 "不适用于有锅炉机械的船舶"——如果未具备STCW规则相关规定的相关知识，及

 .8.4 "仅适用于沿岸航行"——如果未具备STCW规则相关规定的相关知识。

注：如果吨位和功率的限制已列于证书的首行和.9栏，则不在此列出。

.9 本栏所填的职能指STCW规定的以及第Ⅱ、Ⅲ章规定的发证职能；或者，如果合适，是主管机关对于安全配员所规定的职能。

.10 一般限制条款，如值班时须戴上矫正眼镜，也应显著地填写于限制条款栏首，在.10栏签注的限制条款应与.8栏相同。

.11 该栏所填号码应为证书号码，这样，证书与签发的内容就拥有相同的唯一号码，以便于登记证书和签发资料的归档和检索。

.12 该栏填写签发文件原件上的日期。根据不同情况该日期与证件的发放日期可能相同或不同。

.13 授权签发证书的官员的名字应在签名栏下以粗体字填入。

.14 The date of birth shown should be the date confirmed from Administration records or as otherwise verified.

.15 The endorsement should be signed by the seafarer in the presence of an official, or may be incorporated from the seafarer's application form duly completed and verified.

.16 The photograph should be a standard black and white or colour passport type head and shoulders photograph, supplied in duplicate by the seafarer so that one may be kept in or associated with the register of certificates.

.17 If the blocks for revalidation are shown as part of the endorsement form (see section A-I/2, paragraph 1), the Administration may revalidate the endorsement by completing the block after the seafarer has demonstrated continuing proficiency as required by regulation I/11.

2. An endorsement attesting the recognition of a certificate may be attached to and form part of the certificate endorsed, or may be issued as a separate document (see STCW regulation I/2, paragraph 6). All entries made in the form are required to be in Roman characters and Arabic figures (see STCW regulation I/2, paragraph 8). The spaces numbered .1 to .17 in the form which follows the text hereunder are intended to be completed as indicated in paragraph 1 above, except in respect of the following spaces:

.2 where the number assigned by the Party which issued the certificate being recognized should be entered;

.3 where the name entered should be the same as that appearing in the certificate being recognized;

.4 where the name of the Party which issued the certificate being recognized should be entered;

.9 where the capacity or capacities entered should be selected, as appropriate, from those specified in the safe applicable manning requirements of the Administration which is recognizing the certificate;

.11 where the number entered should be unique to the endorsement both for reference and for location in the register of endorsements; and

.12 where the date of original issue of the endorsement should be entered.

3. When replacing a certificate or endorsement which has been lost or destroyed, Parties should issue the replacement under a new number, to avoid confusion with the document to be replaced.

.14 填入的出生日期应为根据主管机关的记录或用其他方法证实的日期。

.15 签发的文件应由该海员当着官员的面签字；或由海员本人在证书申请表上用适当的方法签字和证明。

.16 相片为黑白标准照，或为护照所需格式的含肩彩照 2 张，其中一张与文件一并存档。

.17 如果某个功能"模块"需再有效（见 A-Ⅰ/2 节第 1 段），主管机关应在该海员按公约规则 Ⅰ/11 要求表明其精通该功能"模块"时，给其证书予再有效。

2. 用以证明承认适任证书的签发文件，可能被作为该证书的附属内容附在证书上，或被签发为一个独立的文件（见 STCW 公约规则 A-Ⅰ/2 第 6 章）。所有填入内容的形式应为罗马字体和阿拉伯数字（见 STCW 公约规则 A-Ⅰ/2 第 8 章）。表中从 .1 至 .17 的空栏，除以下所述栏位外，基本上按上述"1."的要求填写：

.2 应填写由承认证书的缔约国发证机构分配的号码；

.3 应填写与被承认的证书上相同的姓名；

.4 应填写承认证书的发证机构的名称；

.9 应根据承认证书的机构的最低安全配员规定选择填入一项或几项适任职能；

.11 所填入的号码应是唯一的，以便于检索和查索签发登记；及

.12 填入签证日期。

3. 给遗失或损坏的证书换证时，机构应签发新证书号码，以免和原证书混淆。

Replacement of Certificates

5. Applications for replacement of lost or destroyed certificates should be carefully screened to ensure that the person to whom the replacement certificate is issued was the lawful holder of the original certificate.

It is important to assign a new or modified number to the replacement certificate and to circulate all relevant information on the certificate which has been reported lost, stolen or destroyed to all officials concerned with checking the manning of ships, so that they are made aware it is null and void.

Enforcement of standards

Administrative instructions

6. In order to achieve the greatest possible uniformity in the conduct of examinations it is necessary to establish a clear set of instructions and guidelines with respect to all aspects of the examination procedure.

All aspects concerning the acceptance of candidates for examination, their examination for medical fitness and the conduct of written and practical tests should be dealt with in the detail necessary to ensure reasonable uniformity of treatment. Exceptional cases should be referred to a central authority so they may be dealt with in a consistent manner and the instructions on guidelines modified accordingly.

An example of guidance provided by a central authority is contained in the appendix at the end of this Part.

Verification of correct manning

7. In general, national legislation places the onus on the shipowner and his representatives, particularly the master, to ensure that, in addition to the master, the officers and crew members are duly certificated according to national law. The function of the Administration is to monitor the manning of ships of its flag for compliance with its national law.

As emphasized in paragraph 12 of Part 1, the 1978 STCW Convention, as amended, does not deal with manning but simply requires that those who are employed in certain positions on board ship must hold requisite certificates.

IMO Assembly resolution—Principles of safe manning—also provides essential guidelines on the application of the recommended principles.

List of invalid certificates

8. As mentioned in paragraph 5, in order to help prevent unlawful use of certificates which may have fallen into the hands of persons other than their lawful holders, it is advisable to circulate all information available on certificates which are reported lost, stolen or destroyed or which have been revoked, cancelled or suspended and which have not been returned to the Administration.

换证

5. 换发遗失、损坏的证书应谨慎从事,以确保换证人是该证书的合法持有人。

   给新换的证书分派号码十分重要,并应将对应的被盗、损坏或遗失的证书的相关信息通知给检查船舶最低配员的检查官员,让他们知道该证书已失效。

执行标准

管理指令

6. 为使考试达到最大程度的一致性,很有必要建立一套关于考试程序的说明和指导。

   对应试者的考试资格审核、体检、笔试、实操等环节应仔细处理,以确保对所有应试者同样对待。异常的情况应报告中心机构,以便他们据此持续改进考试指引和指令。

   该部分结尾处的附录中有一个中心机构提供的考试指引的例子。

查实正确配员

7. 通常,国家法规规定了船东及其代表,特别是船长的责任。他们应确保包括他在内的所有船员依法持有有效证书。主管机关的职能是监控船舶依法配备船员。

   经修订的 STCW 1978 公约第 I 部分第 12 节强调船舶不仅要满足最低数量的船员配备,而且要求所配备船员持有必需的相应证书。

   IMO 大会决议——安全配员原则——也提供了应用推荐原则的必要指引。

无效证书清单

8. 正如第 5 节所提到的,为了防止证书被非法盗用,发布那些据报为丢失、被盗和损坏或被废除、废止或中止而未归还管理中心的证书列一清单,这是明智做法。

Port State Control

9. Article X of the 1978 STCW Convention, as amended, prescribes measures concerning the control of ships of other States visiting the ports of a State Party to the Convention It should be noted that under paragraph (5) of the Article, States Parties to the Convention are required to apply the control provisions as may be necessary to ensure that no more favourable treatment is given to ships entitled to fly the flag of a non-Party than is given to ships entitled to fly the flag of a Party.

10. Because national certificates issued prior to the entry into force of the Convention are recognized for continued use and may not be in a language easily understood by the officer exercising control, the Maritime Safety Committee of IMO, at its fifty-second session, endorsed the recommendation of the Sub-Committee on Standards of Training and Watchkeeping that, for the purposes of the port State control under Article X of the Convention, a document should be issued in respect of each existing certificate by a duly authorized official that indicates, in English, its status, since such certificates would not be endorsed in accordance with regulation I/2 of the Convention (MSC 52/28, paragraph 112). This recommendation was disseminated by STW/Circ. 25.

11. Regulation I/4 of the Convention further amplifies the control procedures which should be applied under Article X. In this connection it should be noted that the harmonized interpretation provided by MSC/Circ. 393 clarifies that, in the case of unsafe watchkeeping under paragraph 2.4 and 2.5 which cannot be construed as a failure under paragraphs 2.1 and 2.3, the Convention provides only that the control officer shall provide written information to the master of the ship and to the appropriate representative of the flag State.

Ensuring implementation of the revised Convention

12. One of the most important aspects of the revised Convention is that it introduces significant measures designed to ensure that the new standards of competence, and other improvements contained in the revised Convention, will be uniformly implemented on a global basis when they enter into force. Some of these measures represent a radical departure from the scope of previous IMO regulations.

    Because there is no single measure that can guarantee that the Convention's standards will be adequately enforced, a "well-balanced package" of controls has been adopted to ensure both compliance by industry and to require effective implementation and enforcement by governments. It is implicit in such a package that there will be more than one layer of measures to ensure compliance and that in some cases there will be a degree of overlap.

港口国检查

9. 经修订的1978年STCW公约第十章规定了缔约国如何管理在其港口的其他缔约国船只。应当注意到该章第5节所述,要求公约缔约国所应用的管理规定,应确保非公约缔约国船旗的船只不会比公约缔约国船旗的船只享有更优惠的待遇。

10. 因为各国早于公约生效日期而签发的证书被认可继续使用,这些证书书写的语言可能是一种不易于被检查官理解的语言。为了实施公约第十章要求的港口国管理,IMO海事安全委员会第52次会议,签署了常务理事会关于培训和值班标准的建议,要求现有的该类证书必须附有一些文件,这些文件由合适的权威机构发行,用英文书写,简要说明该证书情形状况。以后,依照公约规则Ⅰ/2(MSC 52/28第112段)的规定,该类证书不再签发。该建议被编入STCW公约第25号决议。

11. 在公约第十章中,公约规则Ⅰ/4进一步说明了检查程序。同样,应当注意提供相同解释的MSC/Circ.393决议声明:如果出现下列情况,不能按规则2.4和2.5要求保持值班安全又无法按规则2.1和2.3段规定实施,公约所允许的港口国检查官员的权限是他们给该船船长和该船旗国的相应代表提供书面资料。

确保履行经修订的公约

12. 公约最重要的修订之一,是它采纳了一些重要措施来确保新的适任标准和修订的公约中包含的其他改进措施在公约修正案生效后能够在全球范围内被一致履行。其中有些方法甚至表现得和IMO原来规则的内容有根本区别。

   因为没有单一的方法能够保证充分履行公约标准,因而采用一整套充分平衡的控制措施以确保行业依从公约标准、政府有效地实施公约标准。毫无疑问,这一套充分平衡的措施不仅仅包含一个管理层次,而且在某些方面还会出现一定程度上的交叠。

Ensuring compliance by Companies

Penalties

13. In addition to stipulating explicit company responsibilities, the revised Convention reinforces these measures with specific provisions requiring governments to apply penalties to shipping companies and seafarers found to be in breach of the Convention's requirements, Regulation I/5 governing national provisions.

Port state control

14. The responsibilities and obligations of shipping companies under the revised Convention will also be reinforced by provisions expanding the authority of port state control inspectors to verify the qualifications and competence of seafarers.

    As at present, port state control inspectors will be entitled to check:

    — That seafarers hold required certificates or dispensations. But in future this will include flag state endorsements of certificates issued by countries other than the flag state or evidence that applications for such endorsements have been made.

    — That the number and certificates of seafarers on board are in compliance with the flag state's safe manning requirements.

15. Inspectors will also be entitled, as at present, to undertake an assessment of seafarers' abilities if the ship has been involved in a collision, grounding or stranding, if there has been an illegal discharge of substances from the ship, or if it has been manoeuvred in an erratic or unsafe manner.

16. The revised Convention, however, expands the "clear grounds" under which inspectors will be permitted to undertake an assessment of seafarers' abilities to maintain watchkeeping standards to whenever a ship is deemed as "otherwise being operated in such a manner as to pose a threat to persons, properly or the environment".

17. The STCW Code also states in Section A-I/4 that "the assessment...can require the seafarer to demonstrate the related competency at the place of duty. Such demonstration may include verification that operational requirements in respect of watchkeeping standards have been met and that there is a proper response to emergency situations within the seafarer's level of competence".

Ensuring implementation by Governments

18. A particularly important part of the package to restore confidence in the validity of STCW certificates, regardless of where they are issued, is the measures designed to ensure effective implementation of the Convention requirements by governments. These measures include:

确保公司遵行公约规定

处罚

13. 除规定了公司的明确责任外,修订的公约还增加了详细的补充规定,要求政府处罚那些被发现违反公约要求的船公司和船员,相关内容见公约规则 I/5 中国家的规定。

港口国管理

14. 由于港口国管理检查人员对船员的资格和适任实施核查,修订的公约规定中船公司的责任和义务也得到加强。

    目前,PSC 检查官员有权检查:

    — 船员持有所需的证书或特免证书,但将来还包括由船旗国签注并由其他国家颁发的证书的相应证据。

    — 在船的船员人数和证书符合船旗国的配员要求。

15. 如果某船涉及碰撞、搁浅、排泄非法物质、反常和不安全的操纵行为,检查官目前还有权对船员能力进行评估。

16. 修订的公约还详述了这样一种情形——当某船被认为是"如果照此操纵,将会危及生命、财产或环境"的情况下,检查官将被允许对船员的能力和保持安全值班标准做出评估。

17. STCW 规则在 A-I/4 部分规定:"该评估……可以要求该船员示范其所任职务的相关能力。该示范可包括与其适任等级相对应的,值班时所遇各种情况的操作要求和应急情况下的正确反应。"

确保政府履约

18. 确保各履约国政府有效履行公约,使得无论在哪里签发的 STCW 证书其有效性都被信任,这是公约程序的重要内容。这些措施包括:

— Communication of information to IMO Governments issuing STCW certificates will be required to submit to IMO documentary evidence of compliance with the standards of the Convention.

— Quality standards Governments issuing certificates will be obliged to demonstrate that their training and certification regimes incorporate quality standards subject to independent evaluation.

— Flag state responsibilities Flag states will be obliged to accept responsibility for checking the competence of foreign seafarers serving on their ships who hold certificates issued by another state.

Communication of information to IMO

19. Governments issuing STCW certificates will be required to submit detailed reports to IMO including information on:

    — Legal and administrative measures effected nationally to ensure compliance with the Convention with particular regard to training, assessment and the issue of certificates.

    — Details of training courses, examinations and assessment systems.

    — Details of the procedures followed to approve the conduct of training and assessment nationally

    These reports will have to be submitted to IMO by governments before 1 August 1998. With the assistance of "competent persons" appointed by IMO, including at least one person with knowledge of the particular country's training and certification system, these reports will be examined prior to publication by IMO of a list of governments that have provided sufficient documentary evidence.

    — Non-appearance on this IMO list will not in itself be construed as representing a statement by IMO that seafarers holding certificates issued by certain governments are not competent. However:

    — Other governments, through their port state control inspectors, will be entitled to use the list for purposes such as deciding on particular nationalities of crew or ships' flags to target for inspection purposes.

    — Flag states will be entitled to use the list to assist in decisions on matters such as whether to recognise certificates issued by other governments for service by foreign seafarers on board their ships.

    Given that major labour supply countries will be concerned to ensure that demand for their seafarers is not diminished, the provisions concerning the communication of information to IMO should do much to encourage compliance with the requirements of the revised Convention.

— 与IMO部门沟通信息：签发STCW证书的政府应向IMO提交该国已符合公约标准的证明文件。

— 质量标准：签发证书的政府有义务证明他们的培训和发证体系的质量标准是经过独立评估的。

— 船旗国的责任：船旗国有责任检查一些外国船员的证书有效性——这些船员持其他国家签发的证书但服务于船旗国船舶。

与IMO信息沟通

19. 签发STCW证书的政府须向IMO递交详细报告，内容包括：

    — 在法律和行政手段上确保遵从公约关于培训、评估和发证的要求。

    — 培训课程、考试和评估体系细节。

    — 实施培训和评估的国家批准程序细节。

    这些报告须由各有关政府在1998年8月1日前递交IMO。在IMO指定的资深人员，至少包括一个熟悉该国培训和发证体系的人员，在其帮助下审核报告，通过审核，该国方能列入IMO白名单。

    — 然而，IMO白名单并不表明IMO认为那些持有未进入白名单的政府签发的证书的海员是不胜任的。

    — 其他政府，可以通过其PSC检查官，利用白名单确定某国籍船员或某船旗国的船舶成为其检查目标。

    — 船旗国可以利用白名单帮助确定是否承认在其船舶上工作的外籍船员所持的证书是由未列入白名单的政府发行。

主要的劳务输出国会要求确保对其海员的各种要求并非出于歧视。因此，在与IMO进行信息沟通方面需做大量的工作以鼓励这些国家遵从经修订的公约的要求。

Quality standards

20. To reinforce further the implementation of the new STCW standards, there are provisions in the revised Convention that will require governments to demonstrate that the training and certification systems approved in their countries incorporate quality standards which are subjected to independent evaluation.

   In particular, the Convention states that governments must ensure that "... all training, assessment of competence, certification, endorsement and revalidation activities carried out by non-governmental agencies or entities under its authority are continuously monitored through a quality standards system to ensure the achievement of defined objectives, including those concerning the qualifications and experience of instructors and assessors; and where governmental agencies or entities perform such activities, there shall be a quality standards system", Regulation I/8.

21. Governments will be required to ensure that all aspects of their national training and certification regime are subjected to independent evaluation at least every five years. A full report of this evaluation, including details about the qualifications of those undertaking it, will also have to be submitted to IMO as part of the process of communicating documentary evidence of compliance described above.

Flag state responsibilities

22. The final layer of the package of overlapping measures to ensure that the minimum STCW standards are implemented relates to flag state responsibilities regarding the competence of foreign seafarers (i.e seafarers with certificates issued by another state) serving on their ships.

23. Flag states will be required to issue either their own certificates to foreign seafarers or individual endorsements of foreign seafarers' certificates. An endorsement will be issued as a separate document attesting to the recognition of the foreign certificate by the flag state. A three months' period of grace will be permitted between the time when a seafarer joins a "foreign flag" ship and when the endorsement has to be issued by the flag state, provided that documentary proof that an application for an endorsement has been made can be presented.

24. In order to reduce the scope for abuse, the revised Convention requires that in the event that a seafarer is found to be incompetent or holding a bogus certificate and the endorsement is withdrawn, the flag state must inform the government that issued the original certificate.

   Of particular significance, however, is that the amended Convention states that flag states will only be allowed to issue endorsements if:

   Regulation I/10

   The Administration [i.e flag state] has confirmed, through all necessary measures, which may include inspection of facilities and procedures, that the requirements concerning standards of competence, the issue and endorsement of certificates and record keeping are fully complied with.

质量标准

20. 为进一步加强贯彻新的STCW标准,修订的公约要求政府证明他们的经核准的培训和发证体制的质量标准是经过独立评估的。

    公约特别强调,政府应确保"……由其授权的非政府性质的代理机构实施的所有培训、适任评估、发证、签署和证书再有效,包括有关教师和评估员的资格和经验,应在一个质量标准体系下保持连续监控,以确保达到规定的效果;政府性质的代表机构或其授权机构从事这些工作时,他们也必须建立一个质量标准体系",公约规则Ⅰ/8。

21. 有关政府被要求至少每5年对其培训和发证制度进行独立的评估。这些全面的评估报告,包括实施评估的人员的资格的详细报告,作为与IMO信息沟通程序的证明文件的一部分,须提交IMO。

船旗国义务

22. 程序所采取的基本措施是要求船旗国履行确保所有在悬挂该国旗的船上服务的外国海员(即持有其他国家颁发证书的船员)满足STCW公约最低的适任标准职责。

23. 船旗国需要给外国海员签发证书或对外国海员的证书单独进行签证。该签证将由船旗国作为一个独立的证明文件颁发,用以承认外国证书。从一个船员上外国旗船工作到船旗国颁发签证(假如申请签证提出的证明文件能够被批准),允许有3个月的宽限期。

24. 为了减少滥用的机会,公约修正案要求:如果发现海员不适任或者持有伪造证书并已被撤销签证的,船旗国必须通知原始证书签发国政府。

    然而,特殊的意义在于,修订后的公约规定船旗国将只被允许根据如下规定颁发签证:

    公约规则I/10

    船旗国主管机关采用所有必要的可靠措施,包括对设施和程序的检查,确认有关适任标准、证书的颁发和签发以及保持记录的要求得以完全遵守。

25. This requirement incorporates two principles. First, it means that flag states will have to satisfy themselves that foreign governments issuing certificates to officers serving on board their ships are actually doing so in compliance with the Convention's standards. Secondly, the requirement means that flag states will, as a minimum, have to ensure that individual foreign certificates are valid and authentic by making necessary checks with the issuing government. A separate provision in the Convention requires that governments issuing certificates will have to maintain a national register of certificates and answer requests for information received from other maritime administrations.

26. Checking that the authority issuing the certificate appears on the IMO list of governments that have submitted sufficient documentary evidence of compliance (see above) may be one of the "necessary measures" applied by flag states. However, the requirement for criteria for ensuring compliance "through all necessary measures, which may include inspection of facilities and procedures" implies that some additional measures to ensure compliance will also have to be undertaken, as does the fact that flag states will also be required to submit reports to IMO summarising the measures taken to comply with this specific regulation.

Training of examiners

27. After completing this or an equivalent course, those who are to conduct examinations to assess the competency of seafarers should gain experience in setting, selecting and marking or scoring examinations under the general supervision of an experienced examiner.

    Similar experience should be gained in observing the conduct of oral and practical tests by an experienced examiner or examiners.

    Before being authorized to conduct such examinations, the examining authority should ensure by some form of assessment that those who are to conduct examinations are able to conduct them in a fair and uniform manner. The following guidelines provide an example of such an assessment:

    Assessment of New Examiners

    1. All persons who are to act as examiners shall be required to undergo examination by two examiners who must attest to their fitness and competence. No document, examination result or dispensation may be signed by any person who has not been examined at the required level and duly appointed.

    2. The examination or assessment shall not be regarded as a test of technical knowledge. The possession of the required certificate of competency in conjunction with any restrictions imposed regarding the level of examination which may be conducted is considered to satisfy this aspect of the new examiner's fitness.

    3. Before signing an authorization to conduct examinations the two examiners shall be satisfied that the new examiner:

25. 这项要求具体体现了两个原则。首先,这意味着船旗国承认由外国政府发证的、正在本国籍船上服务的船员实际上是符合公约标准的;其次,这项要求意味着船旗国至少应该与颁发国共同实施必要的检查,以确保每一个外国海员的证书是有效并且可信的。在公约中,有一项单独的规定,要求签发国政府要保持证书的国家登记,并向其他海事管理机构提供信息。

26. 核对证书的颁发国是否列在 IMO 白名单上(见上文),可能是船旗国应用的必要手段之一。然而为确保符合"已采用所有可能的必要手段包括对设备和程序的检查"的标准要求,也应采取一些额外的方法,也要求船旗国向 IMO 报告为符合这项特定条款所采用的方法。

考官的培训

27. 在完成了本科目或等效课程后,即将实施海员适任评估考试的人员,应在具有丰富经验的考官的监督下,获得在试题的编制、遴选以及评卷方面的经验。

    类似的经验也能从观摩一位或多位具有丰富经验的考官的口试和实操考试的操作中获取。

    在被批准实际操作这样的考试之前,主考机关应对候任考官进行某种方式的评估以确保他们能够公平一致地实施考试。以下的指引提供了这种评估的例子:

    对新考官的评估

    1. 要求所有即将担任考官的人员要接受由两位业已证明适任和具备能力的考官主持的考试。任何未经要求的水平考核和正式任命的人不能获发任何证明文件、考试成绩或豁免证明。

    2. 这样的考试或评估不应作为技术知识测试。如果新考官拥有所主持的等级考试的适任证书及其任职条件,可以被认为满足技术方面的要求。

    3. 在签署实施考试的授权书之前,两位资深考官应对新考官的以下方面的表现满意:

.1 understands and can apply the instructions relating to the assessment of candidates;

.2 is capable of operating all the instruments, receivers and simulators appropriate to the grades and classes of certificate for which he is to examine;

.3 is generally conversant the various Regulations relating to certificates of competency, efficiency and qualification and related guidance and publications; and

.4 has received sufficient practice in the conduct of oral and practical examinations, so as to:

— adequately cover the prescribed syllabus of examination to an appropriate depth,

— determine weaknesses in a candidate's knowledge,

— draw out information and responses from nervous candidates,

— maintain a reliable record of an applicant's oral and practical performance, and

— arrive at a fair assessment of the candidate.

4. In determining that the criteria listed in paragraph 3. are reached, the new examiner shall mark a sufficient number of written papers and conduct a sufficient number of oral and practical examinations to satisfy the two examiners.

Training and Assessment

28. The revised Convention includes a new Regulation I/6: Training and Assessment.

    Section A-I/6 of the STCW Code states the following:

    Qualifications of instructors, supervisors and assessors

    3. Each Party shall ensure that instructors, supervisors and assessors are appropriately qualified for the particular types and levels of training or assessment of competence of seafarers either on board or ashore, as required under the Convention, in accordance with the provisions of this section.

.1 能理解并应用对考生评估的相关说明；

.2 具有操作适合在他将要实施的等级及种类的证书考试中应用的所有仪器、接收机和模拟器的能力；

.3 应总体熟悉涉及适任证书、职能以及资格的各种规章制度和相关的指南、出版物；及

.4 已经在实施口语及实操考试方面获得足够的实践，能够：

— 充分覆盖考试大纲的要求，设定合适的考试深度，

— 确定考生知识方面的弱项，

— 发现心情紧张的考生并做出反应，

— 保持考生在口语和实操考试中的表现的有效记录，及

— 对所有考生做到公正评价。

4. 为确定达到第3.段中所列的要求，新考官需要操作足够数量的笔试、口试及实操考试以令两位主考官满意。

培训和评估

28. 经修订的公约包含了一条新的公约规则Ⅰ/6：培训和评估。

以下是STCW规则的第A-Ⅰ/6节的规定：

教员、监督员和评估员的资格

3. 各缔约国应按照本节的规定确保教员、监督员和评估员完全胜任公约要求的船上或岸上特定种类和级别的培训或对海员适任能力的评估。

Annex 20-1
Formal investigation of sinking of ANTACUS

Decision of the Commissioner of Maritime Affairs, R.L. and Report of the Formal Investigation in the Matter of the Sinking of the Motor Vessel *ANTACUS*

REPUBLIC OF LIBERIA

DECISION OF THE COMMISSIONER
OF MARITIME AFFAIRS, R.L.

and

REPORT
of the
FORMAL INVESTIGATION

In the Matter of the Sinking of the
Motor Vessel ANTACUS (O.N. 6514)
In the North Atlantic Ocean
On 16 July 1984

PUBLISHED BY THE BUREAU OF MARITIME AFFAIRS
by *Authority of the*
MINISTER OF FINANCE

10 March 1987
Monrovia, Liberia

附件 20-1
关于"ANTACUS"号沉没的正式调查报告

利比里亚共和国海上事务委员会决议,关于机动船"ANTACUS"号沉没事件的正式调查报告

利比里亚共和国

利比里亚共和国海上事务专员裁定文件

及

关于机动船"ANTACUS"号沉没事件的正式调查报告

地点:北大西洋
时间:1984年7月16日

财政部授权海上事务委专员发布
1987年3月10日
利比里亚·蒙罗维亚

REPUBLIC OF LIBERIA
MINISTRY OF FINANCE
MONROVIA, LIBERIA

OFFICE OF THE COMMISSIONER
FOR MARITIME AFFAIRS

Decision of the Commissioner of Maritime Affairs, R.L.
and the Report of Formal Investigation
In the Matter of the Sinking of the
Motor Vessel *ANTACUS* (O.N. 6514)
In the North Atlantic Ocean
On 16 July 1984

AUTHORITY

This Decision is rendered pursuant to the provisions of Sections 11, 18, 258 and 346 of the Liberian Maritime Law and Maritime Regulation 9.258(7).

COMMENT

The bulk carrier *ANTACUS* was abandoned 150 miles northeast of the Azores, at about 0230 16 July 1984, when the Master was unable to control the flooding of holds numbers 4 and 5.

The Chief Engineer shut down the main power plant prior to abandonment, which plunged the vessel into total darkness during that critical operation.

The Radio Officer stated that he had transmitted a distress signal on various frequencies on both the Primary Transmitter and the Emergency Transmitter from 0115 through 0229. He claimed that he activated the automatic keying device on the emergency transmitter prior to abandoning ship.

The distress calls from *ANTACUS* were not acknowledged by any ship or station. The distress message did not provide any indication of the position of *ANTACUS*.

The undersigned views with grave concern that the Radio Officer of *ANTACUS* was unable to effectively transmit a distress signal prior to abandoning ship. The most obvious lesson to be learned from this incident is that the Master should not abandon ship, except in the most extreme conditions, without confidence that his distress call has been acknowledged.

利比里亚共和国
财政部
蒙罗维亚

海上事务委员会

利比里亚共和国海上事务专员裁定文件及关于机动船"ANTACUS"号（O.N.6514）于1984年7月16日在北大西洋沉没事件的正式调查报告

依据

本决议依据利比里亚《海事法律和海事规则》9.258(7)第11条、第18条、第258条和第346条条做出。

评述

由于不能控制4号舱和5号舱的进水，大约在1984年7月16日0230时，散货船"ANTACUS"号船长在亚述尔群岛东北方150海里处弃船。

轮机长在弃船前关闭了主发电机，导致全船在紧要关头处于一片黑暗中。

电报员声称他从0115到0229同时通过主发信机和应急发信机在多个频率上发出了遇险信号，并声称已在弃船前启动了应急电报上的自动发射装置。

从"ANTACUS"号发出的遇险信号未被任何船舶或岸站收悉。遇险信息未提供任何关于"ANTACUS"号的位置信息。

报告签署人深切体会到："ANTACUS"号电报员未能有效地在弃船前发出遇险信号。本次事故中最严重的教训是：除非是在极端情况下，船长不应在遇险呼叫未得到确认之前轻易弃船。

The second lesson to be learned from this incident is that the Radio Officer should in an emergency situation also employ his HF Transmitter to contact any commercial station that he could hear. This would of course be in addition to transmitting on the prescribed distress frequencies.

The undersigned cannot avoid, given the facts, a strong impression that no effective distress signal was ever transmitted from *ANTACUS*.

The Radio Officer did not express any surprise that his calls were not heard. He stated that he was in the "middle of the Atlantic." In fact *ANTACUS* was 700 miles off the coast of Portugal, and most certainly within calling distance of the UK, Belgium, France, and Portugal.

Under these most demanding conditions, the Master failed to exercise the most basic requirements of command. He did not question why the Chief Engineer had shut down the plant. He did not give the Radio Officer the ship's position, or ask the Radio Officer if the distress call had been acknowledged.

The Master also disclaimed any responsibility to load, stow, and trim the cargo of steel products which are known to have a tendency to shift, even when adequately shored. Clause 8 of the amended New York form of charter-party, which was employed for that voyage, provided that "charterers are to load, stow, and trim the cargo... under the supervision and responsibility of the Captain...." Clause 49 of the Time Charter states that "The Stevedores... remain under the direction and control of the Master, who will be responsible for the proper stowage and the seaworthiness of his vessel." This function and responsibility was woefully disregarded.

Neither the Cargo Officer nor the Master inspected the cargo holds once *ANTACUS* was underway from Belgium for the United States. Neither took any action once noise was heard from the cargo holds.

This entire incident appears to reflect a situation where no one was in actual command, and all who could take responsible action accepted the circumstances with a fatalistic attitude.

The entire record of this Formal Investigation having been reviewed, the undersigned takes the following action with respect to the Report of Formal Investigation and its Findings of Fact, Conclusions and Recommendations.

ACTION

1. The Report of Formal Investigation is hereby adopted in full as to its Findings, Conclusions and Recommendations.

2. It is directed that this Decision be published together with the Report of Formal Investigation and its Annexes.

3. As for Recommendations 1, 2 and 3 regarding the status of the Liberian Licenses of the Master, Chief Mate, and Chief Engineer, the proposed action will become effective on the date of this Decision.

第二个教训是:电报员在紧急情况下应该用高频(HF)发信机联系他能收听到的任何民用电台。这当然应作为在规定的遇险频率之外的补充手段。

报告签署人强烈地认为:事实上"ANTACUS"号根本没有发出过有效的遇险信号。

电报员对其发出的呼叫未被收到毫不惊奇。他声称他在"大西洋中部",实际上,"ANTACUS"号是在离葡萄牙海岸700海里处,当然还在英国、比利时、法国和葡萄牙的呼叫范围内。

在最需要情况下,船长未能实施最基本的必要指挥。他不问轮机长为何关掉电源,不给电报员船位,或询问电报员遇险信号是否已被收悉。

船长未能尽到对货物的装载、积载及吃水调整进行管理的责任,而这些钢铁制品货件被公认即使是进行了良好的支撑尚且容易移位的。该船这一航次采用的修正的纽约租船合同文本第8条规定:"……租船人在船长的监督和负责下进行装载、积载及调整平舱……"。期租合同第49条规定:"装卸工人……受船长的控制和指挥,船长负责适当的积载及船舶的适航。"这些职责被可悲地漠视了。

在"ANTACUS"号从比利时到美国的途中,大副和船长一次都没有对货舱进行检查,也没注意到从货舱传来的任何一次响声。

整件事反映出这种情况:没有人在实际指挥,而所有应采取负责行动的人却对事态抱着任其发展的态度。

本调查的全部记录已核查过。以下是本正式调查报告的处理意见及调查结果、结论和建议。

处理

1. 完全采纳正式调查报告的结果、结论及建议。

2. 决定将本决议与调查报告及其附件一起公布。

3. 至于在建议1、2和3点所提到的对船长、大副和轮机长的利比里亚证书的处理情况将在本决议签发之日执行。

4. Liberian License No. 225023 issued to the Master, Captain Ming-Cheng Chen is to be revoked permanently. Mr. Chen is, however, offered the opportunity to apply for a Liberian License in the grade of Chief Mate.

5. The Chief Engineer and the Chief Mate are authorized to apply for a Liberian License in the next lower grade during the period of suspension of their Liberian Licenses.

6. In light of the importance of this Report to the quest for improved safety of life and property at sea, the undersigned will transmit a copy of this Report and Decision to the Secretary-General of the International Maritime Organization, for particular interest of the Sub-Committee on Radiocommunications.

7. The undersigned extends a sincere expression of appreciation to the Captain and crew of the French Yacht SAINT JEAN, the Honduran cargo ship OLANCHO and the Portuguese naval ship AUGUSTO CASTILHO for the rescue of the Master and crew of *ANTACUS*.

8. As a matter of comity, the undersigned will cause a copy of this Report and Decision to be officially transmitted to the Government of Portugal, along with an expression of appreciation to the Search and Rescue organization in the Azores.

Done at Monrovia, Montserrado County, Republic of Liberia
This 10th Day of March, A.D., 1987

Sgd
GEORGE B. COOPER
COMMISSIONER OF MARITIME AFFAIRS, R.L

4. 签发给船长陈明成（音）的编号为No.225023的利比里亚证书被永久注销。对于陈先生，可以给予机会申考利比里亚大副证书。

5. 轮机长和大副可在其利比里亚证书暂停有效期间申考下一等级的证书。

6. 依据本报告对海上人命和财产安全的重要性，将送交一份报告和决议给国际海事组织秘书处，特别是无线电通信分委会。

7. 谨向救助了"ANTACUS"号船长和船员的法籍"SAINT JEAN"号游艇、洪都拉斯货船"OLANCHO"、葡萄牙海军"AUGUSTO CASTILHO"舰的舰船长和船员表达诚挚的感谢。

8. 作为礼节，将正式递送一份报告及决议给葡萄牙政府，同时表达对亚述尔群岛搜救组织的诚挚感谢。

完成于利比里亚共和国Montserrado郡蒙罗维亚
1987年3月10日

签署：
GEOREG B.COOPER
利比里亚海上事务专员

FINDINGS OF FACT

A. Background Material

1. Particulars of Vessel:

Name:	*ANTACUS*
Official Number:	6514
Call Sign:	D5PB
Home Port:	Monrovia, Liberia
Service:	Bulk Carrier
Gross Tons:	16,347
Net Tons:	11,295
Length:	540.5 feet
Breadth:	83.65 feet
Propulsion:	Diesel
Power:	8,650 kW
Year and Place Built:	1973, Scotstoun, Scotland
Class:	100 A1(B) (Lloyd's Register)
Hull Material:	Steel
Cargo Holds:	Five
Pumping Equipment:	Steam bilge pump, 40–50 tons/hr. General service pump, 180 tons/hr. Fire and bilge pump, 120 tons/hr. Sea water cooling pump Ballast pump Emergency fire pump
Life-saving Equipment:	2 motor lifeboats, each with a capacity of 51 persons 2 inflatable life rafts, each with a capacity of 25 persons 1 life raft, 6-person capacity 50 lifejackets

调查事实

A. 背景材料

1. 船舶数据:

船名:	ANTACUS
登记号:	6514
呼号:	D5PB
船籍港:	蒙罗维亚,利比里亚
种类:	散货船
总吨:	16 347
净吨:	11 295
型长:	540.5 英尺
型宽:	83.65 英尺
推进器:	柴油机
功率:	8 650 千瓦
建造年份地点:	1973 年,苏格兰 Scotstoun
船级:	100A1(B)(劳氏船检)
舱材:	钢
货舱数量:	5
泵设备:	蒸汽舱底泵,40~50 吨/小时
	船舶通用泵,180 吨/小时
	消防舱底泵,120 吨/小时
	海水冷却泵
	压载泵
	应急消防泵
救生设备:	2 艘机动救生艇,每艘定员 51 人
	2 艘气胀式救生筏,每艘定员 25 人
	1 具救生筏,定员 6 人
	50 件救生衣

Radio Equipment:
Transmitter:

Mfg.	Type No.		Power Output	Frequencies
Standard	ST1400C	Main	200/400 watts	405–525 kHz
Standard	ST1400C	HF	1200 watts	4,000–26,000 kHz
Standard	ST1400C	Telephony	350/1,500 watts	1,600–23,000 kHz
IMRC	IMR113	Emergency	100 watts	405–525;2,182 kHz
Marconi	Survivor 610	Lifeboat/Port.	1.7–3.8 watts	500/2182/8364 kHz
Standard	STR-65	VHF	25 watts	155.025–157.425 MHz

Receivers & Auxiliary:

Mfg.	Type No.		Frequencies
ITT Marine	IMR5000	Main/HF	100–30,000 kHz
ITT Marine	ST401	Emergency	85–25,000 kHz
Marconi	Warden 4	Radiotelephone Distress Freq. Watchkeeping Rec.	2,182 kHz
ITT Marine	AA204	Auto Alarm Telegraphy	500 kHz
ITT Marine	IMR5400	Auto Keying Device/Telegraphy	
Marconi	Coast Alert	2,182 kHz Radiotelephony Alarm Signal Generating Device	
ITT Marine	ADF2200	Direction Finder	

Owner: Astarte Shipping Company
Monrovia, Liberia

Managers: Chi Yuen Navigation Co. Ltd.
Chien Hsin Building
72, Nanking Road East
Lane 21, Section 2, Taipei
Republic of China

2. A pipe tunnel ran under the cargo holds on the port and starboard sides of the vessel to which there was access via two manholes on the bottom of each cargo hold with the manholes secured by nuts and bolts. A watertight door located on the starboard side forward in the engine room led to the pipe tunnel (299, 302).

无线电设备:
发信机:

生产厂家	型号		输出功率	频率
标准	ST1400C	主发信机	200/400 瓦	405~525 kHz
标准	ST1400C	高频	1 200 瓦	4 000~26 000 kHz
标准	ST1400C	无线电话	350/1 500 瓦	1 600~23 000 kHz
IMRC	IMR113	应急	100 瓦	405~525;2 182 kHz
Marconi	Survivor 610	左舷救生艇	1.7~3.8 瓦	500/2 182/8 364 kHz
标准	STR-65	甚高频无线电话	25 瓦	155.025~157.425 MHz

收信机 & 辅件:

生产厂家	型号		功率
ITT Marine	IMR5000	主/高频	100~30 000 kHz
ITT Marine	ST401	应急	85~25 000 kHz
Marconi	Warden 4	无线电话遇险频率值班记录仪	2 182 kHz
ITT Marine	AA204	自动警报无线电报	500 kHz
ITT Marine	IMR5400	自动拍发无线电报	
Marconi	Coast Alert	2 182 kHz 无线电话警报信号发生器	
ITT Marine	ADF2200	无线电测向仪	

  船东: 阿斯塔特航运公司
       利比里亚蒙罗维亚

  营运人: 齐云海运公司(音)
       中国台北2区21巷
       南京东路72号秦兴大厦

2. 该船左右两舷货舱底层布置一根管隧,通过两个用螺母和螺栓固定的人孔连接。机舱前方右舷有一水密门通向管隧。

3. Chartering Arrangements: *ANTACUS* was on an eight year time charter dated February 10, 1979 to Atlantic Lines and Navigation Company (Exh. 18). *ANTACUS* had a complement of nine officers and ten unlicensed crew members. There were six crew members from the Republic of China and thirteen from the Philippines (Exh. 10). This was Captain Chen's second voyage as Master of *ANTACUS* (78). Captain Chen had served as Master of vessels carrying steel on two prior occasions; on the previous voyage of *ANTACUS*, and once on the *ARION*, the sister ship of *ANTACUS* (76, 77).

B. Loading of *ANTACUS*

4. *ANTACUS*' final voyage, 38-A, involved three load ports, Hamburg, Bremerhaven and Antwerp. At Hamburg, the vessel loaded steel sheets and wire rods in No. 1 hold, steel sheets, wire rods and nails in No. 3 hold, steel plates and steel sheets in No. 4 hold (Exh. 12B, 49). She then sailed on June 30, 1984 for Bremerhaven for further loading.

5. *ANTACUS* arrived at Bremerhaven on July 1, 1984, where bundles of steel pipes were loaded in Nos. 2 and 5 holds and steel girders, steel wires and steel coils were loaded in No. 4 hold. Containers were loaded on deck (49).

6. The preloading surveys at Hamburg (Exh. 12E) and at Bremerhaven (Exh. 12F, 348) each indicated that the holds were clean and fit for cargo. The manhole covers to the pipe tunnel were found secure and no internal damage was reported (481). The filters in the bilge wells in the cargo holds were cleaned and suction was tested (452–453).

7. The superintendent of cargo ("supercargo") for charterers, Captain Tijan, supervised the loading, stowing and securing of cargo by the lashing gangs in all three ports (88–89, 255–256). Captain Tijan informed the Master that the stevedores at Bremerhaven were inexperienced. The Third Mate further testified that the stevedores had not been careful in loading (439, 440).

8. *ANTACUS* sailed from Bremerhaven on July 7, arriving at Antwerp on July 9 (Exh. 13A). Bundles of wire rods, steel sheets, steel plates and other steel products were loaded in No. 5 hold; steel girders, steel "I" beams in No. 4 hold and steel pipes in No. 2 hold.

9. Piping in No. 5 hold was stowed fore and aft (264). The "I" beams in No. 4 hold were also stowed fore and aft on the sides of the hold and athwartship in the middle of the hold (264–266). The steel plates in No. 4 hold were secured by wires with turnbuckles (275); the on-deck containers were stowed on both sides of the vessel and on top of the hatch covers 1 and 2 (286), and the pipes forward in No. 5 hold were secured by wire (311).

10. There was space between the cargo in the forward part of No. 5 hold and the afterpart, and also between the aft cargo and the aft bulkhead in No. 5 hold (333). There was testimony that it is dangerous to have void spaces in cargo holds; if they exist, the spaces should be shored and blocked off to prevent shifting of cargo (958–959). The Chief Mate could not see if there was any shoring in the foregoing spaces but assumed the supercargo placed shoring in the spaces (333–334).

3. 租船安排:"ANTACUS"号自1979年2月10日出租给大西洋班轮海运公司,租期8年。船舶定员9名高级船员,10名普通船员。6名船员来自中国台湾,13名船员来自菲律宾。这是陈船长在该船任船长的第二个航次。陈船长已两次担任运载钢材的船长,一次是在"ANTACUS"号的前一航次,另一次是在其姐妹船"ARION"号上。

B. "ANTACUS"号的货载

4. "ANTACUS"号最后的38-A航次有三个挂靠港:汉堡、不来梅和安特卫普。在汉堡港,该船1号舱装上薄钢板、钢条,3号舱装上薄钢板、钢条和钢钉,4号舱装上薄钢板和钢板。于1984年6月30日开往不来梅港加载。

5. "ANTACUS"号于1984年7月1日抵达不来梅,在那里加载了捆装钢管于2号舱和5号舱,加载钢梁、钢条与卷钢于4号舱。集装箱装于甲板。

6. 在汉堡港与不来梅港商检时,显示每一舱都清洁并适于装货。管隧人孔盖完好并无内部损坏。舱底滤清器清洁并经抽吸试验。

7. 租家的监货员Tijan船长分别在三个港口监督了货物的装载、积载及绑扎。Tijan曾经提醒船长:不来梅港的装卸工人操作不熟练,三副进一步证实:装卸工未能谨慎操作。

8. "ANTACUS"号于7月7日从不来梅港开航,7月9日抵达安特卫普。捆装钢条、钢片、钢板及其他的钢制品装于5号舱,"工"字钢装于4舱,钢管装于2号舱。

9. 5号舱的钢管是纵向积载的。4号舱的"工"字钢在两边是纵向装载而在中间是横向装载的。4号舱的钢板通过带卸扣的钢丝绳固定。甲板的集装箱装在船舷两边及1号、2号舱盖上面。5号舱的钢管用钢丝绳向前固定。

10. 5号舱的前后货载之间、后面货物与舱壁之间存在空隙。实践证明:在货舱中存在空档是非常危险的,若存在空档,应加以支撑及加上联横以防止货物的移动。大副并没有查看是否有任何支撑物支撑上述的空档,仅仅是假想监货员已经这样做了。

11. Captain Tijan gave orders to the stevedore foreman at each of the ports (92, 392), and decided what cargo went into each hold and which tier of cargo went on top of which tier (958). He was not on board during the loading of cargo at all times but frequently left to go to other vessels (332, 333).

    The Master sometimes observed the loading process (96), but did not exercise supervision over the Chief Mate, who had never before been responsible for the loading and stowage of a fabricated steel cargo (250). Although Captain Tijan never reported to the Master (93) and was frequently absent during the loading process (332,392), both the Master and the Chief Mate assumed that Captain Tijan was the person in control of the loading and stowage of the cargo (88-92, 255-257).

12. The Chief Mate worked with Captain Tijan and observed the loading of cargo at all three ports, where he was assisted by the Second and Third Mates, who worked in regular shifts (92, 347, 391).

13. After the cargo was loaded in the holds at each of the loading ports, the Chief Mate went into the holds with the stevedore foreman, checked the lashings and considered them to be satisfactory (257-261,279-280). There were however lashings that he was unable to see or reach (280, 334). According to the Chief Mate and Third Mate, Captain Tijan did not go down into the holds at any time (257, 393).

14. On sailing from Antwerp for New Orleans on July 11, *ANTACUS*' departure drafts were 9.98 meters forward, 10.22 meters midships, and 10.46 meters aft (Exhs. 13A, 12B, 346). The vessel was not loaded beyond her allowable draft and had no discernible list.

C. The Voyage: July 11-15, 1984

15. The weather during the voyage is summarized as follows from entries in the *ANTACUS* log:

Date	Wind Force and Direction	Sea	Barometer (metric readings)
July 11	Wind northwest and east, Force 3-5	Moderate sea and swell	1009-1014
July 12	Wind southwest and west, Force 5-7	Rough sea and heavy swell, vessel pitching and rolling with heavy seas on deck	Rising slightly 1012-1018
July 13	Wind west, Force 6-7	High sea and heavy swell, vessel pitching and rolling heavily with seas on deck	Rising slightly 1021-1029
July 14	Wind west and northwest, Force 6	Same seas and swell as July 13	Steady 1028-1030
July 15	Wind northwest, north, northeast, east northeast, Force 4-6	Rough sea and heavy swell, rolling heavily in morning and moderately in the afternoon	Falling slightly 1030-1028

Exhs. 13, 13A

11. Tijan 船长在每个港口指示工头,决定各舱所装货物,以及哪一层货物应装在哪一层货物的上面。装货期间他并不总在船上,他需要时常到其他船上去。

　　船长偶尔察看一下装载进程,但并未监督大副,而大副此前并未负责过此类多种钢材的装载。尽管 Tijan 在装载过程中未向本船船长报告并经常离开,但船长和大副已假定 Tijan 就是货物装载和积载的负责人。

12. 大副在三个港口都和监货员 Tijan 一起监装货物,二副及三副轮班协助他。

13. 在每一装货港装载完毕后,大副都和工头入舱检查绑扎并认为是符合要求的。然而,有些绑扎是他无法见到的。大副与三副证实,Tijan 监货员从未下过大舱。

14. 7月11日从安特卫普开往新奥尔良,"ANTACUS"号的离港艏吃水是9.98 m,船中吃水10.22 m,艉吃水10.46 m。船舶未超过其允许吃水,没有明显的横倾。

C. 1984年7月11日—15日的航行

15. 以下是从"ANTACUS"号航海日志上摘录的本段航程的天气状况:

日期	风力风向	海况	气压 (度量数据)
7月11日	NE,E 3~5级	中浪,涌浪	1009~1014
7月12日	SW,W 5~7级	大浪,涌浪 船舶纵横摇晃,甲板上浪严重	微升 1012~1018
7月13日	W, 6~7级	狂浪,大涌 船舶纵横摇晃剧烈,甲板上浪	微升 1021~1029
7月14日	W,NW 6级	7月13日	稳定 1028~1030
7月15日	NW,N,NE,ENE 4~6级	大浪,大涌 早上剧烈摇晃下午中等摇晃	微降 1030~1028

The vessel and engine speeds, as recorded in the decklog, are summarized as follows:

Date	RPM		Average Speed (knots)
	Min.	Max.	
July 11	97.0	97.8	10.00
July 12	97.0	98.6	12.04
July 13	98.0	99.0	11.00
July 14	95.4	98.1	11.72
July 15	90.7	98.0	12.16

After departure from Antwerp, the bridge log indicated "Start of sea voyage", at 1142, July 11. *ANTACUS* steered various courses, in a generally westerly direction, until July 12 at 2130 at which time a course of 236° true was set. This course continued until the time of abandonment (Exh. 13).

16. The Carpenter sounded the cargo holds daily, except for No. 1 hold where on deck containers restricted access to the sounding pipe. On July 12-14, he obtained readings of 8-10 centimetres in all the holds except 4 and 5 where he measured 25-30 centimetres. On the morning of July 15 however, the soundings in Nos. 4 and 5 holds were 50-60 centimetres (297, 336-337).

17. There was extensive testimony that during July 13 and 14, dull noises from forward of the crew quariers were heard, while the ship was rolling. The Chief Mate, Third Mate, Bos'n and Second Engineer thought the noises came from either hold No. 4 or 5 (284, 288, 398, 457, 458, 527). The Master also thought that the noises came from a cargo hold, but was unable to state which hold. The Chief Mate, Third Mate and Bos'n recalled that the noises were accompanied by vibrations (284, 399, 457). In fact, the noises were "strong enough for everyone to hear and feel" (399). The noises and vibrations coincided with the rolling of the ship and the Chief Mate, Third Mate and Bos'n thought the noises were caused by cargo hitting the side of the vessel. While most of the crew stated that they had never heard sounds like these before (114, 284, 398), none of them discussed the sounds with each other (289, 400, 459). There was also testimony to the effect that the noises were not reported to the Master because those who heard them assumed the Master had also heard them (289, 400). There are no log entries regarding the noises.

D. The Voyage: July 16, 1986

18. At about 0005-0010 on July 16, 1984, the Second Assistant Engineer opened the watertight door leading to the pipe tunnel as was his regular practice (537) and he observed the water level to be just below the top of the pipe tunnel (536-537, 542). The Second Assistant Engineer closed the door and ordered the oiler to open the suction and discharge valves to the steam bilge pump which he then started (543).

以下是节录于机舱日志的主机转速与船速：

日期	主机转速		平均船速（节）
	最小	最大	
7月11日	97.0	97.8	10.00
7月12日	97.0	98.6	12.04
7月13日	98.0	99.0	11.00
7月14日	95.4	98.1	11.72
7月15日	90.7	98.0	12.16

驶离安特卫普后，航海日志记载：7月11日1142开始"定速航行"，操过多个航向，大致向西。直至7月12日2130，设定真航向236°，此航向一直保持至弃船。

16. 除1号舱由于集装箱挡住测深管外，木匠每天对货舱测量。7月12—14日，测得4号舱和5号舱有25~30厘米积水，其余舱是8~10厘米积水。然而，在7月15日早上，测得4号舱和5号舱的积水达50~60厘米。

17. 有大量的证据证实：7月13、14日，当船舶摇晃时，在船员住舱听到了沉闷的响声。大副、三副、水手长和二管轮认为此响声应从4号舱或5号舱传来的。船长也认为响声是从货舱传来，但未感到振动。事实上，响声是"巨大的，足以让每个人听到、感觉到的"。响声和船舶的摇摆一致，大副和水手长认为响声是由货物撞击舱壁引起的，当时大部分船员都认为从没听到过如此大的响声，但他们都没和其他人谈论此事。他们没将此事报告是因为他们认为船长也应听到了此响声。航海日志中没有关于该噪声的记录。

D. 1984年7月16日的航行

18. 1984年7月16日0005—0010，实习大管轮打开通向管隧的水密门进行例行检查，发现水位处于管隧顶端下方，他关闭水密门并命令加油工打开阀门给舱底蒸汽泵供汽，随后启动了泵。

19. The Second Assistant Engineer then awakened the Chief Engineer and reported to him that there was water in the pipe tunnel. Both proceeded immediately to the watertight door leading to the pipe tunnel in the engine room where the Second Assistant Engineer observed that the water level was about 6″ higher than it had been about 10 minutes before and that the water level was then at the top of the pipe tunnel (545, 583). The door was thereafter closed (546, 583). The Chief Engineer had no knowledge as to whether the door was ever opened again (Exh. 38, p.8).

20. The Chief Engineer changed the fuel from heavy to diesel oil (546–547, 576), and reduced the rpm's (139–140).

21. The Master was awakened by the Second Mate at about 0020 of July 16 and informed that the rpms had been reduced. The Master went to the bridge where the Chief Engineer informed him by telephone that there was a large amount of water in the pipe tunnel and asked that soundings be promptly taken (133, 140). At that time the wind was ENE Beaufort Force 5–6; sea was moderate to rough (134, 138, & Exh. 17A)

22. The Chief Mate reported one meter of water was found in No. 4 hold and four meters in No. 5 hold (140–141). The Chief Mate and Carpenter sounded the wing and hopper tanks and all the cargo holds except the No. 1 hold.

23. About 0045, the Master informed the Chief Engineer of the Chief Mate's report and ordered him to pump the water out of holds 4 and 5. The Chief Engineer ordered the Second Assistant Engineer to use the two electric pumps, the "fire and bilge" pump and the "general service" pump (547–549, Exh. 38, p.6).

24. About 30 minutes later, soundings at Nos. 4 and 5 holds, starboard side, were taken again. Six meters of water were found in No. 5 and over one meter in No. 4 (314–315). These soundings were reported to the master at about 0110 (150, 361).

25. Shortly after the Master had received the report on the second soundings of No. 4 and 5 holds, he ordered the Chief Engineer to continue pumping and ordered the Bos'n to wake up the crew and ready the lifeboat (150–151).

E. Use of the Radio

26. The Master first ordered the Radio Officer to send distress signals about the time he received the second set of soundings (155), i.e. at about 0110 on July 16, 1984.

27. After going into the radio room, the Radio Officer switched on the transmitter to warm it up, then tuned the frequency to 500 kHz until the output light was bright (867). The Radio Officer first transmitted the distress call by using the automatic keying device (754, 756-757, 867-870) for about $1\frac{1}{2}$ minutes to alert stations and vessels at sea (872).

28. The automatic keying device on the transmitting vessel is intended to trigger an alarm automatically on an auto alarm receivers in other vessels' radio rooms, and at coastal radio stations that monitor maritime traffic, thus alerting Radio Officers to listen to the message (765).

19. 实习大管轮随后叫醒轮机长并汇报了管隧内有水的事情。他们立即在机舱内打开了通往管隧的水密门,发现里面的水位已比10分钟前上升了6英寸,处于管隧的顶端了。随后他们关闭了水密门。轮机长不能说明之后是否再次打开过此水密门。

20. 轮机长将主机的重油换成的轻油,并降低了转速。

21. 7月16日0020,二副叫醒了船长并告知他主机已降低转速。船长到达驾驶台,轮机长电话报告管隧里有大量的积水并要求测深。此时风向ENE,风力5~6级;有中到大浪。

22. 大副报告在1号舱有1米水深,5号舱有4米水深。大副和木匠测量了侧边舱、贮水舱和除1号舱外的各舱水深。

23. 0045,船长通知轮机长,告知他大副的报告并命令泵出4号舱和5号舱的积水。轮机长命令实习大管轮启用两台电泵、消防舱底泵和船舶通用泵。

24. 30分钟后,在右舷测量4号舱和5号舱水深。5号舱有6米水深,4号舱有超过1米的水深。这些数据约在0110报告给了船长。

25. 船长在接到4号、5号舱的测深报告后不久,命令轮机长继续排水并命令水手长叫醒所有船员准备救生艇。

E. 电台的使用

26. 船长在收到第二次测深报告后首次命令电报员发送遇险信号,也就是在1984年7月16日0110。

27. 进入电报间后,电报员将发信机打开预热,然后将频率调谐到500 kHz直到输出信号灯亮起来。电报员先是用自动拍发装置发送遇险信号,持续了约1分半钟以提醒岸台及其他海船的注意。

28. 发信船上的自动拍发装置可自动向其他船上的自动收信机及海岸电台的海上交通监视器发出报警,以提醒电报员注意接收信息。

29. The Master wrote down the voice message for the Radio Officer to send: "Mayday. This is motor vessel *ANTACUS*. Water into cargo hold. Very dangerous. Require immediate assistance. Master" (758). The Master's message did not include the position of the vessel(758).

30. Using the 500 kHz transmitter from 0115 to 0130 to send out the SOS, the Radio Officer repeated this process twice in this 15 minute period (870-871). From 0130 to 0140, he used the automatic keying device first and thereafter voice radio 2182, switching to the appropriate antenna beforehand. This process was repeated twice (872).

31. From 0145 to 0159 he used the 500 kHz transmitter three times to send the SOS again switching to the proper antenna beforehand. He again used the automatic keying device before each transmission (873-876).

32. From 0200 to 0214, he used the 2,182 kHz transmitter to send the SOS twice, using the radiotelephone alarm signal generating device beforehand on each occasion.

33. From 0215 to 0229, he used the 500 kHz transmitter following the same procedures before to send the SOS signal three times (877).

34. Every time he used the 500 kHz transmitter the output light was on and the output amperage meter showed a maximum rating, which should have indicated that messages were being transmitted (758-759, 875).

35. The Radio Officer followed the procedure of using the automatic keying device and SOS a total of twelve times before leaving the radio room to abandon the vessel (878).

36. The Radio Officer, whose knowledge of the English language was extremely limited, also tried to call two radio stations in the Azores between 0145 and 0159 without success (759). When the Radio Officer left the radio room, the automatic keying device was still activated to key the emergency transmitter to transmit signals to trigger ships' and stations' auto alarms.

37. No response was received by the *ANTACUS* to any of its SOS transmissions. In fact, the Radio Officer stated that he did not hear a single radio station on either the 500 kHz or 8,364 kHz frequency bands (790-791).

38. There was evidence that *ANTACUS*' radio equipment was working properly prior to July 16, 1984: the Radio Officer had sent out a departure cable at 0050 GMT, July 11, 1984 from Antwerp (866, Exh. 5C, 2F & 2G); a position report at 1335 GMT, July 14— both to Chi Yuen Navigation Co. in Taipei (865-866); and a third message concerning crew change at 1020 GMT, July 15 to Amagansett Radio ITT, New York (867), all of which were received. The Radio Officer had contacted an ITT station in the United States on July 15, 1984 (751). The last time the Radio Officer used the main transmitter was to contact the British weather station at 2330, about one hour and forty minutes before sending the first distress signal July 15 (797); he listened to a station in Belgium at 2205, July 15 (797).

29. 船长写下了口头信息给电报员:"Mayday! 机动船 ANTACUS 呼叫! 货舱进水,需立即援助!"船长的信息里并未包括船位信息。

30. 从 0115 到 0130,15 分钟内电报员用 500 kHz 发信机发送了两次 SOS 信号。随后,从 0130 到 0140,他又使用自动拍发装置并转换天线,在 2182 电台上语音呼叫,此过程重复了两次。

31. 从 0145 到 0159,他又在 500 kHz 上发送了三次 SOS,然后重新调谐和天线,在每次发送信息前都使用了自动拍发装置。

32. 从 0200 到 0214,他用 2 182 kHz 发信机发了两次 SOS,每次都先使用无线电话警报信号发生装置。

33. 从 0215 到 0229,他在发送 SOS 之前在 500 kHz 上重复了三次同样的程序。

34. 他每次使用 500 kHz 发射机发送信息时,输出指示灯都亮着,并且输出安培表都指示最大值,表明信息已发送出去。

35. 在接下来的时间里,直到弃船离开电报室,电报员使用自动拍发装置及 SOS 总共重复了 12 号发信程序。

36. 英语水平很有限的电报员在 0145 到 0159 期间曾试图呼叫亚述尔群岛的两家海岸电台,但未获成功。当他离开电报室时,自动拍发装置仍不断地发送遇险信号。

37. 对于"ANTACUS"号的 SOS 呼叫,没有收到任何应答。实际上,电报员称,无论在 500 kHz 还是在 8 364 kHz 频带上都未听到任何电台的信号。

38. 有证据显示"ANTACUS"号的无线电设备在 1984 年 7 月 16 日前是完好的:电报员在 11 日 0050 GMT 从安特卫普发送了离港电报;14 日 1335 GMT 同时向台北的齐云海运公司发送了船位报告;及 1020 GMT 关于船员调换的电报;15 日向纽约 Amagansett 无线电话公司发送信息,所有这些信息都已收到。电报员曾于 15 日联系过美国一家电信公司的电台。最后一次是在他发第一条遇险信息前 1 小时 40 分钟,2330 他和一家英国天气台站联系过;2205 他收听到比利时一家台站的信息。

F. Abandonment

39. After receiving the second set of soundings at approximately 0100, the Master ordered the Bos'n to wake the crew and prepare the lifeboat. [The Bos'n recalled that he left the bridge to wake up the crew at 0040 (464), whereas the Master stated that he ordered the Bos'n to wake up the crew at 0115 (151-152).]

40. The starboard lifeboat, on the lee side of the vessel, was made ready (153) and lowered to the main deck level where the Second Mate supervised the loading of blankets and food into the lifeboat (466).

41. At about 0220 the Master gave the order to abandon ship because it appeared to him that the ingress of water was continually increasing and the vessel was gradually sinking by the stern, notwithstanding the use of the three pumps (155, 175, 489).

42. Upon notification to abandon ship, the Chief Engineer ordered the engine room crew to report to the starboard lifeboat (550). The Chief Engineer also shut off the main engine and generator (Exh. 35). There was no water in the engine room at that time (Exh. 38, p.7) and all three pumps were reportedly working (570).

43. The Radio Officer abandoned the radio room at about 0230 and took the portable lifeboat radio with him (761-763). [The time the Radio Officer abandoned the radio room was not clearly established. The Radio Officer testified that he left the radio room at 0235 and boarded the lifeboat at 0242 (763). The Radio Officer was neither among the first nor last to board but was somewhere in the middle (467). The Master, who testified he was the last to abandon ship, gave the time he boarded the lifeboat as about 0230 (175).]

44. At 0230 the crew completed boarding the lifeboat, which had been lowered into the water (175). An inflatable lifeboat was placed overboard and secured to the stern of the lifeboat, but not used.

45. At the time of abandonment visibility was good and the winds were force 5-6 (161). The general alarm had been sounded by the Third Mate (152-153).

46. The following items were among the items taken into the lifeboat:

	Transcript
Blankets	(466)
Bridge Log	(156)
Chart	(156)
Extra Clothing	(466)
Liberian Licenses	(430)
Life Jackets	(464), (592)
Lifeboat Radio	(884)
Liquor	(435)
Passports	(430)
Personal Documents	(379)
Seaman's Books	(412), (430)

The radio log, engine log and trim and stability book were not taken.

F. 弃船

39. 约在0100,船长在获得第二次测深数据后,命令水手长叫醒船员准备救生艇。(水手长回忆他是在0040离开驾驶台去叫船员的,而船长称他是在0115命令水手长去叫醒船员的)。

40. 处于下风侧的右舷救生艇已准备好并降到主甲板上,二副监督装上毯子和食物。

41. 尽管用了三台泵往外抽水,由于船舱进水仍在增加导致船尾慢慢下沉,约在0220船长下令弃船。

42. 接获弃船命令后,轮机长命令轮机部船员到右舷救生艇集中。轮机长关闭了主机和发电机。当时机舱还没有进水。据说当时三台泵仍在工作。

43. 0230 电报员离开电报室,带出了手提式艇用电台。(电报员离开电报室的时间并不十分明确,自称是在0235离开电报室而在0242登艇。他既不是最早登艇的也不是最后登艇的,是在中间某个时候登艇的。但船长证明电报员是最后登艇的,并给出0230的登艇时间)。

44. 0230,船员登艇完毕并将艇降到水面。有一个气胀式救生筏固定在救生艇尾外舷,但未被使用。

45. 弃船时能见度良好,风力5~6级。三副拉响了弃船警报。

46. 以下是带进救生艇的物品清单:

	记录编号
毯子	(466)
航海日志	(156)
海图	(156)
额外衣物	(466)
利比里亚船舶证书	(430)
救生衣	(464)(592)
艇用电台	(884)
淡水	(435)
护照	(430)
船员证书	(379)
海员证	(412)(430)

电台日志、轮机日志及稳性报告书未带上艇。

47. At the time the crew abandoned the vessel, the lifeboat was approximately one meter below the level of the main deck on the starboard side near the stern (468).

G. In the Lifeboat

48. After boarding the lifeboat, the Radio Officer transmitted distress signals using 500 kHz frequency band with the portable radio. Two antennas were rigged in the lifeboat (763, 766, Exh. 32). This portable radio had been tested weekly. The Radio Officer stated that he could hear the signal from *ANTACUS*' automatic keying device (885). At one point the Radio Officer stated that the signal from the *ANTACUS* was loud and could be heard throughout the time he was in the lifeboat. He later stated, however, that after five hours in the lifeboat, he either did not hear the *ANTACUS*' signal clearly or could not hear it at all (918).

49. The Master ordered that the lifeboat remain in the vicinity of *ANTACUS* to watch her as long as possible (229, 479-480).

50. *ANTACUS* sank by the stern about midday, July 16, 1984. The lifeboat was 4-6 miles distant from the vessel and drifting (164, 228, 351, 420). The vessel's approximate position at sinking was Lat. 40°50' North, Long. 25°33' West, distant about 150 miles from the Azores (202, 218).

51. At about 2030 on July 16th, the Radio Officer reported that someone had acknowledged his distress signal saying "Regarding your SOS ..." but nothing further (160, 769). He also could hear radio stations at a great distance calling each other (915).

52. The lifeboat was sighted by a yacht, *SAINT JEAN*, on the early morning of July 17. The yacht circled the lifeboat during that day. The Master requested the yacht to send a distress signal on behalf of the lifeboat (166). That message apparently was received by the general cargo ship *OLANCHO*, which rescued the members of the crew at about 1400-1500, July 17, 1984. They were later transferred to a Portuguese warship, *AUGUSTO CASTILHO*, and taken to Ponta Delgada in the Azores on July 18 at 0830 GMT (165, 167, Exh. 17A).

H. Opinions of Ship's Crew as to Cause of Sinking

53. The opinions, as to the cause of the sinking, of those officers and crew who testified was that the steel cargo in hold No. 4 broke its stow, cracking or puncturing the vessel's shell plating (234, 375, 422).

CONCLUSIONS

1. The probable cause of the casualty was that the fabricated steel cargo stowed in either hold No. 4 or hold No. 5 began to shift during the period July 13-14, 1984, due to improper stowage, and became progressively loosened from its lashings, ultimately causing a crack or larger opening through the side shell plating of the vessel, allowing water into the holds. The water found its way into the pipe tunnel through a loosened manhole cover or a crack or other opening in the floor of one or both of holds Nos. 4 and 5.

47. 弃船时,救生艇约在大船船尾右舷主甲板下1米位置。

G. 在救生艇上

48. 登艇后,电报员用手提电台在500 kHz频带发送了遇险信号,救生艇上装有两个天线。该手提电台过去每周都进行检查。电报员称他可听到由"ANTACUS"号自动拍发装置发出的信号。在艇上的所有时间里都可在一个频点听到从"ANTACUS"号发出的响亮信号。然而,后来他又称,在艇上5小时后,他未清晰地听到"ANTACUS"号的信号甚至根本没听到。

49. 船长命令救生艇尽可能长时间地留在"ANTACUS"号附近以察看情况。

50. "ANTACUS"号于1984年7月16日从艉部沉没。救生艇在距离4~6英里处漂航。轮船沉没的概位:(40°50′N, 25°33′W),离亚述尔群岛约150英里。

51. 约在7月16日2030,电报员报告说有人对他的遇险信息回应,说是"收到你的SOS……"但没更多的消息。他甚至可听到远处电台间的通话。

52. 7月17日早上,救生艇被游艇"SAINT JEAN"发现,游艇一直在救生艇周围。船长要求游艇代发一条遇险信息。该信息很快被杂货船"OLANCHO"号收到,并于7月17日1400—1500救起了所有船员。他们后来被转移到葡萄牙军舰"AUGUSTO CASTILHO"号上,于7月18日0830 GMT被送到亚述尔群岛的Ponta Delgada。

H. 船员对于船舶沉没原因的看法

53. 对于船舶沉没的原因,船员的看法是:4号舱的钢材堆垛倒下,刮破或剨穿船舶外板所致。

结论

1. 引起事故的可能原因是:装在4号舱或5号舱的钢材构件由于积载不良,在7月13—14日期间开始移位,绑扎逐渐松散,最后导致船壳板的裂缝或大的开口,船舱进水。水又从松开的人孔盖或4号舱或5号舱的地板裂缝进入管隧中。

2. The shifting of the fabricated steel cargo and consequent damage to the vessel was most likely caused by a combination of the following factors:

   (a) Cargo had been improperly stowed and improperly lashed prior to departure from Antwerp;

   (b) When the cargo began to shift, no action was taken to attempt to mitigate the labouring of the vessel;

   (c) No investigation was made to determine the possibility that some remedial action could be taken to arrest the shifting of the cargo or to mitigate its effects.

3. The standard of care by which the conduct of the Master and the other officers of *ANTACUS* is to be judged is that of reasonable merchant marine officers exercising the degree of skill and judgment to be expected of them in the circumstances in which they found themselves. As will be more fully discussed below, in important respects the conduct of the Master and officers of *ANTACUS* during this voyage did not meet that standard.

4. While a Master may properly delegate the duty of supervising the loading and stowing of cargo to the Chief Mate, such delegation would only have been proper if the Master had actually satisfied himself that the Chief Mate had requisite competence in these areas. The record does not reveal such competence. Regardless of legal responsibility under the terms of the charter party (Exh. 18), (which would be relevant in civillitigation) the proper supervision of loading and stowage of cargo still fell to the Master, Captain Chen, and his designated Cargo Officer, Chief Mate Jean. This was understood by the Master and the Chief Mate, who signed the receipt after cargo was loaded to their satisfaction (312, Exh. 23).

   Compared with the standard practice in the industry, as testified to by Captain McNamara of the National Cargo Bureau (954-963), it is clear that the loading and stowage of this vessel prior to her final departure was lacking in proper supervision.

5. Although, pursuant to the terms of the charter party, the charterer was obliged to load, stow and discharge the cargo, and, in this regard, the supercargo, Captain Tijan, had a duty to the charterer to supervise the loading and stowing of the cargo, this did not relieve the Master and Chief Mate from their duty.

6. The supercargo negligently failed properly to supervise the loading and stowing of all the cargo at the three loading ports, frequently not even being present on board *ANTACUS* during this work.

7. Because of improper loading, the cargo in Nos. 4 and/or 5 holds probably broke its stow in the relatively rough weather on July 13. Although noises were first heard from those holds and vibrations felt when the vessel rolled, neither the Master nor the Chief Mate made any effort to ascertain the reason for those noises. If the stowage had been proper, the cargo should not have broken loose in sea and wind conditions no worse than those prevailing during the voyage. (See above, Findings of Fact, paragraph 15.)

2. 钢材构件的移动及随后的船舶的破损很可能是以下几种因素综合影响的结果：

   (a) 离开安特卫普前，货物未被正确地积载和绑扎；

   (b) 在货物开始移位时，未采取措施减轻船舶的振动；

   (c) 未进行检查以采取一些补救措施阻止货物的移位或减少其影响。

3. 作为商船船员对周围环境的适应技能及判断力水平而言，"ANTACUS"号船长及其他高级船员的行为谨慎程度将在以后详细讨论。但明显地，该船船长及船员在本航次的表现不能符合标准的要求。

4. 虽然船长可将监督货物积载的责任委托给大副，但前提应是船长确认大副在这方面有足够的能力，然而报告显示大副不具备此种能力。不管租船协议上的法定责任如何（这将涉及民事诉讼），保证货物妥善积载的责任仍落在船长陈先生及大副Jean先生的身上。这一点，船长及认为装货情况满意并签署了货物收据的大副应十分清楚。

   国家货物管理局的McNamara船长作证说：从行业惯例来看，很显然，该船最后离港前对货物的装载和积载缺乏正确的监管。

5. 虽然，根据租船协议，承租人对货物的装卸及积载负有责任，在这一点上，代表租船人的监货员Tijan船长有责任监督货物的装载及积载，但这并不免除船长、大副本身的责任。

6. 在三个装货港，监货员都未能对货物的积载进行妥善的监督，装货过程中经常不在现场。

7. 由于不适当的装载，4号舱和/或5号舱的货物在7月13日的大浪中可能坍塌。尽管在船舶摇晃时从货舱里听到了响声并感到振动，船长和大副都没去找出响声的来源。如果货物得到妥善装载，在当时并不比盛行风季海况更恶劣的风浪情况下，货物不至于发生坍塌。（见上文，发现事实，第15段）

8. The Master described the noises as "very heavy and dull," similar to the noise made when cargo was lowered into the holds during loading (113, 114). Although the Master testified that these sounds continued for two days (116), that he thought they came from the cargo hold(s) (115), and that the sound was associated with the rolling of the vessel (113, 114), and although he wondered what was making the sound (114), he did nothing about it.

9. Most importantly, the Master took no action to reduce the labouring of the vessel at any time during the two days that this "very heavy and dull" noise was coming from the vicinity of the cargo holds. The Master could have ordered course changes and/or speed reductions after the noises were heard in an effort to reduce the stress in the vessel, but did not do so. It cannot be dismissed that course changes and/or speed reduction might have reduced the heavy rolling to such an extent that cargo which had broken its stow would have ceased to strike against the shell plating of the vessel. The Chief Mate feeling certain that the Master must have heard these noises (289) gave no order and took no initiative himself. The failure to explore the possibility of reducing stress on the vessel by taking such action constituted gross negligence on the part of both the Master and Chief Mate.

10. After the second set of soundings was taken in 4 and 5 holds at about 0110 on July 16 indicating the water level had increased two meters in about 30 minutes in No. 5 hold and had also increased slightly in No. 4 hold, notwithstanding the use of the steam bilge pump, fire and bilge pump and the general service pump, it was prudent for the Master to order the starboard lifeboat ready and the Chief Engineer to continue the pumping.

11. It was prudent of the Master at this time to order the Radio Officer to send distress messages, although clearly the Master should have given the Radio Officer the vessel's approximate position for inclusion therein.

12. Although *ANTACUS*' Radio Officer appeared to be fully qualified (738-745), as stated above, it was clearly evident from his testimony that his knowledge of the English language was wholly inadequate so that even if his voice transmissions had been received they probably would not have been understood.

13. *ANTACUS*' radio equipment appears to have been in proper operating conditions.

14. The radio equipment was not properly checked. The Radio Officer testified that he checked the condition of the batteries for the emergency transmitter only weekly (751), although such checks are required to be done daily; see 1960 SOLAS Chapter IV, Regulation 9(p). (ANTACUS, because she was built prior to the entry into force of the 1974 SOLAS Convention, falls under 1960 SOLAS.) Although the Radio Officer recalled that he checked the batteries the day before sinking, 15 July 1984, there is no record available to support this recollection (751-752).

8. 船长描述响声是"非常沉闷的",类似于装船时货物跌落舱里的声音。尽管船长证实这些响声持续了两天,他想这是伴随着船舶的摇晃,来自于货舱的声音。虽然他不知道造成这些响声的原因,可他没对此采取任何的行动。

9. 最重要的是,在能听到邻近货舱"非常沉闷"响声的两天时间里,船长未采取任何措施减少船舶的剧烈晃动。其实,在听到响声后,船长应改变航向和/或降低航速以作为降低船舶应力的一种努力,但他没这样做。不可否认,航向改变和/或船速的降低可一定程度上减少船舶的摇晃,坍塌的货物也不致刮伤船壳板。大副认为船长肯定已听到这些响声,他自己也没给出指示和采取主动措施。在这一点上,船长和大副都没积极探究降低船舶应力的可能,而构成了整体疏忽。

10. 大约在7月16日0110,当4号、5号舱的测深数据出来后,意味着5号舱的水位在30分钟内已上升了2米,而4号舱也有轻微上升。尽管已使用蒸汽舱底泵、消防舱底泵和船舶通用泵,船长命令准备右舷救生艇、轮机长保持继续泵水的措施是谨慎的。

11. 虽然他本应该在所给出的信息中包含船舶概位,但当时船长命令电报员发送遇险信息的行为是谨慎的。

12. 如前所述,尽管"ANTACUS"号电报员有职务资格,从其证言可明显看出:他的英语知识是完全不够的,致使他的语音发送信息即使被接收,也可能难于理解。

13. "ANTACUS"号的无线电设备看来是处于正常的工作状态下。

14. 无线电设备未经适当的检查。电报员证实他仅是每周检查应急发信机的电池,而这种检查应该每天进行。见1960 SOLAS公约第Ⅳ章第9(p)条。(因"ANTACUS"号建造于1974 SOLAS公约生效前,故适用SOLAS 1960公约。)尽管电报员回忆说他在船舶沉没前一天,1984年7月15日,检查过发信机电池,但无证据支持。

15. The Radio Officer did not perform his duties with the required skill and competence. While the Radio Officer switched transmissions back and forth between the emergency and main transmitters (754, 757-759, 762-763, 774, 818, 870-871, 873, 875-876), never once did he transmit the vessel's position as part of the distress message. His failure to transmit the vessel's position as part of any distress message [his explanation being that "since we are all very, very busy, I just send out the message as the Captain told me" (758, 759)] does not meet international standards for conduct under such circumstances as summarized in Resolution 7 of the International Convention on Training and Certification of Seafarers, 1978, Annex III ("Recommendation on Basic Guidelines and Operational Guidance Relating to Safety Radio Watchkeeping and Maintenance for Radio Operators"), Sub-part B ("Action to Be Taken in Cases of Distress, Urgency and Safety"). In a distress situation, the very first action to be taken by a Radio Officer is to "obtain from the bridge the ship's actual or estimated position..." [Paragraph 12(a)(i).]

Despite Captain Dorian's observations comparing classical radio transmissions with satellite communications, it is almost unbelievable that if the distress messages had actually been properly sent both from the vessel and its lifeboat, they would not have been received by someone. Although the Radio Officer testified that he heard the words "regarding your SOS" on the lifeboat radio after *ANTACUS* had sunk [either bad weather or "interference to the antennas" prevented him from hearing anything more (769)], it cannot be established that this fragment had anything whatever to do with distress messages from either the *ANTACUS* or the lifeboat. No coastal station within normal range of *ANTACUS* ever picked up a distress message from her (Exh. 14).

Although the failure to comply with the requirements of SOLAS regarding maintenance of the emergency transmitter batteries might not normally be a matter for concern in light of the Radio Officer's testimony that he checked the batteries the day before the sinking and found them fully charged (751), his failure to check them on the required daily basis becomes a serious matter in light of his later testimony that, from the time he began using the lifeboat radio, he could hear at the same time both the autokey transmissions from *ANTACUS* and traffic from other ships, from 0245/0255 onwards (918-919). This is so despite the fact that the lifeboat was at that time close by *ANTACUS*, whose emergency transmitter had a full rated power output of 100 watts (Exh. 8-J, 916). The Radio Officer himself thought that "with 100 watts output transmitter nearby, there will be a disturbance or interference at some time" (919); Mr. Wingrove repeatedly stated that if the emergency transmitter aboard *ANTACUS* had been putting out a signal at rated power, the lifeboat radio "would have been blasted off the air" by these transmissions (822, 834, 856-857). The conclusion to be drawn from the Radio Officer's testimony was either that he had not put the antenna transfer switch over to the emergency transmitter (857, 859, 1128, 1129), or that the batteries driving the emergency transmitter were not fully up to charge. The failure of the Radio Officer to comply with the SOLAS requirements constitutes negligence.

16. It was imprudent and premature for the Master to order the vessel to be abandoned at about 0220, on the rationale that, notwithstanding the pumping with the steam bilge pump, general service pump and fire and bilge pump (with combined capacities of about 350 tons/hr.) the vessel's trim had increased to about 15 by the stern with the surface of the water about one meter below the main deck at the stern. The fact that the abandonment order was premature is evident from the facts that:

15. 电报员未能按要求的技能和适任的能力履行其职责。当他在应急发送与常规发送信息间不断转换时,却没有一次将船位信息在遇险电文中发送出去。[他的解释是:"我们都非常非常忙乱,我只是按船长给我的信息发送了出去。"]按当时环境,不符合《1978年海员培训、发证标准国际公约》大会决议7中,附则Ⅲ("关于电报员的无线电值守安全与维持指导建议与操作指引")、B部分补充("在遇险、紧急与安全情况下的行动")规定的要求。遇险情况下,作为电报员,首要的工作是:"从驾驶台获得准确的或大致的船位……"〔12节(a)(i)〕

    尽管Dorian船长将传统的无线电通信与卫星通信做过比较研究,但如果遇险信息从遇险船和救生艇确实发了出来,但信息未被任何人收到是难以置信的。虽然电报员一再证实他于船舶沉没后在艇用电台上听到"对于你的SOS……"的字句[或者是恶劣的天气或"天线的干扰"阻碍了他进一步的收听],却不能证明有任何无论是发自"ANTACUS"号或救生艇的遇险信息被发送出去。在"ANTACUS"号的通常作用范围内没有岸站收到它的信息。

    虽然电报员的证词声称他在船舶沉没前一天检查过电池并发现它们是充满的,通常不能说他违反了SOLAS公约中对应急电池常规检查的规定。但他其后的证词说明未能按要求的每天检查造成了严重的事故。如其所述,在开始使用艇用电台时,在0245/0255前,他能同时听到"ANTACUS"号的自拍装置发送的信息和过往船舶的通信信息。当时,救生艇离"ANTACUS"号很近,"ANTACUS"号应急电台的最大输出功率为100瓦。电报员认为"附近有100瓦的功率输出时,有时会有干扰";Mingrove先生再三证实:如果"ANTACUS"号的发信机在额定功率情况下发出信号,这些发射的信号会令艇用电台的元件被过载击穿。因此,根据电报员的证词,不管事故是由于电报员未将天线转换开关拨到应急发信机,还是由于应急电池不足造成的,都是电报员未能满足SOLAS公约的要求而构成了疏忽。

16. 船长在0220下达弃船命令显得过早和不够慎重,按照推论,尽管在蒸汽舱底泵、船舶通用泵和舱底消防泵的作用下(总抽水能力约350吨/小时),船舶的纵倾在艉部增加15,船舶尾部的甲板仍高于水面约1米,但以下事实足以证明弃船命令是不够慎重的:

(a) at the time of last observation, the water in the pipe tunnel had not reached the threshold of the water-tight door leading from the engine room into the pipe tunnel; and

(b) the pumps were operating and capable of operation for an indefinite period; and

(c) the vessel could have remained afloat for an additional 15 hours or so if the crew had remained aboard and the pumps continued to operate. She actually sank about 9 $\frac{1}{2}$ to 10 hours after having been abandoned.

17. The Chief Engineer, Mr. Lee, testified on deposition that when he left the engine room he shut down all the machinery, including the generators (Exh. 38A, p.7). This is consistent with his earlier written statement in which he declared this to be his own decision, and that he did so because he felt that "as we were abandoning the vessel everything should be turned off" (Exh. 38B, p.3). Both the Chief Engineer (Exh. 38B, p.3) and the Master (154) agree that the Chief Engineer never received an order from the Master to shut down the power plant. His decision to do so on his own was irresponsible and evidence of incompetence.

    There is testimony that as a result the ship was immediately plunged into darkness. The Chief Engineer testified that he had to use his flashlight to get out of the engine room (Exh. 38B, p.3) and on deck he and others had to use flashlights in order to abandon ship, because the deck lights were off (Exh. 38A, p.7, 154, 436, 468). The testimony is that there were no lights whatever burning on board *ANTACUS* when she was abandoned—not even navigation lights, or more properly, the not-under-command lights which should have been left burning in order to comply with Rule 27(a)(i) of the International Regulations for Preventing Collisions at Sea, 1972, amended. The other major consequence of the premature shutdown of the plant was that the pumps were stopped, and as the Chief Mate testified: "I considered to stop main engine is for the safety of the ship, but the pumps should not be stopped" (368).

    When the Second Assistant Engineer, Mr. Alipis, left the engine room for the last time, there was no water in the engine room, the door to the pipe tunnel was dogged down, and the pumps were still working (550–551). Thereafter, prior to the Chief Engineer leaving the engine room, the watertight door to the pipe tunnel was still dogged down and no water had come into the engine room (Exh. 38, pp.6–8). The Chief Engineer's fear of a possible explosion in the event the engine remained on was unwarranted in view of the fact that the water level was nowhere near the level of the engine room.

18. It is clear that the abandonment order was carried out with unseemly and unnecessary haste. All of the vessel's documents went down with her except the deck log book, the chart in use, and the licenses, passports and seamen's books of the individual crew members (Exh. 13, 429–430). The Master testified that he had no time to open the ship's safe (157), and though he did not take any of his personal belongings off the vessel, other officers and crew members did.

(a) 在最后测深时，管隧内的水位还没到达连接机舱的水密门的门槛上；及

(b) 水泵正在工作并且还可工作一段时间；及

(c) 如果船员还在船上并保持连续泵水，船舶仍可保持漂浮15小时以上。实际上，船是在弃船以后9.5~10个小时才沉没的。

17. 轮机长李先生书面证实他在离开机舱时关闭了所有的机器，包括发电机在内。在早前的书面声明中他说明这是他自己的决定。这样做是他认为"我们弃船时应关闭所有机器"。轮机长和船长都同时承认轮机长并没有接到船长关闭电源的命令。他的自以为是的做法是不负责任的，也是他不适任的证据。

有证据表明，在关闭机器后，全船立即陷入黑暗。轮机长也称他是借助手电筒走出机舱的。由于甲板灯都熄灭了，在甲板上，他和其他人都是借助手电筒登上救生艇的。这有力地证明了，当弃船时，船上没有任何亮着的灯——甚至没有航行灯或其他合适的灯。而在《1972年国际避碰规则》第27(a)(i)条规定：失控船应显示号灯。关闭主电源的其他后果是水泵也停止了工作。轮机长也承认："我认为关闭主机是为了船舶的安全，但水泵工作是不应停止的。"

当实习大管轮Alipis先生最后离开机舱时，机舱内并没有进水，通向管隧的水密门牢牢地关着，水泵仍在工作。其后，到轮机长离开机舱之前，水密门仍牢牢地关着，没有水进入机舱。在水位根本未到达机舱的情况下，轮机长对于机器运行会引发爆炸的担心是毫无根据的。

18. 显然，弃船命令是不恰当、不必要地在匆忙中执行的。除了甲板部航海日志、使用中的海图、船舶证书及船员个人的护照和海员证以外，所有的船舶文件都丢弃了。船长声称他没时间打开船上的保险箱，虽然他并没有带上个人物品离船，但其他高级及普通船员带上了个人物品。

The Master further testified that no log book entries had been made concerning the events of the hours just prior to abandoning the vessel because during that time there was "confusion" (142-144). With the vessel being abandoned in darkness, without any light except flashlights, under the orders of a Master who was indeed in a state of "confusion", it is remarkable that no serious injuries were sustained in the process.

19. While there is no testimony upon which to evaluate the level of communication aboard ship prior to the heavy weather encountered before the sinking, there is much remarkable testimony to the effect that no one aboard the vessel spoke with anyone else concerning repeated loud noises coming from the vicinity of the cargo holds—over a two-day period. The only explanation ever offered for this was that of the Third Mate, Mr. Realigue: "Because this is too obvious to discuss with, sir. Everyone can hear the loud noise. It is loud enough and the vibration you can feel" (429). Yet the Chief Mate, at the end of his testimony, was of the opinion that if the noise had been investigated there might nave been some possibility of saving the ship (375). Of course it is true that such an investigation might have revealed that there was no possibility of saving the ship, but since none was ever made and the matter was never even discussed by the Master with his officers, all possibilities were sacrificed.

20. The Master, Captain Chen, was personally and grossly negligent in:

    (a) failing adequately to supervise the loading and stowage of the cargo; and

    (b) failing to investigate or even discuss investigation of the reason for noises emanating from the vicinity of the cargo holds during heavy weather; and

    (c) failing to alter course or reduce speed so as to lessen the labouring of the ship during the period when the noises were being heard; and

    (d) prematurely ordering the abandonment of the vessel; and

    (e) failing to ensure an orderly abandonment of the vessel.

21. The Chief Mate, Mr. Jean, was personally and grossly negligent in virtually abandoning the loading, stowage and lashing of the cargo to the discretion of the charterers' representative, who was known not to be present at all times during the loading process, and to the stevedores.

22. The Chief Engineer, Mr. Lee, was personally and grossly negligent in prematurely shutting down the power plant, an action which:

    (a) increased the difficulty of abandoning the vessel in darkness; and

    (b) created a navigational hazard during the hours of darkness that the vessel remained afloat; and

    (c) lessened the likelihood that any passing vessel would see *ANTACUS* and come to her rescue; and

船长进一步声称：弃船前几个小时的事情没记入航海日志是因为在此期间是"混乱不堪"的。由于是在黑暗中弃船的，除手电筒外没有任何光线，在确实"混乱"的船长命令之下，整个过程中没出现严重的人员伤害已经是很幸运的。

19. 虽然没有证据去评价船上在沉没前遭遇恶劣天气期间船员的沟通水平，但很显然，在两天时间里，船上没有一个人在听到从货舱附近传来的响声时对此进行过讨论。对此，来自三副Realigue的唯一解释是："因为这事太明显了，先生，每个人都能听到这巨响，它足够响而且你能感到振动。"然而，大副在证言最后持这样的观点：如果调查了这响声的来源，有可能挽救船舶。当然，这样的调查结果也可能会证实没有挽救船舶的可能。但既然没有人采取过这样的行动，船长也没和船员们讨论过这事，所有的可能都不存在了。

20. 船长陈先生，就其个人而言，总的过失在于：

    (a) 未能有效监督货物的装载与积载；及

    (b) 对恶劣天气期间从货舱传来的响声，未做调查；及

    (c) 在听到响声后未采取改变航向或降低航速的措施来减少船舶剧烈晃动；及

    (d) 过早地下达弃船命令；及

    (e) 未能确保弃船过程有序进行。

21. 大副Jean先生，其过错在于将货物监装、积载和绑扎的工作完全依靠在装货期间经常不在场的租船人代表负责，而实际上又由码头工人处理。

22. 轮机长李先生，就其个人而言，总的过错在于过早地关闭了电源开关，导致了：

    (a) 增加了在黑暗中弃船的困难；及

    (b) 增加了船舶在黑暗中漂浮造成的航行危险；及

    (c) 减少了过往船舶发现并救助"ANTACUS"号的可能性；及

(d) inevitably lessened the time that the vessel could remain afloat, thereby lessening any possibility, however remote, of saving the ship and cargo.

23. The Radio Officer, Mr. Lin, was personally and grossly negligent in:

    (a) failing to maintain the emergency transmitter batteries as required by international law; and

    (b) failing to obtain the position of the ship and to include it in the distress messages transmitted.

24. The personal faults of the Master, Chief Mate, Chief Engineer, and Radio Officer all in varying degrees contributed to the loss of the vessel.

25. The evidence of gross fault on the part of those in charge of the vessel during the loading of the cargo and during the voyage is such that there will probably always be lingering doubt as to whether the sinking might have been intentional.

26. The eventual saving of the ANTACUS survivors was a circumstance of sheer good fortune.

（d）　不可避免地降低了船舶保持漂浮的时间,导致减少了挽救船舶与货物的任何可能,即使可能性很小。

23.　电报员林先生,其个人的过错在于：

（a）　未能按国际公约要求维护应急电池；及

（b）　未能获取船位并在遇险信息中发送出去船位等信息。

24.　船长、大副、轮机长及电报员不同程度的个人过失导致了船舶的最终灭失。

25.　在负责船舶的装载过程中、在航行过程中各种过失的证据很可能让人产生这样的疑问：船舶沉没是否是人为故意的?

26.　"ANTACUS"号幸存者的最终获救纯属幸运。

RECOMMENDATIONS

A. The Master

1. It was charged and proved that the Master, Captain Chen, failed to ensure that his Chief Mate was properly discharging the duty to supervise the loading and stowage of the cargo.

2. It was charged and proved that the Master, Captain Chen, failed to investigate the cause of noises coming from the cargo holds, and that he neglected to take effective measures after these noises were heard.

3. It was charged and proved that the Master, Captain Chen, failed to ensure that the Radio Officer was given the position of the ship to include in the SOS message which the Master instructed the Radio Officer to send.

4. It was charged and proved that the Master, Captain Chen, failed to ensure that when the vessel was abandoned her lights (specifically her not-under-command lights) would continue to burn and her pumps continue to operate.

5. It was charged that the Master, Captain Chen, did not organize the abandonment properly, with the result there were a number of defaults and the abandonment was disorganized. This charge also was proved, although there was no injury or loss of life because the fortuitous sighting by the French yacht SAINT JEAN on July 18, 1984 resulted in all hands being saved.

RECOMMENDATION 1
That the license of Captain Chen be permanently revoked.

B. The Chief Mate

1. It was charged and proved that the Chief Mate, Mr. Jean, failed to discharge his duty of adequate supervision of loading and stowage of cargo.

2.. It was charged and proved that the Chief Mate, Mr. Jean, failed to initiate his own investigation of the condition in the cargo holds when noises were heard.

RECOMMENDATION 2
That Mr. Jean's license be suspended for a period of one year, together with a letter of censure and reprimand.

C. The Chief Engineer

It was charged and proved that the Chief Engineer, Mr. Lee, without receiving any order to do so, shut down all power before leaving the engine room with the result that (1) it was impossible for the vessel to pump out any continuing ingress of water; (2) the power to the main radio transmitter was reduced; and (3) there was no power for the deck lights or the not-under-command lights.

建议

A. 船长

1. 被指控并经证实陈船长：未能确保他的大副适当履行其监督货物的装载及积载的责任。

2. 被指控和经证实陈船长：未能调查来自货舱响声的原因，疏于对听到响声采取有效的措施。

3. 被指控和经证实陈船长：没有将船位信息包含在SOS信息中交给电报员发送出去。

4. 被指控和经证实陈船长：未能确保弃船时船上的灯光（特别是"失控船"号灯）保持显示、水泵继续工作。

5. 被指控和经证实陈船长：未能有效组织弃船行动，导致大量的疏忽，弃船行动是紊乱的。尽管幸运地，所有船员于1984年7月18日被法国游艇"SAINT JEAN"发现并最终获救，没有造成人命损伤。

建议1
永久吊销陈氏船长的证书。

B. 大副

1. 被指控和经证实大副Jean先生：未能履行其适当监督货物装载、积载的职责。

2. 被指控和经证实大副Jean先生：在听到货舱传来响声的情况下，未能亲自着手调查。

建议2
暂停有效大副Jean先生的证书一年，并致以惩戒书。

C. 轮机长

被指控和经证实轮机长李先生：在未经授权，离开机舱时关闭电源，致使：(1)船舶不能泵出渗入的海水；(2)供应主发信机的电源中断；及(3)甲板灯及失控号灯无电源供应。

RECOMMENDATION 3
That Mr. Lee's license be suspended for a period of one year.

D. The Radio Officer

1.　It was charged and proved that the Radio Officer, Mr. Lin, failed to properly maintain *ANTACUS*' radio equipment.

2.　It was charged and proved that the Radio Officer, Mr. Lin, failed to insure that the ship's position was transmitted with and as part of the distress message as required by the International Telecommunications Union and Maritime Regulation 2.81 of the Law of Liberia.

RECOMMENDATION 4
That Mr. Lin be sent a letter of censure and reprimand to be placed in his file in addition to the earlier imposed administrative equipment that he satisfactorily pass a test of his English language competence before being reissued a fully valid, full term license as Radiotelegraph Operator.

Gordon W. Paulsen,
Presiding Officer

VADM William F. Rea, III
USCG (Ret.), Assessor

DATED: August 15, 1986

**建议3
暂停李先生有效证书一年。**

D. 电报员

1. 被指控和经证实电报员林先生：未能适当维护"ANTACUS"号的无线电设备。

2. 被指控和经证实电报员林先生：未能根据国际电信联盟及《利比里亚海事法》第2.81条的要求，将船位信息作为遇险信息的一部分发送出去。

**建议4
递送一份惩戒书到其个人档案中。另外，在其获得重新签发无线电操作员的有效和全职证书前，强制要求其令人满意地通过英语能力测试。**

Gordon W.Paulsen,
首席调查官

VADM William F.Rea,Ⅲ
美国海岸警卫队（退役），评估员

日期：1986年8月15日

Annex 20-2
Development of an electronic database for Certification Registration

Requirements

Regulation I/9 of the revised STCW Convention: *Medical standards—Issue and registration of certificates* paragraph 4 states the following:

4. Each Party undertakes to:

   .1 maintain a register or registers of all certificates and endorsements for masters and officers and, as appropriate, ratings, which are issued, have expired or have been revalidated, suspended, cancelled or reported lost or destroyed and of dispensations issued; and

   .2 make available information on the status of such certificates, endorsements and dispensations to other Parties and companies which request verification of the authenticity and validity of certificates produced to them by seafarers seeking recognition of their certificates under regulation I/10 or employment on board ship.

In implementing the requirement in paragraph 4.1 of this regulation for the maintenance of a register of certificates and endorsement, a standard database is not necessary provided that all the relevant information is recorded and available. The database could be in the form of card indexes, manual ledgers or electronic database.

Information required

Information in the database is to be made available to other Parties and shipping companies on request for verification of the authenticity and validity of certificates. It is also available to seafarers seeking recognition of their certificates or employment on board ship.

For electronic registers, Section B-I/9 paragraph 14: *Electronic access to registers* states the following:

14. Where the register or registers of certificates, endorsements and other documents issued by or on behalf of a Party are maintained by electronic means, provision should be made to allow controlled electronic access to such register or registers to allow Administrations and companies to confirm:

   .1 the name of the seafarer to whom a certificate, endorsement or other qualification was issued, its relevant number, date of issue, and date of expiry;

   .2 the capacity in which the holder may serve and any limitations attaching thereto; and

附件 20-2
证书登记数据库的开发

公约要求

STCW公约修正案规则 I/9:健康的标准——证书的签发和登记第4段有如下规定:

4. 缔约国承担下述义务:

   .1 保持对船长和高级船员以及相应的普通船员其所有证书和签证的签发、到期、再有效、暂停有效、注销或报失、损毁以及签发特免证明的登记;及

   .2 当海员向其他缔约国和公司呈交其证书以求根据公约规则 I/10得到承认或被雇用上船工作,而这些国家和公司需要核查证书的可靠性和有效性时,应向其提供这种证书、签证和特免证明状况的资料。

为满足本条规则第4.1段关于保持对证书及签证登记的要求,标准的数据库不必包括所有已记录的及可能记录的相关信息。数据库可以是索引卡片的形式、手工账册形式或电子数据库。

信息要求

数据库中的信息可供其他缔约国和船公司在查询海员证书的可靠性和有效性时使用,也可在海员寻求自己的证书被认可及受雇于船上工作时使用。

对于电子登记,规则第B-I/9节第14段:登记的电子查询,有如下规定:

14. 当使用电子方式对某一缔约国或代表其签发的证书、签证和其他文件进行一种或几种登记时,需制定规定使这种登记具有受控制的电子通道,以便使主管机关和公司确知:

    .1 已被签发证书,签证或其他资格证明的海员姓名,以及这些文件的相应编号、签发日期和失效日期;

    .2 持证人可担任的职务及附带的任何限制;及

.3 the functions the holder may perform, the levels authorized and any limitations attaching thereto.

Note that the keyword is "to allow controlled electronic access", which means that security is of the utmost importance in such a register, since electronic registers with poor security features would be open to abuse and tampering.

The following items of information should be recorded and available either on paper or electronically in accordance with regulation I/9, as a minimum:

.1 *Status of certificate:*
Valid
Suspended
Cancelled
Reported lost
Destroyed
with a record of changes to status to be kept, including dates of changes.

.2 *Certificate details:*
Seafarers' name
Date of birth
Nationality
Sex
Preferably a photograph
Relevant document number
Date of issue
Date of expiry
Last revalidation date
Details of dispensation(s)

.3 *Competency details:*
STCW competency standard (e.g regulation II/1)
Capacity
Function
Level of responsibility
Endorsements
Limitations

.4 *Medical details:*
Date of issue of latest medical certificate relating to the issue or revalidation of the appropriate certificate.

Development of an International electronic register

There are currently 133 Parties to the STCW Convention. Of these, about 80 are anticipated to have significant numbers of seafarers actively working in the international merchant fleet. In a study by ISF/BIMCO in 1995, the numbers of seafarers were estimated to be: 409,000 officers and 825,000 ratings. The information likely to be most important to other adminstrations and shipping companies is that relating to officers.

.3 持证人可履行的职能和所授级别以及附带的任何限制。

注意关键词:"受控的电子通道",意味着在这种电子登记中,安全是极其重要的。因为不安全的电子登记会被滥用及篡改。

根据公约规则 I/9,不论是纸质数据记录还是电子数据,应至少包括以下信息:

.1 证书状态
   有效期
   证书暂停有效
   证书注销
   遗失报告
   证书损毁
   附带一份包括变更日期的状态变更记录

.2 证书细目:
   姓名
   出生日期
   国籍
   性别
   照片
   相关证书编号
   签发日期
   有效期
   上一签证日期
   豁免条目

.3 适任细目:
   STCW适任标准(如:公约规则 II/1)
   职位
   功能
   适任等级
   签注
   限制条件

.4 详细健康情况:
   申请相应证书重有效的最近体检合格证的签发日期。

国际电子登记系统的开发

目前,在STCW公约的133个缔约国中,大概有80多个国家的大量船员活跃在国际营运商船队中,根据ISF/BIMCO 1995年的一份报告,这些船员中有409 000名高级船员及825 000名普通船员。对其他国家的主管机关和船公司而言,高级船员的相关信息更为重要。

As the shipping industry is an international one and seafarers from many nations serve on ships of many other nations, it has been suggested that access to information on seafarers' certificates might be enhanced by the establishment of an INTERNATIONAL database of seafarers' certificates, possibly under the auspices of IMO.

In order to investigate the feasibility of making information on seafarers' certificates readily accessible internationally, IMO is undertaking some research to determine whether the proposal is practicable. With the increasing use of electronic methods of data collection and retrieval, it is inevitable that in future the use of computerised databases by administrations would become the norm. In February 1999, the IMO requested SSPA Maritime Consulting AB of Sweden to study if it is suitable to arrange a common international register covering the intentions of the STCW Convention.

Since the STCW Convention was revised, countries have proceeded with developing their own databases, some of which are electronic. The introduction of an electronic register can facilitate faster retrieval and more effective record-keeping than a manual one. Of course the information capacity of such a system is very large and is very suitable for Administrations with a large number of seafarers. Electronic databases, however, do have their drawbacks:

1. Users have to be computer-literate.

2. Unless the system is simple to use, users might have to undergo some training.

3. Reliable source of power must be available at all times. With unreliable power supply, a backup or Uninterrupted Power Supply (UPS) might be needed.

4. Capital investment in developing the software and purchasing necessary hardware.

5. The system must be secure.

However, these disadvantages can be overcome and an electronic-based system appears to be more suitable than a manual one.

Developing a National electronic register

In developing an electronic register, the following features should be taken into consideration:

1. Security:

    a. Officers who will be able to access and view the database

    b. Officers who will be able to access and edit the database

因为航运业是一个国际化的行业,来自各国的海员服务于不同国家的船舶,要求建立一个针对海员证书的"国际化"电子数据库系统,当然最好是由IMO来主办。

为了论证将海员证书信息纳入国际化的可行性,IMO做了一些调研。随着电子手段在数据收集与检索中越来越多的运用,将来主管机关利用计算机电子数据库也是很正常的。1999年2月,IMO要求瑞典SSPA海事顾问组织研究是否可以建立一个覆盖所有STCW公约缔约国的通用国际登记系统。

自从STCW公约修订以来,很多缔约国已开发了自己的数据库系统,其中有些是电子数据库。比起手工账册,电子数据登记系统将更有利于数据检索及数据保存。当然,信息的容量也会大大增加,便于主管机关对大量的海员信息进行处理。然而,电子数据库系统也有以下一些局限:

1. 使用者须有计算机知识。

2. 除非系统是简单易用的,否则用户须经一定的培训。

3. 任何时候都须有适当的电源供应,否则,应备有不间断电源(UPS)。

4. 在开发软件及购买硬件上须投入基本的资金。

5. 必须保证体系的安全性。

当然,上述这些局限可以克服,电子数据库系统将比手工账册更加适用而且会迅速发展。

开发国家电子登记系统

开发国家电子登记系统时,须考虑以下要点:

1. 安全性:

   a. 授权官员可对数据库数据进行存取

   b. 授权官员可对数据库数据进行修改、编辑

2. Maintenance and Backup facility

If the register is large, the installation of the system can be carried out in stages. During the initial stage, data transfer of ALL existing records from the manual system to the electronic one would be required. Security must be considered during this period in order to ensure that the transfer to electronic medium does not result in unauthorised (false) or erroneous entries. As such, verification of all the records entered is carried out after the data entry. Once the system is in place, new entries for newly-acquired certificate holders can take place. These too must be verified (see below: System Implementation).

The main puroses of the electronic register are;

1. To ensure the **absolute elimination** of misplaced information since all data are available in the system;

2. To help the Administration in ensuring that information is **complete**;

3. To exclude repeated or unreasonable requests; and

4. To analyze certification activities for effective feedback.

Features

The system recently developed by the Maritime and Port Authority of Singapore is MS Windows-based and presently has about 10,000 records. A future version is expected to add features and enhance present ones. Screen examples of the software are featured in this chapter.

General requirements

The system should provide authorized users with the following capabilities:

.1 each user to be able to obtain up-to-date information of all data of a particular person;

.2 easy and quick recording of every new activity;

.3 the system should ensure that the information being recorded is accurate, complete and verifiable;

.4 easy and quick modification of the database structure such as adding new codes or data fields by *authorized users* for the purpose of increasing the system functionality;

.5 auditing of data changes should provide the information of time and author of any changes;

.6 the system should ensure security of the data from unauthorized access and from changes being made by unauthorized users;

2. 易于进行数据维护及备份

如登记数据庞大,建立系统可分步进行,开始时,需将原先的手工账册信息转换为电子数据信息,在此转换过程中,必须保证数据安全,避免有未经批准的或错误的信息录入。数据导入后,应对所有已导入的数据进行详细的核查。一旦系统建立完毕,可以立即将最近签发的证书的持有人的数据录入。这些数据也要进行核查(见以下:系统的实现)。

电子登记的主要目的:

1. 由于所有数据均可从系统获得,可以确保**彻底消除**出错信息;

2. 帮助主管机关确保信息的**完整性**;

3. 拒绝重复的、不合理的请求;及

4. 分析发证事务以得到有效的反馈。

特点

新加坡海运与港口管理局最近开发的系统是以微软视窗系统(MS Windows)为操作平台的,目前约有10 000个记录,以后的版本将增加功能并做进一步改进。本章摘录了一些该软件的界面。

一般要求

系统应为授权用户提供以下功能:

.1 每一用户可获得特定人员的最新资料;

.2 每项新业务可方便快捷记录;

.3 系统应确保输入信息记录的准确、完整及可靠;

.4 可方便快速地改变数据结构,让授权用户可以为增加系统功能而增加新的代码或数据字段;

.5 系统可记录每次信息的修改、修改人及修改时间,以供核查;

.6 系统应确保安全,防止非法数据进入及非法用户修改数据;

.7 enabling data search tools by using various queries;

.8 obtaining statistics on various activities from the system;

.9 the system should be capable of being used by personnel with minimum knowledge or expertise in computer operations i.e. preferably MS Windows-based.

.10 backup facilities should be stipulated in the system to ensure data safety; and

.11 set up and operational costs should be minimized.

Users

Taking into account the importance of the obligations of a responsible Administration, it is expedient to build the system as an Administration-wide system so that anyone who gains access to the Administration network would be able to obtain information from it. However, special access rights should be provided for different users.

Therefore, user groups should be defined according to their access rights:

.1 Anyone—for any user;

.2 Guest—for unauthorized users (public access);

.3 Administration; and

.4 System maintenance and service staff.

Each user may be included into one or several groups and should exercise all rights granted to these groups.

The system should provide different access rights and it should also be able to easily create new user groups and assign them access rights.

Functions

The system should consist of the following sub-systems:

.1 Information sub-system;

.2 Data query sub-system;

.3 Notification sub-system; and

.4 Authentication and security sub-system;

Each sub-system performs an independent set of functions and may be implemented as an independent program or as a part of a unified software package.

.7 可使用多种查询条件实现数据搜索；

.8 获得各种业务的统计信息；

.9 系统应便于操作，即使没多少计算机知识与技能的人也能操作，也就是说，最好使用MS Windows操作平台；

.10 应对系统的数据备份设备做出规定，以确保数据安全；及

.11 应保证较低的安装及操作成本。

用户

考虑到负责的主管机关的义务，将登记系统建成网络系统将更有利于用户登录主管机关的网络并获得所需信息。然而，对不同的用户应有不同的用户权限。

因而，用户群可根据他们的访问权限来划分：

.1 任意用户

.2 访客——未经授权用户（公共登录）；

.3 主管机关；及

.4 系统维护技术组。

每一用户可用以上一组或几组的身份登录，并享有该组的权限。

系统应提供不同的登录权限，可易于创建新的用户并分配其用户权限。

功能

系统应包括以下子系统：

.1 信息子系统；

.2 数据查询子系统；

.3 通告子系统；及

.4 认证与安全子系统。

各子系统可实现独立的功能，可作为单独的程序运行，也可作为整个系统的一部分。

The *information sub-system* is to provide specific information. It should define the structure of tables, types of data fields, validation rules for data fields, tables relations etc. This sub-system should also provide tools for updating data. History of any changes in the data should also be stored.

The *data query sub-system* is to record/allow inquiries and shows/prints the required information in the desired format.

The main purpose of the *notification sub-system* is to allow time or activity based changes being made known to interested users.

The *authentication and security sub-system* is to provide users with the access to the system in accordance with their rights. This system should provide tools to easily add and remove users, create user groups and define their access rights.

Security

It should ensure that only authorized users could access to confidential information and make any changes in the data. Therefore the system structure and a login/password authentication scheme should provide the security system. Consideration should be given to using firewalls and proxies software to prevent unauthorized access to the system resources.

System Implementation

Developing the electronic register should consist of the following stages:

.1 Design statement, including detailed specifications of the database Information subsystem, a code system, an access rights system, data security, statistic reports and defining user groups and rights. The list of available transactions and possible limitations for each user group should be specified preferable before the beginning of system development;

.2 Developing the database software;

.3 Installing and testing software on site;

.4 Developing software documents and manuals;

.5 Training courses; and

.6 Technical and organizational support of software installation and user connection.

The software

The scope of the electronic register captures the following information:

1. a centralised database that captures the personal particulars of the seafarers.

2. the details of the certificates and endorsements.

信息子系统用于提供一些特别的信息。它定义了表的结构形式、字段类型、字段生效条件、表的数据关系等。信息子系统应提供数据更新工具。保存数据改变的所有历史记录。

数据查询子系统可记录数据/允许查询,并可按要求的格式将信息显示/打印出来。

通告子系统的主要目的是向感兴趣的用户知会系统数据变更的时间及业务种类。

认证与安全子系统可让用户按其权限登录系统。同时提供工具,便于对用户进行增删管理,创建新用户并定义其权限。

安全

应确保只有授权用户方可存取机密信息以及对数据进行更改。因而,系统结构和一套登录/密码认证机制可保证体系安全。应使用防火墙和代理服务器软件来阻止非法入侵。

系统实现

开发电子登记系统包括以下阶段:

.1 编制设计书,包括数据库信息子系统、代码系统、登录权限认证、数据安全、统计报告、用户定义及其权限的技术细节;在进行系统开发前,也应对每一用户的处理权力及限制做出特别规定;

.2 开发数据库软件;

.3 在网站中安装和调试软件;

.4 制作软件有关文档及用户手册;

.5 培训课程;及

.6 软件安装的技术支持及客户联系。

软件

电子登记系统包括以下信息:

1. 保存海员个人详细资料的集中数据库。

2. 证书及签证的具体细节。

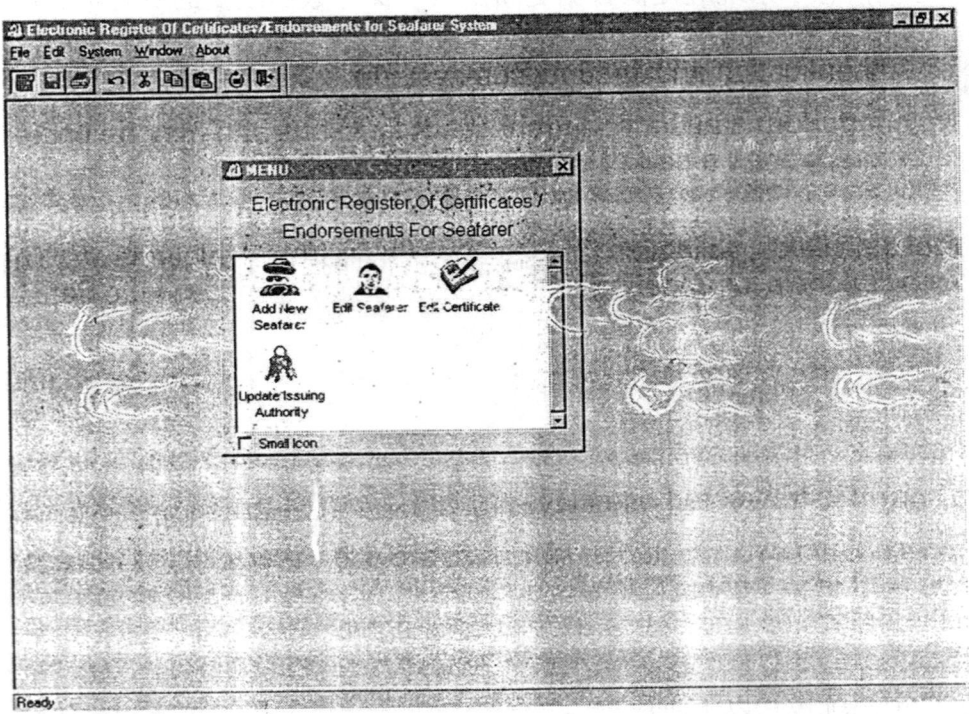

The functions provided are:

1. Creation of new seafarer's record, including data entry of personal particulars

2. Updating facility for maintenance of seafarers' personal and certificates/endorsements records

3. Recording of status of certificates/endorsements which have been revalidated, suspended, cancelled or reported lost, so that the system is up-to-date and complete.

4. Retrieval of information by name or identification number.

Upon the confirmation of the seafarer, a list of all the certificates and endorsements issued to the seafarer will be displayed for selection. Retrieval of certificates/endorsements can also be based on the following data:

    a. Certificate Type

    b. Document Number

The list of certificates captured by the system must be complete, and will include international, national and educational certificates/endorsements. The system will also enable the inclusion of certificates/endorsements or revised certificate structures conceived by future revisions of the STCW Convention.

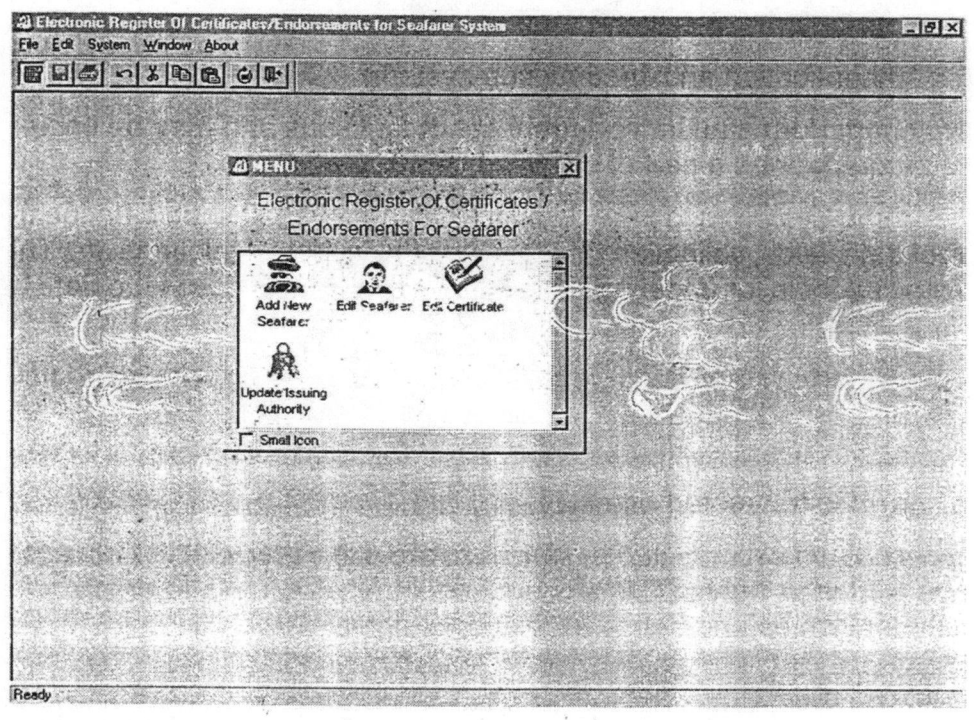

提供的功能:

1. 生成新的海员记录,包括个人详细资料的数据录入。

2. 对海员个人资料及证书/签证记录的更新。

3. 记录海员证书/签证的再有效、暂停有效、注销和报失的状态,以便保证最新和完整的系统记录。

4. 根据姓名或身份证号码检索资料。

在证实海员情况方面,显示签发给海员的所有证书与签证列表供选择查索。证书/签证的检索也可按以下条件进行:

    a.   证书类型

    b.   证书编号

系统所包括的证书列表必须是完整的,包括国际证书、国家证书和学历证书或有关签证。STCW公约将来版本中构思的证书/签证的修正样式,也应包括在内。

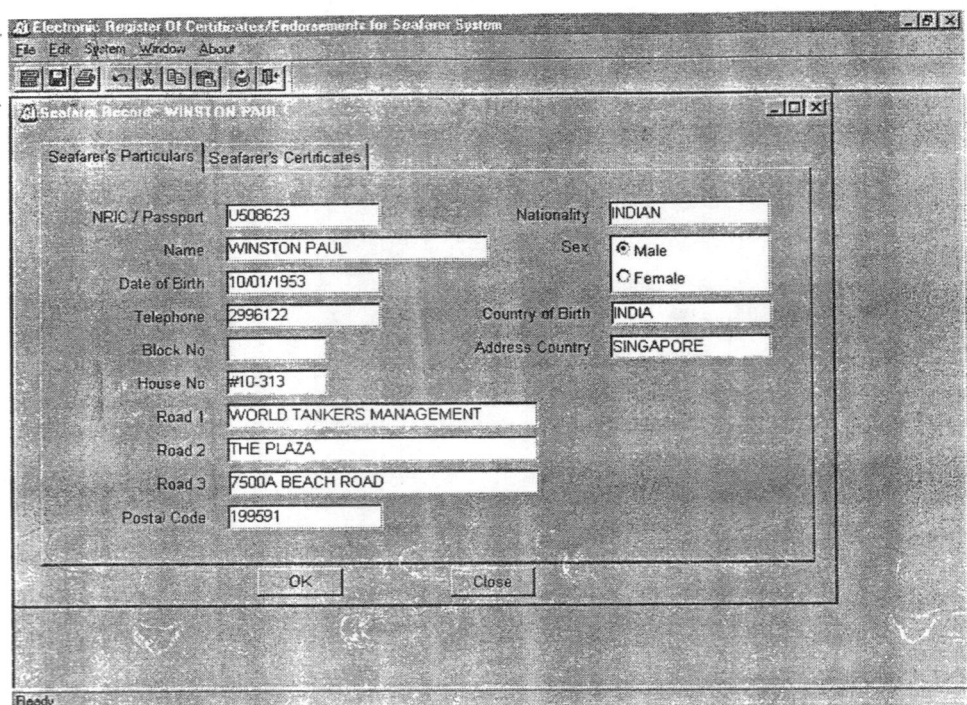

The opening screen for a seafarer's personal particulars is shown above. Fields are editable only to authorised users and changes are tracked by the system. A history of changes made and the persons making the changes is recorded and can be referred to in the event of a dispute.

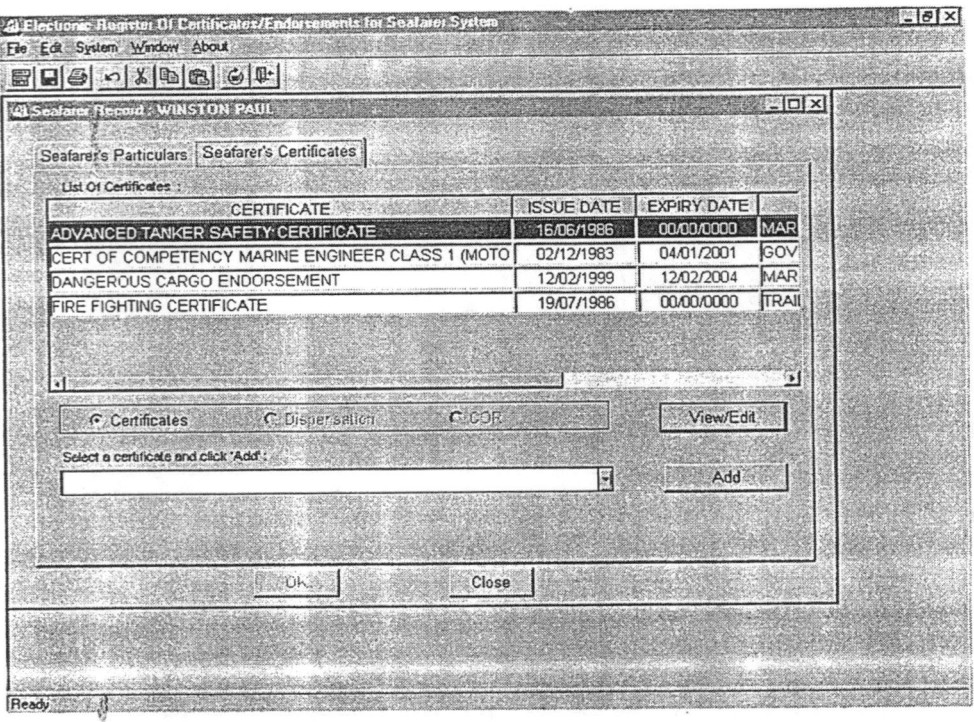

The seafarer's list of certificates and endorsement are shown under "Seafarer's Certificates". Again, the software should be as comprehensive as possible and include options for Dispensation and Certificate of Recognition, as shown above.

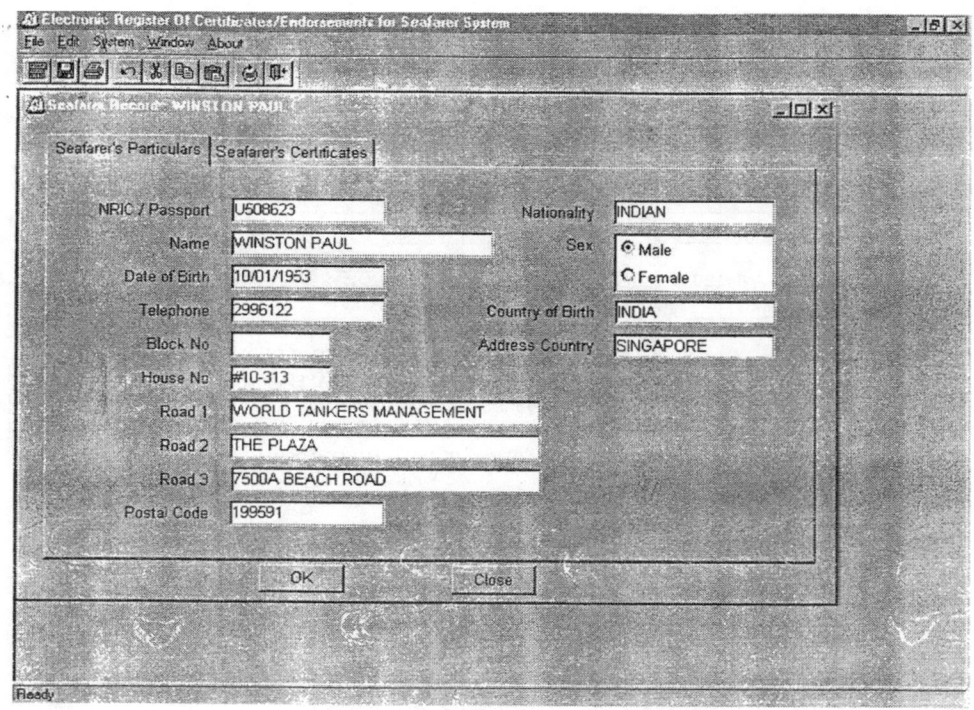

　　以上打开的窗口显示了海员的个人详细资料。仅允许授权用户对字段进行编辑,系统同时记录其编辑过程。将变更的历史及变更处理人记录下来,以便发生争议时查阅。

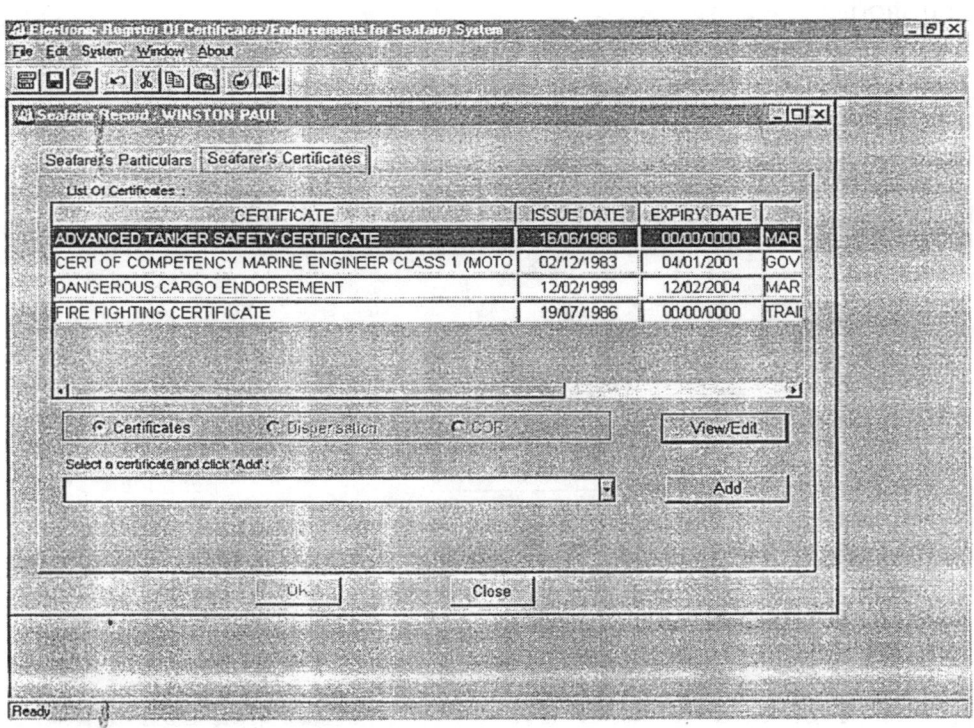

　　有关海员的证书和签证的列表显示在"海员证书"页框下。同时,系统应尽可能全面,包括以上所示的豁免证书和认可的证书,如上所示。

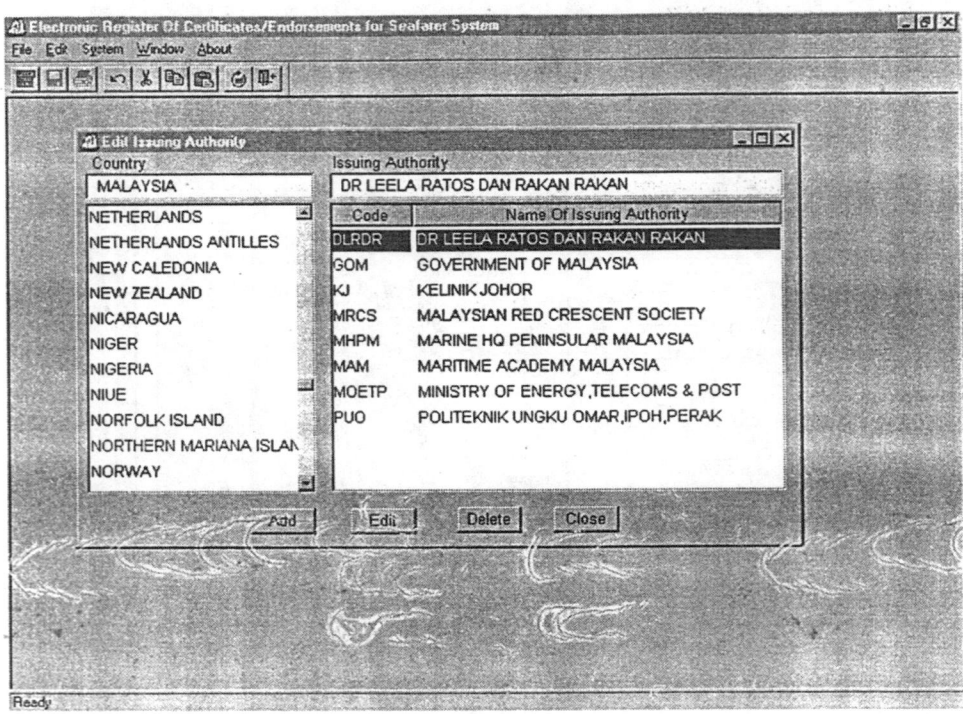

The system should also include a database of issuing authorities of certificates recognised by the Administration.

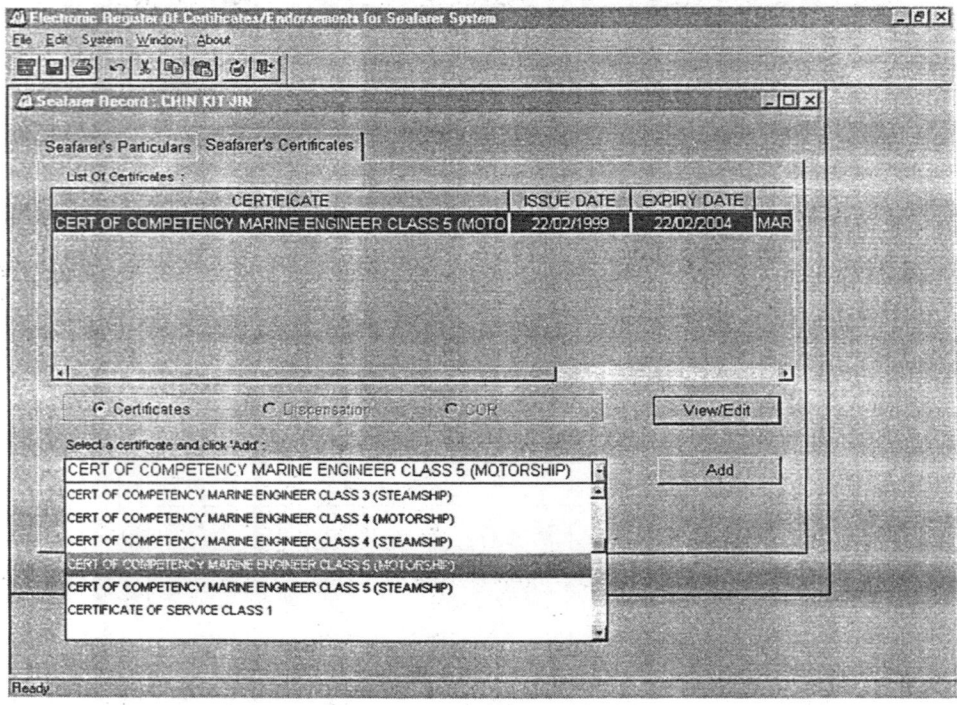

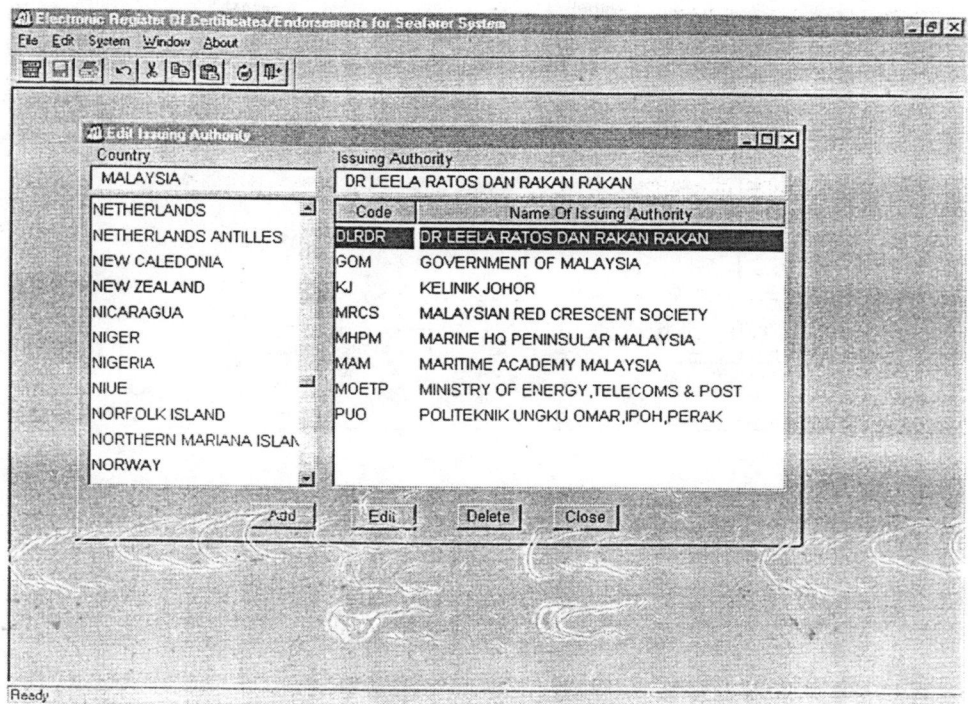

系统还应包括被主管机关承认的证书签发机关的数据资料。

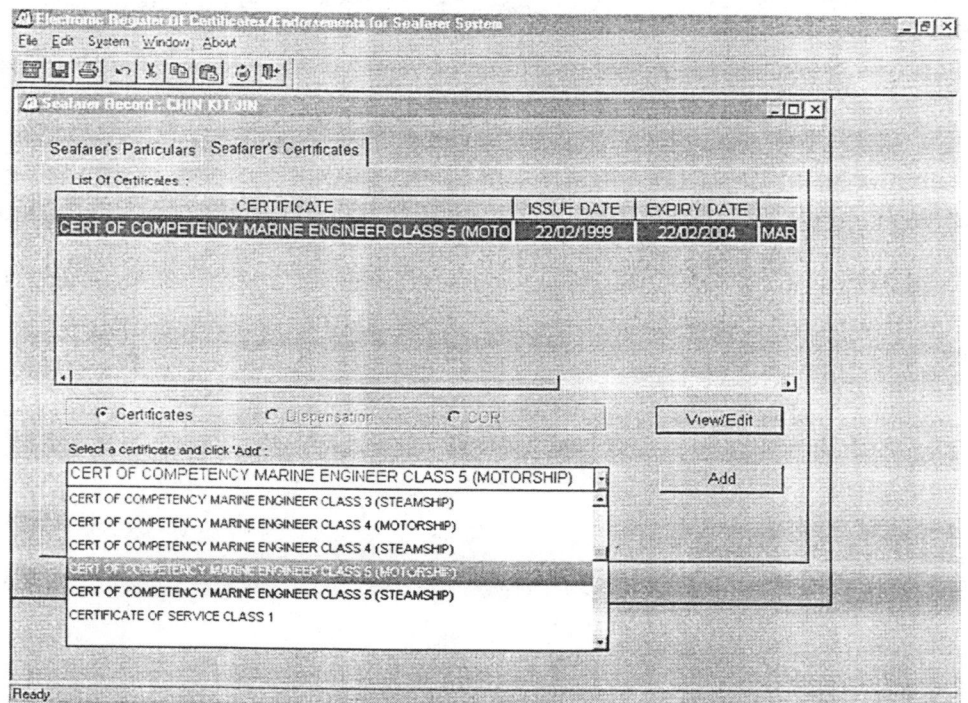

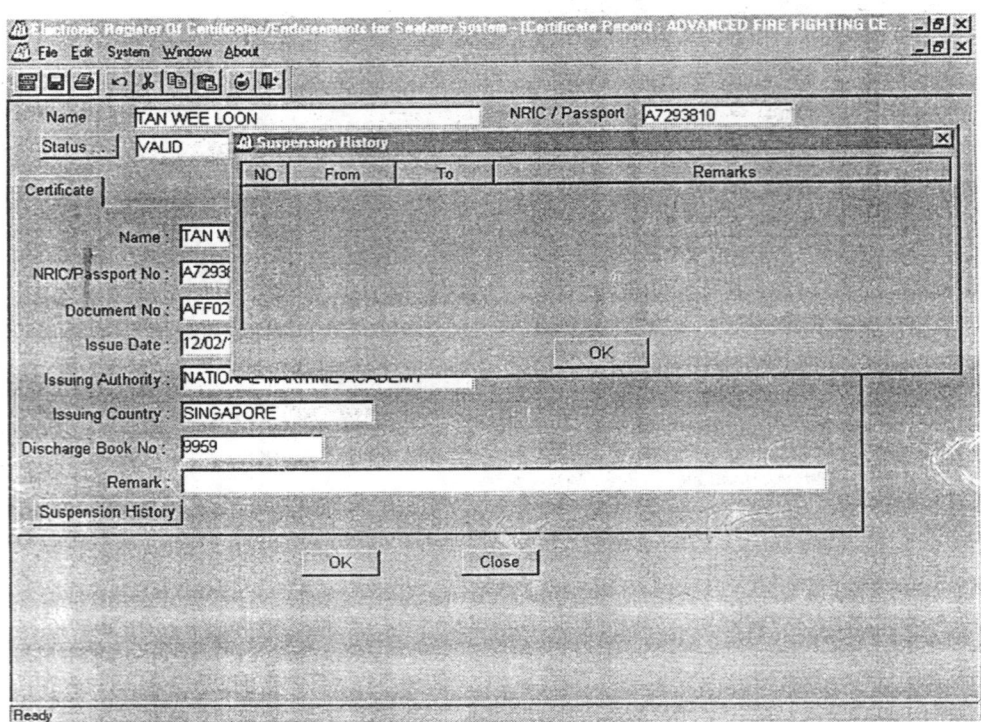

Certificates can be updated and added easily for each seafarer and should include functions typical of Administrations not specifically mentioned in the STCW Convention, e.g suspension. The relationship between the various records held in the system is shown in the following page.

Conclusion

An electronic register is nothing complicated or unusual that a good computer programmer cannot do. Cerlainly there are some features peculiar to certification of seafarers, but other than that, it is simply an ordinary and straightforward database.

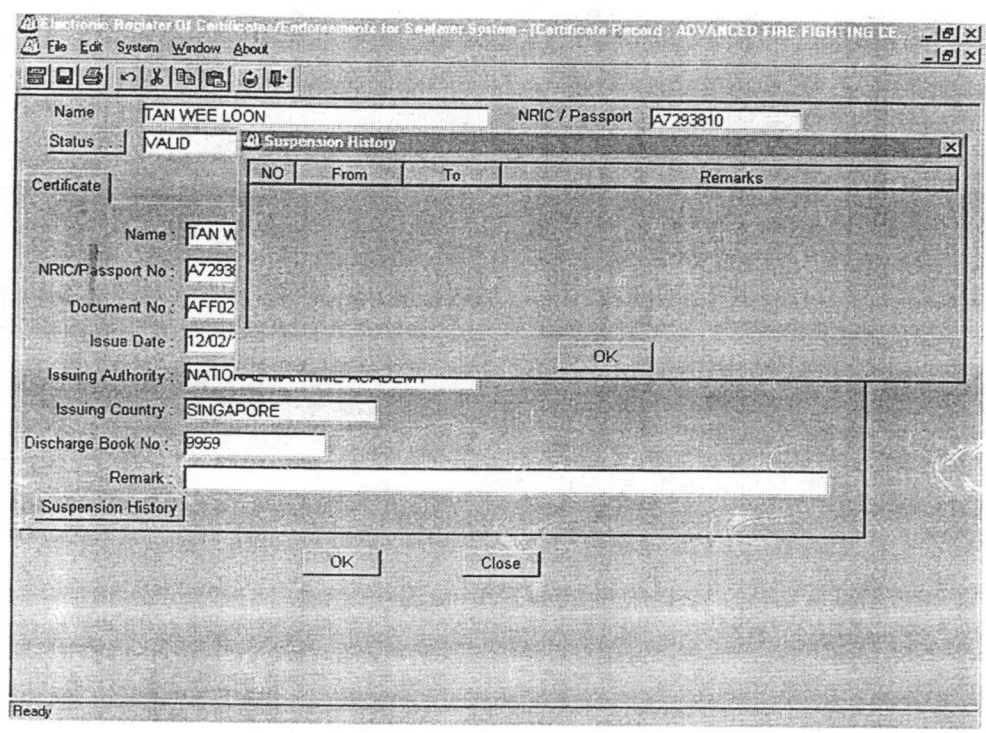

系统应便于对每一海员的证书进行更新及添加内容,包括在STCW公约中未详尽提到的主管机关的典型功能,如:证书的暂停有效。系统中各种记录间的关系如下页所示。

结论

电子登记系统并不复杂,通常一个好的程序设计员就可以完成。当然,它具有一些关于海员证书的固有特点。但除此之外,它是普通、简单、易操作的数据库系统。

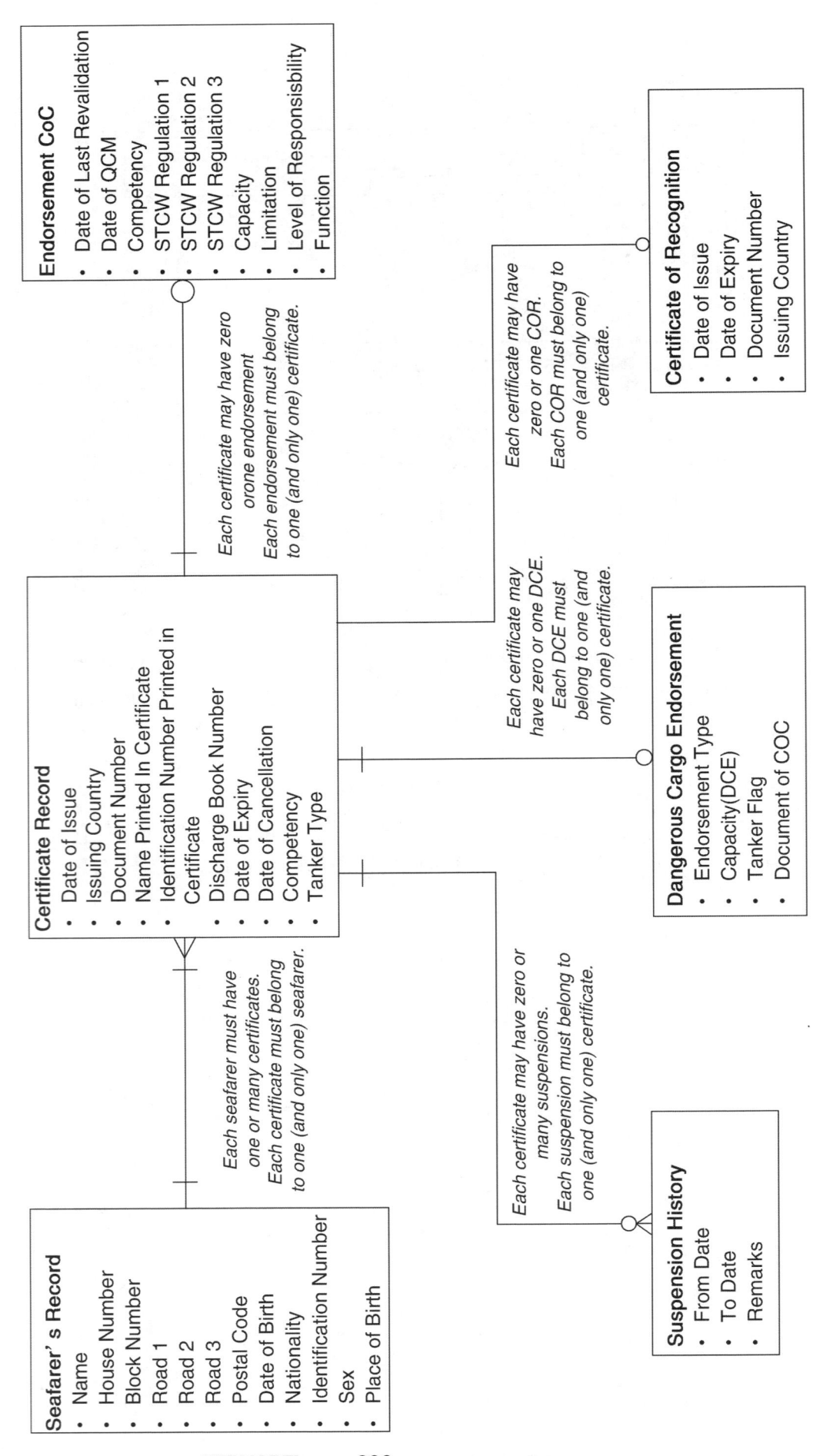

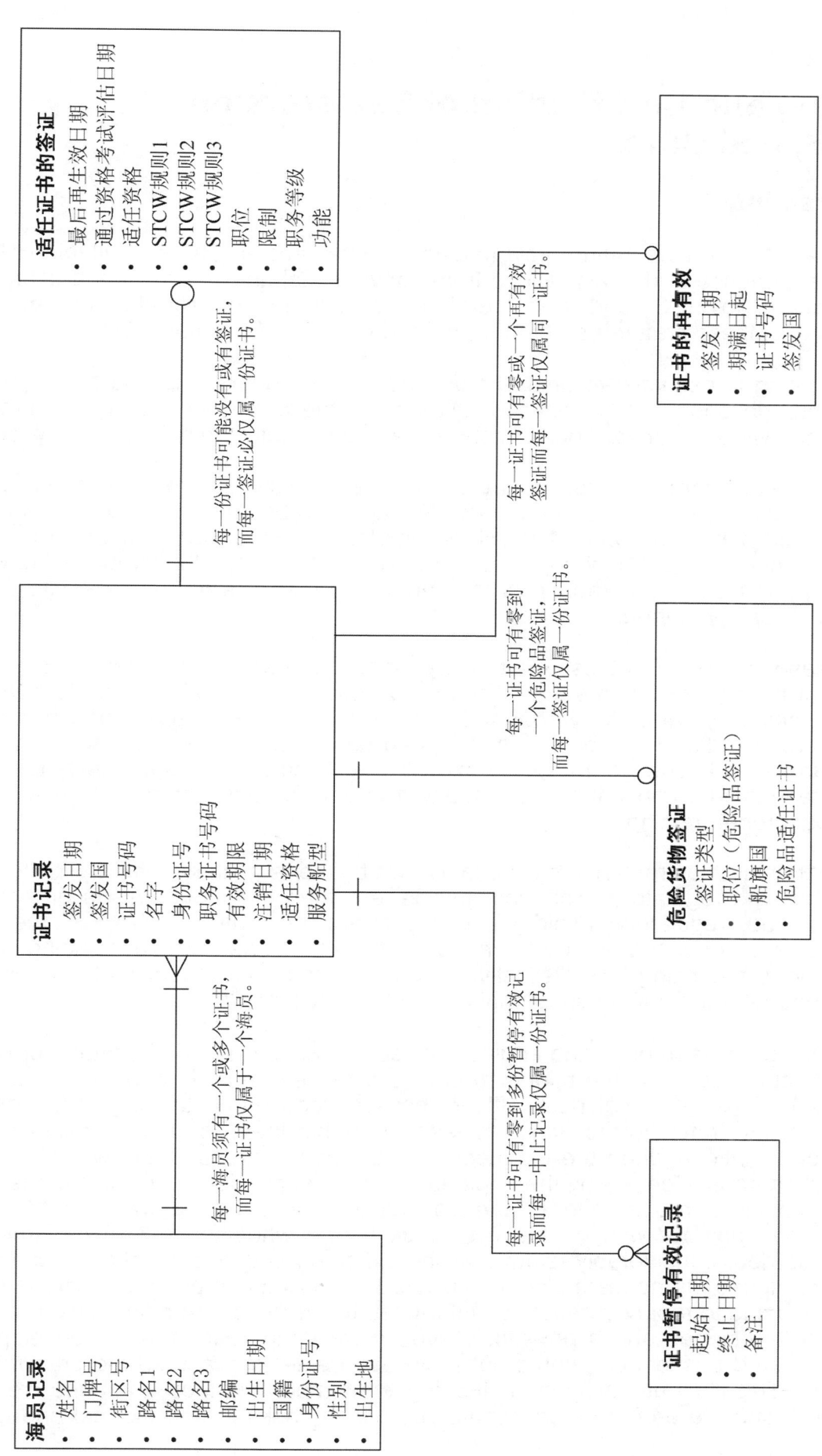

Part 21
Training and Certification of Seafarers on High Speed Craft

Crew Training

It is unlikely that new operating crew (masters, mates and engineers) will join HSC without previous experience and qualifications from conventional ships. This sets a useful baseline for conversion to HSC, and it is therefore possible to concentrate here more on the peculiarities of these craft rather than normal navigation and seamanship etc.

Proper training is essential to ensure safe and efficient operations and hence commercial viability through passenger satisfaction. Without it the quality of the service provided will suffer, so too will the standard of maintenance and eventually the reliability of the craft.

Training is even more important today where the sophistication of high speed passenger craft control systems increase continually by leaps and bounds. If everything is working as intended then it may be argued that it is simpler to control today's generation of craft. However, when things go wrong it can be very difficult for the crew to know what is happening and for them to know how to keep the craft and its passengers safe-unless they have been properly trained.

The increases in speed of these craft also pose far greater problems for the crews than for the craft of twenty or so years ago. These days it is not unusual for craft to operate at 60 knots. By their very nature they operate in confined waters and often in dense traffic, and in some places with large numbers of high speed passenger craft on the same route. It was not unreasonable twenty years ago to expect a new recruit to adapt quickly to high speed craft operations with minimal training, today it is very unreasonable and unsafe to expect this without proper training.

Minimum training requirements may be laid down by the regulatory authority, (1.2.3, 18.1.3.7 & 18.3) but, the regulatory minimum may be less than the requirements of the operating company. The regulatory minimum concentrates on safety, whereas the company requirements may concentrate on the needs of the service as a whole including safety. This dividing line is becoming less distinctive with high speed passenger craft, especially given the wide nature of the IMO International Code of Safety for HSC.

Cross training between deck and engineer officers (18.5.5) is very important for high speed passenger craft. Because the minimum crew are carried and this will often mean only one engineer, it is essential that deck officers have a good understanding of the engineering systems on the craft and the action to take to enable them to keep the craft safe during emergency situations when the engineer may be incapacitated or his workload too great, e.g multiple alarms. Conversely the engineer may assist the deck officers with tasks such as radio communications. In one of the casualties mentioned below, when the accident occurred the engineer was on his way back to the wheelhouse and he arrived at the wheelhouse door considerably faster than he expected and was knocked unconscious, the generators tripped off the main electric bus and the cooling pumps for the generator engines were lost leading to rapid overheating, unfortunately the remaining officers did not know how to stop these engines and a potentially even more dangerous situation developed where seriously injured passengers would not have been able to evacuate the craft if a fire had broken out. This illustrates why cross training is so important. More than one crew member should be trained to perform all essential operational tasks in both normal and emergency situations.

第21章
高速船船员的培训与发证

船员培训

操作高速船的新船员(船长、大副和轮机员)绝大多数具备常规船舶的经验与资格。这给高速船员队伍的转换提供了有益的基础,因而可以更加集中于操纵高速船的特点而不需过多关注常规的航行和操纵技术。

合适的培训对于确保安全和提高操作效率并通过做到令旅客满意来提高商业生存能力,这些都是非常重要的。如不这样,服务质量将蒙受损失,因此,非常有必要维持标准并最终保证高速船的可靠性。

在高速客船控制系统技术飞跃发展的今天,实施船员的培训显得越来越重要。如果船舶一切正常,或许可以说如今的高速船操纵起来是非常简单的。然而,除非船员已经过合适的培训,否则这样的船一旦出现问题,船员想要知道发生了什么,并且想要知道怎样保证快艇和乘客的安全,会是非常困难的。

和20多年前相比,高速船速度的加快也给船员带来值得思考的问题。目前,60节船速的快艇也很常见。同样的,他们会在受限水域、交通繁忙水域,甚至在相同航线上会出现大量高速客船航行的情况。20年前,一个新人可以通过最少的训练很快适应高速船的操作。而现今,未经合适的培训,要一个新人这样做非常不合理并且不安全。

规则(1.2.3、18.1.3.7和18.3)规定了最低限度的培训要求,但是,营运公司的要求可能比规则的最低要求还高。规则最低要求主要集中在安全上,然而公司要求可能集中在总体的服务需要上,其中也包含了安全。对于高速客船这两类规则的分界线越来越不明显,特别是IMO高速船国际安全规则给出了更宽的内容。

对高速客船而言,驾驶员和轮机员(18、5、5)进行交叉训练是非常重要的。因为船上只配备了最少数量的船员并且很多时候只有一名轮机员,驾驶员能够很好地了解船上的轮机系统,并且能够在轮机员不能胜任工作或工作太过繁忙等多种紧急情况下能采取行动保证船舶安全。反过来,轮机员也可以帮助驾驶员执行相关任务,例如进行无线电通信。以下提到了一例关于众多人员伤亡的事故。当时,事故发生在轮机员返回驾驶室的途中,突然撞到舱门上并被撞得不省人事,发电机主电路跳闸,发电机的冷却泵失速导致温度过高。不幸的是,其他驾驶员不知道如何停止这些运行的机器,而潜在的危险情况正在发展,如在那里爆发了火灾,乘客得不到及时疏散将会造成大量的人员伤亡。这个例子说明为什么交叉培训是非常重要的。应有不止一名船员接受训练以执行在日常和紧急情况下的所有重要的操作任务。

The broad training requirements are contained in the IMO International Code of Safety for HSC, upon which Administrations should base their requirements and regulations.

Training can be separated into several parts:
- Type Rating or craft and equipment specific knowledge
- Route training
- Safety training not covered in the Type Rating
- Passenger handling training for both service and safety
- Medical training
- Radar Simulator training
- Maintenance training

Depending on the make up of the Type Rating syllabus, many of the other items may already or to some extent be included, however, the worst case, that Type Rating is the bare minimum, has been assumed here.

Other matters that require consideration include high speed navigation techniques and bridge routines. Again these may or may not form part of the Type Rating.

Type Rating

The term Type Rating has its origins in the aircraft industry and transfer to the marine industry is not surprising when one considers the cross fertilisation between the two industries, initially with the first hovercraft where aircraft construction techniques and technology were used and aircraft pilots were thought suitable as masters, and from Boeing the maker of the Jetfoil hydrofoils.

In many ways the marine industry is taking on the Type Rating concept with e.g tanker and gas carrier endorsements. So the use of Type Rating for HSC is by no means out of step with the rest of the marine industry.

When considering what should be included under Type Rating the requirements of the IMO International Code of Safety for HSC should be considered. But as always the requirements of any particular company may exceed these minimum requirements. Type Rating is achieved following successful training and examination.

Theoretical training

Training may be separated into classroom and underway sections or combined into one on the job training system. Learning the theory in the classroom is arguably a more satisfactory method of learning than doing the same underway, this is because underway the trainers are likely to be the crew who will be unable to devote their complete attention to training and this will cause them extra stress and may distract them from the safe navigation of the voyage. However, some of the training can only be carried out on board, this could be with or without passengers, but of course an HSC underway without passengers is not earning any revenue so this training time will be limited.

船上训练的要求包含在有关IMO的高速船国际公约安全规则中,主管机关应以这些要求和规则为基础制定相应要求。

训练可以被分成几个部分:
- 专门类型船舶适任训练、评估或高速船和仪器的专业知识
- 航线训练
- 在专门类型船舶适任训练、评估中未包含的安全训练
- 基于服务和安全的客船操作训练
- 医疗培训
- 雷达模拟器培训
- 船舶养护培训

依据制定的专门类型船舶适任训练、评估大纲,许多其他的条款可能已经被包含或在某种程度上包含在内。然而,对于最坏的情况,等级评估仅仅是最低的要求。

其他需要考虑的方面包括航海技术和驾驶台规则。这些方面可以选择作为专门类型船舶适任训练、评估的一部分。

专门类型船舶适任训练、评估

专门类型船舶适任训练、评估的条款起源于航空业而后过渡到海运业,两个行业互相渗透并不奇怪。应用航空工业的科技制造第一艘喷射水翼船时,制造商波音公司认为飞行员也适合当船长。

在许多方面,海运行业采用了专门类型船舶适任训练、评估的概念,例如液货船和石油气船的签注。因此高速船的专门类型船舶适任训练、评估无疑将促进航海技术的发展。

应考虑在IMO高速船国际安全规则的要求下,专门类型船舶适任训练、评估应包含什么内容,但是通常公司的要求会超过最低要求。通过成功的培训和考试可以达到专门类型船舶适任训练、评估的要求。

理论培训

培训可以分成课堂和航行两个组成部分或与工作培训系统结合。在课堂学习理论是一种比在航行中学习同样的内容更有效的方法,这是因为航行中担任教师的一般是一名船员,不能集中精力去训练别人,并且这会给他增加额外的压力,也可能干扰他们的安全航行。然而,有些训练只能在船上进行,船上可能有乘客或没有乘客。高速船在没有乘客的航行中没有收入,所以在船上训练的时间会受到限制。

As its name suggests the classroom theory deals with the principles of the craft's various modes of operation and the various systems such as steering, engine control, electricity generation and distribution, emergency systems such as fire detection and extinguishing, hydraulics, pneumatics, fuel, air conditioning, ride control, night vision equipment, navigation aids, bilge pumping, ground tackle, mooring, loading and stability, passenger control, emergency plans, evacuation plans, minimum equipment to sail, action for various breakdowns and other events, route planning under various situations, etc. As can be seen from this list there is an enormous amount of information for a new recruit to absorb.

Practical training

The practical and underway part of the training allows the crew to practice and experiment with the knowledge they learnt in the classroom sessions, so it is ideal to have the practical section last. The practical and underway training are very important not least because it is one of the rare occasions when the crews can gain hands-on experience without passengers. It is not acceptable to practise emergency stops and turns while carrying fare paying passengers. This is normally quite easy to schedule for a new operation, but for a service which has already started it will take some careful planning to ensure passenger service disruption is kept to a minimum, early morning training sessions before passenger service starts is one option. Another important part of the underway training is the ability to test various failure modes, i.e. to disable various pieces of equipment, either with or without the knowledge of the person being trained, to practise their reactions and implant into their minds what action needs to be taken for each of the failure modes. The Failure Mode and Effects Analysis (1.4.19, 1.5.2.1.3 & Annex 4) report for the craft, as required by the IMO International Code of Safety for HSC, is a very useful aid to crew training as it helps to focus-in objectively on the system vulnerabilities in detail.

The exercises to be undertaken should include man overboard manoeuvres, emergency turns, emergency stops, emergency landings where appropriate, anchoring which on many high speed craft is an emergency procedure, rough sea procedures, high speed navigation techniques, berthing techniques and bridge equipment procedures, details of these will be found in the Craft Operating Manual for your particular type of HSC.

Route and bridge procedures familiarisation need to be carefully considered, these could be gained by travelling on normal passenger voyages with an experienced crew, but there is always the danger to watch out for that older masters/engineers will pass on the bad habits they have acquired over the years, a dedicated training crew may be a more suitable source of information.

The crew will be involved in subsets of many items the wheel house crew are trained in, e.g man overboard, mooring, emergency and evacuation procedures and simple tasks involving equipment such as the public address system, pumping bilges and servicing toilets.

So who carries out training? For new operations this is often carried out by the manufacturer's or builder's representative, the larger the operating company is the more likely they are to have dedicated trainers, the trainer is likely to be a senior serving master or engineer. The maintenance staff also have an important contribution to make to the crew training process and this also enables the seeds of a good relationship to be established which is essential. The IMO International Code of Safety for HSC specifies the subjects to be covered in the Maintenance and Servicing Manual, details may be found in Appendix A.

正如训练课程名称所表达的,课堂理论涉及各种高速船和各种系统的操作原理,例如操舵、机舱控制、发电和配电,应急系统如火源探测和灭火、水力学、气体力学、燃料、空调、风浪操纵、夜视设备、助航仪器、污水泵、甲板索具、系泊、装载以及稳性、旅客管理、应急计划、弃船计划、航行最低配备,多种偶然事故和其他事件的行动,多种情况下的航路计划,等等。正如这份列表上看到的一样,一名新人需要吸收大量的信息。

实操培训

实操和航行中的训练使船员可以在实践课堂中学到理论,因此进行实操培训是非常理想的方式。实操与航行培训是非常重要的,船员能够得到少有的机会在没有乘客的情况下获得亲手操作经验,因为在载运付钱乘搭的乘客时练习紧急停车和转向是不可接受的。为新船或新公司制订一份计划表是非常简单的,但是对于已经开始营运的公司,这将需要一些详细的计划来确保对乘客的服务所造成的干扰保持在最小范围,可以利用清晨对乘客开始服务前进行训练。航行中,培训的另外一个重要部分是测试对于各种故障的处理能力。例如,使不同的(无论被培训的人员是否具有相关知识)设备不运作,以训练他们的反应并让他们记住对每种故障应该采取的相应行动。正如IMO高速船国际安全规则所要求的,故障类型和有效的分析报告(见1.4.19、1.5.2.1.3及附件4)有助于使船员客观面对设备的弱点,这对于船员培训是非常有益的。

采用的训练应包含人员落水的操纵,紧急转向,紧急停车,在适合的地方紧急抢滩、抛锚,这些都是高速船的应急操作方法。海况恶劣时的操作、高速航行的操作技术、靠泊技术和驾驶台仪器操作,所有这些方面的详细内容都可以从相应的高速船操作指南中找到。

熟悉航线和驾驶台程序是非常重要的。可以通过与富有经验的船员一起驾驶普通客船来获得这方面知识,但是也要注意资深的船长/轮机员会传授一些他们几十年来养成的坏习惯等此类不利因素,因此一名专门负责培训的船员可能是最合适的传授者。

船员要参与驾驶部船员所需进行的许多项目的训练,例如船员落水、系泊、遇险及弃船程序和有关仪器设备的简单任务,例如全船广播系统、污水泵及生活污水系统的维修。

由谁来实施培训?因为对于新船经常是由工厂或建造者的代表来实施培训的,所以大型的营运公司更需要专职的教练员。教练员最好是高级的船长或轮机长。协调员也很重要,他可以协调船员训练程序,建立必要的各方面良好关系。在IMO高速船国际安全规则中,关于保养和维修手册的内容,详见附录A。

Typically the classroom training will take anything up to three weeks, if carried out on board this time would logically have to be considerably extended to achieve the same number of hours under instruction. The underway section depends on the complexity of the craft, the number of trainees being trained at the same time and the weather conditions. Ideally it is best for a company to train several people at the same time and for them to experience a variety of different weather and sea conditions, this can be achieved by choosing an exercise area with both sheltered and exposed waters.

Night vision equipment

Some areas of operation will warrant the use of night vision equipment for HSC to enable continued safe high speed operations at night (13.10 & 18.1.3.14). However, training for night operations is a separate issue be it with or without night equipment. It is essential for any crew who change to night operations to be very familiar with daytime operations first for the following reasons. Firstly, route familiarisation is essential as navigation can be more difficult at night, at high speed it is of paramount importance that the crew know exactly where they are at all times, a few months on the route during day service should achieve this. Secondly, the crew should be very familiar with the equipment of the craft and the layout of system monitoring and controls in the wheelhouse.

The situation that must be avoided, on a night voyage, is a system malfunction, whether minor or major, that causes an alarm to sound in the wheelhouse, the helmsman's attention (normally the master) is distracted for some time while he tries to identify the source of the alarm and decide what action needs to be taken. With adequate daytime experience and appropriate training the response by the crew should be almost instantaneous and automatic. The alternative is lengthy distractions from the safe navigation of the craft.

This situation can be critical when night vision equipment is in use, which in itself implies that objects that may cause damage to the craft might only be detected with seconds allowed for avoidance manoeuvres. A sustained distraction in the wheelhouse could be disastrous under such circumstances.

Training for night operations differs from normal Type Rating training in that its main purpose is to familiarise the crew with night time wheelhouse procedures as well as the use of any special night vision equipment. Despite its apparent simplicity in comparison to Type Rating, it can in fact take longer. In Hong Kong night training can take one month during which time the crew are not available for other duties.

Without proper training the use of night vision equipment can be quite dangerous and instil a false sense of security in the wheelhouse crew.

典型的课堂培训要占用3周的时间。如果在船上实施培训,应考虑延长时间,以达到要求的相同学习时间。航行中培训应考虑船舶的复杂性、在同一时间内学员的数量和天气条件。对一个公司来说最理想的是能同时培训许多学员并经历多种不同的天气和海况,可以通过选择一个同时具有遮蔽和开阔水域的练习区域来达到目的。

夜视设备

在某些区域可以使用夜视设备以便能够在夜晚保持安全的高速航行(13.10和18.1.3.14)。然而,无论是否有夜视设备,夜航训练都是独立要求的。由于以下原因,转为负责夜航操作的船员应首先熟悉日间航行操作是非常重要的。首先,因为在夜晚航行,对航线的熟悉更加困难,而在高速的情况下船员始终准确地知道他们的位置极为重要,经过几个月的白天航行应该可以达到这个目的。其次,船员应非常熟悉艇船的设备和驾驶室监控系统的位置。

夜航时,无论是主机还是辅机系统的故障,都应极力避免,否则会导致驾驶室的声响警报,为搞清警报的原因和决定需要采取什么行动,舵手的注意力(船长也不例外)会被分散一段时间。通过充分昼航经历和适当的培训,船员的反应应该是即时的、下意识的。犹豫不决不利于船的安全航行。

使用夜航设备其环境是非常紧迫的,因为夜航设备发现危险物体后留给船员避险操纵的时间可能只有几秒钟。在这种情况下,如果操舵船员没有集中精神,会导致很严重的后果。

夜航训练的操作与普通的特殊类型船舶培训有所不同,夜航培训的主要目的是使船员像熟悉所有特殊的夜视设备一样熟悉夜晚驾驶室的操作程序。尽管这表面上看起来比专门类型船舶培训简单,实际上这需要花费更多时间。在香港,夜航培训需花费一个月时间,而在这段时间内船员不允许同时担任其他工作。

没有经过恰当的培训,就使用夜航设备将会非常危险,并且会逐渐造成驾驶室内船员对安全的感觉错误。

Part 22
Group Evaluation

Objective

To provide experience in the preparation, from a detailed teaching syllabus, of a series of tests to evaluate a course outcome, in the field testing of such a test series and in the evaluation of the tests against task criteria.

Action

The exercise will use the syllabus of this model course, "Assessment, Examination and Certification of Seafarers".

1. Each group should appoint one member to act as co-ordinator for the preparation and writing of test questions and their assembly into test papers.

2. The first two hours, approximately, should be spent on drawing up a table of specifications for testing the whole course, deciding which objectives are to be tested and the types of test to be used. Because of the limited time available, the complete test series should require not more than three hours to answer.

3. After deciding which objectives are to be tested, the co-ordinator will arrange the division of the writing of questions between the members of the group who will prepare them, taking into account the weighting for knowledge, comprehension and application shown in the test specification. Marking schemes for essay-type questions will also need to be prepared. Finally, the questions will be assembled to form test papers, which should include full instructions to candidates. It is expected that the above will occupy the remainder of day 11 of the course.

4. Each group will conduct a field test of their test series by setting it for the other group to answer. The morning of the final day of the course is set aside for the field testing.

5. Approximately one hour will be needed to score the completed tests and to examine the results to identify any question which has proved to be unsatisfactory.

6. The final two hours will be devoted to discussion of the evaluation exercise. Be prepared to comment on your own test and on that of the other group, particularly with reference to:

    — the content validity;

    — the item validity of individual questions;

    — the efficiency of the tests from the point of view of their administration and marking;

    — additional or alternative tests which you would have used if more time had been available for preparation;

    — whether the results show any unsatisfactory questions;

    — evaluation against task criteria.

第22章
分组评估

目的

积累根据详细的教学大纲准备评价课程实施成果的系列测试,对试题进行内容审核以及以任务标准为基础对测试进行评价经验。

作用

练习使用本示范教程的大纲:"海员评估、考试及发证"。

1. 每组应指定一名成员来扮演协调人的角色,准备和编写试题然后将他们汇编到试卷中。

2. 开始的大约两个小时应用于草拟整个课程的测试说明,决定测试内容及考试类型。因为可利用的时间有限,整个考试的时间应不超过3个小时。

3. 确定测试科目后,根据测试说明中知识、理解与熟练的比重分配组员准备考题。论述性试题的评分方法也需要准备。最后,试题将被汇编成试卷,试卷应包含所有对考生的说明。以上这些工作预计将会占去课程第11天剩余的所有时间。

4. 每组成员应将试卷给另一组人员用于实施测试。课程的最后一天早上用来实施测试。

5. 大约需要一个小时给试卷评分和检测结果以确定所有不满意的试题。

6. 最后两个小时将用于讨论评估习题。用于准备评论自己和小组其他成员的试题,特别是针对以下方面:

   — 内容有效性;

   — 试题中单个问题的有效性;

   — 试题管理和评分的有效性;

   — 如果考生有充分的准备时间应增加附加题;

   — 是否有不满意的试题;

   — 比对任务标准的评估。